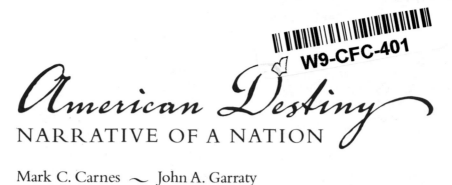

American Destiny
NARRATIVE OF A NATION

Mark C. Carnes ～ John A. Garraty

Custom Edition for
Southern Connecticut State University

With an introduction by Richard Gerber

Taken From:

American Destiny: Narrative of a Nation, Volume 1, Third Edition
by Mark C. Carnes, John A. Garraty

Custom Publishing

New York   Boston   San Francisco
London   Toronto   Sydney   Tokyo   Singapore   Madrid
Mexico City   Munich   Paris   Cape Town   Hong Kong   Montreal

2008300139

WH/TT

Pearson
Custom Publishing
is a division of

www.pearsonhighered.com

ISBN 10: 0-558-10998-5
ISBN 13: 978-0-558-10998-1

MAPS

Maps

To Our Children:

Stephanie and Kathy, Jack, and Sarah

Brief Contents

Taken from *American Destiny: Narrative of a Nation*, Volume 1, Third Edition, by Mark C. Carnes and John A. Garraty

Detailed Contents

Your Mama's Knee

Forward Thoughts

Most students arrive in their introductory American history courses hauling the baggage of inaccurate generalizations, false heroic myths, and other forms of perpetuated bafflegab. We can collect that freight and label it as "Your Mama's Knee." The term derives from the idea that most of you learned about the American experience from the folklore passed down to you from some ancestral authority, matronly or otherwise. From that source you absorbed the legendary anecdotes of some remembered past. Most of that purported information was factually inaccurate and bereft of any critical interpretation.

You survived high school U.S. history, with its outsized pursuit of higher test scores. Perhaps your textbook contained more graphics than words. Students enter HIS 110 with the debris of high school American history still clinging. A sort of intellectual car wash may be needed to cleanse your minds of those curricular fragments that you have not blessedly forgotten. Any genuine appreciation of historical complexity, let alone inspiration and critical historical reasoning, for most of you, remains a rare commodity.

HIS 110, by contrast, is designed to offer students the most recent scholarly historical interpretations of American events, issues and persons of the period from 1763 to 1877. The textbook in your hands, *American Destiny*, is factually accurate and up-to-date. Combining it with the class lectures and the second volume for the course, *Revolution and Union*, permits you to examine the content of this segment of the American past in a *comprehensive, systematic* manner.

"Comprehensive" means that the large significant content areas of American history receive attention. Among the books and the class lectures the important themes are addressed. They are examined in their historical context—as they became critical to the people living in their historical moments. For example, our major consideration of the institution of slavery in America is located within the growing sectionalism of the 1830's, because while slavery had existed in early colonial America and certainly played a part in the formation of the Constitution, the issues surrounding slavery exploded into national prominence during the pre-Civil War generation. Moreover, there are no chronological gaps. In this respect HIS 110 is, indeed, a "comprehensive" survey of the American experience. Emphasis will be placed on government, politics, institutions and ideas.

"Systematic" means that the interpretations put forward in HIS 110 speak with a single voice. There is a certain interpretive consistency through all of the chapters of the books and the various presented lectures. If one decides, for example, that an American president should be judged by how faithfully he kept his campaign promises, then interpretive consistency demands that such an evaluation apply to Thomas Jefferson as well as James K. Polk. If we use a president's capacity to respond to crisis to evaluate him, then interpretive consistency insists that the same standards be applied to John Adams as well as Abraham Lincoln. If we determine that moral character is a valuable yardstick, then interpretive consistency compels Andrew Jackson as well as George Washington to be measured by it. If we use all three, or some others, the principle of interpretive consistency remains the key to historical judgment.

Similarly, interpretive consistency suggests more general criteria which guide the examination and evaluation of changes and continuities within the constitutional system in different moments in time. For illustration, analysis of the content of justice in 1787, and again in 1866, assists students to appreciate the revisions or adjustments which have occurred in that definition over time and what those changes reveal about the development of the American values. Other constructs may include the idea of equality, the idea of right and wrong, the idea of freedom. For this historian interpretive consistency is a virtue. Of course you are welcome to disagree with any of the points of view advanced in HIS 110, but at least you will know just what it is you are challenging.

In addition, the course introduces students to the idea of historical reasoning and the methods of history. Because students frequently take HIS 110 to fulfill a General Education requirement, and hardly intend to major in history, no prior background in American history is expected or anticipated. However, the course is a rigorous and challenging academic venture. No "Mama's Knee" or high school history in HIS 110. Above all, we hope that you will enjoy learning American history—some of you for the first time!

Generations

Students will investigate three of the most crucial generations or periods that shaped the character of the American nation:

- The American Revolution: 1763–1800
- The Emergent Nation: 1801–1848
- The Civil War Era: 1848–1877

American revolutionaries launched the first full-scale republic *in a millennium*. Because today's Americans can imagine no idea of government other than a republic—even a democracy—it is crucial to define this Revolution and place it into its 18th century context. What did it mean to create a nation with no monarch? And no hereditary aristocracy? And no established national religion? And no permanent standing army? How did the revolutionaries define government by consent? What ideological, political and moral values derive from republicanism?

Please note that this idea of revolution extends beyond the protest movements that led to separation from England and the War for Independence that followed.

The ideas about republicanism evolved considerably during the long era from 1763 to 1800. Thus we define the American Revolution by including the conversion from state sovereignty to a national sovereignty in the establishment of the Constitution, the Bill of Rights, the launching of the new nation under Presidents Washington and Adams. The period also includes the critical election of 1800, which did so much to initiate our adversarial two-party system and to advance an alternative new vision for America's future. In this period primary issues to be weighed include the causes and consequences of independence from Great Britain; the shift in sovereignty from the Articles of Confederation to the Constitution and the impact of that shift; the qualities of national leadership; and the beginning of popular participation in American politics.

The second period opens with the presidency of Thomas Jefferson. We consider Jefferson's presidency and the events during the Virginia presidential dynasty (Madison and Monroe). In this period we discuss the development of the American people into a growing form of democratic participation in government and a growing ideology of individualism and rising middle class preeminence under President Andrew Jackson. The delicate political balance between national and sectional interests is also of major consideration, particularly in light of westward expansion and the influence of slavery on American values. The rise of protection for private property rights against popular state-based majorities is examined through considering significant judicial decisions of the Supreme Court under Chief Justice John Marshall of Virginia and then under his successor, Chief Justice Roger B. Taney of Maryland.

The impact of the reform movements of the 1830s is noted and evaluated—a variety of exemplars are examined, from an array of causes, including public education, free homesteads, pacifism, communitarianism, and, of course, abolitionism. These "isms" will be contrasted with the hardening of Southern ideological arteries directed to the protection of the institution of slavery. The defenses for that institution, together with the influence of Southern attitudes on national policy, will be carefully examined. The quality of leadership, as in the first period, remains a major subject for study.

The third period begins with appreciation of the impact of the War against Mexico upon the single most crucial issue leading to the American Civil War, namely the problem of slavery in the territories. Every major event of the 1850s, in the retrospect of some, led inexorably and directly to the bloodiest war in the entire 19th century. From the Compromise of 1850, to the Kansas-Nebraska Act of 1854, to the Dred Scott case three years later, to the election of Abraham Lincoln in 1860, we examine alternative scenarios to this cruel maelstrom.

The Civil War period affirmed national union and sovereignty, ended the institution of slavery, and established civil equality for freed people through the Civil Rights Acts of 1866 and 1875 and, of course, the 13th, 14th and 15th amendments. Investigation also focuses on the relationship between the centralizing tendencies of the Lincoln Administration during the Civil War and the prospects for emancipation. There is significant examination of the variant ideologies and motives of the Republicans who enacted the rights-granting documents for freed people. The content of course concludes with the dramatically altered relationship of the United States and the States in the 14th Amendment and the demise of the Reconstruction process. As in the first two periods the quality of national leadership is again a consideration.

Introduction to the Historian's Process

It has been noted that the presentation of the content of HIS 110 is grounded in interpretive consistency. Students will also learn to develop their own interpretive consistency by understanding the political and moral criteria by which to make historical judgments and apply those criteria at different moments in time about comparable decisions. To achieve interpretive consistency students engage in the practice of historical analysis and evaluation of historical decisions. You learn to ask the questions that professional historians ask. You adopt a historical outlook.

Sometimes students stand outside the past, making historical judgments from the evidence that current perspective provides. You also project yourselves into the time frame of people at earlier contexts in history, into what historians call "historical cosmology," to comprehend how contemporaries viewed the historical drama in which they were participating. Students learn to interpret, analyze and evaluate the significance of events in a consistent manner. How might a woolens importer react to the Stamp Act of 1765? Would a frontier farmer in 1812 favor a war against England? How would humanitarians in Philadelphia in the 1830s feel about moving Indian tribes west of the Mississippi River? Would poor white farmers in Virginia support Southern secession from the United States?

These and a myriad of additional queries will be considered within the context of the time frame in which individuals confronted them. Students in time learn to steer clear of what historians call "presentism," or "present-mindedness," the unrecognized projection of your own 21st values upon those living in the past. You learn to avoid the error of this practice, identified by the French thinker, Voltaire, as "playing tricks on the dead."

Furthermore, students learn a process for presenting their historical ideas. You learn to create thesis statements, to utilize evidence, to detect subjectivity and bias. You learn to distinguish between the concepts of the 21st century and those of earlier moments in time. Through quizzes and exams student hone their ability to organize historical material, to develop an empirical approach, and to write cogently and accurately. The course also introduces ethical standards in research, historical analysis and writing by considering such issues of plagiarism and the validity of internet sources. There is an emphasis on clear, accurate historical writing.

In particular students learn to identify and construct thesis statements and support them with evidence, analyze the nature of evidence, so as to distinguish between a fact and a personal opinion and between significant fact and detail; pinpoint the viewpoint, bias or subjective position of an author or speaker by examining his or her language; write a short coherent essay that poses a thesis and proves it with factual historical evidence; quote, summarize, paraphrase and cite historical sources in writing examination.

Student Learning Outcomes

These three outcomes will be assessed and analyzed in order to determine an appropriate grade for each student. Students know in advance that these are the primary learning outcomes. At the conclusion of HIS 110 you will be able to demonstrate ability to:

- [content] narrate and analyze significant events in American history from 1763 to 1877. Explain what happened, why it happened, and what it means;
- [context] take positions on historical issues from the viewpoint of someone living at the time of an event and examine why that position was taken and others were not;
- [process] write a coherent historical essay that poses a clear thesis and uses factual historical evidence to prove the validity of the thesis.

Use of Internet Sources

Students must be extremely careful in consulting and citing for assignments any web-based sites. Official documents—or other primary sources—are certainly appropriate. But the dangers of internet sources are twofold. First, it is a momentous temptation to copy materials from websites and merely state the name of the site. This is akin to plagiarism, since the genuine source may not be given. Second, Internet sources may be unreliable. In some cases they may be the province of someone with a political agenda or social position. They are all difficult to corroborate. Misuse of internet materials by learners will result in severe academic discredit.

Support for Students in HIS 110

The jumbo size of this version of HIS 110 requires that the material be presented as a set of lectures. It is doubtful that many students have learned history in any class with this number of students. Indeed, it is unlikely that you have experienced sustained lecturing in your collegiate academic experience. The size of this lecture class certainly differs from the cozy personal, interactive discussion classes that most students have experienced. Consequently, certain students may feel that they have lost their identity as individual learners in this large class. Some students, conversely, relish the anonymity the class permits. Some of you may need steady assurance that what you are learning is what you should be learning. Some students need practice in critical thinking. Some need assistance in articulating thoughts in appropriate English. You may want to review your work both before and after you submit it.

No matter who you are the faculty members of HIS 110 want to work with you as individually as you may wish. There are several means to accomplish this end:

- Office Hours: please make an appointment for a conference on any subject (and please keep the appointment). There are numerous times available. Some of you may show up every week. We are delighted to honor all requests for conferences. Sign up and show up!
- E-mail Chatter: at any time, but especially before and after quizzes and exams students are welcome to contact any of us for academic assistance. We will help you, of course, but please do not expect that we will answer the questions for you. *Students who miss class for good reasons may email their quizzes or exams to us. **We will not accept e-mailed work if we think you just blew off the class and are using e-mail as a substitute way of submitting assignments.***
- Rewritten Exams: we encourage you to rewrite your exam if you are dissatisfied with the grade you received. Or if you think you can improve your performance, by all means rewrite the exam or that part of the exam that you wish to improve. This is good practice for developing historical reasoning and for improving your writing prowess. This offer applies to exams but not quizzes

Conclusion

In summary: you are offered constant opportunities to grapple with the growth and development of America as a nation and as a culture over a significant period of time in our history. How can a Constitution written in 1787 still apply in 1877? How could a nation established to meet the needs of the white male leadership of a small and essentially rural and agrarian society remain functionally dynamic in an emerging industrial and increasingly urban nation? How did Americans respond to the explosion of population, the force of territorial expansion, the trial of civil war, the thrust of technology, the impact of economic dislocation, and, indeed, the rise of democracy?

You are cordially invited to inquire into these matters in HIS 110. Bring to this experience your freshest ideas and your most skeptical frame of mind. Trash what you learned on your mama's knee!

Richard Allan Gerber
Professor of History
Southern Connecticut State University

Graphs

Feature Essays

Preface

"AMERICAN DESTINY"—THESE WORDS, SO LADEN WITH PORTENT, may strike some readers as an unsuitable title for a sober work of history. Such words have been invoked on behalf of countless partisan causes and feverish enthusiasms: in John Louis O'Sullivan's 1845 editorial proclaiming it "our manifest destiny to overspread the continent allotted by Providence for the free development of our yearly multiplying millions"; in Daniel Webster's terse repudiation of the looming sectional crisis: "One country, one constitution, one destiny"; in Walt Whitman's celebration, after that crisis had erupted in civil war, of "one common indivisible destiny for ALL"; and in Franklin D. Roosevelt's reference during the Great Depression to his generation's "rendezvous with destiny." Modern politicians have found such expressions irresistible; Ronald Reagan—perhaps unwittingly—invoked puritan theology when he told a Republican gathering: "We will achieve our destiny to be a shining city on a hill for all mankind to see." George W. Bush, in his 2005 inaugural, reaffirmed the nation's commitment to freedom "by making every citizen an agent of his or her own destiny."

Even the nation's critics have been obliged to address the popular belief in an American destiny, if only to repudiate it. For instance, in 1853 Henry David Thoreau bristled that the American people might "go their way to their manifest destiny, a filibustering toward heaven by the great western route"; he intended to look in a different direction. In 1862 Frederick Douglass asserted that "the destiny of America" was also the destiny of black Americans. One hundred and one years later, Martin Luther King, Jr., writing from a jail in Birmingham, Alabama, resurrected Douglass's words: Insofar as "the goal of America is freedom," he declared, "our destiny is tied up with America's destiny." Suffragist Elizabeth Cady Stanton similarly feared for the nation unless it allowed each woman to become "arbiter of her own destiny."

But if most Americans have accepted the concept of a national purpose, they have endlessly debated where the nation was headed and the nature of the force impelling it there. Some have discerned the hand of God lifting the nation up—or perhaps hurling it down. Others have claimed that the nation's destiny was dictated by accident of geography or economics, by the "laws" of social evolution or the "spirit" of democratic liberalism, by the "patterns" of demography or "processes" of modernity, and so on. Our book, however, maintains that no single model explains the complexity of American history. Because historians are poor prophets, we make no attempt to peer into the future. For us, the concept of an American destiny describes a pervasive if inchoate longing that has exerted a powerful hold on the American imagination.

The subtitle—"Narrative of a Nation"—may also strike readers as provocative. Some historians contend that the diverse peoples of the United States cannot be encompassed within the analytical boundaries of a single nation. Consequently, we have not attempted a history of "the American people." Rather, we describe how the voices and actions of its many peoples have produced a particular political structure—the United States, a single nation—and how that nation has in turn influenced the lives of everyone.

Other historians object to the subjectivity of narrative history. But all history is subjective. Historians decide, quite arbitrarily, which stories to tell and how to tell them. Sources are incomplete and biased, our judgments more art than science. We have tried, by digging into the muck of the past, to haul out the bits that make sense, and to present them so as to tell a coherent story. Though some contend that the past is too murky to yield clear meanings, we persist because no one is satisfied with the mud.

But why bother? History, some say, is dead; let it rest in peace so that we can focus on our own lives.

This view is wrong. The past continuously radiates its influence on the present. To underscore this thesis, this edition of *American Destiny* includes a major new feature: Each chapter opens with a discussion of a contemporary issue and shows its relation to the themes of the chapter.

A few examples concern institutions that, though founded long ago, still influence our lives. The copyright provisions of the Constitution, debated over two centuries ago, prevent students from freely downloading songs on the Internet (Chapter 5). The emergence of global corporate behemoths like Wal-Mart, whose revenues exceed the gross national product of Saudi Arabia, was prefigured by the establishment and growth of great industrial corporations during the late nineteenth century (Chapter 17). Our paychecks are smaller because Franklin D. Roosevelt and Congress established Social Security to provide federal protection for the elderly and disabled during the Great Depression (Chapter 26).

Sometimes the past defines the hopes and prospects of entire peoples. The desperate poverty of reservation Indians, and their compensatory ownership of casinos, resulted from the destruction of tribal life during the last half of the nineteenth century (Chapter 16). The decision to use aptitude tests to select officers during World War II led to the Scholastic Aptitude Test (SAT), an obligatory rite of passage for many college students today (Chapter 28).

Sometimes insights about the present inform our thinking about the past. When harassed by telephone solicitors demanding payment of credit card bills, we better appreciate the personal struggles of debtors such as Thomas Jefferson and understand his antipathy to public debt (Chapter 6). Our own frustration with a political discourse that has been truncated into sound bites makes us long for the thoughtful deliberations of Lincoln and Douglas (Chapter 13).

Sometimes knowledge of the past alters our view of contemporary issues. An awareness of the fratricidal slaughter of the American Civil War helps make sense of the "senseless violence" among religious sects in post-Saddam Iraq (Chapter 14). Similarly, the fact that the United States wrested Texas and much of the Southwest from a young Mexican nation deepens our perspective on illegal Mexican immigration today (Chapter 11). We better comprehend the restrictions of freedoms entailed by the Patriot Act following September 11, 2001, in light of restrictions imposed during other wars (Chapter 23).

People have always looked to the past, whether chronicling a hunt for mammoth beasts in a cave painting, or recounting the foundation stories of their civilizations in the Bible or the Mahabharata. Our lives have grown out of the fertile soil of the past, many of whose elements cannot be readily analyzed or even discerned. For us, a less elusive element, but surely an important one, is the American nation, itself the product of the myriad actions, ideas, and forces described in the following pages. By considering its past, we better understand ourselves—and perhaps our own destiny.

New to This Edition

In addition to the new chapter introductions described above, this edition of *American Destiny* differs from its predecessors in several other ways:

- Each chapter has been revised to reflect new scholarship, to offer new perspectives, and to streamline and sharpen the prose. We have also restructured several chapters and compressed others to improve readability. Chapter 10, "The Making of Middle-Class America," combines coverage in the previous edition's Chapters 10 and 11, streamlining less essential detail to make the narrative more manageable for students. Subsequent chapters have been renumbered; in addition to the prologue, there are now 32 chapters, one fewer than in the previous edition. To sharpen the focus of Chapter 16, "The Conquest of the West," sections on post-reconstruction governments have been reorganized and moved to Chapter 20, "Politics: Local, State, and National." Chapter 32, "Misdemeanors and High Crimes," has been significantly updated.

- Archaeologists, anthropologists, and historians have literally unearthed a treasure of knowledge about the earliest inhabitants of what is now the United States. The prologue and first two chapters include vastly expanded sections on American Indians.

- This edition includes two new "Re-Viewing the Past" essays: *Cinderella Man*, a film starring Russell Crowe and Renée Zellweger, about a boxer's unlikely rise to become heavyweight champion during the Great Depression (Chapter 26), and *Good Night, and Good Luck*, a film starring George Clooney, depicting TV broadcaster Edward R. Murrow's confrontation with Wisconsin senator Joseph McCarthy in the 1950s (Chapter 28). We have also added questions for discussion in these features to spark class discussion or writing assignments.

Enduring Features

Debating the Past

Historians argue about nearly every aspect of the nation's complex past, and each chapter includes a "Debating the Past" essay on an important historiographical debate. Because such issues are hard to fix in memory, we have provided a photograph or picture to "trigger" the historiographical essay. For example, the question for Chapter 2—"Were Puritan Communities Peaceable?"—is prefaced by a contemporary painting of a seventeenth-century puritan village, with a river meandering through a nearby meadow. The question for Chapter 11—"Did the Frontier Change Women's Lives?"—commences with a photograph of a farm woman hauling buffalo chips in a wheelbarrow. Each essay concludes with a list of the major works cited. Our final debate—"Do Historians Ever Get It Right?" (Chapter 32)—poses a question that we hope will stimulate discussion.

Re-Viewing the Past

The "Re-Viewing the Past" feature shows how particular movies shape our understanding of history. Directors often spend scores of millions of dollars to show what the past looked like. For example, *The Crucible* (Chapter 2) provides a vivid evocation of puritan Salem, and *Saving Private Ryan* (Chapter 27) of the Normandy invasion of World War II. Yet moviemakers often alter people and events for dramatic purposes. We hope that these "Re-Viewing the Past" essays will provide guidance on which of Hollywood's stories contain some measure of truthfulness, which do not, and how viewers can tell the difference. The essays also serve as reminder that all historical narratives are interpretations, and all contain biases of selection, presentation, voice, and argument. When considering the past, people should be critical of what they see—and read.

Mark C. Carnes
John A. Garraty

Supplements for Instructors and Students

For Qualified College Adopters

Name of Supplement	Available in Print	Available Online	Instructor or Student Supplement	Description
Instructor's Resource Center (IRC)		✓	Instructor Supplement	Web site for downloading relevant supplements. Password protected. Please contact your local Pearson representative for an access code. *www.ablongman.com/irc*
MyHistoryLab		✓	Both	With the best of Longman's multimedia solutions for history in one easy-to-use place, MyHistoryLab offers students and instructors a state-of-the art interactive instructional solution for your U.S. history survey course. Built around a complete e-book version of this text, MyHistoryLab provides numerous study aids, review materials, and activities to make the study of history an enjoyable learning experience. Icons in the e-book link directly to relevant materials in context, many of which are assignable. MyHistoryLab includes several hundred primary source documents, videos, images, and maps, all with accompanying analysis questions. It also includes a History Bookshelf with 50 of the most commonly assigned books in U.S. history courses and a History Toolkit with guided tutorials and helpful links. MyHistoryLab is flexible and easy-to-use as a supplement to a traditional lecture course or to administer as a completely online course. *www.myhistorylab.com*
MyHistoryKit for American History		✓	Both	Online package of study materials, gradable quizzes and over 1,000 primary sources organized generically by typical American history themes to support your U.S. history survey text. Access code required. *www.myhistorykit.com*
American History Study Site		✓	Both	Online package of practice tests, Web links, and flashcards organized generically by major history topics to support your U.S. history survey text. Open access. *www.longmanamericanhistory.com*
Instructor's Manual	✓	✓	Instructor Supplement	Each chapter includes a chapter overview, lecture supplements, and questions for class discussion. Text specific.
Test Bank	✓	✓	Instructor Supplement	Contains thousands of conceptual, objective, and essay questions. Text specific.

(continued)

Name of Supplement	Available in Print	Available Online	Instructor or Student Supplement	Description
Computerized Test Bank	✓	✓	Instructor Supplement	Includes all items in the printed test bank. Questions can be edited, and tests can be printed in several different formats. Text specific.
PowerPoint Presentation		✓	Instructor Supplement	Designed to accompany *The American Nation*, the comprehensive version of this text, these slides contain an outline of each chapter of the text and full-color images of maps and figures.
Digital Transparency Masters		✓	Instructor Supplement	Designed to accompany *The American Nation*, the comprehensive version of this text, these digital transparency masters are available exclusively on the Instructor's Resource Center. *www.ablongman.com/irc*
Comprehensive American History Digital Transparency Masters		✓	Instructor Supplement	Vast collection of American history transparency masters. Available exclusively on the Instructor's Resource Center. *www.ablongman.com/irc*
Discovering American History Through Maps and Views Digital Transparency Masters		✓	Instructor Supplement	Set of 140 full-color digital transparency masters includes cartographic and pictorial maps, views, photos; urban plans and building diagrams; and works of art. Available exclusively on the Instructor's Resource Center. *www.ablongman.com/irc*
History Digital Media Archive	CD		Instructor Supplement	Contains electronic images, interactive and static maps, and video. Available on CD only.
Visual Archives of American History, Updated Edition	CD		Instructor Supplement	Contains dozens of narrated vignettes and videos as well as hundreds of photos and illustrations. Available on CD only.
Study Guide	✓		Student Supplement	Contains chapter overviews, learning objectives, identifications, mapping exercises, multiple-choice and essay questions, and critical thinking exercises. Available in two volumes. Text specific.
Vango Notes		✓	Student Supplement	Downloadable MP3 audio topic reviews. Includes major themes, key terms, practice tests, and rapid reviews. *www.vangonotes.com*
Study Card for American History	✓		Student Supplement	Distills course information down to the basics, helping students quickly master the fundamentals and prepare for exams.
Research Navigator Guide	✓	✓	Student Supplement	A book that contains an access code to EBSCO ContentSelect, *The New York Times*, and "Best of the Web."
Longman American History Atlas	✓		Both	100 full-color maps.

For Qualified College Adopters

Name of Supplement	Available in Print	Available Online	Instructor or Student Supplement	Description
Mapping America: A Guide to Historical Geography	✓		Student Supplement	18 exercises explore the role of geography in history.
Voices of *The American Nation*	✓		Student Supplement	Two-volume collection of primary sources, organized to correspond to the table of contents of *American Destiny*.
America Through the Eyes of Its People	✓		Student Supplement	Two-volume comprehensive anthology of primary sources expertly balances social and political history and includes up-to-date narrative material.
American History Timeline	✓		Student Supplement	Gives students a chronological context to help them understand important political, social, economic, cultural, and technological events.
Sources of the African-American Past	✓		Student Supplement	This collection of primary sources covers key themes in the African-American experience.
Women and the National Experience	✓		Student Supplement	Primary source reader contains both classic and unusual documents describing the history of women in the United States.
Reading the American West	✓		Student Supplement	Primary sources in the history of the American West.
A Short Guide to Writing About History	✓		Student Supplement	Teaches students to write cogent history papers.
American History Firsthand: Working with Primary Sources	✓		Student Supplement	This two-volume collection of loose leaf reproduced primary sources exposes students to archival research.
Longman Penguin Putnam Inc. Value Packs	✓		Student Supplement	A variety of Penguin-Putnam texts are available at discounted prices when bundled with *American Destiny*. Complete list of available titles at www.ablongman.com/penguin.
Library of American Biography Series	✓		Student Supplement	Renowned series of biographies that focus on figures who had a significant impact on American history. Complete list at www.ablongman.com/html/lab.

About the Authors

© 1999 Joel Gordon

MARK C. CARNES received his undergraduate degree from Harvard and his Ph.D. in history from Columbia University, where he studied and trained with Professor John A. Garraty. The Ann Whitney Olin Professor of History at Barnard College, Columbia University, Professor Carnes has chaired both the departments of History and American Studies at Barnard. In addition to this textbook, Carnes and Garraty have co-authored *Mapping America's Past: A Historical Atlas* and are co-general editors of the 24-volume *American National Biography*, for which they were awarded the Waldo Leland Prize of the American Historical Association, the Dartmouth Prize of the American Library Association, and the Hawkins Prize of the American Association of Publishers. In addition, Carnes has published numerous books in American social and cultural history, including *Past Imperfect: History According to the Movies* (1995), *Novel History: Historians and Novelists Confront America's Past (and Each Other)* (2001), and *Invisible Giants: 50 Americans That Shaped the Nation but Missed the History Books* (2002). Carnes also created "Reacting to the Past," which won the Theodore Hesburgh Award, sponsored by TIAA-CREF, as the outstanding pedagogical innovation of 2004.

"Garraty preaches a particular doctrine on historical writing, expounding on the details of a complex process whereby the murky abstractions of the past are distilled into clean, clear narrative. He insists that the writer's sole duty is to readers. This literary alchemy is all the more wondrous for being so devoid of artifice," Carnes observes.

© 1999 Joel Gordon

JOHN A. GARRATY holds a Ph.D. from Columbia University and an L.H.D. from Michigan State University, and is Gouverneur Morris Professor Emeritus of History at Columbia. He is the author, co-author, and editor of scores of books and articles, among them biographies of Silas Wright, Henry Cabot Lodge, Woodrow Wilson, George W. Perkins, and Theodore Roosevelt. Along with Mark Carnes, he is co-editor of the *American National Biography*. Garraty has also contributed a volume—*The New Commonwealth*—to the New American Nation series and edited *Quarrels That Shaped the Constitution*. He was a member of the Board of Directors of *American Heritage* magazine and served as both vice president and head of the teaching division of the American Historical Association. His areas of research interest include the Gilded Age, unemployment (in a historical sense), and the Great Depression of the 1930s. Of his collaboration with Carnes on *American Destiny*, Garraty says, "One of our favorite topics of discussion over these many years has been the craft of historical writing. We share a commitment to clarity and conciseness. We strive to avoid jargon and verbiage. We believe that while the political history of the nation provides a useful narrative framework, its people are what give the story meaning."

AMERICAN DESTINY

Beginnings

IN AUGUST 2005, HURRICANE KATRINA FORMED IN THE CARIBBEAN, swept north, gathered strength in the Gulf of Mexico, and slammed into the Gulf Coast, swamping New Orleans and the surrounding region. Nearly 1,500 people died. Property losses approached $100 billion.

Many blamed the intensity of the hurricane on global warming, a rise in temperatures that most scientists believe is aggravated by burning fossil fuels. They pointed out that hurricanes are fueled by the heat of tropical waters, and that during the 1990s ocean temperatures had increased a full degree Fahrenheit. During the summer of 2005, the hottest on record, the Gulf of Mexico was 5 degrees warmer than usual.

Others responded that evidence of man-made global warming is inconclusive and that any general trend in rising temperatures is part of a natural cycle. They noted that over the past three million years, the earth has experienced alternating cycles of warming and cooling, each cycle lasting about 100,000 years.[1] Many of these cycles predated even the earliest ancestors of man.

While scientists may argue over the causes of current rising temperatures, most agree that dramatic climate changes have altered history. We need only look to our past. The story of America in this sense commences over 100,000 years ago, after the last long period of global warming had ended. During that period, temperatures dropped and a prolonged ice age ensued. Ice sheets near the poles expanded. Some became nearly as broad as Australia and over 10,000 feet thick—the height of ten Empire State Buildings. Giant ice slabs entombed northern Europe and North America. As the slabs moved, they gouged deep holes in the earth's crust, forming the beds of the Great Lakes and Finger Lakes.

About 20,000 years ago the cooling cycle ended and the earth warmed. As the glaciers melted, they unloosed torrents of water that filled the beds of the Great

---

[1]*What causes the cyclical shifts in global temperature is not known for sure. Some point to long-term shifts in the energy output of the sun, wobbles in the earth's orbit, and complicated convergences of other factors.*

Lakes and Finger Lakes and scored the paths of the Mississippi, Missouri, Ohio, and Hudson rivers. The retreating glaciers also left behind huge deposits of rock; examples include Long Island and Staten Island.

Even before any humans had arrived in the Americas, climate had transformed the world they would inhabit. Climatic factors, too, determined who would first set foot in the hemisphere, where they would do so, and how they would survive.

First Peoples

The first human beings emerged in Africa more than two million years ago. Some devised stone tools, thus inaugurating the Paleolithic revolution, a life based on hunting and finding edible nuts, berries, and plants. The Paleolithic people who most resemble us in their aptitude for tools and facility with language appeared more recently, perhaps fewer than 40,000 years ago. They spread through much of Africa, Europe, and Asia, displacing those humans that had preceded them.

For thousands of years the frozen wasteland of Siberia remained impenetrable to these toolmaking humans. But as the supply of big mammals grew increasingly scarce elsewhere in Asia, hunters ventured farther north. What drew them especially were woolly mammoths. Weighing 16,000 pounds, about as much as a large elephant, a single mammoth provided enough meat to feed two dozen hunters nearly all winter. Its fur could be worn as clothing and its fat could be burned for heat. Its bones, when stretched with fur, functioned as simple tents. A woolly mammoth was a kind of movable mall, and hunters regarded it with the avidity of shoppers at a clearance sale. As mammoths moved deeper into the arctic tundra, so did their human predators.

Some of the hunters crossed what is now the Bering Strait to Alaska. What happened next is a matter of conjecture. Eventually these Paleo-Indians came upon lush grasslands, watered by the streams and lakes of the melting ice. Then they happened upon an astonishing scene: vast herds of large mammals. There were plenty of mammoths, but also equally enormous mastodons, with massive legs and stout feet; giant beavers the size of bears; 20-foot-long ground sloths weighing over 6,000 pounds; strange monsters such as glyptodonts, which resembled armadillos but weighed over a ton, and also countless camels, horses, cheetahs, caribou, and deer.

The Demise of the Big Mammals

With so much available game, the hunters' skills improved. They chiseled long stone blades especially designed to penetrate thick hides. Archaeologists have named these hunters after their ingenious blades, first found at Clovis, New Mexico.

WHO—OR WHAT—KILLED THE BIG MAMMALS?

Debating the Past

Paul S. Martin (1984) estimated that Clovis peoples, numbering several hundred thousand at their peak, hunted to extinction some 93 billion pounds of animals throughout the western hemisphere. Critics of what has been dubbed the "overkill" hypothesis insisted that Martin's rendering of a swarm of human predators devouring entire species was far-fetched. Clovis "hunters" were mostly scavengers who rarely succeeded in killing woolly mammoths (see museum reconstruction below) and other huge beasts. The big mammals died off because the climate of North America grew far warmer and drier after 13,000 B.C.E. This damaged the ecosystem on which the big, furry mammals depended. Proponents of the "overkill" hypothesis responded that the big mammals had previously endured millions of years of climate fluctuations, some far more severe than the waning of the last Ice Age. That all these species would vanish during a climate shift that coincided with the arrival of human predators seems an improbable coincidence. And if the climate change was so extreme, why did it not result in the demise of species of birds and fish? Alfred Crosby (1986) also showed that the disappearance of many species of large mammals in Australia coincided with the

arrival of human beings to that continent. This debate has nevertheless raged for nearly a half century. It reminds us that history is not fixed; facts change, as does our way of looking at them.

Paul S. Martin and Richard G. Klein, eds., *Quaternary Extinctions* (1984), which includes Martin's essay and also those of supporters and critics; also Alfred Crosby, *Ecological Imperialism* (1986).

Loosed upon herds of unwary animals, these hunters seemingly slaughtered them almost at will, or stampeded them over cliffs. Archaeologists have found Clovis blades in nearly every state of the United States and even at the southern tip of South America.

And then the big mammals were gone. By about 8000 B.C.E.,[2] most of the large mammals of North America had become extinct, including the mammoths, mastodons, saber-toothed cats, giant beavers, bears, horses, and camels. Whether the hunters had killed off the big mammals or the warming climate caused the blubbery, heavily furred animals to become extinct is a source of debate. (See Debating the Past, "Who—or What—Killed the Big Mammals?" p. 3). What is beyond dispute is that the absence of large mammals profoundly influenced the subsequent course of American history.

The Archaic Period: A World Without Big Mammals

The loss of the big mammals marked the end of the Clovis culture. Descendants of Paleo-Indians had to find new sources of food, clothing, and shelter. The ensuing period, termed "archaic" and comprising about one hundred human generations, was characterized by scarcity. Prolonged droughts or severe winters resulted in starvation. Among the Indians north of Mexico, in what is now the United States, there was little if any population growth.

Eventually the Archaic Indians adapted to particular habitats. In woodland areas east of the Mississippi River, they learned to hunt small animals, like rabbits and beaver, that had previously not been worth the bother; or they learned to find stealthy animals like bear and caribou or to sneak up on skittish ones like elk and deer. On the Great Plains, Indians thrived on bison, which could be stampeded over cliffs.

Most Archaic bands searched for game continuously. They migrated from one place to another according to a seasonal schedule, often returning to the same campsites year after year. In the spring, when fish spawn, Archaic Indians moved to rivers and streams. In the summer, they hunted small animals. In the fall, they shifted to upland woods to gather protein-rich nuts, some of which they hid in caves for emergencies. In winter, they often migrated to forests in search of deer, bear, and caribou.

Often perilously hungry, they discovered that sunflower seeds and sumpweed (a type of spinach) were edible. Over 2,000 years ago, peoples in the Midwest planted sunflower and sumpweed seeds. They were the first inhabitants of what is now the United States to domesticate plants, although most Archaic peoples remained primarily hunters and foragers.

---

[2]B.C.E. *stands for "before the common era," and* C.E. *for "common era." These abbreviations are synonyms for* B.C. *and* A.D., *respectively. In this book dates not followed by* B.C.E. *refer to* C.E.

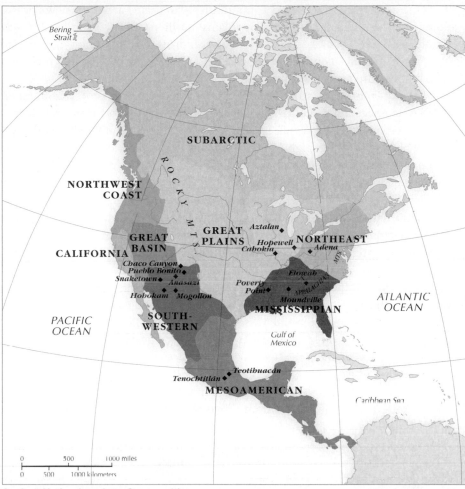

Ancient Native American Communities

The First Sedentary Communities

Some Archaic peoples happened on unusually rich habitats that could sustain them throughout the year. Indians living along the coast and rivers of the Pacific Northwest and Alaska found fish to be so plentiful that they could be scooped up in baskets. These people made nets and fishhooks. Eventually they built boats out of bark and animal skins. Those living along the New England coast discovered a seemingly inexhaustible supply of shellfish. But for even these people, survival was a full-time job.

As tribes remained longer in one area, they began to regard it as their own. They built more substantial habitations, developed pottery to carry water and cook food, and buried the dead with distinctive rituals in special places, often marked with mounds.

One of the earliest sedentary communities was located at what is now Poverty Point, on the Mississippi River floodplains north of Delhi, Louisiana. It was founded around 1500 B.C.E. Poverty Point Indians, like those of the Pacific Northwest, became adept at fishing with nets. They also supplemented their diet with bottle gourd seeds and squash.

Poverty Point peoples filled countless grass baskets with earth and dumped them onto enormous mounds. One mound, shaped like an octagon, had six terraced levels on which were built some 400 to 600 houses. Another was more than 700 feet long and 70 feet high. Viewed from above, it resembled a hawk. In all, the mounds consisted of over a million cubic yards of dirt.

The enormity of their construction projects reveals much about Poverty Point peoples. They could not have diverted so much time and energy to construction if they were not proficient at acquiring food. Moreover, while most Archaic bands were egalitarian, with little differentiation in status, the social structure of Poverty Point was hierarchical. Leaders conceived the plans and directed the labor to build the earthworks.

After about a thousand years, Poverty Point was abandoned. No one knows why. Several hundred years later, scores of smaller mound communities, known as Adena, sprouted in the Ohio and Mississippi river valleys. The inhabitants of these communities were also hunters and foragers who cultivated plants in their spare time. The Adena communities lasted several hundred years.

Around 200 B.C.E., another cluster of mound builders, known as Hopewell, flourished in Ohio and Illinois. Hopewell mounds were often shaped into squares, circles, and cones; some, viewed from above, resembled birds or serpents. Around 400 C.E., the Hopewell sites were abandoned.

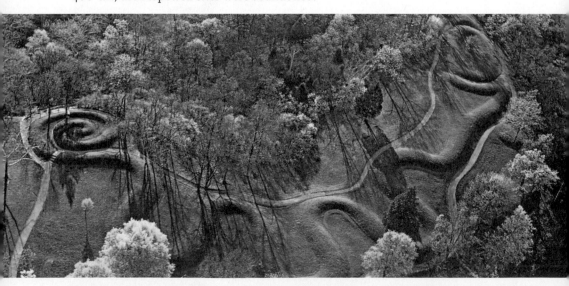

An aerial view of the Great Serpent Mound in Locust Grove, Ohio, built by Mississippian peoples around 1100 C.E. Some Mississippian mounds were in the shape of squares, circles, or cones, but others resembled hawks or panthers, and still others, like this one, depicted a mythical creature or perhaps a snake devouring an egg. Scholars speculate that the shapes reflected religious beliefs or functioned as territorial markers for different clans.

The impermanence of these communities serves as a reminder that the transition from a nomadic existence of hunting and foraging to a settled life based on agriculture was slow and uneven. For the Archaic Indians living north of the Rio Grande, this was about to change. For people living in what is now Central America, it already had.

The Maize Revolution

Maize did not exist seven thousand years ago. But around 5000 B.C.E., perhaps far earlier, Indians in southern Mexico interbred various species of grasses, exploiting subtle changes and perhaps significant mutations. Eventually they created maize. A geneticist writing in *Science* in 2003 declared this to be "arguably man's first, and perhaps his greatest, feat of genetic engineering." The original ears were too small to provide much food value, but within several thousand years farmers in Central America had developed maize that resembled modern corn.

The Neolithic revolution—the transition from hunting and gathering to farming—had come to Central America. Within another thousand years or so, nearly every valley in central Mexico bristled with cornstalks. Population grew and cities emerged. Surplus corn allowed some people to specialize in activities unrelated to food production. By 100 C.E. Teotihuacan, 40 miles north of what is now Mexico City, had a population approaching 100,000 and featured miles of paved streets and a pyramid as large as those of Egypt. Mesoamerica was nearing its classical period, culminating in the great corn-growing civilizations of the Mayans, Aztecs, and Incas.

Eventually corn cultivation leapfrogged the deserts of northern Mexico and was adopted by the Indians of the Southwest: the Hohokam and Mogollon of

Scholars have failed to find any historical evidence of wild corn *(right)*. How, then, did it come to be? Some scientists believe that thousands of years ago Indian farmers somehow genetically engineered the transformation of teosinte *(left)*, a wild grass with tiny seeds, to evolve into maize.

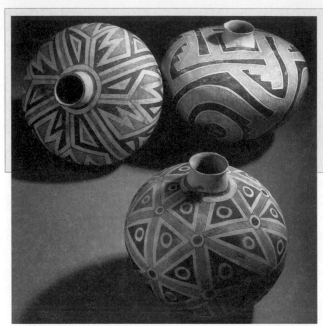

Anasazi earthenware jars, from about 1200 C.E. The development of pottery was part of the ascent of a farming life. Corn could be stored in such jars, warding off starvation in lean winter months. Note the juxtaposition of straight lines and circles, an artistic pattern common among early American peoples.

Arizona and New Mexico; and the Anasazi of the Colorado Plateau. Abandoning their nomadic life, these Indians settled near rivers, built trenches and canals to channel water to the crops, dammed gullies to capture runoff from flash floods, and constructed homes near the cornfields.

Their culture revolved around corn. Sun and water became the focus of their religious beliefs, symbols of life and rebirth. Priest-astronomers carefully measured changes of the seasons. If corn was planted too early, it might shrivel before the late summer rains; if planted too late, it might be destroyed by frost. The centrality of corn to religious beliefs was underscored by the proximity of corn storage to sacred ceremonial pits, known as *kivas*. Corn Mother symbolism, suggesting a relationship between the fertility of the earth and of women, dominated religious practices. Control of the corn surplus was a key to political power.

Despite the aridity and blistering heat of the Southwest, the corn-cultivating peoples increased in number after 800 C.E. The Chaco Canyon, a 22-mile-long gorge in western New Mexico, witnessed the development of a most improbable human habitat. The Anasazi, who grew corn there, carved entire villages into the sandstone and shale cliffs. As population increased, the Anasazi built dozens of towns and villages linked by an elaborate system of roads. The largest of these cliff towns, Pueblo Bonito, had buildings more than five stories tall. The Hohokam constructed an irrigation canal system that spanned hundreds of miles and contained an intricate network of dams, sluices, and headgates. Snaketown, a Hohokam village 250 miles west of modern Phoenix, had a population of several thousand.

These communities were far smaller than those of their mightier neighbors to the south. But the triumph of the corn-growing Anasazi, Hohokam, and Mogollon is measured not by wealth and population figures but by the magnitude of the environmental challenges they overcame.

The Diffusion of Corn

Corn cultivation spread east and north. By 200 C.E., cornfields dotted the southern Mississippi River valley. Thereafter, the advance of corn slowed. Farther north, early cold snaps killed existing varieties of the plant. Moreover, corn cultivation required unremitting labor, and few Indians were eager to subject themselves to its incessant demands. Fields had to be cleared, usually by burning away the undergrowth. Then the soil was hoed using flat stones, clamshells, or the shoulder blades of large animals. After planting, the fields required constant weeding. Ripened corn had to be shucked and dried. Compared to the thrill of the hunt, the taste of game, and the varied tasks associated with a hunting and gathering, farming held little appeal. Males regarded it as a subsidiary activity, a task best relegated to women.

But over time many Indians learned that the alternative to agricultural labor was starvation. Fields farther north and east were cleared and planted with corn, beans, and squash. Old skeletons provide a precise means of tracking corn's advance. When corn is chewed, enzymes in the mouth convert its carbohydrates to sugar, a major cause of dental cavities. Radiocarbon dating of skeletons from the vicinity of what is now St. Louis first shows dental cavities around 700 and those from southern Wisconsin, around 900. By 1000 dental cavities appeared in skeletons throughout the Midwest and the East. Corn had become king.

Population Growth After 800

Corn stimulated population growth. An acre of woodlands fed two or three hunters or foragers; that same acre, planted in corn, provided for as many as 200 people. Hunting and foraging Indians usually found enough to eat in summer and fall, but in winter food sources might disappear. But dried corn, stored in glazed pots or sealed in underground pits, could sustain many people over a long period. Corn cultivators may not have had a particularly nutritious diet, but they could usually survive a long, hard winter.

Corn cultivators also had more children than hunting and gathering peoples. The high caloric corn diet caused women to menstruate at an earlier age, making it possible for them to have more children. Corn also promoted fertility by shortening the duration of breastfeeding. Even toothless infants could be fed a soft mush of boiled corn and could be weaned earlier; once mothers ceased breastfeeding, they were far more likely to become pregnant. Thus while hunter-gathering women would likely conceive no more frequently than once every four years, women who regularly ate corn were likely to have children twice as often.

A sedentary lifestyle promoted population growth in other ways. Infants and toddlers were a nuisance on the trail; some hunting and foraging Indians practiced abortion or even infanticide to ensure mobility and reduce the number of mouths to feed. But farming Indians nearly always could make use of additional hands, even young ones, to help with plowing, hoeing, weeding, and harvesting. Because farmers rarely moved, they built more permanent homes and more successfully sheltered infants from inclement weather and physical dangers.

As in the Southwest, the corn-cultivating peoples of the Mississippi Valley responded to increasing population by clearing more woodland and planting more corn. At first, corn cultivators and hunting-foraging peoples successfully cohabited within the same ecosystem: hunters traded for corn, essential for survival during winter, and corn cultivators traded for game, a source of complex protein. But over time the two groups often came into conflict, and when they did, the much more numerous corn cultivators prevailed.

The corn-cultivating societies expanded west into Dakota, east through the Carolinas, south into Florida, and north into Wisconsin. Their villages consisted of clusters of homes, surrounded by cornfields. They shared a constellation of beliefs and ritual practices. Like the Hopewell, they built burial mounds, but those of the corn cultivators were much larger. Some villages became towns and even small cities. Large temples and granaries and the homes of the governing elite were located on top of the mounds.

The most important and populous of these communities was located in the vicinity of St. Louis. Archaeologists call it Cahokia.

Cahokia: The Hub of Mississippian Culture

By 1000, Cahokia was a major center of trade, shops and crafts, and religious and political activities. It was the first true urban center in what is now the United States. By 1150, at the height of its development, it covered 6 square miles and had about 15,000 inhabitants.

The earthworks at Cahokia included some twenty huge mounds around a downtown plaza, with another 100 large mounds in the outlying areas. The largest mound was 110 feet high, covered 14 acres, and contained 20 million cubic yards of earth. It was probably the largest earthen structure in the Americas. Atop the mound was a 50-foot-high wood-framed temple.

Cahokian society was characterized by sharp class divisions. The elite lived in larger homes and consumed a better and more varied diet (their garbage pits included bones from the best cuts of meat). The corpse of one chieftain was buried upon a bed of 20,000 beaded shells; nearby was a long piece of shaped copper from Lake Superior, several bushels of bird and animal sculptures made of mica, and over 1,000 arrows, many with beautiful quartz or obsidian points.

That the Cahokia had enemies is suggested by the existence of a 3-mile-long wooden palisade surrounding the central core of the city. It consisted of 20,000

An artist's rendering of downtown Cahokia, around 1150 C.E. Cahokia was surrounded by a palisade, made of enormous tree trunks (*left*). On the great mounds within, the elite built homes and performed the ceremonial tasks of Mississippian culture. The open space in the center was probably filled with the stalls of craftspeople.

enormous tree trunks, pounded deep into the ground, interspersed with several dozen watchtowers from which defenders could unloose arrows upon besiegers.

Despite its daunting fortifications, or perhaps because of them, the elite did not command a large army. Its power derived chiefly from its ability to create a compelling religious worldview and express it in tangible symbols. Cahokia was a cultural and religious center rather than a fortress. In the central plaza, skilled workers carved religious figurines from quartz, mica, and galena. Others painted similar symbols on pottery or etched them in copper goods. Lesser chieftains brought corn and other foodstuffs into Cahokia, perhaps as tribute, while the Cahokia rulers reciprocated with gifts of figurines and copper or, in times of famine, grants of surplus corn. In Cahokia, too, priest-astronomers scrutinized the movements of the sun, moon, and stars.

Cahokia dominated a region of several hundred miles. Smaller mound-building communities emerged throughout the eastern woodlands and the Southeast. Two of the largest were Moundville, Alabama, and Etowah, Georgia. Cahokia also established (or perhaps inspired) distant satellite communities. Around 800, Mississippian Indians moved into southern Wisconsin and built Aztalan (in what is now Jefferson County), with similar corn storage depots and large ceremonial mounds surrounding a central plaza.

Like Cahokia, Aztalan erected a massive tree-trunk palisade with watchtowers. Archaeologists have found burned and butchered body parts throughout the ruins, evidence of warfare. Some speculate that the corn-growing Mississippians encroached on the Oneota, a hunting and gathering people, and that the communities long remained hostile.

The Mississippian elites did more than supervise construction of their own massive earthen tombs. They also solved complicated problems of political and social organization.

The Collapse of Urban Centers

Cahokia and Aztalan soon declined. By 1200, Cahokia's population had been reduced to several thousand people; by 1350, it was deserted. Etowah and Moundville went into decline somewhat later.

The major towns and villages of the Southwest civilizations faded as well. By 1200, the inhabitants of Chaco Canyon had vanished and nearly all of the pueblos of the Anasazi had been abandoned. Snaketown and dozens of towns of the Hohokam had become empty ruins, their canals choked with weeds.

What caused the collapse of these communities has long been a source of debate. Some scholars cite protracted droughts during the 1200s and 1300s. Others note that population growth harmed the environment. Slash-and-burn wood clearance thinned the eastern forests, and corn cultivation exhausted the soil. Archaeologists have determined that each Cahokian house required eighty large wooden posts—a half million for the entire city. The palisade at Cahokia consisted of thousands of the trunks of fully grown trees, and it was repeatedly rebuilt. Denuded of big trees, the watershed around Cahokia became susceptible to erosion and flooding, further depleting exhausted topsoils.

The farming Indians of the Southwest also stripped their lands of trees for fuel and for house and kiva construction. The wooden buildings at Chaco Canyon alone required nearly a quarter of a million trees. The irrigation system of the Hohokam harmed the environment in a different way. The canal networks distributed water from the Gila and (aptly named) Salt rivers, and in so doing deposited thousands of tons of mineral salts on cornfields. With little rainfall to leach the soils, the salt residues eventually reached toxic levels.

Crop yields declined as the demand for food in towns and villages was increasing. Studies of human skeletons in Mississippian burial mounds show higher incidences of disease and malnutrition after 1250. What happened next is unclear. Some archaeologists believe that many Mississippian Indians abandoned the cities and villages and quietly reverted to the hunting and foraging life of their Archaic forebears. Others argue that the end was calamitous. Late Mississippian skeletons were smaller and more likely to show signs of disease; they also had more broken bones; often arms, feet, and hands were dismembered. Recurrent famines and disease may have undermined the credibility of elites and the cultural system they supervised, weakening their control of poor urban people as well as chieftains in the hinterlands. The towering log palisades of the Mississippians and the impenetrable cliff dwellings of the Anasazi were manifestations of this collective insecurity.

Warfare became endemic among the corn-growing tribes of the Northeast. By 1300, the Iroquoian peoples of New York and Pennsylvania were building forts with defensive earthworks and palisades. Some tribes joined together to form military alliances. Soil exhaustion, perhaps aggravated by the droughts that had parched the cornfields of the Southwest, may have forced tribes to compete for land and resources. Some scholars propose that gender tensions may have exacerbated these conflicts. Men performed most of the hunting and foraging tasks, while women did most of the work in the cornfields. As corn supplanted game and fish as staples of the diet, women acquired more status and power. To reassert male dominance, men embarked on raids and warfare.

By 1500, nearly all of the large towns had been abandoned. New generations of Indians puzzled over who had inhabited the ruins, or who had erected the massive earthen mounds. The Navajo Indians referred to their predecessors as the "Anasazi," the "Ancient Ones."

The collapse of the cities disrupted trade networks. Some goods continued to move many, many miles, being passed from one tribe to another; but the flow of trade goods slowed to a trickle. Moreover, if the rise of powerful urban communities had forced earlier groups to band together, the demise of the urban communities encouraged the breakup of large groups and tribes. Hundreds, perhaps thousands of small bands lived in relative isolation.

To them, the great Aztec city of Tenochtitlán, beyond the Mexican desert, was only a rumor. Of Europe, Africa, and Asia, they knew nothing. That was about to change.

Eurasia and Africa

If the Neolithic revolution had made but fitful progress north of Mexico by 1500, its advance through Eurasia and Africa was nearly complete. Wheat, first domesticated in Southwest Asia after 9000 B.C.E., spread through the Nile Valley and the Mediterranean and eastward to India and China. Rice, domesticated in China much later, diffused throughout Eurasia. These lead crops were followed by others—oats, peas, olives, grapes, almonds, barley, oranges, lentils, and millet. Several thousand years later, farmers in Africa domesticated sorghum, palm oil, and yams.

The flow of people and crops between Eurasia and Africa was hindered after 4000 B.C.E., when the climate of Africa shifted and the Sahara broadened into a nearly impenetrable desert the size of the United States. The animals of Eurasia were as diverse as its crops. While few large mammals in the Americas survived the Clovis era, the ancient peoples of Eurasia learned how to domesticate horses, pigs, cows, goats, sheep, and oxen. In addition to protein-rich meat, cows and goats provided milk and dairy products such as cheese that could be stored for winter; horses and oxen dragged trees and boulders from fields, pulled ploughs through tough sod, and contributed manure for fertilizer. Eurasians greatly increased the power of oxen and horses by harnessing them to wheeled vehicles. Because of the diversity and nutritional value of its food sources, the Eurasian population increased rapidly.

To accommodate the growing demand for food, Eurasian farmers cut down forests, filled in marshlands, and terraced hillsides. Monarchs joined with merchants and bankers to build port facilities, canals, and fleets of ships to ensure the food supply to urban centers.

If cereal crops and animals dispersed throughout the vast Eurasian land-mass, so did new diseases. New strains of viruses and bacteria appeared in cows, pigs, goats, and sheep and readily spread to the humans that kept them. Diseases also spread readily in large cities, whose sanitation facilities were poor. Recurrent plagues swept across Eurasia. But those who survived acquired biological resistance.

West Africa evolved differently. The grassy savannah just south of the Sahara became the home for mostly herding peoples. Cities emerged in response to the growth of trans-Sahara trade: Finished goods, including cloth from North Africa, were traded for gold, salt, kola—a caffeine rich nut—and slaves. Warlords commanding horse-mounted troops vied for the control of the trade routes, and eventually founded the great kingdoms of Ghana, Mali, and Songhay. By 1500, Timbuktu, the capital of Mali, had become a major city, home to an important Islamic university and library.

Seldom did pastoral and trading empires penetrate far into the tropical regions farther south. The religion of Islam, which had spread through the grass-lands south of the Sahara, also made less progress among Africans on the tropical coast. There the tsetse fly, carrier of sleeping sickness, decimated horse and cattle herds. Malaria, too, discouraged potential invaders.

The village was the main unit of social organization of sub-Saharan Africa. Some villages merged into far-flung kinship networks and even small kingdoms, such as Benin and Congo. Relatively insulated from the imperial struggles farther north, these Africans mostly kept to themselves, growing crops and harvesting the lush vegetation of the forest. By 1500, the lives of these people, too, were about to change.

Europe in Ferment

During the 1400s, Europe's population increased by nearly a third; by 1500, population pressure was acute. When harvests were poor or grain shipments failed to arrive in towns, hunger riots destabilized the political order. Genoa, Italy, for example, was convulsed by fourteen revolutions from 1413 to 1453. Overpopulation was one reason why Jews, a vulnerable minority, were expelled from Spain and Portugal in 1492, and from Sicily in 1493.

Scarcity shook many peasants from the land and drove the urban poor from one city to another. Christoforo Colombo—or Columbus, as we call him—was among the restless youths who left home and took to the sea in search of a better life.

New ideas also unsettled European society. Movable type, which made the printing of books profitable, was perfected during the 1440s. By 1500, over 100 cities in Europe had at least one printing press and as many as 20 million volumes had been published. Books advanced new ideas and weakened the hold of traditional ones. Within a few decades, the treatises of Martin Luther and John Calvin initiated the Protestant Reformation. Books also excited the imagination and gave tangible expression to all manner of dreams and longings. (Columbus's restless curiosity had been stimulated by books on geography and navigation, especially Marco Polo's account of his journey to China.)

Incessant squabbles over land resulted in nearly constant warfare. The military arts advanced accordingly. Improvements in metallurgy made it possible to cast bronze and iron cannon capable of containing charges of gunpowder sufficient to hurl heavy balls great distances. By the early 1500s, cannons weighing a ton or more were mounted in sailing ships or upon carriages pulled by teams of horses. Warfare of this nature was expensive; the cost of constructing fleets, equipping armies, and building massive fortifications required the collective resources of many thousands. No longer an activity of rival cities or contending noblemen, warfare demanded the resources of entire nations.

A restless hunger for land, a population made resistant to biological pathogens, an explosion in communication and knowledge, a new technology and organization of warfare, and the emergence of powerful and contentious nation-states—all imparted a fateful dynamism to late fifteenth-century European society. Plainly, these Europeans had not solved their problems: Population growth exceeded available food sources; poverty undermined political order; and war loomed larger and more ominous. Equally plainly, the people of North America had failed to solve basic social problems: Nomadic Indians who practiced a hunting-gathering lifestyle were vulnerable to starvation as well as to encroachments by the more numerous peoples of the corn-farming tribes. Farming Indians, on the other hand, found it difficult to sustain even small urban communities over a long period. In the absence of writing systems and larger "national" political organizations, few could join in broad enterprises; none possessed military technologies comparable to the Europeans. And the peoples of the Americas lacked the immunity from infectious diseases that so many Europeans had acquired.

Separating these worlds was the impenetrable void of the Atlantic Ocean. Five hundred years earlier a Norseman, Leif Eriksson, had sailed along the coast of Greenland to the shores of Labrador, but little came of his expeditions. But toward the close of the fifteenth century, European sailors of a different type, adept at navigating through the open sea and willing to sail far from land, were about to venture across the expanses of the Atlantic. In so doing they would transform it into a bridge that would join these worlds, and the West African coast as well, bringing all three into fateful collision.

c. 12,000 B.C.E. (perhaps earlier)	Humans from Asia cross Beringia to Alaska
c. 12,000–8000 B.C.E.	Humans diffuse throughout Americas
	Many species of large mammals become extinct in western hemisphere
	Clovis era ends
	Eurasians domesticate wheat
c. 4300 B.C.E.	Mesoamerican peoples cultivate corn and initiate Neolithic revolution
c. 2500 B.C.E.	Peoples of midwestern North America domesticate sunflowers and sumpweed
c. 1700 B.C.E.	First sedentary North American community is founded at today's Poverty Point, Louisiana
c. 1000 B.C.E.	Corn cultivation begins in the Southwest
c. 200 C.E.	Corn cultivation begins in the lower Mississippi Valley
c. 900 C.E.	Corn cultivation begins in Wisconsin
c. 1150 C.E.	Cahokia at its peak
c. 1200s–1300s	Protracted droughts in North America disrupt food supply; urban areas are abandoned

colonies. In most places west of the Appalachians, Indians feared other tribes far more than European interlopers.

By 1750 an immense sea of English-speaking peoples and African slaves had flooded into the eastern portion of the continent. Soon, they would spill beyond the Appalachian Mountains. By sheer force of their numbers, American identity would be strongly associated with the English language. Most, too, were farmers, united by a seemingly inexhaustible craving for land. But these enterprising immigrants also differed in fundamental ways. The cultures the immigrants brought with them varied according to the nationality, social status, and taste of the individual. The newcomers never lost their foreign heritage entirely, but they—and certainly their descendants—became something quite different from their relatives who remained in the Old World. They became what we call Americans.

But not right away.

Milestones

1619	First Africans are sold in Virginia
1636	Puritans found Boston Latin School and Harvard College
1657	Half-Way Covenant leads to rise in puritan church memberships
1676	Western planters launch Bacon's Rebellion in Virginia
1684–1688	Edmund Andros rules Dominion of New England
1689	Leisler's Rebellion in New York seizes control of government
1692	Salem village holds witchcraft trials
1696	Virginia colonists found College of William and Mary
	Rice cultivation is introduced in South Carolina
1701	Connecticut ministers found Yale College
1733	George Oglethorpe leads settlement of Georgia

3 CHAPTER

America in the British Empire

IN 2006 THE AVERAGE AMERICAN PAID ABOUT ONE-THIRD OF HIS or her income to the federal government. Polls show that most Americans believe their taxes are too high. Many cheat. According to a study by the Commerce Department, in 2005 Americans failed to report $1 trillion in income, depriving the government of over $300 billion in tax revenue. Many say that they pay taxes only because they are forced to do so.

Yet most Americans pay, and do so voluntarily. Of the 140 million Americans who owed federal taxes in 2005, 130 million filed returns. And while the tax code includes stern punishments for cheaters, criminal prosecutions are rare. In 2005 the IRS charged fewer than 500 Americans with criminal evasion of their taxes.

In the mid-1700s, by contrast, American colonists paid no more than one-twentieth of their income in taxes, far less than their relatives in England. Yet taxation provoked the colonists more than any other issue. John Adams, a Massachusetts lawyer whose opposition to taxes catapulted him to fame, blamed the American Revolution on England's "enormous taxes, burdensome taxes, oppressive, ruinous, intolerable taxes."

Colonial fury was partly due to a change in how London assessed and collected taxes. During the first half of the eighteenth century, most taxes were set by colonial assemblies and based on landholdings. But after 1763 the British government in London imposed new taxes on trade. When ships entered American ports, captains were required to pay taxes before the "enumerated" (taxable) cargos could be moved from the docks. Whenever Americans bought a bag of nails or a tin of tea, they were making indirect tax payments to London. Tax cheats avoided customs officials by smuggling goods into remote coves at night. But rather than evade the "intolerable" tax burden, colonists increasingly decided to eliminate it altogether.

Resistance to taxation was but one of the sources of ferment in mid-eighteenth-century America. The taxes themselves had been necessitated by war, always a destabilizing force in human affairs. Some people, too, experienced a "great awakening" in religious faith; others looked to the European Enlightenment and its enshrinement of reason and science. Traditional ideas and institutions were being scrutinized more closely. By the 1760s and 1770s, irritation over taxes was symptomatic of a more profound societal unease.

The British Colonial System

In the earliest days of any settlement, the need to rely on home authorities was so obvious that few questioned England's sovereignty. Thereafter, as the fledglings grew strong enough to think of using their own wings, distance and British political inefficiency combined to allow them a great deal of freedom. External affairs were controlled entirely by London, and royal representatives in America tried to direct colonial policy. But in practice the Crown generally yielded the initiative in local matters to the colonies while reserving the right to veto actions it deemed to be against the national interest.

Each colony had a governor. By the eighteenth century he was an appointed official, except in Rhode Island and Connecticut. Governors were chosen by the king in the case of the royal colonies and by the proprietors of Maryland, Delaware, and Pennsylvania. The governors' powers were much like those of the king in Great Britain. They executed the local laws, appointed many minor officials, summoned and dismissed the colonial assemblies, and proposed legislation to them. They possessed the right to veto colonial laws, but in most colonies, again like the king, they were financially dependent on their "subjects."

Each colony also had a legislature. Except in Pennsylvania, these assemblies consisted of two houses. The lower house, chosen by qualified voters, had general legislative powers, including control of the purse. In all the royal colonies members of the upper house, or council, were appointed by the king, except in Massachusetts, where they were elected by the General Court. The councils served primarily as advisors to the governors, but they also had some judicial and legislative powers. Judges were appointed by the king and served at his pleasure. Yet both councilors and judges were normally selected from among the leaders of the local communities; London had neither the time nor the will to investigate their political beliefs. The system therefore tended to strengthen the influence of the entrenched colonials.

Most colonial legislators were practical men. Knowing their own interests, they pursued them steadily, without much regard for political theories or the desires of the royal authorities. They extended their influence by slow accretion. They saw themselves as miniature Houses of Commons, steadily "nibbling" at the authority of the Crown. The king appointed their governors, but governors came and

Lewis Morris, a wealthy landowner, had extensive holdings in the Middle Colonies. He was named New Jersey's first governor when the colony became politically independent from New York in 1738. Honest but overbearing, Morris quarreled constantly with the state assembly over taxation, the militia, and land titles.

went. The lawmakers remained, accumulating experience, building on precedent, widening decade by decade their control over colonial affairs.

The official representatives of the Crown, whatever their powers, whatever their intentions, were prisoners of their surroundings. A royal governor lived thousands of miles from London, alone in a colonial world. Governors had no security of tenure; they served at the whim of the government in London. In their dealings with the assemblies they were often bound by rigid and impractical royal instructions. They had few jobs and favors to offer in their efforts to influence the legislators. Judges might interpret the law according to English precedents, but in local matters colonial juries had the final say. And juries were seldom awed by precedents that clashed with their own conceptions of justice.

Within the British government the king's Privy Council had the responsibility for formulating colonial policy. It could and did disallow (annul) specific colonial laws, but it did not proclaim constitutional principles to which all colonial legislatures must conform. It acted as a court of last appeal in colonial disputes and handled each case individually. One day the council might issue a set of instructions to the governor of Virginia, the next a different set to the governor of South Carolina. No one person or committee thought broadly about the administration of the overseas empire.

At times British authorities, uneasy over their lack of control of the colonies, attempted to create a more effective system. Whenever possible, broadly worded charters were revoked. In the 1680s James II brought New York, New Jersey, and all of New England under one administration, the Dominion of New England; he apparently planned to unify the southern colonies in a similar manner. But James's actions were deeply resented by the colonists, and after the Glorious Revolution and the collapse of the Dominion of New England, no further important efforts at unification were attempted. Instead, the tendency was in the other direction. Delaware was partially separated from Pennsylvania in 1704, and the two Carolinas formally split in 1712.

In 1696 colonial policy was effectively determined by a new Board of Trade, which nominated colonial governors and other high officials. It reviewed all the laws passed by the colonial legislatures, recommending the disallowance of those that seemed to conflict with imperial policy. The efficiency, assiduousness, and wisdom of the Board of Trade fluctuated over the years, but the Privy Council and the Crown nearly always accepted its recommendations.

Colonists naturally disliked having their laws disallowed, but London exercised this power with considerable restraint; only about 5 percent of the laws reviewed were rejected. Furthermore, the board served as an important intermediary for colonists seeking to influence king and Parliament. All the colonies in the eighteenth century maintained agents in London to present the colonial point of view before board members. The most famous colonial agent was Benjamin Franklin, who represented Pennsylvania, Georgia, New Jersey, and Massachusetts at various times during his long career. In general, however, colonial agents were seldom able to exert much influence on British policy.

The British never developed an effective, centralized government for the American colonies. By and large, their American "subjects" ran their own affairs. This fact more than any other explains our present federal system and the wide areas in which the state governments are sovereign and independent.

Mercantilism

The Board of Trade was concerned with commerce as well as colonial administration. According to prevailing European opinion, colonies were important for economic reasons, chiefly as a source of raw materials. To obtain these, British officials developed a number of loosely related policies that later economists called mercantilism. The most important raw materials in the eyes of mercantilists were gold and silver, since these metals, being universally valued and relatively rare, could be exchanged at any time for anything the owner desired or, being durable and compact, stored for future use. For these reasons, how much gold and silver ("treasure" according to mercantilists) a nation possessed was considered the best barometer of its prosperity and power.

Since gold and silver could not be mined in significant amounts in western Europe, every early colonist dreamed of finding "El Dorado." The Spanish were the winners in this search; from the mines of Mexico and South America a treasure in gold and silver poured into the Iberian peninsula. Failing to control the precious metals at the source, the other powers tried to obtain them by guile and warfare (witness the state-supported piracy of Francis Drake).

In the mid-seventeenth century another method, less hazardous and in the long run far more profitable, called itself to the attention of the statesmen of western Europe. If a country could make itself as self-sufficient as possible and also keep its citizens busy producing items sought in other lands, it could sell more goods abroad than it imported. This was known as having "a favorable balance of trade." A country with an unfavorable balance was obliged to make up the

Sea Captains Carousing in Surinam by John Greenwood, a late eighteenth-century oil painting that describes the effects of alcohol—one man guzzles his rum punch straight from the bowl, another vomits onto the floor, while a third pours his punch onto an insensate colleague. Greenwood implicitly denounces as well the trade in sugar (rum) and slaves in which these captains were engaged.

difference by "exporting" gold and silver. Mercantilists regarded colonies as a means of acquiring precious metals by helping the mother country generate a favorable trade balance. Colonists thus were to supply raw materials that would otherwise have to be purchased from foreign sources or colonists were to buy substantial amounts of manufactured goods produced in the mother country.

Of the English colonies in the New World, those in tropical and subtropical climes were valued for their raw materials. The more northerly ones were important as markets, but because they were small in the seventeenth century, in English eyes they took second place. In 1680 the sugar imported from the single West Indian island of Barbados was worth more than the goods sent to England by all the mainland colonies.

If the possession of gold and silver signified wealth, trade was the route that led to riches, and merchants were the captains who would pilot the ship of state to prosperity. "Trade is the Wealth of the World," Daniel Defoe wrote in 1728. One must, of course, have something to sell, so internal production must be stimulated. Parliament encouraged the British people to concentrate on manufacturing by placing tariffs—taxes on trade—on foreign manufactured goods and by subsidizing British-made textiles, iron, and other products.

The Navigation Acts

The nurture of commerce was fundamental. Toward this end Parliament enacted the Navigation Acts. These laws, put into effect over a period of half a century and more, were designed to bring gold and silver into the Royal Treasury, to develop the imperial merchant fleet, to channel the flow of colonial raw materials into England, and to keep foreign goods and vessels out of colonial ports.

The system originated in the 1650s in response to stiff commercial competition by the Dutch, whose sailors roamed the world's oceans in search of business. Before 1650 a large share of the produce of the English colonies in America reached Europe in Dutch vessels; the first slaves in Virginia, it will be recalled, arrived on a Dutch ship and were doubtless paid for in tobacco that was later burned in the clay pipes of the burghers of Amsterdam and Rotterdam.

The Navigation Act of 1660 reserved the entire trade of the colonies to English ships and required that the captain and three-quarters of his crew be English. (Colonists, of course, were English, and their ships were treated on the same terms as those sailing out of London or Liverpool.) The act also provided that certain colonial "enumerated articles"—sugar, tobacco, cotton, ginger, and dyes like indigo (purple) and fustic (yellow)—could not be "shipped, carried, conveyed or transported" outside the empire. Three years later Parliament required that with trifling exceptions all European products destined for the colonies be brought to England before being shipped across the Atlantic. Since trade between England and the colonies was reserved to English vessels, this meant that the goods would have to be unloaded and reloaded in England. Early in the eighteenth century the list of enumerated articles was expanded to include rice, molasses, naval stores, furs, and copper.

The English looked on the empire broadly; they envisioned the colonies as part of an economic unit, not as servile dependencies to be exploited for England's selfish benefit. The growing of tobacco in England was prohibited, and valuable bounties were paid to colonial producers of indigo and naval stores. A planned economy, England specializing in manufacturing and the colonies in the production of raw materials, was the grand design. By and large the system suited the realities of life in an underdeveloped country rich in raw materials and suffering from a chronic labor shortage.

Much has been made by some historians of the restrictions that the British placed on colonial manufacturing. The Wool Act of 1699 prohibited the export (but not the manufacture for local sale) of colonial woolen cloth. A similar law regarding hats was passed in 1732, and in 1750 an Iron Act outlawed the construction of new rolling and slitting mills in America. No other restrictions on manufacturing were imposed.

At most the Wool Act stifled a potential American industry; the law was directed chiefly at Irish woolens rather than American ones. The hat industry cannot be considered a major one. Iron, however, was important; by 1775 the industry was thriving in Virginia, Maryland, New Jersey, and Pennsylvania, and America was turning out one-seventh of the world supply. Yet the Iron Act was designed to steer the American iron industry in a certain direction, not to destroy it. Eager for iron to feed English mills, Parliament eliminated all duties on colonial pig and bar iron entering England, a great stimulus to the basic industry.

The Effects of Mercantilism

Colonists increasingly complained about mercantilism, but did it harm them? The chronic colonial shortage of hard money was superficially caused by the flow of specie—gold and silver—to England to meet the "unfavorable" balance of trade. The rapidly growing colonial economy consumed far more manufactured products than it could pay for out of current production. To be "in debt" to England really meant that the English were investing capital in America, a state of affairs that benefited lender and borrower alike.

Important colonial products for which no market existed in England (such as fish, wheat, and corn) were never enumerated and moved freely and directly to foreign ports. Most colonial manufacturing was untouched by English law. Shipbuilding benefited from the Navigation Acts, since many English merchants bought vessels built in the colonies. Between 1769 and 1771, Massachusetts, New Hampshire, and Rhode Island yards constructed perhaps 250 ships of 100 to 400 tons for transatlantic commerce and twice that many sloops and schooners for fishermen and coastal traders.

Two forces that worked in opposite directions must be considered before arriving at any judgment about English mercantilism. While the theory presupposed a general imperial interest above that of both colony and mother country, when conflicts of interest arose the latter nearly always predominated. Whenever Parliament or the Board of Trade resolved an Anglo-American disagreement, the colonists tended to lose.

Complementary interests conspired to keep conflicts at a minimum, but in the long run, as the American economy became more complex, the colonies would have been seriously hampered and much more trouble would have occurred had the system continued to operate.

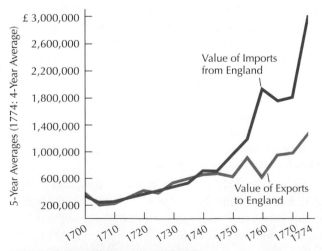

Colonial Trade with England, 1700–1774

On the other hand, the restrictions of English mercantilism were greatly lessened by inefficiency. The king and his ministers handed out government posts to win political favor or to repay political debts, regardless of the recipient's ability to perform the duties of the office.

Transported to remote America, this bumbling and cynical system scarcely functioned at all when local opinion resisted it. Smuggling became a respected profession, bribery of English officials standard practice. Despite a supposedly prohibitive duty of sixpence a gallon imposed by the Molasses Act of 1733, molasses from the French West Indies continued to be imported. The duty was seldom collected.

Mercantilist policies hurt some colonists such as the tobacco planters, who grew far more tobacco than British consumers could smoke. Tobacco planters wanted to ship directly to Dutch or French ports. But the policies helped others, and most people proved adept at getting around those aspects of the system that threatened them. In any case, the colonies enjoyed almost continuous prosperity, as even so dedicated a foe of mercantilist restrictions as Adam Smith admitted.

By the same token, England profited greatly from its overseas possessions. With all its inefficiencies, mercantilism worked. Prime Minister Sir Robert Walpole's famous policy of "salutary neglect," which involved looking the other way when Americans violated the Navigation Acts, was partly a bowing to the inevitable, partly the result of complacency. English manufactures were better and cheaper than those of other nations. This fact, together with ties of language and a common heritage, predisposed Americans toward doing business in England. All else followed naturally; the mercantilist laws merely steered the American economy in a direction it had already taken.

The Great Awakening

Although a majority of the settlers were of English, Scottish, or Scots-Irish descent, and their interests generally coincided with those of their cousins in the mother country, people in the colonies were beginning to recognize their common interests and character. Their loyalties were still predominantly local, but by 1750 the word *American*, used to describe something characteristic of all the British possessions in North America, had entered the language. Events in one part of America were beginning to have direct effects on other regions. One of the first of these developments was the so-called Great Awakening.

By the early eighteenth century, religious fervor had slackened in all the colonies. Prosperity turned many colonists away from their forebears' preoccupation with the rewards of the next world to the more tangible ones of this one. John Winthrop invested his faith in God and his own efforts in the task of creating a spiritual community; his grandsons invested in Connecticut real estate.

The proliferation of religious denominations made it impracticable to enforce laws requiring regular religious observances. Even in South Carolina, the colony that came closest to having an "Anglican Establishment," only a minority were

Debating the Past

WAS ECONOMIC GAIN THE COLONISTS' MAIN MOTIVATION?

This bustling New York farm scene was painted in 1732 on a wood plank. Were those who first placed it above their mantelpiece enshrining their prosperity or their family? Perhaps the first important account of the eighteenth century was by James Truslow Adams (1927), a Wall Street broker who amassed a fortune, retired at age 34, and turned to history. The colonists, he believed, were likewise consumed with acquiring better and more abundant food, clothing, furnishings, housing, and the status such goods signified. He doubted that they cared much about anything else. In the 1950s many scholars, flush with post–World War II patriotism, insisted that the colonists cared deeply about religious, political, and family values. Edmund Morgan (1958) best exemplified this viewpoint. But Adams's position resurfaced several decades later. James Lemon (1972) claimed that Pennsylvania attracted middle-class immigrants who quickly became profit-maximizing farmers. Jack Greene (1988) and Alan Kulikoff (1992) showed that farmers in the Chesapeake and the South had almost from the start been pre-occupied with money and land. The studies of colonial towns during the 1970s transformed the debate. Philip Greven (1970) and others discovered that while nearly everyone craved land, they did so chiefly for their families. Parents sought enough land to give or bequeath to their many children, who otherwise, on attaining adulthood, would be forced to scatter. This focus on parents and family life also spotlighted the central role of women in colonial society, a theme that was developed by Linda Kerber (1980), Mary Beth Norton (1980), and many others.

James Truslow Adams, *Provincial Society* (1927), Edmund Morgan, *A Puritan Dilemma* (1958), James Lemon, *Best Poor Man's Country* (1972), Jack Greene, *Pursuits of Happiness* (1988), Alan Kulikoff, *Agrarian Origins of American Capitalism* (1992), Philip Greven, *Four Generations* (1970), Linda Kerber, *Women of the Republic* (1980), Mary Beth Norton, *Liberty's Daughters* (1980).

churchgoers. Settlers in frontier districts lived beyond the reach of church or clergy. The result was a large and growing number of "persons careless of all religion."

This state of affairs came to an abrupt end with the Great Awakening of the 1740s. The Awakening began in the Middle Colonies as the result of religious developments that originated in Europe. In the late 1720s two newly arrived ministers, Theodore Frelinghuysen, a Calvinist from Westphalia, and William Tennent, an Irish-born Presbyterian, sought to instill in their sleepy Pennsylvania and New Jersey congregations the evangelical zeal and spiritual enthusiasm they had witnessed among the Pietists in Germany and the Methodist followers of John Wesley in England. Their example inspired other clergymen, including Tennent's two sons.

In this painting evangelist George Whitefield appears to be cross-eyed. This is the fault of John Wollaston, the painter. Whitefield had eye problems; his detractors called him "Dr. Squintum." The woman's rapturous gaze is unaffected by Whitefield's own curious visage.

A more significant surge of religious enthusiasm followed the arrival in 1738 in Georgia of the Reverend George Whitefield, a young Oxford-trained Anglican minister. Whitefield was a marvelous pulpit orator and no mean actor. He played on the feelings of his audience the way a conductor directs a symphony. Whitefield undertook a series of fund-raising tours throughout the colonies. The most successful began in Philadelphia in 1739. Benjamin Franklin, not a very religious person and not easily moved by emotional appeals, heard one of these sermons. "I silently resolved he should get nothing from me," he later recalled.

> I had in my Pocket a Handful of Copper Money, three or four silver Dollars, and five Pistoles in Gold. As he proceeded I began to soften and concluded to give the Coppers. Another Stroke of his Oratory . . . determin'd me to give the Silver; and he finish'd so admirably that I emply'd my Pocket wholly into the Collector's Dish.

Whitefield's visit changed the "manners of our inhabitants," Franklin added.

Wherever Whitefield went he filled the churches. If no local clergyman offered his pulpit, he attracted thousands to meetings out of doors. During a three-day visit to Boston, 19,000 people (more than the population of the town) thronged to hear him. His oratorical brilliance aside, Whitefield succeeded in releasing an epidemic of religious emotionalism because his message was so well suited to American ears. By preaching a theology that one critic said was "scaled down to the comprehension of twelve-year-olds," he spared his audiences the rigors of hard thought. Though he usually began by chastising his listeners as sinners, "half animals and half devils," he invariably took care to leave them with the hope that eternal salvation could be theirs. While not denying the doctrine of predestination, he preached a God responsive to good intentions. He disregarded sectarian differences and encouraged his listeners to do the same. "God help us to forget party names and become Christians in deed and truth," he prayed.

Some churches split into factions. Those who supported the incumbent minister were called, among Congregationalists, "Old Lights," and among Presbyterians, "Old Sides," while those who favored revivalism were known as "New Lights" and "New Sides." These splits often ran along class lines. The richer, better-educated, and more influential members of the church tended to stay with the traditional arrangements.

But many were deeply moved by the new ideas. Persons chafing under the restraints of puritan authoritarianism, or feeling guilty over their preoccupation with material goods, now found release in religious ferment. For some the release was more than spiritual; Timothy Cutler, a conservative Anglican clergyman, complained that as a result of the Awakening "our presses are forever teeming with books and our women with bastards." Whether or not Cutler was correct, the Great Awakening helped some people to rid themselves of the idea that disobedience to authority entailed damnation. Anything that God justified, human law could not condemn. The Great Awakening did not entail opposition to British tax policies; but it did undermine traditional conceptions of authority.

Other institutions besides the churches were affected by the Great Awakening. In 1741 the president of Yale College criticized the theology of itinerant ministers who imitated Whitefield. One of these promptly retorted that a Yale faculty member had no more divine grace than a chair! Other revivalists called on the New Light churches of Connecticut to withdraw their support from Yale and endow a college of their own. The result was the College of New Jersey (now Princeton), founded in 1746 by New Side Presbyterians. Three other educational by-products of the Great Awakening followed: the College of Rhode Island (Brown), founded by Baptists in 1765; Queen's College (Rutgers), founded by Dutch Reformers in 1766; and Dartmouth, founded by New Light Congregationalists in 1769.

The Rise and Fall of Jonathan Edwards

Jonathan Edwards, the most famous native-born revivalist of the Great Awakening, was living proof that the evangelical temperament need not be hostile to learning. Edwards, though deeply pious, was passionately devoted to intellectual pursuits. But in 1725, four years after graduating from Yale, he was offered the position of assistant at his grandfather Solomon Stoddard's church in Northampton, Massachusetts. He accepted, and when Stoddard died two years later, Edwards became pastor.

During his six decades in Northampton, Stoddard had so dominated the ministers of the Connecticut Valley that some referred to him as "pope." His prominence came in part from the "open enrollment" admission policy he adopted for his own church. Evidence of saving grace was neither required nor expected of members: mere good behavior sufficed. As a result, the grandson inherited a congregation whose members were possessed of an "inordinate engagedness after this world." How ready they were to meet their Maker in the next was another question.

For all his learning and intellectual brilliance, Edwards did not stick at dramatizing what unconverted listeners had to look forward to. The heat of Hell's consuming fires and the stench of brimstone became palpable at his rendering. In his most famous sermon, "Sinners in the Hands of an Angry God," delivered at Enfield, Connecticut, in 1741, he pulled out all the stops, depicting a "dreadfully provoked" God holding the unconverted over the pit of Hell, "much as one holds a spider, or some loathsome insect." Later, on the off-chance that his listeners did not recognize themselves among the "insects" in God's hand, he declared that "this is the dismal case of every soul in this congregation that has not been born again, however moral and strict, sober and religious, they may otherwise be." A great moaning reverberated through the church. People cried out, "What must I do to be saved?"

Unfortunately for some church members, Edwards's warnings about the state of their souls caused much anxiety. One disconsolate member, Joseph Hawley, slit his throat. Edwards took the suicide calmly. "Satan seems to be in a great rage," he declared. But for some of Edwards's most prominent parishioners, Hawley's death roused doubts. They began to miss the forgiving God of Solomon Stoddard.

Rather than soften his message, Edwards persisted, and in 1749 his parishioners voted unanimously to dismiss him. He became a missionary to some Indians in Stockbridge, Massachusetts. In 1759 he was appointed president of Princeton, but he died of smallpox before he could take office.

By the early 1750s a reaction had set in against religious "enthusiasm" in all its forms. Except in the religion-starved South, where traveling New Side Presbyterians and Baptists continued their evangelizing efforts, the Great Awakening had run its course. Whitefield's tour of the colonies in 1754 attracted little notice.

Although it caused divisions, the Great Awakening also fostered religious toleration. If one group claimed the right to worship in its own way, how could it deny to other Protestant churches equal freedom? The Awakening was also the first truly national event in American history. It marks the time when the previously distinct histories of New England, the Middle Colonies, and the South began to intersect. Powerful links were being forged. As early as 1691 there was a rudimentary intercolonial postal system. In 1754, not long after the Awakening, the far-sighted Benjamin Franklin advanced his Albany Plan for a colonial union to deal with common problems, such as defense against Indian attacks on the frontier. Thirteen once-isolated colonies, expanding to the north and south as well as westward, were merging.

The Enlightenment in America

The Great Awakening pointed ahead to an America marked by religious pluralism; by the 1740s many colonists were rejecting not only the stern Calvinism of Edwards but even the easy Arminianism of Solomon Stoddard in favor of a far less forbidding theology, one more in keeping with the ideas of the European Enlightenment.

The Enlightenment, whose proponents enshrined reason and scientific inquiry, had an enormous impact in America. The founders of the colonies were contemporaries of the astronomer Galileo Galilei (1564–1642), the philosopher-mathematician René Descartes (1596–1650), and Sir Isaac Newton (1642–1727), the genius who revealed to the world the workings of gravity and other laws of motion. American society developed amid the excitement generated by these great discoverers, who provided both a new understanding of the natural world and a mode of thought that implied that impersonal, scientific laws governed the behavior of all matter, animate and inanimate. Earth and the heavens, human beings and the lower animals—all seemed parts of an immense, intricate machine. God had set it all in motion and remained the master technician (the divine watchmaker) overseeing it, but He took fewer and fewer occasions to interfere with its immutable operation. If human reasoning powers and direct observation of natural phenomena rather than God's revelations provided the key to knowledge, it followed that knowledge of the laws of nature, by enabling people to understand the workings of the universe, would enable them to control their earthly destinies and to have at least a voice in their eternal destinies.

Most creative thinkers of the European Enlightenment realized that human beings were not entirely rational and that a complete understanding of the physical world was beyond their grasp. They did, however, believe that human beings were becoming more rational and would be able, by using their rational powers, to discover the laws governing the physical world. Their faith in these ideas produced the so-called Age of Reason. And while their confidence in human rationality now seems naive and the "laws" they formulated no longer appear so mechanically perfect (the universe is far less orderly than they imagined), they added immensely to knowledge.

Many churchgoing colonists, especially better educated ones, accepted the assumptions of the Age of Reason wholeheartedly. Some repudiated the doctrine of original sin and asserted the benevolence of God. Others came to doubt the divinity of Christ and eventually declared themselves Unitarians. Still others, among them Benjamin Franklin, embraced Deism, a faith that revered God for the marvels of His universe rather than for His power over humankind.

The impact of Enlightenment ideas went far beyond religion. The writings of John Locke and other political theorists found a receptive audience. So did the work of the Scottish philosophers Francis Hutcheson and David Hume and the French *philosophes*, particularly Montesquieu and Voltaire. Ideas generated in Europe often reached America with startling speed. No colonial political controversy really heated up in America until all involved had published pamphlets citing half a dozen European authorities. Radical ideas that in Europe were discussed only by an intellectual elite became almost commonplace in the colonies.

As the topics of learned discourse expanded, ministers lost their monopoly on intellectual life. By the 1750s, only a minority of Harvard and Yale graduates were becoming ministers. The College of Philadelphia (later the University of Pennsylvania), founded in 1751, and King's College (later Columbia), founded in New York in 1754, added two institutions to the growing ranks of American colleges, which were never primarily training grounds for clergymen.

Lawyers, who first appeared in any number in colonial towns in the 1740s, swiftly asserted their intellectual authority in public affairs. Physicians and the handful of professors of natural history declared themselves better able to make sense of the new scientific discoveries than clergymen. Yet because fields of knowledge were far less specialized than in modern times, self-educated amateurs could also make useful contributions.

The most famous instances of popular participation occurred in Philadelphia. It was there, in 1727, that 21-year-old Benjamin Franklin founded the Junto, a club at which he and other young artisans gathered on Friday evenings to discuss "any point of morals, politics, or natural philosophy." In 1743 Franklin established an expanded version of the Junto, the American Philosophical Society, which he hoped would "cultivate the finer arts and improve the common stock of knowledge."

Colonial Scientific Achievements

America produced no Galileo or Newton, but colonists contributed significantly to the collection of scientific knowledge. The unexplored continent provided a laboratory for the study of natural phenomena. The Philadelphia Quaker John Bartram, a "down right plain Country Man," ranged from Florida to the Great Lakes during the middle years of the eighteenth century, gathering and classifying hundreds of plants. Bartram also studied Indians closely, speculating about their origins and collecting information about their culture.

Benjamin Franklin is most often depicted as he looked in later life, with his own thinning hair rather than the wig that was de rigueur for an eighteenth-century man of good family. In this 1767 portrait, a younger Franklin follows the fashion.

Benjamin Franklin's far-ranging curiosity extended to science. "No one of the present age has made more important discoveries," Thomas Jefferson declared. Franklin's studies of electricity, which he capped in 1752 with his famous kite experiment, established him as a scientist of international stature. He also invented the lightning rod, the iron Franklin stove (a far more efficient way to heat a room than an open fireplace), bifocal spectacles, and several other ingenious devices. In addition he served 14 years (1751–1764) in the Pennsylvania assembly. He founded a circulating library and helped to get the first hospital in Philadelphia built. He came up with the idea of a lottery to raise money for public purposes. In his spare time he taught himself Latin, French, Spanish, and Italian.

Involvement at even the most marginal level in the intellectual affairs of Europe gave influential New Englanders, Middle Colonists, and Southerners a chance to get to know one another. Like the spread of evangelical religion, Enlightenment values created new forms of community in English America. Men who in 1750 were discussing botany, physics, and natural phenomena would also soon be exchanging ideas about governance.

Repercussions of Distant Wars

The British colonies were part of a great empire that was part of a still larger world. Seemingly isolated in their remote communities, scattered like a broken string of beads between the wide Atlantic and the trackless Appalachian forests, Americans were constantly affected by outside events both in the Old World and in the New. Under the spell of mercantilist logic, the western European nations competed fiercely for markets and colonial raw materials. War—hot and cold, declared and undeclared—was almost a permanent condition of seventeenth- and eighteenth-century life, and when the powers clashed they fought wherever they could get at one another, in America, in Europe, and elsewhere.

Although the American colonies were minor pieces in the game and were sometimes casually exchanged or sacrificed by the masterminds in London, Paris, and Madrid in pursuit of some supposedly more important objective, the colonists quickly generated their own international animosities. Frenchmen and Spaniards clashed savagely in Florida as early as the sixteenth century. Before the landing of the Pilgrims, Samuel Argall of Virginia was sacking French settlements in Maine and carrying off Jesuit priests into captivity at Jamestown. Instead of fostering tranquility and generosity, the abundance of America seemed to make the settlers belligerent and greedy.

The North Atlantic fisheries quickly became a source of trouble between Canadian and New England colonists, despite the fact that the waters of the Grand Banks teemed with cod and other fish. To dry and salt their catch the fishermen needed land bases, and French and English Americans struggled constantly over the harbors of Maine, Nova Scotia, and Newfoundland.

Even more troublesome was the fur trade. The yield of the forest was easily exhausted by indiscriminate slaughter, and traders contended bitterly to control valuable hunting grounds. The French in Canada conducted their fur trading through tribes such as the Algonquin and the Huron. This brought them into conflict with the Five Nations, the powerful Iroquois confederation of central New York. As early as 1609 the Five Nations were at war with the French and their Indian allies. For decades this struggle flared sporadically, the Iroquois more than holding their own both as fighters and as traders. The Iroquois brought quantities of beaver pelts to the Dutch at Albany, some obtained by their own trappers, others taken by ambushing the fur-laden canoes of their enemies. They preyed on and ultimately destroyed the Huron in the land north of Lake Ontario and dickered with Indian trappers in far-off Michigan. When the English took over the New Amsterdam colony they eagerly adopted the Iroquois as allies, buying their furs and supplying them with trading goods and guns.

By the last decade of the seventeenth century it had become clear that the Dutch lacked the strength to maintain a big empire and that Spain was fast declining. The future, especially in North America, belonged to England and France. In the wars of the next 125 years European alliances shifted dramatically, yet the English and what the Boston lawyer John Adams called "the turbulent Gallicks" were always on opposite sides.

In the first three of these conflicts colonists played only minor parts. The fighting in America consisted chiefly of sneak attacks on isolated outposts. In King William's War (1689–1697), the American phase of the War of the League of Augsburg, French forces raided Schenectady in New York and frontier settlements in New England. English colonists retaliated by capturing Port Royal, Nova Scotia, only to lose that outpost in a counterattack in 1691. The Peace of Ryswick in 1697 restored all captured territory in America to the original owners.

The next struggle was the War of the Spanish Succession (1702–1713), fought to prevent the union of Spain and France under the Bourbons. The Americans named this conflict Queen Anne's War. French-inspired Indians razed Deerfield, Massachusetts. A party of Carolinians burned St. Augustine in Spanish Florida. The New Englanders retook Port Royal. In the Treaty of Utrecht in 1713, France yielded Nova Scotia, Newfoundland, and the Hudson Bay region to Great Britain.

If the colonies were mere pawns in these wars, battle casualties were proportionately high and the civilian population of New England (and of Canada) paid heavily because of the fighting. Many frontier settlers were killed in the raids. Hundreds of townspeople died during the campaigns in Nova Scotia. Massachusetts taxes went up sharply and the colony issued large amounts of paper currency to pay its bills, causing an inflation that ate into the living standards of wage earners.

The American phase of the third Anglo-French conflict, the War of the Austrian Succession (1740–1748), was called King George's War. The usual Indian raids were launched in both directions across the lonely forests that separated the St. Lawrence settlements from the New York and New England frontier. A New England force captured the strategic fortress of Louisbourg on Cape Breton Island, guarding the entrance to the Gulf of St. Lawrence. The Treaty of Aix-la-Chapelle in 1748, however, required the return of Louisbourg, much to the chagrin of the New Englanders.

As this incident suggests, the colonial wars generated a certain amount of trouble between England and the colonies; matters that seemed unimportant in London might loom large in American eyes, and vice versa. But the conflicts were seldom serious. The wars did, however, increase the bad feelings between settlers north and south of the St. Lawrence. Every Indian raid was attributed to French provocateurs, although more often than not the English colonists themselves were responsible for the Indian troubles. Conflicting land claims further aggravated the situation. Massachusetts, Connecticut, and Virginia possessed overlapping claims to the Ohio Valley, and Pennsylvania and New York also had pretensions in the region. Yet the French, ranging broadly across the midcontinent, insisted that the Ohio country was exclusively theirs.

The Great War for the Empire

In this beautiful, almost untouched land, a handful of individuals determined the future of the continent. Over the years the French had established a chain of forts and trading posts running from Mackinac Island in northern Michigan to Kaskaskia on the Mississippi River and Vincennes on the Wabash River, and from Niagara in the east to the Bourbon River, near Lake Winnipeg, in the west. By the 1740s, however, Pennsylvania fur traders, led by George Croghan, a rugged Irishman, were setting up posts north of the Ohio River and bargaining with Miami and Huron Indians, who ordinarily sold their furs to the French. In 1748 Croghan built a fort at Pickawillany, deep in the Miami country, in what is now western Ohio. That same year agents of a group of Virginia land speculators who had recently organized what they called the Ohio Company reached this area.

With trifling exceptions, an insulating band of wilderness had always separated the French and English in America. Now the two powers came into contact. The immediate result was a showdown battle for control of North America, the "great war for the empire." Thoroughly alarmed by the presence of the English on land they had long considered their own, the French struck hard. Attacking suddenly in 1752, they wiped out Croghan's post at Pickawillany and drove his traders back into Pennsylvania. Then they built a string of barrier forts south from Lake Erie along the Pennsylvania line: Fort Presque Isle, Fort Le Boeuf, Fort Venango.

The Pennsylvania authorities chose to ignore this action, but Lieutenant Governor Robert Dinwiddie of Virginia (who was an investor in the Ohio Company) dispatched a 21-year-old surveyor named George Washington to warn the French that they were trespassing on Virginia territory.

Washington, a gangling, inarticulate, and intensely ambitious young planter, made his way northwest in the fall of 1753 and delivered Dinwiddie's message to the commandant at Fort Le Boeuf. It made no impression. "[The French] told me," Washington reported, "that it was their absolute Design to take Possession of the Ohio, and by G— they would do it." Governor Dinwiddie thereupon promoted Washington to lieutenant colonel and sent him back in the spring of 1754 with 150

This, the first portrait of George Washington, was done by Charles Willson Peale in 1772. Washington's right hand is inside his vest, a convention later associated with Napoleon; his left hand is behind his back. Perhaps this was to spare the painter of the trouble of rendering hands and fingers, always a challenge.

men to seize a strategic junction south of the new French forts, where the Allegheny and Monongahela rivers join to form the Ohio.

Eager but inexperienced in battle, young Washington botched his assignment. As his force labored painfully through the tangled mountain country southeast of the fork of the Ohio, he received word that the French had already occupied the position and were constructing a powerful post, Fort Duquesne. Outnumbered by perhaps four to one, Washington foolishly pushed on. He surprised and routed a French reconnaissance party, but this brought on him the main body of enemy troops.

Hastily he threw up a defensive position, aptly named Fort Necessity, but the ground was ill chosen; the French easily surrounded the fort and Washington had to surrender. After tricking the young officer, who could not read French, into signing an admission that he had "assassinated" the leader of the reconnaissance party, his captors, with the gateway to the Ohio country firmly in their hands, permitted him and his men to march off. Nevertheless, Washington returned to Virginia a hero, for although still undeclared, this was war, and he had struck the first blow against the hated French.

In the resulting conflict, which historians call the French and Indian War (to the colonists it was simply "the French War"), the English outnumbered the French by about 1.5 million to 90,000. But the English were divided and disorganized, the French disciplined and united. The French controlled the disputed territory, and most of the Indians took their side. As a colonial official wrote, together they made formidable forest fighters, "sometimes in our Front, sometimes in our Rear, and often on all sides of us, Hussar Fashion, taking the Advantage of every Tree and Bush." With an ignorance and arrogance typical of eighteenth-century colonial administration, the British mismanaged the war and failed to make effective use of local resources. For several years they stumbled from one defeat to another.

General Edward Braddock, a competent but uninspired soldier, was dispatched to Virginia to take command. In June 1755 he marched against Fort Duquesne with 1,400 Redcoats and a smaller number of colonials, only to be decisively defeated by a much smaller force of French and Indians. Braddock died bravely in battle, and only 500 of his men, led by Colonel Washington, who was serving as his aide-de-camp, made their way back to Virginia.

Elsewhere Anglo-American arms fared little better in the early years of the war. Expeditions against Fort Niagara, key to all French defenses in the west, and Crown Point, gateway to Montréal, bogged down. Meanwhile Indians, armed by the French, bathed the frontier in blood. Venting the frustration caused by 150 years of white advance, they attacked defenseless outposts with unrestrained brutality.

The most feared of the "French" Indians were the Delaware, a once-peaceful Pennsylvania tribe that had been harried from their homelands by English and Iroquois. General Braddock paid his Indian allies only £5 each for French scalps but offered £200 for the hair of Shinngass, the Delaware chieftain.

In 1756 the conflict spread to Europe to become the Seven Years' War. Prussia sided with Great Britain, Austria with the French. On the world stage, too, things went badly for the British. Finally, in 1758, as defeat succeeded defeat, King George II was forced to allow William Pitt, whom he detested, to take over leadership of the war effort. Pitt, grandson of "Diamond" Pitt, a nouveau riche East India merchant, was an unstable man who spent much of his life on the verge of madness, but he was a brilliant strategist and capable of inspiring the nation in its hour of trial.

Pitt recognized, as few contemporaries did, the potential value of North America. Instead of relying on the tightfisted and shortsighted colonial assemblies for men and money, he poured regiment after regiment of British regulars and the full resources of the British treasury into the contest, mortgaging the future recklessly to secure the prize. Grasping the importance of sea power in fighting a war on the other side of the Atlantic, he used the British navy to bottle up the enemy fleet and hamper French communications with Canada. He possessed a keen eye for military genius, and when he discovered it, he ignored seniority and the outraged feelings of mediocre generals and promoted talented young officers to top commands. (His greatest find was James Wolfe, whom he made a brigadier at age 31.)

In the winter of 1758, as Pitt's grand strategy matured, Fort Duquesne fell. It was appropriately renamed Fort Pitt, the present Pittsburgh. The following summer Fort Niagara was overrun. General Jeffrey Amherst took Crown Point, and Wolfe sailed up the St. Lawrence to Québec. There General Louis Joseph de Montcalm had prepared formidable defenses, but after months of probing and planning, Wolfe found and exploited a chink in the city's armor and captured it. Both he and Montcalm died in the battle. In 1760 Montréal fell and the French abandoned all Canada to the British. The British also won major victories against Spanish forces in Cuba and Manila, and against the French in the West Indies and India.

Britain Victorious: The Peace of Paris

Peace was restored in 1763 by the Treaty of Paris. Its terms were moderate considering the extent of the British triumph. France abandoned all claim to North America except for two small islands near Newfoundland; Great Britain took over Canada and the eastern half of the Mississippi Valley. Spain got back both the Philippine Islands and Cuba, but in exchange ceded East and West Florida to Great Britain. In a separate treaty, Spain also got New Orleans and the huge area of North America west of the Mississippi River.

"Half the continent," the historian Francis Parkman wrote, "had changed hands at the scratch of a pen." From the point of view of the English colonists in America, the victory was overwhelming. All threat to their frontiers seemed to have been swept away. Surely, they believed in the first happy moments of victory, their peaceful and prosperous expansion was ensured for countless generations.

No honest American could deny that the victory had been won chiefly by British troops and with British gold. Colonial militiamen fought well in defense of their homes or when some highly prized objective seemed ripe for the plucking; they lacked discipline and determination when required to fight far from home and under commanders they did not know. As one American official admitted, it was difficult to get New Englanders to enlist "unless assurances can be given that they shall not march to the southward of certain limits."

British Successes, 1758–1763

Colonials were delighted that scarlet-clad British regulars had borne the brunt of the fighting and happier still that the Crown had shouldered most of the financial burden of the long struggle. The local assemblies contributed to the cost, but except for Massachusetts and Virginia their outlays were trivial compared with the £82 million poured into the worldwide conflict by the British.

Little wonder that the great victory produced a burst of praise for king and mother country throughout America. Parades, cannonading, fireworks, banquets, the pealing of church bells—these were the order of the day in every colonial town. "Nothing," said Thomas Pownall, wartime governor of Massachusetts and a student of colonial administration, "can eradicate from [the colonists'] hearts their natural, almost mechanical affection to Great Britain." A young South Carolinian who had been educated in England claimed that the colonists were "more wrapped up in a king" than any people he had ever heard of.

Burdens of an Expanded Empire

In London peace proved a time for reassessment; that the empire of 1763 was not the same as the empire of 1754 was obvious. The new, far larger dominion would be much more expensive to maintain. Pitt had spent a huge sum winning and securing it, much of it borrowed money. Great Britain's national debt had doubled between 1754 and 1763. Now this debt must be serviced and repaid, and the strain that this would place on the economy was clear to all. Furthermore, the day-to-day cost of administering an empire that extended from the Hudson Bay to India was far larger than that which the already burdened British taxpayer could be expected to bear. Before the great war for the empire, Britain's North American possessions were administered for about £70,000 a year; after 1763 the cost was five times as much.

The American empire had also become far more complex. A system of administration that treated it as a string of separate plantations struggling to exist on the edge of the forest would no longer suffice. The war had been fought for control of the Ohio Valley. Now that the prize had been secured, ten thousand hands were eager to make off with it. The urge to expand was, despite the continent's enormous empty spaces, an old American drive. As early as the 1670s eastern stay-at-homes were lamenting the "insatiable desire after Land" that made people willing to "live like Heathen, only that so they might have Elbow-room enough in the world." Frontier warfare had frustrated this urge for seven long years. How best could it be satisfied now that peace had come?

Conflicting colonial claims, based on charters drafted by men who thought the Pacific lay over the next hill, threatened to make the Ohio valley a battleground once more. The Indians remained "unpacified." Rival land companies contested for charters, while fur traders strove to hold back the wave of settlement that must inevitably destroy the world of the beaver and the deer.

Apparently only Great Britain could deal with these problems and rivalries, for when Franklin had proposed a rudimentary form of colonial union—the Albany

European Claims in All of North America, 1763

Plan of 1754—it was rejected by almost everyone. Unfortunately, the British government did not rise to the challenge. Perhaps this was to be expected. A handful of aristocrats (fewer than 150 peers were active in government affairs) dominated British politics, and they were more concerned with local offices and personal advantage than with large questions of policy. An American who spent some time in London in 1764 trying to obtain approval for a plan for the development of the West reported: "The people hear Spend thire time in Nothing but abuseing one Another and Striveing who shall be in power with a view to Serve themselves and Thire friends." King George III was not a tyrant, as once was commonly believed, but he was an inept politician and the victim of frequent bouts of illness.

Serene in their ignorance, most English leaders insisted that colonials were uncouth and generally inferior beings. During the French and Indian War, British commanders repeatedly expressed contempt for colonial militiamen, whom they considered fit only for "fatigue" duties such as digging trenches, chopping wood, and other noncombat tasks. General Wolfe characterized colonial troops as the "most contemptible cowardly dogs you can conceive," and another English officer, annoyed by their unsanitary habits, complained that they "infect the air with a disagreeable stink." The British officers failed to understand that colonial soldiers were volunteers who had formally contracted to serve under specific conditions. Lord Loudoun, the British commander-in-chief during the French and Indian War, was flabbergasted to discover that New England troops refused to obey one of his direct orders on the ground that it violated their contracts.

Many English people resented Americans simply because the colonies were rapidly becoming rich and powerful. They were growing at an extraordinary rate. Between 1750 and 1770 the population of British America increased from 1 million to more than 2 million. As early as 1751, Benjamin Franklin predicted that in a century "the greatest number of Englishmen will be on this Side of the Water." (His guess was nearly on the mark: in 1850 the population of Great Britain was 20.8 million, that of the United States 23.1 million, including some 4 million slaves and others who were not of British descent.) If the English did not say much about this possibility, they too considered it from time to time—without Franklin's complacency.

Tightening Imperial Controls

The attempt of the inefficient, ignorant, and indignant British government to deal with the intricate colonial problems that resulted from the great war for the empire led to the American Revolution. Trouble began when the British decided after the French and Indian War to intervene more actively in American affairs. Theoretically the colonies were entirely subordinate to Crown and Parliament, yet except for the disastrous attempt to centralize control of the colonies in the 1680s,

This engraving depicts Pontiac confronting Colonel Henry Bouquet. Pontiac had good reason to be angry. In a letter dated July 16, 1763, Sir Jeffrey Amherst, commander of British forces in North America, advised Bouquet to infect Pontiac's Indians with smallpox: "You will do well to try to Innoculate the Indians by means of Blanketts, as well as to try Every other method that can serve to Extirpate this Execrable Race." Bouquet responded a week later: "All your directions will be observed."

Proclamation of 1763

George III's Proclamation of 1763 in effect reserved for the Indians the vast area across the Appalachians (except for the new royal colonies of Québec, East Florida, and West Florida) as far west as Spanish Louisiana and as far north as the Hudson Bay Company preserve.

they had been allowed a remarkable degree of freedom to manage their own affairs. Of course they had come to expect this as their right.

Parliament had never attempted to tax American colonists. "Compelling the colonies to pay money without their consent would be rather like raising contributions in an enemy's country than taxing Englishmen for their own benefit," Benjamin Franklin wrote. Sir Robert Walpole, initiator of the policy of salutary neglect, recognized the colonial viewpoint. He responded to a suggestion that Parliament tax the colonies by saying: "I will leave that for some of my successors, who may have more courage than I have." Nevertheless, the *legality* of parliamentary taxation, or of other parliamentary intervention in colonial affairs, had not been seriously contested. During King George's War and again during the French and Indian War many British officials in America suggested that Parliament tax the colonies.

Despite the peace treaty of 1763, the American colonies continued to be a drain on the British treasury. Mostly this was due to the cost of fighting Indians. Freed of the restraint posed by French competition, Englishmen and colonists increased their pressure on the Indians. Fur traders cheated them outrageously, while callous military men hoped to exterminate them like vermin. One British officer expressed the wish that they could be hunted down with dogs.

Led by an Ottawa chief named Pontiac, the tribes made one last effort to drive the whites back across the mountains. What the whites called Pontiac's "Rebellion" caused much havoc, but it failed. By 1764 most of the western tribes had accepted the peace terms offered by a royal commissioner, Sir William Johnson, one of the few whites who understood and sympathized with them. The British government then placed fifteen regiments, some 6,000 soldiers, in posts along the entire arc of the frontier, as much to protect the Indians from the settlers as the settlers from the Indians. It proclaimed a new western policy: no settlers were to cross the Appalachian divide. Only licensed traders might do business with the Indians beyond that line. The purchase of Indian land was forbidden. In compensation, three new colonies—Québec, East Florida, and West Florida—were created, but they were not permitted to set up local assemblies.

This Proclamation of 1763 excited much indignation in America. The frustration of dozens of schemes for land development in the Ohio Valley angered many influential colonists. Colonel Washington referred to the proclamation contemptuously as "a temporary expedient to quiet the minds of Indians," and he continued to stake out claims to western lands.

Originally the British had intended the proclamation to be temporary. With the passage of time, however, checking westward expansion seemed a good way to save money, prevent trouble with the Indians, and keep the colonies tied closely to the mother country. The proclamation line, the Board of Trade declared, was "necessary for the preservation of the colonies in due subordination."[1] Naturally this attitude caused resentment in America. To close off the West temporarily in order to pacify the Indians made some sense; to keep it closed was like trying to contain a tidal wave.

The Sugar Act

Americans disliked the new western policy but realized that the problems were knotty and that no simple solution existed. Their protests were somewhat muted. Great Britain's effort to raise money in America to help support the increased cost of colonial administration caused far more vehement complaints. George Grenville, who became prime minister in 1763, was a fairly able man, although long-winded and rather narrow in outlook. His reputation as a financial expert was based chiefly on his eagerness to reduce government spending. Under his leadership Parliament passed, in April 1764, the so-called Sugar Act. This law placed tariffs on sugar, coffee,

---

[1]The British were particularly concerned about preserving the colonies as markets for their manufactures. They feared that the spread of population beyond the mountains would stimulate local manufacturing because the high cost of land transportation would make British goods prohibitively expensive.

wines, and other things imported into America in substantial amounts. At the same time, measures aimed at enforcing all the trade laws were put into effect. Those accused of violating the Sugar Act were to be tried before British naval officers in vice admiralty courts. Grenville was determined to end smuggling, corruption, and inefficiency. Soon the customs service was collecting each year fifteen times as much in duties as it had before the war.

More alarming was the nature of the Sugar Act and the manner of its passage. The Navigation Act duties had been intended to regulate commerce, and the sums collected had not cut deeply into profits. Indeed, the Navigation Acts might well be considered an instrument of imperial foreign policy, an area of government that everyone willingly conceded to London. Yet few Americans were willing to concede that Parliament had the right to tax them. As *Englishmen* they believed that no one should be deprived arbitrarily of property and that, as James Otis put it in his stirring pamphlet *The Rights of the British Colonies Asserted and Proved* (1764), everyone should be "free from all taxes but what he consents to in person, or by his representative." John Locke had made clear in his *Second Treatise on Government* (1690) that property ought never be taken from people without their consent, not because material values transcend all others but because human liberty can never be secure when arbitrary power of any kind exists. "If our Trade may be taxed why not our Lands?" the Boston town meeting asked when news of the Sugar Act reached America. "Why not the produce of our Lands and every Thing we possess or make use of?"

American Colonists Demand Rights

To most people in Great Britain the colonial protest against taxation without representation seemed a hypocritical quibble, and it is probably true that in 1764 many of the protesters had not thought the argument through. The distinction between tax laws and other types of legislation was artificial, the British reasoned. Either Parliament was sovereign in America or it was not, and only a fool or a traitor would argue that it was not. If the colonists were loyal subjects of George III, as they claimed, they should bear cheerfully their fair share of the cost of governing his widespread dominions. As to representation, the colonies *were* represented in Parliament; every member of that body stood for the interests of the entire empire. If Americans had no say in the election of members of Commons, neither did most English subjects.

This concept of "virtual" representation accurately described the British system. But it made no sense in America, where from the time of the first settlements members of the colonial assemblies had represented the people of the districts in which they stood for office. The confusion between virtual and actual (geographically based) representation revealed the extent to which colonial and British political practices had diverged over the years.

The British were correct in concluding that selfish motives influenced colonial objections to the Sugar Act. The colonists denounced taxation without representation, but an offer of a reasonable number of seats in Parliament would not have satisfied them. They would probably have complained about paying taxes to support imperial administration even if imposed by their own assemblies. American abundance and the simplicity of colonial life had enabled them to prosper without assuming any considerable tax burden. Now their maturing society was beginning to require communal rather than individual solutions to the problems of existence. Not many of them were prepared to face up to this hard truth.

Over the course of colonial history Americans had taken a narrow view of imperial concerns. They had avoided complying with the Navigation Acts whenever they could profit by doing so. Colonial militiamen had compiled a sorry record when asked to fight for Britain or even for the inhabitants of colonies other than their own. True, most Americans professed loyalty to the Crown, but not many would voluntarily open their purses except to benefit themselves. In short they were provincials, in attitude and in fact.

Although the colonists were opposed in principle to taxation without representation, they only failed to agree on a common plan of resistance. Many of the assemblies drafted protests, but these varied in force as well as in form. Merchant groups that tried to organize boycotts of products subject to the new taxes met with indifferent success. Then in 1765 Parliament provided the flux necessary for welding colonial opinion by passing the Stamp Act.

The Stamp Act: The Pot Set to Boiling

The Stamp Act placed stiff excise taxes on all kinds of printed matter. No one could sell newspapers or pamphlets, or convey licenses, diplomas, or legal papers without first buying special stamps and affixing them to the printed matter. Stamp duties were intended to be relatively painless to pay and cheap to collect; in England similar taxes brought in about £100,000 annually. Grenville hoped the Stamp Act would produce £60,000 a year in America, and the law provided that all revenue should be applied to "defraying the necessary expenses of defending, protecting, and securing, the . . . colonies."

Hardly a farthing was collected. As the Boston clergyman Jonathan Mayhew explained, "Almost every British American . . . considered it as an infraction of their rights, or their dearly purchased privileges." The Sugar Act had been related to Parliament's uncontested power to control colonial trade, but the Stamp Act was a direct tax. When Parliament ignored the politely phrased petitions of the colonial assemblies, more vigorous protests quickly followed.

Virginia took the lead. In late May 1765 Patrick Henry introduced resolutions asserting redundantly that the Burgesses possessed "the only and sole and exclusive right and power to lay taxes" on Virginians and suggesting that Parliament had no legal authority to tax the colonies at all. Henry spoke for what the royal governor called the "Young, hot and Giddy Members" of the legislature (most of whom, incidentally, had absented themselves from the meeting). The more extreme of Henry's resolutions were defeated, but the debate they occasioned attracted wide

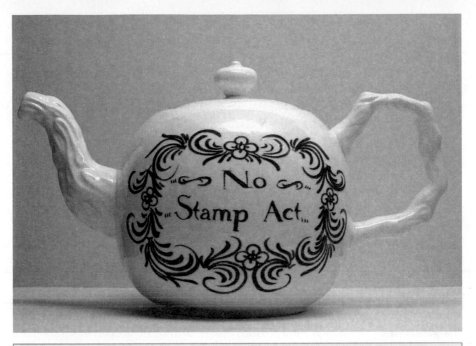

By the mid-eighteenth century, tea had become a staple of the colonists' diet. (In 1766, for example, the residents of the Philadelphia poorhouse demanded that they be served Bohea tea rather than cheaper substitutes.) But colonial ceramics could not withstand boiling water. Thus tea cups and tea pots were manufactured in Staffordshire, England, which had perfected high-temperature ceramics. This "No Stamp Tax" teapot—ironically—was manufactured in England.

and favorable attention. On June 6 the Massachusetts assembly proposed an inter-colonial Stamp Act Congress, which, when it met in New York City in October, passed another series of resolutions of protest. The Stamp Act and other recent acts of Parliament were "burthensome and grievous," the delegates declared. "It is un-questionably essential to the freedom of a people . . . that no taxes be imposed on them but with their own consent."

During the summer irregular organizations known as Sons of Liberty began to agitate against the act. Far more than anyone realized, this marked the start of the revolution. For the first time extralegal organized resistance was taking place, dis-tinct from protest and argument conducted by constituted organs of government like the House of Burgesses and the Massachusetts General Court.

Although led by men of character and position, the "Liberty Boys" frequently resorted to violence to achieve their aims. In Boston they staged vicious riots, loot-ing and vandalizing the houses of the stamp master and his brother-in-law, Lieutenant Governor Thomas Hutchinson. In Connecticut stamp master Jared Ingersoll, a man of great courage and dignity, faced an angry mob demanding his resignation. When threatened with death if he refused, he coolly replied that he was prepared to die "perhaps as well now as another Time." Probably his life was not really in danger, but the size and determination of the crowd convinced him that resistance was useless, and he capitulated.

The stamps were printed in England and shipped to stamp masters (all Americans) in the colonies well in advance of November 1, 1765, the date the law was to go into effect. The New York stamp master had resigned, but the stamps were stored in the city under military guard. Radicals distributed placards reading: "The first Man that either distributes or makes use of Stampt Paper let him take care of his House, Person, and Effects. We dare." When Major Thomas James, the British officer who had charge of the stamps, promised that "the stamps would be crammed down New Yorkers' throats," a mob responded by breaking into his house, drinking all his wine, and smashing his furniture and china.

In some colonies the stamps were snatched by mobs and put to the torch amid rejoicing. Elsewhere they were locked up in secret by British officials or held on shipboard. For a time no business requiring stamped paper was transacted; then, gradually, people began to defy the law by issuing and accepting unstamped documents. Threatened by mob action should they resist, British officials stood by helplessly. The law was a dead letter.

The looting associated with this crisis alarmed many colonists, including some prominent opponents of the Stamp Act. "When the pot is set to boil," the lawyer John Adams remarked sadly, "the scum rises to the top." Another Bostonian called the vandalizing of Thomas Hutchinson's house a "flagrant instance of to what a pitch of infatuation an incensed populace can rise." Such people worried that the protests might be aimed at the wealthy and powerful in America as well as at British tyranny. This does not mean that they disapproved of crowd protests, or even the destruction of property during such protests, as distinct from stealing. Many such people took part in the rioting. "State-quakes," John Adams also said, this time complacently, were comparable to "earth-quakes" and other kinds of natural violence.

Rioters or Rebels?

That many of the poor resented the colonial elite goes without saying, as does the fact that in many instances the rioting got out of hand and took on a social as well as a political character. Times were hard, and the colonial elite, including most of the leading critics of British policy, had little compassion for the poor, whom they feared could be corrupted by anyone who offered them a square meal or a glass of rum. Once roused, laborers and artisans may well have directed their energies toward righting what they considered local wrongs.

Yet the mass of the people, being owners of property and capable of influencing political decisions, were not social revolutionaries. They might envy and resent the wealth and power of the great landowners and merchants, but there is little evidence that they wished to overthrow the established order.

The British were not surprised that Americans disliked the Stamp Act. They had not anticipated, however, that Americans would react so violently and so unanimously. Americans did so for many reasons. Business continued to be poor in

1765, and at a time when 3 shillings was a day's wage for an urban laborer, the stamp tax was 2 shillings for an advertisement in a newspaper, 5 shillings for a will, and 20 shillings for a license to sell liquor. The taxes would hurt the business of lawyers, merchants, newspaper editors, and tavernkeepers. Even clergymen dealt with papers requiring stamps. The protests of such influential and articulate people had a powerful impact on public opinion.

The greatest cause of concern to the colonists was Great Britain's flat rejection of the principle of no taxation without representation. This alarmed them for two closely related reasons. First of all, *as Americans* they objected to being taxed by a legislative body they had not been involved in choosing. To buy a stamp was to surrender all claim to self-government. Secondly, as *British subjects* they valued what they called "the rights of Englishmen." They saw the Stamp Act as only the worst in a series of arbitrary invasions of these rights.

Already Parliament had passed still another measure, the Quartering Act, requiring local legislatures to house and feed new British troops sent to the colonies. Besides being a form of indirect taxation, a standing army was universally deemed to be a threat to liberty. Why were Redcoats necessary in Boston and New York where there was no foreign enemy for thousands of miles in any direction? In hard times, soldiers were particularly unwelcome because, being miserably underpaid, they took any odd jobs they could get in their off hours, thus competing with unemployed colonists.

Reluctantly, many Americans were beginning to fear that the London authorities had organized a conspiracy to subvert the liberties of all British subjects.

Taxation or Tyranny?

In the eighteenth century the English were universally recognized to be the freest people in the world. In Mozart's opera, *The Abduction from the Seraglio* (1782), when the Turk Osmin tells the kidnapped Blonda that she is his slave, a "gift" from his master, she replies contemptuously: "A slave! I am an Englishwoman, born to freedom." Americans, like their English cousins, attributed their freedom to what they called their balanced government. In Britain power appeared to be shared by the Crown, the House of Lords (representing the aristocracy), and the House of Commons (representing the rest of the realm). The governors, councils, and assemblies seemed to play analogous roles in the colonies.

In reality this balance of separate forces never existed, either in Britain or in America. The apparent harmony of society was in both instances the product of a lack of seriously divisive issues, not of dynamic tension between rival forces. But the new laws seemed to Americans to threaten the balance, and this idea was reinforced by their observations of the corruption of English elections. Benjamin Franklin, being a colonial agent in London, knew British politics well. He complained that the entire country was "at market" and "might be bought . . . by the Devil himself" for about £12 million. A clique seeking unlimited power was trying to destroy balanced government in Britain and in America, or so many colonists thought.

There was no such conspiracy, yet no certain answer can be made to the question, Were American rights actually in danger? Grenville and his successors were English politicians, not tyrants. They looked down on bumptious colonials but surely had no wish to destroy them or their prosperity. The British attitude was like that of a parent making a recalcitrant youngster swallow a bitter medicine: protests were understandable, but in the patient's own interest they must be ignored. Franklin reported one high official in London as saying: "His Majesty's Instructions . . . are the LAW OF THE LAND; *they are*, the Law of the Land, and as such *ought to be* OBEYED."

At the same time, British leaders believed that the time had come to assert royal authority and centralize imperial power at the expense of colonial autonomy. The need to maintain a substantial British army in America to control the western Indians tempted the government to use some of the troops to "control" white Americans as well. This attitude probably had as much to do with the coming of the revolution as any specific act of Parliament because it flew in the face of the reality that the colonies had progressed beyond the "childhood" stage. They were no longer entirely dependent on "the mother country." This did not mean breaking away from the Empire. However, it surely meant dealing with Great Britain on terms approaching equality.

Besides refusing to use stamps, Americans responded to the Stamp Act by boycotting British goods. Nearly a thousand merchants signed nonimportation agreements. These struck British merchants hard in their pocketbooks, and they began to pressure Parliament for repeal. After a hot debate—Grenville, whose ministry had fallen over another issue, advocated using the army to enforce the act—the hated law was repealed in March 1766. In America there was jubilation at the news. The ban on British goods was lifted and the colonists congratulated themselves on having stood fast in defense of principle.

The Declaratory Act

The great controversy over the constitutional relationship of colony to mother country was only beginning. The same day that it repealed the Stamp Act, Parliament passed a Declaratory Act stating that the colonies were "subordinate" and that Parliament could enact any law it wished "to bind the colonies and people of America."

To most Americans this bald statement of parliamentary authority seemed unconstitutional—a flagrant violation of their understanding of how the British imperial system was supposed to work. Actually the Declaratory Act highlighted the degree to which British and American views of the system had drifted apart. The English and the colonials were using the same words but giving them different meanings. Their conflicting definitions of the word *representation* was a case in point. Another involved the word *constitution*, the term that James Otis had used in his attack on writs of assistance. To the British the Constitution meant the totality of laws, customs, and institutions that had developed over time and under which the nation functioned. In America, partly because governments were based on specific charters, the word meant a written document or contract spelling out, and thus limiting, the powers of government. If a law were unconstitutional, it simply had no force.

Even more basic were the differing meanings that English and Americans were giving to the word *sovereignty*. Eighteenth-century English political thinkers believed that sovereignty (ultimate political power) could not be divided. Government and law being based ultimately on force, some "final, unqualified, indivisible" authority had to exist if social order was to be preserved. The Glorious Revolution in England had settled the question of where sovereignty resided—in Parliament. The Declaratory Act, so obnoxious to Americans, seemed to the English the mere explication of the obvious. That colonial governments had passed local laws the English did not deny, but they had done so at the sufferance of the sovereign legislative power, Parliament.

Given these ideas and the long tradition out of which they had sprung, one can sympathize with the British failure to follow the colonists' reasoning (which had not yet evolved into a specific proposal for constitutional reform). But most responsible British officials refused even to listen to the American argument.

The Townshend Duties

Despite the repeal of the Stamp Act, the British did not abandon the policy of taxing the colonies. If direct taxes were inexpedient, indirect ones like the Sugar Act certainly were not. To persuade Parliament to repeal the Stamp Act, some Americans (most notably Benjamin Franklin) had claimed that the colonists objected only to direct taxes.

Therefore, in June 1767, the chancellor of the exchequer, Charles Townshend, introduced a series of levies on glass, lead, paints, paper, and tea imported into the colonies. Townshend was a charming man experienced in colonial administration, but he was something of a playboy (his nickname was Champagne Charlie), and he lacked both integrity and common sense. He liked to think of Americans as ungrateful children; he once said he would rather see the colonies turned into "Primitive Desarts" than treat them as equals.

By this time the colonists were thoroughly on guard, and they responded quickly to the Townshend levies with a new boycott of British goods. In addition they made elaborate efforts to stimulate colonial manufacturing. By the end of 1769 imports from the mother country had been almost halved. Meanwhile, administrative measures enacted along with the Townshend duties were creating more ill will. A Board of Customs Commissioners, with headquarters in Boston, took charge of enforcing the trade laws, and new vice admiralty courts were set up at Halifax, Boston, Philadelphia, and Charleston to handle violations. These courts operated without juries, and many colonists considered the new commissioners rapacious racketeers who systematically attempted to obtain judgments against honest merchants in order to collect the huge forfeitures—one-third of the value of ship and cargo—that were their share of all seizures.

The struggle forced Americans to do some deep thinking about both American and imperial political affairs. The colonies' common interests and growing economic and social interrelationships probably made some kind of union inevitable. Trouble with England speeded the process. In 1765 the Stamp Act Congress (another extralegal organization and thus a further step in the direction of revolution) had brought the delegates of nine colonies to New York. Now, in 1768, the Massachusetts General Court took the next step. It sent the legislatures of the other colonies a "Circular Letter" expressing the "humble opinion" that the Townshend Acts were "Infringements of their natural & constitutional Rights."

The question of the limits of British power in America was much debated, and this too was no doubt inevitable, again because of change and growth. Even in the late seventeenth century the assumptions that led Parliament to pass the Declaratory Act would have been unrealistic. By 1766 they were absurd.

After the passage of the Townshend Acts, John Dickinson, a Philadelphia lawyer, published "Letters from a Farmer in Pennsylvania to the Inhabitants of the British Colonies." Dickinson considered himself a loyal British subject trying to find a solution to colonial troubles. "Let us behave like dutiful children, who have received unmerited blows from a beloved parent," he wrote. Nevertheless, he stated plainly that Parliament had no right to tax the colonies. Another moderate Philadelphian, John Raynell, put it this way: "If the Americans are to be taxed by a Parliament where they are not . . . Represented, they are no longer Englishmen but Slaves."

Some Americans were much more radical than Dickinson. Samuel Adams of Boston, a genuine revolutionary agitator, believed by 1768 that Parliament had no right at all to legislate for the colonies. If few were ready to go that far, fewer still accepted the reasoning behind the Declaratory Act.

The British ignored American thinking. The Massachusetts Circular Letter had been framed in moderate language and clearly reflected the convictions of most of the people in the Bay Colony, yet when news of it reached England, the secretary of state for the colonies, Lord Hillsborough, ordered the governor to dissolve the legislature. Two regiments of British troops were transferred from the frontier to Boston, part of the aforementioned policy of bringing the army closer to the centers of colonial unrest.

The Boston Massacre

These acts convinced more Americans that the British were conspiring to destroy their liberties. Resentment was particularly strong in Boston, where the postwar depression had come on top of two decades of economic stagnation. Crowding 4,000

This portrait is from 1772, when Samuel Adams was furious over the Boston Massacre. The painter was John Singleton Copley. Although his parents were impoverished Irish immigrants, Copley had recently married the daughter of a rich Tory merchant. Did Copley side with his father-in-law, who detested Adams as a tribune of the "mob," or with Adams?

tough British soldiers into a town of 16,000 people, many of them as capable of taking care of themselves when challenged as any Redcoat, was a formula for disorder.

How many brawls and minor riots took place in the waterfront taverns and darkened alleys of the colonial ports that winter is lost to history. In January 1770 scuffles between Liberty Boys and Redcoats in the Golden Hill section of New York City resulted in a number of injuries. Then, in Boston on March 5, 1770, real trouble erupted. Late that afternoon a crowd of idlers began tossing snowballs at a company of Redcoats guarding the Custom House. Some of these missiles had been carefully wrapped around suitably sized rocks. Gradually the crowd increased in size and its mood grew meaner. The soldiers panicked and began firing their muskets. When the smoke cleared, five Bostonians lay dead and dying on the bloody ground.

This so-called Boston Massacre infuriated the populace. The violence played into the hands of radicals like Samuel Adams. But just as at the time of the Stamp Act riots, cooler heads prevailed. Announcing that he was "defending the rights of man and unconquerable truth," John Adams volunteered his services to make sure the soldiers got a fair trial. Most were acquitted; the rest were treated leniently by the standards of the day. In Great Britain, confrontation also gave way to adjustment. In April 1770 all the Townshend duties except a threepenny tax on tea were repealed. The tea tax was maintained as a matter of principle.

A kind of postmassacre truce settled over Boston and the rest of British America. During the next two years no serious crisis erupted. Imports of British goods were nearly 50 percent higher than before the nonimportation agreement. So long as the British continued to be conciliatory, the colonists seemed satisfied with their place in the empire.

This engraving of the Boston Massacre (1770) became the most reprinted depiction of the event, and probably the most inaccurate. It was done by Paul Revere, engraver, silversmith, and eventual patriot. The British soldiers did not form ranks and fire on command at the crowd. The judge at the subsequent trial of the British soldiers warned jurors not to be influenced by "the prints exhibited in our houses" that added "wings to fancy"—prints, specifically, such as this one. The jury of colonists acquitted all the British soldiers but two, who received mild punishments.

The Pot Spills Over

In 1772 this informal truce ended and new troubles broke out. The first was plainly the fault of the colonists involved. Early in June the British patrol boat *Gaspee* ran aground in Narragansett Bay, south of Providence, while pursuing a suspected smuggler. The *Gaspee*'s commander, Lieutenant Dudingston, had antagonized everyone in the area by his officiousness and zeal; that night a gang of local people boarded the helpless *Gaspee* and put it to the torch. This action was clearly criminal, but when the British attempted to bring the culprits to justice no one would testify against them. The British, frustrated and angry, were strengthened in their conviction that the colonists were utterly lawless.

Then Thomas Hutchinson, now governor of Massachusetts, announced that henceforth the Crown rather than the local legislature would pay his salary. Since control over the salaries of royal officials gave the legislature a powerful hold on them, this development was disturbing. Groups of radicals formed "committees of correspondence" and stepped up communications with one another, planning joint action in case of trouble. This was another monumental step along the road to revolution; an organized colony-wide resistance movement, lacking in any "legitimate" authority but ready to consult and act in the name of the public interest, was taking shape.

The Tea Act Crisis

In the spring of 1773 an entirely unrelated event precipitated the final crisis. The British East India Company held a monopoly of all trade between India and the rest of the empire. This monopoly had yielded fabulous returns, but decades of corruption and inefficiency together with heavy military expenses in recent years had weakened the company until it was almost bankrupt.

Among the assets of this venerable institution were some 17 million pounds of tea stored in English warehouses. The decline of the American market, a result first of the boycott and then of the smuggling of cheaper Dutch tea, partly accounted for the glut. Normally, East India Company tea was sold to English wholesalers. They in turn sold it to American wholesalers, who distributed it to local merchants for sale to the consumer. A substantial British tax was levied on the tea as well as the threepenny Townshend duty. Now Lord North, the new prime minister, decided to remit the British tax and to allow the company to sell directly in America through its own agents. The savings would permit a sharp reduction of the retail price and at the same time yield a nice profit to the company. The Townshend tax was retained, however, to preserve (as Lord North said when the East India Company directors suggested its repeal) the principle of Parliament's right to tax the colonies.

The company then shipped 1,700 chests of tea to colonial ports. Though the idea of high-quality tea offered at bargain prices was tempting, after a little thought nearly everyone in America appreciated the dangers involved in buying it. If Parliament could grant the East India Company a monopoly of the tea trade, it could parcel out all or any part of American commerce to whomever it pleased. More important, the act appeared utterly diabolical, a dastardly trick to trap them into paying the tea tax. The plot seemed obvious: the real price of Lord North's tea was American submission to parliamentary taxation.

Public indignation was so great in New York and Philadelphia that when the tea ships arrived, the authorities ordered them back to England without attempting to unload. The tea could be landed only "under the Protection of the Point of the Bayonet and Muzzle of the Cannon," the governor of New York reported. "Even then," he added, "I do not see how the Sales or Consumption could be effected."

The situation in Boston was different. The tea ship *Dartmouth* arrived on November 27. The radicals, marshaled by Sam Adams, were determined to prevent it from landing its cargo; Governor Hutchinson (who had managed to have two of his sons appointed to receive and sell the tea) was equally determined to collect the tax and enforce the law. For days the town seethed. Crowds milled in the streets, harangued by Adams and his friends, while the *Dartmouth* and two later arrivals swung with the tides on their moorings. Then, on the night of December 16, as Hutchinson was preparing to seize the tea for nonpayment of the duty, a band of colonists disguised as Indians rowed out to the ships and dumped the hated tea chests into the harbor.

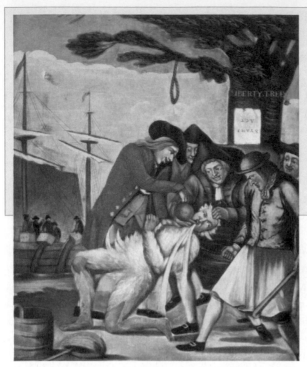

A noose hanging from a "Liberty Tree" reveals this artist's bias: the "tar-and-feathering" of a British official would doubtless culminate in greater violence. As historian Gordon Wood points out, however, the mob actions of the colonists often "grew out of folk festivals and traditional popular rites." A "tar-and-feathering," though painful and occasionally dangerous, was mostly a humiliation. By the early 1770s, though, the mockery was becoming tinged with violence.

The destruction of the tea was a serious crime and it was obvious that a solid majority of the people of Boston approved of it. The painted "Patriots" who jettisoned the chests were a veritable cross-section of society, and a huge crowd gathered at wharfside and cheered them on. The British burned with indignation when news of the "Tea Party" reached London. People talked (fortunately it was only talk) of flattening Boston with heavy artillery. Nearly everyone, even such a self-described British friend of the colonists as Edmund Burke, agreed that the colonists must be taught a lesson. George III himself said, "We must master them or totally leave them to themselves."

What particularly infuriated the British was the certain knowledge that no American jury would render a judgment against the criminals. The memory of the *Gaspee* affair was fresh in everyone's mind in England, as undoubtedly it was in the minds of those Bostonians who, wearing the thinnest of disguises, brazenly destroyed the tea.

From Resistance to Revolution

Parliament responded in the spring of 1774 by passing a series of acts known as the Coercive Acts. The Boston Port Act closed the harbor of Boston to all commerce until its citizens paid for the tea. The Administration of Justice Act provided for the transfer of cases to courts outside Massachusetts when the governor felt that an impartial trial could not be had within the colony. The Massachusetts Government Act revised the colony's charter drastically, strengthening the power of the governor, weakening that of the local town meetings, making the council appointive rather than elective, and changing the method by which juries were selected. These were unwise laws—they cost Great Britain an empire. All of them, and especially the Port Act, were unjust laws as well. Parliament was punishing the entire community for the crimes of individuals. Even more significant, they marked a drastic change in British policy—from legislation and strict administration to treating colonial protesters as criminals, from attempts to persuade and conciliate to coercion and punishment.

The Americans named the Coercive Acts the Intolerable Acts. That the British answer to the crisis was coercion the Americans found unendurable. Although neither the British nor the colonists yet realized it, the American Revolution had begun.

Step by step, in the course of a single decade, a group of separate political bodies, inhabited by people who (if we put aside the slaves who were outside the political system) were loyal subjects of Great Britain, had been forced by the logic of events—by new British policies and by a growing awareness of their common interests—to take political power into their own hands and to unite with one another to exercise that power effectively. Ordinary working people, not just merchants, lawyers, and other well-to-do people, played increasingly more prominent roles in public life as crisis after crisis roused their indignation. This did not yet mean that most Americans wanted to be free from British rule. Nearly every colonist was willing to see Great Britain continue to control, or at least regulate, such things as foreign relations, commercial policy, and other matters of general American interest. Parliament, however—and in the last analysis George III and most Britishers—insisted that their authority over the colonies was unlimited. Behind their stubbornness lay the arrogant psychology of the European: "*Colonists are inferior. . . . We own you.*"

Lord North directed the Coercive Acts at Massachusetts alone because he assumed that the other colonies, profiting from the discomfiture of Massachusetts, would not intervene, and because of the British tendency to think of the colonies as separate units connected only through London. His strategy failed because his assumption was incorrect: the colonies began at once to act in concert.

Extralegal political acts now became a matter of course. In June 1774 Massachusetts called for a meeting of delegates from all the colonies to consider common action. This First Continental Congress met at Philadelphia in September; only Georgia failed to send delegates. Many points of view were represented, but even the so-called conservative proposal, introduced by Joseph Galloway of Pennsylvania, called for a thorough overhaul of the empire. Galloway suggested an *American* government, consisting of a president general appointed by the king and a grand council chosen by the colonial assemblies, that would manage intercolonial affairs and possess a veto over parliamentary acts affecting the colonies.

This was not what the majority wanted. If taxation without representation was tyranny, so was all legislation. Therefore Parliament had no right to legislate in any way for the colonies. John Adams, while prepared to *allow* Parliament to regulate colonial trade, now believed that Parliament had no inherent right to control it. "The foundation . . . of all free government," he declared, "is a right in the people to participate in their legislative council." Americans "are entitled to a free and exclusive power of legislation in their several provincial legislatures."

Propelled by the reasoning of Adams and others, the Congress passed a declaration of grievances and resolves that amounted to a complete condemnation of Britain's actions since 1763. A Massachusetts proposal that the people take up arms to defend their rights was endorsed. The delegates also organized a "Continental Association" to boycott British goods and to stop all exports to the empire. To enforce this boycott, committees were appointed locally "to observe the conduct of all persons touching this association" and to expose violators to public scorn.

If the Continental Congress reflected the views of the majority—there is no reason to suspect that it did not—it is clear that the Americans had decided that drastic changes must be made. It was not merely a question of mutual defense against the threat of British power, not only (in Franklin's aphorism) a matter of hanging together lest they hang separately. A nation was being born.

Looking back many years later, one of the delegates to the First Continental Congress made just these points. He was John Adams of Massachusetts, and he said: "The revolution was complete, in the minds of the people, and the Union of the colonies, before the war commenced."

The furious American resistance to the new taxes baffled British officials. In 1774 Lord North declared that colonial opposition betrayed a "distempered state of turbulence." Some members of Parliament declared that the Americans had gone "stark staring mad" over taxes any reasonable person would pay willingly.

But what had begun as a dispute over taxes had shifted to a struggle over sovereignty. Colonists were not against taxes in principle—and their descendants would willingly (if not happily) pay taxes that most colonists would have regarded as base enslavement. The colonists insisted, however, that they also have a say in their governance. Their "madness," originally manifested in bitter opposition to trade taxes, would become a feverish commitment to war.

1650–1696	Parliament enacts Navigation Acts
1689–1697	King William's War (War of the League of Augsburg)
1699–1750	Parliament enacts laws regulating colonial manufacturing
1702–1713	Queen Anne's War (War of the Spanish Succession): France loses Nova Scotia, Newfoundland, and Hudson Bay to Britain
1733	Molasses Act's duty leads to smuggling
1738–1742	Religious enthusiasm surges during Great Awakening
1740–1748	King George's War (War of the Austrian Succession)
1743	Benjamin Franklin founds American Philosophical Society
1752	Franklin discovers nature of lightning
1754	Albany Congress paves way for Stamp Act Congress and Continental Congress
1754–1763	British and American Colonists fight French and Indians in French and Indian War (Seven Years' War)
1760	George III becomes king of England
1763	George III's Proclamation forbids settlement beyond Appalachians
1764	Sugar Act places tariffs on sugar, coffee, wines, and other imports
1765	Stamp Act places excise taxes on all printed matter, leads to Stamp Tax Congress
1766	Stamp Act is repealed; Declaratory Act asserts parliamentary authority over colonies
1767	Townshend Duties lead to Massachusetts Circular Letter
1770	Five American colonists die in Boston Massacre
1772	Colonists burn *Gaspee*
1773	Tea Act leads to Boston Tea Party
1774	Coercive Acts lead to First Continental Congress

The American Revolution

IN THE SPRING OF 2006, THE SAMUEL ADAMS BREWERY IN BOSTON announced its "Patriot Collection" of beers, each named for a Founding Father. "James Madison Dark Wheat" celebrated James Madison, who so loved beer that he "considered a proposal for a national brewery." "Ginger Honey Ale" was inspired by Thomas Jefferson and his wife, who together "brewed 15 gallons of ginger beer with fresh lemons and honey every two weeks." "George Washington Porter," a blend of aged and freshly brewed ales, honored the father of the nation's favorite beer. "Just as the founding fathers took America's destiny into their hands," the company declared, "so it was with their brewing."

The Founders are so deeply embedded in our culture that their names, in addition to appearing on beer bottles, can be spotted almost everywhere. "Washington" is the name of thirty-one counties and forty-two cities. Iowa and Indiana together have nearly a hundred "Washington" townships; California has twenty-eight "Washington Elementary Schools." After "Main Street," Washington is the most common street name in the United States. Schoolchildren relish his name: Since Washington's birthday was declared a national holiday in 1968, most states have chosen to honor him by keeping students home from school.

Indeed, the Founders now loom so large that it may seem they were invincible, their victory over the British empire a foregone conclusion. But in order for us to understand the American Revolution, we must examine it from the perspective of the past, before the names of the Founders adorned beer bottles and elementary schools, before the United States had become a mighty nation. The simple truth is that the American Revolution was accomplished by men and women who did not know whether they would succeed. At the outset, they did not even know whether they sought British concessions or independence, whether most colonists would side with them or remain loyal to His Majesty's government, whether foreign powers such as France could be enlisted to provide support, whether rebellion against political authority in London would undermine social order in America, or whether the many different peoples of the colonies could be knitted into a single nation. The revolutionaries did know, however, that if they failed they would likely face arrest, imprisonment, and even death.

As the colonial rebellion transformed into a full-scale war for independence, the colonists faced the challenges of creating and financing an army that could succeed against the Empire. In the midst of fighting, and in the wake of freedom from British rule, they faced an even greater challenge—the founding of a new nation, with a new government and a new national spirit.

The Shot Heard Round the World

The actions of the First Continental Congress led the British authorities to force a showdown with their bumptious colonial offspring. "The New England governments are in a state of rebellion," George III announced. "Blows must decide whether they are to be subject to this country or independent." General Thomas Gage, veteran of Braddock's ill-fated expedition against Fort Duquesne and now commander-in-chief of all British forces in North America, had already been appointed governor of Massachusetts. Some 4,000 Redcoats were concentrated in Boston, camped on the town common once peacefully reserved for the citizens' cows.

Parliament echoed with demands for a show of strength in America. After the Tea Party the general impression was that resistance to British rule was concentrated in Massachusetts. Based on the behavior of colonial militia in the French and Indian War, most Britishers did not think people in the other colonies would be inclined to fight outside their own region. General James Grant announced that with 1,000 men he "would undertake to go from one end of America to the other, and geld all the males, partly by force and partly by a little coaxing." Some opposed the idea of crushing the colonists, and others believed that it could not be easily managed, but they were a small minority. The House of Commons listened to Edmund Burke's magnificent speech on conciliating the colonies and then voted 270 to 78 against him.

The London government decided to use troops against Massachusetts in January 1775, but the order did not reach General Gage until April. In the interim both sides were active. Parliament voted new troop levies and declared Massachusetts to be in a state of rebellion. The Massachusetts Patriots, as they were now calling themselves, formed an extralegal provincial assembly, reorganized the militia, and began training "Minute Men" and other fighters. Soon companies armed with anything that would shoot were drilling on town commons throughout Massachusetts and in other colonies too.

When Gage received his orders on April 14, he acted swiftly. The Patriots had been accumulating arms at Concord, some 20 miles west of Boston. On the night of April 18, Gage dispatched 700 crack troops to seize these supplies. The Patriots were prepared. Paul Revere and other horsemen rode off to alert the countryside and warn John Hancock and Sam Adams, leaders of the provincial assembly, whose arrests had been ordered.

When the Redcoats reached Lexington early the next morning, they found the common occupied by about seventy Minute Men. After an argument, the Americans began to withdraw. Then someone fired a shot. There was a flurry of gunfire and the Minute Men fled, leaving eight of their number dead. The British then marched on to Concord, where they destroyed whatever supplies the Patriots had been unable to carry off.

But militiamen were pouring into the area from all sides. A hot skirmish at Concord's North Bridge forced the Redcoats to yield that position. Becoming alarmed, they began to march back to Boston. Soon they were being subjected to a withering fire from American irregulars along their line of march. A strange battle developed on a "field" 16 miles long and only a few hundred yards wide. Gage was obliged to send out an additional 1,500 soldiers, and total disaster was avoided only by deploying skirmishers to root out snipers hiding in barns and farmhouses along the road to Boston. When the first day of the Revolutionary War ended, the British had sustained 273 casualties, the Americans fewer than 100. "The Rebels are not the despicable rabble too many have supposed them to be," General Gage admitted.

For a brief moment of history tiny Massachusetts stood alone at arms against an empire that had humbled France and Spain. Yet Massachusetts assumed the offensive! The provincial government organized an expedition that captured Fort Ticonderoga and Crown Point, on Lake Champlain. The other colonies rallied quickly to the cause, sending reinforcements to Cambridge. When news of the battle reached Virginia, George Washington wrote sadly, "A brother's sword has been sheathed in a brother's breast and the once happy and peaceful plains of America are either to be drenched in blood or inhabited by a race of slaves." And then he added: "Can a virtuous man hesitate in his choice?"

Two weeks after the battle of Lexington and Concord, Ralph Earl, a colonial militiaman from Connecticut, was ordered to make sketches and paintings of what had transpired. Earl revisited the battlefield and interviewed those who had fought. He was an accurate painter. Note that each of the British formations, facing officers, contains exactly twenty-five men.

The Second Continental Congress

On May 10, 1775, the day Ticonderoga fell, the Second Continental Congress met in Philadelphia. It was a distinguished group, more radical than the First Congress. Besides John and Sam Adams, Patrick Henry and Richard Henry Lee of Virginia, and Christopher Gadsden of South Carolina, all holdovers from the First Congress, there was Thomas Jefferson, a lanky, sandy-haired young planter from Virginia. Jefferson had recently published "A Summary View of the Rights of British America," an essay criticizing the institution of monarchy and warning George III that "kings are the servants, not the proprietors of the people." The Virginia convention had also sent George Washington, who knew more than any other colonist about commanding men and who wore his buff-and-blue colonel's uniform, a not-too-subtle indication of his willingness to place this knowledge at the disposal of the Congress. The renowned Benjamin Franklin was a delegate, moving rapidly to the radical position.

The Boston merchant John Hancock was chosen president of the Congress, which, like the first, had no legal authority. Yet the delegates had to make agonizing decisions under the pressure of rapidly unfolding military events, with the future of every American depending on their actions. Delicate negotiations and honeyed words might yet persuade king and Parliament to change their ways, but precipitate, bold effort was essential to save Massachusetts.

In this predicament the Congress naturally dealt first with the military crisis. It organized the forces gathering around Boston into the so-called Continental Army and appointed George Washington commander in chief. After Washington and his staff left for Massachusetts on June 23, the Congress turned to the task of requisitioning men and supplies.

The Battle of Bunker Hill

Meanwhile, in Massachusetts, the first major battle of the war had been fought. The British position on the peninsula of Boston was impregnable to direct assault, but high ground north and south, at Charlestown and Dorchester Heights, could be used to pound the city with artillery. When the Continentals seized Bunker Hill and Breed's Hill at Charlestown and set up defenses on the latter, Gage determined at once to drive them off. This was accomplished on June 17. Twice the Redcoats marched in close ranks, bayonets fixed, up Breed's Hill, each time being driven back after suffering heavy losses. Stubbornly they came again, and this time they carried the redoubt, for the defenders had run out of ammunition.

The British then cleared the Charlestown peninsula, but the victory was really the Americans', for they had proved themselves against professional soldiers and had exacted a terrible toll. More than 1,000 Redcoats had fallen in a couple of hours, out of a force of some 2,500, while the Continentals lost only 400 men, most of them cut down by British bayonets after the hill was taken. "The day ended in glory," a British officer wrote, "but the loss was uncommon in officers for the number engaged."

The Battle of Bunker Hill, as it was called for no good reason, greatly reduced whatever hope remained for a negotiated settlement. The spilling of so much blood left each side determined to force the other's submission. The British recalled General Gage, replacing him with General William Howe, a respected veteran of the French and Indian War, and George III formally proclaimed the colonies to be "in open rebellion." The Continental Congress dispatched one last plea to the king (the Olive Branch Petition), but this was a sop to the moderates. Immediately thereafter it adopted the Declaration of the Causes and Necessity of Taking Up Arms, which condemned everything the British had done since 1763. Americans were "a people attacked by unprovoked enemies"; the time had come to choose between "submission" to "tyranny" and "resistance by force." The Congress then ordered an attack on Canada and created committees to seek foreign aid and to buy munitions abroad. It authorized the outfitting of a navy under Commodore Esek Hopkins of Rhode Island.

The Great Declaration

The Congress (and the majority of the people) still hung back from a break with the Crown. To declare for independence would be to burn the last bridge, to become traitors in the eyes of the mother country. Aside from the word's ugly associations, everyone knew what happened to traitors when their efforts failed. It was sobering to think of casting off everything that being English meant: love of king, the traditions of a great nation, pride in the power of a mighty empire. "Where shall we find another Britain?" John Dickinson had asked at the time of the Townshend Acts crisis. "Torn from the body to which we are united by religion, liberty, laws, affections, relation, language and commerce, we must bleed at every vein."

Then, too, rebellion might end in horrors worse than submission to British tyranny. The disturbances following the Stamp Act and the Tea Act had revealed an alarming fact about American society. The organizers of those protests, mostly persons of wealth and status, had thought in terms of "ordered resistance." They countenanced violence only as a means of forcing the British authorities to pay attention to their complaints. But protest meetings and mob actions had brought thousands of ordinary citizens into the struggle for local self-government. Some of the upper-class leaders among the Patriots, while eager to have their support, were concerned about what they would make of actual independence. In addition, not all the property that had been destroyed belonged to Loyalists and British officials. Too much exalted talk about "rights" and "liberties" might well give the poor (to say nothing of the slaves) an exaggerated impression of their importance.

Finally, in a world where every country had some kind of monarch, could common people *really* govern themselves? The most ardent defender of American rights might well hesitate after considering all the implications of independence.

Yet independence was probably inevitable by the end of 1775. The belief that George III had been misled by evil or stupid advisers on both sides of the Atlantic became progressively more difficult to sustain. Mistrust of Parliament—indeed, of the whole of British society—grew apace.

Two events in January 1776 pushed the colonies a long step toward a final break. First came the news that the British were sending hired Hessian soldiers to fight against them. Colonists associated mercenaries with looting and rape and feared that the German-speaking Hessians would run amok among them. Such callousness on the part of Britain made reconciliation seem out of the question.

The second decisive event was the publication of *Common Sense*. This tract was written by Thomas Paine, a one-time English corsetmaker and civil servant turned pamphleteer, a man who had been in America scarcely a year. *Common Sense* called boldly for complete independence. It attacked not only George III but the idea of monarchy itself. Paine applied the uncomplicated logic of the zealot to the recent history of America. Where the colonists had been humbly petitioning George III and swallowing their resentment when he ignored them, Paine called George a "Royal Brute" and "the hardened sullen-tempered Pharaoh of England." Many Americans had wanted to control their own affairs but feared the instability of untried republican government. To them Paine said: "We have it in our power to begin the world again." "A government of our own is our natural right," he insisted. "O! ye that love mankind! Ye that dare oppose not only tyranny but the tyrant, stand forth!"

The tone of the debate changed sharply as Paine's slashing attack took effect. In March 1776 the Congress unleashed privateers against British commerce; in April it opened American ports to foreign shipping; in May it urged the Patriots who had set up extralegal provincial conventions to frame constitutions and establish state governments.

On June 7 Richard Henry Lee of Virginia introduced a resolution of the Virginia Convention:

> RESOLVED: *That these United Colonies are, and of right ought to be, free and independent States, that they are absolved from all allegiance to the British Crown, and that all political connection between them and the State of Great Britain is, and ought to be, totally dissolved.*

This momentous resolution was not passed until July 2; the Congress first appointed a committee consisting of Thomas Jefferson, Benjamin Franklin, John Adams, Roger Sherman, and Robert Livingston to frame a suitable justification of independence.

Thomas Jefferson was probably placed on the committee because politics required that a Virginian be included and because of his literary skill and general intelligence. Aside from writing *A Summary View of the Rights of British America*, he had done little to attract notice. At age 33 he was the youngest member of the Continental Congress and was only marginally interested in its deliberations. He had been slow to take his seat in the fall of 1775, and he had gone home to Virginia before Christmas. He put off returning several times and arrived in Philadelphia

WAS THE AMERICAN REVOLUTION ROOTED IN CLASS STRUGGLE?

This 1795 engraving by John Trumbull of a Stamp Act protest delineates a class division. The three British Tories—one is suspended, the others are sprawled below—are wealthy. They wear wigs, stockings, and breeches; one has buckles on his shoes. The Patriots wear cloth hats, pants, and shoes with laces. Historian Carl Becker (1909) declared that the Revolution was fought "not only about home rule but also about who should rule at home." In his view, leaders of the Revolution sought not only to defeat the Crown in England but also the rabble in Boston and New York—the Patriots as depicted in the picture above. Arthur Schlesinger Sr. (1918) wrote that commercial elites "instigated" popular opposition to British policies, grew alarmed at the "engulfing tide of radicalism" that led to war, and then turned against the farmers and workers who did most of the fighting. Edmund Morgan (1956) rejected the notion that the Revolution grew out of class divisions. It did not constitute a victory of the rich over the poor, but "a union of three million cantankerous colonists into a new nation." Historians during the tumultuous 1960s underscored the divisions in American society. Gary B. Nash (1989) showed how declining opportunities had radicalized urban workers. Other social historians found yet other cleavages: Mary Beth Norton (1996) between men and women; Sylvia R. Frey (1991) between masters and slaves; Colin Calloway (1995) between colonists and Indians.

Carl Becker, *History of Political Parties in the Province of New York* (1909), Arthur M. Schlesinger Sr., *The Colonial Merchants and the American Revolution* (1918), Edmund Morgan, *The Birth of the Republic* (1956), Gary B. Nash, *The Urban Crucible* (1989), Mary Beth Norton, *Founding Mothers and Fathers* (1996), Sylvia R. Frey, *Water from the Rock* (1991), Colin Calloway, *American Revolution in Indian Country* (1995).

only on May 14. Had he delayed another month, someone else would have written the Declaration of Independence.

The committee asked Jefferson to prepare a draft. The result, with a few amendments made by Franklin and Adams and somewhat toned down by the whole Congress, was officially adopted by the delegates on July 4, 1776, two days after the delegates had voted for the decisive break with Great Britain.

Jefferson's Declaration of Independence (see the text of the document in the Appendix, pp. A-3–A-5) consisted of two parts. The first, introductory part justified the abstract right of any people to revolt and described the theory on which the Americans based their creation of a new, republican government. The second, much longer section was a list of the "injuries and usurpations" of George III, a bill of indictment explaining why the colonists felt driven to exercise the rights outlined in the first part of the document. Here Jefferson stressed the monarch's interference with the functioning of representative government in America, his harsh administration of colonial affairs, his restrictions on civil rights, and his maintenance of troops in the colonies without their consent.

Jefferson sought to marshal every possible evidence of British perfidy, and he made George III, rather than Parliament, the villain because the king was the personification of the nation against which America was rebelling. He held the monarch responsible for Parliament's efforts to tax the colonies and restrict their trade, for many actions by subordinates that George III had never deliberately authorized, and for some things that never happened. He even blamed the king for the existence of slavery in the colonies, a charge the Congress cut from the document not entirely because of its concern for accuracy. The long bill of particulars reads more like a lawyer's brief than a careful analysis, but it was intended to convince the world that the Americans had good reasons for exercising their right to form a government of their own.

This 1857 painting depicts the destruction of a statue of King George III during the Revolution. This rendering purges the "mob" action of its menacing violence: the arm gestures are celebratory rather than threatening, and the women and children are well-to-do. This is a middle-class view of the American Revolution, bloodless, public-spirited, and consensual.

Jefferson's general statement of the right of revolution has inspired oppressed peoples all over the world for more than 200 years:

> We hold these truths to be self-evident, that all men are created equal, that they are endowed by their Creator with certain unalienable Rights, that among these are Life, Liberty and the pursuit of Happiness. That to secure these rights, Governments are instituted among Men, deriving their just powers from the consent of the governed, That whenever any Form of Government becomes destructive of these ends, it is the Right of the People to alter or to abolish it, and to institute new Government. . . .

The Declaration was intended to influence foreign opinion, but its proclamation had little immediate effect outside Great Britain, and there it only made people angry and determined to subdue the rebels. A substantial number of European military men offered their services to the new nation, and a few of these might be called idealists, but most were adventurers and soldiers of fortune, thinking mostly of their own advantage. Why, then, has the Declaration had so much influence on modern history? Not because the thought was original with Jefferson. As John Adams later pointed out—Adams viewed his great contemporary with a mixture of affection, respect, and jealousy—the basic idea was commonplace among eighteenth-century liberals. "I did not consider it any part of my charge to invent new ideas," Jefferson explained, "but to place before mankind the common sense of the subject, in terms so plain and firm as to command their assent. . . . It was intended to be an expression of the American mind."

Revolution was not new, but the spectacle of a people solemnly explaining and justifying their right, in an orderly manner, to throw off their oppressors and establish a new system on their own authority was almost without precedent. Soon the French would be drawing on this example in their revolution, and rebels everywhere have since done likewise. And if Jefferson did not create the concept, he gave it a nearly perfect form.

1776: The Balance of Forces

A formal declaration of independence merely cleared the way for tackling the problems of founding a new nation. Lacking both traditions and authority based in law, the Congress had to create political institutions and a new national spirit, all in the midst of war.

Always the military situation took precedence, for a single disastrous setback might make everything else meaningless. At the start the Americans already possessed their lands (except for the few square miles occupied by British troops). Although thousands of colonists fought for George III, the British soon learned that to put down the American rebellion they would have to bring in men and supplies from bases on the other side of the Atlantic. This was a most formidable task.

Certain long-run factors operated in America's favor. Although His Majesty's soldiers were brave and well disciplined, the army was as inefficient and ill directed

A 1797 engraving of Deborah Sampson, the first woman to serve as a soldier in the Revolution. Born in 1760, Sampson in 1782 put on men's clothes and enlisted in the Massachusetts Militia under the name of Timothy Thayer. Her imposture was discovered and she was expelled. She then enlisted as Robert Shurtlieff in the Continental army. At a battle against Loyalists at Tarrytown, New York, she was wounded in the thigh. Rather than let a doctor treat her—and discover her gender—she extracted the musket ball herself. After the war, she continued to wear men's clothing until she married and had children.

as the rest of the British government. Whereas nearly everyone in Great Britain wanted to crack down on Boston after the Tea Party, many boggled at engaging in a full-scale war against all the colonies. Aside from a reluctance to spill so much blood, there was the question of expense. Finally, the idea of dispatching the cream of the British army to America while powerful enemies on the Continent still smarted from past defeats seemed risky. For all these reasons the British approached gingerly the task of subduing the rebellion. When Washington fortified Dorchester Heights overlooking Boston, General Howe withdrew his troops to Halifax rather than risk another Bunker Hill.

For a time, the initiative remained with the Americans. An expedition under General Richard Montgomery captured Montréal in November 1775, and another small force under Benedict Arnold advanced to the gates of Québec after a grueling march across the wilderness from Maine. Montgomery and Arnold attempted to storm the Québec defenses on December 31, 1775, but were repulsed with heavy losses. Even so, the British troops in Canada could not drive the remnants of the American army—perhaps 500 men in all—out of the province until reinforcements arrived in the spring.

Awareness of Britain's problems undoubtedly spurred the Continental Congress to the bold actions of the spring of 1776. However, on July 2, 1776, the same day that Congress voted for independence, General Howe was back on American soil, landing in force on Staten Island in New York harbor in preparation for an assault on the city. Soon Howe had at hand 32,000 well-equipped troops and a powerful fleet commanded by his brother, Richard, Lord Howe. If the British controlled New York City and the Hudson River, they could, as Washington realized, "stop intercourse between the northern and southern Colonies, upon which depends the Safety of America."

Suddenly the full strength of the empire seemed to have descended on the Americans. Superior British resources (a population of 9 million to the colonies' 2.5 million, large stocks of war materials and the industrial capacity to boost them further, mastery of the seas, a well-trained and experienced army, a highly centralized and, when necessary, ruthless government) were now all too evident.

The demonstration of British might in New York harbor accentuated American military and economic weaknesses: Both money and the tools of war were continually in short supply in a predominantly agricultural country. Many of Washington's soldiers were armed with weapons no more lethal than spears and tomahawks. Few had proper uniforms. Even the most patriotic resisted conforming to the conventions of military discipline; the men hated drilling and all parade-ground formality. And all these problems were complicated by the fact that Washington had to create an army organization out of whole cloth at the same time that he was fighting a war.

Supply problems were handled inefficiently and often corruptly. Few officers knew much about such mundane but vital matters as how to construct and maintain proper sanitary facilities when large numbers of soldiers were camped at one place for extended periods of time. What was inelegantly known as "the itch" afflicted soldiers throughout the war.

Loyalists

Behind the lines, the country was far from united. Whereas nearly all colonists had objected to British policies, many still hesitated to take up arms against the mother country. Even Massachusetts harbored many Loyalists, or Tories, as they were called; about a thousand Americans left Boston with General Howe, abandoning their homes rather than submit to the rebel army.

No one knows exactly how the colonists divided on the question of independence. John Adams's off-the-cuff estimate was that a third of the people were ardent Patriots, another third loyal to Great Britain, and the rest neutral or tending to favor whichever side seemed to be winning. This guess is probably as useful as any, although in keeping with Adams's character he may have understated the number who agreed with him and overstated those opposed to his position. Most historians think that about a fifth of the people were Loyalists and about two-fifths Patriots, but there are few hard figures to go by. What is certain is that large elements, perhaps a majority of the people, were more or less indifferent to the conflict or, in Tom Paine's famous phrase, were summer soldiers and sunshine patriots—they supported the Revolution when all was going well and lost their enthusiasm in difficult hours.

The divisions cut across geographical, social, and economic lines. A high proportion of those holding royal appointments and many Anglican clergymen remained loyal to King George, as did numbers of merchants with close connections in Britain. There were important pockets of Tory strength in rural sections of New

York, in the North Carolina backcountry, and among persons of non-English origin and other minority groups who tended to count on London for protection against the local majority.

The Tories lacked organization. While Patriot leaders worked closely together, many of the Tory "leaders" did not even know one another. They had no central committee to lay plans or coordinate their efforts. When the revolutionaries took over a colony, some Tories fled; others sought the protection of the British army; others took up arms; and still others accommodated themselves silently to the new regime.

If the differences separating Patriot from Loyalist are unclear, feelings were nonetheless bitter. Individual Loyalists were often set upon by mobs, tarred and feathered, and otherwise abused. Some were thrown into jail for no legitimate reason; others were exiled and their property confiscated. Battles between Tory units and the Continental Army were often exceptionally bloody. "Neighbor was against neighbor, father against son and son against father," one Connecticut Tory reported. "He that would not thrust his own blade through his brother's heart was called an infamous villain."

Early British Victories

General Howe's campaign against New York brought to light another American weakness—the lack of military experience. Washington, expecting Howe to attack New York, had moved south to meet the threat immediately after Howe had abandoned Boston. But both he and his men failed badly in this first major test. Late in August Howe crossed from Staten Island to Brooklyn. In the Battle of Long Island he easily outflanked and defeated Washington's army. Had he acted decisively, he could probably have ended the war on the spot, but Howe could not make up his mind whether to be a peacemaker or a conqueror. This hesitation in consolidating his gains permitted Washington to withdraw his troops to Manhattan Island.

Howe could still have trapped Washington simply by using his fleet to land troops on the northern end of Manhattan; instead he attacked New York City directly, leaving the Americans an escape route to the north. Again Patriot troops proved no match for British regulars. Although Washington threw his hat to the ground in a rage and threatened to shoot cowardly Connecticut soldiers as they fled the battlefield, he could not stop the rout and had to fall back on Harlem Heights in upper Manhattan. Yet once more Howe failed to pursue his advantage promptly.

Still, Washington refused to see the peril in remaining on an island while the enemy commanded the surrounding waters. Only when Howe shifted a powerful force to Westchester, directly threatening his rear, did Washington move north to the mainland. Finally, after several narrow escapes, he crossed the Hudson River and marched south to New Jersey, where the British could not use their naval superiority against him.

New York and New Jersey Campaigns, 1776–1777

The battles in and around New York City seemed to presage an easy British triumph. Yet somehow Washington salvaged a moral victory from these ignominious defeats. He learned rapidly; seldom thereafter did he place his troops in such vulnerable positions. And his men, in spite of repeated failure, had become an army. In November and December 1776 they retreated across New Jersey and into Pennsylvania. General Howe then abandoned the campaign, going into winter quarters in New York but posting garrisons at Trenton, Princeton, and other strategic points.

The troops at Trenton were hated Hessian mercenaries, and Washington decided to attack them. He crossed the ice-clogged Delaware River with 2,400 men on Christmas night during a wild storm. The little army then marched nine miles to Trenton, arriving at daybreak in the midst of a sleet storm. The Hessians were taken by surprise. Those who could fled in disorder; the rest—900 of them—surrendered.

The Hessians were first-class professional soldiers, probably the most competent troops in Europe at that time. The victory gave a boost to American morale. A few days later Washington outmaneuvered General Cornwallis, who had rushed to Trenton with reinforcements, and won another battle at Princeton. These engagements had little strategic importance, since both armies then went into winter quarters. Without them, however, there might not have been an army to resume the war in the spring.

Saratoga and the French Alliance

When spring reached New Jersey in April 1777, Washington had fewer than 5,000 men under arms. Great plans—far too many and too complicated, as it turned out—were afoot in the British camp. The strategy called for General John Burgoyne to lead a large army from Canada down Lake Champlain toward Albany while a smaller force under Lieutenant Colonel Barry St. Leger pushed eastward toward Albany from Fort Oswego on Lake Ontario. General Howe was to lead a third force north up the Hudson. The Patriots would be trapped and the New England states isolated from the rest.

As a venture in coordinated military tactics, the British campaign of 1777 was a fiasco. General Howe had spent the winter in New York wining and dining his officers and prominent local Loyalists and having a torrid affair with the wife of the

The British generals were criticized at home for their losses during the Revolutionary War. This 1779 cartoon shows a British commander in America relaxing in his command tent while his defeated colleagues surrender at Saratoga.

officer in charge of prisoners of war. He was less attentive to his responsibilities for the British army advancing south from Canada.

General "Gentleman Johnny" Burgoyne, a charming if somewhat bombastic character, part politician, part poet, part gambler, part ladies' man, yet also a brave soldier, had begun his march from Canada in mid-June. By early July his army, which consisted of 500 Indians, 650 Loyalists, and 6,000 regulars, had captured Fort Ticonderoga at the southern end of Lake Champlain. He quickly pushed beyond Lake George but then bogged down. Burdened by a huge baggage train that included 138 pieces of generally useless artillery, more than thirty carts laden with his personal wardrobe and supply of champagne, and his mistress, he could advance at but a snail's pace through the dense woods north of Saratoga.[1] Patriot militia impeded his way by felling trees across the forest trails.

St. Leger was also slow in carrying out his part of the grand design. He did not leave Fort Oswego until July 26, and when he stopped to besiege a Patriot force at Fort Stanwix, General Benedict Arnold had time to march west with 1,000 men from the army resisting Burgoyne and drive him back to Oswego.

Meanwhile, with magnificent disregard for the agreed-on plan, Howe wasted time trying to trap Washington into exposing his army in New Jersey. This enabled Washington to send some of his best troops to buttress the militia units opposing Burgoyne. Then, just when St. Leger was setting out for Albany, Howe took the bulk of his army off by sea to attack Philadelphia, leaving only a small force commanded by General Sir Henry Clinton to aid Burgoyne.

When Washington moved south to oppose Howe, the Britisher taught him a series of lessons in tactics, defeating him at the Battle of Brandywine, then luring him out of position and moving unopposed into Philadelphia. But by that time it was late September, and disaster was about to befall General Burgoyne.

The American forces under Philip Schuyler and later under Horatio Gates and Benedict Arnold had erected formidable defenses immediately south of Saratoga. Burgoyne struck at this position twice and was thrown back both times with heavy losses. Each day more local militia swelled the American forces. Soon Burgoyne was under siege, his troops pinned down by withering fire from every direction, unable even to bury their dead. The only hope was General Clinton, who had finally started up the Hudson from New York. Clinton got as far as Kingston, about 80 miles below Saratoga, but on October 16 he decided to return to New York for reinforcements. The next day, at Saratoga, Burgoyne surrendered. Some 5,700 British prisoners were marched off to Virginia.

This overwhelming triumph changed the course and character of the war. France would probably have entered the war in any case; the country had never reconciled itself to its losses in the Seven Years' War and for years had been build-

---

[1]*Many soldiers, enlisted men as well as officers, were accompanied by their wives or other women on campaigns. More than 2,000 accompanied the Burgoyne expedition. At one point Washington complained of "the multitude of women . . . especially those who are pregnant, or have children [that] clog upon every movement." Actually, women in eighteenth-century armies worked hard, doing most of the cooking, washing, and other "housekeeping" tasks.*

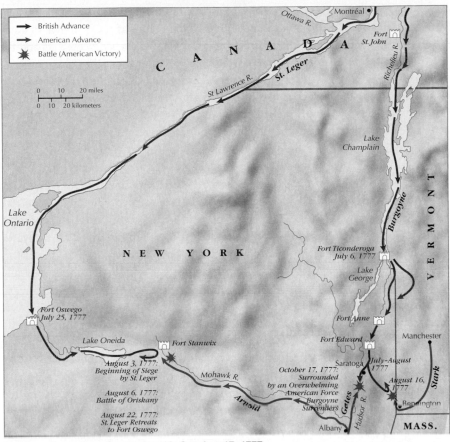

Saratoga Campaign, September 19–October 17, 1777

ing a navy capable of taking on the British. Helping the Americans was simply another way of weakening their British enemy. As early as May 1776 the Comte de Vergennes, France's foreign minister, had persuaded Louis XVI to authorize the expenditure of 1 million livres for munitions for America, and more was added the next year. Spain also contributed, not out of sympathy for the Revolution but because of its desire to injure Great Britain. Soon vital supplies were being funneled secretly to the rebels through a dummy company, Roderigue Hortalez et Cie. When news of the victory at Saratoga reached Paris, the time seemed ripe and Louis XVI recognized the United States. Then Vergennes and three American commissioners in Paris, Benjamin Franklin, Arthur Lee, and Silas Deane, drafted a commercial treaty and a formal treaty of alliance. The two nations agreed to make "common cause and aid each other mutually" should war "break out" between France and Great Britain. Meanwhile, France guaranteed "the sovereignty and independence absolute and unlimited" of the United States. The help of Spain and France, Washington declared, "will not fail of establishing the Independence of America in a short time."

When the news of Saratoga reached England, Lord North realized that a Franco-American alliance was almost inevitable. To forestall it, he was ready to give in on all the issues that had agitated the colonies before 1775. Both the Coercive Acts and the Tea Act would be repealed; Parliament would pledge never to tax the colonies.

Instead of implementing this proposal promptly, Parliament delayed until March 1778. Royal peace commissioners did not reach Philadelphia until June, a month after Congress had ratified the French treaty. The British proposals were icily rejected, and while the peace commissioners were still in Philadelphia, war broke out between France and Great Britain.

The American Revolution, however, had yet to be won. After the loss of Philadelphia, Washington had settled his army for the winter at Valley Forge, 20 miles to the northwest. The army's supply system collapsed. Often the men had nothing to eat but "fire cake," a mixture of ground grain and water molded on a stick or in a pan and baked in a campfire. According to the Marquis de Lafayette, one of many Europeans who volunteered to fight on the American side, "the unfortunate soldiers . . . had neither coats, nor hats, nor shirts, nor shoes; their feet and legs froze till they grew black, and it was often necessary to amputate them."

To make matters worse, there was grumbling in Congress over Washington's failure to win victories and talk of replacing him as commander-in-chief with Horatio Gates, the "hero" of Saratoga. (In fact, Gates was an indifferent soldier, lacking in decisiveness and unable to instill confidence in his subordinates.)

As the winter dragged on, the Continental Army melted away. So many officers resigned that Washington was heard to say that he was afraid of "being left Alone with the Soldiers only." Since enlisted men could not legally resign, they deserted by the hundreds. Yet the army survived. Gradually the soldiers who remained became a tough, professional fighting force.

The War Moves South

Spring brought a revival of American hopes in the form of more supplies, new recruits, and, above all, word of the French alliance. In May 1778 the British replaced General Howe as commander with General Clinton, who decided to transfer his base back to New York. While Clinton was moving across New Jersey, Washington attacked him at Monmouth Court House. The fight was inconclusive, but the Americans held the field when the day ended and were able to claim a victory.

Thereafter British strategy changed. Fighting in the northern states degenerated into skirmishes and other small-unit clashes. Instead, relying on sea power, the supposed presence of many Tories in the South, and the possibility of obtaining the help of slaves, the British concentrated their efforts in South Carolina and Georgia. Savannah fell to them late in 1778, and most of the settled parts of Georgia were overrun during 1779. In 1780 Clinton led a massive expedition against Charleston. When the city surrendered in May, more than 3,000 soldiers were captured, the most overwhelming American defeat of the war. Leaving General Cornwallis and some 8,000 men to carry on the campaign, Clinton then sailed back to New York.

The Tories in South Carolina and Georgia came closer to meeting British expectations than in any other region, but the callous behavior of the British troops persuaded large numbers of hesitating citizens to join the Patriot cause. Guerrilla bands led by Francis Marion, the "Swamp Fox," Thomas Sumter, after whom Fort Sumter, famous in the Civil War, was named, and others like them provided a nucleus of resistance in areas that had supposedly been subdued.

But the tide soon turned. In 1779 the Spanish governor of Louisiana, José de Gálvez, administered a stinging defeat to British troops in Florida, and in 1780 and 1781 he captured the British-held Gulf ports of Pensacola and Mobile. More important, in June 1780 Congress placed Horatio Gates in charge of a southern army consisting of the irregular militia units and a hard core of Continentals transferred from Washington's command. Gates encountered Cornwallis at Camden, South Carolina. Foolishly, he entrusted a key sector of his line to untrained militiamen, who panicked when the British charged with fixed bayonets. Gates suffered heavy losses and had to fall back. Congress then recalled him, sensibly permitting Washington to replace him with General Nathanael Greene, a first-rate officer.

A band of militiamen had trapped a contingent of Tories at King's Mountain and forced its surrender. Greene, avoiding a major engagement with Cornwallis's superior numbers, divided his troops and staged a series of raids on scattered points. In January 1781, at the Battle of Cowpens in northwestern South Carolina, General Daniel Morgan inflicted a costly defeat on Colonel Banastre Tarleton, one of Cornwallis's most effective officers. Cornwallis pursued Morgan hotly, but the American rejoined Greene, and at Guilford Court House they again inflicted heavy losses on the British. Then Cornwallis withdrew to Wilmington, North Carolina, where he could rely on the fleet for support and reinforcements. Greene's Patriots quickly regained control of the Carolina backcountry.

Victory at Yorktown

Seeing no future in the Carolinas and unwilling to vegetate at Wilmington, Cornwallis marched north into Virginia, where he joined forces with troops under Benedict Arnold. (Disaffected by what he considered unjust criticism of his generalship, Arnold had sold out to the British in 1780. He intended to betray the bastion of West Point on the Hudson River. The scheme was foiled when incriminating papers were found on the person of a British spy, Major John André. Arnold fled to the British and André was hanged.) As in the Carolina campaign, the British had numerical superiority at first but lost it rapidly when local militia and Continental forces concentrated against them. Cornwallis soon discovered that Virginia Tories were of little help in such a situation. "When a Storm threatens, our friends disappear," he grumbled.

General Clinton ordered Cornwallis to establish a base at Yorktown, where he could be supplied by sea. It was a terrible mistake. The British navy in American waters far outnumbered American and French vessels, but the Atlantic is wide, and in those days communication was slow. The French had a fleet in the West Indies under Admiral François de Grasse and another squadron at Newport, Rhode Island,

Legend:
- British Army Assembly Area, Jan. 1781
- American Army Assembly Area, Jan. 1781
- British Advance
- British Outpost, 1781
- American Clearing Operation, Late 1781
- Town Still Held by British, End 1781
- British Victory
- American Victory

PENNSYLVANIA

MARYLAND

NEW JERSEY

DEL.

Chesapeake Bay

VIRGINIA

Monticello · *Detachment*

Richmond

Petersburg · Yorktown

Guilford Court House
March 15, 1781

Kings Mountain
Oct. 7, 1880

Cowpens
Jan. 17, 1781

Charlotte

NORTH CAROLINA

Cheraw Hill

Winnsboro · Camden
Aug. 16, 1780

Wilmington

Augusta

SOUTH CAROLINA

Georgetown

GEORGIA

Charleston
Captured, May 12, 1780

Savannah

Clinton sails with Cornwallis from New York, Dec. 1779

ATLANTIC OCEAN

SPANISH TERRITORY

0   50   100 miles
0   50   100 kilometers

Campaign in the South, 1779–1781

where a French army was stationed. In the summer of 1781 Washington, de Grasse, and the Comte de Rochambeau, commander of French land forces, designed and carried out with an efficiency unparalleled in eighteenth-century warfare a complex plan to bottle up Cornwallis.

The British navy in the West Indies and at New York might have forestalled this scheme had it moved promptly and in force. But Admiral Sir George Rodney sent only part of his Indies fleet. As a result, de Grasse, after a battle with a British fleet commanded by Admiral Thomas Graves, won control of the Chesapeake and cut Cornwallis off from the sea.

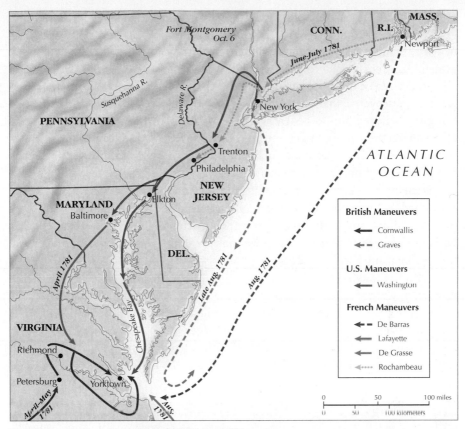

The Yorktown Campaign, April–September 1781

The next move was up to Washington, and this was his finest hour as a commander. He desperately wanted to attack the British base at New York, but at the urging of Rochambeau he agreed instead to strike at Yorktown. After tricking Clinton into thinking he was heading for New York, he pushed boldly south. In early September he reached Yorktown and joined up with an army commanded by Lafayette and troops from de Grasse's fleet. He soon had nearly 17,000 French and American veterans in position.

Cornwallis was helpless. He held out until October 17 and then asked for terms. Two days later more than 7,000 British soldiers marched out of their lines and laid down their arms. Then the jubilant Lafayette ordered his military band to play "Yankee Doodle."

Negotiating a Favorable Peace

The British gave up trying to suppress the rebellion after Yorktown, but the event that confirmed the existence of the United States as an independent nation was the signing of a peace treaty with Great Britain.

The Continental Congress appointed John Adams, Benjamin Franklin, John Jay, Thomas Jefferson, and Henry Laurens as a commission to conduct peace talks in Paris, France. Franklin and Jay did most of the actual negotiating. Congress, grateful for French aid during the Revolution, had instructed the commissioners to rely on the advice of the Comte de Vergennes. In Paris, however, the commissioners soon discovered that Vergennes was not the perfect friend of America that Congress believed him to be. He was, after all, a French official, and France had other interests far more important than concern for its American ally. Vergennes "means to keep his hand under our chin to prevent us from drowning," Adams complained, "but not to lift our head out of the water."

Franklin, whose fame as a scientist and sage had spread to Europe, was wined and dined by the cream of Paris and petted and fussed over by some of the city's most beautiful women. He did not press the American point of view as forcefully as he might have. But this was because he took the long view, which was to achieve a true reconciliation with the British, not simply to drive the hardest bargain possible. John Jay was somewhat more tough-minded. But on basic issues all the Americans were in agreement.

By the end of November 1782 a preliminary treaty had been signed. "His Britannic Majesty," Article 1 began, "acknowledges the said United States . . . to be free, sovereign and independent States." Other terms were equally in line with American hopes and objectives. The boundaries of the nation were set at the Great

The surrender of Cornwallis at Yorktown on October 19, 1781, painted by John Trumbull in 1820. In 1789 Trumbull, who had served as an aide to Washington, wrote to Thomas Jefferson that he wanted to make paintings "to preserve and diffuse the memory of the noblest series of actions which have e'er presented themselves to the history of man"—the American Revolution. The next year he went to London to study painting with Benjamin West; he was promptly arrested as an American spy. Fortunately, West had made connections with King George III and managed to spare Trumbull from the gallows.

Lakes, the Mississippi River, and 31° north latitude (roughly the northern boundary of Florida, which the British turned over to Spain).[2] Britain recognized the right of Americans to take fish on the Grand Banks off Newfoundland and, far more important, to dry and cure their catch on unsettled beaches in Labrador and Nova Scotia. The British agreed to withdraw their troops from American soil "with all convenient speed." On the touchy problem of Tory property seized during the Revolution, the Americans agreed only that Congress would "earnestly recommend" that the states "provide for the restitution of all estates, rights and properties which have been confiscated." They promised to prevent further property confiscation and prosecutions of Tories—certainly a wise as well as a humane policy—and they agreed not to impede the collection of debts owed British subjects. Vergennes was flabbergasted by the success of the Americans. "The English buy the peace more than they make it," he wrote. "Their concessions . . . exceed all that I should have thought possible."

The American commissioners obtained these favorable terms because they were shrewd diplomats and because of the rivalries that existed among the great European powers. In the last analysis, Britain preferred to have a weak nation of English-speaking people in command of the Mississippi Valley rather than France or Spain.

From their experience at the peace talks, the American leaders learned the importance of playing one power against another without committing themselves completely to any. This policy demanded constant contact with European affairs and skill at adjusting policies to changes in the European balance of power. It enabled the United States, a young and relatively feeble country, to grow and prosper.

National Government Under the Articles of Confederation

Independence was won on the battlefield and at the Paris Peace Conference, but it could not have been achieved without the work of the Continental Congress and the new state governments. The delegates recognized that the Congress was essentially a legislative body rather than a complete government and from the start they struggled to create a workable central authority. But their effort was handicapped by much confusion and bickering, and early military defeats sapped their energy and morale. In July 1776 John Dickinson prepared a draft national constitution, but it could not command much support. The larger states objected to equal representation of all the states, and the states with large western land claims refused to cede them to the central government. It was not until

(text continues on page 150)

---

[2]*Much of this vast region, of course, was controlled not by the British but by various Indian tribes.*

The Patriot

As the opening credits roll, Benjamin Martin (played by Mel Gibson) pries open a wooden box. It contains yellowing papers, a few medals and a tomahawk. He lifts the tomahawk, fingers its handle gingerly, and stares at the blade. "I had long feared that my sins would revisit me," a voice intones, "and the cost is more than I can bear." The viewer suspects—rightly, it turns out—that Martin's sins were violent, and that they had something to do with hacking people apart. But at the outset of *The Patriot*, Hollywood's $100-million blockbuster on the American Revolution, Martin is more pacifist than patriot. When the South Carolina legislature votes to go to war with Great Britain, he publicly declares that his chief obligation is to his family: "I will not fight."

He soon changes his mind after the British capture Charleston (1780), which brings onto the scene a villainous British cavalry officer, Colonel Tavington. Ordered by General Cornwallis to subdue the insurrection in the countryside, Tavington ransacks plantations, forces slaves into the King's service, and hounds the rebel militia. He also arrests Gabriel (Heath Ledger), Martin's oldest son, and orders the boy's execution as a spy. When Gabriel's younger brother tries to intervene, Tavington shoots the boy dead. Overcome with rage, Martin races to his room, grabs the hatchet, and proceeds to bury it—repeatedly—into the chests and skulls of countless British soldiers. He takes command of the militia, recruits more Patriots, and harries the British at every turn.

Mel Gibson as a Patriot leader with Jason Isaacs as Colonel Tavington, a barbarous British officer.

Tavington responds by intensifying his campaign against the rebels. His culminating barbarity is to round up the villagers of Wakefield (including Gabriel's fiancé), herd them into a church, and set it ablaze. All perish in unimaginable (and mercifully unfilmed) agony. Martin checks his rage long enough to plot the defeat of Cornwallis's army. This occurs at the Battle of Cowpens, where the militia holds its position despite being blasted by British artillery and decimated by repeated fusillades. When Tavington leads a cavalry charge, Martin's eyes widen and he reaches for the tomahawk. Tavington dies at Martin's hands, and Cornwallis is routed, too; the latter's subsequent surrender at Yorktown is now a foregone conclusion.

Historians have found much to criticize in the movie's retelling of the war in the South. There was no such person as Benjamin Martin, though elements of his story can be found in the exploits of guerrilla leaders such as Francis Marion ("the Swamp Fox"), Thomas Sumter, Andrew Pickens, and General Daniel Morgan, who commanded the Continentals at Cowpens. Although the British cavalry wear red uniforms in the movie, they were known as the Green Dragoons for a reason that seemingly eluded the filmmakers. The movie's version of the Battle of Cowpens featured a glorious display of fireworks, though neither army's artillery in South Carolina was capable of firing explosive shells. Cornwallis was not humiliated at Cowpens because he was not there. In the movie the British are caricatured as either evil geniuses or bungling twits; and the Patriots, as big-hearted rogues or pious patriarchs. The real combatants doubtless adhered less predictably to type. The most serious deviation from the historical record was the incineration of the occupied church: there is no record of any such event. "*The Patriot* is to history what Godzilla was to biology," declared historian David Hackett Fischer.

However, *The Patriot* raises and thoughtfully addresses an important historical issue: How can any society reconcile peaceable virtues—love for family, neighborliness, cooperation—with the violence of war? In *The Patriot*, the dilemma is symbolized by

Colonel Banastre Tarleton, on whom Tavington was based.

Martin's tomahawk. This weapon helps free his captured son and vanquish the evil Tavington; and yet it is also a manifestation of Martin's savage, even pathological, rage. Martin's secret shame, alluded to in the opening scene, was his dismembering corpses after a particularly brutal battle during the French and Indian War.

Eighteenth-century Europeans were in fact preoccupied with reconciling the violence of war with the need for social order. Their particular refinement of the military arts was the ordered massing of musket fire. The technology of warfare required intense discipline; and the new penchant for order imposed seeming coherence upon the chaos of the battlefield.

The Patriot provides a vivid rendering of this juxtaposition. Soldiers in beautifully colored uniforms march in straight, regular columns to the steady cadence of drums while officers bark precise commands: "Circle right. Face forward. Lift weapons . . ." These stately preliminaries, depicted on ripening fields beneath a summer sun, provide an unsettling backdrop for the ensuing violence: volleys of musket fire shatter the formations; low-velocity cannon balls decapitate soldiers; and bayonets pierce their chests.

Martin concludes that the British cannot be defeated in this type of battle. And they seldom were. Martin advocates guerrilla tactics, as did many southern Patriot militiamen. The British had good reason to doubt the legitimacy of this type of warfare. When men went wild on the battlefield, or fired shots and then hid among civilians, they were criminals, not soldiers. If such behavior were condoned, warfare would become barbarity.

The movie develops this point at considerable length. During a truce, Martin confers with Cornwallis, who complains that the

Patriot militia aimed at officers at the beginning of battles. Such behavior was inconsistent with "civilized warfare." The movie's debate over the nature of "civilized" warfare parallels an ongoing debate at the time. At the outset of the war, British officers took an oath affirming the British Articles of War, which protected citizens and soldiers who had surrendered. The American Congress also adopted the British Articles of War as the basis for discipline and military justice. But with the outbreak of guerrilla warfare in the South, both sides frequently ignored these rules.

"Colonel Tavington" was obviously based on Banastre Tarleton, the actual commander of the Green Dragoons. Tarleton became notorious after his soldiers raped three plantation women and killed several militiamen who had surrendered. This behavior worried Cornwallis, who sent a dispatch that, while commending his subordinate's courage and zeal, also included a warning: "Use your utmost endeavors to prevent the troops under your command from committing irregularities." In a subsequent engagement at Waxhaws, however, Tarleton again lost control of his men, who stabbed and slashed vanquished foes. An American officer discovered that the American corpses at Waxhaws had each received, on the average, sixteen wounds.

British and American officers sought to affirm that the war could be civilized. But such high-minded notions were repeatedly subverted during tomahawk-wielding guerrilla warfare and by excessively zealous commanders. The question then remained, as it does today, whether unchecked aggression is, among soldiers, a virtue or a vice. *The Patriot* raises these issues but does not resolve them. Martin, surely, should have kept his tomahawk in its locked box; but if he had, would the Patriots have won?

Questions for Discussion

- Do you think that the justice of a cause warrants the use of violence to attain it?
- Was guerrilla warfare in the South morally justified?
- In general, how can filmmakers contribute to understanding the past? How are they likely to alter the past to suit cinematic purposes?

November 1777 that the Articles of Confederation were submitted to the states for ratification. The approval of all the states was required before the Articles could go into effect. All acted fairly promptly but Maryland, which did not ratify the document until 1781.

The Articles merely provided a legal basis for authority that the Continental Congress had already been exercising. Each state, regardless of size, was to have but one vote; the union it created was only a "league of friendship." Article 2 defined the limit of national power: "Each state retains its sovereignty, freedom, and independence, and every Power, jurisdiction, and right, which is not by this confederation expressly delegated to the United States, in Congress assembled." Time proved this an inadequate arrangement, chiefly because the central government lacked the authority to impose taxes and had no way of enforcing the powers it did have.

Financing the War

In practice, Congress and the states carried on the war cooperatively. General officers were appointed by Congress, lesser ones locally. The Continental Army, the backbone of Washington's force, was supported by Congress. The states raised militia chiefly for short-term service. Militiamen fought well at times but often proved unreliable, especially when asked to fight at any great distance from their homes. Washington continually fretted about their "dirty mercenary spirit" and their "intractable" nature, yet he could not have won the war without them.

The fact that Congress's requisitions of money often went unhonored by the states does not mean that the states failed to contribute heavily to the war effort. Altogether they spent about $5.8 million in hard money, and they met Congress's demands for beef, corn, rum, fodder, and other military supplies. In addition, Congress raised large sums by borrowing. Americans bought bonds worth between $7 and $8 million during the war. Foreign governments lent another $8 million, most of this furnished by France. Congress also issued more than $240 million in paper money, the states over $200 million more. This currency fell rapidly in value, resulting in an inflation that caused hardship and grumbling. The people, in effect, paid much of the cost of the war through the depreciation of their savings, but it is hard to see how else the war could have been financed, given the prejudice of the populace against paying taxes to fight a war against British taxation.

At about the time the Articles of Confederation were ratified, Congress established Departments of Foreign Affairs, War, and Finance, with individual heads responsible to it. The most important of the new department heads was the superintendent of finance, Robert Morris, a Philadelphia merchant. When Morris took office, the Continental dollar was worthless, the system of supplying the army chaotic, the credit of the government exhausted. He set up an efficient method of obtaining food and uniforms for the army, persuaded Congress to

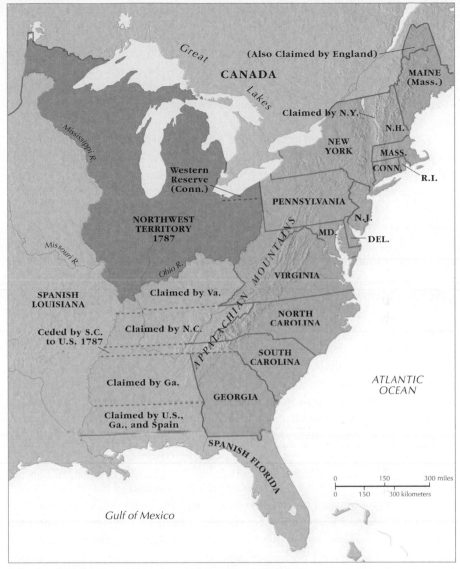

The United States Under the Articles of Confederation, 1787

New York and Virginia gave up their claims to the vast area that became the Northwest Territory and thus set a precedent for trans-Appalachian land policy. By 1802 the various state claims had been ceded to the national government. The original Northwest Territory (the Old Northwest) was bounded by the Ohio River, the Mississippi, and the Great Lakes.

charter a national Bank of North America, and aided by the slackening of military activity after Yorktown, got the country back on a hard money basis. New foreign loans were obtained, partly because Morris's efficiency and industry inspired confidence.

State Republican Governments

However crucial the role of Congress, in an important sense the real revolution occurred when the individual colonies broke their ties with Great Britain. Using their colonial charters as a basis, the states began framing new constitutions even before the Declaration of Independence. By early 1777 all but Connecticut and Rhode Island, which continued under their colonial charters well into the nineteenth century, had taken this decisive step.

On the surface the new governments were not drastically different from those they replaced. The most significant change was the removal of outside control, which had the effect of making the governments more responsive to public opinion. Gone were the times when a governor could be appointed and maintained in office by orders from London. The new constitutions varied in detail, but all provided for an elected legislature, an executive, and a system of courts. In general the powers of the governor and of judges were limited, the theory being that elected rulers no less than those appointed by kings were subject to the temptations of authority, that, as one Patriot put it, all men are "tyrants enough at heart." The typical governor had no voice in legislation and little in appointments. Pennsylvania went so far as to eliminate the office of governor, replacing it with an elected council of twelve.

Power was concentrated in the legislature, which the people had come to count on to defend their interests. In addition to the lawmaking authority exercised by the colonial assemblies, the state constitutions gave the legislatures the power to declare war, conduct foreign relations, control the courts, and perform many other essentially executive functions. While continuing to require that voters be property owners or taxpayers, the constitution makers remained suspicious even of the legislature.

They rejected the British concept of virtual representation. They saw legislators as representatives, that is, agents reflecting the interests of the voters of a particular district rather than superior persons chosen to decide public issues according to their own best judgment. Where political power was involved, the common American principle was every man for himself, but also everyone for the nation, the republic. People were no longer subjects, but citizens, *parts* of government, obedient to its laws, but not blindly subordinate to governmental authority epitomized in the monarch.

A majority of the constitutions contained bills of rights (such as the one George Mason wrote for Virginia) protecting the people's civil liberties against all branches of the government. In Britain such guarantees checked only the Crown; the Americans invoked them against their elected representatives as well.

The state governments combined the best of the British system, including its respect for status, fairness, and due process, with the uniquely American stress on individualism and a healthy dislike of too much authority. The idea of drafting written frames of government—contracts between the people and their representatives that carefully spelled out the powers and duties of the latter—grew out of the experience of the colonists after 1763, when the vagueness of the unwritten British constitution had caused so much controversy, and from the compact principle, the heart of republican government as described so eloquently in the Declaration of Independence. This constitutionalism represented one of the most important innovations of the Revolutionary era: a peaceful method for altering the political system. In the midst of violence, the states changed their frames of government in an orderly, legal manner—a truly remarkable achievement that became a beacon of hope to reformers all over the world. The states' example, the Reverend Simeon Howard of Massachusetts predicted, "will encourage the friends and rouse a spirit of liberty through other nations."

Social Reform

Many states seized the occasion of constitution making to introduce important political and social reforms. In Pennsylvania, Virginia, North Carolina, and other states the seats in the legislature were reapportioned in order to give the western districts their fair share. Primogeniture, entail (the right of an owner of property to prevent heirs from ever disposing of it), and quitrents were abolished wherever they had existed. Steps toward greater freedom of religion were taken, especially in states where the Anglican Church had enjoyed a privileged position. In Virginia the movement to separate church and state was given the force of law by Jefferson's Statute of Religious Liberty, enacted in 1786. "Our civil rights have no dependence on our religious opinions, any more than our opinions in physics or geometry," the statute declared. "Truth is great and will prevail if left to herself."

Many states continued to support religion; Massachusetts did not end public support of Congregational churches until the 1830s. But after the Revolution the states usually distributed the money roughly in accordance with the numerical strength of the various Protestant denominations.

A number of states moved tentatively against slavery. In attacking British policy after 1763, colonists had frequently claimed that Parliament was trying to make slaves of them. No less a personage than George Washington wrote in 1774: "We must assert our rights, or submit to every imposition, that can be heaped upon us, till custom and use shall make us tame and abject slaves." However exaggerated the language, such reasoning led to denunciations of slavery, often vague but significant in their effects on public opinion. The fact that practically every important thinker of the European Enlightenment (Montesquieu, Voltaire, Diderot, and Rousseau in France, David Hume, Samuel Johnson, and Adam Smith in England, to name the most important) had criticized slavery on moral and economic grounds also had an impact on educated opinion. Then, too, the forthright statements in the Declaration of Independence about liberty and equality seemed impossible to reconcile with slaveholding. "How is it," asked Dr. Johnson, who opposed independence vehemently, "that we hear the loudest yelps for liberty among the drivers of negroes?"

The war opened direct paths to freedom for some slaves. In November 1775 Lord Dunmore, the royal governor of Virginia, proclaimed that all slaves "able and willing to bear arms" for the British would be liberated. In fact, the British treated slaves as captured property, seizing them by the thousands in their campaigns in the South. The fate of these blacks is obscure. Some ended up in the West Indies, still slaves. Others were evacuated to Canada and liberated, and some of them settled the British colony of Sierra Leone in West Africa, founded in 1787. Probably many more escaped from bondage by running away during the confusion accompanying the British campaigns in the South.

About 5,000 blacks served in the Patriot army and navy. Most black soldiers were assigned noncombat duties, but there were some black soldiers in every major battle from Lexington to Yorktown.

Beginning with Pennsylvania in 1780, the northern states all did away with slavery. In most cases slaves born after a certain date were to become free on reaching maturity. Since New York did not pass a gradual emancipation law until 1799 and New Jersey not until 1804, there were numbers of slaves in the so-called free states well into the nineteenth century—more than 3,500 as late as 1830. But the institution was on its way toward extinction. All the states prohibited the importation of slaves from abroad, and except for Georgia and South Carolina, the southern states passed laws removing restrictions on the right of individual owners to free their slaves. The greatest success of voluntary emancipation came in Virginia, where, between 1782 and 1790, as many as 10,000 blacks were freed.

These advances encouraged foes of slavery to hope that the institution would soon disappear. But slavery died only where it was not economically important. Except for owners whose slaves were "carried off" by the British, only in Massachusetts, where the state supreme court ruled slavery unconstitutional in 1783, were owners deprived of existing slaves against their will.

Despite the continuing subordination of blacks, there is no question that the Revolution permanently changed the tone of American society. In the way they dressed, in their manner of speech, and in the way they dealt with one another in public places, Americans paid at least lip service to the idea of equality.

After the publication of *Common Sense* and the Declaration of Independence, with their excoriations of that "Royal Brute," King George III, it became fashionable to denounce the granting of titles of nobility, all "aristocrats," and any privilege based on birth. In 1783 a group of army officers founded a fraternal organization, the Society of Cincinnati. Although the revered George Washington was its president, many citizens found the mere existence of a club restricted to officers alarming; the fact that membership was to be hereditary, passing on the death of a member to his oldest son, caused a furor.

Nevertheless, little of the social and economic upheaval usually associated with revolutions occurred, before, during, or after 1776. At least part of the urban violence of the period (just how large a part is difficult to determine at this distance) had no social objective. America had its share of criminals, mischievous youths eager to flex their muscles, and other people unable to resist the temptation to break the law when it could be done without much risk of punishment. Certainly there was no wholesale proscription of any class, faith, or profession.

The property of Tories was frequently seized by the state governments, but almost never with the idea of redistributing wealth or providing the poor with land. While some large Tory estates were broken up and sold to small farmers, others passed intact to wealthy individuals or to groups of speculators. The war disrupted many traditional business relationships. Some merchants were unable to cope with the changes; others adapted well and grew rich. But the changes occurred without regard for the political beliefs or social values of either those who profited or those who lost.

During the war, conflicts erupted over economic issues involving land and taxation, yet no single class or interest triumphed in all the states or in the national government. In Pennsylvania, where the western radical element was strong, the constitution was extremely democratic; in Maryland and South Carolina the conservatives maintained control handily. Throughout the country, many great landowners were ardent Patriots, but others became Tories—and so did many small farmers.

Finally, the new governments became more responsive to public opinion, no matter what the particular shape of their political institutions. This was true principally because *Common Sense*, the Declaration of Independence, and the experience of participating in a revolution had made people conscious of their rights in a republic and of their power to enforce those rights. Conservatives swiftly discovered that state constitutions designed to insulate legislators and officials from popular pressures were ineffective when the populace felt strongly about any issue.

Effects of the Revolution on Women

In the late eighteenth century there was a trend in the Western world, barely perceptible at the time, toward increasing the legal rights of women. This movement was strengthened in America by the events leading up to the break with Great Britain and still more by the Declaration of Independence. When Americans began to think and talk about the rights of the individual and the evils of arbitrary rule, subtle effects on relations between the sexes followed. For example, it became somewhat easier for women to obtain divorces. In colonial times divorces were relatively rare, but easier for men to obtain than for women. After the Revolution the difference did not disappear, but it became considerably smaller. In Massachusetts, before the 1770s no woman is known to have obtained a divorce on the ground of her husband's adultery. Thereafter, successful suits by wives against errant husbands were not unusual. In 1791 a South Carolina judge went so far as to say that the law protecting "the absolute dominion" of husbands was "the offspring of a rude and barbarous age." The "progress of civilization," he continued, "has tended to ameliorate the condition of women, and to allow even to wives, something like personal identity."

As the tone of this "liberal" opinion indicates, the change in male attitudes that took place in America because of the Revolution was small. Courts in New York and Massachusetts refused to take action against Tory women whose husbands

Abigail Adams, in asking her husband John to "remember the ladies" when reforming society, was not advocating political rights for women. Rather, she wanted fairer treatment for women within the family. "Do not put such unlimited power into the hands of the husbands," she wrote him. "Remember all men would be tyrants if they could."

were Tories on the ground that it was the duty of women to obey their husbands, and when John Adams's wife Abigail warned him in 1776 that if he and his fellow rebels did not "remember the ladies" when reforming society, the women would "foment a Rebellion" of their own, he treated her remarks as a joke. Adams believed that voting (and as he wrote on another occasion, writing history) was "not the Province of the Ladies."[3]

However, the war effort increased the influence of women in several ways. With so many men in uniform, women took over the management of countless farms, shops, and businesses, and they became involved in the handling of other day-to-day matters that men had normally conducted. Their experiences made both them and in many cases their fathers and husbands more aware of their ability to take on all sorts of chores previously considered exclusively masculine in character. At the same time, women wanted to contribute to the winning of independence, and their efforts to do so made them conscious of their importance. Furthermore, the rhetoric of the Revolution, with its stress on liberty and equality, affected women in the same way that it caused many whites of both sexes to question the morality of slavery.

---

[3]Adams's distaste for women historians may have been based on the fact that in his friend Mercy Otis Warren's History of the Rise, Progress, and Termination of the American Revolution (1805) Warren claimed that Adams sometimes allowed his "prejudices" to distort his judgment.

Attitudes toward the education of women also changed because of the Revolution. According to the best estimates, at least half the white women in America could not read or write as late as the 1780s. In a land of opportunity like the United States, women seemed particularly important, not only because they themselves were citizens, but because of their role in training the next generation. "You distribute 'mental nourishment' along with physical," one orator told the women of America in 1795. "The reformation of the world is in your power. . . . The solidity and stability of your country rest with you." The idea of female education began to catch on. Schools for girls were founded, and the level of female literacy gradually rose.

Growth of a National Spirit

The growth of American nationalism was an important result of the Revolution. Most modern revolutions have been *caused* by nationalism and have *resulted* in independence. In the case of the American Revolution, the desire to be free antedated any intense national feeling. The colonies entered into a political union not because they felt an overwhelming desire to bring all Americans under one rule but because unity offered the only hope of winning a war against Great Britain. That they remained united after throwing off British rule reflects the degree to which nationalism had developed during the conflict.

By the middle of the eighteenth century the colonists had begun to think of themselves as a separate society distinct from Europe and even from Britain. Benjamin Franklin described himself not as a British subject but as "an American subject of the King," and in 1750 a Boston newspaper could urge its readers to drink "American" beer in order to free themselves from being "beholden to Foreigners" for their alcoholic beverages. Little political nationalism existed before the Revolution, however, in part because most people knew little about life outside their own colony. When a delegate to the first Continental Congress mentioned "Colonel Washington" to John Adams soon after the Congress met, Adams had to ask him who this "Colonel Washington" was. He had never heard the name before.

The new nationalism arose from a number of sources and expressed itself in different ways. Common sacrifices in war certainly played a part; the soldiers of the Continental Army fought in the summer heat of the Carolinas for the same cause that had led them to brave the ice floes of the Delaware in order to surprise the Hessians. Such men lost interest in state boundary lines; they became Americans.

The war caused many people to move from place to place. Soldiers traveled as the tide of war fluctuated; so too—far more than in earlier times—did prominent leaders. Members of Congress from every state had to travel to Philadelphia; in the process they saw much of the country and the people who inhabited it. Listening to their fellows and serving with them on committees almost inevitably broadened these men, most of them highly influential in their local communities.

With its thirteen stars and thirteen stripes representing the states, the American flag symbolized national unity and reflected the common feeling that such a symbol was necessary. Yet the flag had separate stars and stripes; local interests and local loyalties remained extremely strong, and these could be divisive when conflicts of interest arose.

Certain practical problems that demanded common solutions also drew the states together. No one seriously considered having thirteen postal systems or thirteen sets of diplomatic representatives abroad. Every new diplomatic appointment, every treaty of friendship or commerce signed, committed all to a common policy and thus bound them more closely together. And economic developments had a unifying effect. Deprived of English goods, Americans manufactured more things themselves, stimulating both interstate trade and national pride.

The Great Land Ordinances

The lands west of the Appalachians, initially a source of dispute, became a force for unity once they had been ceded to the national government. Everyone realized what a priceless national asset they were, and all now understood that no one state could determine the future of the West.

The politicians argued hotly about how these lands should be developed. Some advocated selling the land in township units in the traditional New England manner to groups or companies; others favored letting individual pioneers stake out farms in the helter-skelter manner common in the colonial South. The decision was a compromise. The Land Ordinance of 1785 provided for surveying western territories into 6-mile-square townships before sale. Every other township was to be further subdivided into thirty-six sections of 640 acres (1 square mile) each. The land was sold at auction at a minimum price of $1 an acre. The law favored speculative land-development companies, for even the 640-acre units were far too large and expensive for the typical frontier family. But the fact that the land was to be surveyed and sold by the central government was a nationalizing force. It ensured orderly development of the West and simplified the task of defending the frontier in the event of Indian attack. Congress set aside the sixteenth section of every township for the maintenance of schools, another farsighted decision.

Still more significant was the Northwest Ordinance of 1787, which established governments for the West. As early as 1775 settlers in frontier districts were petitioning Congress to allow them to enter the Union as independent states, and in 1780 Congress had resolved that all lands ceded to the nation by the existing states should be "formed into distinct republican States" with "the same rights of sovereignty, freedom and independence" as the original thirteen. In 1784 a committee headed by Thomas Jefferson worked out a plan for doing this, and in 1787 it was enacted into law. The area bounded by the Ohio, the Mississippi, and the Great Lakes was to be carved into not fewer than three or more than five territories. Until the adult male population of the entire area reached 5,000, it was to be ruled by a governor and three judges, all appointed by Congress. When 5,000 men of voting age had settled in the territory, the Ordinance authorized them to elect a legislature,

The Land Ordinance of 1785 called for surveying and dividing the Western Territories into one-mile square mile subdivisions—640 acres. These were further subdivided and sold as 40-acre tracts. Few pieces of legislation have left a more visible imprint upon the landscape. Nowadays the Midwest, as seen from an airplane, resembles a patchwork quilt of 40-acre squares, like this section of Kansas.

which could send a nonvoting delegate to Congress. Finally, when 60,000 persons had settled in any one of the political subdivisions, it was to become a state. It could draft a constitution and operate in any way it wished, save that the government had to be "republican" and that slavery was prohibited.

Seldom has a legislative body acted more wisely. That the western districts must become states everyone conceded from the start. The people had had their fill of colonialism under British rule, and the rebellious temper of frontier settlers made it impossible even to consider maintaining the West in a dependent status. (When North Carolina ceded its trans-Appalachian lands to the United States in 1784, the settlers there, uncertain how they would fare under federal rule, hastily organized an extralegal state of Franklin, and it was not until 1789 that the national government obtained control.) But it would have been unfair to turn the territories over to the firstcomers, who would have been unable to manage such large domains and would surely have taken advantage of their priority to dictate to later arrivals. A period of tutelage was necessary, a period when the "mother country" must guide and nourish its growing offspring.

The system worked well and was applied to nearly all the regions absorbed by the nation as it advanced westward. Together with the Ordinance of 1785, which branded its checkerboard pattern on the physical shape of the West, this law gave the growing country a unity essential to the growth of a national spirit.

National Heroes

The Revolution further fostered nationalism by giving the people their first commonly revered heroes. Benjamin Franklin was widely known before the break with Great Britain through his experiments with electricity, his immensely successful *Poor Richard's Almanack,* and his invention of the Franklin stove. His staunch support of the Patriot cause, his work in the Continental Congress, and his diplomatic successes in France, where he was extravagantly admired, added to his fame. Franklin demonstrated, to Europeans and to Americans themselves, that not all Americans need be ignorant rustics.

Washington, however, was "the chief human symbol of a common Americanism." Stern, cold, a man of few words, the great Virginian did not seem a likely candidate for hero worship. "My countenance never yet revealed my feelings," he himself admitted. Yet he had qualities that made people name babies after him and call him "the Father of His Country" long before the war was won: his personal sacrifices in the cause of independence, his integrity, and above all, perhaps, his obvious desire to retire to his Mount Vernon estate (for many Americans feared any powerful leader and worried lest Washington seek to become a dictator).

As a general, Washington was not a brilliant strategist like Napoleon. Neither was he a tactician of the quality of Caesar or Robert E. Lee. But he was a remarkable organizer and administrator—patient, thoughtful, conciliatory. In a way, his lack of genius made his achievements all the more impressive. He held his forces together in adversity, avoiding both useless slaughter and catastrophic defeat. People of all sections, from every walk of life, looked on Washington as the embodiment of American virtues: a man of deeds rather than words; a man of substance accustomed to luxury yet capable of enduring great hardships stoically and as much at home in the wilderness as an Indian; a bold Patriot, quick to take arms against British tyranny, yet eminently respectable. The Revolution might have been won without Washington, but it is unlikely that the free United States would have become so easily a true nation had he not been at its call.

1774	Thomas Jefferson writes *A Summary View of the Rights of British America*
	General Thomas Gage, commander-in-chief of British army in North America, is named governor of Massachusetts
1775	Colonists fight British in Battles of Lexington and Concord
	Second Continental Congress names George Washington commander-in-chief (of Continental Army)
	Gage is replaced as British commander by General Sir William Howe after Battle of Bunker Hill
1776	Thomas Paine publishes *Common Sense*
	Washington's troops occupy Boston
	Second Continental Congress issues Declaration of Independence
	Washington's troops are defeated in Battle of Long Island
	Washington evacuates New York City
	Washington's victory at Battle of Trenton boosts morale
1777	Washington's troops win Battle of Princeton
	American victory at Saratoga turns the tide and leads to alliance with France
	British occupy Philadelphia after Battle of Germantown
1777–1778	Continental Army winters at Valley Forge
1778	British capture Savannah
1780	British capture Charleston
1781	States ratify Articles of Confederation
	General Cornwallis surrenders at Yorktown
1783	Great Britain recognizes independence of United States by signing Peace of Paris
1785	Congress passes Land Ordinance of 1785
1787	Northwest Ordinance establishes governments for the West

The Federalist Era: Nationalism Triumphant

ON APRIL 3, 2003, THE PHONE RANG IN THE DORM ROOM OF JESSE Jordan, a freshman at Rensselaer Polytechnic Institute. Jordan had no idea that the Constitution of the United States was about to crash into his life. Jordan's dean was on the line. The nation's record companies, the dean explained, had filed a lawsuit against Jordan for copyright infringement. Jordan had illegally downloaded and shared files of Christina Aguilera's "Genie in a Bottle," Busta Rhymes's "Break Ya Neck," and hundreds of other songs. Because copyright law set fines of $150,000 or more for each infringement, Jordan owed the record companies $15 million, or so the lawsuit claimed.

That same day brought even worse news to Joseph Nievelt, a sophomore at Michigan Technological University. Because Nievelt had downloaded and shared thousands of songs, his fine was set at $97.8 billion. Jordan eventually turned over his life savings—$12,000—to settle the lawsuit. Nievelt paid $15,000.

If the Articles of Confederation had remained the law of the land, Jordan and Nievelt would have done nothing illegal. The Articles included no mention of copyright. In the 1780s, moreover, only a couple of states had made it illegal to copy an invention or print someone else's book. But James Madison observed that if inventors did not "own" their inventions, they would have little incentive to invent. Authors, too, could expect no profit if their books could be freely reprinted by others. The economy would suffer and knowledge would languish. Thomas Jefferson, on the other hand, observed that in England copyright laws allowed businesses to monopolize inventions and books. This drove prices up and restricted dissemination of ideas. He argued that ideas, once divulged, should swiftly and freely be made available to the public.

Eventually the framers reached a compromise and added it to the Constitution of the United States. Article 1, Section 8 empowered Congress to "promote the Progress of Science and the Useful Arts" by providing "authors and inventors" the "exclusive right" to their creations; however, this right would endure for a "limited" time only. Then the invention or book would become public property.

Although Jesse Jordan and Joseph Nievelt may not have been very happy with the Constitution on the particular point of copyright infringement, they, like most Americans today, appreciate the many important provisions of the Constitution, including the protection of the rights of individuals and the enumeration of the powers and responsibilities (and limitations) of the federal government. In the 1780s, however, many Americans were satisfied with the federal government under the Articles of Confederation. Whatever its weaknesses, it had negotiated the treaty ending the Revolutionary War, adopted humane and farsighted land policies, and established a rudimentary bureaucracy to manage routine affairs. If, as Washington said, that government had moved "on crutches . . . tottering at every step," it moved forward nevertheless. Yet the country's evolution placed demands on the national government that its creators had not anticipated. Dissatisfaction with the Articles mounted; the Founders sought solutions that through a process of conflict and compromise would finally result in the Constitution.

Inadequacies of the Articles of Confederation

Following the Revolutionary War and the peace settlement at Paris, the United States faced new challenges. The new nation struggled to achieve control of its own territory, to define the nature of its trade relationships with Europe, and to overcome crippling economic depression and the specter of inflation. If the Articles had proved adequate in achieving victory in the war, they proved less so in addressing these new concerns.

Both Great Britain and Spain stood in the way of the United States winning control of its borders. Although the British kept their promise to withdraw their troops from American soil promptly, they refused to abandon seven military posts beyond the periphery of the original thirteen states. Pressing against America's exposed frontier like hot coals, these posts seared national pride. The inability to eject the British seemed a national disgrace. In 1784, moreover, the Spaniards had closed the lower Mississippi River to American commerce. This harmed settlers beyond the Appalachians who depended on the Mississippi and its network of tributaries to get their corn, tobacco, and other products to eastern and European markets. Many reasoned that a stronger central government might have dealt with Britain and Spain more forcefully and effectively.

Another key problem concerned trade. After hostilities had ended, British merchants, eager to regain markets closed to them during the Revolution, poured low-priced manufactured goods of all kinds into the United States. Americans, long deprived of British products, rushed to take advantage of the bargains. Soon imports of British goods were approaching the levels of the early 1770s, while exports to the empire reached no more than half their earlier volume.

The influx of British goods aggravated the situation just when the economy was suffering a dislocation as a result of the ending of the war. From 1784 to 1786 the country went through a period of bad times. The inability of Congress to find money to pay the nation's debts undermined public confidence. Veterans who had still not been paid, and private individuals and foreign governments that had lent the government money during the Revolution, were clamoring for their due. In some regions crop failures compounded the difficulties.

An obvious way of dealing with these problems would have been to place tariffs on British goods in order to limit British imports, but the Confederation lacked the authority to do this. When individual states erected tariff barriers, British merchants easily got around them by bringing their goods in through states that did not. That the central government lacked the power to control commerce disturbed merchants, other businessmen, and the ever-increasing number of national-minded citizens in every walk of life.

Thus a movement developed to give the Confederation the power to tax imports, and in 1781 Congress sought authority to levy a 5 percent tariff duty. This would enable Congress to pay off some of its obligations and also put pressure on the British to relax their restrictions on American trade with the West Indies. Every state but Rhode Island agreed, but the measure required the unanimous consent of the states and therefore failed.

Defeat of the tariff pointed to the need for revising the Articles of Confederation, for here was a case where a large percentage of the states were ready to increase the power of the national government yet were unable to do so. Although many individuals in every region were worried about creating a centralized monster that might gobble up the sovereignty of the states, the practical needs of the times convinced many others that this risk must be taken.

Daniel Shays's "Little Rebellion"

The Massachusetts legislature was determined to pay off the state debt and maintain a sound currency. Taxes amounting to almost £1.9 million were levied between 1780 and 1786, the burden falling most heavily on those of moderate income. The average Massachusetts farmer paid about a third of every year's income in taxes. Bad times and deflation led to many foreclosures, and the prisons were crowded with honest debtors. "Our Property is torn from us," one town complained, "our Gaols filled & still our Debts are not discharged."

This broadside lauds Daniel Shays *(left)*, who headed the armed rebellion against Massachusetts, which was cracking down on debtors. Shays is pictured in his Continental uniform. For his efforts at the Battle of Saratoga in 1777, Marquis de Lafayette had presented Shays with a ceremonial sword, pictured here. Shays sold the sword to pay off his debts.

In the summer of 1786 throngs of disgruntled farmers in the western communities began to stop foreclosures by forcibly preventing the courts from holding their sessions. Under the leadership of Daniel Shays, a veteran of Bunker Hill, Ticonderoga, and Saratoga, the "rebels" marched on Springfield and prevented the state supreme court from meeting. When the state government sent troops against them, the rebels attacked the Springfield arsenal. They were routed, and the uprising then collapsed. Shays fled to Vermont.

As Thomas Jefferson observed at safe remove from the trouble in Paris, where he was serving as minister to France, Shays's uprising was only "a *little* rebellion" and as such "a medicine necessary for the sound health of government." But Shays and his followers were genuinely exasperated by the refusal of the government even to try to provide relief for their troubles. By taking up arms they forced the authorities to heed them: At its next session the legislature made some concessions to their demands.

Unlike Jefferson, most well-to-do Americans considered Shays's uprising "Liberty run mad." "What, gracious God, is man! that there should be such inconsistency and perfidiousness in his conduct?" the usually unexcitable George Washington asked when news of the riots reached Virginia. "We are fast verging to anarchy and confusion!" During the crisis private persons had had to subscribe funds to put the rebels down, and when Massachusetts had appealed to Congress for help there was little Congress could legally do. The lessons seemed plain: Liberty must not become an excuse for license; greater authority must be vested in the central government.

To Philadelphia, and the Constitution

If most people wanted to increase the power of Congress, they were also afraid to shift the balance too far lest they destroy the sovereignty of the states and the rights of individuals. The machinery for change established in the Articles of Confederation, which required the unanimous consent of the states for all amendments, posed a particularly delicate problem. Experience had shown it unworkable, yet to bypass it would be revolutionary and therefore dangerous.

The first fumbling step toward reform was taken in March 1785 when representatives of Virginia and Maryland, meeting at the home of George Washington to settle a dispute over the improvement of navigation on the Potomac River, suggested a conference of all the states to discuss common problems of commerce.

Among the delegates was a young New York lawyer named Alexander Hamilton, a brilliant, imaginative, and daring man who was convinced that only drastic centralization would save the nation from disintegration. Hamilton described himself as a "nationalist." While the war still raged he contrasted the virtues of "a great Federal Republic" with the existing system of "petty states with the appearance only of union, jarring, jealous, and perverse." Instead of giving up, he proposed calling another convention to meet at Philadelphia to deal generally with constitutional reform. Delegates should be empowered to work out a broad plan for correcting "such defects as may be discovered to exist" in the Articles of Confederation.

The Annapolis group approved Hamilton's suggestion, and Congress reluctantly endorsed it. This time all the states but Rhode Island sent delegates. On May 25, 1787, the convention opened its proceedings at the State House in Philadelphia and unanimously elected George Washington its president. When it adjourned four months later, it had drafted the Constitution.

The Great Convention

Collectively the delegates possessed a rare combination of talents. Most of them had had considerable experience in politics, and the many lawyers among them were skilled in logic and debate. Furthermore, the times made them acutely aware of their opportunities. It was "a time when the greatest lawgivers of antiquity would have wished to live," an opportunity to "establish the wisest and happiest government that human wisdom can contrive," John Adams wrote. "We . . . decide for ever the fate of republican government," James Madison said during the deliberations.

If these remarks overstated the importance of their deliberations, they nonetheless represented the opinion of most of those present. They were boldly optimistic about their country. "We are laying the foundation of a great empire," Madison predicted. At the same time the delegates recognized the difficulties they faced. The ancient Roman republic was one model, and all knew that it had been overthrown by tyrants and eventually overrun by barbarians. The framers were also familiar with Enlightenment thinkers such as John Locke, Thomas Hobbes, and Montesquieu, and also with the ideas that swirled around the great disputes between Parliament and the Stuart monarchs during the seventeenth century.

Fortunately, they were nearly all of one mind on basic questions. That there should be a federal system, with both independent state governments and a national government with limited powers to handle matters of common interest, was accepted by all but one or two of them. Republican government, drawing its

Independence Hall in Philadelphia, where the Declaration of Independence was adopted (1776) and where the Constitution was drafted and signed (1787). Despite stifling heat, delegates kept the windows shut to keep their deliberations secret.

authority from the people and remaining responsible to them, was a universal assumption. A measure of democracy followed inevitably from this principle, for even the most aristocratic delegates agreed that ordinary citizens should share in the process of selecting those who were to make and execute the laws.

All agreed that no group within society, no matter how numerous, should have unrestricted authority. They looked on political power much as we today view nuclear energy: a force with tremendous potential value for humankind, but one easily misused and therefore dangerous to unleash. People meant well and had limitless possibilities, the constitution makers believed, but they were selfish by nature and could not be counted on to respect the interests of others. The ordinary people—small farmers, artisans, any taxpayer—should have a say in government in order to be able to protect themselves against those who would exploit their weakness, and the majority must somehow be prevented from plundering the rich, for property must be secure or no government could be stable. No single state or section must be allowed to predominate, nor should the legislature be supreme over the executive or the courts. Power, in short, must be divided, and the segments must be balanced one against the other.

At the outset the delegates decided to keep the proceedings secret. That way no one was tempted to play to the gallery or seek some personal political advantage at the expense of the common good. Next they agreed to go beyond their instructions to revise the Articles of Confederation and draft an entirely new form of government. This was a bold, perhaps illegal act, but it was in no way irresponsible

Debating the Past

WHAT IDEAS SHAPED THE CONSTITUTION?

In this 1788 cartoon, the angel "Concord" presents the Constitution to "Columbia"—an embodiment of the United States; a Greek temple sits in the background, its thirteen pillars representing the colonies. Were the people who drafted the Constitution inspired by classical antiquity? No, declared historian Charles A. Beard (1913). He argued that their chief concerns were to protect their property and business interests.

Few historians found much confirmation of Beard's thesis; but, what, then *were* the Founders thinking? Daniel Boorstin (1948) regarded the Founders as practical men who sought "a refuge from the diversity of ideas in the satisfying concreteness of experience." In 1967 Bernard Bailyn rejected this argument. His research revealed that the revolutionary leaders learned to cherish republican virtue and citizenship from ancient Roman philosophers such as Plutarch and Tacitus, from thinkers of the European Enlightenment, and from critics of eighteenth-century British monarchs. Joyce Appleby (1984) countered that if ideas were at the heart of the Constitution, they came from John Locke, a seventeenth-

century philosopher who enshrined property rights and the individual. The Constitution was a blueprint for capitalist development. Jack Rakove (1996) concluded that the Founders lacked any clear "original intent." They favored a government strong enough to protect people and promote their interests; they also favored individual rights and freedom. Which mattered more, they could not agree.

Charles A. Beard, *An Economic Interpretation of the Constitution of the United States* (1913), Daniel Boorstin, *The Lost World of Thomas Jefferson* (1948), Bernard Bailyn, *The Ideological Origins of the American Revolution* (1967), Gordon Wood, *The Creation of the American Republic* (1969), Joyce Appleby, *Capitalism and a New Social Order* (1984), Jack Rakove, *Original Meanings* (1996).

because nothing the convention might recommend was binding on anyone, and it was absolutely essential because under the Articles a single state could have prevented the adoption of any change. Alexander Hamilton captured the mood of the gathering when he said: "We can only propose and recommend—the power of ratifying or rejecting is still in the States. . . . We ought not to sacrifice the public Good to narrow Scruples."

The Compromises That Produced the Constitution

The delegates voted on May 30, 1787 that "a national Government ought to be established." They then set to work hammering out a specific plan. Furthermore, the delegates believed that the national government should have separate executive and judicial branches as well as a legislature. But two big questions had to be answered. The first—*What powers should this national government be granted?*—occasioned relatively little discussion. The right to levy taxes and to regulate interstate and foreign commerce was assigned to the central government almost without debate. So was the power to raise and maintain an army and navy and to summon the militia of the states to enforce national laws and suppress insurrections. With equal absence of argument, the states were deprived of their rights to issue money, to make treaties, and to tax either imports or exports without the permission of Congress. Thus, in summary fashion, was brought about a massive shift of power, a shift made necessary by the problems that had brought the delegates to Philadelphia and made practicable by the new nationalism of the 1780s.

The second major question—*Who shall control the national government?*—proved more difficult to answer in a manner satisfactory to all. Led by Virginia, the larger states pushed for representation in the national legislature based on population. The smaller states wished to maintain the existing system of equal representation for each state regardless of population. The large states rallied behind the Virginia Plan, drafted by James Madison and presented to the convention by Edmund Randolph, governor of the state. The small states supported the New Jersey Plan, prepared by William Paterson, a former attorney general of that state. The question was important; equal state representation would have been undemocratic, whereas a proportional system would have effectively destroyed the influence of all the states as states. But the delegates saw it in terms of combinations of large or small states, and this old fashioned view was unrealistic: When the states combined, they did so on geographic, economic, or social grounds that seldom had anything to do with size. Nevertheless, the debate was long and heated, and for a time it threatened to disrupt the convention.

Day after day in the stifling heat of high summer, the weary delegates struggled to find a suitable compromise. Madison and a few others had to use every weapon in their arsenal of argument to hold the group together. (All told, during the 88 sessions of the convention, a total of 569 votes were taken.) July 2 was perhaps the most fateful day of the whole proceedings. "We are at full stop," said Roger Sherman of Connecticut, who had been one of the drafters of the Declaration of Independence. "If we do not concede on both sides," a North Carolina delegate warned, "our business must soon be at an end."

But the delegates did "concede on both sides," and the debates went on. Again on July 17 collapse threatened as the representatives of the larger states caucused to consider walking out of the convention. Fortunately they did not walk out, and finally the delegates adopted what is known as the Great Compromise. In the lower branch of the new legislature—the House of Representatives—places were to be assigned according to population and filled by popular vote. In the upper house—the Senate—each state was to have two members, elected by its legislature.

Then a complicated struggle took place between northern and southern delegates, occasioned by the institution of slavery and the differing economic interests of the regions. About one American in seven in the 1780s was a slave. Northerners contended that slaves should be counted in deciding each state's share of direct federal taxes. Southerners, of course, wanted to exclude slaves from the count. Yet Southerners wished to include slaves in determining each district's representation in the House of Representatives, although they had no intention of permitting the slaves to vote. In the Three-fifths Compromise it was agreed that "three-fifths of all other Persons" should be counted for both purposes. (As it turned out, the compromise was a victory for the Southerners, for direct taxes were only rarely levied by Congress before the Civil War.) Settlement of the knotty issue of the African slave trade was postponed by a clause making it illegal for Congress to outlaw the trade before 1808.

The final document (see the text of the Constitution in the Appendix, pp. A-6–A-13), signed on September 17, established a legislature of two houses; an executive branch, consisting of a president with wide powers and a vice president whose only function was to preside over the Senate; and a national judiciary consisting of a Supreme Court and such "inferior courts" as Congress might decide to create. The lower, popularly elected branch of the Congress was supposed to represent especially the mass of ordinary citizens. It was given the sole right to introduce bills for raising revenue. The twenty-six-member Senate was looked on by many as a sort of advisory council similar to the upper houses of the colonial legislatures. Its consent was required before any treaty could go into effect and for major presidential appointments. The Founders also intended the Senate to represent in Congress the interests not only of the separate states but of what Hamilton called "the rich and the well-born" as contrasted with "the great mass of the people."

The creation of a powerful president was the most drastic departure from past experience, and it is doubtful that the Founders would have gone so far had everyone not counted on Washington, a man universally esteemed for character, wis-

James Madison was a key figure at the Great Convention of 1787. He not only influenced the shaping of the Constitution but also kept the most complete record of the proceedings. "Every person," wrote one delegate, "seems to acknowledge his greatness."

dom, and impartiality, to be the first to occupy the office. Besides giving him general responsibility for executing the laws, the Constitution made the president commander-in-chief of the armed forces of the nation and general supervisor of its foreign relations. He was to appoint federal judges and other officials, and he might veto any law of Congress, although his veto could be overridden by a two-thirds majority of both houses. While not specifically ordered to submit a program of legislation to Congress, he was to deliver periodic reports on the "State of the Union" and recommend "such Measures as he shall judge necessary and expedient." Most modern presidents have interpreted this requirement as authorizing them to submit detailed legislative proposals and to use the full power and prestige of the office to get Congress to enact them.

Looking beyond Washington, whose choice was sure to come about under any system, the Constitution established a cumbersome method of electing presidents. Each state was to choose "electors" equal in number to its representation in Congress. The electors, meeting separately in their own states, were to vote for two persons for president. Supposedly the procedure would prevent anyone less universally admired than Washington from getting a majority in the "electoral college," in which case the House of Representatives would choose the president from among the leading candidates, each state having but one vote. However, the swift rise of national political parties prevented the expected fragmentation of the electors' votes, and only two elections have ever gone to the House for settlement.

The national court system was set up to adjudicate disputes under the laws and treaties of the United States. No such system had existed under the Articles, a major weakness. Although the Constitution did not specifically authorize the courts to declare laws void when they conflicted with the Constitution, the courts soon exercised this right of "judicial review" in cases involving both state and federal laws.

The Founders believed that since the new powers of government might easily be misused, each should be held within safe limits by some countervailing force. The Constitution is full of ingenious devices ("checks and balances") whereby one power controls and limits another without reducing it to impotence. "Let Congress Legislate, let others execute, let others judge," John Jay suggested. This separation of legislative, executive, and judicial functions is the fundamental example of the principle. Other examples are the president's veto; Congress's power of impeachment, cleverly divided between House and Senate; the Senate's power over treaties and appointments; and the balance between Congress's right to declare war and the president's control of the armed forces.

Ratifying the Constitution

Influenced by the widespread approval of the decision of Massachusetts to submit its state constitution of 1780 to the voters for ratification, the framers of the Constitution provided (Article VII) that their handiwork be ratified by special state conventions.

Such a complex and controversial document as the Constitution naturally excited argument throughout the country. Those who favored it called themselves Federalists, thereby avoiding the more accurate but politically unattractive label of Centralizers. Their opponents thus became the Anti-Federalists.

It is difficult to generalize about the members of these groups. The Federalists tended to be substantial individuals, members of the professions, well-to-do, active in commercial affairs, and somewhat alarmed by the changes wrought by the Revolution. They were more interested, perhaps, in orderly and efficient government than in safeguarding the maximum freedom of individual choice.

The Anti-Federalists were more often small farmers, debtors, and persons to whom free choice was more important than power and who resented those who sought and held power. "Lawyers and men of learning and money men . . . expect to be the managers of the Const[itution], and get all the power and all the money into their own hands," a Massachusetts Anti-Federalist complained. "Then they will swallow up all us little folks . . . just as the whale swallowed up *Jonah*." But many rich and worldly citizens opposed the Constitution, and many poor and obscure persons were for it. It seems likely that most did not support or oppose the new system for narrowly selfish reasons.

Very little of the opposition to the Constitution grew out of economic issues. Most people wanted the national debt paid off; nearly everyone opposed an unstable currency; most favored uniform trade policies; most were ready to give the new government a chance if they could be convinced that it would not destroy the states. When backers agreed to add amendments guaranteeing the civil liberties of the people against challenge by the national government and reserving all unmentioned power to the states, much of the opposition disappeared. Sam Adams ended up voting for the Constitution in the Massachusetts convention after the additions had been promised.

The Constitution met with remarkably little opposition in most of the state ratifying conventions, considering the importance of the changes it instituted. Delaware acted first, ratifying unanimously on December 7, 1787. Pennsylvania followed a few days later, voting for the document by a 2 to 1 majority. New Jersey approved unanimously on December 18; so did Georgia on January 2, 1788. A week later Connecticut fell in line, 128 to 40.

The Massachusetts convention provided the first close contest. Early in February, after an extensive debate, the delegates ratified by a vote of 187 to 168. In April, Maryland accepted the Constitution by nearly 6 to 1, and in May, South Carolina approved, 149 to 73. New Hampshire came along on June 21, voting 57 to 47 for the Constitution. This was the ninth state, making the Constitution legally operative.

Before the news from New Hampshire had spread throughout the country, the Virginia convention debated the issue. Virginia, the largest state and the home of so many prestigious figures, was absolutely essential if the Constitution was to succeed. With unquestioned patriots like Richard Henry Lee and Patrick Henry opposed, the result was not easy to predict. But when the vote came on June 25, Virginia ratified, 89 to 79. Aside from Rhode Island, this left only New York and North Carolina outside the Union.

New York politics presented a complex and baffling picture. Resistance to independence had been strong there in 1776 and remained a problem all through the war. Although New York was the third largest state, with a population rapidly approaching 340,000, it sided with the small states at Philadelphia, and two of its three delegates (Hamilton was the exception) walked out of the convention and took the lead in opposing ratification. A handful of great landowning and mercantile families dominated politics, but they were divided into shifting factions. In general, New York City, including most ordinary working people as well as the merchants, favored ratification and the rural areas were against it.

The Anti-Federalists, well organized and competently led in New York by Governor George Clinton, won 46 of the 65 seats at the ratifying convention. The New York Federalists had one great asset in the fact that so many states had already ratified and another in the person of Alexander Hamilton. Although contemptuous of the *weakness* of the Constitution, Hamilton supported it with all his energies as being incomparably stronger than the old government. Working with Madison and John Jay, he produced the *Federalist Papers*, a series of brilliant essays explaining and defending the new system. In his articles, Hamilton stressed the need for a strong federal executive, while Madison sought to allay fears that the new national government would have too much power by emphasizing the many checks and balances in the Constitution. The essays were published in the local press and later in book form. Although generations of judges and lawyers have treated them almost as parts of the Constitution, their impact on contemporary public opinion was probably slight. Open-minded members of the convention were undoubtedly influenced, but few delegates were open-minded.

Hamilton became a kind of one-man army in defense of the Constitution, plying hesitating delegates with dinners and drinks, facing obstinate ones with the threat that New York City would secede from the state if the Constitution were rejected. Once New Hampshire and Virginia had ratified, opposition in New York became a good deal less intransigent. In the end, by promising to support a call for a second national convention to consider amendments, the Federalists carried the day, 30 to 27. With New York in the fold, the new government was free to get under way. North Carolina finally ratified in November 1789, Rhode Island the following year, in May 1790.

Washington as President

Elections took place in the states during January and February 1789, and by early April enough congressmen had gathered in New York, the temporary national capital, to commence operation. The ballots of the presidential electors were officially counted in the Senate on April 6, Washington being the unanimous choice. John Adams, with 34 electoral votes, won the vice-presidency.

When he left Mount Vernon for the eight-day trip to New York for his inauguration, Washington's progress was a series of celebrations. In every town he was met by bands, honor guards, local dignitaries, and crowds of cheering citizens. The

80°   75°   70°

40°

Lake Huron

Lake Ontario

VERMONT

NEW YORK   NEW
HAMPSHIRE

Lake Erie   MASSACHUSETTS

CONN.   R.I.

PENNSYLVANIA

40°

NEW
JERSEY

MARYLAND

DELAWARE

VIRGINIA   ATLANTIC
OCEAN

KENTUCKY

35°

TENNESSEE

NORTH CAROLINA

SOUTH
CAROLINA

0   50   100 miles

0   50   100 kilometers

GEORGIA

Majority for Constitution

Majority Against Ratification

Even

Not Voting

Ratification of the Constitution

people were informally ratifying the decision to create a new and more powerful United States. On April 30 Washington took the oath of office at New York's Federal Hall.

Washington made a firm, dignified, conscientious, but cautious president. His acute sense of responsibility led him to face the task "with feelings not unlike those of a culprit who is going to the place of his execution." Each presidential action must of necessity establish a precedent. "The eyes of Argus are upon me," he complained, "and no slip will pass unnoticed." Hoping to make the presidency appear respectable in the eyes of the world, he saw to it that his carriage was drawn by six cream-colored horses, and when he rode (he was a magnificent horseman), it was on a great white charger, with the saddle of leopard skin and the cloth edged in gold. Twenty-one servants (seven of them slaves) attended his needs at the presidential mansion on Broadway.

Washington meticulously avoided treading on the toes of Congress, for he took seriously the principle of the separation of powers. Never would he speak for or against a candidate for Congress, nor did he think that the president should push or even propose legislation. When he knew a controversial question was to be discussed in Congress, he avoided the subject in his annual message. The veto, he believed, should be employed only when the president considered a bill unconstitutional.

Although the Constitution said nothing about a presidential Cabinet, Washington established the system of calling his department heads together for general advice, a practice that was followed by his successors. In selecting these department heads and other important administrators, he favored no particular faction. He insisted only that appointees be competent and "of known attachment to the Government we have chosen." He picked Hamilton for secretary of the treasury, Jefferson for secretary of state, General Henry Knox of Massachusetts for secretary of war, and Edmund Randolph for attorney general. He called on them for advice according to the logic of his particular needs and frequently without regard for their own specialties. Thus he sometimes consulted Jefferson about financial matters and Hamilton about foreign affairs. This system caused resentment and confusion, especially when rival factions began to coalesce around Hamilton and Jefferson.

Despite his respect for the opinions of others, Washington was a strong chief executive. As Hamilton put it, he "consulted much, pondered much, resolved slowly, resolved surely." His stress on the dignity of his office suited the needs of a new country whose people tended to be perhaps too informal. It was indeed important that the first president be particularly concerned about establishing precedents. His scrupulous care lest he overstep the bounds of presidential power helped erase the prejudices of those who feared that republican government must inevitably succumb to dictatorship and tyranny. When each step is an experiment, when foreign dangers loom at the end of every errant path, it is surely wise to go slowly. And no one should forget that Washington's devotion to duty did not always come easily. Occasionally he exploded. Thomas Jefferson has left us a graphic description of the president at a Cabinet meeting, in a rage because of some unfair criticism, swearing that "by god he had rather be on his farm than to be made emperor of the world."

Congress Under Way

By September 1789 Congress had created the State, Treasury, and War departments and passed a Judiciary Act establishing thirteen federal district courts and three circuit courts of appeal. The number of Supreme Court justices was set at six, and Washington named John Jay the chief justice.

True to Federalist promises—for a large majority of both houses were friendly to the Constitution—Congress prepared a list of a dozen amendments (ten were ratified) guaranteeing what Congressman James Madison, who drafted the amendments, called the "great rights of mankind." These amendments, known as the Bill of Rights (see Amendments to the Constitution in the Appendix, pp. A-14–A-20), provided that Congress should make no law infringing freedom of speech, the press, or religion. The right of trial by jury was reaffirmed, the right to bear arms guaranteed. No one was to be subject to "unreasonable" searches or seizures or compelled to testify against himself or herself in a criminal case. No one was to "be deprived of life, liberty, or property, without due process of law."

Despite Washington's reluctance to interfere with the activities of Congress, he urged acceptance of these amendments so that the "rights of freemen" would be "impregnably fortified." The Bill of Rights was unique; the English Bill of Rights of 1689 was much less broad-gauged and, being an act of Parliament, was subject to repeal by Parliament at any time. The Tenth Amendment—not, strictly speaking, a part of the Bill of Rights—was designed to mollify those who feared that the states would be destroyed by the new government. It provided that powers not delegated to the United States or denied specifically to the states by the Constitution were to reside either in the states or in the people.

As experts pointed out, the amendments were not logically necessary because the federal government had no authority to act in such matters to begin with. But many had wanted to be reassured. Experience has proved repeatedly that whatever the logic of the situation, the protection afforded individuals by the Bill of Rights has been anything but unnecessary.

The Bill of Rights did much to convince doubters that the new government would not become too powerful. More complex was the task of proving that it was powerful enough to deal with those national problems that the Confederation had not been able to solve: the threat to the West posed by the British, Spaniards, and Indians; the disruption of the pattern of American foreign commerce resulting from independence; and the collapse of the financial structure of the country.

Hamilton and Financial Reform

One of the first acts of Congress in 1789 was to employ its new power to tax. The simplest means of raising money seemed to be that first attempted by the British after 1763, a tariff on foreign imports. Congress levied a 5 percent duty on all foreign products entering the United States, applying higher rates to certain products, such as hemp, glass, and nails, as a measure of protection for American producers. The Tariff Act of 1789 also placed heavy tonnage duties on all foreign shipping, a mercantilist measure designed to stimulate the American merchant marine.

Raising money for current expenses was a small and relatively simple aspect of the financial problem faced by Washington's administration. The nation's debt was large, its credit shaky, its economic future uncertain. In October 1789

New Yorkers honor Hamilton during a parade marking ratification of the Constitution. That Hamilton stood on a ship was fitting, not only because he sought to strengthen the federal "ship of state" but also because New York merchants were among his staunchest backers.

Congress deposited on the slender shoulders of Secretary of the Treasury Hamilton the task of straightening out the fiscal mess and stimulating the country's economic development.

Hamilton at age 34 had already proved himself a remarkable man. Born in the British West Indies, the illegitimate son of a shiftless Scot who was little better than a beachcomber, and raised by his mother's family, he came to New York in 1773 to attend King's College. When the Revolution broke out, he joined the Continentals. At 22 he was a staff colonel, aide-de-camp to Washington. Later, at Yorktown, he led a line regiment, displaying a bravery approaching foolhardiness. He married the daughter of Philip Schuyler, a wealthy and influential New Yorker, and after the Revolution he practiced law in that state.

Hamilton was a bundle of contradictions. Witty, charming, possessed of a mind like a sharp knife, he was sometimes the soul of practicality, sometimes an incurable romantic. No more hardheaded realist ever lived, yet he was quick to resent any slight to his honor, even—tragically—ready to fight a duel though he abhorred the custom of dueling. A self-made man, he admired aristocracy and disparaged the abilities of the common run of mankind who, he said, "seldom judge or determine right." Although granting that Americans must be allowed to govern themselves, he was as apprehensive of the "turbulence" of the masses as a small boy passing a graveyard in the dark. "No popular government was ever without its

Catilines and its Caesars," he warned—a typical example of that generation's concern about the fate of the Roman republic.

The country, Hamilton insisted, needed a strong national government. "I acknowledge," he wrote in one of the *Federalist Papers*, "my aversion to every project that is calculated to disarm the government of a single weapon, which in any possible contingency might be usefully employed for the general defense and security." He avowed that government should be "a great Federal Republic," not "a number of petty states, with the appearance only of union, jarring, jealous, perverse, without any determined direction." He wished to reduce the states to mere administrative units, like English counties.

As secretary of the treasury, Hamilton proved to be a farsighted economic planner. The United States, a "Hercules in the cradle," needed capital to develop its untapped material and human resources. To persuade investors to commit their funds in America, the country would have to convince them that it would meet every obligation in full. His *Report on the Public Credit* outlined a plan for the federal government to borrow money to pay all of its debts as well as those of the states.

While most members of Congress agreed, albeit somewhat grudgingly, that the debt should be paid in full, they had misgivings as to who should get those payments. Many of the soldiers, farmers, and merchants who had been forced to accept government securities in lieu of cash for goods and services had sold their securities for a fraction of their face value to speculators; under Hamilton's proposal, the speculators—now paid for the full value of the securities—would make a killing. To the argument for divided payment, Hamilton answered coldly: "[The speculator] paid what the commodity was worth in the market, and took the risks. . . . He . . . ought to reap the benefit of his hazard."

Hamilton was essentially correct, and in the end Congress had to go along. After all, the speculators had not caused the securities to fall in value; indeed, as a group they had favored sound money and a strong government. The best way to restore the nation's credit was to convince investors that the government would honor all obligations in full. What infuriated his contemporaries and still attracts the scorn of many historians was Hamilton's motive. He deliberately intended his plan to give a special advantage to the rich. The government would be strong, he thought, only if well-to-do Americans enthusiastically supported it. What better way to win them over than to make it worth their while financially to do so?

In part, opposition to the funding plan was sectional, for citizens of the northern states held more than four-fifths of the national debt. The scheme for assuming the state debts aggravated the controversy, since most of the southern states had already paid off much of their Revolutionary War obligations. For months Congress was deadlocked. Finally, in July 1790, Hamilton worked out a compromise with Representative James Madison and Secretary of State Jefferson. The two Virginians swung a few southern votes, and Hamilton induced some of his followers to support the southern plan for locating the permanent capital of the Union on the Potomac River.

Jefferson later claimed that Hamilton had hoodwinked him. Having only recently returned from Europe, he said, "I was really a stranger to the whole subject." Hamilton had persuaded him to "rally around" by the false tale that "our Union" was threatened with dissolution. This was nonsense; Jefferson agreed to the compromise because he expected that Virginia and the rest of the South would profit from having the capital so near at hand.

The assumption bill passed, and the entire funding plan was a great success. Soon the United States had the highest possible credit rating in the world's financial centers. Foreign capital poured into the country.

Hamilton next proposed that Congress charter a national bank. Such an institution would provide safe storage for government funds and serve as an agent for the government in the collection, movement, and expenditure of tax money. Most important, because of its substantial resources a bank could finance new and expanding business enterprises, greatly speeding the economic growth of the nation. It would also be able to issue bank notes, thereby providing a vitally needed medium of exchange for the specie-starved economy. This Bank of the United States was to be partly owned by the government, but 80 percent of the $10 million stock issue was to be sold to private individuals.

The country had much to gain from such a bank, but again—Hamilton's cleverness was never more in evidence—the well-to-do commercial classes would gain still more. Government balances in the bank belonging to all the people would earn dividends for a handful of rich investors. Manufacturers and other capitalists would profit from the bank's credit facilities. Public funds would be invested in the bank, but control would remain in private hands, since the government would appoint only five of the twenty-five directors. Nevertheless, the bill creating the bank passed both houses of Congress with relative ease in February 1791.

President Washington, however, hesitated to sign it, for the bill's constitutionality had been questioned during the debate in Congress. Nowhere did the Constitution specifically authorize Congress to charter corporations or engage in the banking business. As was his wont when in doubt, Washington called on Jefferson and Hamilton for advice.

Hamilton defended the legality of the bank by enunciating the doctrine of "implied powers." If a logical connection existed between the purpose of the bill and powers clearly stated in the Constitution, he wrote, the bill was constitutional.

> If the end be clearly comprehended within any of the specified powers, and if the measure have an obvious relation to that end . . . it may safely be deemed to come within the compass of the national authority . . . . A bank has a natural relation to the power of collecting taxes—to that of regulating trade—to that of providing for the common defence.

Jefferson disagreed. Congress could only do what the Constitution specifically authorized, he said. The "elastic clause" granting it the right to pass "all Laws which shall be necessary and proper" to carry out the specified powers must be interpreted literally or Congress would "take possession of a boundless field of power, no longer susceptible to any definition." Because a bank was obviously not neces-sary, it was not authorized.

Although not entirely convinced, Washington accepted Hamilton's reasoning and signed the bill. He could just as easily have followed Jefferson, for the Constitution is not clear. If one stresses *proper* in the "necessary and proper" clause in Article I, Section 8 of the Constitution, one ends up a Hamiltonian; if one stresses *necessary,* then Jefferson's view is correct. Historically (and this is the important point) politicians have nearly always adopted the "loose" Hamiltonian "implied powers" interpretation when they favored a measure and the "strict" Jeffersonian one when they do not. Jefferson disliked the bank; therefore, he claimed it was un-constitutional. Had he approved, he doubtless would have taken a different tack.

In 1819 the Supreme Court officially sanctioned Hamilton's construction of the "necessary and proper" clause, and in general that interpretation has prevailed. Because the majority tends naturally toward an argument that increases its free-dom of action, the pressure for this view has been continual and formidable. The Bank of the United States succeeded from the start. When its stock went on sale, investors snapped up every share in a matter of hours. People eagerly accepted its bank notes at face value. Business ventures of all kinds found it easier to raise new capital. Soon state-chartered banks entered the field. There were only three state banks in 1791; by 1801, there were thirty-two.

Hamilton had not finished. In December 1791 he submitted his *Report on Manufactures,* a bold call for economic planning. He called for government tariffs, subsidies, and awards to encourage American manufacturing. He hoped to change an essentially agricultural nation into one with a complex, self-sufficient economy. Once again business and commercial interests in particular would benefit. A ma-jority of the Congress, however, balked at so broad-gauged a scheme. Hamilton's *Report* was set aside, although many of the specific tariffs he recommended were enacted into law in 1792.

Nevertheless, the secretary of the treasury had managed to transform the fi-nancial structure of the country and to prepare the ground for an economic revolu-tion. The constitutional reforms of 1787 had made this possible, and Hamilton turned possibility into reality.

The Ohio Country: A Dark and Bloody Ground

Trouble came swiftly when white settlers moved onto the land north of the Ohio River in large numbers. The Indians, determined to hold this country at all costs, struck hard at the invaders. In 1790 the Miami chief Little Turtle, a gifted strategist, inflicted a double defeat on militia units commanded by General Josiah Harmar. The next year Little Turtle and his men defeated the forces of General Arthur St. Clair still more convincingly. Both Harmar and St. Clair resigned from the army, their careers ruined, but the defeats led Congress to authorize raising a regular army of 5,000 men.

By early 1792 the Indians had driven the whites into "beachheads" at Marietta and Cincinnati on the Ohio. Resentment of the federal government in the western counties of every state from New York to the Carolinas mounted, the people feeling that it was ignoring their interests. They were convinced that the British were inciting the Indians to attack them, yet the supposedly powerful national government seemed unable to force Great Britain to surrender its forts in the West.

Still worse, the Westerners believed, was the way the government was taxing them. In 1791, as part of his plan to take over the debts of the states, Hamilton had persuaded Congress to adopt an excise tax of 8 cents a gallon on American-made whiskey. Excise taxes were particularly disliked by most Americans. A duty on imported products was collected from merchants and passed on to consumers as part of the price, and it was by its nature imposed only on foreign-made products. People who did not want to pay it usually could find a domestic alternative. But the collection of excise taxes on American goods required hordes of tax collectors, armed with the power to snoop into one's affairs. Westerners, who were heavy drinkers and who turned much of their grain into whiskey in order to cope with the high cost of transportation, were especially angered by the tax on whiskey.

Knowing that the tax would be unpopular, Hamilton promised that the distillers would "be secured from every species of injury by the misconduct of the officers to be employed" in collecting it. But he was determined to enforce the law. To western complaints, he coolly suggested that farmers drank too much to begin with. If they found the tax oppressive, they should cut down on their consumption. Of course this did nothing to reduce western opposition to the tax. Resistance was especially intense in western Pennsylvania. When treasury agents tried to collect it there, they were forcibly prevented from doing so.

Revolution in France

Momentous events in Europe were also affecting the situation. In 1789 the French Revolution erupted, and four years later war broke out between France and Great Britain and most of the rest of Europe. With France fighting Great Britain and Spain, there arose the question of America's obligations under the Alliance of 1778. That treaty required the United States to defend the French West Indies "forever against all other powers." Suppose the British attacked Martinique; must America then go to war? Morally the United States was so obligated, but no responsible American statesman urged such a policy. With the British in Canada and Spanish forces to the west and south, the nation would be in serious danger if it entered the war. Instead, in April 1793, Washington issued a proclamation of neutrality committing the United States to be "friendly and impartial" toward both sides in the war.

Meanwhile the French had sent a special representative, Edmond Charles Genet, to the United States to seek support. Quickly concluding that the proclamation of neutrality was "a harmless little pleasantry designed to throw dust in the eyes of the British," he began, in plain violation of American law, to license

American vessels to operate as privateers against British shipping and to grant French military commissions to a number of Americans in order to mount expeditions against Spanish and British possessions in North America.

Washington received Genet coolly, and soon thereafter demanded that he stop his illegal activities. Genet, whose capacity for self-deception was monumental, appealed to public opinion over the president's head and continued to commission privateers. Washington then requested his recall.

The Genet affair was incidental to a far graver problem. Although the European war increased the foreign demand for American products, it also led to attacks on American shipping by both France and Great Britain. Each power captured American vessels headed for the other's ports whenever it could. In 1793 and 1794 about 600 United States ships were seized.

The British attacks caused far more damage, both physically and psychologically, because the British fleet was much larger than France's, and France at least professed to be America's friend and to favor freedom of trade for neutrals. Pouncing without warning, British warships captured about 250 American vessels and sent them off as prizes to British ports. The merchant marine, one American diplomat declared angrily, was being "kicked, cuffed, and plundered all over the Ocean."

The attacks roused a storm in America, reviving hatreds that had been smoldering since the Revolution. The continuing presence of British troops in the Northwest (in 1794 the British began to build a new fort in the Ohio country) and the restrictions imposed on American trade with the British West Indies raised tempers still further. To try to avoid a war, for he wisely believed that the United States should not become embroiled in the Anglo-French conflict, Washington sent Chief Justice John Jay to London to seek a settlement with the British.

Federalists and Republicans: The Rise of Political Parties

The furor over the violations of neutral rights focused attention on a new development, the formation of political parties. Why national political parties emerged after the ratification of a Constitution that made no provision for such organizations is a question that has long intrigued historians. Probably the main reason was the obvious one: By creating a strong central government the Constitution produced national issues and a focus for national discussion and settlement of these issues. Furthermore, by failing to create machinery for nominating candidates for federal offices, the Constitution left a vacuum, which informal party organizations filled. That the universally admired Washington headed the government was a force limiting partisanship, but his principal advisers, Hamilton and Jefferson, were in sharp disagreement, and they soon became the leaders around which parties coalesced.

In the spring of 1791 Jefferson and James Madison began to sound out other politicians about forming an informal political organization. Jefferson also appointed the poet Philip Freneau to a minor state department post and Freneau then began publishing a newspaper, the *National Gazette,* to disseminate the views of what became known as the Republican party. The *Gazette* was soon describing Jefferson as a "Colossus of Liberty" and flailing away editorially at Hamilton's policies. Hamilton hit back promptly, organizing his own followers in the Federalist party, the organ of which was John Fenno's *Gazette of the United States.*

At the start Hamilton had the ear of the president, and his allies controlled a majority in Congress. Jefferson, who disliked controversy, avoided a direct confrontation as long as he could. He went along with Hamilton's funding plan and traded the assumption of state debts for a capital on the Potomac. However, when Hamilton proposed the Bank of the United States, he dug in his heels. It seemed designed to benefit the northeastern commercial classes at the expense of southern and western farmers. He sensed a dastardly plot to milk the producing masses for the benefit of a few capitalists.

The growing controversy over the French Revolution and the resulting war between France and Great Britain widened the split between the parties. After the radicals in France executed Louis XVI and instituted the Reign of Terror, American conservatives were horrified. The Jeffersonians were also deeply shocked. However, they continued to defend the Revolution. Great southern landlords whose French counterparts were losing their estates—some their heads—extolled "the glorious successes of our Gallic brethren." In the same way the Federalists began to idealize the British, whom they considered the embodiment of the forces that were resisting French radicalism.

1794: Crisis and Resolution

During the summer of 1794 several superficially unrelated events brought the partisan conflicts of the period to a peak. For the better part of two years the government had been unable to collect Hamilton's whiskey tax in the West. In Pennsylvania, mobs had burned the homes of revenue agents, and several men had been killed. Late in July, 7,000 "rebels" converged on Pittsburgh, threatening to set fire to the town. They were turned away by the sight of federal artillery and the liberal dispensation of whiskey by the frightened inhabitants.

Early in August President Washington determined "to go to every length that the Constitution and laws would permit" to enforce the law. He mustered an enormous army of nearly 13,000 militiamen. This had the desired effect; when the troops arrived in western Pennsylvania, rebels were nowhere to be seen. The expected Whiskey Rebellion simply did not happen. Good sense had triumphed. Moderates in the region (not everyone, after all, was a distiller) agreed that even unpopular laws should be obeyed.

More important, perhaps, than the militia in pacifying the Pennsylvania frontier was another event that occurred while that army was being mobilized. This was the Battle of Fallen Timbers in Ohio near present-day Toledo, where the

In 1792 farmers in western Pennsylvania, outraged over Hamilton's tax on liquor, rose up in rebellion against tax collectors. Their banners included the slogan of the French revolutionaries: "Liberty, Equality, and Fraternity!" Washington crushed the rebellion in 1794.

regular army troops of Major General "Mad Anthony" Wayne won a decisive victory over the Indians. Wayne's victory opened the way for white settlement of the region. Some 2,000 of the whiskey tax rebels simply pulled up stakes and headed for Ohio after the effort to avoid the excise collapsed.

Jay's Treaty

Still more significant was the outcome of President Washington's decision to send John Jay to England to seek a treaty settling the conflicts that vexed relations between the two nations. The British genuinely wanted to reach an accommodation with the United States—as one minister quipped, the Americans "are so much in debt to this country that we scarcely dare to quarrel with them." Jay was received by both the King and Queen and wined and dined by the foreign secretary, the prime minister, and other officials. The British also feared that the two new republics, France and the United States, would draw together in a battle against Europe's monarchies. On the other hand, the British were riding the crest of a wave of important victories in the war in Europe and were not disposed to make concessions to the Americans simply to avoid trouble.

The treaty that Jay brought home did contain a number of concessions. The British agreed to evacuate the posts in the West. They also promised to compensate American shipowners for seizures in the West Indies and to open up their colonies in Asia to American ships. They conceded nothing, however, to American demands that the rights of neutrals on the high seas be respected; no one really expected them to do so in wartime. A provision opening the British West Indies to American commerce was so hedged with qualifications limiting the size of American vessels and the type of goods allowed that the United States refused to accept it.

Jay also committed the United States to paying pre-Revolutionary debts still owed British merchants, a slap in the face to many states whose courts had been impeding their collection. Yet nothing was said about the British paying for the slaves they had "abducted" during the fighting in the South.

Although Jay might have driven a harder bargain, this was a valuable treaty for the United States. But it was also a humiliating one. Most of what the United States gained already legally belonged to it, and the treaty sacrificed principles of importance to a nation dependent on foreign trade. When the terms became known, they raised a storm of popular protest. It seemed possible that President Washington would repudiate the treaty or that if he did not, the Senate would refuse to ratify it.

1795: All's Well That Ends Well

Washington did not repudiate Jay's Treaty and after long debate the Senate ratified it in June 1795. After a bitter debate, with most Republicans opposing the measure, the House passed the requisite funding resolution. The treaty marked an important step toward the regularization of Anglo-American relations, which in the long run was essential for both the economic and political security of the nation. And the evacuation of the British forts in the Northwest was of enormous immediate benefit.

Still another benefit was totally unplanned. Unexpectedly, Jay's Treaty enabled the United States to solve its problems on its southeastern frontier. During the early 1790s Spain had entered into alliances with the Cherokee, Creek, and other Indian tribes hostile to the Americans and built forts on territory ceded to the United States by Great Britain in the Treaty of Paris. In 1795, however, Spain intended to withdraw from the European war against France. Fearing a joint Anglo-American attack on Louisiana and its other American possessions, it decided to improve relations with the United States. Therefore the king's chief minister, Manuel de Godoy, known as "the Prince of Peace," offered the American envoy Thomas Pinckney a treaty that granted the United States the free navigation of the Mississippi River and the right of deposit at New Orleans that western Americans so urgently needed. This Treaty of San Lorenzo, popularly known as Pinckney's Treaty, also accepted the American version of the boundary between Spanish Florida and the United States.

The Senate ratified Jay's Treaty in June. Pinckney signed the Treaty of San Lorenzo in October that same year. These agreements put an end, at least temporarily, to European pressures in the trans-Appalachian region. Between the signings, in August 1795, as an aftermath of the Battle of Fallen Timbers, twelve tribes signed the Treaty of Greenville. The Indians surrendered huge sections of their lands, thus ending a struggle that had consumed a major portion of the government's revenues for years.

After the events of 1794 and 1795, settlers poured into the West as water bursts through a broken dike. "I believe scarcely anything short of a Chinese Wall or a line of Troops will restrain . . . the Incroachment of Settlers, upon the Indian Territory," President Washington explained in 1796. Kentucky had become a state in 1792; now, in 1796, Tennessee was admitted. Two years later the Mississippi Territory was organized, and at the end of the century, the Indiana Territory. The great westward flood reached full tide.

Washington's Farewell

Settlement of western problems did not, however, put an end to partisan strife. Even the sainted Washington was neither immune to attack nor entirely above the battle. On questions of finance and foreign policy he usually sided with Hamilton and thus increasingly incurred the anger of the Jeffersonians. But he was, after all, a Virginian. Only the most rabid partisan could think him a tool of northern commercial interests. He remained as he intended himself to be, a symbol of national unity. But he was determined to put away the cares of office at the end of his second term. In September 1796 he announced his retirement in a "Farewell Address" to the nation.

Washington found the acrimonious rivalry between Federalists and Republicans most disturbing. Hamilton advocated national unity, yet he seemed prepared to smash any individual or faction that disagreed with his vision of the country's future. Jefferson had risked his neck for independence, but he opposed the economic development needed to make America strong enough to defend that independence. Washington was less brilliant than either Hamilton or Jefferson but wiser. He appreciated how important it was that the new nation should remain at peace—with the rest of the world and with itself. In his farewell he deplored the "baneful effects of the spirit of party" that led honest people to use unscrupulous means to win a mean advantage over fellow Americans. He tried to show how the North benefited from the prosperity of the South, the South from that of the North, and the East and West also, in reciprocal fashion.

Washington urged the people to avoid both "inveterate antipathies" and "passionate attachments" to any foreign nation. Nothing had alarmed him more than the sight of Americans dividing into "French" and "English" factions. Furthermore, France had repeatedly interfered in American domestic affairs. "Against the insidious wiles of foreign influence," Washington now warned, "the jealousy of a free people ought to be constantly awake." America should develop its foreign trade but steer clear of foreign political connections as far as possible. "Permanent alliances" should be avoided, although "temporary alliances for extraordinary emergencies" might sometimes be useful.

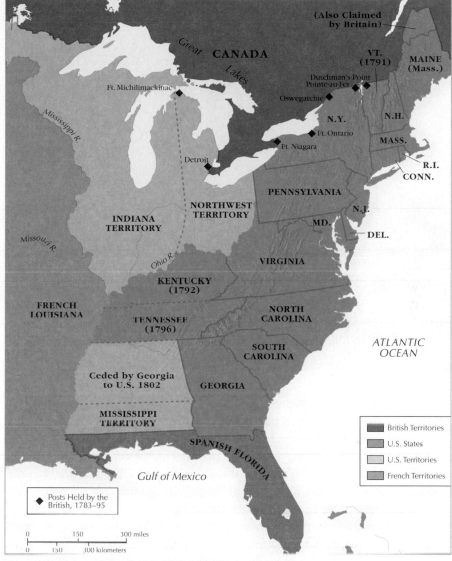

The United States and Its Territories, 1787–1802

In 1804 Georgia's cession became part of the Mississippi Territory. The seven British western forts were evacuated as a result of Jay's Treaty (1795).

Map labels:
(Also Claimed by Britain)
CANADA
Great Lakes
VT. (1791)
MAINE (Mass.)
Ft. Michilimackinac
Dutchman's Point
Pointe-au-Fer
Oswegatchie
Mississippi R.
N.Y.
N.H.
Ft. Ontario
MASS.
Ft. Niagara
Detroit
R.I.
CONN.
PENNSYLVANIA
N.J.
NORTHWEST TERRITORY
INDIANA TERRITORY
MD.
DEL.
Missouri R.
Ohio R.
VIRGINIA
KENTUCKY (1792)
FRENCH LOUISIANA
TENNESSEE (1796)
NORTH CAROLINA
ATLANTIC OCEAN
SOUTH CAROLINA
Ceded by Georgia to U.S. 1802
GEORGIA
MISSISSIPPI TERRITORY
SPANISH FLORIDA
Gulf of Mexico

Legend:
British Territories
U.S. States
U.S. Territories
French Territories

◆ Posts Held by the British, 1783–95

0   150   300 miles
0   150   300 kilometers

The Election of 1796

Washington's Farewell Address was destined to have a long and important influence on American thinking, but its immediate impact was slight. He had intended it to cool political passions. Instead, in the words of Federalist congressman Fisher Ames, people took it as "a signal, like dropping a hat, for the party racers to start." By the time the 1796 presidential campaign had ended, many Federalists and Republicans were refusing to speak to one another.

This portrait of John Adams by William Winstanley was done in 1798. Jeffersonian newspapers referred to Adams derisively as "His Rotundity." Benjamin Bache, editor of the Philadelphia *Aurora*, described him as "blind, bald, toothless, querulous," which was three-quarters true but irrelevant.

Jefferson was the only Republican candidate seriously considered in 1796. The logical Federalist was Hamilton, but, as was to happen so often in American history with powerful leaders, he was not considered "available" because his controversial policies had made him many enemies. Gathering in caucus, the Federalists in Congress nominated Vice President John Adams for the top office and Thomas Pinckney of South Carolina, negotiator of the popular Spanish treaty, for vice president. In the election the Federalists were victorious.

Hamilton, hoping to run the new administration from the wings, preferred Pinckney to Adams. He arranged for some of the Federalist electors from South Carolina to vote only for Pinckney. (Pinckney, who was on the high seas at the time, did not even know he was running for vice president!) Catching wind of this, a number of New England electors retaliated by cutting Pinckney. As a result, Adams won in the electoral college, 71 to 68, over *Jefferson*, who thus became vice president. Pinckney got only 59 electoral votes.

That Adams would now be obliged to work with a vice president who led the opposition seemed to presage a decline in partisanship. Adams actually preferred the Virginian to Pinckney for the vice presidency, while Jefferson said that if Adams would "relinquish his bias to an English constitution," he might make a fine chief executive. The two had in common a distaste for Hamilton—a powerful bond.

However, the closeness of the election indicated a trend toward the Republicans, who were making constant and effective use of the charge that the

Federalists were "monocrats" (monarchists) determined to destroy American liberty. Without Washington to lead them, the Federalist politicians were already quarreling among themselves; honest, able, hardworking John Adams was too caustic and too scathingly frank to unite them. Everything seemed to indicate a Republican victory at the next election.

The XYZ Affair

At this point occurred one of the most remarkable reversals of public feeling in American history. French attacks on American shipping, begun out of irritation at the Jay Treaty and in order to influence the election, continued after Adams took office. Hoping to stop them, Adams appointed three commissioners (Charles Pinckney, U.S. minister to France, and elder brother of Thomas; John Marshall, a Virginia Federalist lawyer; and Elbridge Gerry of Massachusetts, who was not closely identified with either party) to try to negotiate a settlement. They were instructed to seek a moderate settlement, to "terminate our differences . . . without referring to the merits."

Their mission was a fiasco. Talleyrand, the French foreign minister, sent an agent later spoken of as X to demand "something for the pocket," a "gratification," (that is, a bribe) as the price of making a deal. Later two other Tallyrand agents, Y and Z, made the same demand. The Americans refused, more because they suspected Talleyrand's good faith than because of any particular distaste for bribery. "No, no, not a sixpence," Pinckney later told X. The talks broke up, and in April 1798 President Adams released the commissioners' reports.

They caused a sensation. Americans' sense of national honor, perhaps overly tender because the country was so young and insecure, was outraged. Pinckney's laconic refusal to pay a bribe was translated into the grandiose phrase "Millions for defense, but not one cent for tribute!" and broadcast throughout the land. John Adams, never a man with mass appeal, suddenly found himself a national hero. Federalist hotheads burned for a fight. Congress unilaterally abrogated the French Alliance, created a Navy Department, and appropriated enough money to build forty-odd warships and triple the size of the army. Washington came out of retirement to lead the forces, with Hamilton, now a general, as second in command. On the seas American privateers began to attack French shipping.

Adams did not much like the French and he could be extremely stubborn. A declaration of war would have been immensely popular. But perhaps—it is not an entirely illogical surmise about John Adams, who later in life described himself with some relish as "obnoxious, suspected, and unpopular"—the president did not want to be popular. Instead of calling for war, he contented himself with approving the buildup of the armed forces.

The Republicans, however, committed to friendship with France, did not appreciate Adams's moderation. Although angered by the XYZ Affair, they tried, one

William Russel Birch engraving of the construction of the twenty-eight-gun frigate *Philadelphia* in that city. The *Philadelphia* was one of the larger ships built during the heightened tensions with France after the XYZ affair.

Federalist complained, "to clog the wheels of government" by opposing the military appropriations. John Daly Burk of the New York *Time Piece* called Adams a "mock Monarch" surrounded by a "court composed of tories and speculators," which of course was a flat lie.

Many Federalists expected the Republicans to side with France if war broke out. Hysterical and near panic, they easily persuaded themselves that the danger of subversion was acute. The French Revolution and the resulting war were churning European society to the depths, stirring the hopes of liberals and striking fear in the hearts of conservatives. Refugees of both persuasions were flocking to the United States. Suddenly the presence of these foreigners seemed threatening to "native" Americans.

The Alien and Sedition Acts

Conservative Federalists saw in this situation a chance to smash the opposition. In June and July 1798 they pushed through Congress a series of repressive measures known as the Alien and Sedition Acts. The Alien Enemies Act gave the president the power to arrest or expel aliens in time of "declared war," but since the quasi-war with France was never declared, this measure had no practical importance. The

Alien Act authorized the president to expel all aliens whom he thought "dangerous to the peace and safety of the United States." (Adams never invoked this law, but a number of aliens left the country out of fear that he might.)

Finally, there was the Sedition Act. Its first section, making it a crime "to impede the operation of any law" or to attempt to instigate a riot or insurrection, was reasonable enough; but the act also made it illegal to publish, or even to utter, any "false, scandalous and malicious" criticism of high government officials. Although milder than British sedition laws, this proviso rested, as James Madison said, on "the exploded doctrine" that government officials "are the masters and not the servants of the people."

As the election of 1800 approached, the Federalists made a systematic attempt to silence the leading Republican newspapers. Twenty-five persons were prosecuted and ten convicted, all in patently unfair trials. In typical cases, the editor Thomas Cooper, an English-born radical, later president of the University of South Carolina, was sentenced to six months in jail and fined $400; the editor Charles Holt got three months and a $200 fine; and the editor James Callender got nine months and a $200 fine.

The Kentucky and Virginia Resolves

While Thomas Jefferson did not object to state sedition laws, he believed that the Alien and Sedition Acts violated the First Amendment's guarantees of freedom of speech and the press and were an invasion of the rights of the states. In 1798 he and Madison decided to draw up resolutions arguing that the laws were unconstitutional. Madison's draft was presented to the Virginia legislature and Jefferson's to the legislature of Kentucky.

Jefferson argued that since the Constitution was a compact made by sovereign states, each state had "an equal right to judge for itself" when the compact had been violated. Thus a state could declare a law of Congress unconstitutional. Madison's Virginia Resolves took an only slightly less forthright position.

Neither Kentucky nor Virginia tried to implement these resolves or to prevent the enforcement of the Alien and Sedition Acts. Jefferson and Madison were protesting Federalist high-handedness and firing the opening salvo of Jefferson's campaign for the presidency, not advancing a new constitutional theory of extreme states' rights. "Keep away all show of force," Jefferson advised his supporters.

This was sound advice, for events were again playing into the hands of the Republicans. Talleyrand had never wanted war with the United States. When he discovered how vehemently the Americans had reacted to his little attempt to replenish his personal fortune, he let Adams know that new negotiators would be properly received.

President Adams quickly grasped the importance of the French change of heart. Other leading Federalists, however, had lost their heads. By shouting about the French danger, they had roused the country against radicalism, and they did not intend to surrender this advantage tamely. Hamilton in particular wanted war at almost any price—if not against France, then against Spain. He saw himself at the head of the new American army sweeping first across Louisiana and the Floridas, then on to the South. "We ought to squint at South America," he suggested. "Tempting objects will be within our grasp."

But the Puritan John Adams was a specialist at resisting temptation. At this critical point his intelligence, his moderate political philosophy, and his stubborn integrity stood him in good stead. He would neither go to war merely to destroy the political opposition in America nor follow "the fools who were intriguing to plunge us into an alliance with England . . . and wild expeditions to South America." Instead he submitted to the Senate the name of a new minister plenipotentiary to France, and when the Federalists tried to block the appointment, he threatened to resign. That would have made Jefferson president! So the furious Federalists had to give in, although they forced Adams to send three men instead of one.

Napoleon had taken over France by the time the Americans arrived, and he drove a harder bargain than Talleyrand would have. But in the end he signed an agreement (the Convention of 1800) abrogating the Franco-American treaties of 1778. Nothing was said about the damage done to American shipping by the French, but the war scare was over.

The Kentucky and Virginia Resolves, however, had raised an issue that would loom large in the next century. If Congress passed laws that particular states thought to be unconstitutional, did states have the right to ignore those laws—or to withdraw from the Constitution altogether?

1781	States fail to approve Congress's tariff
1786	Rhode Island Supreme Court upholds state legal tender act (*Trevett* v. *Weeden*)
	Shays's Rebellion collapses in Springfield, Massachusetts
	Only five states send delegates to Annapolis Convention
1787	Delegates meet at Philadelphia Constitutional Convention
1787–1788	All states but North Carolina and Rhode Island ratify Constitution
1789	President Washington is inaugurated
	Storming of Bastille in Paris begins French Revolution
1790	Hamilton issues his *Report on Public Credit*
1791	Hamilton issues his *Report on Manufactures*
	First Ten Amendments (Bill of Rights) to the Constitution are ratified
	Republican and Federalist political parties are organized
	Philip Freneau's *National Gazette* and John Fenno's *Gazette of the United States* are founded
1793	French revolutionaries execute King Louis XVI
	Washington issues Declaration of Neutrality
1794	"Mad Anthony" Wayne's troops defeat Indians at Battle of Fallen Timbers
	Washington's militiamen thwart Whiskey Rebellion in Pennsylvania
1795	Senate ratifies humiliating Jay Treaty
1796	Washington announces his retirement in Farewell Address
	John Adams is elected president
1798	French demand bribe during XYZ Affair
	Congress passes Alien and Sedition Acts
1798–1799	Jefferson presents Kentucky Resolutions
	Madison presents Virginia Resolutions

Jeffersonian Democracy

DURING THEIR FIRST WEEK IN COLLEGE, FRESHMEN ON AVERAGE receive eight applications for credit cards. Credit card companies target college students because they have a lifetime to acquire debt—and pay it off. A recent government study showed that the average college senior had a credit card balance of $3,200. One in five college students had credit card debt between $3,000 and $7,000. Many cope with such debt by cutting expenses, taking jobs, or skipping school; some do not cope. A 2006 documentary film described the plight of two college students in Oklahoma who, awash in credit card debt, committed suicide.

Many college students incur debt responsibly, most often to pay for college. College graduates owe on the average $20,000 in student loans, but this usually pays off—literally: In 2004 college graduates on the average earned $51,500, while individuals with only a high school education earned $28,600.

Many of the Founders of the nation were also entangled in personal debt. In 1798 Robert Morris, the financier who had devised the funded debt to pay and equip George Washington's army, was imprisoned for personal debt. He languished in the Prune Street debtor's prison in Philadelphia for three years. Thomas Jefferson, on paper one of the richest men in Virginia, owner of thousands of acres of land and 200 slaves, was also plagued by debt. His financial woes mounted as he built additions to Monticello, his home, and acquired more books for his library, one of the finest in the nation. Creditors harassed him. "I am miserable till I shall owe not a shilling," he wrote in 1787. When he died, he was bankrupt. His slaves were sold to pay creditors.

Jefferson's antipathy to debt influenced his ideas about government. He opposed federal expenditures because they could lead to indebtedness. His parsimony left the nation vulnerable to foreigners, whether high-handed European rulers or pirate states in northern Africa. On a few occasions—such as the chance to acquire the Louisiana Territory—he splurged, but soon recanted. On leaving office he urged his successor to pay off the federal deficit.

Jefferson Elected President

Once the furor over war and subversion subsided, public attention focused on the presidential contest between Adams and Jefferson. Because of his stand for peace, Adams personally escaped the brunt of popular indignation against the Federalist party. His solid qualities had a strong appeal to conservatives, and fear that the Republicans would introduce radical "French" social reforms did not disappear when the danger of war with France ended. Many nationalist-minded voters worried that the Republicans, waving the banner of states' rights, would weaken the strong government established by the Federalists. The economic progress stimulated by Hamilton's financial reforms also seemed threatened. But when the electors' votes were counted in February 1801, the Republicans were discovered to have won narrowly, 73 to 65.

But which Republican was to be president? The Constitution did not distinguish between presidential and vice presidential candidates; it provided only that each elector vote for two candidates, the one with the most votes becoming president and the runner-up vice president. The development of national political parties made this system impractical. The vice presidential candidate of the Republicans was Aaron Burr of New York, a former senator and a rival of Hamilton in law and politics. But Republican party solidarity had been perfect; Jefferson and Burr received seventy-three votes each. Because of the tie, the Constitution required that the House of Representatives (voting by states) choose between them.

In the House the Republicans could control only eight of the sixteen state delegations. On the first ballot Jefferson got these eight votes, one short of election, while six states voted for Burr. Two state delegations, being evenly split, lost their votes. Through thirty-five ballots the deadlock persisted; the Federalist congressmen, fearful of Jefferson's supposed radicalism, voted solidly for Burr.

In the end, Alexander Hamilton decided who would be the next president. Although he considered Jefferson "too much in earnest in his democracy" and "not very mindful of truth," he detested Burr. He exerted his considerable influence on Federalist congressmen on Jefferson's behalf. Finally, on February 17, 1801, Jefferson was elected. Burr became vice president.

To make sure that this deadlock would never be repeated, the Twelfth Amendment was drafted, providing for separate balloting in the Electoral College for president and vice president. This change was ratified in 1804, shortly before the next election.

The Federalist Contribution

On March 4, 1801, in the raw new national capital on the Potomac River named in honor of George Washington, the Father of his Country, Thomas Jefferson took the presidential oath and delivered his inaugural address.[1] His goal was to recapture the simplicity and austerity—the "pure republicanism"—that had characterized "the spirit of '76." The new president believed that a revolution as important as that heralded by his immortal Declaration of Independence had occurred, and for once most of his political enemies agreed with him.

Certainly an era had ended. In the years between the Peace of Paris and Jay's Treaty, the Federalists had practically monopolized the political good sense of the nation. They were "right" in strengthening the federal government, in establishing a sound fiscal system, in trying to diversify the economy, in seeking an accommodation with Great Britain, and in refusing to be carried away with enthusiasm for France despite the bright dreams inspired by the French Revolution.

But the Federalists were unable to face up to defeat. When they saw the Republicans gathering strength by developing clever new techniques of party organization and propaganda, mouthing slogans about liberty, attacking "monocrats," glorifying both the past with its satisfying simplicity and the future with its promise of a glorious day when all men would be free, equal, and brothers, they panicked. Abandoning the sober wisdom of their great period, they fought to save themselves at any cost. The effort turned defeat into rout. The Republican victory, close in the Electoral College, approached landslide proportions in the congressional elections, where popular feeling expressed itself directly.

Jefferson erred, however, in calling this triumph a revolution. The real upheaval had been attempted in 1798; it was Federalist-inspired, and it failed. In 1800 the voters expressed a preference for the old over the new; that is, for individual freedom and limited national power. And Jefferson, despite Federalist fears that he would destroy the Constitution and establish a radical social order, presided instead over a regime that confirmed the great achievements of the Federalist era.

What was most significant about the election of 1800 was that it was *not* a revolution. After a bitter contest, the Jeffersonians took power and proceeded to change the policy of the government. They did so peacefully. Thus American republican government passed a crucial test: Control of its machinery had changed hands in a democratic and orderly way. And only slightly less significant, the informal party system had demonstrated its usefulness. The Jeffersonians had organized popular dissatisfaction with Federalist policies, formulated a platform of reform, chosen leaders to put their plans into effect, and elected those leaders to office.

---

[1]*In 1790, when Jefferson balked at having the federal government assume the obligation of paying state debts and creditors with claims on the Continental Congress, Hamilton agreed to place the national capital in Virginia.*

Thomas Jefferson: Political Theorist

Much as Jefferson worried that an indebted nation could become enslaved to its creditors, he feared banks because they too deprived debtors of true liberty. He believed *all* government a necessary evil at best, for by its nature it restricted the freedom of the individual. For this reason, he wanted the United States to remain a society of small independent farmers. Such a nation did not need much political organization.

Jefferson's main objection to Alexander Hamilton was that Hamilton wanted to commercialize and centralize the country; Hamilton embraced public debt so as to initiate public projects and promote investment. This Jefferson feared, for it would mean that financial speculators and creditors would acquire economic power. Moreover, a commercial economy would lead to the growth of cities, which would complicate society and hence require more regulation. "The mobs of great cities add just as much to the support of pure government," he said, "as sores do to the strength of the human body." Later in life he warned a nephew to avoid "populous cities" because, he said, in such places young men acquire "habits and partialities which do not contribute to the happiness of their afterlife." Like Hamilton, he believed that city workers were easy prey for demagogues. "I consider the class of artificers as the panderers of vice, and the instruments by which the liberties of a country are usually overturned," he said. "Those who labor in the earth," he also said, "are the chosen people of God, if ever He had a chosen people."

Jefferson objected to what he considered Hamilton's pro-British orientation. Despite his support of the American Revolution, Hamilton admired English society and the orderliness of the British government, and he modeled much of his financial program on the British example. To the author of the Declaration of Independence, these attitudes passed all understanding. Jefferson thought English society immoral and decadent, the British system of government fundamentally corrupt. Toward France, the two took opposite positions. Jefferson was in Paris when the French Revolution broke out; he was delighted to see another blow struck at tyranny. To Hamilton, the violence and social disruption caused by the French Revolution were anathema.

Like Hamilton, Jefferson thought human beings basically selfish. "Lions and tigers are mere lambs compared with men," he once said. Although he claimed to have some doubts about the subject, he suspected that blacks were "inferior to whites in the endowments both of body and mind." (Hamilton, who also owned slaves, stated flatly of blacks: "Their natural faculties are as good as ours.") Jefferson's pronouncements on race are yet more troubling in light of recent research, including DNA studies that point to the likelihood that he fathered one or more children by Sally Hemings, one of his slaves.

Yet like a good child of the Enlightenment, Jefferson believed that "no definite limits can be assigned to the improvability of the human race" and that unless people were free to follow the dictates of reason, the march of civilization would grind quickly to a halt. "To preserve the freedom of the human mind," he wrote, "every

DID THOMAS JEFFERSON FATHER A CHILD BY HIS SLAVE?

The photo below *(left)* shows Thomas Jefferson's bedroom at Monticello. He designed the alcove to ensure privacy. A page from his farm accounts *(right)* in his own writing lists as slaves Sally Hemings and several of her children, including Madison, born in 1805, and Eston, born in 1808. In 1787, Sally Hemings, a young slave from the Jefferson plantation, was sent to Paris to serve Thomas Jefferson, U.S. minister to France, and his two daughters. Jefferson's wife had died five years earlier. After Jefferson was elected president in 1800, a newspaper claimed that he had fathered all of Hemings's children. Jefferson ignored the charges and his political allies denounced them as lies. In 1873 Madison Hemings told an Ohio reporter that his mother, Sally Hemings, had said that his father was Thomas Jefferson. Few took the story seriously. Jefferson scholar Merrill Peterson (1960) was the first to mention Madison Hemings's story, which he attributed to Federalists seeking to embarrass Jefferson and abolitionists seeking to discredit slavery. Dumas Malone (1948–1981), the preeminent Jefferson biographer, flatly

rejected the possibility of a Jefferson-Hemings liaison. Among scholars, Malone's views went mostly unchallenged for decades. But Annette Gordon-Reed (1997), a lawyer, accumulated considerable evidence in support of Madison Hemings's story, though she did not think it proven. The next year a forensic pathologist compared a DNA sample of a descendant of Field Jefferson, Thomas Jefferson's uncle, to that of a descendant of Eston Hemings. A genetic sequence matched. Eston had been fathered by a Jefferson. Some scholars pointed to Jefferson's younger brother, Randolph, as the father, but most Jefferson scholars concluded that Thomas Jefferson was the more likely father. No such revelations could diminish Jefferson's significance as statesman, but they further complicate our understanding of one of the nation's foremost apostles of freedom.

Merrill Peterson, *The Jefferson Image in the American Mind* (1960), Dumas Malone, *Jefferson and His Time*, 6 volumes (1948–1981), Annette Gordon-Reed, *Thomas Jefferson and Sally Hemings* (1997). See also Joseph Ellis, *American Sphinx* (1998).

spirit should be ready to devote itself to martyrdom." Democracy seemed to him not so much an ideal as a practical necessity. If people could not govern themselves, how could they be expected to govern their fellows? He had no patience with Hamilton's fondness for magnifying the virtues of the rich and the well-born. He believed that "genius" was a rare quality but one "which nature has shown as liberally among poor as rich." When a very old man he wrote:

"The mass of mankind has not been born with saddles on their backs, nor a favored few booted and spurred, ready to ride them legitimately, by the grace of God."

Jefferson as President

The novelty of the new administration lay in its style and its moderation. Jefferson saw to it that the whiskey tax and other Federalist excises were repealed, and he made sharp cuts in military and naval expenditures to keep the budget in balance. The Naturalization Act of 1798 was repealed, and the old five-year residence requirement for citizenship restored. The Sedition Act and the Alien Act expired of their own accord in 1801 and 1802.

The changes were not drastic. Jefferson made no effort to tear down the fiscal structure that Hamilton had erected. "We can pay off his debt," the new president confessed, "but we cannot get rid of his financial system." Nor did the author of the Kentucky Resolves try to alter the balance of federal-state power.

Yet there was a different tone to the new regime. Jefferson had no desire to surround himself with pomp and ceremony; the excessive formality of the Washington and Adams administrations had been distasteful to him. From the moment of his election, he played down the ceremonial aspects of the presidency. He asked that he be notified of his election by mail rather than by a committee, and he would have preferred to have taken the oath at Charlottesville, near Monticello, his home, rather than at Washington. After the inauguration, he returned to his boardinghouse on foot and took dinner in his usual seat at the common table.

In the White House he often wore a frayed coat and carpet slippers, even to receive the representatives of foreign powers when they arrived, resplendent with silk ribbons and a sense of their own importance, to present their credentials. At social affairs he paid little heed to the status and seniority of his guests. When dinner was announced, he offered his arm to whichever lady he was talking to at the moment and placed her at his right; other guests were free to sit wherever they found an empty chair. During business hours congressmen, friends, foreign officials, and plain citizens coming to call took their turn in the order of their arrival. "The principle of society with us," Jefferson explained, "is the equal rights of all. . . . Nobody shall be above you, nor you above anybody, *pell-mell* is our law."

Jefferson made effective use of his close supporters in Congress and of Cabinet members as well, in persuading Congress to go along with his proposals. His state papers were models of reason, minimizing conflicts, stressing areas where all honest people must agree. After all, as he indicated in his inaugural address, nearly all Americans believed in having both a federal government and a republican system. No great principle divided them into irreconcilable camps. Jefferson set out to bring them all into *his* camp, and he succeeded so well in four years that when he ran for reelection against Charles Pinckney, he got 162 of the 176 electoral votes cast. Eventually even John Quincy Adams, son of the second president, became a Jeffersonian.

At the same time, Jefferson was anything but nonpartisan in the sense that Washington had been. His Cabinet consisted exclusively of men of his own party. He exerted almost continuous pressure on Congress to make sure that his legislative program was enacted into law. He did not remove many Federalist officeholders, and at one point he remarked ruefully that government officials seldom died and never resigned. But when he could, he used his power of appointment to reward his friends and punish his enemies.

Jefferson's Attack on the Judiciary

Although notably open-minded and tolerant, Jefferson had a few stubborn prejudices. One was against kings, another against the British system of government. A third was against judges, or rather, against entrenched judicial power. While recognizing that judges must have a degree of independence, he feared what he called their "habit of going out of the question before them, to throw an anchor ahead, and grapple further hold for future advances of power." The biased behavior of Federalist judges during the trials under the Sedition Act had enormously increased this distrust, and it burst all bounds when the Federalist majority of the dying Congress rammed through the Judiciary Act of 1801.

The Judiciary Act created six new circuit courts, presided over by sixteen new federal judges and a small army of attorneys, marshals, and clerks. The expanding country needed the judges, but with the enthusiastic cooperation of President Adams, the Federalists made shameless use of the opportunity to fill all the new positions with conservative members of their own party. The new appointees were dubbed "midnight justices" because Adams had stayed up until midnight on March 3, his last day as president, feverishly signing their commissions.

The Republicans retaliated as soon as the new Congress met by repealing the Judiciary Act of 1801, but on taking office Jefferson had discovered that in the confusion of Adams's last hours, the commissions of a number of justices of the peace for the new District of Columbia had not been distributed. While these were small fry indeed, Jefferson was so angry that he ordered the commissions held up even though they had been signed by Adams.

One of the appointees, William Marbury, then petitioned the Supreme Court for a writ of mandamus (Latin for "we order") directing the new secretary of state, James Madison, to give him his commission.

The case of *Marbury* v. *Madison* (1803) placed Chief Justice John Marshall, one of Adams's "midnight" appointments, in an embarrassing position. Marbury had a strong claim; if Marshall refused to issue a mandamus, everyone would say he dared not stand up to Jefferson, and the prestige of the Court would suffer. If he issued the writ, however, he would place the Court in direct conflict with the executive. Jefferson particularly disliked Marshall. He would probably tell Madison to ignore the order, and in the prevailing state of public opinion nothing could be done about it. This would be a still more staggering blow to the judiciary. What should the chief justice do?

Marshall had studied law only briefly and had no previous judicial experience, but in this crisis he first displayed the genius that was to mark him as a great judge. By right Marbury should have his commission, he announced. However, the Court could not require Madison to give it to him. Marbury's request for a mandamus had been based on an ambiguous clause in the Judiciary Act of 1789. That clause was unconstitutional, Marshall declared, and therefore void. Congress could not legally give the Supreme Court the right to issue writs of mandamus in such circumstances.

With the skill and foresight of a chess grand master, Marshall turned what had looked like a trap into a triumph. By sacrificing the pawn, Marbury, he established the power of the Supreme Court to invalidate federal laws that conflicted with the Constitution. Jefferson could not check him because Marshall had *refused* power instead of throwing an anchor ahead, as Jefferson had feared. Yet he had certainly grappled a "further hold for future advances of power," and the president could do nothing to stop him.

The *Marbury* ruling made Jefferson more determined to strike at the Federalist-dominated courts. He decided to press for the impeachment of some of the more partisan judges. First he had the House of Representatives bring charges against District Judge John Pickering. Pickering was clearly deranged—he had frequently delivered profane and drunken harangues from the bench—and the Senate quickly voted to remove him. Then Jefferson went after a much larger fish, Samuel Chase, associate justice of the Supreme Court.

Chase had been prominent for decades, an early leader of the Sons of Liberty, a signer of the Declaration of Independence, active in the affairs of the Continental Congress. Washington had named him to the Supreme Court in 1796, and he had delivered a number of important opinions. But his handling of cases under the Sedition Act had been outrageously high-handed. Defense lawyers had become so exasperated as to throw down their briefs in disgust at some of his prejudiced rulings. However, the trial demonstrated that Chase's actions had not constituted the "high crimes and misdemeanors" required by the Constitution to remove a judge. Even Jefferson became disenchanted with the efforts of some of his more extreme followers and accepted Chase's acquittal with equanimity.

The Barbary Pirates

The North African Arab states of Morocco, Algiers, Tunis, and Tripoli had for decades made a business of piracy, seizing vessels all over the Mediterranean and holding crews and passengers for ransom. The European powers found it simpler to pay them annual protection money than to crush them. Under Washington and Adams, the United States joined in the payment of this tribute; while large, the sums were less than the increased costs of insurance for shippers when the protection was not purchased.

Such spinelessness ran against Jefferson's grain. "When this idea comes across my mind, my faculties are absolutely suspended between indignation and impatience," he said. When the pasha of Tripoli tried to raise the charges, he balked. Tripoli then declared war in May 1801, and Jefferson dispatched a squadron to the Mediterranean.

But the pirates were not overwhelmed, and a major American warship, the frigate *Philadelphia,* had to be destroyed after running aground off the Tripolitan coast. The payment of tribute continued until 1815. Just the same, America, though far removed from the pirate bases, was the only maritime nation that tried to resist the blackmail. Although the war failed to achieve Jefferson's purpose of ending the payments, the pasha agreed to a new treaty more favorable to the United States, and American sailors, led by Commodore Edward Preble, won valuable experience and a large portion of fame. The greatest hero was Lieutenant Stephen Decatur, who captured two pirate ships, led ten men in a daring raid on another in which he took on a gigantic sailor in a wild battle of cutlass against boarding pike, and snatched the stricken *Philadelphia* from the pirates by sneaking aboard and setting it afire.

The Louisiana Purchase

The major achievements of Jefferson's first term had to do with the American West, and the greatest by far was the acquisition of the huge area between the Mississippi River and the Rocky Mountains. In a sense the purchase of this region, called Louisiana, was fortuitous, an accidental by-product of European political adjustments and the whim of Napoleon Bonaparte. Certainly Jefferson had not planned it, for in his inaugural address he had expressed the opinion that the country already had all the land it would need "for a thousand generations." It was nonetheless the perfectly logical—one might almost say inevitable—result of a long series of events in the history of the Mississippi Valley.

Along with every other American who had even a superficial interest in the West, Jefferson understood that the United States must have access to the mouth of the Mississippi and the city of New Orleans or eventually lose everything beyond the Appalachians. "There is on the globe one single spot, the possessor of which is our natural and habitual enemy," he was soon to write. "It is New Orleans." Thus when he learned shortly after his inauguration that Spain had given Louisiana back to France, he was immediately on his guard. Control of Louisiana by Spain, a "feeble" country with "pacific dispositions," could be tolerated; control by a resurgent France dominated by Napoleon, the greatest military genius of the age, was entirely different. Did Napoleon have designs on Canada? Did he perhaps mean to resume the old Spanish and British game of encouraging the Indians to torment the American frontier? And what now would be the status of Pinckney's precious treaty?

Deeply worried, the president instructed his minister to France, Robert R. Livingston, to seek assurances that American rights in New Orleans would be respected and to negotiate the purchase of West Florida in case that region had also been turned over to France.

Jefferson's concern was well founded; France was indeed planning new imperial ventures in North America. Immediately after settling its difficulties with the United States through the Convention of 1800, France signed the secret Treaty of San Ildefonso with Spain, which returned Louisiana to France. Napoleon hoped to use this region as a breadbasket for the French West Indian sugar plantations, just as colonies like Pennsylvania and Massachusetts had fed the British sugar islands before the Revolution.

However, the most important French island, Saint Domingue (Hispaniola), at the time occupied entirely by the nation of Haiti, had slipped from French control. During the French Revolution, the slaves of the island had revolted. In 1793 they were granted personal freedom, but they fought on under the leadership of the "Black Napoleon," a self-taught genius named Toussaint Louverture, and by 1801 the island was entirely in their hands. The original Napoleon, taking advantage of the slackening of war in Europe, dispatched an army of 20,000 men under General Charles Leclerc to reconquer it.

When Jefferson learned of the Leclerc expedition, he had no trouble divining its relationship to Louisiana. His uneasiness became outright alarm. In April 1802 he again urged Minister Livingston to attempt the purchase of New Orleans and Florida or, as an alternative, to buy a tract of land near the mouth of the Mississippi where a new port could be constructed. Of necessity, the mild-mannered, idealistic president now became an aggressive realist. If the right of deposit could not be preserved through negotiation, it must be purchased with gunpowder, even if that meant acting in conjunction with the despised British. "The day that France takes possession of New Orleans," he warned, "we must marry ourselves to the British fleet and nation."

In October 1802 the Spanish, who had not yet actually turned Louisiana over to France, heightened the tension by suddenly revoking the right of deposit at New Orleans. We now know that the French had no hand in this action, but it was beyond reason to expect Jefferson or the American people to believe it at the time. With the West clamoring for relief, Jefferson appointed his friend and disciple James Monroe minister plenipotentiary and sent him to Paris with instructions to offer up to $10 million for New Orleans and Florida. If France refused, he and Livingston should open negotiations for a "closer connection" with the British.

The tension broke before Monroe even reached France. General Leclerc's Saint Domingue expedition ended in disaster. Although Toussaint surrendered, Haitian resistance continued. Yellow fever raged through the French army; Leclerc himself fell to the fever, which wiped out practically his entire force.

When news of this calamity reached Napoleon early in 1803, he began to have second thoughts about reviving French imperialism in the New World. Without Saint Domingue, the wilderness of Louisiana seemed of little value. Napoleon was

The 1790 slave rebellion in Haiti, led by Toussaint Louverture, caused thousands of French to flee the island; many settled in South Carolina. Their stories fueled fears of a slave uprising in the South.

preparing a new campaign in Europe. He could no longer spare troops to recapture a rebellious West Indian island or to hold Louisiana against a possible British attack, and he needed money.

For some weeks the commander of the most powerful army in the world mulled the question without consulting anyone. Then, with characteristic suddenness, he made up his mind. On April 10 he ordered Foreign Minister Talleyrand to offer not merely New Orleans but all of Louisiana to the Americans. The next day Talleyrand summoned Livingston to his office on the rue du Bac and dropped this bombshell. Livingston was almost struck speechless but quickly recovered his composure. When Talleyrand asked what the United States would give for the province, he suggested the French equivalent of about $5 million. Talleyrand pronounced the sum "too low" and urged Livingston to think about the subject for a day or two.

Livingston faced a situation that no modern diplomat would ever have to confront. His instructions said nothing about buying an area almost as large as the entire United States, and there was no time to write home for new instructions. The offer staggered the imagination. Luckily, Monroe arrived the next day to share the responsibility. The two Americans consulted, dickered with the French, and finally

New Orleans in 1803, when the city was acquired—along with much of the modern United States—in the Louisiana Purchase. It was known as the Crescent City because of the way it hugged a curved section of the Mississippi River. In 1803, its population was about 8,000, including 4,000 whites, 2,700 slaves, and about 1,300 free "persons of color."

agreed—they could scarcely have done otherwise—to accept the proposal. Early in May they signed a treaty. For 60 million francs—about $15 million—the United States was to have all of Louisiana.

No one knew exactly how large the region was or what it contained. When Livingston asked Talleyrand about the boundaries of the purchase, he replied: "I can give you no direction. You have made a noble bargain for yourselves, and I suppose you will make the most of it." Never, as the historian Henry Adams wrote, "did the United States government get so much for so little."

Napoleon's unexpected concession caused consternation in America, though there was never real doubt that the treaty would be ratified. Jefferson did not believe that the government had the power under the Constitution to add new territory or to grant American citizenship to the 50,000 residents of Louisiana by executive act, as the treaty required. He even drafted a constitutional amendment: "The province of Louisiana is incorporated with the United States and made part thereof," but his advisers convinced him that it would be dangerous to delay approval of the treaty until an amendment could be acted on by three-fourths of the states. Jefferson then suggested that the Senate ratify the treaty and submit an amendment afterward "confirming an act which the nation had not previously authorized." This idea was so obviously illogical that he quickly dropped it. Finally, he came to believe "that the less we say about constitutional difficulties the better." Since what he called "the good sense of our country" clearly wanted Louisiana, he decided to "acquiesce with satisfaction" while Congress overlooked the "metaphysical subtleties" of the problem and ratified the treaty.

It was ironic—and a man as perceptive as Hamilton must surely have recognized the irony—that the acquisition of Louisiana ensured Jefferson's reelection and further contributed to the downfall of the Federalists. The purchase was popular even in the New England bastions of that party. While the negotiations were progressing in Paris, Jefferson had written of partisan political affairs: "If we can settle happily the difficulties of the Mississippi, I think we may promise ourselves smooth seas during our time." These words turned out to be no more accurate than most political predictions, but the Louisiana Purchase drove another spike into the Federalists' coffin.

The Federalists Discredited

The West and South were solidly for Jefferson, and the North was rapidly succumbing to his charm. The addition of new western states would soon further reduce New England's power in national affairs. So complete did the Republican triumph seem that a handful of diehard Federalists in New England began to think of secession. Led by former secretary of state Timothy Pickering, a sour, implacable conservative, a group known as the Essex Junto organized in 1804 a scheme to break away from the Union and establish a "northern confederacy."

Even within the dwindling Federalist ranks the junto had little support. Nevertheless, Pickering and his friends pushed ahead, drafting a plan whereby, having captured political control of New York, they would take the entire Northeast out of the Union. Since they could not begin to win New York for anyone in their own ranks, they hit on the idea of supporting Vice President Aaron Burr, who was running against the "regular" Republican candidate for governor of New York. Although Burr did not promise to bring New York into their confederacy if elected, he encouraged them enough to win their backing. The foolishness of the plot was revealed in the April elections: Burr was overwhelmed by the regular Republican. The junto's scheme collapsed.

The incident, however, had a tragic aftermath. Hamilton had campaigned against Burr, whom he considered "an embryo Caesar." When he continued after the election to cast aspersions on Burr's character (not a very difficult assignment, since Burr, despite being a grandson of the preacher Jonathan Edwards, frequently violated both the political and sexual mores of the day), Burr challenged him to a duel. It was well known that Hamilton opposed dueling in principle, his own son having been slain in such an encounter, and he certainly had no need to prove his courage. But he believed that his honor was at stake. The two met with pistols on July 11, 1804, at Weehawken, New Jersey, across the Hudson River from New York City. Hamilton made no effort to hit the challenger, but Burr took careful aim. Hamilton fell, wounded; he died the next day. Thus a great, if enigmatic, man was

Pistols used in the duel between Aaron Burr and Alexander Hamilton. Before the duel Hamilton's lawyer drew up a contract specifying the terms: The duelists were to shoot from ten paces, and the barrels of the guns were to be no longer than 11 inches. Taking deadly aim, Burr fired a .54-caliber ball that hit Hamilton in the chest. It ricocheted off his rib, punctured his liver, and lodged in his backbone. He died the next day.

cut off in his prime. His work, in a sense, had been completed, and his philosophy of government was being everywhere rejected, yet the nation's loss was large.

Lewis and Clark

While the disgruntled Federalists dreamed of secession, Jefferson was planning the exploration of Louisiana and the region beyond. He especially hoped to find a water route to connect the upper Mississippi or its tributaries with the Pacific Ocean. Early in 1803 he got $2,500 from Congress and obtained the permission of the French to send his exploring party across Louisiana. To command the expedition he appointed his private secretary, Meriwether Lewis, a young Virginian who had seen considerable service with the army in the West and who possessed, according to Jefferson, "a great mass of accurate information on all the subjects of nature." Lewis chose as his companion officer William Clark, another soldier (he had served with General Anthony Wayne at the Battle of Fallen Timbers) who had much experience in negotiating with Indians.

Lewis and Clark gathered a group of forty-eight experienced men near St. Louis during the winter of 1803–1804. In the spring they made their way slowly up the Missouri River in a 55-foot keelboat and two dugout canoes, called pirogues. By late fall they had reached what is now North Dakota, where they built a small station, Fort Mandan, and spent the winter there. In April 1805, having shipped back to the president more than thirty boxes of plants, minerals, animal skins and bones, and Indian artifacts, they struck out again toward the mountains, accompanied by a Shoshone woman, Sacagawea, and her French-Canadian husband, Toussaint Charbonneau, who acted as interpreters and guides. They passed the Great Falls of the Missouri and then clambered over the Continental Divide at Lemhi Pass in

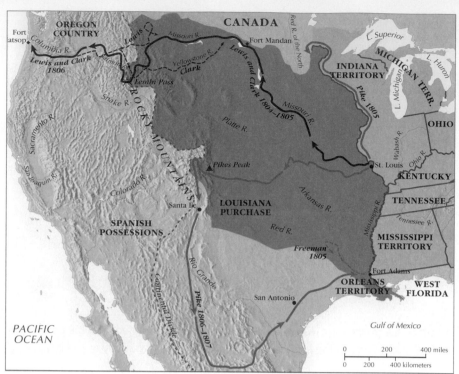

Exploring the Louisiana Purchase

southwestern Montana. Soon thereafter the going became easier, and they descended to the Pacific by way of the Clearwater and Columbia Rivers, reaching their
destination in November. They had hoped to return by ship, but during the long,
damp winter not a single vessel appeared. In the spring of 1806 they headed back
by land, reaching St. Louis on September 23.

The country greeted the news of their return with delight. Besides locating several passes across the Rocky Mountains, Lewis and Clark had established friendly relations with a great many Indian tribes to whom they presented gifts, medals, American
flags, and a sales talk designed to promote peace and the fur trade. They brought back
a wealth of data about the country and its resources. The journals kept by members of
the group were published and, along with their accurate maps, became major sources
for scientists, students, and future explorers. To Jefferson's great personal satisfaction,
Lewis provided him with many specimens of the local wildlife, including two grizzly
bear cubs, which he kept for a time in a stone pit in the White House lawn.

The success of Lewis and Clark did not open the gates of Louisiana very wide.
Other explorers sent out by Jefferson accomplished far less. Thomas Freeman, an
Irish-born surveyor, led a small party up the Red River but ran into a powerful
Spanish force near the present junction of Arkansas, Oklahoma, and Texas and was
forced to retreat. Between 1805 and 1807 Lieutenant Zebulon Pike explored the upper Mississippi Valley and the Colorado region. (He discovered but failed to scale
the peak south of Denver that bears his name.) Pike eventually made his way to

The "Flat Head" (Chinook) Indians acquired their name through shaping in infancy, as shown in a diagram from the Lewis and Clark journals. More remarkable to the explorers than the shape of the Indian heads was the tribeswomen's open sexuality. "The young females are fond of the attention of our men and appear to meet the sincere approbation of their friends and connections for thus obtaining their favors," Captain Clark confided in his diary.

Santa Fe and the upper reaches of the Rio Grande, but he was not nearly so careful and acute an observer as Lewis and Clark were and consequently brought back much less information. By 1808 fur traders based at St. Louis were beginning to invade the Rockies, and by 1812 there were 75,000 people in the southern section of the new territory, which was admitted to the Union that year as the state of Louisiana. The northern region lay almost untouched until much later.

The Burr Conspiracy

Republican virtue seemed to have triumphed. But Jefferson soon found himself in trouble at home and abroad.

In part his difficulties arose from the extent of the Republican victory. In 1805 his Federalist opponents had no useful ideas, no intelligent leadership, no effective numbers. They held only a quarter of the seats in Congress. As often happens in such situations, lack of opposition weakened party discipline and encouraged factionalism among the Republicans.

The Republican who caused Jefferson the most trouble was Aaron Burr, and the president was partly to blame for the difficulty. After their contest for the presidency in 1801, Jefferson pursued Burr vindictively, depriving him of federal patronage in New York and replacing him as the 1804 Republican vice presidential candidate with Governor George Clinton, Burr's chief rival in the state.

While still vice president, Burr began to flirt with treason. He approached Anthony Merry, the British minister in Washington, and offered to "effect a separation of the Western part of the United States." His price was £110,000 and the support of a British fleet off the mouth of the Mississippi. The British did not fall in with his scheme, but Burr went ahead nonetheless. Exactly what he had in mind has long been in dispute. Certainly he dreamed of acquiring a western empire for himself; whether he intended to wrest it from the United States or from Spanish territories beyond Louisiana is unclear. He joined forces with General James Wilkinson, whom Jefferson had appointed governor of the Louisiana Territory, who was secretly in the pay of Spain.

The opening of the Ohio and Mississippi valleys had not totally satisfied land-hungry Westerners. In 1806 Burr and Wilkinson had no difficulty raising a small force at a place called Blennerhassett Island, in the Ohio River. Some six dozen men began to move downriver toward New Orleans under Burr's command. Whether the objective was New Orleans or some part of Mexico, the scheme was clearly illegal. For some reason, however—possibly because he was incapable of loyalty to anyone[2]—Wilkinson betrayed Burr to Jefferson at the last moment. Burr tried to escape to Spanish Florida but was captured in February 1807, brought to Richmond, Virginia, under guard, and charged with high treason.

Any president will deal summarily with traitors, but Jefferson's attitude during Burr's trial reveals the depth of his hatred. He "made himself a party to the prosecution," personally sending evidence to the U.S. attorney who was handling the case and offering blanket pardons to associates of Burr who would agree to turn state's evidence. In stark contrast, Chief Justice Marshall, presiding at the trial in his capacity as judge of the circuit court, repeatedly showed favoritism to the prisoner.

In this contest between two great men at their worst, Jefferson as a vindictive executive and Marshall as a prejudiced judge, the victory went to the judge. Organizing "a military assemblage," Marshall declared on his charge to the jury, "was not a levying of war." To "advise or procure treason" was not in itself treason. Unless two independent witnesses testified to an overt act of treason as thus defined, the accused should be declared innocent. The jury, deliberating only 25 minutes, found Burr not guilty.

Throughout the trial, Burr never lost his self-possession. He seemed to view the proceedings with amiable cynicism. Then, since he was wanted either for murder or for treason in six states, he went into exile in Europe. Some years later he returned to New York, where he spent an unregenerate old age, fathering two illegitimate children in his seventies and being divorced by his second wife on grounds of adultery at 80.

The Burr affair was a blow to Jefferson's prestige; it left him more embittered against Marshall and the federal judiciary, and it added nothing to his reputation as a statesman.

---

[2]*John Randolph said of him: "Wilkinson is the only man that I ever saw who was from the bark to the very core a villain."*

The Battle of Trafalgar, by Nicholas Pocock (1808), showing two flotillas of English ships attacking a combined fleet of French and Spanish ships (1805). Seventeen French and Spanish ships surrendered or were sunk; the English fleet lost no ships, although its commander, Admiral Nelson, died in the battle.

Napoleon and the British

Jefferson's difficulties with Burr may be traced at least in part to the purchase of Louisiana, which, empty and unknown, excited the greed of men like Burr and Wilkinson. But problems infinitely more serious were also related to Louisiana.

Napoleon had jettisoned Louisiana to clear the decks before resuming the battle for control of Europe. This war had the effect of stimulating the American economy, for the warring powers needed American goods and American vessels. Shipbuilding boomed; foreign trade, which had quintupled since 1793, nearly doubled again between 1803 and 1805. By the summer of 1807, however, the situation had changed: a most unusual stalemate had developed in the war.

In October 1805 Britain's Horatio Nelson demolished the combined Spanish and French fleets in the Battle of Trafalgar, off the coast of Spain. Napoleon, now at the summit of his powers, quickly redressed the balance, smashing army after army thrown against him by Great Britain's continental allies. By 1807 he was master of Europe, while the British controlled the seas around the Continent. Neither nation could strike directly at the other.

They therefore resorted to commercial warfare, striving to disrupt each other's economy. Napoleon struck first with his Berlin Decree (November 1806), which made "all commerce and correspondence" with Great Britain illegal. The British retaliated with a series of edicts called Orders in Council, blockading most continental ports and barring from them all foreign vessels unless they first stopped at a British port and paid customs duties. Napoleon then issued his Milan Decree (December 1807), declaring any vessel that submitted to the British rules "to have become English property" and thus subject to seizure.

When war first broke out between Britain and France in 1792, the colonial trade of both sides had fallen largely into American hands because the danger of capture drove many belligerent merchant vessels from the seas. This commerce had engaged Americans in some devious practices. For example, American merchants carried sugar from the French colony of Martinique first to the United States, a legal peacetime voyage under French mercantilism. Then they reshipped it to France as American sugar. Since the United States was a neutral nation and sugar was not contraband of war, the Americans expected the British to let their ships pass with impunity. Continental products likewise reached the French West Indies by way of United States ports, and the American government encouraged the traffic in both directions by refunding customs duties on foreign products reshipped within a year. Between 1803 and 1806 the annual value of foreign products reexported from the United States jumped from $13 million to $60 million! In 1806 the United States exported 47 million pounds of coffee—none, of course, of local origin.

This underhanded commerce irritated the British. In the cases of the *Essex* and the *William* (1805–1806), a British judge, Sir William Grant, decreed that American ships could no longer rely on "mere voluntary *ceremonies*" to circumvent the Rule of 1756. Thus just when Britain and France were cracking down on direct trade by neutrals, Britain determined to halt the American reexport trade, thereby gravely threatening American prosperity.

The Impressment Controversy

More dismaying were the cruel indignities being visited on American seamen by the British practice of impressment. Under British law any able-bodied subject could be drafted for service in the Royal Navy in an emergency. Normally, when the commander of a warship found himself shorthanded, he put into a British port and sent a "press gang" ashore to round up the necessary men in harborside pubs. When far from home waters, he might hail any passing British merchant ship and commandeer the necessary men, though this practice was understandably unpopular in British maritime circles. He might also stop a *neutral* merchant vessel on the high seas and remove any British subject. Since the United States owned by far the largest merchant fleet among the neutrals, its vessels bore the brunt of this practice.

Impressment had been a cause of Anglo-American conflict for many years; American pride suffered every time a vessel carrying the flag of the United States was forced to heave to at the command of a British man-of-war. Still more galling was the contemptuous behavior of British officers when they boarded American ships. In 1796 an American captain named Figsby was stopped twice by British warships while carrying a cargo of poultry and other livestock to Guadeloupe. First a privateer, the *Sea Nymph*, impressed two of his crew, confiscated most of his chickens, "abused" him, and stole his ship's flag. Two days later HMS *Unicorn* took another of Figsby's men, the rest of his poultry, four sheep, and three hogs.

Many British captains made little effort to be sure they were impressing British subjects; any likely looking lad might be taken when the need was great. Furthermore, there were legal questions in dispute. When did an English immigrant become an American? When he was naturalized, the United States claimed. Never, the British retorted; "once an Englishman, always an Englishman."

The Jefferson administration conceded the right of the British to impress their own subjects from American merchant ships. When naturalized Americans were impressed, however, the administration was irritated, and when native-born Americans were taken, it became incensed. Impressment, Secretary of State Madison said in 1807, was "anomalous in principle . . . grievous in practice, and . . . abominable in abuse." Between 1803 and 1812 at least 5,000 sailors were snatched from the decks of U.S. vessels and forced to serve in the Royal Navy. Most of them—estimates run as high as three out of every four—were Americans.

The British did not claim the right to impress native-born Americans, and when it could be proved that boarding officers had done so, the men in question were released by higher authority. During the course of the controversy, the British authorities freed 3,800 impressed Americans, which suggests that many more were seized. However, the British refused to abandon impressment.

The combination of impressment, British interference with the reexport trade, and the general harassment of neutral commerce instituted by both Great Britain and France would have perplexed the most informed and hardheaded of leaders, and in dealing with these problems Jefferson was neither informed nor hardheaded. He believed it much wiser to stand up for one's rights than to compromise, yet he hated the very thought of war. Instead of building a navy that other nations would have to respect, he relied on a tiny fleet of frigates and a swarm of gunboats that were useless against the Royal Navy—"a macabre-monument," in the words of one historian, "to his hasty, ill-digested ideas" about defense.[3]

The Embargo Act

The frailty of Jefferson's policy became obvious once the warring powers began to attack neutral shipping in earnest. Between 1803 and 1807 the British seized more than 500 American ships, Napoleon more than 200 more. The United States, with only a handful of large ships, could do nothing.

The ultimate in frustration came on June 22, 1807, off Norfolk, Virginia. The American 46-gun frigate *Chesapeake* had just left port for patrol duty in the Mediterranean. Among its crew were a British sailor who had deserted from HMS *Halifax* and three Americans who had been illegally impressed by the captain of

[3]*The gunboats had performed effectively against the Barbary pirates, but Jefferson was enamored of them mainly because they were cheap. A gunboat cost about $10,000 to build, a big frigate over $300,000.*

The Ograbme ("embargo" spelled backward), a unique snapping turtle created by cartoonist Alexander Anderson, effectively frustrates an American tobacco smuggler.

HMS *Melampus* and had later escaped. The *Chesapeake* was barely out of sight of land when the 56-gun HMS *Leopard* approached and signaled the *Chesapeake* to heave to. Thinking that *Leopard* wanted to make some routine communication, Captain James Barron did so. A British officer came aboard and demanded that the four "deserters" be handed over to him. Barron refused, whereupon as soon as the officer was back on board, *Leopard* opened fire on the unsuspecting American ship, killing three sailors. Barron had to surrender. The "deserters" were seized, and then the crippled *Chesapeake* was allowed to limp back to port.

The attack was in violation of international law, for no nation claimed the right to impress sailors from warships. The British government admitted this, though it delayed making restitution for years. The American press clamored for war, but the country had nothing to fight with. Jefferson contented himself with ordering British warships out of American territorial waters. However, he was determined to put a stop to the indignities being heaped on the flag by Great Britain and France. The result was the Embargo Act.

The Embargo Act prohibited all exports. American vessels could not clear for any foreign port, and foreign vessels could do so only if empty. Importing was not forbidden, but few foreign ships would come to the United States if they had to return without a cargo. Although the law was sure to injure the American economy, Jefferson hoped that it would work in two ways to benefit the nation. By keeping U.S. merchant ships off the seas, it would end all chance of injury to them and to the national honor. By cutting off American goods and markets, it would put great economic pressure on Britain and France to moderate policies toward American shipping. The fact that boycotts had repeatedly wrested concessions from the British during the crises preceding the Revolution was certainly in Jefferson's mind when he devised the embargo.

Seldom has a law been so bitterly resented and resisted by a large segment of the public. It demanded of the maritime interests far greater sacrifices than they could reasonably be expected to make. Massachusetts-owned ships alone were

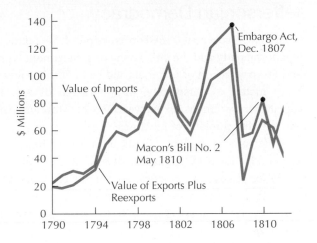

American Foreign Trade, 1790–1812

The embargo's effects are shown graphically here. The space between the upper (import) and the lower (export) line indicates a persistent foreign-trade deficit.

earning over $15 million a year in freight charges by 1807, and Bay State merchants were making far larger gains from the buying and selling of goods. Foreign commerce was the most expansive force in the economy, the chief reason for the nation's prosperity. As John Randolph remarked in a typical sally, the administration was trying "to cure the corns by cutting off the toes."

The Embargo Act had catastrophic effects. Exports fell from $108 million in 1807 to $22 million in 1808, imports from $138 million to less than $57 million. Prices of farm products and manufactured goods reacted violently; seamen were thrown out of work; merchants found their businesses disrupted.

Surely the embargo was a mistake. The United States ought either to have suffered the indignities heaped on its vessels for the sake of profits or, by constructing a powerful navy, made it dangerous for the belligerents to treat its merchant ships so roughly. Jefferson was too proud to choose the former alternative, too frugal to choose the latter. Instead he applied harsher and harsher regulations in a futile effort to accomplish his purpose. Militiamen patrolled the Canadian border; revenuers searched out smuggled goods without proper warrants. The illegal trade continued, and in his last months as president Jefferson simply gave up. Even then he would not admit that the embargo was a fiasco and urge its repeal. Only in Jefferson's last week in office did a leaderless Congress finally abolish it, substituting the Non-Intercourse Act, which forbade trade only with Great Britain and France and authorized the president to end the boycott against either power by proclamation when and if it stopped violating the rights of Americans.

Thus Jefferson's political career ended on a sour note. Several weeks after he had left office and returned to Monticello, he privately advised his successor, James Madison, to trust his own judgment to govern because the people readily succumbed to "the floating lies of the day."

Jeffersonian Democracy

Yet, Jefferson completed the construction of the political institution known as the Republican party and the philosophy of government known as Jeffersonian democracy. From what sort of materials had he built this polity? In part Jefferson's success was a matter of personality; in the march of American democracy he stood halfway, temperamentally, between Washington and Andrew Jackson, perfectly in tune with the thinking of his times.

Jefferson's marvelous talents as a writer help explain his success. He expounded his ideas in language that few people could resist. He had a remarkable facility for discovering practical arguments to justify his beliefs—as when he suggested that by letting everyone vote, elections would be made more honest because with large numbers going to the polls, bribery would become prohibitively expensive.

Jefferson prepared the country for democracy by proving that a democrat could establish and maintain a stable regime. The Federalist tyranny of 1798 was compounded of selfishness and stupidity, but it was also based in part on honest fears that an egalitarian regime would not protect the fabric of society from hotheads and crackpots.

Jefferson calmed these fears. "Pell-mell" might scandalize the British and Spanish ministers and a few locals, but it was scarcely revolutionary. The most partisan Federalist was hard put to see a Robespierre, leader during the Reign of Terror in France, in the amiable president scratching out state papers at his desk or chatting with a Kentucky congressman at a "republican" dinner party. Furthermore, Jefferson accepted Federalist ideas on public finance, even learning to live with Hamilton's bank. As a good democrat, he drew a nice distinction between his own opinions and the wishes of the majority, which he felt must always take priority. Even in his first inaugural he admitted that manufacturing and commerce were, along with agriculture, the "pillars of our prosperity," and while believing that these activities would thrive best when "left most free to individual enterprise," he accepted the principle that the government should protect them when necessary from "casual embarrassments." During his term the country grew and prospered, the commercial classes sharing in the bounty along with the farmers so close to Jefferson's heart. Blithely he set out to win the support of all who could vote. "It is material to the safety of Republicanism," he wrote in 1803, "to detach the mercantile interests from its enemies and incorporate them into the body of its friends."

Thus Jefferson undermined the Federalists all along the line. They had said that the country must pay a stiff price for prosperity and orderly government, and they demanded prompt payment in full, both in cash (taxes) and in the form of limitations on human liberty. Under Jefferson these much-desired goals had been achieved cheaply and without sacrificing freedom. A land whose riches could only be guessed at had been obtained without firing a shot and without burdening the people with new taxes. "What farmer, what mechanic, what laborer, ever sees a tax-gatherer of the United States?" the president could ask in 1805, without a single Federalist rising to challenge him. Order without discipline, security without a large military establishment, prosperity without regulatory legislation, freedom without license—truly the Sage of Monticello appeared to have led his fellow Americans into a golden age.

Jefferson insisted that one of his chief accomplishments had been to reduce the national debt from $83 million to $57 million. Writing from Monticello shortly after leaving office, he urged his successors to eliminate the remainder. "The discharge of the public debt," he warned Treasury Secretary Gallatin, "is vital to the destinies of our government."

Yet Jefferson had also learned the perils of an inadequately funded government. His unwillingness to build a real navy had rendered the nation vulnerable to foreign states. Conversely, he had exulted in the purchase of Louisiana, and he backed modest proposals for spending federal money on roads, canals, and other projects that, according to his political philosophy, ought to have been left to the states and private individuals. Jefferson had even learned to live with Hamilton's bank. Debt, Jefferson accepted, was sometimes good policy.

Milestones

1800	Jefferson is elected president (Revolution of 1800)	
1801	Judiciary Act of 1801 allows Adams to appoint many Federalist judges	
1801–1805	United States wages war against Barbary pirates in North Africa	
1803	Supreme Court declares part of Judiciary Act of 1789 unconstitutional (*Marbury* v. *Madison*)	
	Jefferson negotiates Louisiana Purchase with France	
1804	Aaron Burr kills Alexander Hamilton in duel	
	Jefferson is reelected	
1804–1806	Lewis and Clark explore West	
1806	Aaron Burr schemes to take land in West during Burr Conspiracy	
1806–1807	Napoleon issues Berlin and Milan decrees in order to disrupt British shipping and economy	
1807	HMS *Leopard* attacks USS *Chesapeake*	
	Embargo Act prohibits all exports	
1809	Non-Intercourse Act forbids trade with Great Britain and France	

7 CHAPTER

National Growing Pains

IN RECENT YEARS, THE STICKER PRICE OF BICYCLES SOLD IN THE United States has been inflated by about $5 to cover the import tax—tariff—on foreign-made bicycles. In 2005, 99 percent of the 20 million bikes sold in the United States were manufactured abroad and thus subject to the tariff. (Of these, over 90 percent were made in China.)

Tariffs protect domestic manufacturers from foreign competition and generate revenue for the federal government. In 2005, for example, the bicycle tariff yielded $100 million; federal income from all tariffs approached $23 billion. But this was a mere drop in the mighty stream of federal revenue, which in that year exceeded $2.1 trillion. Of this sum, nearly $1 trillion came from individual income taxes, $280 billion from corporate income taxes, and $800 billion from payments to the Social Security system.

It was different 200 years ago. In 1809, the total revenue of the U.S. Treasury fell short of $8 million.[1] Of that, more than $7 million was generated by the tariff. The sale of public lands and of postage stamps provided most of the balance.

Without income from the tariff, the federal government could have done little more than deliver the mail. Tariff taxes, by raising the cost of cloth and metal goods produced by large British factories, protected American manufacturers of those goods. But this meant that farmers would pay more for clothing and farm implements. Worse, Britain and other foreign nations could retaliate against high American tariffs by setting their own tariffs on American imports to *their* countries—chiefly tobacco, cotton, wheat, and other foodstuffs mostly grown in the South and West.

---

[1]*The revenue figures for 1809 and those for 2005 are not adjusted for inflation. That is because the nature of most goods has changed so much that comparison is meaningless.*

The tariff pitted one section of the nation against another. The North, increasingly a manufacturing region, supported high tariffs, while the South, chiefly an exporter of farm products, opposed them. The West was divided on the matter, opposing higher prices for manufactured goods but requiring federal help for economic development and defense.

From 1809 to 1828, Americans repeatedly decided to expand the role of the federal government. Armies and navies were raised to subdue the Indians and defend the nation from European predators; highways were built to encourage trade and promote settlement of the Louisiana territories. The federal budget tripled. As costs went up, so did the tariff. The 1828 "Tariff of Abominations" was the highest to that time. That year, of the total revenue, more than 90 percent came from the tariff. The growth of the nation—and of the national government—came at a price.

Madison in Power

It is a measure of Jefferson's popularity and of the political ineptitude of the Federalists that the Republicans won the election of 1808 handily despite the embargo. James Madison got 122 of the 173 electoral votes for the presidency, and the party carried both houses of Congress, although by reduced majorities.

In his inaugural address, Madison observed that the "present situation" of the United States was "full of difficulties" and that war continued to rage among European powers. Yet he assumed the presidency, he said, "with no other discouragement than what springs from my own inadequacy." The content of the speech was as modest as its delivery; virtually no one could hear it.

Madison was a small, neat, rather precise person, narrower in his interests than Jefferson but in many ways a deeper thinker. He was more conscientious in the performance of his duties and more consistent in adhering to his principles. Ideologically, however, they were as close as two active and intelligent people could be. Madison had no better solution to offer for the problem of the hour than had Jefferson. The Non-Intercourse Act proved difficult to enforce—once an American ship left port, there was no way to prevent the skipper from steering for England or France—and it exerted little economic pressure on the British, who continued to seize American vessels.

Because prudent captains remained in port, trade stagnated. Federal revenue declined. In 1809, Secretary of the Treasury Albert Gallatin was alarmed by the growing federal deficit. He urged Representative Nathaniel Macon of North Carolina to introduce legislation to remove all restrictions on commerce with France and Britain. Known as Macon's Bill No. 2, it authorized the president to reapply the principle of nonintercourse to either of the major powers if the other should "cease to violate the neutral commerce of the United States." This bill became law in May 1810.

The volume of United States commerce with the British Isles swiftly zoomed to pre-embargo levels. The mighty British fleet controlled the seas. Napoleon therefore announced that he had repealed his decrees against neutral shipping.

Madison, seeking concessions from Britain, closed American ports to British ships and goods. Napoleon, despite his announcement to the contrary, continued to seize American ships and cargoes whenever it suited him to do so.

The British grimly refused to modify the Orders in Council. Madison could not afford either to admit that Napoleon had deceived him or to reverse American policy still another time. Reluctantly he came to the conclusion that unless Britain repealed the Orders, the United States must declare war.

Tecumseh and Indian Resistance

There were other reasons for fighting besides British violations of neutral rights. The Indians were again restive, and western farmers believed that the British in Canada were egging them on. This had been true in the past but was no longer the case in 1811 and 1812. American domination of the southern Great Lakes region was no longer in question.

American political leaders tended to believe that Indians should be encouraged to become farmers and to copy the "civilized" ways of whites. However, no government had been able to control the frontiersmen, who by bribery, trickery, and force were driving the tribes back year after year from the rich lands of the Ohio Valley. General William Henry Harrison, governor of the Indiana Territory, a tough, relentless soldier, kept constant pressure on them. He wrested land from one tribe by promising it aid against a traditional enemy, from another as a penalty for having murdered a white man, from others by corrupting a few chiefs. Harrison justified his sordid behavior by citing the end in view—that "one of the fairest portions of the globe" be secured as "the seat of civilization, of science, and of true religion." The "wretched savages" should not be allowed to stand in the path of this worthy objective. As early as 1805 it was clear that unless something drastic was done, Harrison's aggressiveness, together with the corroding effects of white civilization, would soon obliterate the tribes.

At this point the Shawnee chief, Tecumseh, made a bold and imaginative effort to reverse the trend by binding all the tribes east of the Mississippi into a great confederation. Traveling from the Wisconsin country to the Floridas, he persuaded tribe after tribe to join him. "Let the white race perish," Tecumseh declared. "They seize your land; they corrupt your women. . . . Back whence they came, upon a trail of blood, they must be driven!"

To Tecumseh's political movement his brother Tenskwatawa, known as "The Prophet," added the force of a moral crusade. Instead of copying white customs, the Prophet said, Indians must give up white ways, white clothes, and white liquor and reinvigorate their own culture. Ceding lands to the whites must stop because the Great Spirit intended that the land be used in common by all.

The Prophet was a fanatic who saw visions and claimed to be able to control the movement of heavenly bodies. Tecumseh, however, possessed true genius. A powerful orator and a great organizer, he had deep insight into the needs of his people. Harrison himself said of Tecumseh: "He is one of those uncommon

As a young man Tecumseh *(left)* was a superb hunter and warrior; his younger brother, Tenskwatawa *(right)* was awkward and inept with weapons; he accidentally gouged out his right eye with an arrow. In 1805 he had a religious vision, became known as "The Prophet," and inspired Tecumseh's warriors.

geniuses which spring up occasionally to produce revolutions and overturn the established order of things." The two brothers made a formidable team. By 1811 thousands of Indians were organizing to drive the whites off their lands. Alarm swept through the West.

With about a thousand soldiers, General Harrison marched boldly against the brothers' camp at Prophetstown, where Tippecanoe Creek joins the Wabash River, in Indiana. Tecumseh was away recruiting men, and the Prophet recklessly ordered an assault on Harrison's camp outside the village on November 7, 1811. When the white soldiers held their ground despite the Prophet's magic, the Indians lost confidence and fell back. Harrison then destroyed Prophetstown.

While the Battle of Tippecanoe was pretty much a draw, it disillusioned the Indians and shattered their confederation. Frontier warfare continued, but in the disorganized manner of former times. Like all such fighting it was brutal and bloody.

Unwilling as usual to admit that their own excesses were the chief cause of the trouble, the settlers directed their resentment at the British in Canada. "This combination headed by the Shawanese prophet is a British scheme," a resolution adopted by the citizens of Vincennes, Indiana, proclaimed. As a result, the cry for war with Great Britain rang along the frontier.

Depression and Land Hunger

Some Westerners pressed for war because they were suffering an agricultural depression. The prices they received for their wheat, tobacco, and other products in the markets of New Orleans were falling, and they attributed the decline to the loss of foreign markets and to plunder by the British. American commercial restrictions had more to do with the western depression than the British, and in any case the slow and cumbersome transportation and distribution system that western farmers were saddled with was the major cause of their difficulties. But the farmers were no more inclined to accept these explanations than they were to absolve the British from responsibility for the Indian difficulties. If only the seas were free, they reasoned, costs would go down, prices would rise, and prosperity would return.

To some extent western expansionism also heightened the war fever. The West contained immense tracts of virgin land, but Westerners wanted more. Canada would surely fall to American arms in the event of war, the frontiersmen believed. So, apparently, would Florida, for Spain was now Britain's ally. Florida in itself provided no cause for a war, for it was sure to fall into American hands before long. In 1810 Madison had snapped up the extreme western section without eliciting any effective response from Spain.

But Westerners, and many Easterners too, were more patriots than imperialists or merchants in 1811 and 1812. When the "War Hawks" (their young leaders in Congress) called for war against Great Britain, they did so because they saw no other way to defend the national honor and force repeal of the Orders in Council. The choice seemed to lie between war and surrender of true independence. As Madison put it, to bow to British policy would be to "recolonize" American foreign commerce.

Opponents of War

Large numbers of people, however, thought that a war against Great Britain would be a national calamity. Some Federalists would have resisted anything the administration proposed; Congressman Josiah Quincy of Massachusetts declared that he "could not be kicked" into the war, which he considered a cowardly, futile, and unconstitutional business designed primarily to ensure the reelection of Madison. According to Quincy the War Hawks were "backwoodsmen" willing to wage a "cruel, wanton, senseless and wicked" war in order to swallow up Canada.

But other people based their objections on economics and a healthy realism. No shipowner could view with equanimity the idea of taking on the largest navy in the world. Such persons complained sincerely enough about impressment and the Orders in Council, but war seemed worse to them by far. Self-interest led them to urge patience.

Such a policy would have been wise, for Great Britain did not represent a real threat to the United States. British naval officers were high-handed, officials in London complacent, British diplomats in Washington second-rate and obtuse. Yet

HOW DID INDIANS AND SETTLERS INTERACT?

Two Indians *(below)* gaze at a frontier settlement. In 1893 historian Frederick Jackson Turner, the most important historian of his era, credited the frontier for the individualistic ethos that made the United States distinctive. In his view, the frontier had not been a particular zone or region, but "the outer edge of the wave—the meeting point between savagery and civilization." The nature of the interaction between Indians and settlers was one-sided: the Indians fell back. But in recent decades, historians have challenged this concept not only because it disparaged Indian societies and cultures, but also because it ignored the many ways in which Indians and settlers interacted. Abandoning the concept of an Indian-settler frontier, Richard White (1991) described a "middle ground" and James Merrell (1999) the "edge of the woods," a region where Indians and settlers resolved disputes, traded goods, and exchanged ideas. The concept of a "middle ground" put Indians and settlers on equal footing. But that also may be its chief difficulty. Daniel K. Richter (2001) and Jane T. Merritt (2003) showed that while

Indians preferred to co-exist with the settlers rather than fight them, by the eighteenth century raw power prevailed—as did, usually, the settlers.

Frederick Jackson Turner, "The Significance of the Frontier in American History" (1893), Patricia Nelson Limerick, *The Legacy of Conquest* (1987), Richard White, *The Middle Ground* (1991), James Merrell, *Into the Woods* (1999), Daniel K. Richter, *Facing East from Indian Country* (2001), Jane T. Merritt, *At the Crossroads* (2003).

language, culture, and strong economic ties bound the two countries. Napoleon, on the other hand, represented a tremendous potential danger. He had offhandedly turned over Louisiana, but even Jefferson, the chief beneficiary of his largesse, hated everything he stood for. Jefferson called Napoleon "an unprincipled tyrant who is deluging the continent of Europe with blood."

What made the situation even more unfortunate was the fact that by 1812 conditions had changed in England in a way that made a softening of British maritime policy likely. A depression caused chiefly by the increasing effectiveness of Napoleon's Continental System was plaguing the country. (The Continental System, based on Napoleon's Berlin and Milan decrees, forbade neutral countries or French allies from trading with Britain or its colonies.) Manufacturers, blaming the slump on the loss of American markets, were urging repeal of Britain's Orders in Council. Gradually, though with exasperating slowness, the British government prepared to yield. On June 23, after a change of ministries, the new foreign secretary, Lord Castlereagh, suspended the Orders. Five days earlier, alas, the United States had declared war.

The War of 1812

The illogic of the War Hawks in pressing for a fight was exceeded only by their ineffectiveness in planning and managing the struggle. By what possible strategy could the ostensible objective of the war be achieved? To construct a navy capable of challenging the British fleet would have been the work of many years and a more expensive proposition than the War Hawks were willing to consider. So hopeless was that prospect that Congress failed to undertake any new construction in the first year of the conflict. Several hundred merchant ships lashed a few cannon to their decks and sailed off as privateers to attack British commerce. The navy's seven modern frigates, built during the war scare after the XYZ affair, put to sea. But these forces could make no pretense of disputing Britain's mastery of the Atlantic.

For a brief moment the American frigates held center stage, for they were faster, tougher, larger, and more powerfully armed than their British counterparts. Barely two months after the declaration of war, Captain Isaac Hull in USS *Constitution* chanced upon HMS *Guerrière* in mid-Atlantic, outmaneuvered *Guerrière* brilliantly, brought down its mizzenmast with his first volley, and then gunned it into submission, a hopeless wreck. In October USS *United States,* captained by Stephen Decatur, hero of the war against the Barbary pirates, caught HMS *Macedonian* off the Madeiras, pounded it unmercifully at long range, and forced the British ship to surrender. *Macedonian* was taken into New London as a prize; over a third of the 300-man crew were casualties, while American losses were but a dozen. Then, in December, *Constitution*, now under Captain William Bainbridge, took on the British frigate *Java* off Brazil. "Old Ironsides" shot away *Java's* mainmast and reduced it to a hulk too battered for salvage.

These victories had little influence on the outcome of the war. The Royal Navy had thirty-four frigates, seven more powerful ships of the line, and dozens of smaller vessels. As soon as these forces could concentrate against them, the American frigates were immobilized, forced to spend the war gathering barnacles at their moorings while powerful British squadrons ranged offshore. The privateering merchantmen were more effective because they were so numerous; they captured more than 1,300 British vessels during the war. The best of them—vessels like *America* and *True-Blooded Yankee*—were redesigned, given more sail to increase their speed, and formidably armed. *America* captured twenty-six prizes valued at more than a million dollars. *True-Blooded Yankee* took twenty-seven vessels and destroyed seven more in a Scottish harbor.

Great Britain's one weak spot seemed to be Canada. The colony had but half a million inhabitants to oppose 7.5 million Americans. Only 2,257 British regulars guarded the long border from Montréal to Detroit. The Canadian militia was feeble, and many of its members, being American-born, sympathized with the "invaders." According to the War Hawk congressman Henry Clay of Kentucky, the West was one solid horde of ferocious frontiersmen, armed to the teeth and thirsting for Canadian blood. Yet such talk was mostly brag and bluster; when Congress authorized increasing the army by 25,000 men, Kentucky produced 400 enlistments.

With a few exceptions, American forces in the War of 1812 were ill-trained and ill-led, and poor strategy resulted in several disgraceful defeats. Here, a resplendently dressed militia officer consults a map.

American military leadership proved extremely disappointing. Madison showed poor judgment by relying on officers who had served with distinction in the Revolution. Instead of a concentrated strike against Canada's St. Lawrence River lifeline, which would have isolated Upper Canada, the generals planned a complicated three-pronged attack. It failed dismally. In July 1812 General William Hull, veteran of the battles of Trenton, Saratoga, and Monmouth and now governor of the Michigan Territory, marched forth with 2,200 men against the Canadian positions facing Detroit. Hoping that the Canadian militia would desert, he delayed his assault, only to find his communications threatened by hostile Indians led by Tecumseh. Hastily he retreated to Detroit, and when the Canadians, under General Isaac Brock, pursued him, he surrendered the fort without firing a shot! In October another force attempted to invade Canada from Fort Niagara. After an initial success it was crushed by superior numbers, while a large contingent of New York militiamen watched from the east bank of the Niagara River, unwilling to fight outside their own state.

The third arm of the American "attack" was equally unsuccessful. Major General Henry Dearborn, who had fought honorably in the Revolution from Bunker Hill to Yorktown, but who had now grown so fat that he needed a specially designed cart to get from place to place, set out from Plattsburgh, New York, at the head of an army of militiamen. Their objective was Montréal, but when they reached the border, the troops refused to cross. Dearborn meekly marched them back to Plattsburgh.

Meanwhile, the British had captured Fort Michilimackinac in northern Michigan, and the Indians had taken Fort Dearborn (now Chicago), massacring 85 captives. Instead of sweeping triumphantly through Canada, the Americans found themselves trying desperately to keep the Canadians out of Ohio.

Stirred by these disasters, Westerners rallied somewhat in 1813. General Harrison, the victor of Tippecanoe, headed an army of Kentuckians in a series of inconclusive battles against British troops and Indians led by Tecumseh. He found it impossible to recapture Detroit because a British squadron controlling Lake Erie threatened his communications. President Madison therefore assigned Captain Oliver Hazard Perry to the task of building a fleet to challenge this force. In September 1813, at Put-in-Bay near the western end of the lake, Perry destroyed the British vessels in a bloody battle in which 85 of the 103 men on Perry's flagship were casualties. "We have met the enemy and they are ours," he reported. About a quarter of Perry's 400 men were blacks, which led him to remark that "the color of a man's skin" was no more an indication of his worth than "the cut and trimmings" of his coat. With the Americans in control of Lake Erie, Detroit became untenable for the British, and when they fell back, Harrison gave chase and defeated them at the Thames River, some 60 miles northeast of Detroit. Although little more than a skirmish, this battle had large repercussions. Tecumseh was among the dead (an eccentric American colonel, Richard Mentor Johnson, was to base a long and successful political career, culminating in his election as vice president of the United States in 1836, on his claim of having personally done in the great chief), and without him the Indians lost heart. But American attempts to win control of Lake Ontario and to invade Canada in the

In the heat of the Battle of Lake Erie, Perry had to abandon his flagship, the *Lawrence*, which had been shot to pieces by enemy fire. (Over three-fourths of the ship's crew were killed or wounded.) He was rowed to the Niagara, from which he directed the rest of the engagement.

Niagara region were again thrown back. Late in 1813 the British captured Fort Niagara and burned the town of Buffalo. The conquest of Canada was as far from realization as ever.

Britain Assumes the Offensive

Until 1814 the British put relatively little effort into the American war, being concerned primarily with the struggle against Napoleon. However, in 1812 Napoleon had invaded Russia and been thrown back; thereafter, one by one, his European satellites rose against him. Gradually he relinquished his conquests; the Allies—his enemies—marched into France, Paris fell, and in April 1814 the emperor abdicated. Then the British, free to strike hard at the United States, dispatched some 14,000 veterans to Canada.

By the spring of 1814 British strategists had devised a master plan for crushing the United States. One army, 11,000 strong, was to march from Montréal, tracing the route that General Burgoyne had followed to disaster in the Revolution. A smaller amphibious force was to make a feint at the Chesapeake Bay area, destroying coastal towns and threatening Washington and Baltimore. A third army was to assemble at Jamaica and sail to attack New Orleans and bottle up the West.

It is necessary, in considering the War of 1812, to remind oneself repeatedly that in the course of the conflict many brave young men lost their lives. Without this sobering reflection it would be easy to dismiss the conflict as a great farce compounded of stupidity, incompetence, and brag. The British, despite their years of experience against Napoleon, were scarcely more effective than the Americans when they assumed the offensive. They achieved significant success only in the diversionary attack in the Chesapeake Bay area.

While the main British army was assembling in Canada, some 4,000 veterans under General Robert Ross sailed from Bermuda for the Chesapeake. After making a rendezvous with a fleet commanded by Vice Admiral Sir Alexander Cochrane and Rear Admiral Sir George Cockburn, which had been terrorizing the coast, they landed in Maryland at the mouth of the Patuxent River, southeast of Washington. A squadron of gunboats "protecting" the capital promptly withdrew upstream; when the British pursued, their commander ordered them blown up to keep them from being captured.

The British troops marched rapidly toward Washington. At Bladensburg, on the outskirts of the city, they came upon an army twice their number, commanded by General William H. Winder, a Baltimore lawyer who had already been captured and released by the British in the Canadian fighting. While President Madison and other officials watched, the British charged—and Winder's army turned tail almost without firing a shot. The British swarmed into the capital and put most public buildings to the torch. Before personally setting fire to the White House, Admiral Cockburn took one of the president's hats and a cushion from Dolley Madison's chair as souvenirs, and, finding the table set for dinner, derisively drank a toast to "Jemmy's health," adding, an observer coyly recalled, "pleasantries too vulgar for me to repeat."

This was the sum of the British success. When they attempted to take Baltimore, they were stopped by a formidable line of defenses devised by General Samuel Smith, a militia officer. General Ross fell in the attack. The fleet then moved up the Patapsco River and pounded Fort McHenry with its cannon, raining 1,800 shells upon it in a 25-hour bombardment on September 13 and 14.

"The Star Spangled Banner"

While this attack was in progress, an American civilian, Francis Scott Key, who had been temporarily detained on one of the British ships, watched anxiously through the night. Key had boarded the vessel before the attack in an effort to obtain the release of an American doctor who had been taken into custody in Washington. As twilight faded, Key had seen the Stars and Stripes flying proudly over the battered fort. During the night the glare of rockets and bursting of bombs gave proof that the defenders were holding out. Then, by the first light of the new day, Key saw again the flag, still waving over Fort McHenry. Drawing an old letter from his pocket, he dashed off the words to "The Star Spangled Banner," which, when set to music, was to become the national anthem of the United States.

The War of 1812

To Key that dawn seemed a turning point in the war. He was roughly correct, for in those last weeks of the summer of 1814 the struggle began to move toward resolution. Unable to crack the defenses of Baltimore, the British withdrew to their ships; shortly after, they sailed to Jamaica to join the forces preparing to attack New Orleans.

The destruction of Washington had been a profound shock. Thousands came forward to enlist in the army. The new determination and spirit were strengthened

The Bombardment of Fort McHenry by John Bower, with the Stars and Stripes flying over the fort *(center)*. The British fleet fired 1,800 bombs and red-glaring incendiary rockets. The fort did not return fire because the British ships were beyond the range of its cannon. Although "The Star Spangled Banner" celebrates the "home of the brave," the defenders of Fort McHenry sensibly fled the ramparts and took cover below during the bombardment; they sustained only thirty casualties.

by news from the northern front, where General Sir George Prevost had been leading the main British invasion force south from Montréal. At Plattsburgh, on the western shore of Lake Champlain, his 1,000 Redcoats came up against a well-designed defense line manned by 3,300 Americans under General Alexander Macomb. Prevost called up his supporting fleet of four ships and a dozen gunboats. An American fleet of roughly similar strength under Captain Thomas Macdonough, a youthful officer who had served with Decatur against the Barbary pirates, came forward to oppose the British. On September 11, in a brutal battle at point-blank range, Macdonough destroyed the British ships and drove off the gunboats. With the Americans now threatening his flank, Prevost lost heart and retreated to Canada.

The Treaty of Ghent

The war might as well have ended with the battles of Plattsburgh, Washington, and Baltimore, for later military developments had no effect on the outcome. Earlier in 1814 both sides had agreed to discuss peace terms. Commissioners were appointed and negotiations begun during the summer at Ghent, in Belgium. The British were in no hurry to sign a treaty, believing that their three-pronged offensive in 1814 would swing the balance in their favor. But news of the defeat at Plattsburgh modified their ambitions, and when the Duke of Wellington advised that from a military point of view they had no case for territorial concessions so long as the United States controlled the Great Lakes, they agreed to settle for *status quo ante bellum*, to leave things as they were before the war. The other issues, everyone suddenly realized, had simply evaporated. The mighty war triggered by the French Revolution seemed finally over. The seas were free to all ships, and the Royal Navy no longer had need to snatch sailors from the vessels of the United States or of any other power. On Christmas Eve 1814 the treaty, which merely ended the state of hostilities, was signed. Although, like other members of his family, he was not noted for tact, John Quincy Adams rose to the spirit of the occasion. "I hope," he said, "it will be the last treaty of peace between Great Britain and the United States." And so it was.

The Hartford Convention

Before news of the treaty could cross the Atlantic, two events took place that had important effects but that would not have occurred had the news reached America more rapidly. The first was the Hartford Convention, a meeting of New England Federalists held in December 1814 and January 1815 to protest the war and to plan for a convention of the states to revise the Constitution.

Sentiment in New England had opposed the war from the beginning. The governor of Massachusetts titled his annual address in 1813 "On the Present Unhappy War," and the General Court went on record calling the conflict "impolitic, improper, and unjust." The Federalist party had been quick to employ the discontent to revive its fortunes. Federalist-controlled state administrations refused to provide militia to aid in the fight and discouraged individuals and banks from lending money to the hard-pressed national government.

Their attitude toward the war made the Federalists even more unpopular with the rest of the country, and this in turn encouraged extremists to talk of seceding from the Union. After Massachusetts summoned the meeting of the Hartford Convention, the fear was widespread that the delegates would propose a New England Confederacy, thereby striking at the Union in a moment of great trial.

Luckily for the country, moderate Federalists controlled the convention. They approved a statement that in case of "deliberate, dangerous and palpable infractions of the Constitution" a state has the right "to interpose its authority" to protect itself. This concept, similar to that expressed in the Kentucky and Virginia resolutions by the Republicans when they were in the minority, was accompanied by a list of proposed constitutional amendments designed to make the national government conform more closely to the New England ideal. These would have (1) repealed the Three-fifths Compromise on representation and direct taxes, which favored the slaveholding states; (2) required a two-thirds vote of Congress for the admission of new states and for declaring war; (3) reduced Congress's power to restrict trade by measures such as an embargo; (4) limited presidents to a single term; and (5) made it illegal for naturalized citizens to hold national office.

Nothing formally proposed at Hartford was treasonable, but the proceedings were kept secret, and rumors of impending secession were rife. In this atmosphere came the news from Ghent of an honorable peace. The Federalists had been denouncing the war and predicting a British triumph; now they were discredited.

The Battle of New Orleans

Still more discrediting to Federalists was the second event that would not have happened had communications been more rapid: the Battle of New Orleans. During the fall of 1814 the British had gathered an army at Negril Bay in Jamaica, commanded by Major General Sir Edward Pakenham, brother-in-law of the Duke of Wellington. Late in November an armada of sixty ships set out for New Orleans with 11,000 soldiers. Instead of sailing directly up from the mouth of the Mississippi as the Americans expected, Pakenham approached the city by way of Lake Borgne, to the east. Proceeding through a maze of swamps and bayous, he advanced close to the city's gates before being detected. Early on the afternoon of December 23, three mud-spattered local planters burst into the headquarters of General Andrew Jackson, commanding the defenses of New Orleans, with the news.

For once in this war of error and incompetence the United States had the right man in the right place at the right time. After his Revolutionary War experiences, Jackson had studied law, then moved West, settling in Nashville, Tennessee. He served briefly in both houses of Congress and was active in Tennessee affairs. Jackson was a hard man and fierce-tempered, frequently involved in brawls and duels, but honest and, by western standards, a good public servant. When the war broke out, he was named major general of volunteers. Almost alone among nonprofessional troops during the conflict, his men won impressive victories, savagely crushing the Creek Indians in a series of battles in Alabama.

Jackson's success was due to his toughness and determination. Discipline based on fear, respect, and their awareness of his genuine concern for their well-being made his individualistic frontier militiamen into an army. His men called Jackson Old Hickory; the Indians called him Sharp Knife.

Following these victories, Jackson was assigned the job of defending the Gulf Coast against the expected British strike. Although he had misjudged Pakenham's destination, he was ready when the news of the British arrival reached him. "By the Eternal," he vowed, "they shall not sleep on our soil." "Gentlemen," he told his staff officers, "the British are below, we must fight them tonight."

While the British rested and awaited reinforcements, planning to take the city the next morning, Jackson rushed up men and guns. At 7:30 P.M. on December 23 he struck hard, taking the British by surprise. But Pakenham's veterans rallied quickly, and the battle was inconclusive. With Redcoats pouring in from the fleet, Jackson fell back to a point 5 miles below New Orleans and dug in.

He chose his position wisely. On his right was the Mississippi, on his left an impenetrable swamp, to the front an open field. On the day before Christmas (while the commissioners in Ghent were signing the peace treaty), Jackson's army, which included a segregated unit of free black militiamen, erected an earthen parapet about 10 yards behind a dry canal bed. Here the Americans would make their stand.

For two weeks Pakenham probed the American line. Jackson strengthened his defenses daily. At night, patrols of silent Tennesseans slipped out with knife and tomahawk to stalk British sentries. They called this grim business "going hunting." On January 8, 1815, Pakenham ordered an all-out frontal assault. The American position was formidable, but these were men who had defeated Napoleon. At dawn, through the lowland mists, the Redcoats moved forward with fixed bayonets. Pakenham assumed that the undisciplined Americans—about 4,500 strong— would run at the sight of bare steel.

The Americans did not run. Perhaps they feared the wrath of their commander more than enemy bayonets. Artillery raked the advancing British, and when the range closed to about 150 yards, the riflemen opened up. Jackson had formed his men in three ranks behind the parapet. One rank fired, then stepped down as another took its place. By the time the third had loosed its volley, the first had reloaded and was ready to fire again. Nothing could stand against this rain of lead. General Pakenham was wounded twice, then killed by a shell fragment while calling up his last reserves. During the battle a single brave British officer reached the top of the parapet. When retreat was finally sounded, the British had suffered almost 2,100 casualties, including nearly 300 killed. Thirteen Americans lost their lives, and fifty-eight more were wounded or missing.

Victory Weakens the Federalists

Word of Jackson's magnificent triumph reached Washington almost simultaneously with the good news from Ghent. People found it easy to confuse the chronology and consider the war a victory won on the battlefield below New Orleans instead of the standoff it had been. Jackson became the "Hero of New Orleans"; his proud fellow citizens rated his military abilities superior to those of the Duke of Wellington. The nation rejoiced. One sour Republican complained that the Federalists of Massachusetts had fired off more powder and wounded more men celebrating the victory than they had during the whole course of the conflict. The Senate ratified the peace treaty unanimously, and the frustrations and failures of the past few years were forgotten.

The nation had suffered relatively few casualties and little economic loss, except to the shipping interests. The Indians were the main losers in the contest.

When Jackson defeated the Creeks, for example, he forced them to surrender 23 million acres, constituting three-fifths of what is now Alabama and one-fifth of Georgia.

The war completed the destruction of the Federalist party. It soon disappeared even in New England, swamped beneath a wave of patriotism that flooded the land.

The chief reason for the happy results of the war had little to do with American events. After 1815 Europe settled down to what was to be a century of relative peace. With peace came an end to serious foreign threats to America and a revival of commerce. European emigration to the United States, long held back by the troubled times, spurted ahead, providing the expanding country with its most valuable asset—strong, willing hands to do the work of developing the land. The mood of Jefferson's first term, when democracy had reigned amid peace and plenty, returned with a rush. And the nation, having had its fill of international complications, turned in on itself as Jefferson had wished. The politicians, ever sensitive to public attitudes, had learned what seemed at the time a valuable lesson. Foreign affairs were a potent cause of domestic conflict. The volatile character of sectional politics was thus another reason why America should escape from involvement in European affairs.

Anglo-American Rapprochement

There remained a few matters to straighten out with Great Britain, Spain, and Europe generally. Since no territory had changed hands at Ghent, neither signatory had reason to harbor a grudge. There was no sudden flowering of Anglo-American friendship. Yet for years no serious trouble marred Anglo-American relations. The war had taught the British to respect Americans, if not to love them.

In this atmosphere the two countries worked out peaceful solutions to a number of old problems. American trade was becoming ever more important to the British, that of the sugar islands less so. In July 1815 they therefore signed a commercial convention ending discriminatory duties and making other adjustments favorable to trade. Boundary difficulties also moved toward resolution. At Ghent the diplomats had created several joint commissions to settle the disputed boundary between the United States and Canada. Many years were to pass before the line was finally drawn, but establishing the principle of defining the border by negotiation was important. In time, a line extending over 3,000 miles was agreed to without the firing of a single shot.

Immediately after the war the British reinforced their garrisons in Canada and began to rebuild their shattered Great Lakes fleet. The United States took similar steps. But both nations found the cost of rearming more than they cared to bear. When the United States suggested demilitarizing the lakes, the British agreed. The Rush-Bagot Agreement of 1817 limited each country to one 100-ton vessel armed with a single 18-pounder on Lake Champlain and another on Lake Ontario. They were to have two each for all the other Great Lakes.

The Kingsley plantation, on Ford George Island in Jacksonville, Florida. Zephaniah Kingsley, the owner, bought Anta, a 13-year-old slave, in 1806. Although they never had a legal marriage ceremony, Zephaniah described Anta—now Anna—as his wife. He freed her and all five of her children, whom he recognized as his heirs. Anna managed the plantation until 1821, when Spain finally transferred Florida to the United States. Unwilling to live under the harsh slave laws that prevailed in the South, Kingsley emigrated to Haiti with Anna and their children. The slave quarters are on the right.

Gradually, as an outgrowth of this decision, the entire border was demilitarized, a remarkable achievement. In the Convention of 1818 the two countries agreed to the 49th parallel as the northern boundary of the Louisiana Territory between the Lake of the Woods and the Rocky Mountains, and to the joint control of the Oregon country for ten years.

The Transcontinental Treaty

The acquisition of Spanish Florida and the settlement of the western boundary of Louisiana were also accomplished as an aftermath of the War of 1812, but in a far different spirit. Spain's control of the Floridas was feeble. West Florida had passed into American hands by 1813, and frontiersmen in Georgia were eyeing East Florida greedily. Indians struck frequently into Georgia from Florida, then fled to sanctuary across the line. American slaves who escaped across the border could not be recovered. In 1818 James Monroe, who had been elected president in 1816, ordered General Andrew Jackson to clear raiding Seminole Indians from American soil and to pursue them into Florida if necessary. Seizing on these instructions, Jackson marched into Florida and easily captured two Spanish forts.

Although Jackson eventually withdrew from Florida, the impotence of the Spanish government made it obvious even in Madrid that if nothing were done, the United States would soon fill the power vacuum by seizing the territory. The Spanish minister to the United States, Luis de Onís, undertook to negotiate a treaty with Monroe's Secretary of State John Quincy Adams. Adams pressed Onís mercilessly on the question of Louisiana's western boundary, and eventually the minister agreed to accept a boundary that followed the Sabine, Red, and Arkansas Rivers to the Continental Divide and the 42nd parallel to the Pacific, thus abandoning Spain's claim to a huge area beyond the Rockies that had no connection at all with the Louisiana Purchase. The United States obtained Florida in return for a mere $5 million, and that paid not to Spain but to Americans who held claims against the Spanish government.

This "Transcontinental Treaty," also known as the Adams-Onís Treaty, was signed in 1819, although ratification was delayed until 1821. Most Americans at the time thought the acquisition of Florida the most important part of the treaty, but Adams, whose vision of America's future was truly continental, knew better. "The acquisition of a definite line of boundary to the [Pacific] forms a great epoch in our history," he recorded in his diary.

The Monroe Doctrine

Concern with defining the boundaries of the United States did not reflect a desire to limit expansion; rather, the feeling was that there should be no more quibbling and quarreling with foreign powers that might distract the people from the great task of national development. The classic enunciation of this point of view, the completion of America's withdrawal from Europe, was the Monroe Doctrine.

Two separate strands met in this pronouncement. The first led from Moscow to Alaska and down the Pacific Coast to the Oregon country. Beginning with the explorations of Vitus Bering in 1741, the Russians had maintained an interest in fishing and fur trading along the northwest coast of North America. In 1821 the Russian czar extended his claim south to the 51st parallel and forbade the ships of other powers to enter coastal waters north of that point. This announcement was disturbing.

The second strand ran from the courts of the European monarchs to Latin America. Between 1817 and 1822 practically the entire region from the Rio Grande to the Strait of Magellan had won its independence. Spain, former master of all the area except Brazil, was too weak to win it back by force, but Austria, Prussia, France, and Russia decided at the Congress of Verona in 1822 to try to regain the area for Spain in the interests of "legitimacy." There was talk of sending a large French army to South America. This possibility also caused grave concern in Washington.

To the Russian threat, Monroe and Secretary of State Adams responded with a terse warning: "The American continents are no longer subjects for any new European colonial establishments." This statement did not impress the Russians, but they had no intention of colonizing the region. In 1824 they signed a treaty with the United States abandoning all claims below the present southern limit of Alaska (54° 40' north latitude) and removing their restrictions on foreign shipping.

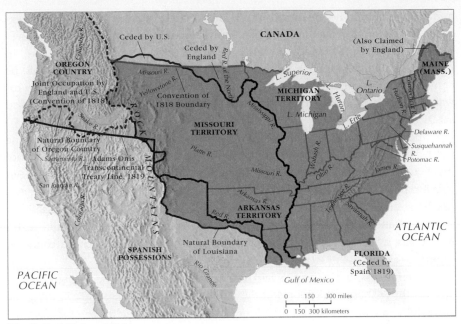

The United States, 1819

The Latin American problem was more complex. In 1823 the British foreign minister, George Canning, suggested to the American minister in London that the United States and Britain issue a joint statement opposing any French interference in South America, pledging that they themselves would never annex any part of Spain's old empire, and saying nothing about recognition of the new republics that were emerging in Latin America. This proposal of joint action with the British was flattering to the United States but scarcely in its best interests. The United States had already recognized the new republics, and it had no desire to help Great Britain retain its South American trade. As Secretary Adams pointed out, to agree to the proposal would be to abandon the possibility of someday adding Cuba or any other part of Latin America to the United States. America should act independently, Adams urged. "It would be more candid, as well as more dignified, to avow our principles explicitly . . . than to come in as a cockboat in the wake of the British man-of-war."

Monroe heartily endorsed Adams's argument and decided to include a statement of American policy in his annual message to Congress in December 1823. "The American continents," he wrote, "by the free and independent condition which they have assumed and maintain, are henceforth not to be considered as subjects for future colonization by any European powers." Europe's political system was "essentially different" from that developing in the New World, and the two should not be mixed. The United States would not interfere with existing European colonies in North or South America and would avoid involvement in strictly European affairs, but any attempt to extend European control to countries in the hemisphere that had already won their independence would be considered, Monroe warned, "the manifestation of an unfriendly disposition toward the United States" and consequently a threat to the nation's "peace and safety."

This policy statement—it was not dignified with the title Monroe Doctrine until decades later—attracted little notice in Europe or Latin America and not much more at home. Obviously the United States, whose own capital had been overrun by a mere raiding party less than ten years before, could not police the entire Western Hemisphere. European statesmen dismissed Monroe's message as "arrogant" and "blustering," worthy only of "the most profound contempt." Latin Americans, while appreciating the intent behind it, knew better than to count on American aid in case of attack.

Nevertheless, the principles laid down by President Monroe so perfectly expressed the wishes of the people of the United States that when the country grew powerful enough to enforce them, there was little need to alter or embellish his pronouncement. However understood at the time, the doctrine may be seen as the final stage in the evolution of American independence.

From this perspective, the famous Declaration of 1776 merely began a process of separation and self-determination. The peace treaty ending the Revolutionary War was a further step, and Washington's Declaration of Neutrality in 1793 was another, demonstrating as it did the capacity of the United States to determine its own best interests despite the treaty of alliance with France. The removal of British troops from the northwest forts, achieved by the otherwise ignominious Jay Treaty, marked the next stage. Then the Louisiana Purchase made a further advance toward true independence by ensuring that the Mississippi River could not be closed to the commerce so vital to the development of the western territories.

The standoff War of 1812 ended any lingering British hope of regaining control of America, the Latin American revolutions further weakened colonialism in the Western Hemisphere, and the Transcontinental Treaty pushed the last European power from the path of westward expansion. Monroe's "doctrine" was a kind of public announcement that the sovereign United States had completed its independence and wanted nothing more than to be left alone to concentrate on its own development. Better yet if Europe could be made to allow the entire hemisphere to follow its own path.

The Era of Good Feelings

The person who gave his name to the so-called doctrine was an unusually lucky man. James Monroe lived a long life in good health and saw at close hand most of the great events in the history of the young republic. At the age of 18 he shed his blood for liberty at the Battle of Trenton. He was twice governor of Virginia, a United States senator, and a Cabinet member. He was at various times the nation's representative in Paris, Madrid, and London. Elected president in 1816, his good fortune continued. The world was finally at peace, the country united and prosperous. A person of good feeling who would keep a steady hand on the helm and hold to the present course seemed called for, and Monroe possessed exactly the qualities that the times required. "He is a man whose soul might be turned wrongside outwards, without discovering a blemish," Jefferson said, and John Quincy Adams, a harsh critic of public figures, praised Monroe's courtesy, sincerity, and sound judgment.

Courtesy and purity of soul do not always suffice to make a good president. In more troubled times Monroe might well have brought disaster, for he was neither an outstanding intellect nor a forceful leader. He blazed few paths, organized no personal machine. The Monroe Doctrine, by far the most significant achievement of his administration, was as much the work of Secretary of State Adams as his own. No one ever claimed that Monroe was much better than second-rate, yet when his first term ended, he was reelected without organized opposition.

By 1817 the divisive issues of earlier days had vanished. Monroe dramatized their disappearance by beginning his first term with a goodwill tour of New England, heartland of the opposition. The tour was a triumph. Everywhere the president was greeted with tremendous enthusiasm. After he visited Boston, once the headquarters and now the graveyard of Federalism, a Federalist newspaper, the *Columbian Centinel*, gave the age its name. Pointing out that the celebrations attending Monroe's visit had brought together in friendly intercourse many persons "whom party politics had long severed," it dubbed the times the "Era of Good Feelings."

The Jeffersonian balance between individual liberty and responsible government, having survived both bad management and war, had justified itself to the opposition. The new unity was symbolized by the restored friendship of Jefferson and John Adams. In 1801 Adams had slipped sulkily out of Washington without waiting to attend his successor's inauguration, but after ten years of icy silence, the two old collaborators effected a reconciliation. Although they continued to disagree vigorously about matters of philosophy and government, the bitterness between them disappeared entirely. By Monroe's day, Jefferson was writing long letters to "my dear friend," ranging over such subjects as theology, the proper reading of the classics, and agricultural improvements, and receiving equally warm and voluminous replies. "Whether you or I were right," Adams wrote amiably to Jefferson, "Posterity must judge."

When political divisions appeared again, as they soon did, it was not because the old balance had been shaky. Few of the new controversies challenged Republican principles or revived old issues. Instead, these controversies were children of the present and the future, products of the continuing growth of the country. From 1790 to 1820, the area of the United States doubled, but very little of the Louisiana Purchase had been settled. More significant, the population of the nation had more than doubled, from 4 million to 9.6 million. The pace of the westward movement had also quickened; by 1820 the moving edge of the frontier ran in a long, irregular curve from Michigan to Arkansas.

New Sectional Issues

Sectional tensions led to many disputes over the tariff, banking, federal land policy, and internal improvements. Overshadowing all of these was the debate over slavery.

The War of 1812 and the depression that struck the country in 1819 had shaped many of the controversies. The tariff question was affected by both. To meet the added expenses occasioned by the War of 1812, Congress doubled all tariffs. In 1816, when the revenue was no longer needed, a new act kept duties close to wartime levels to protect the nation's infant industries, especially textiles, from foreign competitors.

Initially there was backing for high duties in every section except New England, which had suffered little from foreign competition and therefore supported free trade. But with the passage of time the South rejected protection almost completely. Industry failed to develop, and since Southerners exported most of their cotton and tobacco, they soon concluded that besides increasing the cost of nearly everything they bought, high duties on imports would limit the foreign market for southern staples by inhibiting international exchange. As this fact became clear, the West tended to divide on the tariff question: the Northwest and much of Kentucky, which had a special interest in protecting its considerable hemp production, favored high duties; the Southwest, where cotton was the major crop, favored low duties.

National banking policy was another important political issue affected by the war and the depression. Presidents Jefferson and Madison had managed to live with the Bank of the United States despite its dubious constitutionality, but its charter was not renewed when it expired in 1811. Aside from the constitutional question, the major opposition to recharter came from state banks eager to take over the business of the Bank for themselves. The fact that English investors owned most of the Bank's stock was also used as an argument against recharter.

Many more state banks were created after 1811, and most extended credit recklessly. When the British raid on Washington and Baltimore in 1814 sent panicky depositors scurrying to convert their deposits into gold or silver, the overextended financiers could not oblige them. All banks outside New England suspended specie payments; that is, they stopped exchanging their bank notes for hard money on demand. Paper money immediately fell in value; a paper dollar was soon worth only 85 cents in coin in Philadelphia, less in Baltimore. Government business also suffered from the absence of a national bank. In October 1814 Secretary of the Treasury Alexander J. Dallas submitted a plan for a second Bank of the United States, and after considerable wrangling over its precise form, the institution was authorized in April 1816.

Capitalized at $35 million, the new Bank was much larger than its predecessor. However, unlike Hamilton's creation, the second Bank was badly managed at the start. But the appointment in 1819 of Langdon Cheves of South Carolina as president of the Bank restored the bank's reputation. Cheves restricted credit, issuing far fewer loans than his predecessor. This infuriated many borrowers. "The Bank was saved," the contemporary economist William Gouge wrote somewhat hyperbolically, "and the people were ruined." Indeed, the bank reached a low point in public favor. Irresponsible state banks resented it, as did the advocates of hard money.

Regional lines were less sharply drawn on the Bank issue than on the tariff. Northern congressmen voted against the Bank 53 to 44 in 1816—many of them because they objected to the particular proposal, not because they were against any national bank. Those from other sections favored it, 58 to 30. The economic depression of the Panic of 1819 produced further opposition to the institution in the West.

Land policy in the West also caused sectional controversy. No one wished to eliminate the system of survey and sale, but there was continuous pressure to reduce the price of public land and the minimum unit offered for sale. Sectional attitudes toward the public lands were fairly straightforward. The West wanted cheap land; the North and South tended to look on the national domain as an asset that should be converted into as much cash as possible. Northern manufacturers feared that cheap land in the West would drain off surplus labor and force wages up, while Southern planters were concerned about the competition that would develop when new lands in the Southwest were put to the plow to grow cotton. The West, however, was ready to fight to the last line of defense over land policy, while the other regions would usually compromise on the issue to gain support for their own vital interests.

Sectional alignments on the question of internal improvements were similar to those on land policy, but this issue, soon to become very important, had not greatly agitated national affairs before 1820. The only significant federal internal improvement project undertaken before that date was the National Road.

The most divisive sectional issue was slavery. After the compromises affecting the "peculiar institution" made at the Constitutional Convention, it caused remarkably little conflict in national politics before 1819. Although the importation of blacks rose in the 1790s, Congress abolished the African slave trade in 1808 without major incident. As the nation expanded, free and slave states were added to the Union in equal numbers—free states of Ohio, Indiana, and Illinois being balanced by the slave states of Louisiana, Mississippi, and Alabama. In 1819 there were twenty-two states, eleven slave and eleven free. The expansion of slavery occasioned by the cotton boom led Southerners to support it more aggressively, which tended to irritate many Northerners, but most persons considered slavery mainly a local issue. To the extent that it was a national question, the North opposed it and the South defended it ardently. The West leaned toward the southern point of view, for in addition to the southwestern slave states, the Northwest was sympathetic, partly because much of its produce was sold on southern plantations and partly because at least half of its early settlers came from Virginia, Kentucky, and other slave states.

The Missouri Compromise

The sectional concerns of the 1820s repeatedly influenced politics. The depression of 1819 to 1822 increased people's tensions over the issues of the day. For example, manufacturers who wanted high tariffs in 1816 were more vehemently in favor of protection in 1820 when their business fell off. Even when economic conditions improved, geographic alignments on key issues tended to solidify.

One of the first and most critical of the sectional questions concerned the admission of Missouri as a slave state. When Louisiana entered the Union in 1812, the rest of the Louisiana Purchase was organized as the Missouri Territory. Building on a nucleus of Spanish and French inhabitants, the region west and north of St. Louis grew rapidly, and in 1817 the Missourians petitioned for statehood. A large percentage of the settlers—the population exceeded 60,000 by 1818—were Southerners who had moved into the valleys of the Arkansas and Missouri rivers. Since many of them owned slaves, Missouri would become a slave state.

The admission of new states had always been a routine matter, in keeping with the pattern established by the Northwest Ordinance. But during the debate on the Missouri Enabling Act in February 1819, Congressman James Tallmadge of New York introduced an amendment prohibiting "the further introduction of slavery" and providing that all slaves born in Missouri after the territory became a state should be freed at age 25.

While Tallmadge was merely seeking to apply in the territory the pattern of race relations that had developed in the states immediately east of Missouri, his amendment represented, at least in spirit, something of a revolution. The Northwest Ordinance had prohibited slavery in the land between the Mississippi and the Ohio, but that area had only a handful of slaveowners in 1787 and little prospect of attracting more. Elsewhere no effort to restrict the movement of slaves into new territory had been attempted. If one assumed (as whites always had) that the slaves themselves should have no say in the matter, it appeared democratic to let the settlers of Missouri decide the slavery question for themselves. Nevertheless, the Tallmadge amendment passed the House, the vote following sectional lines closely. The Senate, however, resoundingly rejected it. The less populous southern part of Missouri was then organized separately as the Arkansas Territory, and an attempt to bar slavery there was stifled. The Missouri Enabling Act failed to pass before Congress adjourned.

When the next Congress met in December 1819, the Missouri issue came up at once. The vote on Tallmadge's amendment had shown that the rapidly growing North controlled the House of Representatives. It was vital, Southerners felt, to preserve a balance in the Senate. Yet Northerners objected to the fact that Missouri extended hundreds of miles north of the Ohio River, which they considered slavery's natural boundary. Angry debate raged in Congress for months.

The debate did not turn on the morality of slavery or the rights of blacks. Northerners objected to adding new slave states because under the Three-fifths Compromise these states would be overrepresented in Congress (60 percent of their slaves would be counted in determining the size of the states' delegations in the House of Representatives) and because they did not relish competing with slave labor. Since the question was political influence rather than the rights and wrongs of slavery, a compromise was worked out in 1820. Missouri entered the

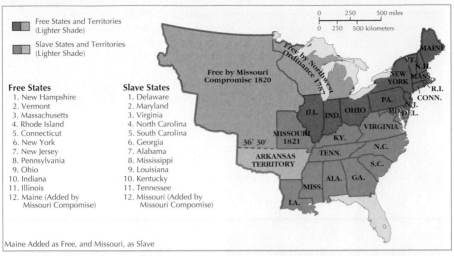

Free States and Territories (Lighter Shade)

Slave States and Territories (Lighter Shade)

Free States	Slave States
1. New Hampshire	1. Delaware
2. Vermont	2. Maryland
3. Massachusetts	3. Virginia
4. Rhode Island	4. North Carolina
5. Connecticut	5. South Carolina
6. New York	6. Georgia
7. New Jersey	7. Alabama
8. Pennsylvania	8. Mississippi
9. Ohio	9. Louisiana
10. Indiana	10. Kentucky
11. Illinois	11. Tennessee
12. Maine (Added by Missouri Compomise)	12. Missouri (Added by Missouri Compomise)

Maine Added as Free, and Missouri, as Slave

The Missouri Compromise, 1820

The Missouri Compromise temporarily put aside the congressional debate over slavery, with the slave states (12) and free states (12) being in perfect balance. This meant, of course, that the Senate was evenly divided as well. But what would happen when other parts of the Missouri Territory sought admission to the Union as states?

Union as a slave state and Maine, having been separated from Massachusetts, was admitted as a free state to preserve the balance in the Senate.

To prevent further conflict, Congress adopted the proposal of Senator Jesse B. Thomas of Illinois, which "forever prohibited" slavery in all other parts of the Louisiana Purchase north of 36° 30' latitude, the westward extension of Missouri's southern boundary. Although this division would keep slavery out of most of the territory, Southerners accepted it cheerfully. The land south of the line, the present states of Arkansas and Oklahoma, seemed ideally suited for the expanded plantation economy, and most persons considered the treeless northern regions little better than a desert. One northern senator, decrying the division, contemptuously described the land north and west of Missouri, today one of the world's richest agricultural regions, as "a prairie without food or water."

The Missouri Compromise did not end the crisis. When Missouri submitted its constitution for approval by Congress (the final step in the admission process), the document, besides authorizing slavery and prohibiting the emancipation of any slave without the consent of the owner, required the state legislature to pass a law barring free blacks and mulattos from entering the state "under any pretext whatever." This provision plainly violated Article IV, Section 2, of the U.S. Constitution: "The Citizens of each State shall be entitled to all Privileges and Immunities of Citizens in the several States." It did not, however, represent any more of a break with established racial patterns, North or South, than the Tallmadge amendment; many states east of Missouri barred free blacks without regard for the Constitution.

Nevertheless, northern congressmen hypocritically refused to accept the Missouri constitution. Once more the debate raged. Again, since few Northerners cared to defend the rights of blacks, the issue was compromised. In March 1821

Henry Clay of Kentucky. "Life itself is but a compromise between death and life," Clay said, a principle he applied to politics.

Congressman Henry Clay of Kentucky found a face-saving formula: Out of respect for the "supreme law of the land," Congress accepted the Missouri constitution with the notation that no law passed in conformity to it should be construed as violating Article IV, Section 2 of the U.S. Constitution.

Every thinking person recognized the political dynamite inherent in the Missouri controversy. The sectional lineup had been terrifyingly compact. What meant the Union if so trivial a matter as one new state could so divide the people? Moreover, despite the timidity and hypocrisy of the North, everyone realized that the rights and wrongs of slavery lay at the heart of the conflict. "We have the wolf by the ears, and we can neither safely hold him, nor safely let him go," Jefferson wrote a month after Missouri became a state. The dispute, he said, "like a fire bell in the night, awakened and filled me with terror." Jefferson knew that the compromise had not quenched the flames ignited by the Missouri debates. "This is a reprieve only," he said. John Quincy Adams called it the "title page to a great tragic volume." Yet one could still hope that the fire bell was only a false alarm, that Adams's tragic volume would remain unread.

The Election of 1824

Other controversies that aroused strong feelings did not seem to divide the country so deeply. The question of federal internal improvements caused endless debate that split the country on geographical lines. In 1816 the nationalist-minded Congressman John C. Calhoun of South Carolina had pressed a plan to set up a $1.5 million fund for roads and canals. Congress approved this despite strong opposi-

Eyes like "anthracite furnaces," the English historian Thomas Carlyle remarked of Daniel Webster; this is the "Black Dan" portrait by Francis Alexander (1835).

tion in New England and a divided South. In 1822 a bill providing money for the upkeep of the National Road caused another sectional split. Both measures were vetoed, but in 1824 Monroe approved a differently worded internal improvement act. Such proposals excited intense reactions. Congressman John Randolph of Virginia, opposing the 1824 bill with his usual ferocity, threatened to employ "every . . . means short of actual insurrection" to defeat it. Yet no one—not even Randolph, it will be noted—threatened the Union on this issue.

The tariff continued to divide the country. When a new, still higher tariff was enacted in 1824, the slave states voted almost unanimously against it, the North and Northwest in favor, and New England remained of two minds. Daniel Webster of Massachusetts (after conducting a poll of business leaders before deciding how to vote) made a powerful speech against the act, but the measure passed without creating a major storm.

The presidential fight was waged on personal grounds, although the heat generated by the contest began the process of reenergizing party politics. Besides Calhoun the candidates were Andrew Jackson, hero of the Battle of New Orleans, William Crawford of Georgia, John Quincy Adams, and Henry Clay of Kentucky. The maneuvering among them was complex, the infighting savage. In March 1824, Calhoun, who was young enough to wait for the White House, withdrew and declared for the vice presidency, which he won easily. Crawford, who had the support of many congressional leaders, seemed the likely winner, but he suffered a series of paralytic strokes that gravely injured his chances.

Despite the bitterness of the contest, it attracted relatively little public interest; barely a quarter of those eligible took the trouble to vote. In the Electoral College Jackson led with 99, Adams had 84, Crawford 41, and Clay 37. Since no one had a majority, the contest was thrown into the House of Representatives, which, under the Constitution, had to choose from among the three leaders, each state delegation having one vote. By employing his great influence in the House, Clay swung the balance. Not wishing to advance the fortunes of a rival Westerner like Jackson and feeling, with reason, that Crawford's health made him unavailable, Clay gave his support to Adams, who was thereupon elected.

John Quincy Adams as President

Adams, who took a Hamiltonian view of the future of the country, hoped to use the national authority to foster all sorts of useful projects. He asked Congress for a federal program of internal improvements so vast that even Clay boggled when he realized its scope. He came out for aid to manufacturing and agriculture, for a national university, and even for a government astronomical observatory. For a nationalist of unchallengeable Jeffersonian origins like Clay or Calhoun to have pressed for so extensive a program would have been politically risky. For the son of John Adams to do so was disastrous; every doubter remembered his Federalist background and decided that he was trying to overturn the glorious "Revolution of 1800."

Adams proved to be his own worst enemy, for he was an inept politician. Although capable on occasion of turning a phrase—in his first annual message to Congress he described astronomical observatories as "light-houses of the skies"—his general style of public utterance was bumbling and cumbersome. Knowing that many citizens considered things like observatories impractical extravagances, he urged Congress not to be "palsied by the will of our constituents." To persuade Americans, who were almost pathological on the subject of monarchy, to support his road building program, he cited with approval the work being done abroad by "the nations of Europe and . . . their rulers," which revived fears that all Adamses were royalists at heart. He was insensitive to the ebb and flow of public feeling; even when he wanted to move with the tide, he seldom managed to dramatize and publicize his stand effectively. There was wide support in the country for a federal bankruptcy law, but instead of describing himself in plain language as a friend of poor debtors, Adams called for the "amelioration" of the "often oppressive codes relating to insolvency" and buried the recommendation at the tail end of a dull state paper.

Calhoun's *Exposition and Protest*

The tariff question added to the president's troubles. High duties, increasingly more repulsive to the export-conscious South, attracted more and more favor in the North and West. Besides manufacturers, lead miners in Missouri, hemp raisers in Kentucky, wool growers in New York, and many other interests demanded protection against foreign competition. The absence of party discipline provided an

This striking portrait of John C. Calhoun was painted sometime between 1818 and 1825, probably by Charles Bird King. Calhoun was in his thirties.

ideal climate for "logrolling" in Congress. Legislators found themselves under pressure from their constituents to raise the duties on products of local importance; to satisfy these demands, they traded votes with other congressmen similarly situated. In this way massive "support" for protection was generated.

In 1828 a new tariff was hammered into shape by the House Committee on Manufactures. Northern and western agricultural interests were in command; they wrote into the bill extremely high duties on raw wool, hemp, flax, fur, and liquor. New England manufacturers protested vociferously, for although their products were protected, the proposed law would increase the cost of their raw materials. This gave Southerners, now hopelessly in the minority on the tariff question, a chance to block the bill. When the New Englanders proposed amendments lowering the duties on raw materials, the Southerners voted nay, hoping to force them to reject the measure on the final vote. This desperate strategy failed. New England had by this time committed its future to manufacturing, a change signaled by the somersault of Webster, who, ever responsive to local pressures, now voted for protection. After winning some minor concessions in the Senate, largely through the intervention of Martin Van Buren of New York, enough New Englanders accepted the so-called Tariff of Abominations to ensure its passage.

Vice President Calhoun believed that the new tariff would impoverish the South. He warned Jackson that relief from high import taxes must soon be provided or the Union would be shaken to its foundations. Then he returned to his South Carolina plantation and wrote an essay, *The South Carolina Exposition and Protest*, repudiating the nationalist philosophy he had previously championed.

The South Carolina legislature released this document to the country in December 1828, along with eight resolutions denouncing the protective tariff as unfair and unconstitutional. The theorist Calhoun, however, was not content with outlining the case against the tariff. His *Exposition* provided an ingenious defense of the right of the people of a state to reject a law of Congress. Starting with John Locke's revered concept of government as a contractual relationship, he argued that since the states had created the Union, logic dictated that they be the final arbiters of the meaning of the Constitution. If a special state convention, representing the sovereignty of the people, decided that an act of Congress violated the Constitution, it could interpose its authority and "nullify" the law within its boundaries. Calhoun did not seek to implement this theory in 1828, for he hoped that the next administration would lower the tariff and make nullification unnecessary.

The Meaning of Sectionalism

The sectional issues that occupied the energies of politicians and strained the ties between the people of the different regions were produced by powerful forces that actually bound the sections together. Growth caused differences that sometimes led to conflict, but growth itself was the product of prosperity. People were drawn to the West by the expectation that life would be better there, as more often than not it was, at least in the long run. Henry Clay proclaimed his support for an "American System" where each section of the nation would specialize economically, thus benefiting the nation as a whole. He argued plausibly that western farmers would profit by selling their crops to eastern city dwellers and that spending public money on building roads and other internal improvements would make transportation and communication less expensive and thus benefit everyone.

Another force unifying the nation was patriotism; the increasing size and prosperity of the nation made people proud to be part of a growing, dynamic society. Still another was the uniqueness of the American system of government and the people's knowledge that their immediate ancestors had created it. John Adams and Thomas Jefferson died on the same day, July 4, 1826, the fiftieth anniversary of the signing of the Declaration of Independence. People took this not as a remarkable coincidence, but as a sign from the heavens, an indication that God looked with favor on the American experiment.

1808	James Madison is elected president
1810	Macon's Bill No. 2 removes all restrictions on commerce with Britain and France
1811	Battle of Tippecanoe shatters Indian confederation
1812	James Madison is reelected president
	Congress declares war on Great Britain
	USS *Constitution* and *United States* win naval victories
1813	Oliver Hazard Perry destroys British fleet in Battle of Lake Erie
	William Henry Harrison defeats British in Battle of the Thames
	Tecumseh dies at Battle of the Thames
1814	British burn Washington, D.C.
	Francis Scott Key writes "The Star Spangled Banner" during bombardment of Fort McHenry
	New England Federalists meet at Hartford Convention
	Treaty of Ghent officially ends war of 1812
1815	Andrew Jackson defeats British at Battle of New Orleans
1816	James Monroe is elected president
1817	Rush-Bagot Agreement limits American and British forces on Lake Champlain and Great Lakes
1819	United States signs Transcontinental Treaty with Spain
1819–1822	United States experiences economic depression
1820	James Monroe is reelected president
1820–1821	Missouri Compromise closes Missouri Territory to slavery, but opens Arkansas Territory to slavery
1820–1850	Cities and manufacturing grow rapidly
1823	Monroe Doctrine says U.S. will consider future European colonization in western hemisphere a threat to America
1824–1825	House of Representatives decides election of 1824 in favor of John Quincy Adams
1828	Congress passes Tariff of Abominations
	South Carolina legislature releases Calhoun's *Exposition and Protest*, leading to debate over nullification

Toward a National Economy

THE PURSUIT OF HAPPYNESS (2006), A MOVIE STARRING WILL Smith, tells the story of Chris Gardner, a struggling salesman who dreams of a better life. Early in the film, while musing about Thomas Jefferson and the Declaration of Independence, Gardner raises the theme of the movie's (misspelled) title: "The passage about our right to life, liberty, and the pursuit of happiness—How did he know to put the pursuit part in there? That happiness?"

Gardner covets wealth. His heart flutters when he sees a Porsche. To own such a car would be happiness. Then, after losing both his job and wife, he careens into abject poverty. He and his young son sleep on the floors of public bathrooms; sometimes they go hungry. Gardner takes a job as an unpaid intern; once he reports for work without shoes. Happiness now means a plateful of food, a warm bed, and decent clothing. The movie ends happily; as in real life, Gardner gets a job with the brokerage, rises to the top, and makes a fortune.

Gardner's insight about Jefferson and the pursuit of happiness was on target. The Founding Fathers did not regard political rights merely as abstract philosophies but as a means to satisfy human desires. And in terms of food, clothing, and shelter, most Americans in the early 1800s were far better off than their counterparts in Europe. But Americans wanted more. During the early decades of the nineteenth century, they initiated the dynamic transformation of the economy. They built factories and devised machines to produce more goods at a lower cost. They recruited immigrants, women, and children to take low-paying jobs and they bought more slaves. They imposed new forms of discipline on all workers. They constructed turnpikes and canals. They built cities to distribute the wealth of the regions. They concocted legal structures to protect corporations and channel wealth into productive enterprises.

Did the booming economy generate happiness? By the mid-1800s, many observers had doubts. "I have never thought America a happy country," Thomas Law Nichols, a physician and health reformer, wrote at midcentury. "Every little ragged boy dreams of being a John Jacob Astor" (a reference to perhaps the wealthiest man in New York). "The dream may be a pleasant one while it lasts, but what of the excited, restless, feverish life spent in the pursuit of phantoms?"

Gentility and the Consumer Revolution

The democratic revolution was accompanied by widespread emulation of aristocratic behavior. On his trip to Paris in 1778 on behalf of the Continental Congress, John Adams denounced the splendor of the houses, furniture, and clothing. "I cannot help suspecting that the more Elegance, the less Virtue," he concluded. Yet despite the constraints of war, Adams purchased a lavish carriage. On returning to America, he bought a three-story mansion and furnished it with Louis XV chairs and, among other extravagances, an ornate wine cooler from Vincennes, France.

Among aristocratic circles in Europe, gentility was the product of ancestry and cultivated style; but in America it was largely defined by possession of material goods. Houses with parlors, dining rooms, and hallways bulged with countless articles of consumption: porcelain plates, silver tea services, woolen carpets, walnut tables. By the mid-eighteenth century the "refinement of America" had touched the homes of some southern planters and urban merchants; but a half century later porcelain plates made by English craftsman Josiah Wedgwood and mahogany washstands by Thomas Chippendale were appearing even in frontier communities. Americans were demanding more goods than such craftsmen could turn out. Everywhere producers sought to expand their workshops, hire and train more artisans, and acquire large stocks of materials and labor-saving machines.

Americans enshrined the simple life and a homespun equality; yet they coveted the cultural markers of aristocracy, such as imported porcelain tea services. This one, made in France, was given to Alexander Hamilton. Gentility spread, historian Richard Bushman writes, "because people longed to be associated with the 'best society.'"

But first they had to locate the requisite capital, find ways to supervise large numbers of workers, and discover how to get raw materials to factories and products to customers. The solutions to these problems, taken together, constituted the "market revolution" of the early nineteenth century. The "industrial revolution" came on its heels.

Birth of the Factory

By the 1770s British manufacturers, especially those in textiles, had made astonishing progress in mechanizing their operations, bringing workers together in buildings called factories where waterpower, and later steam, supplied the force to run new spinning and weaving devices that increased productivity and reduced labor costs.

Because machine-spun cotton was cheaper and of better quality than that spun by hand, producers in other countries were eager to adopt British methods. Americans had depended on Great Britain for such products until the Revolution cut off supplies; then the new spirit of nationalism gave impetus to the development of local industry. A number of state legislatures offered bounties to anyone who would introduce the new machinery. The British, however, guarded their secrets vigilantly. It was illegal to export any of the new machines or to send their plans abroad. Workers skilled in their construction and use were forbidden to leave the country. These restrictions were effective for a time; the principles on which the new machines were based were simple enough, but to construct workable models without plans was another matter. Although a number of persons tried to do so, it was not until Samuel Slater installed his machines in Pawtucket, Rhode Island, that a successful factory was constructed.

Slater, born in England, was more than a skilled mechanic. Attracted by stories of the rewards offered in the United States, he slipped out of England in 1789. Not daring to carry any plans, he depended on his memory and his mechanical sense for the complicated specifications of the necessary machines. Moses Brown brought Slater to Rhode Island to help run his textile-manufacturing operation. Slater insisted on scrapping the crude machinery Brown's company had assembled. Then, working in secrecy with a carpenter who was "under bond not to steal the patterns nor disclose the nature of the work," Slater built and installed his machinery. In December 1790 the first American factory began production.

It was a humble beginning indeed. Slater's machines made only cotton thread, which Brown's company sold in its Providence store and "put out" to individual artisans, who, working for wages, wove it into cloth in their homes. The machines were tended by a labor force of nine children, for the work was simple and the pace slow. The young operatives' pay ranged from 33 to 67 cents a week, about what a youngster could earn in other occupations.[1]

---

[1]This labor pattern persisted for several decades. In 1813 a cotton manufacturer placed the following advertisement in the Utica (N.Y.) Patriot: "A few sober and industrious families of at least five children each, over the age of eight years are wanted at the Cotton Factory. Widows with large families would do well to attend this notice."

The factory was profitable from the start. Slater soon branched out on his own, and others trained by him opened their own establishments. By 1800 seven mills possessing 2,000 spindles were in operation; by 1815, after production had been stimulated by the War of 1812, there were 130,000 spindles turning in 213 factories. Many of the new factories were inefficient, but the well-managed ones earned large profits. Slater began with almost nothing. When he died in 1835 he owned mill properties in Rhode Island, Massachusetts, Connecticut, and New Hampshire in addition to other interests. By the standards of the day he was a rich man.

Before long the Boston Associates, a group of merchants headed by Francis Cabot Lowell, added a new dimension to factory production. Beginning at Waltham, Massachusetts, where the Charles River provided the necessary water-power, between 1813 and 1850 they revolutionized textile production. Some early factory owners had set up hand looms in their plants, but the weavers could not keep pace with the whirring spinning jennies. Lowell, after an extensive study of British mills, smuggled the plans for an efficient power loom into America. His Boston Manufacturing Company at Waltham, capitalized at $300,000, combined machine production, large-scale operation, efficient management, and centralized marketing procedures. It concentrated on the mass production of a standardized product.

Lowell's cloth, though plain and rather coarse, was durable and cheap. His profits averaged almost 20 percent a year during the Era of Good Feelings. In 1823 the Boston Associates began to harness the power of the Merrimack River, setting up a new $600,000 corporation at the sleepy village of East Chelmsford, Massachusetts (population 300), where there was a fall of 32 feet in the river. Within three years the town, appropriately renamed Lowell, had 2,000 inhabitants.

An Industrial Proletariat?

As machines displaced skilled labor, the ability of laborers to influence working conditions declined. If skilled, they either became employers and developed entrepreneurial and managerial skills, or they descended into the mass of wage earners. Simultaneously, the changing structure of production widened the gap between owners and workers and blurred the distinction between skilled and unskilled labor.

These trends might have been expected to generate hostility between workers and employers. To some extent they did. There were strikes for higher wages and to protest work speedups throughout the 1830s and again in the 1850s. Efforts to found unions and to create political organizations dedicated to advancing the interests of workers were also undertaken. But well into the 1850s Americans displayed less evidence of the class solidarity common among European workers.

Why America did not produce a self-conscious working class is a question that has long intrigued historians. As with most such large questions, no single answer has been forthcoming. Some historians argue that the existence of the frontier siphoned off displaced and dissatisfied workers. The number of urban laborers who went West could not have been large, but the fact that the expanding economy created many opportunities for laborers to rise out of the working class was surely another reason why so few of them developed strong class feelings.

Other historians believe that ethnic and racial differences kept workers from seeing themselves as a distinct class with common needs and common enemies. The influx of needy immigrants willing to accept almost any wage was certainly resented by native-born workers. The growing number of free blacks in northern cities—between 1800 and 1830 the number tripled in Philadelphia and quadrupled in New York—also inhibited the development of a self-identified working class.

These answers help explain the relative absence of class conflict during the early stages of the industrial revolution in America, but so does the fact that conditions in the early shops and factories represented an improvement for the people who worked in them. This was the case with nearly all European immigrants, though less so for urban free blacks, since in the South many found work in the skilled trades.

Most workers in the early textile factories were drawn from outside the regular labor market. Relatively few artisan spinners and weavers became factory workers; indeed, some of them continued to work as they had, for it was many years before the factories could even begin to satisfy the ever-increasing demand for cloth. Nor did immigrants attend the new machines. Instead, the mill owners relied chiefly on women and children. They did so because machines lessened the need for skill and strength and because the labor shortage made it necessary to tap unexploited sources. By the early 1820s about half the cotton textile workers in the factories were under 16 years of age.

Most people of that generation considered this a good thing. They reasoned that the work was easy and that it kept youngsters busy at useful tasks while providing their families with extra income. Roxanna Foote, whose daughter, Harriet Beecher Stowe, wrote *Uncle Tom's Cabin,* came from a solid middle-class family in Guilford, Connecticut. Nevertheless, she worked full-time before her marriage in her grandfather's small spinning mill. "This spinning-mill was a favorite spot," a relative recalled many years later. "Here the girls often received visitors, or read or chatted while they spun." Roxanna explained her daily regimen as a mill girl matter-of-factly: "I generally rise with the sun, and, after breakfast, take my wheel, which is my daily companion, and the evening is generally devoted to reading, writing, and knitting."

This seems an idealized picture, or perhaps working for one's grandfather made a difference. Another young girl, Emily Chubbock, later a well-known writer, had a less pleasant recollection of her experience as an 11-year-old factory hand earning $1.25 a week. "My principal recollections . . . are of noise and filth, bleeding hands and aching feet, and a very sad heart." In any case, a society accustomed to seeing the children of fairly well-to-do farmers working full-time in the fields was not shocked by the sight of children working all day in mills. In factories where laborers were hired in family units, no member earned very much, but with a couple of adolescent daughters and perhaps a son of 9 or 10 helping out, a family could take home enough to live decently. For most working Americans, then as now, that was success enough.

The first mill operations performed only the task of spinning wool, cotton, and other fibers into thread; soon weaving was also mechanized, so that fabric ready to be cut and sewn was manufactured. Note the child at left, working under the spindles where an adult could not stand.

Lowell's Waltham System: Women as Factory Workers

Instead of hiring children, the Boston Associates developed the "Waltham System" of employing young, unmarried women in their new textile mills. For a generation after the opening of the Merrimack Manufacturing Company in 1823, the thriving factory towns of Lowell, Chicopee, and Manchester provided the background for a remarkable industrial idyll. Young women came from farms all over New England to work for a year or two in the mills. They were lodged in company boardinghouses, which, like college dormitories, became centers of social life. Unlike modern college dormitories, the boardinghouses were strictly supervised; straitlaced New Englanders did not hesitate to permit their daughters to live in them. The regulations laid down by one company, for example, required that all employees "show that they are penetrated by a laudable love of temperance and virtue." "Ardent spirits" were banished from company property, "games of hazard and cards" prohibited. A 10 P.M. curfew was strictly enforced.

The women earned between $2.50 and $3.25 a week, about half of which went for room and board. Some of the remainder they sent home, the rest (what there was of it) they could spend as they wished.

Most of these young women did not have to support themselves. They worked to save up for their marriage, to help educate a younger brother, or simply for the experience and excitement of meeting new people and escaping the confining environment of the farm. "The feeling that at this new work, the few hours they had of every-day leisure was entirely their own was a satisfaction to them," one Lowell worker recalled. Anything but an industrial proletariat, they filled the windows of the factories with flowering plants, organized sewing circles, edited their own literary periodicals, and attended lectures on edifying subjects. That such activity was possible on top of a 70-hour work week is a commentary on both the resiliency of youth and the leisurely pace of these early factories. The English novelist Charles Dickens, though scarcely enchanted by other American ways, was impressed by his visit to Lowell, which he compared most favorably to "those great haunts of misery," the English manufacturing towns. "They were all well dressed," he wrote of the workers. "They were healthy in appearance, many of them remarkably so, and had the manners and deportment of young women. . . . The rooms in which they worked were as well ordered as themselves."

Life in the mills was not all it might have been. Although they made up 85 percent of the workforce, women were kept out of supervisory positions. In 1834 workers in several mills "turned out" to protest cuts in their wages and a hike in what they paid for board. This work stoppage did not force a reversal of management policy. Another strike two years later in response to a work speedup was somewhat more successful. But when a drop in prices in the 1840s led the owners to introduce new rules designed to increase production, workers lacked the organizational strength to block them. By then young women of the kind that had flocked to the mills in the 1820s and 1830s were beginning to find work as schoolteachers and clerks. Mill owners turned increasingly to Irish immigrants to operate their machines.

Irish and German Immigrants

Between 1790 and 1820 the population of the United States had more than doubled to 9.6 million. The most remarkable feature of this growth was that it resulted almost entirely from natural increase. The birthrate in the early nineteenth century exceeded 50 per 1,000 population, a rate as high as that of any country in the world today. Fewer than 250,000 immigrants entered the United States between 1790 and 1820. European wars, the ending of the slave trade, and doubts about the viability of the new republic slowed the flow of humanity across the Atlantic to a trickle.

But soon after the final defeat of Napoleon in 1815, immigration picked up. In the 1820s, some 150,000 European immigrants arrived; in the 1830s, 600,000; in the 1840s, 1.7 million. The 1850 census, the first to make the distinction, estimated that of the nation's population of 23 million, more than 10 percent were foreign-born. In the Northeast the proportion exceeded 15 percent.

Most of this human tide came from Germany and Ireland, but substantial numbers also came from Great Britain and the Scandinavian countries. As with earlier immigrants, most were drawn to America by what are called "pull" factors:

the prospect of abundant land, good wages, and economic opportunity generally, or by the promise of political and religious freedom. But many came because of "push" factors: to stay where they were meant to face starvation. This was particularly true of those from Ireland, where a potato blight triggered the flight of tens of thousands. This Irish exodus continued; by the end of the century there were more people of Irish origin in America than in Ireland.

Once ashore in New York, Boston, or Philadelphia, most relatively prosperous immigrants pushed directly westward. Others found work in the new factory towns along the route of the Erie Canal, in the lower Delaware Valley southeast of Philadelphia, or along the Merrimack River north of Boston. But most of the Irish immigrants, "the poorest and most wretched population that can be found in the world," one of their priests called them, lacked the means to go West. Aside from the cost of transportation, starting a farm required far more capital than they could raise. Like it or not, they had to settle in the eastern cities.

Viewed in historical perspective, this massive wave of immigration stimulated the American economy. In the short run, the influx of the 1830s and 1840s depressed living standards and strained the social fabric. For the first time the nation had acquired a culturally distinctive, citybound, and propertyless class. The poor Irish immigrants had to accept whatever wages employers offered them. By doing so they caused resentment among native workers, resentment exacerbated by the unfamiliarity of the Irish with city ways and by their Roman Catholic faith, which the Protestant majority associated with European authoritarianism and corruption.

The Persistence of the Household System

Since technology affected American industry unevenly, contemporaries found the changes difficult to evaluate. Interchangeable firing pins for rifles did not lead at once even to matching pairs of shoes. More than 15 years passed after John Fitch built and launched the world's first regularly scheduled steamboat in 1790 before it was widely accepted. Few people in the 1820s appreciated how profound the impact of the factory system would be. The city of Lowell seemed remarkable and important but not necessarily a herald of future trends.

Yet in nearly every field apparently minor changes were being made. Beginning around 1815, small improvements in the design of waterwheels, such as the use of leather transmission belts and metal gears, made possible larger and more efficient machinery in mills and factories. The woolen industry gradually became as mechanized as the cotton. Iron production advanced beyond the stage of the blacksmith's forge and the small foundry only slowly; nevertheless, by 1810 machines were stamping out nails at a third of the cost of the hand-forged type, and a few years later sheet iron, formerly hammered out laboriously by hand, was being produced in efficient rolling mills. At about this time the puddling process for refining pig iron made it possible to use coal for fuel instead of expensive charcoal.

Key improvements were made soon after the War of 1812 in the manufacture of paper, glass, and pottery. The commercial canning of sterilized foods in airtight containers began about 1820. The invention in that year of a machine for cutting ice, which reduced the cost by over 50 percent, had equally important effects on urban eating habits.

Rise of Corporations

Mechanization required substantial capital investment, and capital was chronically in short supply. The modern method of organizing large enterprises, the corporation, was slow to develop. Between 1781 and 1801 only 326 corporations were chartered by the states, and only a few of them were engaged in manufacturing.

The general opinion was that only quasi-public projects, such as roads and waterworks, were entitled to the privilege of incorporation. Anyone interested in organizing a corporation had to obtain a special act of a state legislature. And even among businessmen there was a tendency to associate corporations with monopoly, with corruption, and with the undermining of individual enterprise.

While the growth of industry did not suddenly revolutionize American life, it reshaped society in various ways. For a time it lessened the importance of foreign commerce. Some relative decline from the lush years immediately preceding Jefferson's embargo was no doubt inevitable, especially in the fabulously profitable reexport trade. But American industrial growth reduced the need for foreign products and thus the business of merchants. Only in the 1850s, when the wealth and population of the United States were more than three times what they had been in the first years of the century, did the value of American exports climb back to the levels of 1807. As the country moved closer to self-sufficiency (a point it never reached), nationalistic and isolationist sentiments were subtly augmented. During the embargo and the War of 1812 a great deal of capital had been transferred from commerce to industry; afterward new capital continued to prefer industry, attracted by the high profits and growing prestige of manufacturing. The rise of manufacturing affected farmers too, for as cities grew in size and number, the need to feed the populace caused commercial agriculture to flourish. Dairy farming, truck gardening, and fruit growing began to thrive around every manufacturing center.

Cotton Revolutionizes the South

By far the most important indirect effect of industrialization occurred in the South, which soon began to produce cotton to supply the new textile factories of Great Britain and New England. The possibility of growing large amounts of this crop in America had not been seriously considered in colonial times, but by the 1780s the demand for raw cotton to feed the voracious British mills was causing many

American farmers to experiment with the crop. Most of the world's cotton at this time came from Egypt, India, and the East Indies. The plant was considered tropical, most varieties being unable to survive the slightest frost. Alexander Hamilton, who missed nothing that related to the economic growth of the country, reported: "It has been observed . . . that the nearer the place of growth to the equator, the better the quality of the cotton."

Beginning in 1786, "sea-island" cotton was grown successfully in the mild, humid lowlands and offshore islands along the coasts of Georgia and South Carolina. This was a high-quality cotton, silky and long-fibered like the Egyptian. But its susceptibility to frost severely limited the area of its cultivation. Elsewhere in the South, "green-seed," or upland, cotton flourished, but this plant had little commercial value because the seeds could not be easily separated from the lint. When sea-island cotton was passed between two rollers, its shiny black seeds simply popped out; with upland cotton the seeds were pulled through with the lint and crushed, the oils and broken bits destroying the value of the fiber. To remove the seeds by hand was laborious; a slave working all day could clean scarcely a pound of the white fluff. This made it an uneconomical crop. In 1791 the usually optimistic Hamilton admitted in his *Report on Manufactures* that "the extensive cultivation of cotton can, perhaps, hardly be expected."

This was the situation in the spring of 1793, when Eli Whitney was a guest at Mulberry Grove, the plantation of Catherine Greene, widow of General Nathanael Greene, some dozen miles from Savannah.[2] Whitney had accepted a position as private tutor at 100 guineas a year with a nearby family and had stopped to visit a friend, Phineas Miller, who was overseer of the Greene plantation. While at Mulberry Grove, Whitney, who had never seen a cotton plant before, met a number of the local landowners.

> I heard [he wrote his father] much of the extreme difficulty of ginning Cotton, that is, separating it from its seed. There were a number of very respectable Gentlemen at Mrs. Greene's who all agreed that if a machine could be invented that would clean the Cotton with expedition, it would be a great thing both to the Country and to the inventor.

Whitney thought about the problem for a few days and then "struck out a plan of a machine." He described it to Miller, who enthusiastically offered to finance the invention. Since Whitney had just learned that his job as tutor would pay only 50 guineas, he accepted Miller's proposal.

Within ten days he had solved the problem that had baffled the planters. His gin (engine) consisted of a cylinder covered with rows of wire teeth rotating in a box filled with cotton. As the cylinder turned, the teeth passed through narrow slits in a metal grating. Cotton fibers were caught by the teeth and pulled through the

---

[2] *The property, formerly owned by a prominent Georgia Tory, had been given to Greene by the state in gratitude for his having driven out the British during the Revolution.*

Eli Whitney's cotton gin made it easier to process cotton; this stimulated cotton production and greatly increased the demand for slaves to farm and collect it, as the picture suggests.

slits. The seeds, too thick to pass through the openings, were left behind. A second cylinder, with brushes rotating in the opposite direction to sweep the cotton from the wires, prevented matting and clogging.

This "absurdly simple contrivance" almost instantly transformed southern agriculture. With a gin a slave could clean fifty times as much cotton as by hand; soon larger models driven by mules and horses were available. The machines were so easy to construct (once the basic idea was understood) that Whitney and Miller were never able to enforce their patent rights effectively. Rival manufacturers shamelessly pirated their work, and countless farmers built gins of their own. Cotton production increased from 3,000 bales in 1790 to well over 400,000 bales a year in the early 1820s. The South boomed.

Upland cotton would grow wherever there were 200 consecutive days without frost and 24 inches of rain. The crop engulfed Georgia and South Carolina and spread north into parts of Virginia. After Andrew Jackson smashed the southwestern Indians during the War of 1812, the rich "Black Belt" area of central Alabama and northern Mississippi and the delta region along the lower Mississippi River were rapidly taken over by the fluffy white staple. In 1821 Alabama alone raised 40,000 bales. Central Tennessee also became important cotton country.

Cotton stimulated the economy of the rest of the nation as well. Most of it was exported, the sale paying for much-needed European products. The transportation, insurance, and final disposition of the crop fell largely into the hands of northern merchants, who profited accordingly. And the surplus corn and hogs of western farmers helped feed the slaves of the new cotton plantations. Cotton was the major force in the economy for a generation, beginning about 1815.

Revival of Slavery

Amid the national rejoicing over this prosperity, one aspect both sad and ominous was easily overlooked. Slavery, a declining or at worst stagnant institution in the decade of the Revolution, was revitalized in the following years.

Libertarian beliefs inspired by the Revolution ran into the roadblock of race prejudice as soon as some of the practical aspects of freedom for blacks became apparent. As disciples of John Locke, the Revolutionary generation had a deep respect for property rights; in the last analysis most white Americans placed these rights ahead of the personal liberty of black Americans. Forced abolition of slavery therefore attracted few recruits. Moreover, the rhetoric of the Revolution had raised the aspirations of blacks. Increasing signs of rebelliousness appeared among them, especially after the slave uprising in Saint Domingue, which culminated, after a great bloodbath, in the establishment of the black Republic of Haiti in 1804. This example of a successful slave revolt filled white Americans with apprehension. Their fears were irrational (Haitian blacks outnumbered whites and mulattos combined by seven to one) but nonetheless real. And fear led to repression; the exposure in 1801 of a plot to revolt in Virginia, led by the slave Gabriel, resulted in some three dozen executions even though no actual uprising had occurred.

The mood of the Revolutionary decade had led a substantial number of masters to free their slaves. Unfortunately this led many other whites to have second thoughts about ending slavery. "If the blacks see all of their color slaves, it will seem to them a disposition of Providence, and they will be content," a Virginia legislator, apparently something of an amateur psychologist, claimed. "But if they see others like themselves free . . . they will repine." As the number of free blacks rose, restrictions on them were everywhere tightened.

In the 1780s many opponents of slavery began to think of solving the "Negro problem" by colonizing freed slaves in some distant region—in the western districts or perhaps in Africa. The colonization movement had two aspects. One, a manifestation of an embryonic black nationalism, reflected the disgust of black Americans with local racial attitudes and their interest in African civilization. Paul Cuffe, a Massachusetts Quaker, managed to finance the emigration of thirty-eight of his fellow blacks to British Sierra Leone in 1815, but few others followed. Most influential northern blacks, the most conspicuous among them the Reverend Richard Allen, bishop of the African Methodist Church, opposed the idea vigorously.

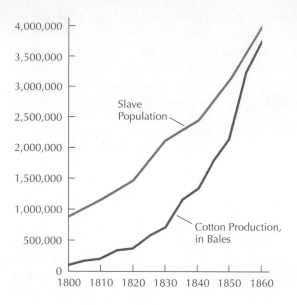

Cotton Production and Slave Population, 1800–1860

The other colonization movement, led by whites, was paternalistic. Some white colonizationists genuinely abhorred slavery. Others could not stomach living with free blacks; to them colonization was merely a polite word for deportation. Most white colonizationists were conservatives who considered themselves realists.

The colonization idea became popular in Virginia in the 1790s, but nothing was achieved until after the founding of the American Colonization Society in 1817. The society purchased African land and established the Republic of Liberia. However, despite the cooperation of a handful of black nationalists and the patronage of many important white Southerners, including Presidents Madison and Monroe and Chief Justice Marshall, it accomplished little. Although some white colonizationists expected former slaves to go to Africa as Christian missionaries to convert and "civilize" the natives, few blacks wished to migrate to a land so alien to their own experience. Only about 12,000 went to Liberia, and the toll taken among them by tropical diseases was large. As late as 1850 the black American population of Liberia was only 6,000.

The cotton boom of the early nineteenth century acted as a brake on the colonization movement. As cotton production expanded, the need for labor in the South grew apace. The price of slaves doubled between 1795 and 1804. As it rose, the inclination of even the most kindhearted masters to free their slaves began to falter. Although the importation of slaves from abroad had been outlawed by all the states, perhaps 25,000 were smuggled into the country in the 1790s. In 1804 South Carolina reopened the trade, and between that date and 1808, when the constitutional prohibition of importation became effective, some 40,000 were brought in. Thereafter the miserable traffic in human beings continued clandestinely, though on a lesser scale.

Prices for Cotton and for Slaves, 1802–1860

The vertical axis on the left shows cents, and the curve for the price of cotton should be read against it; the right vertical axis shows dollars, and the price of slaves should be read against it. These prices are from New Orleans records. The rising trend of slave prices (and a growing slave population) shows the continuing profitability and viability of slavery up to 1860.

The cotton boom triggered an internal trade in slaves that frequently ripped black families apart. While it had always been legal for owners to transport their own slaves to a new state if they were settling there, many states forbade, or at least severely restricted, interstate commercial transactions in human flesh. A Virginia law of 1778, for example, prohibited the importation of slaves for purposes of sale, and persons entering the state with slaves had to swear that they did not intend to sell them. Once cotton became important, these laws were either repealed or systematically evaded. There was a surplus of slaves in one part of the United States and an acute shortage in another. A migration from the upper South to the cotton lands quickly sprang up. Slaves from "free" New York and New Jersey and even from New England began to appear on the auction blocks of Savannah and Charleston. Early in the Era of Good Feelings, newspapers in New Orleans were carrying reports such as: "Jersey negroes appear to be particularly adapted to this market. . . . We have the right to calculate on large importations in the future, from the success which hitherto attended the sale."

By about 1820 the letter of the law began to be changed. Soon the slave trade became an organized business, cruel and shameful, frowned on by the "best" people of the South, managed by the depraved and the greedy, yet patronized by nearly anyone who needed labor. "The native land of Washington, Jefferson, and Madison," one disgusted Virginian told a French visitor, "[has] become the Guinea of the United States."

The lot of African Americans in the northern states was almost as bad as that of southern free blacks. Except in New England, where there were few blacks to begin with, most were denied the vote, either directly or by extralegal pressures. They could not testify in court, intermarry with whites, obtain decent jobs or housing, or get even a rudimentary education. Most states segregated blacks in theaters, hospitals, and churches and on public transportation facilities. They were barred from hotels and restaurants patronized by whites.

Northern blacks could at least protest and try to convince the white majority of the injustice of their treatment. These rights were denied their southern brethren.

They could and did publish newspapers and pamphlets, organize for political action, petition legislatures and the Congress for redress of grievance—in short, they applied methods of peaceful persuasion in an effort to improve their position in society.

Roads to Market

Inventions and technological improvements were extremely important in the settlement of the West. On superficial examination, this may not seem to have been the case, for the hordes of settlers who struggled across the mountains immediately after the War of 1812 were no better equipped than their ancestors who had pushed up the eastern slopes in previous generations. Many plodded on foot over hundreds of miles, dragging crude carts laden with their meager possessions. More fortunate pioneers traveled on horseback or in heavy, cumbersome wagons, the best known being the canvas-topped Conestoga "covered wagons," pulled by horses or oxen.

In many cases the pioneers followed trails and roads no better than those of colonial days—quagmires in wet weather, rutted and pitted with potholes a good part of the year. When they settled down, their way of life was no more advanced than that of the Pilgrims. At first they were creatures of the forest, feeding on its abundance, building their homes and simple furniture with its wood, clothing themselves in the furs of forest animals. They usually planted the first crop in a natural glade; thereafter, year by year, they pushed back the trees with ax and saw and fire until the land was cleared. Any source of power more complicated than an ox was beyond their ken. Until the population of the territory had grown large enough to support town life, settlers were as dependent on crude household manufacturers as any earlier pioneer.

The spread of settlement into the Mississippi Valley created challenges that required technological advances if they were to be met. In the social climate of that age in the United States, these advances were not slow in coming. Most were related to transportation, the major problem for Westerners. Without economical means of getting their produce to market, they were condemned to lives of crude self-sufficiency. Everyone recognized that an efficient transportation network would increase land values, stimulate domestic and foreign trade, and strengthen the entire economy.

The Mississippi River and its tributaries provided a natural highway for western commerce and communication, but it was one that had grave disadvantages. Farm products could be floated down to New Orleans on rafts and flatboats, but the descent along the Ohio River from Pittsburgh to the Mississippi took at least a month. Transportation upstream was out of the question for anything but the lightest and most valuable products, and even for them it was extremely expensive. In any case, the natural flow of trade was be-

This stagecoach, having just passed over a solid road of made of tree trunks, must now make its way across an all-dirt road. Already its wheels have sunk several inches into the mud.

tween East and West. That is why, from early in the westward movement, much attention was given to building roads linking the Mississippi Valley to the eastern seaboard.

Constructing decent roads over the rugged Appalachians was a formidable task. The steepest grades had to be reduced by cutting through hills and filling in low places, all without modern blasting and earth-moving equipment. Streams had to be bridged. Drainage ditches were essential if the roads were not to be washed out by the first rains, and a firm foundation of stones, topped with a well-crowned gravel dressing, had to be provided if they were to stand up under the pounding of heavy wagons. The skills required for building roads of this quality had been developed in Great Britain and France, and the earliest American examples, constructed in the 1790s, were similar to good European highways. The first such road, connecting Philadelphia and Lancaster, Pennsylvania, opened to traffic in 1794.

In heavily populated sections the volume of traffic made good roads worth their cost, which ran to as much as $13,000 a mile where the terrain was difficult, though the average was perhaps half that figure. In some cases good roads ran into fairly remote areas. In New York, always a leading state in the movement for improved transportation, an excellent road had been built all the way from Albany to Lake Erie by the time of the War of 1812, and by 1821 the state had some 4,000 miles of good roads.

Transportation and the Government

Most of the improved highways and many bridges were built as business ventures by private interests. Promoters charged tolls, the rates being set by the states. Tolls were collected at gates along the way; hinged poles suspended across the road were turned back by a guard after receipt of the toll. Hence these thoroughfares were known as turnpikes, or simply pikes.

The profits earned by a few early turnpikes, such as the one between Philadelphia and Lancaster, caused the boom in private road building, but even the most fortunate of the turnpike companies did not make much money. Maintenance was expensive, traffic spotty.

Despite much talk about individual self-reliance and free enterprise, local, state, and national governments contributed heavily to the development of what in the jargon of the day were called "internal improvements." They served as "primary entrepreneurs," supplying capital for risky but socially desirable enterprises, with the result that a fascinating mixture of private and public energy went into the building of these institutions. At the federal level even the parsimonious Jeffersonians became deeply involved.

Logically, the major highways, especially those over the mountains, should have been built by the national government. Strategic military requirements alone would have justified such a program. One major artery, the Old National Road, running from Cumberland, Maryland, to Wheeling, in western Virginia, was constructed by the United States between 1811 and 1818. In time it was extended as far west as Vandalia, Illinois. However, further federal road building was hampered by political squabbles in Congress, usually phrased in constitutional terms but in fact based on sectional rivalries and other economic conflicts. Thus no comprehensive highway program was undertaken in the nineteenth century.

While the National Road, the New York Pike, and other, rougher trails such as the Wilderness Road into the Kentucky country were adequate for the movement of settlers, they did not begin to answer the West's need for cheap and efficient transportation. Wagon freight rates averaged at least 30 cents a ton-mile around 1815. At such rates, to transport a ton of oats from Buffalo to New York would have cost twelve times the value of the oats! To put the problem another way, four horses could haul a ton and a half of oats about 18 or 20 miles a day over a good road. If they could obtain half their feed by grazing, the horses would still consume about 50 pounds of oats a day. It requires little mathematics to figure out how much oats would be left in the wagon when it reached New York City, almost 400 miles away.

Until the coming of the railroad, which was just being introduced in England in 1825, the cost of shipping bulky goods by land over the great distances common in America was prohibitive. Businessmen and inventors concentrated instead on improving water transport, first by designing better boats and then by developing artificial waterways.

Development of Steamboats

Rafts and flatboats were adequate for downstream travel, but the only practical solution to upstream travel was the steamboat. One early enthusiast was John Stevens, a wealthy New Jerseyite, who designed an improved steam boiler for which he received one of the first patents issued by the United States. Stevens got his brother-in-law, Robert R. Livingston, interested in the problem, and the latter used his political influence to obtain an exclusive charter to operate steamboats on New York waters. In 1802, while in France trying to buy New Orleans from Napoleon, Livingston got to know Robert Fulton, a young American artist and engineer who was experimenting with steam navigation, and agreed to finance his work. In 1807, after returning to New York, Fulton constructed the *North River Steam Boat*, famous to history as the *Clermont*.

The *Clermont* was 142 feet long, 18 feet abeam, and drew 7 feet of water. With its towering stack belching black smoke, its side wheels could push it along at a steady 5 miles an hour. Nothing about it was radically new, but Fulton brought the essentials—engine, boiler, paddle wheels, and hull—into proper balance and thereby produced an efficient vessel.

No one could patent a steamboat; soon the new vessels were plying the waters of every navigable river from the Mississippi east. After 1815 steamers were making the run from New Orleans as far as Ohio. By 1820 at least sixty vessels were operating between New Orleans and Louisville, and by the end of the decade there were more than 200 steamers on the Mississippi.

The day of the steamboat had dawned, and although the following generation would experience its high noon, even in the 1820s its major effects were clear. The great Mississippi Valley, in the full tide of its development, was immensely enriched. Produce poured down to New Orleans, which soon ranked with New York and Liverpool among the world's great ports. Only 80,000 tons of freight reached New Orleans from the interior in 1816 and 1817, more than 542,000 tons in 1840 and 1841. Upriver traffic was affected even more spectacularly. Freight charges plummeted, in some cases to a tenth of what they had been after the War of 1812. Around 1818 coffee cost 16 cents a pound more in Cincinnati than in New Orleans, a decade later less than 3 cents more. The Northwest emerged from self-sufficiency with a rush and became part of the national market.

The Canal Boom

While the steamboat was conquering western rivers, canals were being constructed that further improved the transportation network. Since the midwestern rivers all emptied into the Gulf of Mexico, they did not provide a direct link with the eastern seaboard. If an artificial waterway could be cut between the great central valley and some navigable stream flowing into the Atlantic, all sections would profit immensely.

Canals were more expensive than roads, but so long as the motive power used in overland transportation was the humble horse, they offered enormous economic advantages to shippers. Because there is less friction to overcome, a team plodding along a towpath could pull a canal barge with a 100-ton load and make better time over long distances than it could pulling a single ton in a wagon on the finest road.

Although canals were as old as Egypt, only about 100 miles of them existed in the United States as late as 1816. Construction costs aside, in a rough and mountainous country canals presented formidable engineering problems. To link the Mississippi Valley and the Atlantic meant somehow circumventing the Appalachian Mountains. Most people thought this impossible.

Mayor DeWitt Clinton of New York believed that such a project was feasible in New York State. In 1810, while serving as state canal commissioner, he traveled across central New York and convinced himself that it would be practicable to dig a canal from Buffalo, on Lake Erie, to the Hudson River. The Mohawk Valley cuts through the Appalachian chain just north of Albany, and at no point along the route to Buffalo does the land rise more than 570 feet above the level of the Hudson. Marshaling a mass of technical, financial, and commercial information (and making effective use of his political influence), Clinton placed his proposal before the New York legislature.

In 1817 New York State began construction along a route 363 miles long, most of it across densely forested wilderness. At the time the longest canal in the United States ran less than 28 miles!

The Erie, completed in 1825, was an immediate financial success. Together with the companion Champlain Canal, which linked Lake Champlain and the Hudson, it brought in over half a million dollars in tolls in its first year. Soon its entire $7 million cost had been recovered, and it was earning profits of about $3 million a year. The effect of this prosperity on New York State was enormous. Buffalo, Rochester, Syracuse, and half a dozen lesser towns along the canal flourished.

New York City: Emporium of the Western World

The Erie Canal cemented New York's position as the national metropolis. Most European-manufactured goods destined for the Mississippi Valley entered the country at New York and passed on to the West over the canal. The success of the Erie also sparked a nationwide canal-building boom. Most canals were constructed either by the states, as in the case of the Erie, or as "mixed enterprises" that combined public and private energies.

No state profited as much from this construction as New York, for none possessed New York's geographic advantages. The rocky hills of New England discouraged all but fanatics. Canals were built connecting Worcester and Northampton, Massachusetts, with the coast, but they were financial failures. The Delaware and Hudson Canal, running from northeastern Pennsylvania across northern New Jersey and lower New York to the Hudson, was completed by private interests in

DID A "MARKET REVOLUTION" TRANSFORM EARLY NINETEENTH-CENTURY AMERICA?

In this 1847 painting by George Caleb Bingham, a steamboat in the distance has run aground. The men in the flatboat are considering, perhaps, whether to help lighten its load. Their faces brim with satisfaction. *They* are not soot-begrimed wage slaves who shovel coal into smoke-belching machines. *They* work when and where they wish, moved only by the pull of the current and the sweat of their muscles. And yet the viewer senses that their satisfaction will be fleeting. The steamboat will get going again. George Rogers Taylor (1951) proposed that the key factor in the transformation of the economy during the early nineteenth century was a "transportation revolution," the development of a system of canals, steamboats, and railroads. But in the 1990s other scholars suggested that the "transportation revolution" was merely a component of a larger and more powerful process: a "market revolution." The thesis was proposed by Charles Sellers (1991), Harry Watson (1990), and others. They argued that early in the nineteenth century some well-connected entrepreneurs used public funds to establish banks

and corporations and to construct the nation's transportation infrastructure. This transformed craftsmen into factory workers and subsistence farmers into petty capitalists. In the frenzy to make money, such people turned their backs on family and community. The "market revolution" thesis has provoked many debates, not the least of which is whether it was a good thing. Sellers was sure that its effects were harmful. "Capitalism commodifies and exploits all life," he declared. But the only judgment that matters was that of the people such as those depicted above. If the steamboat captain had offered them higher wages and steady work, would they have accepted?

George Rogers Taylor, *The Transportation Revolution* (1951), Charles Sellers, *The Market Revolution* (1991), Harry Watson, *Liberty and Power* (1990).

A view of New York's Broadway in 1835. The broad avenue was home to many of the large, modern stores that helped make New York City the commercial center of the nation.

1828. It managed to earn respectable dividends by barging coal to the eastern seaboard, but it made no attempt to compete with the Erie for the western trade. Pennsylvania, desperate to keep up with New York, engaged in an orgy of construction. In 1834 it completed a complicated system, part canal and part railroad, over the mountains to Pittsburgh. This Mainline Canal cost a staggering sum for that day. With its 177 locks and cumbersome "inclined-plane railroad" it was slow and expensive to operate and never competed effectively with the Erie. Efforts of Maryland to link Baltimore with the West by water failed utterly.

Beyond the mountains there was even greater zeal for canal construction in the 1820s and still more in the 1830s. Once the Erie opened the way across New York, farmers in the Ohio country demanded that links be built between the Ohio River and the Great Lakes so that they could ship their produce by water directly to the East. Local feeder canals seemed equally necessary; with corn worth 20 cents a bushel at Columbus selling for 50 cents at Marietta, on the Ohio, the value of cheap transportation became obvious to Ohio farmers.

Even before the completion of the Erie, Ohio had begun construction of the Ohio and Erie Canal running from the Ohio River to Cleveland. Another, from Toledo to Cincinnati, was begun in 1832. Meanwhile, Indiana had undertaken the 450-mile Wabash and Erie Canal. These canals were well conceived, but the western states overextended themselves building dozens of feeder lines, trying, it sometimes seemed, to supply all farmers west of the Appalachians with water connections from their barns to the New York docks. Politics made such programs almost inevitable, for in order to win support for their pet projects, legislators had to

Canals and Roads, 1820–1850

back the schemes of their fellows. The result was frequently financial disaster. There was not enough traffic to pay for all the waterways that were dug. By 1844, $60 million in state "improvement" bonds were in default. Nevertheless, the canals benefited both western farmers and the national economy.

The Marshall Court

The most important legal advantages bestowed on business in the period were the gift of Chief Justice John Marshall. Historians have tended to forget that Chief Justice John Marshall had six colleagues on the Supreme Court, and that is easy to understand. Marshall's particular combination of charm, logic, and forcefulness made the Court during his long reign, if not a rubber stamp, remarkably submissive to his view of the Constitution. Marshall's belief in a powerful central government explains his tendency to hand down decisions favorable to manufacturing and business interests. He also thought that "the business community was the agent of order and progress" and tended to interpret the Constitution in a way that would advance its interests.

Many important cases came before the Court between 1819 and 1824, and in each one Marshall's decision was applauded by most of the business community. The cases involved two major principles: the "sanctity" of contracts and the supremacy of federal legislation over the laws of the states. Marshall shared the conviction of the Revolutionary generation that property had to be protected against arbitrary seizure if liberty was to be preserved. Contracts between private individuals and between individuals and the government must be strictly enforced, he believed, or chaos would result. He therefore gave the widest possible application to the constitutional provision that no state could pass any law "impairing the Obligation of Contracts."

In *Dartmouth College* v. *Woodward* (1819), which involved an attempt by New Hampshire to alter the charter granted to Dartmouth by King George III in 1769, Marshall held that such a charter was a contract and might not be canceled or altered without the consent of both parties. The state had sought not to destroy the college but to change it from a private to a public institution, yet Marshall held that to do so would violate the contract clause.

Marshall's decisions concerning the division of power between the federal government and the states were even more important. The question of the constitutionality of a national bank, first debated by Hamilton and Jefferson, had not been submitted to the courts during the life of the first Bank of the United States. By the time of the second Bank there were many state banks, and some of them felt that their interests were threatened by the national institution. Responding to pressure from local banks, the Maryland legislature placed an annual tax of $15,000 on "foreign" banks, including the Bank of the United States! The Maryland branch of the Bank of the United States refused to pay, whereupon the state brought suit against its cashier, James W. McCulloch. *McCulloch* v. *Maryland* was crucial to the Bank, for five other states had levied taxes on its branches, and others would surely follow suit if the Maryland law were upheld.

Marshall extinguished the threat. The Bank of the United States was constitutional, he announced in phrases taken almost verbatim from Hamilton's 1791 memorandum to Washington on the subject; its legality was implied in many of the powers specifically granted to Congress. Full "discretion" must be allowed Congress in deciding exactly how its powers "are to be carried into execution." Since the Bank was legal, the Maryland tax was unconstitutional. Marshall found a "plain repugnance" in the thought of "conferring on one government a power to control the constitutional measures of another." He put this idea in the simplest possible language: "The power to tax involves the power to destroy . . . the power to destroy may defeat and render useless the power to create." The long-range significance of the decision lay in its strengthening of the implied powers of Congress and its con-

The artist Chester Harding painted John Marshall in 1828, during the Chief Justice's twenty-seventh year on the Supreme Court. "The unpretentious dignity [and] the sober factualism" of Harding's style (as art historian Oliver Larkin describes it) was well suited to Marshall's character.

firmation of the Hamiltonian or "loose" interpretation of the Constitution. By establishing the legality of the Bank, it also aided the growth of the economy.

In 1824 Marshall handed down an important decision involving the regulation of interstate commerce. This was the "steamboat case," *Gibbons* v. *Ogden*. In 1815 Aaron Ogden, former United States senator and governor of New Jersey, had purchased the right to operate a ferry between Elizabeth Point, New Jersey, and New York City from Robert Fulton's backer, Robert R. Livingston, who held a New York monopoly of steamboat navigation on the Hudson. When Thomas Gibbons, who held a federal coasting license, set up a competing line, Ogden sued him. Ogden argued in effect that Gibbons could operate his boat (whose captain was Cornelius Vanderbilt, later a famous railroad magnate) on the New Jersey side of the Hudson but had no right to cross into New York waters. After complicated litigation in the lower courts, the case reached the Supreme Court on appeal. Marshall decided in favor of Gibbons, effectively destroying the New York monopoly. A state can regulate commerce which begins and ends in its own territory but not when the transaction involves crossing a state line; then the national authority takes precedence. "The act of Congress," he said, "is supreme; and the law of the state . . . must yield to it."

This decision threw open the interstate steamboat business to all comers, and since an adequate 100-ton vessel could be built for as little as $7,000, dozens of small operators were soon engaged in it. Their competition tended to keep rates low and service efficient, to the great advantage of the country. More important in the long run was the fact that in order to include the ferry business within the federal government's power to regulate interstate commerce, Marshall had given the word the widest possible meaning. "Commerce, undoubtedly, is traffic, but it is something more,—it is intercourse." By construing the "commerce" clause so broadly, he made it easy for future generations of judges to extend its coverage to include the control of interstate electric power lines and even radio and television transmission.

Many of Marshall's decisions aided the economic development of the country in specific ways, but his chief contribution lay in his broadly national view of economic affairs. When he tried consciously to favor business by making contracts inviolable, his influence was important but limited—and, as it worked out, impermanent. In the steamboat case and in *McCulloch* v. *Maryland*, where he was really deciding between rival property interests, his work was more truly judicial in spirit and far more lasting. In such matters his nationalism enabled him to add form and substance to Hamilton's vision of the economic future of the United States.

Marshall and his colleagues firmly established the principle of judicial limitation on the power of legislatures and made the Supreme Court a vital part of the American system of government. In an age plagued by narrow sectional jealousies, Marshall's contribution was of immense influence and significance, and on it rests his claim to greatness.

John Marshall died in 1835. Two years later, in the *Charles River Bridge* case, the court handed down another decision that aided economic development. The state of Massachusetts had built a bridge across the Charles River between Boston and Cambridge that drew traffic from an older, privately owned toll bridge nearby. Since no tolls were collected from users of the state bridge after construction costs were recovered, owners of the older bridge sued for damages on the ground that the free bridge made the stock in their company worthless. They argued that in building the bridge, Massachusetts had violated the contract clause of the Constitution.

The Court, however, now speaking through the new Chief Justice, Roger B. Taney, decided otherwise. The state had a right to place "the comfort and convenience" of the whole community over that of a particular company, Taney declared. "Improvements" that add to public "wealth and property" take precedence. How John Marshall would have voted in this case, in which he would have had to choose between his Dartmouth College and steamboat case arguments, will never be known. But like most of the decisions of the Court that were made while Marshall was Chief Justice, the Charles River Bridge case advanced the interests of those who favored economic development. Whether they were pursuing political advantage or economic, the Americans of the early nineteenth century seemed committed to a policy of compromise and accommodation.

1790	Samuel Slater sets up first American factory
1793	Eli Whitney invents cotton gin
1794	Philadelphia–Lancaster turnpike is built
1807	Robert Fulton constructs *North River Steam Boat (Clermont)*
1808	Constitutional prohibition of importation of slaves goes into effect
1813	Boston Manufacturing Company opens in Waltham, Massachusetts
1816	Second Bank of the United States is created
1817	American Colonization Society is founded in order to establish republic of Liberia for freed slaves
1819	Chief Justice John Marshall asserts "sanctity" of contracts in *Dartmouth College* v. *Woodward*
	Chief Justice Marshall strengthens implied powers of Congress in *McCulloch* v. *Maryland* (Bank of United States)
1824	Chief Justice Marshall defends supremacy of federal government over states in *Gibbons* v. *Ogden* (steamboat case)
1825	Erie Canal is completed
1837	Chief Justice Roger B. Taney rules in favor of the whole community over a particular company in *Charles River Bridge* v. *Warren Bridge*

Jacksonian Democracy

PUNDITS COMPLAIN OF THE POLITICAL APATHY OF AMERICANS, AND of young people in particular. The critics point to the fact that even in the hotly contested 2004 presidential campaign, only 58 percent of the eligible voting-age population went to the polls.

Such criticisms assume that it was different in the days of the Founding Fathers. But this is not true. During the early 1800s, a much lower proportion of eligible voters went to the polls. In the 1824 presidential election, for example, only 27 percent of the eligible voters cast ballots, a total of 350,000; the vote was divided among four candidates.

But this apathy evaporated during the heated campaign leading to the 1828 presidential election. Andrew Jackson transformed his supporters—called Jacksonians— into the Democratic party, built a rudimentary bureaucracy to manage its affairs, and appealed directly—and effectively—to voters. That year, a total of 1.1 million votes were cast, 58 percent of the eligible voters.

Jackson won in a landslide. During the next few decades, his opponents had little choice but to emulate his strategy and build a rival party. The American political system emerged in consequence. Its central features included a consistent turnout of over half the electorate, at least during presidential elections, and a two-party culture that inhibited formation of additional parties.

Almost from the start, however, Jackson's more inclusive politics encountered new challenges and obstacles. Victorious campaign workers clamored for government jobs. Energized voters, seeking cheap land, ignored the plight of the Indians, not to mention legal rights secured by treaties. As more people voted, too, politicians were obliged to "represent" a vast electorate, which made it difficult to broker deals. Sectional tensions intensified; campaigns acquired a new stridency occasionally tinged with demagoguery. The new politics of democratic engagement were not without costs; within several decades, these would include civil war.

"Democratizing" Politics

At 11 A.M. on March 4, 1829, a bright sunny day, Andrew Jackson, hatless and dressed severely in black, left his quarters at Gadsby's Hotel. Accompanied by a few close associates, he walked up Pennsylvania Avenue to the Capitol. At a few minutes after noon he emerged on the East Portico with the justices of the Supreme Court and other dignitaries. Before a throng of more than 15,000 people he delivered an almost inaudible and thoroughly commonplace inaugural address and then took the presidential oath. The first man to congratulate him was Chief Justice Marshall, who had administered the oath. The second was "Honest George" Kremer, a Pennsylvania congressman best known for the leopardskin coat that he affected, who led the cheering crowd that brushed past the barricade and scrambled up the Capitol steps to wring the new president's hand.

Jackson shouldered his way through the crush, mounted a splendid white horse, and rode off to the White House. A reception had been announced, to which "the officially and socially eligible as defined by precedent" had been invited. The day was unseasonably warm after a hard winter, and the streets of Washington were muddy. As Jackson rode down Pennsylvania Avenue, the crowds that had turned out to see the Hero of New Orleans followed-on horseback, in rickety wagons, and on foot. Nothing could keep them out of the executive mansion, and the result was chaos. Long tables laden with cakes, ice cream, and orange punch had been set up in the East Room, but these scarcely deflected the well-wishers. Jackson was pressed back helplessly as men tracked mud across valuable rugs and clambered up on delicate chairs to catch a glimpse of him. The White House shook with their shouts. Glassware splintered, furniture was overturned, women fainted.

Jackson was a thin old man despite his toughness, and soon he was in danger. Fortunately, friends formed a cordon and managed to extricate him through a rear door. The new president spent his first night in office at Gadsby's hotel.

Only a generation earlier Jefferson had felt obliged to introduce pell-mell to encourage informality in the White House (see p. 199). Now a man whom John Quincy Adams called "a barbarian" held Jefferson's office, and, as one Supreme Court justice complained, "The reign of King 'Mob' seemed triumphant."

Jackson's inauguration, and especially this celebration in the White House, symbolized the triumph of "democracy," the achievement of place and station by "the common man." Having been taught by Jefferson that all men are created equal, the Americans of Jackson's day (conveniently ignoring males with black skins, to say nothing of women, regardless of color) found it easy to believe that every person was as competent and as politically important as his neighbor.

The difference between Jacksonian democracy and the Jefferson variety was more one of attitude than of practice. Jefferson had believed that ordinary citizens could be educated to determine what was right. Jackson insisted that they knew what was right by instinct. Jefferson's pell-mell encouraged the average citizen to hold up his head; by the time of Jackson, the "common man" gloried in ordinariness and made mediocrity a virtue. The slightest hint of distinctiveness or servility became suspect. That President Washington required his footmen to wear uniforms was taken as a matter of course in the 1790s, but the British minister in Jackson's day found it next to impossible to find Americans willing to don his splendid livery. While most middle-class families could still hire people to do their cooking and housework, the word *servant* itself fell out of fashion, replaced by the egalitarian *help*.

Even the presidency, designed to be removed from direct public control by the Electoral College, felt the impact of the new thinking. By Jackson's time only two states, Delaware and South Carolina, still provided for the choice of presidential electors by the legislature; in all others they were selected by popular vote. The system of permitting the congressional caucus to name the candidates for the presidency came to an end before 1828. Jackson and Adams were put forward by state legislatures, and soon thereafter the still more democratic system of nomination by national party conventions was adopted. Officeholders began to stress the fact that they were *representatives* as well as leaders and to appeal more openly and much more intensively for votes. The public responded. At each succeeding presidential election, more people went to the polls. Eight times as many people voted in 1840 as in 1824.

As voting became more important, so did competition among candidates, and this led to changes in the role and structure of political parties. Running campaigns and getting out the vote required money, people, and organized effort. Party managers, often holders of relatively minor offices, held rallies, staged parades, dreamed up catchy slogans, and printed broadsides, party newspapers, and ballots containing the names of the party's nominees for distribution to their supporters. Parties became powerful institutions that instilled loyalty among adherents.

1828: The New Party System in Embryo

The new system could scarcely have been imagined in 1825 while John Quincy Adams ruled over the White House; Adams was not well equipped either to lead King Mob or to hold it in check. Indeed, it was the battle to succeed Adams that caused the system to develop. The campaign began almost on the day of his selection by the House of Representatives. Jackson felt that he, the man who had received the largest number of votes, had been cheated of the presidency in 1824 by "the corrupt bargain" that he believed Adams had made with Henry Clay, and he sought vindication.

Relying heavily on his military reputation and on Adams's talent for making enemies, Jackson avoided taking a stand on issues and on questions where his

Rachel Jackson, wife of Andrew Jackson. At 17 she had married Lewis Robards, but theirs was a tempestuous marriage. After two years she returned to her family in Natchez, Mississippi. Robards sued for divorce in Virginia on grounds of desertion. Several months later she married Jackson in Mississippi. But, unbeknownst to Jackson, Robards would not finalize the divorce until a year after Rachel's marriage to Jackson. In defending Rachel's honor from a charge of bigamy, Jackson killed a man in a duel. During the 1824 and 1828 presidential campaigns, critics denounced their marriage as immoral. Rachel died in December 1828, weeks before her husband was inaugurated.

views might displease one or another faction. The political situation thus became chaotic, one side unable to marshal support for its policies, the other unwilling to adopt policies for fear of losing support.

The campaign was disgraced by character assassination and lies of the worst sort. Administration supporters denounced Jackson as a bloodthirsty military tyrant, a drunkard, and a gambler. His wife Rachel, ailing and shy, was dragged into the campaign by an Adams pamphleteer who branded her a "convicted adultress." (See picture above.)

Furious, the Jacksonians (now calling themselves Democrats) replied in kind. They charged that while serving as American minister to Russia, Adams had supplied a beautiful American virgin for the delectation of the czar. Discovering that Adams had purchased a chess set and a billiard table for the White House, they accused him of squandering public money on gambling devices. They translated his long and distinguished public service into the statistic that he had received over the years a sum equal to $16 for every day of his life in government pay. The great questions of the day were largely ignored.

All this was inexcusable, and both sides must share the blame. But as the politicians noticed when the votes were counted, their efforts had certainly brought out the electorate. *Each* candidate received far more votes than all four candidates had received in the preceding presidential election.

When inauguration day arrived, Adams refused to attend the ceremonies because Jackson had failed to pay the traditional pre-inaugural courtesy call on him at the White House, but the Old Puritan may have been equally, if unconsciously, motivated by shame at tactics he had countenanced during the campaign. Jackson felt vindication, not shame, but in any case, deep personal feelings were uppermost in everyone's mind at the formal changing of the guard. The real issues, however, remained. Andrew Jackson would now have to deal with them.

The Jacksonian Appeal

Although Jackson's supporters liked to cast him as the political heir of Jefferson, he was in many ways like the conservative Washington: a soldier first, an inveterate speculator in western lands, the owner of a fine plantation and of many slaves, a man with few intellectual interests and only sketchily educated.

Nor was Jackson quite the rough-hewn frontier character he sometimes seemed. True, he could not spell (again, like Washington), he possessed the unsavory habits of the tobacco chewer, and he had a violent temper. But his manners and lifestyle were those of a southern planter. Jackson's judgment was intuitive yet usually sound; his frequent rages were often feigned, designed to accomplish some carefully thought-out purpose.

Whatever his personal convictions, Jackson stood as the symbol for a new, democratically oriented generation. That he was both a great hero and in many ways a most extraordinary person helps explain his mass appeal. He had defeated a mighty British army and killed hosts of Indians, but he acted on hunches and not always consistently, shouted and pounded his fist when angry, put loyalty to old comrades above efficiency when making appointments, distrusted "aristocrats" and all special privilege. Perhaps he was rich, perhaps conservative, but he was a man of the people, born in a frontier cabin, familiar with the problems of the average citizen.

Jackson epitomized many American ideals. He was intensely patriotic, generous to a fault, natural and democratic in manner (at home alike in the forest and in the ballroom of a fine mansion). He admired good horseflesh and beautiful women, yet no sterner moralist ever lived; he was a fighter, a relentless foe, but a gentleman in the best American sense. That some special providence watched over him (as over the United States) appeared beyond argument to those who had followed his career. He seemed, in short, both an average and an ideal American, one the people could identify with and still revere.

For these reasons Jackson drew support from every section and every social class: western farmers and southern planters, urban workers and bankers and merchants. In this sense he was profoundly democratic—and in the sense, too, that whatever his position on public issues, he believed in equality of opportunity, distrusted entrenched status of every sort, and rejected no free American because of humble origins or inadequate education.

The Spoils System

Jackson took office with the firm intention of punishing the "vile wretches" who had attacked him so viciously during the campaign. (Rachel Jackson died shortly after the election, and her devoted husband was convinced that the indignities heaped on her by Adams partisans had hastened her decline.) The new concept of political office as a reward for victory seemed to justify a housecleaning in Washington.

Eager for the "spoils," an army of politicians invaded Washington. There was nothing especially innovative about this invasion, for the principle of filling offices with one's partisans was almost as old as the republic. However, the long lapse of time since the last real political shift, and the recent untypical example of John Quincy Adams, who rarely removed or appointed anyone for political reasons, made Jackson's policy appear revolutionary. His removals were not entirely unjustified, for many government workers had grown senile and others corrupt. A number of officials were found to be short in their accounts; a few were hopeless drunks. Jackson was determined to root out the thieves. Even Adams admitted that some of those Jackson dismissed deserved their fate.

Aside from going along with the spoils system and eliminating crooks and incompetents, Jackson advanced another reason for turning experienced government employees out of their jobs: the principle of rotation. "No man has any more intrinsic right to official station than another," he said. Those who hold government jobs for a long time "are apt to acquire a habit of looking with indifference upon the public interests and of tolerating conduct from which an unpracticed man would revolt." By "rotating" jobholders periodically, more citizens could participate in the tasks of government, and the danger of creating an entrenched bureaucracy would be eliminated. The problem was that the constant replacing of trained workers by novices was not likely to increase the efficiency of the government. Jackson's response to this argument was typical: "The duties of all public officers are . . . so plain and simple that men of intelligence may readily qualify themselves for their performance."

Contempt for expert knowledge and the belief that ordinary Americans can do anything they set their minds to became fundamental tenets of Jacksonian democracy. To apply them to present-day government would be to court disaster, but in the early nineteenth century it was not so preposterous, because the role that government played in American life was simple and nontechnical.

Spoilsmen roamed the capital in force during the spring of 1829, seeking, as the forthright Jackson said, "a tit to suck the treasury pap." Their philosophy was well summarized by a New Yorker: "No d——d rascal who made use of his office . . . for the purpose of keeping Mr. Adams in, and Genl. Jackson out of power is entitled to the least lenity or mercy. . . . Whether or not I shall get anything in the general scramble for plunder, remains to be proven, but I rather guess I shall."

President of All the People

More than any earlier president, Jackson conceived of himself as the direct representative of all the people and therefore the embodiment of national power. From Washington to John Quincy Adams, his predecessors together had vetoed only

This painting of Jackson is by Ralph E. W. Earl (1833), whose father, a soldier, had been assigned to do accurate paintings of the battles of Lexington and Concord. The son married a niece of Andrew Jackson and completed this imposing portrait.

nine bills, all on the ground that they believed the measures unconstitutional. Jackson vetoed a dozen, some simply because he thought the legislation inexpedient. Yet he had no ambition to expand the scope of federal authority at the expense of the states. Basically he was a Jeffersonian; he favored a "frugal," constitutionally limited national government. Furthermore, he was a poor administrator, given to penny-pinching and lacking in imagination. His strong prejudices and his contempt for expert advice, even in fields such as banking where his ignorance was almost total, did him no credit and the country considerable harm.

Jackson's great success (not merely his popularity) was primarily the result of his personality. A shrewd French observer, Michel Chevalier, after commenting on "his chivalric character, his lofty integrity, and his ardent patriotism," pointed out what was probably the central element in Jackson's appeal. "His tactic in politics, as well as in war," Chevalier wrote in 1824, "is to throw himself forward with the cry of *Comrades, follow me!*" Sometimes he might be wrong, but always he was a leader.

Jackson: "The Bank . . . I Will Kill It!"

In the fall of 1832 Jackson was reelected president, handily defeating Henry Clay. The main issue in this election, aside from Jackson's personal popularity, was the president's determination to destroy the second Bank of the United States. In this "Bank war," Jackson won a complete victory, yet the effects of his triumph were anything but beneficial to the country.

After *McCulloch* v. *Maryland* had presumably established its legality and the conservative Langdon Cheves had gotten it on a sound footing, the Bank of the

United States had flourished. In 1823 Cheves was replaced as president by Nicholas Biddle, who managed it brilliantly. A talented Philadelphian, only 37 when he took over the Bank, Biddle was experienced in literature, the law, and diplomacy as well as in finance. Almost alone in the United States, Biddle realized that his institution could act as a rudimentary central bank, regulating the availability of credit throughout the nation by controlling the lending policies of the state banks. Small banks, possessing limited amounts of gold and silver, sometimes overextended themselves in making large amounts of bank notes available to borrowers in order to earn interest. All this paper money was legally convertible into hard cash on demand, but in the ordinary run of business people seldom bothered to convert their notes so long as they thought the issuing bank was sound.

Bank notes passed freely from hand to hand and from bank to bank in every section of the country. Eventually much of the paper money of the local banks came across the counter of one or another of the twenty-two branches of the Bank of the United States. By collecting these notes and presenting them for conversion into coin, Biddle could compel the local banks to maintain adequate reserves of gold and silver—in other words, make them hold their lending policies within bounds. "The Bank of the United States," he explained, "has succeeded in keeping in check many institutions which might otherwise have been tempted into extravagant and ruinous excesses."

Biddle's policies in the 1820s were good for the Bank of the United States, which earned substantial profits, for the state banks, and probably for the country. Pressures on local bankers to make loans were enormous. The nation had an insatiable need for capital, and the general mood of the people was optimistic. Everyone wanted to borrow, and everyone expected values to rise, as in general they did. But by making liberal loans to produce merchants, for example, rural bankers indirectly stimulated farmers to expand their output beyond current demand, which eventually led to a decline in prices and an agricultural depression. In every field of economic activity, reckless lending caused inflation and greatly exaggerated the ups and downs of the business cycle. It can be argued, however, that by restricting the lending of state banks, Biddle was slowing the rate of economic growth and that in a predominantly agricultural society an occasional slump was not a large price to pay for rapid economic development.

Biddle's policies acted to stabilize the economy, and many interests, including a substantial percentage of state bankers, supported them. They also provoked a great deal of opposition. In part the opposition originated in pure ignorance: Distrust of paper money did not disappear, and people who disliked all paper saw the Bank as merely the largest (and thus the worst) of many bad institutions. At the other extreme, some bankers chafed under Biddle's restraints because by discouraging them from lending freely, he was limiting their profits. Few financiers realized what Biddle was trying to accomplish. What was "sound" banking practice? Honest people disagreed, and many turned against the ideas of Nicholas Biddle.

Jackson's Bank Veto

Opposition to the Bank was diffuse and unorganized until Andrew Jackson brought it together. When he did, the Bank was quickly destroyed. Jackson can be included among the ignorant enemies of the institution, a hard-money man suspicious of all commercial banking. "I think it right to be perfectly frank with you," he told Biddle in 1829. "I do not dislike your Bank any more than all banks. But ever since I read the history of the South Sea Bubble I have been afraid of banks."

Jackson's attitude dismayed Biddle. It also mystified him, since the Bank was the country's best defense against a speculative mania like the eighteenth-century South Sea Bubble, in which hundreds of naive British investors had been fleeced. Almost against his will, Biddle found himself gravitating toward Clay and the new National Republican party, offering advantageous loans and retainers to politicians and newspaper editors in order to build up a following. Thereafter, events moved inevitably toward a showdown, for the president's combative instincts were easily aroused. "The Bank," he told Van Buren, "is trying to kill me, *but I will kill it!*"

Henry Clay, Daniel Webster, and other prominent National Republicans hoped to use the Bank controversy against Jackson. They reasoned that the institution was so important to the country that Jackson's opposition to it would undermine his popularity. They therefore urged Biddle to ask Congress to renew the Bank's charter. The charter would not expire until 1836, but by pressing the issue before the 1832 presidential election, they could force Jackson either to approve the recharter bill or to veto it (which would give candidate Clay a lively issue in the campaign). The banker yielded to this strategy and a recharter bill passed Congress early in July 1832. Jackson promptly vetoed it.

Jackson's message explaining why he had rejected the bill was immensely popular, but it adds nothing to his reputation as a statesman. Being a good Jeffersonian—and no friend of John Marshall—he insisted that the Bank was unconstitutional. (*McCulloch* v. *Maryland* he brushed aside, saying that as president he had sworn to uphold the Constitution as *he* understood it.) The Bank was inexpedient, he argued. A dangerous private monopoly that allowed a handful of rich men to accumulate "many millions" of dollars, the Bank was making "the rich richer and the potent more powerful." Furthermore, many of its stockholders were foreigners: "If we must have a bank . . . it should be *purely American*.".[1]

Biddle considered Jackson's veto "a manifesto of anarchy," its tone like "the fury of a chained panther biting the bars of his cage." A large majority of the voters, however, approved of Jackson's hard-hitting attack.

Buttressed by his election triumph, Jackson acted swiftly. "Until I can strangle this hydra of corruption, the Bank, I will not shrink from my duty," he said. Shortly after the start of his second term, he decided to withdraw the government funds deposited in its vaults. Under the law only the secretary of the treasury could re-

---

[1]*The country needed all the foreign capital it could attract. Foreigners owned only $8 million of the $35 million stock, and in any case they could not vote their shares.*

move the deposits. When Secretary Louis McLane refused to do so, believing that the alternative depositories, the state banks, were less safe, Jackson promptly "promoted" him to secretary of state and appointed William J. Duane, a Pennsylvania lawyer, to the treasury post. Foolishly, he failed to ask Duane his views on the issue before appointing him. Too late he discovered that the new secretary agreed with McLane! It would not be "prudent" to entrust the government's money to "local and irresponsible" banks, Duane said.

Believing that Cabinet officers should obey the president as automatically as a colonel obeys a general, Jackson dismissed Duane, replacing him with Attorney General Roger B. Taney, who had been advising the president closely on Bank affairs. Taney carried out the order by depositing new federal receipts in seven state banks in eastern cities while continuing to meet government expenses with drafts on the Bank of the United States.

The situation was confused and slightly unethical. Set on winning the Bank war, Jackson lost sight of his fear of unsound paper money. Taney, however, knew exactly what he was doing. One of the state banks receiving federal funds was the Union Bank of Baltimore. Taney owned stock in this institution, and its president was his close friend. Little wonder that Jackson's enemies were soon calling the favored state banks "pet" banks. This charge was not entirely fair because Taney took pains to see that the deposits were placed in financially sound institutions.

"King Andrew the First," standing atop the U.S. Constitution—a scepter in one hand, and a veto in another. Compare this drawing to the one of Queen Elizabeth on page 30.

BORN TO COMMAND.

OF VETO MEMORY.

HAD I BEEN CONSULTED.

KING ANDREW THE FIRST.

Furthermore, by 1836 the government's funds had been spread out reasonably equitably in about ninety banks. But neither was the charge entirely unfair; the administration certainly favored institutions whose directors were politically sympathetic to it.

When Taney began to remove the deposits, the government had $9,868,000 to its credit in the Bank of the United States; within three months the figure fell to about $4 million. Faced with the withdrawal of so much cash, Biddle had to contract his operations. He decided to exaggerate the contraction, pressing the state banks hard by presenting all their notes and checks that came across his counter for conversion into specie and drastically limiting his own bank's business loans. He hoped that the resulting shortage of credit would be blamed on Jackson and that it would force the president to return the deposits. "Nothing but the evidence of suffering . . . will produce any effect," he reasoned.

For a time the strategy appeared to be working. Paper money became scarce, specie almost unobtainable. A serious panic threatened. New York banks were soon refusing to make any loans at all. "Nobody buys; nobody can sell," a French visitor to the city observed. Memorials and petitions poured in on Congress. Worried and indignant delegations of businessmen began trooping to Washington seeking "relief." Clay, Webster, and John C. Calhoun thundered against Jackson in the Senate.

The president would not budge. "I am fixed in my course as firm as the Rockey Mountain," he wrote Vice President Van Buren. No "frail mortals" who worshiped "the golden calf" could change his mind. To others he swore he would sooner cut off his right arm and "undergo the torture of ten Spanish inquisitions" than restore the deposits. When delegations came to him, he roared: "Go to Nicholas Biddle. . . . Biddle has all the money!" And in the end—because he was right—business leaders began to take the old general's advice. Pressure on Biddle mounted swiftly, and in July 1834 he suddenly reversed his policy and began to lend money freely. The artificial crisis ended.

Jackson Versus Calhoun

Although southern-born, Jackson had devoted too much of his life to fighting for the entire United States to countenance disunion. Therefore, in April 1830, when the states' rights faction invited him to a dinner to celebrate the anniversary of Jefferson's birth, he came prepared. The evening reverberated with speeches and toasts of a states' rights tenor, but when the president was called on to volunteer a toast, he raised his glass, fixed his eyes on John C. Calhoun, and said: "Our *Federal* Union: It must be preserved!" Calhoun took up the challenge at once. "The Union," he retorted, "next to our liberty, most dear!"

It is difficult to measure the importance of the animosity between Jackson and Calhoun in the crisis to which this clash was a prelude. Calhoun wanted very much to be president. He had failed to inherit the office from John Quincy Adams and had accepted the vice presidency again under Jackson in the hope of succeeding him at the end of one term, if not sooner, for Jackson's health was known to be frail. Yet Old Hickory showed no sign of passing on or retiring. Jackson also seemed to place special confidence in the shrewd Van Buren, who, as secretary of state, also had claim to the succession.

A silly social fracas in which Calhoun's wife appeared to take the lead in the systematic snubbing of Peggy Eaton, wife of the secretary of war, had estranged Jackson and Calhoun. (Peggy was supposed to have had an affair with Eaton while she was still married to another man, and Jackson, undoubtedly sympathetic because of the attacks he and Rachel had endured, stoutly defended her good name.) Then, shortly after the Jefferson Day dinner, Jackson discovered that in 1818, when he had invaded Florida, Calhoun, then secretary of war, had recommended to President Monroe that Jackson be summoned before a court of inquiry and charged with disobeying orders. Since Calhoun had repeatedly led Jackson to believe that he had supported him at the time, the revelation convinced the president that Calhoun was not a man of honor.

The personal difficulties are worth stressing because Jackson and Calhoun were not far apart ideologically except on the ultimate issue of the right of a state to overrule federal authority. Jackson was a strong president, but he did not believe that the area of national power was large or that it should be expanded. His interests in government economy, in the distribution of federal surpluses to the states, and in interpreting the powers of Congress narrowly were all similar to Calhoun's. Like most Westerners, he favored internal improvements, but he preferred that local projects be left to the states. In 1830 he vetoed a bill providing aid for the construction of the Maysville Road because the route was wholly within Kentucky. There were political reasons for this veto, which was a slap at Kentucky's hero, Henry Clay, but it could not fail to please Calhoun.

Indian Removals

The president also took a states' rights position in the controversy that arose between the Cherokee Indians and Georgia. Jackson subscribed to the theory, advanced by Jefferson, that Indians were "savage" because they roamed wild in a trackless wilderness. The "original inhabitants of our forests" were "incapable of self-government," Jackson claimed, ignoring the fact that the Cherokee lived settled lives and had governed themselves without trouble before the whites arrived.

The Cherokee inhabited a region coveted by whites because it was suitable for growing cotton. Since most Indians preferred to maintain their tribal ways, Jackson pursued a policy of removing them from the path of white settlement. This policy seems heartless to modern critics, but since few Indians were willing to adopt the white way of life, most contemporary whites considered removal the only humane solution if the nation was to continue to expand. Jackson insisted that the Indians receive fair prices for their lands and that the government bear the expense of resettling them. He believed that moving them beyond the Mississippi River would

Indian Removals

protect them from the "degradation and destruction to which they were rapidly hastening . . . in the States."

Many tribes resigned themselves to removal without argument. Between 1831 and 1833, some 15,000 Choctaw migrated from their lands in Mississippi to the region west of the Arkansas Territory.

In *Democracy in America*, the Frenchman Alexis de Tocqueville described "the frightful sufferings that attend these forced migrations," and he added sadly that the migrants "have no longer a country, and soon will not be a people." He vividly described a group of Choctaw crossing the Mississippi River at Memphis in the dead of winter:

> *The cold was unusually severe; the snow had frozen hard upon the ground, and the river was drifting huge masses of ice. The Indians had their families with them, and they brought in their train the wounded and the sick, with children newly born and old men upon the verge of death. They possessed neither tents nor wagons, but only*

their arms and some provisions. I saw them embark to pass the mighty river, and never will that solemn spectacle fade from my remembrance. No cry, no sob, was heard among the assembled crowd; all were silent.

Tocqueville was particularly moved by the sight of an old woman whom he described in a letter to his mother. She was "naked save for a covering which left visible, at a thousand places, the most emaciated figure imaginable. . . . To leave one's country at that age to seek one's fortune in a foreign land, what misery!"

A few tribes, such as Black Hawk's Sauk and Fox in Illinois and Osceola's Seminole in Florida, resisted removal and were subdued by troops. One Indian nation, the Cherokee, sought to hold on to their lands by adjusting to white ways. They took up farming and cattle raising, developed a written language, drafted a constitution, and tried to establish a state within a state in northwestern Georgia. Several treaties with the United States seemed to establish the legality of their government. But Georgia would not recognize the Cherokee Nation. It passed a law in 1828 declaring all Cherokee laws void and the region part of Georgia.

The Indians challenged this law in the Supreme Court. When a Cherokee named Corn Tassel, convicted in a Georgia court of the murder of another Indian, appealed on the ground that the crime had taken place in Cherokee territory, Chief Justice John Marshall agreed and declared the Georgia action unconstitutional.

Jackson backed Georgia's position. No independent nation could exist within the United States, he insisted. Georgia thereupon hanged Corn Tassel. In 1838, after Jackson had left the White House, the United States forced 15,000 Cherokee to leave Georgia for Oklahoma. At least 4,000 of them died on the way; the route has been aptly named the Trail of Tears.

Jackson's willingness to allow Georgia to ignore decisions of the U.S. Supreme Court persuaded extreme southern states' righters that he would not oppose the doctrine of nullification should it be formally applied to a law of Congress. They deceived themselves egregiously. Jackson did not challenge Georgia because he approved of the state's position. He spoke of "the poor deluded . . . Cherokees" and called William Wirt, the distinguished lawyer who defended their cause, a "truly wicked" man. Jackson was not one to worry about being inconsistent. When South Carolina revived the talk of nullification in 1832, he acted in quite a different manner.

The Nullification Crisis

The proposed alliance of South and West to reduce the tariff and the price of land had not materialized, partly because Webster had discredited the South in the eyes of western patriots and partly because the planters of South Carolina and Georgia, fearing the competition of fertile new cotton lands in Alabama and Mississippi, opposed the rapid exploitation of the West almost as vociferously as northern manufacturers did. When a new tariff law was passed in 1832, it lowered duties much less than the Southerners desired. At once talk of nullifying it began to be heard in South Carolina.

In addition to the economic woes of the up-country cotton planters, the great planter-aristocrats of the rice-growing Tidewater, though relatively prosperous, were troubled by northern criticisms of slavery. In the rice region, blacks outnumbered whites two to one; it was the densest concentration of blacks in the United States. Thousands of these slaves were African-born, brought in during the burst of importations before Congress outlawed the trade in 1808. Controlled usually by overseers of the worst sort, the slaves seemed to their masters like savage beasts straining to rise up against their oppressors. In 1822 the exposure in Charleston of a planned revolt organized by Denmark Vesey, who had bought his freedom with money won in a lottery, had alarmed many whites. News of a far more serious uprising in Virginia led by the slave Nat Turner in 1831, just as the tariff controversy was coming to a head, added to popular concern. Radical South Carolinians saw protective tariffs and agitation against slavery as the two sides of one coin; against both aspects of what appeared to them the tyranny of the majority, nullification seemed the logical defense. Yield on the tariff, editor Henry L. Pinckney of the influential *Charleston Mercury* warned, and "abolition will become the order of the day."

President Jackson brushed aside Calhoun's mental gymnastics; intuitively he realized the central reality: If a state could nullify a law of Congress, the Union could not exist. "Tell . . . the Nullifiers from me that they can talk and write resolutions and print threats to their hearts' content," he warned a South Carolina representative when Congress adjourned in July 1832. "But if one drop of blood be shed there in defiance of the laws of the United States, I will hang the first man of them I can get my hands on to the first tree I can find."

The warning was not taken seriously in South Carolina. In October the state legislature provided for the election of a special convention, which, when it met, contained a solid majority of nullifiers. On November 24, 1832, the convention passed an ordinance of nullification prohibiting the collection of tariff duties in the state after February 1, 1833. The legislature then authorized the raising of an army and appropriated money to supply it with weapons.

Jackson quickly began military preparations of his own, telling friends that he would have 50,000 men ready to move in a little over a month. He also made a statesmanlike effort to end the crisis peaceably. First he suggested to Congress that it lower the tariff further. On December 10 he delivered a "Proclamation to the People of South Carolina." Nullification could only lead to the destruction of the Union, he said. "The laws of the United States must be executed. I have no discretionary power on the subject. . . . Those who told you that you might peaceably prevent their execution deceived you." Old Hickory added sternly: "Disunion by armed force is *treason*. Are you really ready to incur its guilt?" Jackson's reasoning profoundly shocked even opponents of nullification. If South Carolina did not back down, the president's threat to use force would mean civil war and possibly the destruction of the Union he claimed to be defending.

Calhoun sought desperately to control the crisis. By prearrangement with Senator Hayne, he resigned as vice president and was appointed to replace Hayne in the Senate, where he led the search for a peaceful solution. Having been de-

A South Carolina belle sewing—albeit languorously—a palmetto (a stylized palm leaf) onto a "nullification hat."

feated in his campaign for the presidency, Clay was a willing ally. In addition, many who admired Jackson nonetheless, as Van Buren later wrote, "distrusted his prudence," fearing that he would "commit some rash act." They believed in dealing with the controversy by discussion and compromise.

As a result, administration leaders introduced both a new tariff bill and a Force Bill granting the president additional authority to execute the revenue laws. Jackson was perfectly willing to see the tariff reduced but insisted that he was determined to enforce the law. As the February 1 deadline approached, he claimed that he could raise 200,000 men if needed to suppress resistance. "Union men, fear not," he said. "*The Union will be preserved.*"

Jackson's determination sobered the South Carolina radicals. Their appeal for the support of other southern states fell on deaf ears: All rejected the idea of nullification. The unionist minority in South Carolina added to the radicals' difficulties by threatening civil war if federal authority were defied. Calhoun, though a brave man, was alarmed for his own safety, for Jackson had threatened to "hang him as high as Haman" if nullification were attempted. Observers described him as "excessively uneasy." He was suddenly eager to avoid a showdown.

Ten days before the deadline, South Carolina postponed nullification pending the outcome of the tariff debate. Then, in March 1833, Calhoun and Clay pushed a compromise tariff through Congress. As part of the agreement Congress also passed the Force Bill, mostly as a face-saving device for the president.

And so the Union weathered the storm. Having stepped to the brink of civil war, the nation had drawn hastily back. The South Carolina legislature professed to be satisfied with the new tariff (in fact it made few immediate reductions, providing for a gradual lowering of rates over a ten-year period) and repealed the Nullification Ordinance, saving face by nullifying the Force Act, which was now a dead letter. But the radical South Carolina planters were becoming convinced that only secession would protect slavery. The nullification fiasco had proved that they could not succeed without the support of other slave states. Thereafter they devoted themselves ceaselessly to obtaining it.

Boom and Bust

During 1833 and 1834 Secretary of the Treasury Taney insisted that the pet banks maintain large reserves. But other state banks began to offer credit on easy terms, aided by a large increase in their reserves of gold and silver resulting from causes unconnected with the policies of either the government or Biddle's Bank. A decline in the Chinese demand for Mexican silver led to increased exports of the metal to the United States, and the rise of American interest rates attracted English capital into the country. Heavy English purchases of American cotton at high prices also increased the flow of specie into American banks. These developments caused bank notes in circulation to jump from $82 million in January 1835 to $120 million in December 1836. Bank deposits rose even more rapidly.

Much of the new money flowed into speculation in land; a mania to invest in property swept the country. The increased volume of currency caused prices to soar 15 percent in six months, buoying investors' spirits and making them ever more optimistic about the future. By the summer of 1835 one observer estimated that in New York City, which had about 250,000 residents, enough house lots had been laid out and sold to support a population of 2 million. Chicago at this time had only 2,000 to 3,000 inhabitants, yet most of the land for 25 miles around had been sold and resold in small lots by speculators anticipating the growth of the area. Throughout the West farmers borrowed money from local banks by mortgaging their land, used the money to buy more land from the government, and then borrowed still more money from the banks on the strength of their new deeds.

So long as prices rose, the process could be repeated endlessly. In 1832, while the Bank of the United States still regulated the money supply, federal income from the sale of land was $2.6 million. In 1834 it was $4.9 million; in 1835, $14.8 million. In 1836 it rose to $24.9 million, and the government found itself totally free of debt and with a surplus of $20 million!

Finally Jackson became alarmed by the speculative mania. In the summer of 1836 he issued the Specie Circular, which provided that purchasers must henceforth pay for public land in gold or silver. At once the rush to buy land came to a halt. As demand slackened, prices sagged. Speculators, unable to dispose of lands mortgaged to the banks, had to abandon them to the banks, but the banks could not realize enough on the foreclosed property to recover their loans. Suddenly the public mood changed. Commodity prices tumbled 30 percent between February and May.

Hordes of depositors sought to withdraw their money in the form of specie, and soon the banks exhausted their supplies. Panic swept the country in the spring of 1837 as every bank in the nation was forced to suspend specie payments. The boom was over.

Major swings in the business cycle can never be attributed to the actions of a single person, however powerful, but there is no doubt that Jackson's war against the Bank exaggerated the swings of the economic pendulum, not so much by its direct effects as by the impact of the president's ill-considered policies on popular thinking. His Specie Circular did not prevent speculators from buying land—at most it caused purchasers to pay a premium for gold or silver. But it convinced potential buyers that the boom was going to end and led them to make decisions that in fact ended it. Old Hickory's combination of impetuousness, combativeness, arrogance, and ignorance rendered the nation he loved so dearly a serious disservice.

The Jacksonians

Jackson's personality had a large impact on the shape and tone of American politics and thus with the development of the second party system. When he came to office, nearly everyone professed to be a follower of Jefferson. By 1836 being a Jeffersonian no longer meant much; what mattered was how one felt about Andrew Jackson. He had ridden to power at the head of a diverse political army, but he left behind him an organization with a fairly cohesive, if not necessarily consistent, body of ideas. This Democratic party contained rich citizens and poor, Easterners and Westerners, abolitionists as well as slaveholders. It was not yet a close-knit national organization, but—always allowing for individual exceptions—the Jacksonians agreed on certain underlying principles. These included suspicion of special privilege and large business corporations, both typified by the Bank of the United States; freedom of economic opportunity, unfettered by private or governmental restrictions; absolute political freedom, at least for white males; and the conviction that any ordinary man is capable of performing the duties of most public offices.

Jackson's ability to reconcile his belief in the supremacy of the Union with his conviction that national authority should be held within narrow limits tended to make the Democrats the party of those who believed that the powers of the states should not be diminished. Tocqueville caught this aspect of Jackson's philosophy perfectly: "Far from wishing to extend Federal power," he wrote, "the president belongs to the party that wishes to limit that power."

Although the radical Locofoco[2] wing of the party championed the idea, nearly all Jacksonians, like their leader, favored giving the small man his chance—by supporting public education, for example, and by refusing to place much weight on a

---

[2] A locofoco was a type of friction match. The name was first applied in politics when a group of New York Jacksonians used these matches to light candles when a conservative faction tried to break up their meeting by turning off the gaslights.

person's origin, dress, or manners. "One individual is as good as another" (for accuracy we must insert the adjective *white*) was their axiom. This attitude helps explain why immigrants, Catholics, and other minority groups usually voted Democratic. However, the Jacksonians showed no tendency either to penalize the wealthy or to intervene in economic affairs to aid the underprivileged. The motto "That government is best which governs least" graced the masthead of the chief Jacksonian newspaper, the *Washington Globe*, throughout the era.

Rise of the Whigs

The opposition to Jackson was far less cohesive. Henry Clay's National Republican party provided a nucleus, but Clay never dominated that party as Jackson dominated the Democrats. Its orientation was basically anti-Jackson. It was as though the American people were a great block of granite from which some sculptor had just fashioned a statue of Jackson, the chips scattered about the floor of the studio representing the opposition.

While Jackson was president, the impact of his personality delayed the formation of a true two-party system, but as soon as he surrendered power, the opposition, taking heart, began to coalesce. Many Democrats could not accept the odd logic of Jacksonian finance. As early as 1834 they, together with the Clay element, the extreme states' righters who followed Calhoun, and other dissident groups, were calling themselves Whigs. The name harkened back to the Revolution. It implied patriotic distaste for too-powerful executives, expressed specifically as resistance to the tyranny of "King Andrew."

This coalition possessed great resources of wealth and talent. Anyone who understood banking was almost obliged to become a Whig unless he was connected with one of Jackson's "pets." Those spiritual descendants of Hamilton who rejected the administration's refusal to approach economic problems from a broadly national perspective also joined in large numbers. Those who found the coarseness and "pushiness" of the Jacksonians offensive were another element in the new party. The anti-intellectual and antiscientific bias of the administration (Jackson rejected proposals for a national university, an observatory, and a scientific and literary institute) drove many ministers, lawyers, doctors, and other well-educated people into the Whig fold.

The philosopher Ralph Waldo Emerson was no doubt thinking of these types when he described the Whigs as "the enterprizing, intelligent, well-meaning and wealthy part of the people," but Whig arguments also appealed to ordinary voters who were predisposed to favor strong governments that would check the "excesses" of unrestricted individualism.

The Whigs were slow to develop effective party organization. They had too many generals and not enough troops. The issues that defined the Whigs varied from one state to another. For the most part, the sole unifying principle was oppo-

FOR WHOM DID JACKSON FIGHT?

In 1837, his last year as president, Jackson here distributes hunks of a 1,400-pound cheese, a gift from New York farmers. They thought it the best present the "farming class" could give to someone who so forcefully had represented "their interest." In 1855 historian George Bancroft maintained that Jackson himself embodied America, for he "shared and possessed all the creative ideas of his country and his time." (This is the sort of twaddle that gives nineteenth-century historians a bad name.) In 1945 Arthur M. Schlesinger Jr.—son of the progressive historian—praised Jackson for battling on behalf of farmers and workers against big business. Jackson approached politics in terms of class rather than geography, and in that sense anticipated Franklin Delano Roosevelt. In both eras, Schlesinger observed, "the business community" had brought "national affairs to a state of crisis." Richard Hofstadter (1948) conceded that Jackson's fight against business had "many superficial points in common" with Roosevelt's. But Jackson had been no friend of the "common man," for he had consistently promoted the interests of well-to-do farmers and local entrepreneurs. This point received some confirmation from Edward Pessen's (1969) study

of wealth accumulation during the Jacksonian era, which showed that the rich grew richer and the poor, poorer. Robert Remini (1984), on the other hand, argued that Jackson adhered to republican ideals: he did what was good for the nation as a whole. Whatever the reality, many different people *believed* that Jackson represented them. Note that at the public reception shown above, some wore formal attire and others, work clothes. But all got cheese.

George Bancroft, *Literary and Historical Miscellanies* (1855), Arthur M. Schlesinger Jr., *Age of Jackson* (1945), Richard Hofstadter, *The American Political Tradition* (1948), Edward Pessen, *Jacksonian America* (1969), Lee Benson, *The Concept of Jacksonian Democracy* (1961), Robert Remini, *Andrew Jackson and the Course of American Democracy* (1984).

sition to Jackson. Furthermore, they stood in conflict with the major trend of the age: the glorification of the common man.

Lacking a dominant leader in 1836, the Whigs relied on "favorite sons," hoping to throw the presidential election into the House of Representatives. Daniel Webster ran in New England. For the West and South, Hugh Lawson White of Tennessee, a former friend who had broken with Jackson, was counted on to carry the fight. General William Henry Harrison was supposed to win in the Northwest and to draw support everywhere from those who liked to vote for military heroes. This sorry strategy failed; Jackson's handpicked candidate, Martin Van Buren, won a majority of both the popular and the electoral votes.

Martin Van Buren: Jacksonianism Without Jackson

Van Buren's brilliance as a political manipulator—the Red Fox, the Little Magician—has tended to obscure his statesmanlike qualities and his engaging personality. He made a powerful argument, for example, that political parties were a force for unity, not for partisan bickering. In addition, high office sobered him, and improved his judgment. He fought the Bank of the United States as a monopoly, but he also opposed irresponsible state banks. Van Buren believed in public construction of internal improvements, but he favored state rather than national programs, and he urged a rational approach: Each project must stand on its own as a useful and profitable public utility.

He continued to equivocate spectacularly on the tariff—in his *Autobiography* he described two of his supporters walking home after listening to him talk on the tariff, each convinced that it had been a brilliant speech, but neither having obtained the slightest idea as to where Van Buren stood on the subject—but he was never in the pocket of any special interest group or tariff lobbyist. He accounted himself a good Jeffersonian, tending to prefer state action to federal, but he was by no means doctrinaire. Basically he approached most questions rationally and pragmatically.

Van Buren had outmaneuvered Calhoun easily in the struggle to succeed Jackson, winning the old hero's confidence and serving him well. In 1832 he was elected vice president and thereafter was conceded to be the "heir apparent." In 1835 the Democratic National Convention unanimously nominated him for president.

Van Buren took office just as the Panic of 1837 struck the country. Its effects were frightening but short-lived. When the banks stopped converting paper money into gold and silver, they outraged conservatives but in effect eased the pressure on the money market: Interest rates declined and business loans again became relatively easy to obtain. In 1836, at the height of the boom in land sales, Congress had voted to "distribute" the new treasury surplus to the states, and this flow of money, which the states promptly spent, also stimulated the revival. Late in 1838 the banks resumed specie payments.

But in 1839 a bumper crop caused a sharp decline in the price of cotton. Then a number of state governments that had overextended themselves in road- and canal-building projects were forced to default on their debts. This discouraged investors, particularly foreigners. A general economic depression ensued that lasted until 1843.

Van Buren was not responsible for the panic or the depression, but his manner of dealing with economic issues was scarcely helpful. He saw his role as being concerned only with problems plaguing the government, ignoring the economy as a whole. "The less government interferes with private pursuits the better for the general prosperity," he pontificated. As Daniel Webster scornfully pointed out, Van Buren was following a policy of "leaving the people to shift for themselves," one that many Whigs rejected.

Van Buren's chief goal was finding a substitute for the state banks as a place to keep federal funds. The depression and the suspension of specie payments embarrassed the government along with private depositors. He soon settled on the idea of "divorcing" the government from all banking activities. His independent treasury bill called for the construction of government-owned vaults where federal revenues could be stored until needed. To ensure absolute safety, all payments to the government were to be made in hard cash. After a battle that lasted until the summer of 1840, the Independent Treasury Act passed both the House and the Senate.

Opposition to the Independent Treasury Act had been bitter, and not all of it was partisan. Bankers and businessmen objected to the government's withholding so much specie from the banks, which needed all the hard money they could get to support loans that were the lifeblood of economic growth. It seemed irresponsible for the federal government to turn its back on the banks, which so obviously performed a semipublic function. These criticisms made good sense, but through a lucky combination of circumstances, the system worked reasonably well for many years.

By creating suspicion in the public mind, officially stated distrust of banks acted as a damper on their tendency to overexpand. No acute shortage of specie developed because heavy agricultural exports and the investment of much European capital in American railroads beginning in the mid-1840s brought in large amounts of new gold and silver. After 1849 the discovery of gold in California added another important source of specie. The supply of money and bank credit kept pace roughly with the growth of the economy, but through no fault of the government. "Wildcat" banks proliferated. Fraud and counterfeiting were common, and the operation of everyday business affairs was inconvenienced in countless ways. The disordered state of the currency remained a grave problem until corrected by Civil War banking legislation.

The Log Cabin Campaign

It was not his financial policy that led to Van Buren's defeat in 1840. The depression naturally hurt the Democrats, and the Whigs were far better organized than in 1836. The Whigs also adopted a different strategy. The Jacksonians had come to power on

The 1840 presidential campaign was the first to use circus hoopla and the techniques of mass appeal that came to characterize political contests in the United States. This photograph is of a log cabin with a "hard cider" keg that was carried on a pole at rallies for William Henry Harrison.

the coattails of a popular general whose views on public questions they concealed or ignored. They had maintained themselves by shouting the praises of the common man. Now the Whigs seized on these techniques and carried them to their logical—or illogical—conclusion. Not even bothering to draft a program, and passing over Clay and Webster, whose views were known and therefore controversial, they nominated General William Henry Harrison for president. The "Hero of Tippecanoe" was counted on to conquer the party created in the image of the Hero of New Orleans. To "balance" the ticket, the Whigs chose a former Democrat, John Tyler of Virginia, an ardent supporter of states' rights, as their vice presidential candidate.

Harrison came from a distinguished family, being the son of Benjamin Harrison, a signer of the Declaration of Independence and a former governor of Virginia. He was well educated and in at least comfortable financial circumstances. The Whigs ignored these facts. The log cabin and the cider barrel became their symbols, which every political meeting saw reproduced in a dozen forms. The leading Whig campaign newspaper, edited by a vigorous New Englander named Horace Greeley, was called the *Log Cabin*. Cartoons, doggerel, slogans, and souvenirs were everywhere substituted for argument.

The Democrats used the same methods as the Whigs and were equally well organized, but they had little heart for the fight. The best they could come up with was the fact that their vice presidential candidate, Richard Mentor Johnson, had killed Tecumseh, not merely defeated him. Van Buren tried to focus public attention on issues, but his voice could not be heard above the huzzahs of the Whigs. When the Whigs chanted "Tippecanoe and Tyler too!" and "Van, Van, is a used-up man" and rolled out another barrel of hard cider, the best the Democrats could come up with was:

Rumpsey, Dumpsey,
Colonel Johnson
Killed Tecumseh.

A huge turnout (four-fifths of the eligible voters) carried Harrison to victory by a margin of almost 150,000. The electoral vote was 234 to 60.

The Democrats had been blown up by their own bomb. In 1828 they had portrayed John Quincy Adams as a bloated aristocrat and Jackson as a simple farmer. The lurid talk of Van Buren dining off golden plates was no different from the stories that made Adams out to be a passionate gambler. If Van Buren was a lesser man than Adams, Harrison was a pale imitation indeed of Andrew Jackson.

The Whigs continued to repeat history by rushing to gather the spoils of victory. Washington was again flooded by office seekers; the political confusion was monumental. Harrison had no ambition to be an aggressive leader. He believed that Jackson had misused the veto and professed to put as much emphasis as had Washington on the principle of the separation of legislative and executive powers. This delighted the Whig leaders in Congress, who had had their fill of the "executive usurpation" of Jackson. Either Clay or Webster seemed destined to be the real ruler of the new administration, and soon the two were squabbling over their old general like sparrows over a crust.

At the height of their squabble, less than a month after his inauguration, Harrison fell gravely ill. Pneumonia developed, and on April 4 he died. John Tyler of Virginia, honest and conscientious but doctrinaire, became president of the United States. The political climate of the country was changed dramatically. Events began to march in a new direction.

Milestones

1828	Andrew Jackson is elected president
1829	Crowds cause chaos at Jackson's White House inaugural reception
1830	Jackson vetoes the Maysville Road Bill
1831	Nat Turner leads slave rebellion in Virginia
1831–1838	Southern Indians are removed to Oklahoma
1832	South Carolina defends states' rights in Ordinance of Nullification
	Force Bill grants president authority to execute revenue laws
	Jackson vetoes Bank Recharter Bill
	Jackson is reelected president
1833	Treasury Secretary Roger B. Taney orders Treasury funds removed from Bank of the United States
	Calhoun and Clay push through Compromise Tariff
1836	Jackson issues Specie Circular to control speculation
	Martin Van Buren is elected president
1837–1838	Panic sweeps nation, ending economic boom
1838	4,000 Cherokee die on Trail of Tears to Oklahoma
1840	Independent Treasury Act divorces federal government from all banking activities
	"Log Cabin" Campaign is first to use "hoopla"
	William Henry Harrison is elected president
1841	Harrison dies one month after inauguration; John Tyler becomes president

The Making of Middle-Class America

"THE AMERICAN FAMILY IS IN A STATE OF CRISIS"—THE PHRASE IS trumpeted by countless politicians and pollsters. The statistics seem to prove them right. Today, nearly a third of all children are born to unwed mothers; half of all marriages end in divorce; a third of all families are headed by a single parent; more than half of all single mothers with children younger than six work outside the home. Only a fourth of all households fit the "traditional" conception of family: a husband, a wife who does not work outside the home, and children.

But complaints about a "crisis" in the family have provoked cries of alarm for over a century, when divorce rates first began to rise. If ever the traditional "ideal" prevailed in America, it was during decades after 1820. In 1830 divorce was rare; the overwhelming majority of families had two parents; only one in fifteen women worked outside the home, and when these women married they almost always quit their jobs. With the exception of slave families, the traditional family structure had become normative.

Whether such families were "happier" or "stronger" than now is a different matter. Divorce was rare partly because it was hard to attain. South Carolina recognized no legal grounds for divorce. Many other states granted divorce only if a spouse committed adultery. Many couples thus endured loveless, unhappy marriages.

But after 1820, the family was perceived as a new and dynamic force in American society. Middle-class women, especially those freed from the drudgery of farm chores, were especially influential. Sarah Hale, the leading female journalist of the era, pronounced women to be "God's appointed agents of morality." Such women organized religious revivals, spearheaded efforts to improve prisons and mental asylums, and campaigned for temperance, abolitionism, and women's rights. Young middle-class women, too, were avid readers, and their patronage stimulated publication of books and magazines. These women shaped society and culture even more directly by serving as teachers in the common schools that extended public education to much of the nation.

The reformers of the era decried the pessimism of their Calvinist forebears and enshrined human sensibilities. Romanticism in the arts and literature was the cultural expression of a spirit affirming that Americans and their institutions could—and would—grow and change for the better.

Tocqueville: Democracy in America

On May 12, 1831, two French aristocrats, Alexis de Tocqueville and Gustave de Beaumont, arrived in New York City from Le Havre on the packet *President*. Their official purpose was to make a study of American prisons for the French government. But they really came, as Tocqueville explained, "to see what a great republic is like."

Tocqueville and Beaumont believed that Europe was passing from its aristocratic past into a democratic future. How better to prepare for the change, they believed, than by studying the United States, where democracy was already the "enduring and normal state" of the land. The visit provided the material for Tocqueville's classic *De la Démocratie en Amérique*, published in France in 1835 and a year later in an English translation. *Democracy in America* has been the starting point for virtually all subsequent writers who have tried to describe what Tocqueville called "the creative elements" of American institutions.

The gist of *Democracy in America* is contained in the book's first sentence: "No novelty in the United States struck me more vividly during my stay there than the equality of conditions." Tocqueville meant not that Americans lived in a state of total equality, but that the inequalities that did exist among white Americans were

Rural Versus Urban Population, 1820–1860

As the balance of rural and urban population began to shift during the years from 1820 to 1860, the number of cities with populations over 100,000 grew from one in 1820—New York—to nine in 1870, including southern and western cities like New Orleans and San Francisco.

not enforced by institutions or supported by public opinion. Moreover, the inequalities paled when compared with those of Europe. "In America," he concluded, "men are nearer equality than in any other country in the world." The circumstances of one's birth meant little, one's education less, and one's intelligence scarcely anything. Economic differences, while real and certainly "paraded" by those who enjoyed "a pre-eminence of wealth," were transitory. "Such wealth," Tocqueville assured his readers, "is within reach of all."

Despite a blindness to the growing gap between rich and poor, Tocqueville realized that America was undergoing some fundamental social changes. These changes, he wrote, were being made by "an innumerable crowd who are . . . not exactly rich nor yet quite poor [and who] have enough property to want order and not enough to excite envy." In his notes he put it even more succinctly: "The whole society seems to have turned into one middle class."

The Family Recast

Tocqueville was particularly struck by the character of the family. Americans, he wrote, showed an "equal regard" for husbands and wives, but defined their roles differently. This was made possible by the growth of the market economy, which undermined the home and family as the basic unit of economic production. More and more people did their work in shops, in offices, or on factory floors. Whether a job was skilled or unskilled, white-collar or blue-collar, or strictly professional, it took the family breadwinner out of the house during working hours six days a week. This did not mean that the family necessarily ceased to be an economic unit. But the labor of the father and any children with jobs came home in the form of cash, thus at least initially in the custody of the individual earners. The social consequences of this change were enormous for the traditional "head of the family" and for his wife and children.

Because he was away so much, the husband had to surrender to his wife some of the power in the family that he had formerly exercised, if for no other reason than that she was always there. Noah Webster explained that the ideal father's authority was "like the mild dominion of a limited monarch, and not the iron rule of an austere tyrant." It certainly explains why Tocqueville concluded that "a sort of equality reigns around the domestic hearth" in America.

The new power and prestige that wives and mothers enjoyed were not obtained without cost. Since they were exercising day-to-day control over household affairs, they were expected to tend only to those affairs. Expanding their interest to other fields of human endeavor was frowned on. Where the typical wife had formerly been a partner in a family enterprise, she now left earning a living entirely to her husband. She was certainly not encouraged to have an independent career as, say, a lawyer or doctor. Time spent away from home or devoted to matters unrelated to the care of husband and family was, according to the new normative doctrine of "separate spheres," time misappropriated.

Joseph Moore and His Family (1839), by Erastus Salisbury Field, reflects the emerging middle-class family. Although the painting is named after the father, the mother is carefully placed in a precisely equivalent position; each child has a space of his or her own.

This trend widened the gap between the middle and lower classes. For a middle-class wife and mother to take a job or, still worse, to devote herself to any "frivolous" activity outside the home was considered a dereliction of duty. Such an attitude could not possibly develop in lower-class families where everyone had to work simply to keep food on the table.

Some women objected to making a cult out of "womanhood": by placing an ideal on so high a pedestal, all real women would fall short. Others escaped its more suffocating aspects by forming close friendships with other women. But most women, including such forceful proponents of women's rights as Hale and the educator Catharine Beecher, subscribed to the view that a woman's place was in the home. "The formation of the moral and intellectual character of the young is committed mainly to the female hand," Beecher wrote in *A Treatise on Domestic Economy for the Use of Young Ladies* (1841). "The mother forms the character of the future man."

Another reason for the shift in domestic influence from husbands to wives was that women began to have fewer children. Here again, the change happened earliest and was most pronounced among families in the rapidly urbanizing Northeast. On the frontier, where middle-class norms lagged behind, couples generally had larger families. But the birthrate gradually declined all over the country. People married later than in earlier periods. Long courtships and broken engagements were common, probably because prospective marriage partners were becoming more selective. On average, women began having their children two or three years later than their mothers had, and they stopped two or three years sooner. Apparently many middle-class couples made a conscious effort to limit family size, even when doing so required sexual abstinence.

Having fewer children led parents to value children more highly, or so it would seem from the additional time and affection lavished on them. Here again, the mother provided most of both. Child rearing fell within her "sphere" and occupied the time that earlier generations of mothers had devoted to such tasks as weaving, sewing, and farm chores. Not the least of these new responsibilities was overseeing the children's education, both secular and religious.

The Second Great Awakening

The inclination to set aside other Calvinist tenets, such as predestination, became more pronounced as a new wave of revivalism took shape in the 1790s. This Second Great Awakening began as a counteroffensive to the deistic thinking and other forms of "infidelity" that New England Congregationalists and southern Methodists alike identified with the French Revolution. Prominent New England ministers, who considered themselves traditionalists but also revivalists, men such as Yale's president, Timothy Dwight, and Dwight's student, the Reverend Lyman Beecher, placed less stress in their sermons on God's arbitrary power over mortals, more on the promise of the salvation of sinners because of God's mercy and "disinterested benevolence." When another of Dwight's students, Horace Bushnell, declared in a sermon on "Christian nurture" in 1844 that Christian parents should prepare their children "for the skies," he meant that parents could contribute to their children's salvation.

Calvinism came under more direct assault from Charles Grandison Finney, probably the most effective of a number of charismatic evangelists who brought the Second Great Awakening to its crest. In 1821 Finney abandoned a promising career as a lawyer and became an itinerant preacher. His most spectacular successes occurred during a series of revivals conducted in towns along the Erie Canal, a region Finney called "the burned-over district" because it had been the site of so many revivals before his own. From Utica, where his revival began in 1826, to Rochester, where it climaxed in 1831, he exhorted his listeners to take their salvation into their own hands. He insisted that people could control their own fate. He dismissed Calvinism as a "theological fiction." Salvation was available to anyone. But the day of judgment was just around the corner; there was little time to waste.

During and after Finney's efforts in Utica, conversions increased sharply. In Rochester, church membership doubled in six months. Elsewhere in the country, churches capitalized on the efforts of other evangelists to fill their pews. In 1831 alone, church membership grew by 100,000, an increase, according to a New England minister, "unparalleled in the history of the church." The success of the evangelists of the Second Great Awakening stemmed from the timeliness of their

Religious revivals stirred passions, as this rendering of an 1839 camp meeting suggests: people are gesticulating, swooning, and writhing on the ground. Finney endorsed such "excitements" as essential for conversion. But some doubted the wisdom of eliciting passions so as to persuade people to exercise more restraint and sin less often.

assault on Calvinist doctrine and even more from their methods. Finney, for example, consciously set out to be entertaining as well as edifying. The singing of hymns and the solicitation of personal testimonies provided his meetings with emotional release and human interest. Prominent among his innovations was the "anxious bench," where leading members of the community awaited the final prompting from within before coming forward to declare themselves saved.

Women, and especially the wives of the business leaders of the community, felt particularly responsible for the Christian education of their children, which fell within their separate sphere. Many women had servants and thus had time and energy to devote to their own and their offsprings' salvation.

Paradoxically, this caused many of them to venture out of that sphere—and out of the shadow of their husbands. They founded the Oneida County Female Missionary Society, an association that did most of the organizing and a good deal of the financing of the climactic years of the Second Awakening. The Female Missionary Society raised more than $1,000 a year (no small sum at that time) to support the revival in Utica, in its environs, and throughout the burned-over district. Apparently without consciously intending to do so, women challenged the authority of the paternalistic, authoritarian churches they so fervently embraced. Then, by mixtures of exhortation, example, and affection, they set out to save the souls of their loved ones, first their children and ultimately their husbands too.

The Shakers segregated the sexes and enforced celibacy. Pent-up sexual tensions were released in religious ecstasy expressed through church dances, as the lines of men and women approached each other—but never touched.

Backwoods Utopias

Rather than save individual souls, some Americans sought to reform society or, more venturesome, withdraw from workaday American society and establish experimental communities. The first communitarians were religious reformers. In a sense the Pilgrims fall into this category, along with a number of other groups in colonial times, but only in the nineteenth century did the idea flourish.

One of the most influential of the earlier communities were the Shakers, founded by Ann Lee, an Englishwoman who came to America in 1774. Mother Ann, as she was called, saw visions that convinced her that Christ would come to earth again as a woman and that she was that woman. With a handful of followers she founded a community near Albany, New York. The group grew rapidly, and after Ann Lee's death in 1784 her movement continued to expand. By the 1830s her followers had established about twenty successful communities.

The Shakers practiced celibacy; believing that the millennium was imminent, they saw no reason for perpetuating the human race. Each group lived in a large Family House, the sexes strictly segregated. Property was held in common but controlled by a ruling hierarchy. So much stress was placed on equality of labor and reward and on voluntary acceptance of the rules, however, that the system does not seem to have been oppressive.

The Shaker religion, joyful and fervent, was marked by much group singing and dancing, which provided the members with emotional release from their tightly controlled regimen. An industrious, skillful people, they made a special virtue of simplicity; some of their designs for buildings and, especially, furniture achieved a classic beauty seldom equaled among untutored artisans. Despite their customs, the Shakers were universally tolerated and even admired.

There were many other religious colonies, such as the Amana Community, which flourished in New York and Iowa in the 1840s and 1850s, and John Humphrey Noyes's Oneida Community, where the members practiced "complex" marriage—a form of promiscuity based on the principle that every man in the group was married to every woman. They prospered by developing a number of manufacturing skills.

The most important of the religious communitarians were the Mormons. A remarkable Vermont farm boy, Joseph Smith, founded the religion in western New York in the 1820s. Smith saw visions; he claimed to have discovered and translated an ancient text, the Book of Mormon, written in hieroglyphics on plates of gold, which described the adventures of a tribe of Israelites that had populated America from biblical times until their destruction in a great war in 400 C.E. With a small band of followers, Smith established a community in Ohio in 1831. The Mormons' dedication and economic efficiency attracted large numbers of converts, but their unorthodox religious views and their exclusivism, a product of their sense of being a chosen people, caused some non-Mormons to resent and persecute Smith and his followers. The Mormons were forced to move first to Missouri and then back to Illinois, where in 1839 they founded the town of Nauvoo.

Nauvoo flourished—by 1844 it was the largest city in the state, with a population of 15,000—but once again the Mormons ran into local trouble. They quarreled among themselves, especially after Smith secretly authorized polygamy (he called it "celestial marriage") and a number of other unusual rites for members of the "Holy Order," the top leaders of the church.[1] They created a paramilitary organization, the Nauvoo Legion, headed by Smith, envisaging themselves as a semi-independent state within the Union. Smith announced that he was a candidate for president of the United States. Rumors circulated that the Mormons intended to take over the entire Northwest for their "empire." Once again local "gentiles" rose against them. Smith was arrested, then murdered by a mob.

Under a new leader, Brigham Young, the Mormons sought a haven beyond the frontier. In 1847 they marched westward, pressing through the mountains until they reached the desolate wilderness on the shores of the Great Salt Lake. There, at last, they established their Zion and began to make their truly significant impact on American history. Irrigation made the desert flourish, precious water wisely being treated as a community asset. Hard, cooperative, intelligently directed effort

---

[1]One justification of polygamy, paradoxically, was that marriage was a sacred, eternal state. If a man remarried after his wife's death, eventually he would have two wives in Heaven. Therefore why not on earth?

Persecution forced the Mormons to move from New York to Ohio to Missouri, before settling for a time in Nauvoo, Illinois. There, in 1844 Joseph Smith, the Mormon leader, announced his candidacy for president of the United States. Smith and his brother Hyrum were arrested by local authorities and murdered in their jail cell by a hostile mob.

spelled growth and prosperity; more than 11,000 people were living in the area when it became part of the Utah Territory in 1850. In time the communal Mormon settlement broke down, but the religion has remained—known as the Church of Latter-Day Saints, a major force in the shaping of the West. The Mormon Church is still by far the most powerful single influence in Utah and is a thriving organization in many other parts of the United States and in Europe.

Despite their many common characteristics, the religious communities varied enormously; subordination of the individual to the group did not destroy group individualism. Their sexual practices, for example, ranged from the "complex marriage" of the Oneidans through Mormon polygamy and ordinary monogamy to the reluctant acceptance of sexual intercourse by the Amana Community and the celibacy of the Shakers. The communities are significant as reflections of the urgent reform spirit of the age.

The communities had some influence on reformers who wished to experiment with social organization. When Robert Owen, a British utopian socialist who believed in economic as well as political equality and who considered competition debasing, decided to create an ideal community in America, he purchased the Rappite settlement at New Harmony, Indiana. Owen's advocacy of free love and "enlightened atheism" did not add to the stability of his group or to its popularity among outsiders. The colony was a costly failure.

The American followers of Charles Fourier, a French utopian socialist who proposed that society should be organized in cooperative units called phalanxes, fared better. Fourierism did not seek to tamper with sexual and religious mores. Its advocates included important journalists such as Horace Greeley of the *New York Tribune* and Parke Godwin of the *New York Evening Post*. In the 1840s several dozen Fourierist colonies were established in the northern and western states. Members worked at whatever tasks they wished and only as much as they wished. Wages were paid according to the "repulsiveness" of the tasks performed; the person who "chose" to clean out a cesspool would receive more than someone hoeing corn or mending a fence or engaging in some task requiring complex skills. As might be expected, none of the communities lasted very long.

The Age of Reform

The communitarians were the most colorful of the reformers, their proposals the most spectacular. More effective, however, were the many individuals who took on themselves responsibility for caring for the physically and mentally disabled and for the rehabilitation of criminals. The work of Thomas Gallaudet in developing methods for educating deaf people reflects the spirit of the times. Gallaudet's school in Hartford, Connecticut, opened its doors in 1817; by 1851 similar schools for the deaf had been established in fourteen states.

Dr. Samuel Gridley Howe did similar work with the blind, devising means for making books with raised letters (Louis Braille's system of raised dots was not introduced until later in the century) that the blind could "read" with their fingers. Howe headed a school for the blind in Boston, the pioneering Perkins Institution, which opened in 1832. Of all that Charles Dickens observed in America, nothing so favorably impressed him as Howe's success in educating 12-year-old Laura Bridgman, who was deaf, mute, and blind. Howe was also interested in trying to educate the mentally disabled and in other causes, including antislavery. "Every creature in human shape should command our respect," he insisted. "The strong should help the weak, so that the whole should advance as a band of brethren."

One of the most striking aspects of the reform movement was the emphasis reformers placed on establishing special institutions for dealing with social problems. In the colonial period, orphans, indigent persons, the insane, and the feeble-minded were usually cared for by members of their own families or boarded in a neighboring household. They remained part of the community. Even criminals were seldom "locked away" for extended jail terms, punishment commonly consisted of whipping, being placed in stocks in the town square, or (for serious crimes) execution. But once persuaded that people were primarily shaped by their surroundings, reformers demanded that deviant and dependent members of the community be taken from their present corrupting circumstances and placed in specialized institutions where they could be trained or rehabilitated. Almshouses, orphanages, reformatories, prisons, and "lunatic asylums" sprang up throughout the United States.

The rationale for this movement was scientific; elaborate statistical reports attested to the benefits that such institutions would bring to both inmates and society as a whole. The motivating spirit of the founders of these asylums was humane, although many of the institutions seem anything but humane to the modern eye.

Debating the Past

DID ANTEBELLUM REFORM MOVEMENTS IMPROVE SOCIETY?

The Eastern State Penitentiary in Philadelphia was built in the 1820s. The lithograph *(below left)* was done by Samuel Cowperthwaite, Convict # 2954. Eastern State consisted of seven rows of cells radiating out from the central tower. The design ensured continuous supervision and isolation. The reformers who conceived of the prison thought it would teach an inmate to "listen to the reproaches of his conscience." The dessert plate *(below right)* commemorating the jail is proof that some people believed in its mission. After visiting the prison, however, Charles Dickens described its system of confinement as "rigid, strict and hopeless." In *Madness and Civilization* (1961) and *Discipline and Punish* (1975), the French philosopher Michel Foucault similarly regarded such institutions as part of the process whereby modern societies squelched individuality. Those who refused to accept the discipline of teachers, employers, and government officials were labeled "deviants" and sent to institutions that would "reform" them through the imposition of order, a thesis that David J. Rothman (1971) applied to antebellum

penitentiaries and asylums. Before Foucault, most scholars had endorsed antebellum reforms. Now these reforms were reassessed more critically. Michael B. Katz (1968) and Stanley K. Schultz (1973) argued that the public schools were means for preparing the young for industrial labor by instilling discipline and regimentation. Movements to promote temperance and suppress prostitution, similarly, were increasingly viewed as unwarranted intrusions on private matters. But in the 1980s women's historians altered this debate. Mary Ryan (1981) and others showed that women dominated nearly all antebellum reform movements, and for good reason. The child who could not attend a school was often subjected to the ceaseless drudgery of farm or factory. The exuberant individualist who tarried at the tavern sometimes beat his wife on returning home. The Eastern State Penitentiary and the antebellum insane asylums were fearsome places, but would their inmates have been better off on the streets? Excessive discipline erodes individuality; excessive individuality erodes social cohesion.

Michel Foucault, *Madness and Civilization* (1961) and *Discipline and Punish* (1975), Michael B. Katz, *The Irony of Early School Reform* (1968), Stanley K. Schultz, *The Culture Factory* (1973), David J. Rothman, *The Discovery of the Asylum* (1971), Mary Ryan, *Cradle of the Middle Class* (1981).

The highly regarded Philadelphia prison system was based on strict solitary confinement, which was supposed to lead culprits to reflect on their sins and then reform their ways. The prison was literally a penitentiary, a place to repent. In fact, the system drove some inmates mad, and soon a rival Auburn system was introduced in New York State, which allowed for some social contact among prisoners and for work in shops and stone quarries. Absolute silence was required at all times. The prisoners were herded about in lockstep and punished by flogging for the slightest infraction of the rules. Regular "moral and religious instruction" was provided, which the authorities believed would lead inmates to reform their lives. Tocqueville and Beaumont, in their report on American prisons, concluded that the Philadelphia system produced "the deepest impression on the soul of the convict," while the Auburn system made the convict "more conformable to the habits of man in society." (See also Debating the Past, p. 310)

The hospitals for mental patients were intended to cure inmates, not merely to confine them. The emphasis was on isolating them from the pressures of society; on order, quiet, routine; on control but not on punishment. The unfortunates were seen as deranged; the task was to arrange their lives in a rational manner. In practice, shortages of trained personnel, niggardly legislative appropriations, and the inherent difficulty of managing violent and irrational patients often produced deplorable conditions in the asylums.

This situation led Dorothea Dix, a woman of almost saintlike selflessness, to devote thirty years of her life to a campaign to improve the care of the insane. She traveled to every state in the Union, and as far afield as Turkey and Japan, inspecting asylums and poorhouses. Insane persons in Massachusetts, she wrote in a memorial intended to shock state legislators into action, were being kept in cages and closets, "chained, naked, beaten with rods, and lashed into obedience!" Her reports led to some improvement in conditions in Massachusetts and other states, but in the long run the bright hopes of the reformers were never realized. Institutions founded to uplift the deviant and dependent all too soon became places where society's "misfits" might safely be kept out of sight.

"Demon Rum"

Women did much of the work in all antebellum reforms, but they were especially active in the temperance movement. The husband who squandered his earnings on booze, or who came home drunk and debauched, imperiled the family. Thus middle-class women who believed that a woman's place was in the home were obliged to take on a public role to protect the family.

Alcohol—"demon rum"—was perhaps foremost among those threats. By the 1820s Americans were consuming prodigious amounts of alcohol, more than ever before or since. Not that the colonists had been teetotalers. Liquor, mostly in the form of rum or hard apple cider, was cheap and everywhere available; taverns were an integral part of colonial society. There were alcoholics in colonial America, but because neither political nor religious leaders considered drinking dangerous, there was no alcohol "problem." Most doctors recommended the regular consumption of alcohol as healthy. John Adams, certainly the soul of propriety, drank a tankard of hard cider every day for breakfast. Dr. Benjamin Rush's *Inquiry into the Effects of Ardent Spirits* (1784), which questioned the medicinal benefits of alcohol, fell on deaf ears.

However, alcohol consumption increased markedly in the early years of the new republic, thanks primarily to the availability of cheap corn and rye whiskey distilled in the new states of Kentucky and Tennessee. In the 1820s the per capita consumption of hard liquor reached 5 gallons, well over twice what it is today. Since small children and many grown people did not drink that much, others obviously drank a great deal more. Many women drank, if mostly at home; and reports of carousing among 14-year-old college freshmen show that youngsters did too. But the bulk of the heavy drinking occurred when men got together, at taverns or grogshops and at work. Many prominent politicians, including Clay and Webster, were heavy consumers. Webster is said to have kept several thousand bottles of wine, whiskey, and other alcoholic beverages in his cellar.

Artisans and common laborers regarded their twice-daily "dram" of whiskey as part of their wages. In workshops, masters were expected to halt production periodically to drink with their apprentices and journeymen. Trips to the neighborhood grogshop also figured into the workaday routine. In 1829 Secretary of War John Eaton estimated that three-quarters of the nation's laborers drank at least 4 ounces of distilled spirits a day.

The foundation of the American Temperance Union in 1826 signaled the start of a national crusade against drunkenness. Employing lectures, pamphlets, rallies, essay contests, and other techniques, the union set out to persuade people to "sign the pledge" not to drink liquor. Primitive sociological studies of the effects of drunkenness (reformers were able to show a high statistical correlation between alcohol consumption and crime) added to the effectiveness of the campaign.

In 1840 an organization of reformed alcoholics, the Washingtonians, set out to reclaim alcoholics. One of the most effective Washingtonians was John B. Gough, rescued by the organization after seven years in the gutter. "Crawl from the slimy ooze, ye drowned drunkards," Gough would shout, "and with suffocation's blue and livid lips speak out against the drink!"

Revivalist ministers like Charles Grandison Finney argued that alcohol was one of the great barriers to conversion, which helps explain why Utica, a town of fewer than 13,000 residents in 1840, supported four separate temperance societies in that year. Employers all over the country also signed on, declaring their businesses henceforward to be "cold-water" enterprises. Soon the temperance movement claimed a million members.

The temperance people aroused bitter opposition, particularly after they moved beyond calls for restraint to demands for prohibition of all alcohol. German and Irish immigrants, for the most part Catholics, and also members of Protestant sects that used wine in their religious services, objected to being told by reformers that their drinking would have to stop. But by the early 1840s the reformers had secured legislation in many states that imposed strict licensing systems and heavy liquor taxes. Local option laws permitted towns and counties to ban the sale of alcohol altogether.

In 1851 Maine passed the first effective law prohibiting the manufacture and sale of alcoholic beverages. The leader of the campaign was Mayor Neal Dow of Portland, a businessman who became a prohibitionist after seeing the damage done by drunkenness among workers in his tannery. By 1855 a dozen other states had passed laws based on the Maine statute, and the nation's per capita consumption of alcohol had plummeted to 2 gallons a year.

The Abolitionist Crusade

No reform movement of this era was more significant, more ambiguous, or more provocative of later historical investigation than the drive to abolish slavery. That slavery should have been a cause of indignation to reform-minded Americans was inevitable. Humanitarians were outraged by the master's whip and by the practice of disrupting families. Democrats protested the denial of political and civil rights to slaves. Perfectionists of all stripes deplored the fact that slaves had no chance to improve themselves. However, well into the 1820s, the abolitionist cause attracted few followers because there seemed to be no way of getting rid of slavery short of revolution. While a few theorists argued that the Fifth Amendment, which provides that no one may be "deprived of life, liberty, or property, without due process of law," could be interpreted to mean that the Constitution outlawed slavery, the great majority believed that the institution was not subject to federal control.

Particularly in the wake of the Missouri Compromise, antislavery Northerners neatly compartmentalized their thinking. Slavery was wrong; they would not tolerate it in their own communities. But since the Constitution obliged them to tolerate it in states where it existed, they felt no responsibility to fight it. The issue was explosive enough even when limited to the question of the expansion of slavery into the territories. People who advocated any kind of forced abolition in states where it was legal were judged irresponsible in the extreme.

More provocative and less accommodating to local sensibilities were people such as William Lloyd Garrison of Massachusetts, who called for "immediate" abolition. When his extreme position made continued residence in Baltimore impossible, he returned to Boston, where in 1831 he established his own newspaper, *The Liberator*. "I am in earnest," he announced in the first issue. "I will not equivocate—I will not excuse—I will not retreat a single inch—and I will be heard."

Garrison's position, and that espoused by the New England Anti-Slavery Society, which he organized in 1831, was absolutely unyielding: Slaves must be freed immediately and treated as equals; compensated emancipation was unacceptable, colonization unthinkable. Because the U.S. government countenanced slavery, Garrison refused to engage in political activity to achieve his ends. Burning a copy of the Constitution—that "agreement with hell"—became a regular feature at Society-sponsored public lectures.

Few white Americans found Garrison's line of argument convincing, and many were outraged by his confrontational tactics. Whenever he spoke in public, he risked being mobbed by what newspaper accounts approvingly described as "gentlemen of property and standing." In 1833 a Garrison meeting in New York City was broken up by colonizationists. Two years later a mob dragged Garrison through the streets of his own Boston. That same day a mob broke up the convention of the New York Anti-Slavery Society in Utica.

In the wake of this violence some of Garrison's backers had second thoughts about his call for an immediate end to slavery. The wealthy New York businessmen Arthur and Lewis Tappan, who had subsidized *The Liberator,* turned instead to Theodore Dwight Weld, a young minister who was part of Charles Grandison Finney's "holy band" of revivalists. Weld and his followers spoke of "immediate" emancipation "gradually" achieved, and they were willing to engage in political activity to achieve that goal.

In 1840 the Tappans and Weld broke with Garrison over the issue of involvement in politics and the participation of female abolitionists as public lecturers. Garrison, mindful of women's central role in other reforms, supported the women. "The destiny of the slaves is in the hands of American women," he had declared in 1833. Weld thought women lecturers would needlessly antagonize would-be supporters.

Many blacks were abolitionists long before the white movement began to attract attention. In 1830 some fifty black antislavery societies existed, and thereafter these groups grew in size and importance, being generally associated with the Garrisonian wing. White abolitionists eagerly sought out black speakers, especially runaway slaves, whose heartrending accounts of their experiences aroused sympathies and who, merely by speaking clearly and with conviction, stood as living proof that blacks were neither animals nor fools.

The first prominent black abolitionist was David Walker, whose powerful *Appeal to the Coloured Citizens of the World* (1829) is now considered one of the roots of the modern black nationalist movement. Walker was born free and had experienced American racism extensively in both the South and the North. He denounced white talk of democracy and freedom as pure hypocrisy and predicted that when God finally brought justice to America white "tyrants will wish they were never born!"

Frederick Douglass, a former slave who had escaped from Maryland, was one of the most remarkable Americans of his generation. While a bondsman he had received a full portion of beatings and other indignities, but he had been allowed to learn to read and write and to master a trade, opportunities denied the vast majority of slaves. Settling in Boston, he became an agent of the Massachusetts Anti-Slavery Society and a featured speaker at its public meetings.

Frederick Douglass in 1847, having escaped from slavery nine years earlier. He attracted large audiences as an antislavery lecturer, though his white supporters worried that he neither looked nor sounded like a former slave. Lest audiences think him an imposter, William Lloyd Garrison counseled him to not sound too "learned." Another thought it would be better if he had "a little of the plantation in his speech." Douglass rejected such suggestions.

Douglass was a tall, majestically handsome man who radiated determination and indignation. Slavery, he told white audiences, "brands your republicanism as a sham, your humanity as a base pretense, your Christianity as a lie." In 1845 he published his *Narrative of the Life of Frederick Douglass*, one of the most gripping autobiographical accounts of a slave's life ever written. Douglass insisted that freedom for blacks required not merely emancipation but full equality, social and economic as well as political. Not many white Northerners accepted his reasoning, but few who heard him or read his works could afterward maintain the illusion that all blacks were dull-witted or resigned to inferior status.

At first Douglass was, in his own words, "a faithful disciple" of Garrison, prepared to tear up the Constitution and destroy the Union to gain his ends. In the late 1840s, however, he changed his mind, deciding that the Constitution, created to "establish Justice, insure domestic Tranquility . . . and secure the Blessings of Liberty," as its preamble states, "could not well have been designed at the same time to maintain and perpetuate a system of rapine and murder like slavery." Thereafter he fought slavery and race prejudice from within the system, something Garrison was never willing to do.

Garrison's importance cannot be measured by the number of his followers, which was never large. Unlike more moderately inclined enemies of slavery, he recognized that abolitionism was a revolutionary movement, not merely one more middle-class reform. He also understood that achieving racial equality, not merely "freeing" the slaves, was the only way to reach the abolitionists' professed objective: full justice for blacks. And he saw clearly that few whites, even among abolitionists, believed that blacks were their equals.

Women's Rights

The question of slavery was related to another major reform movement of the era, the crusade for women's rights. The relationship was personal and ideological, direct and indirect, simple and profound. Superficially, the connection can be explained in this way: Women were as likely as men to find slavery offensive and to protest against it. When they did so, they ran into even more adamant resistance, the prejudices of those who objected to abolitionists being reinforced by their feelings that women should not speak in public or participate in political affairs. Thus female abolitionists, driven by the urgencies of conscience, were almost forced to become advocates of women's rights. "We have good cause to be grateful to the slave," the feminist Abby Kelley wrote. "In striving to strike his irons off, we found most surely, that we were manacled ourselves."

At a more profound level, the reference that abolitionists made to the Declaration of Independence to justify their attack on slavery radicalized women with regard to their own place in society. Were only all men created equal and endowed by God with unalienable rights? For many women the question was a consciousness-raising experience; they began to believe that, like blacks, they were imprisoned from birth in a caste system, legally subordinated and assigned menial social and economic roles that prevented them from developing their full potentialities. Such women considered themselves in a sense worse off than blacks, who had at least the psychological advantage of confronting an openly hostile and repressive society rather than one concealed behind the cloying rhetoric of romantic love.

With the major exception of Margaret Fuller, whose book *Women in the Nineteenth Century* (1844) made a frontal assault on all forms of sexual discrimination, the leading advocates of equal rights for women began their public careers in the abolitionist movement. Among the first were Sarah and Angelina Grimké, South Carolinians who abandoned their native state and the domestic sphere to devote themselves to speaking out against slavery. (In 1841 Angelina married Theodore Dwight Weld.) Male objections to the Grimkés' activities soon made them advocates of women's rights. Similarly, the refusal of delegates to the World Anti-Slavery Convention held in London in 1840 to let women participate in their debates precipitated the decision of two American abolitionists, Lucretia Mott and Elizabeth Cady Stanton, to turn their attention to the women's rights movement.

Slavery aside, there were other aspects of feminist consciousness-raising. Some women rejected the idea that they should confine themselves to a sphere of activity consisting mostly of child rearing and housekeeping. The very effort to enforce this kind of specialization made women aware of their second-class citizenship and thus more likely to be dissatisfied. They lacked not merely the right to vote, of which they did not make a major issue, but if married, the right to own property or to make a will. Lydia Maria Child, a popular novelist, found this last restriction particularly offensive. It excited her "towering indignation" that her husband had to sign her will.

The subordination of women was as old as most civilizations. The attack on it came not because of any new discrimination but for the same reasons that moti-

Anna Elizabeth Klumpke's portrait of Elizabeth Cady Stanton (1887). In 1848 Stanton helped draft the Declaration of Sentiments, spelling out the injustices of man to woman. The conclusion: "He has endeavored, in every way he could, to destroy her confidence in her own powers, to lessen her self-respect, and to make her willing to lead a dependent and abject life."

vated reformers against other forms of injustice: belief in progress, a sense of personal responsibility, and the conviction that institutions could be changed and that the time for changing them was limited.

When women sought to involve themselves in reform, they became aware of perhaps the most serious handicap that society imposed on them—the conflict between their roles as wives and mothers and their urge to participate in the affairs of the larger world. Elizabeth Cady Stanton has left a striking description of this dilemma. She lived in the 1840s in Seneca Falls, a small town in central New York. Her husband was frequently away on business; she had a brood of growing children and little domestic help. When, stimulated by her interest in abolition and women's rights, she sought to become active in the movements, her family responsibilities made it almost impossible even to read about them.

"I now fully understood the practical difficulties most women had to contend with," she recalled in her autobiography, *Eighty Years and More* (1898):

The general discontent I felt with woman's portion as wife, mother, housekeeper, physician, and spiritual guide, the chaotic condition into which everything fell without her constant supervision, and the wearied, anxious look of the majority of women, impressed me with the strong feeling that some active measures should be taken.

Active measures she took. Together with Lucretia Mott and a few others of like mind, she organized a meeting, the Seneca Falls Convention (July 1848), and drafted a Declaration of Sentiments patterned on the Declaration of Independence. "We hold these truths to be self-evident: that all men and women are created equal," it stated, and it went on to list the "injuries and usurpations" of men, just as Jefferson had outlined those of George III.

From this seed the movement grew. During the 1850s a series of national conventions was held, and more and more reformers, including William Lloyd Garrison, joined the cause. Of the recruits, Susan B. Anthony was the most influential, for she was the first to see the need for thorough organization if effective pressure was to be brought to bear on male-dominated society. Her first campaign, mounted in 1854 and 1855 in behalf of a petition to the New York legislature calling for reform of the property and divorce laws, accumulated 6,000 signatures. But the petition did not persuade the legislature to act. Indeed, the feminists achieved very few practical results during the Age of Reform. Their leaders, however, were persevering types, most of them extraordinarily long-lived. Their major efforts lay in the future.

The Romantic View of Life

The spreading belief that human institutions were improving had a profound effect on the arts and literature. In the Western world, it gave rise to romanticism, a revolt against the bloodless logic of the Age of Reason. It was a noticeable if unnamed point of view in Germany, France, and England as early as the 1780s and in America a generation later; by the second quarter of the nineteenth century, few intellectuals were unmarked by it. "Romantics" believed that change and growth were the essence of life, for individuals and for institutions. They valued feeling and intuition over pure thought, and they stressed the differences between individuals and societies rather than the similarities. Ardent love of country characterized the movement; individualism, optimism, ingenuousness, and emotion were its bywords. Romanticism, too, drew much from the religious sensibilities of mothers. Children were innately good; pernicious influences led to their corruption.

The romantic way of thinking found its greatest American expression in transcendentalism, a New England creation that is difficult to describe because it emphasized the indefinable and the unknowable. It was a mystical, intuitive way of looking at life that subordinated facts to feelings. Its literal meaning was "to go beyond the world of the senses," by which the transcendentalists meant the material and observable world. To the transcendentalists, human beings were truly divine because they were part of nature, itself the essence of divinity. Their intellectual capacities did not define their capabilities, for they could "transcend" reason by having faith in themselves and in the fundamental benevolence of the universe. Transcendentalists were complete individualists, seeing the social whole as no more than the sum of its parts. Organized religion, indeed all institutions were unimportant if not counterproductive; what mattered was the single person and that people aspire, stretch *beyond* their known capabilities. Failure resulted only from lack of effort. The expression "Hitch your wagon to a star" is of transcendentalist origin.

Emerson and Thoreau

The leading transcendentalist thinker was Ralph Waldo Emerson. Born in 1803 and educated at Harvard, Emerson became a minister, but in 1832 he gave up his pulpit, deciding that "the profession is antiquated." After traveling in Europe he settled in Concord, Massachusetts, where he had a long career as an essayist, lecturer, and sage.

Emerson's philosophy was at once buoyantly optimistic and rigorously intellectual, self-confident, and conscientious. In "The American Scholar," a notable address he delivered at Harvard in 1837, he urged Americans to put aside their devotion to things European and seek inspiration in their immediate surroundings. Emerson saw himself as pitting "spiritual powers" against "the mechanical powers and the mechanical philosophy of this time." The new industrial society of New England disturbed him profoundly.

Because he put so much emphasis on self-reliance, Emerson disliked powerful governments. "The less government we have the better," he said. In a sense he was the prototype of some modern alienated intellectuals, so repelled by the world as it was that he would not actively try to change it. Nevertheless he thought strong leadership essential. Emerson also had a strong practical streak. He made his living by lecturing, tracking tirelessly across the country, talking before every type of audience for fees ranging from $50 to several hundreds.

Closely identified with Emerson was his Concord neighbor Henry David Thoreau. After graduating from Harvard in 1837, Thoreau taught school for a time and helped out in a small pencil-making business run by his family. He was a strange man, gentle, a dreamer, content to absorb the beauties of nature almost intuitively, yet stubborn and individualistic to the point of selfishness. The hectic scramble for wealth that Thoreau saw all about him he found disgusting—and alarming, for he believed it was destroying both the natural and the human resources of the country.

Like Emerson, Thoreau objected to many of society's restrictions on the individual. "That government is best which governs not at all," he said, going both Emerson and the Jeffersonians one better. He was perfectly prepared to see himself as a majority of one. "When were the good and the brave ever in a majority?" Thoreau asked. "If a man does not keep pace with his companions," he wrote on another occasion, "perhaps it is because he hears a different drummer."

In 1845 Thoreau decided to put to the test his theory that a person need not depend on society for a satisfying existence. He built a cabin at Walden Pond on some property owned by Emerson and lived there alone for two years. The best fruit of this period was that extraordinary book *Walden* (1854). Superficially, *Walden* is the story of Thoreau's experiment, movingly and beautifully written. It is also an acid indictment of the social behavior of the average American, an attack on unthinking conformity, on subordinating one's own judgment to that of the herd.

The most graphic illustration of Thoreau's confidence in his own values occurred while he was living at Walden. At that time the Mexican War was raging.

Thoreau considered the war immoral because it advanced the cause of slavery. To protest, he refused to pay his Massachusetts poll tax. For this he was arrested and lodged in jail, although only for one night because an aunt promptly paid the tax for him. His essay "Civil Disobedience," explaining his view of the proper relation between the individual and the state, resulted from this experience. Like Emerson, however, Thoreau refused to participate in practical reform movements. "I love Henry," one of his friends said, "but I cannot like him; and as for taking his arm, I should as soon think of taking the arm of an elm tree."

Edgar Allan Poe

The work of all the imaginative writers of the period reveals romantic influences, and it is possibly an indication of the affinity of the romantic approach to American conditions that a number of excellent writers of poetry and fiction first appeared in the 1830s and 1840s. Edgar Allan Poe, one of the most remarkable, seems almost a caricature of the romantic image of the tortured genius. Poe was born in Boston in 1809, the son of poor actors who died before he was three years old. He was raised by a wealthy Virginian, John Allan.

Few persons as neurotic as Poe have been able to produce first-rate work. In college he ran up debts of $2,500 in less than a year and had to withdraw. He won an appointment to West Point but was discharged after a few months for disobedience and "gross neglect of duty." He was a lifelong alcoholic and an occasional taker of drugs. He married a child of 13.

Poe was obsessed with death. Once he attempted to poison himself; repeatedly he was down and out, even to the verge of starvation. He was haunted by melancho-

In 1845 Edgar Allan Poe, impoverished and an alcoholic, was living in the "greatest wretchedness." His young wife was dying of tuberculosis. That same year he wrote "The Raven," a poem about an ill-omened bird that intrudes on a young man's grief over the death of his beloved. "Take thy beak from out of my heart" the man screams. Quoth the raven—famously— "Nevermore."

lia and hallucinations. Yet he was an excellent magazine editor, a penetrating critic, a poet of unique if somewhat narrow talents, and a fine short story writer. Although he died at age 40, he turned out a large volume of serious, highly original work.

Poe responded strongly to the lure of romanticism. His works abound with examples of wild imagination and fascination with mystery, fright, and the occult. If he did not invent the detective story, he perfected it; his tales "The Murders in the Rue Morgue" and "The Purloined Letter" stressed the thought processes of a clever detective in solving a mystery by reasoning from evidence.

Although dissolute in his personal life, when Poe touched pen to paper, he became a disciplined craftsman. The most fantastic passages in his works are the result of careful, reasoned selection; not a word, he believed, could be removed without damage to the whole. And despite his rejection of most of the values prized by middle-class America, Poe was widely read in his own day. His poem "The Raven" won instantaneous popularity when it was published in 1845. Had he been a little more stable, he might have made a good living with his pen—but in that case he might not have written as he did.

Nathaniel Hawthorne

Another product of the prevailing romanticism was Nathaniel Hawthorne, born in 1804 in Salem, Massachusetts. When Hawthorne was a small child, his father died and his grief-stricken mother became a recluse. Left largely to his own devices, he grew to be a lonely, introspective person. Wandering about New England by himself in summertime, he soaked up local lore, which he drew on in writing short stories.

Hawthorne's early stories, originally published in magazines, were brought together in *Twice-Told Tales* (1837). They made excellent use of New England culture and history for background but were concerned chiefly with the struggles of individuals with sin, guilt, and especially the pride and isolation that often afflict those who place too much reliance on their own judgment. His greatest works were two novels written after the Whigs turned him out of his government job in 1849. *The Scarlet Letter* (1850), a grim yet sympathetic analysis of adultery, condemned not the woman, Hester Prynne, but the people who presumed to judge her. *The House of the Seven Gables* (1851) was a gripping account of the decay of an old New England family brought on by the guilt feelings of the current owners of the house, caused by the way their ancestors had cheated the original owners of the property.

Herman Melville

In 1850, while Hawthorne was writing *The House of the Seven Gables,* his publisher introduced him to another writer who was in the midst of a novel. The writer was Herman Melville; the book, *Moby Dick.* Hawthorne and Melville became good friends at once, for despite their dissimilar backgrounds, they had a great deal in common. Melville was a New Yorker, born in 1819, one of eight children of a merchant of distinguished lineage. His father, however, lost all his money and died when the boy was 12. Herman left school at 15, worked briefly as a bank clerk, and in 1837 went to sea. For 18 months, in 1841 and 1842, he was crewman on the whaler *Acushnet*. Then he jumped ship in the South Seas. For a time he lived among a tribe of cannibals in the Marquesas; later he made his way to Tahiti, where he idled away nearly a year. After another year at sea he returned to America in the fall of 1844.

Although he had never before attempted serious writing, in 1846 he published *Typee*, an account of his life in the Marquesas. The book was a great success, for Melville had visited a part of the world almost unknown to Americans, and his descriptions of his bizarre experiences suited the taste of a romantic age. Success inspired him to write a sequel, *Omoo* (1847); other books followed quickly.

Experience made Melville too aware of the evil in the world to be a transcendentalist. His dark view of human nature culminated in *Moby Dick* (1851). This book, Melville said, was "broiled in hellfire." Against the background of a whaling voyage (no better account of whaling has ever been written), he dealt subtly and symbolically with the problems of good and evil, of courage and cowardice, of faith, stubbornness, pride. In Captain Ahab, driven relentlessly to hunt down the huge white whale Moby Dick, which had destroyed his leg, Melville created one of the great figures of literature; in the book as a whole, he produced one of the finest novels written by an American, comparable to the best in any language.

As Melville's work became more profound, it lost its appeal to the average reader, and its originality and symbolic meaning escaped most critics. *Moby Dick*, his masterpiece, received little attention and most of that unfavorable. He kept on writing until his death in 1891 but was virtually ignored. Only in the 1920s did the critics rediscover him and give him his merited place in the history of American literature. His "Billy Budd, Foretopman," now considered one of his best stories, was not published until 1924.

Walt Whitman

Walt Whitman, whose *Leaves of Grass* (1855) was the last of the great literary works of this brief outpouring of genius, was the most romantic and by far the most distinctly American writer of his age. He was born on Long Island, outside New York City, in 1819. At 13 he left school and worked for a printer; thereafter he held a succession of newspaper jobs in the metropolitan area.

Although genuinely a "common man," thoroughly at home among tradesmen and laborers, he was surely not an ordinary man. Deeply introspective, he read omnivorously, if in a rather disorganized fashion, while working out a new, intensely personal mode of expression. During the early 1850s, while employed as a carpenter and composing the poems that made up *Leaves of Grass*, he regularly carried a book of Emerson in his lunch box. "I was simmering, simmering, simmering," he later recalled. "Emerson brought me to a boil." The transcendental

Some scholars regard Walt Whitman as the poet of nature, and others, of the body—a reference to erotic lines such as: "Without shame the man I like knows and avows the deliciousness of his sex, / Without shame the woman I like knows and avows hers." Whitman's *Leaves of Grass* had every leaf in nature, complained critic E. P. Whipple, except the fig leaf.

idea that inspiration and aspiration are at the heart of all achievement captivated him. Poets could best express themselves, he believed, by relying uncritically on their natural inclinations without regard for rigid metrical forms.

Leaves of Grass consisted of a preface, in which Whitman made the extraordinary statement that Americans had "probably the fullest poetical nature" of any people in history, and twelve poems in free verse: rambling, uneven, appearing to most readers shocking both in the commonplace nature of the subject matter and the coarseness of the language. Emerson, Thoreau, and a few others saw a fresh talent in these poems, but most readers and reviewers found them offensive. Indeed, the work was so undisciplined and so much of it had no obvious meaning that it was easy to miss the many passages of great beauty and originality.

Whitman's work was more authentically American than that of any contemporary. His egoism—he titled one of his finest poems "Song of Myself"—was tempered by his belief that he was typical of all humanity:

> *I celebrate myself and sing myself*
> *And what I assume you shall assume,*
> *For every atom belonging to me as good belongs to you.*

He had a remarkable ear for rendering common speech poetically, for employing slang, for catching the breezy informality of Americans and their faith in themselves:

> *Earth! you seem to look for something at my hands,*
> *Say, old top-knot, what do you want?*
> *I bequeath myself to the dirt to grow from the grass I love,*
> *If you want me again look for me under your boot-soles.*

Because of these qualities and because in his later work, especially during the Civil War, he occasionally struck a popular chord, Whitman was never as neglected as Melville. When he died in 1892, he was, if not entirely understood, at least widely appreciated.

Education for Democracy

The literary flowering of the mid-nineteenth century did not reach a broad audience; apart from Whitman, none of the great writers of the day found a large reading audience. But although few Americans aspired to the intellectual refinement found among some European elites, literacy was expanding markedly in the United States.

Except on the edge of the frontier and in the South, most youngsters between the ages of five and ten attended a school for at least a couple of months of the year. These schools, however, were privately run and charged fees. Attendance was not required and fell off sharply once children learned to read and do their sums well enough to get along in day-to-day life. The teachers were usually young men waiting for something better to turn up.

All this changed with the rise of the common school movement. At the heart of the movement was the belief, widely expressed in the first days of the republic, that a government based on democratic rule must provide the means, as Jefferson put it, to "diffuse knowledge throughout the mass of the people." This meant free tax-supported schools, which all children were expected to attend. It also came to mean that such an educational system should be administered on a statewide basis and that teaching should become a profession that required formal training.

The two most effective leaders of the common school movement were Henry Barnard and Horace Mann. Both were New Englanders, Whigs, trained in the law, and in other ways conservative types. They shared an unquenchable faith in the improvability of the human race through education. Mann drafted the 1837 Massachusetts law creating a state school board and then became its first secretary. Over the next decade Mann's annual reports carried the case for common schools to every corner of the land. Seldom given to understatement, Mann called common schools "the greatest discovery ever made by man." He encouraged young women to become teachers while commending them to school boards by claiming that they could get along on lower salaries than men.

Young women adhered to the call. By 1860, women comprised 78 percent of the common school teachers in Massachusetts, a trend that prefigured developments elsewhere. The influx of young women invigorated the common schools and brought missionary zeal to the enterprise. Harriet Beecher Stowe, who once taught at the Hartford Seminary, explained that male teachers lacked the "patience, the long-suffering, and gentleness necessary to superintend the formation of character."

By the 1850s every state outside the South provided free elementary schools and supported institutions for training teachers. Many extended public education to include high schools, and Michigan and Iowa even established publicly supported colleges.

In addition to common schools, thousands of female seminaries were built between 1820 and 1850, many of them by evangelical denominations. During the Revolutionary Era, it was thought that half as many women were literate as men; but the Census of 1850 revealed that women's literacy equaled that of men.

The State of the Colleges

Unlike common schools, with their democratic overtones, private colleges had at best a precarious place in Jacksonian America. For one thing, there were too many of them. Any town with pretensions of becoming a regional center felt it had to have a college. Ohio had twenty-five in the 1850s, Tennessee sixteen. Many of these institutions were short-lived. Of the fourteen colleges founded in Kentucky between 1800 and 1850, only half were still operating in 1860.

The problem of supply was compounded by a demand problem—too few students. Enrollment at the largest, Yale, never topped 400 until the mid-1840s. On the eve of the Civil War the largest state university, North Carolina, had fewer than 500. Higher education was beyond the means of the average family. Although most colleges charged less than half the $55 tuition required by Harvard, that was still too much for most families, wages being what they were. So desperate was the shortage that colleges accepted applicants as young as 11 and 12 and as old as 30.

Once enrolled, students had little worry about making the grade, not least because grades were not given. Since students were hard to come by and classwork was considered relatively unimportant, discipline was lax. Official authority was frequently challenged, and rioting was known to break out over such weighty matters as the quality of meals. A father who visited his son's college dormitory in 1818 found it inhabited by "half a dozen loungers in a state of oriental lethargy, each stretched out upon two or three chairs, with scarce any indication of life in them [other] than the feeble effort to keep up the fire of their cigars."

The typical college curriculum, dominated by the study of Latin and Greek, had almost no practical relevance except for future clergymen. The Yale faculty, most of them ministers, defended the classics as admirably providing for both "the discipline and the furniture of the mind," but these subjects commended themselves to college officials chiefly because they did not require costly equipment or a faculty that knew anything else. Professors spent most of their time in and out of the classroom trying to maintain a semblance of order, "to the exclusion of any great literary undertakings to which their choice might lead them," one explained. "Our country is yet too young for old professors," a Bostonian informed a foreign visitor in the 1830s, "and, besides, they are too poorly paid to induce first rate men to devote themselves to the business of lecturing. . . . We consider professors as secondary men."

Fortunately for the future of higher education, some college officials recognized the need for a drastic overhaul of their institutions. President Francis Wayland of Brown University used his 1842 address, "On the Present Collegiate System," to call for a thorough revamping of the curriculum to make it responsive to the economic realities of American society. This meant more courses in science, economics (where Wayland's own *Elements of Political Economy* might be used), modern history, and applied mathematics; fewer in Hebrew, biblical studies, Greek, and ancient history.

Yale established a separate school of science in 1847, which it hoped would attract serious-minded students and research-minded professors. At Harvard, which also opened a scientific school, students were allowed to choose some of their courses and were compelled to earn grades as a stimulus to study. Colleges in the West and the South began to offer mechanical and agricultural subjects relevant to their regional economies. Oberlin enrolled four female students in 1837, and the first women's college, the Georgia Female College, opened its doors in 1839.

These reforms slowed the downward spiral of colleges; they did not restore them to the honored place they had enjoyed in the Revolutionary era. Of the first six presidents of the United States, only Washington did not graduate from college. Beginning in 1829, seven of the next eleven did not. In this presidents Jackson, Van Buren, Harrison, Taylor, Fillmore, Lincoln, and Johnson were like 98 of every 100 white males, all blacks and Indians, and all but a handful of white women in mid-nineteenth-century America. Going to college had yet, in Wayland's words, to "commend itself to the good sense and patriotism of the American people."

1774	Mother Ann Lee founds first Shaker community
1784	Dr. Benjamin Rush's *Inquiry into the Effects of Ardent Spirits* questions alcohol's benefits
1826	American Temperance Union begins campaign against drunkenness
1829	Black abolitionist David Walker publishes *Appeal to the Coloured Citizens of the World*
1830s	Second Great Awakening stresses promise of salvation
	Prison reformers debate Auburn versus Philadelphia system
1830–1850	Utopian communities flourish
1830	Joseph Smith shares his "vision" in *Book of Mormon*
1831	Abolitionist William Lloyd Garrison founds *The Liberator* and the New England Anti-Slavery Society
1831–1832	Alexis de Tocqueville and Gustave de Beaumont tour America
1832	Perkins Institution for the Blind opens in Boston
1837	Illinois abolitionist Elijah Lovejoy is murdered
	Ralph Waldo Emerson delivers "The American Scholar" at Harvard
	Horace Mann and Henry Barnard call for common schools
1843	Dorothea Dix exposes treatment of the insane in *Memorial to the Legislature of Massachusetts*
1844	Margaret Fuller condemns sexual discrimination in *Women in the Nineteenth Century*
	Nauvoo mob murders Joseph Smith
1845	Frederick Douglass describes slave life in *Narrative of the Life of Frederick Douglass*
1847	Brigham Young leads Mormon migration to Great Salt Lake
1848	Elizabeth Cady Stanton and Lucretia Mott organize Seneca Falls Convention and draft Declaration of Sentiments
1850	Nathaniel Hawthorne publishes *The Scarlet Letter*
1851	Maine bans alcoholic beverages
	Herman Melville publishes *Moby Dick*
1854	Henry David Thoreau attacks conformity in *Walden*
1854–1855	Susan B. Anthony leads petition campaign against New York property and divorce laws
1855–1892	Walt Whitman publishes *Leaves of Grass* (various editions)

CHAPTER

Westward Expansion

IN OCTOBER 2006, PRESIDENT GEORGE W. BUSH SIGNED THE Secure Fence Act, which provided for construction of a 700-mile fence stretching from Brownsville, Texas, to a western point near San Diego, California. "We must keep our borders secure," Bush explained. Every year since 2000, nearly a half million Mexicans entered the United States illegally. By 2007, the number of illegal aliens in the United States exceeded 11 million. "Ours is a nation of immigrants," Bush added, "but we're also a nation of laws." Congress concurred; the Secure Fence Act passed in the House of Representatives by a margin of 101 votes.

But throughout the debate, several historical facts went virtually unnoticed. Most ironic was the fact that the fence was to be built to prevent Mexicans from passing into lands that had once belonged to Mexico. The American Southwest, of course, had previously been occupied by Indians and their ancestors, a region that was subsequently claimed by Spain. In 1821 Mexico secured independence from Spain and claimed ownership of all of New Spain. By then, however, American settlers were flocking into the Southwest, especially Texas. In 1830, the Mexican government outlawed further American immigration into the region.

Initially the Mexican government ignored the flood of American immigrants; but by the mid-1830s it stepped up border patrols and sent an army to drive illegal immigrants from Texas. This led to clashes that culminated in war. Mexico's defeat caused a shift in boundaries. Now the Southwest belonged to the United States. Mexicans who entered the region were trespassing; in time, they would become illegal immigrants.

The Mexican War was just one of the unintended consequences of the settlement of the West. Another concerned slavery. As the United States acquired more territory and created more states, would slavery expand as well? Would the "peculiar institution" eventually stretch from the Atlantic to the Pacific and span the entire continent? The prospect disquieted many.

Tyler's Troubles

John Tyler, who became president in 1841 after the death of William Henry Harrison, was a thin, rather delicate-appearing man with pale blue eyes and a long nose. Courteous, tactful, soft-spoken, he gave the impression of being weak, an impression reinforced by his professed belief that the president should defer to Congress in the formulation of policy. This was a false impression; John Tyler was stubborn and proud, and these characteristics combined with an almost total lack of imagination to make him worship consistency, as so many second-raters do. He had turned away from Jackson because of the aggressive way the president had used his powers of appointment and the veto, but he also disagreed with Henry Clay and the northern Whigs about the Bank, protection, and federal internal improvements. Being a states' rights Southerner, he considered such measures unconstitutional. Nevertheless, he was prepared to cooperate with Clay as the leader of what he called the "more immediate representatives" of the people, the members of Congress. But he was not prepared to be Clay's puppet. He asked all of Harrison's Cabinet to remain in office.

Tyler and Clay did not get along, and for this Clay was chiefly to blame. He behaved in an overbearing manner that was out of keeping with his nature, probably because he resented having been passed over by the Whigs in 1840. In Congress, Clay announced a comprehensive program that ignored Tyler's states' rights view of the Constitution. Most important was his plan to set up a new Bank of the United States. A bill to repeal the Independent Treasury Act caused no difficulty, but when Congress passed a new Bank bill, Tyler vetoed it. The entire Cabinet except Secretary of State Daniel Webster thereupon resigned in protest.

John Tyler posed for a daguerreotypist about 1850, after he had retired from public life. Never fully committed to the cause of the party that put him in power, he proved to be an ineffective president.

Abandoned by the Whigs, Tyler attempted to build a party of his own. He failed to do so, and for the remainder of his term the political squabbling in Washington was continuous.

The Webster-Ashburton Treaty

Webster's decision to remain in the Cabinet was motivated in part by his desire to settle the boundary between Maine and New Brunswick. The intent of the peace treaty of 1783 had been to award the United States all land in the area drained by rivers flowing into the Atlantic rather than into the St. Lawrence, but the wording was obscure and the old maps conflicting. In 1842 the British sent a new minister, Lord Ashburton, to the United States to try to settle all outstanding disputes. Ashburton and Webster easily worked out a compromise boundary. Lord Ashburton, gratified by having obtained a portion of the disputed lands to build a military road, made concessions elsewhere along the Canadian and American border. British dependence on foreign foodstuffs was increasing; America's need for British capital was rising. War, or even unsettled affairs, would have injured vital business relations and produced no compensating gains.

The Texas Question

The settlement with Great Britain won support in every section of the United States, but the same could not be said for Tyler's attempt to annex the Republic of Texas, for this involved the question of slavery. In the Transcontinental Treaty of 1819 with Spain, the boundary of the United States had been drawn in such a way as to exclude Texas. This seemed unimportant at the time, yet within months of the treaty's ratification in February 1821, Americans led by Stephen F. Austin had begun to settle in the area. Almost simultaneously Mexico threw off the last vestiges of Spanish rule.

Cotton flourished on the fertile Texas plains, and for a time, the new Mexican authorities offered free land and something approaching local autonomy to groups of settlers from the United States. By 1830 there were some 20,000 white Americans in Texas, about 2,000 slaves, and only a few thousand Mexicans.

As soon as the Mexican government began to restrict them, the Texans began to seek independence. In 1835 a series of skirmishes escalated into a full-scale rebellion. The Mexican president, Antonio López de Santa Anna, marched north with 6,000 soldiers to subdue the rebels. Late in February 1836 he reached San Antonio.

A force of 187 men under Colonel William B. Travis held the city. They took refuge behind the stout walls of a former mission called the Alamo. For ten days they beat off Santa Anna's assaults, inflicting terrible casualties on the attackers. Finally, on March 6, the Mexicans breached and scaled the walls. Once inside they killed everyone, even the wounded. Among the dead were the legendary Davy Crockett and Jim Bowie, inventor of the Bowie knife.

After the Alamo and a similar slaughter at another garrison at Goliad, southeast of San Antonio, peaceful settlement of the dispute between Texas and Mexico was impossible. Meanwhile, on March 2, 1836, Texas had declared its independence. Sam Houston, a former congressman and governor of Tennessee and an experienced Indian fighter, was placed in charge of the rebel army. For a time Houston retreated before Santa Anna's troops, who greatly outnumbered his own. At the San Jacinto River he took a stand. On April 21, 1836, shouting "Forward! Charge! Remember the Alamo! Remember Goliad!" his troops routed the Mexican army, which soon retreated across the Rio Grande. In October, Houston was elected president of the Republic of Texas, and a month later a plebiscite revealed that an overwhelming majority favored annexation by the United States.

President Jackson hesitated. To take Texas might lead to war with Mexico. Assuredly it would stir up the slavery controversy. On his last day in office he recognized the republic, but he made no move to accept it into the Union, nor did his successor, Van Buren. Texas thereupon went its own way, which involved developing friendly ties with Great Britain. An independent Texas suited British tastes perfectly, for it could provide an alternative supply of raw cotton and a market for manufactures unfettered by tariffs.

These events caused alarm in the United States, especially among Southerners, who dreaded the possibility that a Texas dominated by Great Britain might abolish slavery. As a Southerner, Tyler shared these feelings; as a beleaguered politician, spurned by the Whigs and held in contempt by most Democrats, he saw in annexation a chance to revive his fortunes. When Webster resigned as secretary of state in 1843, Tyler replaced him with a fellow Virginian, Abel P. Upshur, whom he ordered to seek a treaty of annexation. The South was eager to take Texas, and in the West and even the Northeast the patriotic urge to add such a magnificent new territory to the national domain was great. Counting noses, Upshur convinced himself that the Senate would approve annexation by the necessary two-thirds majority. He negotiated a treaty in February 1844, but before he could sign it he was killed by the accidental explosion of a cannon on the USS *Princeton* during a weapons demonstration.

To ensure the winning of Texas, Tyler appointed John C. Calhoun secretary of state. This was a blunder; by then Calhoun was so closely associated with the South and with slavery that his appointment alienated thousands of Northerners who might otherwise have welcomed annexation. Suddenly Texas became a hot political issue. Clay and Van Buren, who seemed assured of the 1844 Whig and Democratic presidential nominations, promptly announced that they opposed annexation, chiefly on the ground that it would probably lead to war with Mexico. With a national election in the offing, northern and western senators refused to vote for annexation, and in June the Senate rejected the treaty, 35 to 16. The Texans were angry and embarrassed, the British eager again to take advantage of the situation.

Manifest Destiny

The Senate, Clay, and Van Buren had all misinterpreted public opinion. Where pioneers had once stood in awe before the majesty of the Blue Ridge, then hesitated to venture from the protective shadows of the forest into the open prairies of Illinois, they now shrugged their shoulders at great deserts and began to talk of the Rocky Mountains as "mere molehills" along the road to the Pacific. After 200 years of westward expansion had brought them as far as Missouri and Iowa, Americans perceived their destined goal. *The whole continent was to be theirs!* Theirs to exploit, and theirs to make into one mighty nation, a land of opportunity, a showcase to display the virtues of democratic institutions, living proof that Americans were indeed God's chosen people. A New York journalist, John L. O'Sullivan, captured the new mood in a sentence. Nothing must interfere, he wrote in 1845, with "the fulfillment of our *manifest destiny* to overspread the continent allotted by Providence for the free development of our yearly multiplying millions."

The expansion, stimulated by the natural growth of the population and by a revived flood of immigration, was going on in every section and with little regard for political boundaries. New settlers rolled westward in hordes. Between 1830 and 1835, some 10,000 entered "foreign" Texas, and this was a trickle compared to what the early 1840s were to bring. The politicians did not sense the new mood in 1844; even Calhoun, who saw the acquisition of Texas as part of a broader program, was thinking of balancing sectional interests rather than of national expansion.

Life on the Trail

The romantic myths attached by later generations to this mighty human tide have obscured the adjustments forced on the pioneers and focused attention on the least significant of the dangers they faced and the hardships they endured. For example, Indians could of course be deadly enemies, but pioneers were more likely to complain that the Indians they encountered were dirty, lazy, and pitiably poor than to worry about the danger of Indian attack. Women tended to fear their strangeness, not their actual behavior. One reported that Indian men were commonly "guiltless of clothing."

The greater dangers were accidents on the trail, particularly to children, and also unsanitary conditions and exposure to the elements. "Going west" had always been laborious, but in the 1840s the distances covered were longer by far and the comforts and conveniences of "civilization" that had to be left behind, being more extensive than those available to earlier generations, tended to be more painful to surrender.

Travel on the plains west of the Mississippi was especially taxing for women. Some assumed tasks traditionally performed by men. "I keep close to my gun and dog," a woman from Illinois wrote in her diary. But most found the experience disillusioning. Guidebooks promised them that "regular exercise, in the open air . . .

DID THE FRONTIER CHANGE WOMEN'S ROLES?

Ada McColl here gathers buffalo chips to be burned for fuel. She and all other frontier women were missing from Frederick Jackson Turner's famous argument (1893) on the centrality of the frontier to American history. Subsequent scholars provided some anecdotal accounts of women on the frontier, but it was not until the 1970s, when feminism moved to the center of national debate, that scholars flocked to the subject. In a study of letters and diaries, John Mack Faragher (1979) concluded that women on the overland trail had not experienced feminist liberation but had instead been exploited. The men's tasks of herding animals and overcoming streams and boulders allowed occasional respites, but women worked ceaselessly—preparing meals, caring for children, cleaning clothes—in nearly impossible conditions. That same year Julie Roy Jeffrey drew a similar picture. Although women were "co-partners in the frontier adventure," husbands still made the "major decisions." Equally important, frontier women themselves endorsed the "cult of true womanhood": the woman's role was to elevate human affairs. Such women sought to civilize the frontier. Sandra L. Myres (1982), on the

other hand, argued that while frontier women accepted traditional women's roles, they also sought to "enlarge the scope of women's place" and in so doing undermined traditions. Research in the 1990s has altered this picture. On the frontier, land was power. Elaine Lindgren (1991) and Katherine Harris (1993) have shown that women often acquired land and managed it effectively.

333

Frederick Jackson Turner, "The Significance of the Frontier in American History" (1893), John Mack Faragher, *Women and Men on the Overland Trail* (1979), Julie Roy Jeffrey, *Frontier Women* (1979), Sandra L. Myres, *Westering Women and the Frontier Experience* (1982), Elaine Lindgren, *Land in Her Own Name* (1991), Katherine Harris, *Long Vistas* (1993).

gives additional vigor and strength." But the books did not prepare women for collecting dried buffalo dung for fuel, for the heat and choking dust of summer, for the monotony, the dirt, the cramped quarters. Caring for an infant or a two-year-old in a wagon could be torture week after week on the trail.

In their letters and journals pioneer women mostly complained of being bone weary. "It is impossible to keep anything clean," one recorded. "Oh dear," another wrote in her journal, "I do so want to get there, it is now almost four months since we have slept in a house." What sort of a house a pioneer family would actually sleep in when they reached their destination is a question this woman did not record, which was probably fortunate for her peace of mind.

California and Oregon

By 1840 many Americans had settled far to the west in California, which was unmistakably Mexican territory, and in the Oregon country, jointly claimed by the United States and Great Britain; and it was to these distant regions that the pioneers were going in increasing numbers as the decade progressed. California was a sparsely settled land of some 7,000 Spanish-speaking ranchers and a handful of "Anglo" settlers from the United States. Until the 1830s, when their estates were broken up by the anticlerical Mexican government, twenty-one Catholic missions, stretching north from San Diego to San Francisco, controlled more than 30,000 Indian converts, who were little better off than slaves.

Oregon, a vaguely defined area between California and Russian Alaska, proved still more alluring to Americans. Captain Robert Gray had sailed up the Columbia River in 1792, and Lewis and Clark had visited the region on their great expedition. In 1811 John Jacob Astor's Pacific Fur Company had established trading posts on the Columbia. Two decades later Methodist, Presbyterian, and Catholic missionaries began to find their way into the Willamette Valley, a green land of rich soil, mild climate, and tall forests teeming with game. Gradually a small number of settlers followed, until by 1840 there were about 500 Americans in the Willamette area.

In the early 1840s, fired by the spirit of manifest destiny, the country suddenly burned with "Oregon fever." In dozens upon dozens of towns, societies were founded to collect information and organize groups to make the march to the Pacific. Land hunger (stimulated by glowing reports from the scene) drew the new migrants most powerfully, but the patriotic concept of manifest destiny gave the trek across the 2,000 miles of wilderness separating Oregon from the western edge of American settlement in Missouri the character of a crusade. In 1843 nearly 1,000 pioneers made the long trip.

The Oregon Trail began at the western border of Missouri and followed the Kansas River and the perverse, muddy Platte ("a mile wide and six inches deep") past Fort Laramie to the Rockies. It crossed the Continental Divide by the relatively easy South Pass, veered south to Fort Bridger, on Mexican soil, and then ran north and west through the valley of the Snake River and eventually, by way of the Columbia, to Fort Vancouver, a British post guarding the entrance to the Willamette Valley.

Over this tortuous path wound the canvas-covered caravans with their scouts and their accompanying herds. Each group became a self-governing community on the march, with regulations democratically agreed on "for the purpose of keeping good order and promoting civil and military discipline." Most of the travelers consisted of young families, some from as far away as the east coast cities, more from towns and farms in the Ohio Valley. Few could be classified as poor because the cost of the trip for a family of four was about $600, no small sum at that time. (The faster and less fatiguing trip by ship around South America cost about $600 per person.)

For large groups Indians posed no great threat (though constant vigilance was necessary), but the five-month trip was full of labor, discomfort, and uncertainty. "It became so monotonous after a while that I would have welcomed an Indian fight if

Trails West

The Old Spanish Trail was the earliest of the trails west. Part of it was mapped in 1776 by a Franciscan missionary. The Santa Fe Trail came into use after 1823. The Oregon Trail was pioneered by trappers and missionaries. The Mormon Trail was first traversed in 1847, while the Oxbow Route, developed under a federal mail contract, was used from 1858 to 1861.

awake," one man wrote. And at the end lay the regular tasks of pioneering. The spirit of the trailblazers is caught in an entry from the diary of James Nesmith:

> *Friday, October 27.—Arrived at Oregon City at the falls of the Willamette.*
> *Saturday, October 28.—Went to work.*

The Election of 1844

In the spring of 1844 expansion did not seem likely to affect the presidential election. The Whigs nominated Clay unanimously and ignored Texas in their party platform. When the Democrats gathered in convention at Baltimore in May, Van

Buren appeared to have the nomination in his pocket. He too wanted to keep Texas out of the campaign. John C. Calhoun, however, was determined to make Texas a campaign issue.

That a politician of Van Buren's caliber, controlling the party machinery, could be upset at a national convention seemed unthinkable. But upset he was, for the southern delegates rallied round the Calhoun policy of taking Texas to save it for slavery. "I can beat Clay and Van Buren put together on this issue," Calhoun boasted. "They are behind the age." With the aid of a few northern expansionists the Southerners forced through a rule requiring that a candidate must be approved by a two-thirds majority. Van Buren could not muster that much support. After a brief deadlock, a "dark horse," James K. Polk of Tennessee, swept the convention.

Polk was a good Jacksonian; his supporters called him "Young Hickory." He opposed high tariffs and was dead set against establishing another national bank. But he believed in taking Texas, and he favored expansion generally.

Texas was now in the campaign. When Clay sensed the new expansionist sentiment of the voters, he tried to hedge on his opposition to annexation, but by doing so he probably lost as many votes as he gained. The election was extremely close. The campaign followed the pattern established in 1840, with stress on parades, mass meetings, and slogans. Polk carried the country by only 38,000 of 2.7 million votes. In the Electoral College the vote was 170 to 105.

Polk's narrow victory was nevertheless taken as a mandate for expansion. Tyler promptly called on Congress to take Texas by joint resolution, which would avoid the necessity of obtaining a two-thirds majority in the Senate. This was done a few days before Tyler left the White House. Under the resolution, if the new state agreed, as many as four new states might be carved from its territory. Polk accepted this arrangement, and in December 1845 Texas became a state.

Polk as President

President Polk, a slightly built, erect man with grave, steel-gray eyes, was approaching 50 years of age. His mind was not of the first order, for he was too tense and calculating to allow his intellect free rein, but he was an efficient, hard worker with a strong will and a tough skin, qualities that stood him in good stead in the White House, and he made politics his whole life.

Oregon was the first order of business. In his inaugural address Polk stated the American claim to the entire region in the plainest terms, but he informed the British minister in Washington, Richard Pakenham, that he would accept a boundary following the 49th parallel to the Pacific. Pakenham rejected this proposal without submitting it to London, and Polk thereupon decided to insist again on the whole area. When Congress met in December 1845, he asked for authority to give the necessary one year's notice for abrogating the 1818 treaty of joint occupation. "The only way to treat John Bull," he told one congressman, "was to look him straight in the eye." Following considerable discussion, Congress complied and in May 1846 Polk notified Great Britain that he intended to terminate the joint occupation.

The British then decided to compromise. Officials of the Hudson's Bay Company had become alarmed by the rapid growth of the American settlement in the Willamette Valley. By 1845 there were some 5,000 people there, whereas the country north of the Columbia contained no more than 750 British subjects. A clash between the groups could have but one result. The company decided to shift its base from the Columbia to Vancouver Island. And British experts outside the company reported that the Oregon country could not possibly be defended in case of war. Thus, when Polk accompanied the one-year notice with a hint that he would again consider a compromise, the British foreign secretary, Lord Aberdeen, hastily suggested Polk's earlier proposal, dividing the Oregon territory along the 49th parallel. Polk, abandoning his belligerent attitude, agreed. The treaty followed that line from the Rockies to Puget Sound, but Vancouver Island, which extends below the line, was left entirely to the British, so that both nations retained free use of the Strait of Juan de Fuca. Although some northern Democrats accused Polk of treachery because he had failed to fight for all of Oregon, the treaty so obviously accorded with the national interest that the Senate approved it by a large majority in June 1846. Polk was then free to take up the Texas question in earnest.

War with Mexico

One reason for the popularity of the Oregon compromise was that the country was already at war with Mexico and wanted no trouble with Great Britain. The war had broken out in large measure because of the expansionist spirit, and the confidence born of its overwhelming advantages of size and wealth certainly encouraged the United States to bully Mexico. In addition, Mexico had defaulted on debts owed the United States, which caused some people to suggest using force to obtain the money. But Mexican pride was also involved. Texas had been independent for the better part of a decade, and Mexico had made no serious effort to reconquer it; nevertheless, Mexico never recognized its independence and promptly broke off diplomatic relations when the United States annexed the republic.

Polk then ordered General Zachary Taylor into Texas to defend the border. However, the location of that border was in dispute. Texas claimed the Rio Grande; Mexico insisted that the boundary was the Nueces River, which emptied into the Gulf of Mexico about 150 miles to the north. Taylor reached the Nueces in July 1845 with about 1,500 troops and crossed into the disputed territory. He stopped on the southern bank at Corpus Christi, not wishing to provoke the Mexicans by marching to the Rio Grande.

Polk had already ordered Taylor to advance to the Rio Grande. By late March 1846 the army, swelled to about 4,000, had taken up positions near the Mexican town of Matamoros. The Mexicans crossed the river on April 25 and attacked an American mounted patrol. They were driven back easily, but when news of the fighting reached Washington, Polk asked Congress to declare war. He treated the matter as a *fait accompli:* "War exists," he stated flatly. Congress accepted this reasoning and without actually declaring war voted to raise and supply an additional 50,000 troops.

From the first battle, the outcome of the Mexican War was never in doubt. At Palo Alto, north of the Rio Grande, 2,300 Americans scattered a Mexican force more than twice their number. Then, hotly pursuing, 1,700 Americans routed 7,500 Mexicans at Resaca de la Palma. Fewer than fifty U.S. soldiers lost their lives in these engagements, while Mexican losses in killed, wounded, and captured exceeded 1,000. Within a week of the outbreak of hostilities, the Mexicans had been driven across the Rio Grande and General Taylor had his troops firmly established on the southern bank.

To the Halls of Montezuma

President Polk insisted not only on directing grand strategy (he displayed real ability as a military planner) but on supervising hundreds of petty details, down to the purchase of mules and the promotion of enlisted men. But he allowed party considerations to control his choice of generals. This partisanship caused unnecessary turmoil in army ranks. He wanted, as Thomas Hart Benton said, "a small war, just large enough to require a treaty of peace, and not large enough to make military reputations dangerous for the presidency."

Unfortunately for Polk, both Taylor and Winfield Scott, the commanding general in Washington, were Whigs. Polk, who tended to suspect the motives of anyone who disagreed with him, feared that one or the other would make political capital of his popularity as a military leader. The examples of his hero, Jackson, and of General Harrison loomed large in Polk's thinking.

The dust had barely settled on the field of Buena Vista when Whig politicians began to pay Taylor court. "Great expectations and great consequences rest upon

This 1846 daguerreotype is the earliest known American war photograph. U.S. General John E. Wood poses with his staff in Saltillo, Mexico.

you," a Kentucky politician explained to him. "People everywhere begin to talk of converting you into a political leader, when the War is done."

Polk's concern was heightened because domestic opposition to the war was growing. Many Northerners feared that the war would lead to the expansion of slavery. Others—among them an obscure Illinois congressman named Abraham Lincoln—felt that Polk had misled Congress about the original outbreak of fighting and that the United States was the aggressor. The farther from the Rio Grande one went in the United States, the less popular "Mr. Polk's war" became; in New England opposition was almost as widespread as it had been to "Mr. Madison's war" in 1812.

Polk's design for prosecuting the war consisted of three parts. First, he would clear the Mexicans from Texas and occupy the northern provinces of Mexico. Second, he would take possession of California and New Mexico. Finally, he would march on Mexico City. Proceeding west from the Rio Grande, Taylor swiftly overran Mexico's northern provinces. In June 1846, American settlers in the Sacramento Valley seized Sonoma and raised the Bear Flag of the Republic of California. Another group, headed by Captain John C. Frémont, leader of an American exploring party that happened to be in the area, clashed with the Mexican authorities around Monterey, California, and then joined with the Sonoma rebels. A naval squadron under Commodore John D. Sloat captured Monterey and San Francisco in July 1846, and a squadron of cavalry joined the other American units in mopping-up operations around San Diego and Los Angeles. By February 1847 the United States had won control of nearly all of Mexico north of the capital city.

The campaign against Mexico City was the most difficult of the war. Fearful of Taylor's growing popularity and entertaining certain honest misgivings about his ability to oversee a complicated campaign, Polk put Winfield Scott in charge of the offensive.

Scott landed his army south of Vera Cruz, Mexico, on March 9, 1847, laid siege to the city, and obtained its surrender in less than three weeks with the loss of only a handful of his 10,000 men. Marching westward through hostile country, he maintained effective discipline, avoiding atrocities that might have inflamed the countryside against him. Finding his way blocked by well-placed artillery and a large army at Cerro Gordo, where the National Road rose steeply toward the central highlands, Scott outflanked the Mexican position and then carried it by storm, capturing more than 3,000 prisoners and much equipment. By mid-May he had advanced to Puebla, only 80 miles southeast of Mexico City.

After delaying until August for the arrival of reinforcements, he pressed on, won two hard-fought victories at the outskirts of the capital, and on September 14 hammered his way into the city. In every engagement the American troops had been outnumbered, yet they always exacted a far heavier toll from the defenders than they themselves were forced to pay. In the fighting on the edge of Mexico City, for example, Scott's army sustained about 1,000 casualties, for the Mexicans defended their capital bravely. But 4,000 Mexicans were killed or wounded in the

The War with Mexico, 1846–1848

engagements, and 3,000 (including eight generals, two of them former presidents of the republic) were taken prisoner. No less an authority than the Duke of Wellington, the conqueror of Napoleon, called Scott's campaign the most brilliant of modern times.

The Treaty of Guadalupe Hidalgo

The Mexicans were thoroughly beaten, but they refused to accept the situation. Early in February the Treaty of Guadalupe Hidalgo was completed. By its terms Mexico accepted the Rio Grande as the boundary of Texas and ceded New Mexico and Upper California to the United States. In return the United States agreed to pay Mexico $15 million and to take on the claims of American citizens against Mexico, which by that time amounted to another $3.25 million.

The relatively easy military victory made some people ashamed that their country was crushing a weaker neighbor. Abolitionists, led by William Lloyd Garrison, called it an "invasion . . . waged solely for the detestable and horrible purpose of extending and perpetuating American slavery." The Senate, subject to the same pressures as the president, ratified the agreement by a vote of 38 to 14.

The Fruits of Victory: Further Enlargement of the United States

The Mexican War, won quickly and at relatively small cost in lives and money, brought huge territorial gains. The Pacific coast from south of San Diego to the 49th parallel and all the land between the coast and the Continental Divide had become the property of the American people. Immense amounts of labor and capital would have to be invested before this new territory could be made to yield its bounty, but the country clearly had the capacity to accomplish the job.

PLUCKED: OR,

THE MEXICAN EAGLE BEFORE THE WAR!   THE MEXICAN EAGLE AFTER THE WAR!

An 1847 cartoon chortling over Mexico's defeat. Sam Houston captured the jingoistic sentiment of the moment: "The Mexicans, are no better than Indians," he said, "and I see no reason why we should not go on in the same course now, and take their land."

In this atmosphere came what seemed a sign from the heavens. In January 1848, while Scott's veterans rested on their victorious arms in Mexico City, a mechanic named James W. Marshall was building a sawmill on the American River in the Sacramento Valley east of San Francisco. One day, while supervising the deepening of the millrace, he noticed a few flecks of yellow in the bed of the stream. These he gathered up and tested. They were pure gold.

Other strikes had been made in California and been treated skeptically or as matters of local curiosity; since the days of Jamestown, too many pioneers had run fruitlessly in search of El Dorado, and too much fool's gold had been passed off as the real thing. Yet this discovery produced an international sensation. The gold was real and plentiful—$200 million of it was extracted in four years—but equally important was the fact that everyone was ready to believe the news. The gold rush reflected the heady confidence inspired by Guadalupe Hidalgo; it seemed the ultimate justification of manifest destiny. Surely an era of continental prosperity and harmony had dawned.

Slavery: The Storm Clouds Gather

Prosperity came in full measure but harmony did not, for once again expansion brought the nation face to face with the divisive question of slavery. This giant chunk of North America, most of it vacant, its future soon to be determined—should it be slave or free? The question, in one sense, seems hardly worth the national crisis it provoked. Slavery appeared to have little future in New Mexico and California, none in Oregon. Why did the South fight so hard for the right to bring slaves into a region that seemed so poorly suited to their exploitation?

Narrow partisanship provides part of the explanation. In districts where slavery was entrenched, a congressman who zealously defended the institution against the most trivial slight usually found himself a popular hero. In the northern states, the representatives who were vigilant in what they might describe as "freedom's cause" seldom regretted it on election day. But slavery raised a moral question. Most Americans tried to avoid confronting this truth; as patriots they assumed that any sectional issue could be solved by compromise. However, while the majority of whites had little respect for blacks, slave or free, few persons, northern or southern, could look upon the ownership of one human being by another as simply an alternative form of economic organization and argue its merits as they would those of the protective tariff or a national bank. Twist the facts as they might, slavery was either right or it was wrong; being on the whole honest and moral, they could not, having faced that truth, stand by unconcerned while the question was debated.

The question could come up in Congress only indirectly, for the Constitution did not give the federal government any control over slavery in the states. But Congress had complete control in the territories. Therefore the fact that slavery had no future in the Mexican cession was unimportant—in fact, for the foes of slavery, it was an advantage. By attacking slavery where it did not and probably never could exist, they could conceal from the slaveholders—and perhaps even from themselves—their hope ultimately to extinguish the institution.

Slavery had complicated the Texas problem from the start, and it beclouded the future of the Southwest even before the Mexican flag had been stripped from the staffs at Santa Fe and Los Angeles. On August 8, 1846, during the debate on a bill appropriating money for the conduct of the war, Democratic Congressman David Wilmot of Pennsylvania introduced an amendment that provided "as an express and fundamental condition to the acquisition of any territory from the Republic of Mexico" that "neither slavery nor involuntary servitude shall ever exist in any part of said territory".

Southerners found the Wilmot Proviso particularly insulting. Nevertheless, it passed the House, where northern congressmen outnumbered southern. But it was defeated in the Senate, where Southerners held the balance. To counter the Proviso, Calhoun, once again serving as senator from South Carolina, introduced resolutions in 1846 arguing that Congress had no right to bar slavery from any territory; because territories belonged to all the states, slave and free, all should have equal rights in them. From this position it was only a step (soon taken) to demanding that Congress guarantee the right of slave owners to bring slaves into the territories and establish federal slave codes in the territories. Most Northerners considered this proposal as repulsive as Southerners found the Wilmot Proviso.

Calhoun's resolutions could never pass the House of Representatives, and Wilmot's Proviso had no chance in the Senate. Yet their very existence threatened the Union; as Senator Benton remarked, they were like the blades of a pair of scissors, ineffective separately, an efficient cutting tool taken together.

To resolve the territorial problem, two compromises were offered. One, eventually backed by President Polk, would extend the Missouri Compromise line to the Pacific. The majority of Southerners were willing to go along with this scheme, but most Northerners would no longer agree to the reservation of any new territory for slavery. The other possibility, advocated by Senator Lewis Cass of Michigan, called for organizing new territories without mention of slavery, thus leaving it to local settlers, through their territorial legislatures, to determine their own institutions. Cass's "popular sovereignty," known more vulgarly as "squatter sovereignty," had the superficial merit of appearing to be democratic. Its virtue for the members of Congress, however, was that it allowed them to escape the responsibility of deciding the question themselves.

The Election of 1848

Plainly the time had come, in a democracy, to go to the people. The coming presidential election seemed to provide an ideal opportunity.

The opportunity was missed. The politicians of the parties hedged, fearful of losing votes in one section or another. With the issues blurred, voters had no real choice. That the Whigs should behave in such a manner was perhaps to be expected of the party of "Tippecanoe and Tyler Too," but in 1848 they outdid even their 1840 performance, nominating Zachary Taylor for president. They chose the general despite his lack of political sophistication and after he had flatly refused to state his opinion on any current subject. The party offered no platform. Taylor was a brave man and a fine general; the Democrats had mistreated him; he was a common, ordinary fellow, unpretentious and warmhearted. Such was the Whig "argument." Taylor's contribution to the campaign was so naive as to be pathetic. "I am a Whig, *but not an ultra Whig*. . . . If elected . . . I should feel bound to administer the government untrammeled by party schemes."

The Democratic nominee was Lewis Cass, the father of popular sovereignty, but the party did not endorse that or any other solution to the territorial question. Cass was at least an experienced politician, having been governor of the Michigan Territory, secretary of war, minister to France, and senator.

The Van Buren wing of the Democratic party was known as the Barnburners to call attention to their radicalism—supposedly they would burn down the barn to get rid of the rats. The Barnburners could not stomach Cass's willingness to countenance the extension of slavery into new territories. Combining with the antislavery Liberty party, they formed the Free Soil party and nominated Van Buren.

Van Buren knew he could not be elected, but he believed the time had come to take a stand. "The minds of nearly all mankind have been penetrated by a conviction of the evils of slavery," the onetime "Fox" and "Magician" declared. The Free Soil party polled nearly 300,000 votes, about 10 percent of the total, in a very dull campaign. Offered a choice between the honest ignorance of Taylor and the cynical opportunism of Cass, the voters—by a narrow margin—chose the former, Taylor receiving 1.36 million votes to Cass's 1.22 million. Taylor carried eight of the fifteen slave states and seven of the fifteen free states, proof that the sectional issue had been avoided. The chief significance of the election was the growing strength of the antislavery forces; in the next decade, this would bring about the collapse of the second party system.

The Gold Rush

The question of slavery in the territories could no longer be deferred. The discovery of gold had brought an army of prospectors into California. By the summer of 1848 San Francisco had become almost a ghost town, and an estimated two-thirds of the adult males of Oregon had hastened south to the gold fields. After President Polk confirmed the "extraordinary character" of the strike in his annual message of December 1848, there was no containing the gold seekers. During 1849, some 25,000 Americans made their way to California from the East by ship; more than 55,000 others crossed the continent by overland routes. About 8,000 Mexicans, 5,000 South Americans, and numbers of Europeans joined the rush.

The rough limits of the gold country had been quickly marked out. For 150 miles and more along the western slope of the Sierra stretched the great mother lode. Along the expanse any stream or canyon, any ancient gravel bed might conceal a treasure in nuggets, flakes, or dust. Armed with pickaxes and shovels, with washing pans, even with knives and spoons, eager prospectors hacked and dug and sifted, each accumulating a hoard, some great, some small, of gleaming yellow metal.

The impact on the region was enormous. Between 1849 and 1860 about 200,000 people, nearly all of them males, crossed the Rockies to California and thousands more reached California by ship via Cape Horn. Almost overnight the Spanish American population was reduced to the status of a minority. Disregarding justice and reason alike, the newcomers from the East, as one observer noted, "regarded every man but a native [North] American as an interloper." They referred to people of Latin American origin as "greasers" and sought by law and by violence to keep them from mining for gold. Even the local Californians (now American citizens) were discriminated against. The few free blacks in California and the several thousand more who came in search of gold were treated no better. As for the far larger Indian population, it was almost wiped out. There were about 150,000 Indians in California in the mid-1840s but only 35,000 in 1860.

The ethnic conflict was only part of the problem. Rough, hard men, separated from women, lusting for gold in a strange wild country where fortunes could be made in a day, gambled away in an hour, or stolen in an instant—the situation demanded the establishment of a territorial government. President Taylor appreciated this, and in his gruff, simple-hearted way he suggested an uncomplicated answer: admit California directly as a state, letting the Californians decide for themselves about slavery. The rest of the Mexican cession could be formed into another state. No need for Congress, with its angry rivalries, to meddle at all, he believed. In this way the nation could avoid the divisive effects of sectional debate.

The Californians reacted favorably to Taylor's proposal. They were overwhelmingly opposed to slavery, though not for humanitarian reasons. On the contrary, they tended to look on blacks as they did Mexicans and feared that if slavery were permitted, white gold seekers would be disadvantaged. "They would be unable," one delegate to the California constitutional convention predicted, "to compete with the bands of negroes who would be set to work under the direction of capitalists. It would become a monopoly." By October 1849 they had drawn up a constitution that outlawed slavery, and by December the new state government was functioning.

Taylor was the owner of a large plantation and more than 100 slaves; Southerners had assumed (without bothering to ask) that he would fight to keep the territories open to slavery. But being a military man, he was above all a nationalist; he disliked the divisiveness that partisan discussion of the issue was producing. Southerners were horrified by the president's reasoning. To admit California

Gold prospectors used a "long Tom" to wash gold from gravel in a stream. The California gold rush brought mostly men—along with a few women—west in search of their fortunes.

would destroy the balance between free and slave states in the Senate; to allow all the new land to become free would doom the South to wither in a corner of the country, surrounded by hostile free states. Should that happen, how long could slavery sustain itself, even in South Carolina? Radicals were already saying that the South would have to choose between secession and surrender. Taylor's plan played into the hands of extremists.

The Compromise of 1850

This was no longer a squabble over territorial governments. With the Union itself at stake, Henry Clay rose to save the day. He had been as angry and frustrated when the Whigs nominated Taylor as he had been when they passed him over for Harrison. Now, well beyond age 70 and in ill health, he put away his ambition and his resentment and for the last time concentrated his remarkable vision on a great, multifaceted national problem. California must be free and soon admitted to the Union, but the South must have some compensation. For that matter, why not seize the opportunity to settle every outstanding sectional conflict related to slavery? Clay wondered long and hard, drew up a plan, then consulted his old Whig rival Webster and obtained his general approval. On January 29, 1850, he laid his proposal, "founded upon mutual forbearance," before the Senate. A few days later he defended it on the floor of the Senate in the last great speech of his life.

California should be brought directly into the Union as a free state, he argued. The rest of the Southwest should be organized as a territory without mention of slavery: The Southerners would retain the right to bring slaves there, while in fact none would do so. "You have got what is worth more than a thousand Wilmot Provisos," Clay pointed out to his northern colleagues. "You have nature on your side." Empty lands in dispute along the Texas border should be assigned to the New Mexico Territory, Clay continued, but in exchange the United States should take over Texas's preannexation debts. The slave trade should be abolished in the District of Columbia (but not slavery itself), and a more effective federal fugitive slave law should be enacted and strictly enforced in the North.

Clay's proposals occasioned one of the most magnificent debates in the history of the Senate. Every important member had his say. Calhoun, perhaps even more than Clay, realized that the future of the nation was at stake and that his own days were numbered (he died four weeks later). He was so feeble that he could not deliver his speech himself. He sat impassive, wrapped in a great cloak, gripping the arms of his chair, while Senator James M. Mason of Virginia read it to the crowded Senate. Calhoun thought his plan would save the Union, but his speech was an argument for secession; he demanded that the North yield completely on every point, ceasing even to discuss the question of slavery. Clay's compromise was unsatisfactory; he himself had no other to offer. If you will not yield, he said to the northern senators, "let the States . . . agree to separate and part in peace. If you are unwilling we should part in peace, tell us so, and we shall know what to do."

Three days later, on March 7, Daniel Webster took the floor. He too had begun to fail. Years of heavy drinking and other forms of self-indulgence had taken their toll. The brilliant volubility and the thunder were gone, and when he spoke his face was bathed in sweat and there were strange pauses in his delivery. But his argument was lucid. Clay's proposals should be adopted. Since the future of all the territories had already been fixed by geographic and economic factors, the Wilmot Proviso was unnecessary. The North's constitutional obligation to yield fugitive slaves, he said, braving the wrath of New England abolitionists, was "binding in honor and conscience." (A cynic might say that once again Webster was placing property rights above human rights.) The Union, he continued, could not be sundered without bloodshed. At the thought of that dread possibility, the old fire flared: "Peaceable secession!" Webster exclaimed, "Heaven forbid! Where is the flag of the republic to remain? Where is the eagle still to tower?" The debate did not end with the aging giants. Every possible viewpoint was presented, argued, rebutted, rehashed. Senator William H. Seward of New York, a new Whig leader, close to Taylor's ear, caused a stir while arguing against concessions to the slave interests by saying that despite the constitutional obligation to return fugitive slaves, a "higher law" than the Constitution, the law of God, forbade anything that countenanced the evil of slavery.

The majority clearly favored some compromise, but nothing could have been accomplished without the death of President Taylor on July 9, 1850. Obstinate,

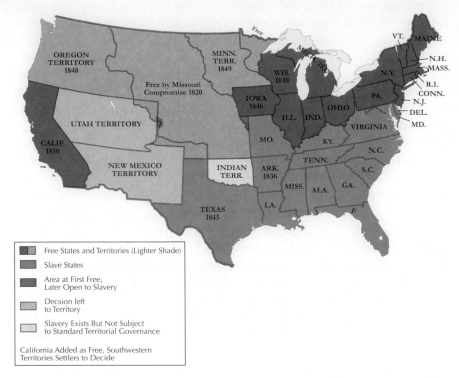

Free by Missouri
Compromise 1820

Free States and Territories (Lighter Shade)

Slave States

Area at First Free,
Later Open to Slavery

Decsion left
to Territory

Slavery Exists But Not Subject
to Standard Territorial Governance

California Added as Free, Southwestern
Territories Settlers to Decide

Compromise of 1850

probably resentful because few people paid him half the heed they paid Clay and other prominent members of Congress, the president had insisted on his own plan to bring both California and New Mexico directly into the Union. When Vice President Millard Fillmore, who was a politician, not an ideologue, succeeded Taylor, the deadlock between the White House and Capitol Hill was broken.

In the Senate and then in the House, tangled combinations pushed through the separate measures, one by one. California became the thirty-first state. The rest of the Mexican cession was divided into two territories, New Mexico and Utah, each to be admitted to the Union when qualified, "with or without slavery as [its] constitution may prescribe." Texas received $10 million to pay off its debt in return for accepting a narrower western boundary. The slave trade in the District of Columbia was abolished as of January 1, 1851. The Fugitive Slave Act of 1793 was amended to provide for the appointment of federal commissioners with authority to issue warrants, summon posses, and compel citizens under pain of fine or imprisonment to assist in the capture of fugitives. Commissioners who decided that an accused person was a runaway received a larger fee than if they declared the person legally free. The accused could not testify in their own defense. They were to be returned to the South without jury trial merely on the submission of an affidavit by their "owner."

In this piecemeal fashion the Union was preserved. The credit belongs mostly to Clay, whose original conceptualization of the compromise enabled lesser minds to understand what they must do.

Everywhere sober and conservative citizens sighed with relief. Mass meetings throughout the country "ratified" the result. Hundreds of newspapers gave the compromise editorial approval. In Washington patriotic harmony reigned. "You would suppose that nobody had ever thought of disunion," Webster wrote. "All say they always meant to stand by the Union to the last." When Congress met again in December it seemed that party discord had been buried forever. "I have determined never to make another speech on the slavery question," Senator Douglas told his colleagues. "Let us cease agitating, stop the debate, and drop the subject." If this were done, he predicted, the compromise would be accepted as a "final settlement." With this bit of wishful thinking the year 1850 passed into history.

Milestones

1835	Alamo falls to Santa Anna's Mexican army
1836	Sam Houston routs Santa Anna at Battle of San Jacinto
1837	U.S. recognizes Republic of Texas
1841	William Henry Harrison is elected president
	William Henry Harrison dies; Vice President John Tyler becomes president
1842	Webster-Ashburton Treaty determines Maine boundary
1843	Oregon Trail opens
1844	James K. Polk is elected president
1845	U.S. annexes Texas
	John L. O'Sullivan coins the expression *manifest destiny*
1846	U.S. and Britain settle Oregon boundary dispute
1846–1848	U.S. wages "Mr. Polk's War" with Mexico
1846	House of Representatives adopts Wilmot Proviso prohibiting slavery in Mexican cession, but Senate defeats it
1847	General Winfield Scott captures Mexico City
1848	James W. Marshall discovers gold at Sutter's Mill, California
	Treaty of Guadalupe Hidalgo brings U.S. huge territorial gains
	Zachary Taylor is elected president
1850	Taylor dies; Vice President Millard Fillmore becomes president
	Henry Clay's Compromise of 1850 preserves Union

The Sections Go Their Ways

Dearborn, Michigan, headquarters of the Ford Motor Company, is in many ways the prototypical American city. Yet nearly a third of its 100,000 residents are Arab-speaking immigrants from Lebanon, Iraq, Yemen, and Palestine.

Lowell, Massachusetts, whose textile mills employed young women from New England farms during the 1820s and 1830s, is now the home to some 20,000 Cambodians, refugees from the regime of Pol Pot, a Communist dictator who killed 2 million of his people.

About 10,000 Sudanese, refugees from a genocidal war in Africa, have flocked to Omaha, Nebraska, to work in its meatpacking plants. Nearly as many Bosnians, refugees from a civil war in the Balkans, have settled in Boise, Idaho.

The United States, long a nation of immigrants, remains so. And while some immigrant groups still settle together in tightly knit local communities, they are not concentrated primarily in port cities or border towns as many new immigrants were in the early nineteenth century. Immigrants today move throughout the United States, following opportunity. Although recent Hispanic immigrants constitute a large proportion of the workforce in much of the South and Southwest, they have settled throughout the nation. Even in Maine and Utah, people of Hispanic origin constitute the largest minority.

But during the first half of the nineteenth century, each section of the nation had a distinctive workforce. Immigrants who sought work in factories generally settled in the Northeast, while those interested in farming were drawn to the West. The culture of the South was in large part shaped by its unwilling immigrants, the slaves.

Improvements in transportation after 1830 reduced the differences among the sections. The Northeast and the West became economically interdependent. The

South, whose transportation infrastructure lagged, nevertheless benefited from the development of the steamship, which greatly reduced the cost of shipping to Europe. By the 1850s the nation remained divided—chiefly between the slave economy of the South and the nominally "free" labor of the North. But as the nation was knit together more tightly, the incompatibility of those systems could no longer be ignored.

The Economics of Slavery

The increased importance of cotton in the South strengthened the hold of slavery on the region. The price of slaves rose until by the 1850s a prime field hand was worth as much as $1,800, roughly three times the cost in the 1820s. While the prestige value of owning this kind of property affected prices, the rise chiefly reflected the increasing value of the South's agricultural output. "Crop value per slave" jumped from less than $15 early in the century to more than $125 in 1859.

In the cotton fields of the Deep South slaves brought several hundred dollars per head more than in the older regions; thus the tendency to sell them "down the river" continued. Mississippi took in some 10,000 slaves a year throughout the period; by 1830 the black population of the state exceeded the white. The westward shift of cotton cultivation was accompanied by the forcible transfer of more than a million African American slaves from the seaboard states to the dark, rich soil of

Price, Birch & Company of Virginia, "dealers in Slaves." Such companies not only sold slaves but also arranged for them to work in nearby shops and factories.

regions watered by the Mississippi and Arkansas rivers and their tributaries. This "second great migration" of blacks greatly surpassed the original uprooting of blacks from Africa to the United States.

Slave trading became a big business. In the 1850s there were about fifty dealers in Charleston and 200 in New Orleans. The largest traders were Isaac Franklin and John Armfield, who collected slaves from Virginia and Maryland at their "model jail" in Alexandria and shipped them by land and sea to a depot near Natchez. Each of the partners cleared half a million dollars before retiring, and some smaller operators did proportionately well.

The impact of the trade on the slaves was frequently disastrous. Husbands were often separated from wives, parents from children. This was somewhat less likely to happen on large, well-managed plantations than on small farms, but it was common enough everywhere. According to one study, one-third of all slave first "marriages" in the upper South were broken by forced separation and nearly half of all children were separated from at least one parent. Families were torn apart less frequently in the lower South, where far more slaves were bought than sold.

Because the business was so profitable, the prejudice against slave traders abated as the price of slaves rose. Men of high social status became traders, and persons of humble origin who had prospered in the trade had little difficulty in buying land and setting up as respectable planters.

As blacks became more expensive, the ownership of slaves became more concentrated. In 1860 only about 46,000 of the 8 million white residents of the slave states had as many as twenty slaves. When one calculates the cost of twenty slaves and the land to keep them profitably occupied, it is easy to understand why this figure is so small. The most efficient size of a plantation worked by gangs of slaves ranged between 1,000 and 2,000 acres. In every part of the South the majority of farmers cultivated no more than 200 acres, in many sections fewer than 100 acres. On the eve of the Civil War only one white family in four in the South owned any slaves at all. A few large plantations and many small farms—this was the pattern.

There were few genuine economies of scale in southern agriculture. Small farmers grew the staple crops; and many of them owned a few slaves, often working beside them in the fields. These yeomen farmers were hardworking, self-reliant, and moderately prosperous, quite unlike the poor whites of the pine barrens and the remote valleys of the Appalachians who scratched a meager subsistence from substandard soils and lived in ignorance and squalor.

Well-managed plantations yielded annual profits of 10 percent and more, and, in general, money invested in southern agriculture earned at least a modest return. Considering the way the workforce was exploited, this is hardly surprising. Recent estimates indicate that after allowing for the cost of land and capital, the average plantation slave "earned" cotton worth $78.78 in 1859. It cost masters about $32 a year to feed, clothe, and house a slave. In other words, almost 60 percent of the product of slave labor was expropriated by the masters.

Foreign observers in New England frequently noted the alertness and industriousness of ordinary laborers and attributed this, justifiably, to the high level of literacy. Nearly everyone in New England could read and write. Correspondingly, the stagnation and inefficiency of southern labor could be attributed in part to the high degree of illiteracy, for over 20 percent of *white* Southerners could not read or write, another tragic squandering of human resources.

The Sociology of Slavery

It is difficult to generalize about slavery because so much depended on the individual master's behavior. Although some former slaves told of masters who refused to whip them, Bennet Barrow of Louisiana, a harsh master, averaged one whipping a month. "The great secret of our success," another planter recalled years later, "was the great motive power contained in that little instrument." Overseers were commonly instructed to give twenty lashes for ordinary offenses, such as shirking work or stealing, and thirty-nine for more serious offenses, such as running away. Sometimes slaves were whipped to death; however, by 1821, all southern states had

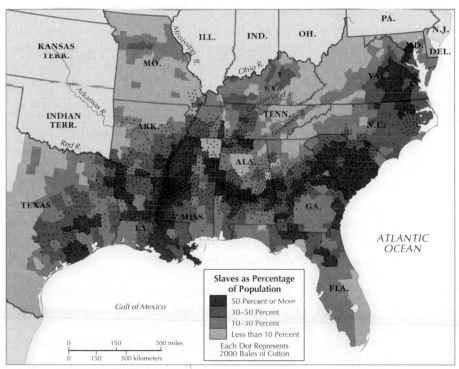

Cotton and Slaves in the South, 1860
Not surprisingly, the areas of greatest cotton production were also the areas with the highest proportion of slaves in the population. Note the concentrations of both in the Piedmont, the Alabama Black Belt, and the lower Mississippi Valley, and the relative absence of both in the Appalachian Mountains.

passed laws allowing a master to be charged with murder if he caused a slave's death from excessive punishment. Conviction normally resulted in a fine. In 1840 a South Carolina woman convicted of killing a slave was fined $214.28.

Most owners provided adequate clothing, housing, and food for their slaves. Only a fool or a sadist would fail to take care of such valuable property. However, vital statistics indicate that infant mortality among slaves was twice the white rate, life expectancy at least five years less.

On balance, it is significant that the United States was the only nation in the Western Hemisphere where the slave population grew by natural increase. After the ending of the slave trade in 1808, the black population increased at nearly the same rate as the white. Put differently, during the entire period from the founding of Jamestown to the Civil War, only a little more than half a million slaves were imported into the country, about 5 percent of the number of Africans carried by slavers to the New World. Yet in 1860 there were about 4 million blacks in the United States.

Most owners felt responsibilities toward their slaves, and slaves were dependent on and in some ways imitative of white values. However, powerful fears and resentments, not always recognized, existed on both sides. The plantation environment forced the two races to live in close proximity. From this circumstance could arise every sort of human relationship. One planter, using the appropriate pseudonym Clod Thumper, could write: "Africans are nothing but brutes, and they will love you better for whipping, whether they deserve it or not." Another, describing a slave named Bug, could say: "No one knows but myself what feeling I have for him. Black as he is we were raised together." One southern white woman tended a dying servant with "the kindest and most unremitting attention." Another, discovered crying after the death of a slave she had repeatedly abused, is said to have explained her grief by complaining that she "didn't have nobody to whip no more."

Such diametrically conflicting sentiments often existed within the same person. And almost no white Southerners had any difficulty exploiting the labor of slaves for whom they felt genuine affection.

Slaves were without rights; they developed a distinctive way of life by attempting to resist oppression and injustice while accommodating themselves to the system. Their marriages had no legal status, but their partnerships seem to have been loving and stable. Even families whose members were sold to different masters often maintained close ties over considerable distances.

Slave religion, on the surface an untutored form of Christianity tinctured with some African survivals, seemed to most slave owners a useful instrument for teaching meekness and resignation and for providing harmless emotional release, which it sometimes was and did. However, religious meetings, secret and open, provided slaves with the opportunity to organize, which led at times to rebellions and more often to less drastic ways of resisting white domination. Religion also sustained the slaves' sense of their own worth as beings made in the image of God, and it taught them, therefore, that while human beings can be enslaved in body, their spirits cannot be enslaved without their consent.

Observing that slaves often seemed happy and were only rarely overtly rebellious, whites persuaded themselves that most blacks accepted the system without resentment and indeed preferred slavery to the uncertainties of freedom. There was much talk about "loyal and faithful servants." The Civil War, when slaves flocked to the Union lines once assured of freedom and fair treatment, would disabuse them of this illusion.

As the price of slaves rose and as northern opposition to the institution grew more vocal, the system hardened perceptibly. White Southerners made much of the danger of insurrection. When a plot was uncovered or a revolt took place, instant and savage reprisals resulted. In 1822, after the conspiracy of Denmark Vesey was exposed by informers, thirty-seven slaves were executed and another thirty-odd deported, although no overt act of rebellion had occurred. After an uprising in Louisiana, sixteen blacks were decapitated, their heads left to rot on poles along the Mississippi as a grim warning.

The Nat Turner revolt in Virginia in 1831 was the most sensational of the slave uprisings; fifty-seven whites lost their lives before it was suppressed. White Southerners treated runaways almost as brutally as rebels, although they posed no real threat to whites. The authorities tracked down fugitives with bloodhounds and subjected captives to merciless lashings.

After the Nat Turner revolt, interest in doing away with slavery vanished in the white South. The southern states made it increasingly difficult for masters to free their slaves; during 1859 only about 3,000 in a slave population of nearly 4 million were given their freedom.

Slavery did not flourish in urban settings, and cities did not flourish in societies where slavery was important. Most southern cities were small, and within them, slaves made up a small fraction of the labor force. The existence of slavery goes a long way toward explaining why the South was so rural and why it had so little industry. Blacks were much harder to supervise and control in urban settings. Individual slaves were successfully employed in southern manufacturing plants, but they made up only an insignificant fraction of the South's small industrial labor supply.

Southern whites considered the existence of free blacks undesirable, no matter where they lived. The mere fact that they could support themselves disproved the notion that blacks were by nature childlike and shiftless, unable to work efficiently without white guidance. From the whites' point of view, free blacks set a bad example for slaves. In a petition calling for the expulsion of free blacks from the state, a group of South Carolinians noted that slaves

continualy have before their eyes, persons of the same color . . . freed from the control of masters, working where they please, going where they please, and expending their money how they please.

At a minimum, as another Southerner said, the sight of "a vile and lazy free negro lolling in the sun-shine" might make slaves envious. Still worse, it might encourage them to try to escape, and worst of all, the free blacks might help them do so.

Many southern states passed laws aimed at forcing free blacks to emigrate, but these laws were not well enforced. There is ample evidence that the white people of, say, Maryland, would have liked to get rid of the state's large free black population. Free blacks were barred from occupations in which they might cause trouble—no free black could be the captain of a ship, for example—and they were required by law to find a "respectable" white person who would testify as to their "good conduct and character." But whites, who needed slave labor, did not try very hard to expel them.

Psychological Effects of Slavery

The injustice of slavery needs no proof; less obvious is the fact that it had a corrosive effect on the personalities of Southerners, slave and free alike. By "the making of a human being an animal without hope," the system bore heavily on all slaves' sense of their own worth. Some found the condition absolutely unbearable. They became the habitual runaways who collected whip scars like medals, the "loyal" servants who struck out in rage against a master knowing that the result would be certain death, and the leaders of slave revolts.

Denmark Vesey of South Carolina, even after buying his freedom, could not stomach the subservience demanded of slaves by the system. When he saw Charleston slaves step into the gutter to make way for whites, he taunted them: "You deserve to remain slaves!" For years he preached resistance to his fellows, drawing his texts from the Declaration of Independence and the Bible and promising help from black Haiti. So vehemently did he argue that some of his followers claimed they feared Vesey more than their masters, even more than God. He planned his uprising for five years, patiently working out the details, only to see it aborted at the last moment when a few of his recruits lost their nerve and betrayed him. For Denmark Vesey, death was probably preferable to living with such rage as his soul contained.

Yet Veseys were rare. Most slaves appeared at least resigned to their fate. Many seemed even to accept the whites' evaluation of their inherent abilities and place in society. Of course in most instances it is impossible to know whether this apparent subservience was feigned in order to avoid trouble.

Slaves had strong family and group attachments and a complex culture of their own, maintained, so to speak, under the noses of their masters. By a mixture of subterfuge, accommodation, and passive resistance, they erected subtle defenses against exploitation, achieving a sense of community that helped sustain the psychic integrity of individuals. But slavery discouraged, if it did not extinguish, independent judgment and self-reliance. These qualities are difficult enough to develop in human beings under the best of circumstances; when every element in white society encouraged slaves to let others do their thinking for them, to avoid questioning the status quo, to lead a simple life, many did so willingly enough. Was this not slavery's greatest shame?

Whites, too, were harmed by the slave system. Associating working for others with servility discouraged many poor white Southerners from hiring out to earn a

Debating the Past

DID SLAVES AND MASTERS FORM EMOTIONAL BONDS?

Slavery, Ulrich Bonnell Phillips (1918) declared, was a benign institution. "Severity was clearly the exception, and kindliness the rule," he remarked. Kenneth Stampp (1956), writing as the civil rights movement of the 1950s was gaining momentum, repudiated Phillips's thesis. Slavery ripped apart families, reduced human beings to chattel, and eroded the slave's sense of self. The kindness of some slave masters was that of a father toward a "fawning dependent," he argued. Stanley Elkins (1959) went further still, comparing southern slavery to the subjugation of inmates in Nazi concentration camps. Slavery was so absolute that the psyche of African Americans was crushed for generations. Two major works in the 1970s challenged this rendering of slavery but in different ways. Eugene D. Genovese (1974) argued that masters and slaves were locked in a system of mutual dependence. Slaves were bound to their owners "in an organic relationship so complex and ambivalent that neither could express the simplest human feelings without reference to each other." Their emotional ties, however complicated, were real. Herbert Gutman (1976) insisted that slaves did not bond with their masters. Slave parents, children, and other relatives formed lasting ties that endured. Because it is hard to know what people really felt, the issue resists historical analysis: Did the slave girl in this photograph know for sure how she felt about the child in her arms?

Ulrich Bonnell Phillips, *American Negro Slavery* (1918), Kenneth Stampp, *The Peculiar Institution* (1956), Stanley Elkins, *Slavery* (1959), Eugene D. Genovese, *Roll, Jordan, Roll* (1974), Herbert Gutman, *The Black Family in Slavery and Freedom* (1976).

stake. Slavery provided the weak, the shiftless, and the unsuccessful with a scapegoat that made their own miserable state easier to bear but harder to escape.

More subtly, the patriarchal nature of the slave system reinforced the already existing tendency toward male dominance over wives and children typical of the larger society. For men of exceptional character, the responsibilities of ownership could be ennobling, but for hotheads, alcoholics, or others with psychological problems, the power could be brutalizing, with terrible effects on the whole plantation community, whites and blacks alike.

Aside from its fundamental immorality, slavery caused basically decent people to commit countless petty cruelties. "I feel badly, got very angry and whipped Lavinia," one Louisiana woman wrote in her diary. "O! for government over my temper." But for slavery, she would surely have had better self-control. The finest white Southerners were often warped by the institution. Even those who abhorred slavery sometimes let it corrupt their thinking: "I consider the labor of a breeding woman as no object, and that a child raised every 2 years is of more profit than the crop of the best laboring man." This cold calculation came from the pen of Thomas Jefferson, author of the Declaration of Independence, a man who, it now seems likely, fathered at least one child by a slave.

Manufacturing in the South

Although the temper of southern society discouraged business and commercial activities, considerable manufacturing developed. Small flour and lumber mills flourished. There were important rope-making plants in Kentucky and commercial cotton presses, used to compact cotton into 500-pound bales, in many southern cities. Iron and coal were mined in Virginia, Kentucky, and Tennessee. In the 1850s the Tredegar Iron Works in Richmond did an annual business of about $1 million.

Less than 15 percent of all the goods manufactured in the United States in 1860 came from the South; the region did not really develop an industrial society. Its textile manufacturers depended on the North for machinery, for skilled workers and technicians, for financing, and for insurance. When the English geologist Charles Lyell visited New Orleans in 1846, he was astounded to discover that the thriving city supported not a single book publisher. Even a local guidebook that he purchased bore a New York imprint.

The Northern Industrial Juggernaut

The most obvious change in the North in the decades before the Civil War was the rapid growth of industry. The best estimates suggest that immediately after the War of 1812 the United States was manufacturing less than $200 million worth of goods annually. In 1859 the northeastern states alone produced $1.27 billion of the national total of almost $2 billion.

Manufacturing expanded in so many directions that it is difficult to portray or to summarize its evolution. The factory system made great strides. The development of rich anthracite coal fields in Pennsylvania was particularly important in this connection. The coal could be floated cheaply on canals to convenient sites and used to produce both heat for smelting and metalworking and steam power to drive machinery. Steam permitted greater flexibility in locating factories and in organizing work within them, and since waterpower was already being used to capacity, steam was essential for the expansion of output.

American industry displayed a remarkable receptivity to technological change. The list of inventions and processes developed between 1825 and 1850 included—besides such obviously important items as the sewing machine, the vulcanization of rubber, and the cylinder press—the screw-making machine, the friction match, the lead pencil, and an apparatus for making soda water.

In the 1820s a foreign visitor noted: "Everything new is quickly introduced here, and all the latest inventions. . . . The moment an American hears the word 'invention' he pricks up his ears." Twenty years later a Frenchman wrote: "If they continue to work with the same ardor, they will soon have nothing more to desire or to do. All the mountains will be flattened, the valleys filled, all matter rendered productive." By 1850 the United States led the world in the manufacture of goods that required the use of precision instruments, and in certain industries the country was well on the way toward modern mass production methods. American clocks, pistols, rifles, and locks were outstanding.

In the 1850s the earlier prejudice against the corporation began to break down; by the end of the decade the northern and northwestern states had all passed general incorporation laws. Of course, the corporate device made possible larger accumulations of capital. While the federal government did not charter business corporations, two actions of Congress illustrate the shift in public attitudes. In 1840 a group of scientists sought a federal charter for a National Institution for the Promotion of Science. They were turned down on constitutional grounds; if Congress "went on erecting corporations in this way," one legislator said, "they would come, at last, to have corporations for everything." In 1863, however, the bill creating the National Academy of Science passed both houses without debate.

Industrial growth led to a great increase in the demand for labor. The effects, however, were mixed. Skilled artisans, technicians, and toolmakers earned good wages and found it relatively easy to set themselves up first as independent craftsmen, later as small manufacturers. The expanding frontier drained off much agricultural labor that might otherwise have been attracted to industry, and the thriving new towns of the West absorbed large numbers of eastern artisans of every kind. At the same time, the pay of an unskilled worker was never enough to support a family decently, and the new machines weakened the bargaining power of artisans by making skill less important.

Many other forces acted to stimulate the growth of manufacturing. Immigration increased rapidly in the 1830s and 1840s. An avalanche of strong backs, willing hands, and keen minds descended on the country from Europe. European investors poured large sums into the booming American economy, and the savings of millions of Americans and the great hoard of new California gold added to the supply of capital. Improvements in transportation, population growth, the absence of internal tariff barriers, and the relatively high per capita wealth all meant an ever-expanding market for manufactured goods.

A Nation of Immigrants

Rapid industrialization influenced American life in countless ways, none more significant than its effect on the character of the workforce and consequently on the structure of society. The jobs created by industrial expansion attracted European immigrants by the tens of thousands. It is a truism that America is a nation of immigrants—recall that even the ancestors of the Indians came to the New World from Asia. But only with the development of nationalism, that is, with the establishment of the independent United States, did the word *immigrant*, meaning a foreign-born resident, come into existence.

The "native" population (native in this case meaning those whose ancestors had come from Europe rather than Native Americans, the Indians) tended to look down on immigrants, and many of the immigrants, in turn, developed prejudices of their own. The Irish, for example, disliked blacks, with whom they often competed for work. One Irish leader in the old country, Daniel O'Connell, admitted that the American Irish were "among the worst enemies of the colored race." And of course blacks responded with equal bitterness. "Every hour sees us elbowed out of some employment to make room for some newly arrived emigrant from the Emerald Isle, whose hunger and color entitle him to special favor," one of them complained. Antiblack prejudice was less noticeable among other immigrant groups but by no means absent; most immigrants adopted the views of the local majority, which was often unfriendly to African Americans.

Social and racial rivalries aside, unskilled immigrants caused serious disruptions of economic patterns wherever they appeared. Their absorption into the factories of New England speeded the disintegration of the system of hiring young farm women. Already competition and technical advances in the textile industry were increasing the pace of the machines and reducing the number of skilled workers needed to run them. Fewer young farm women were willing to work under these conditions. Recent immigrants, who required less "coddling" and who seemed to provide the mills with a "permanent" working force, replaced the women in large numbers. By 1860 Irish immigrants alone made up more than 50 percent of the labor force in the New England mills.

How Wage Earners Lived

In the early factory towns, most working families maintained small vegetable gardens and a few chickens; low wage rates did not necessarily reflect a low standard of living. But in the new industrial slums even a blade of grass was unusual. In 1851 the editor Horace Greeley's *New York Tribune* published a minimum weekly budget for a family of five. The budget, which allowed nothing for savings, medical bills, recreation, or other amenities (Greeley did include 12 cents a week for newspapers), came to $10.37. Since the weekly pay of a factory hand seldom reached $5, the wives and children of most male factory workers also had to labor in the factories merely

A strike by 800 women shoemakers in Lynn, Massachusetts, 1860. In 1851 a Lynn shoemaker had adapted a Howe sewing machine so that it could pierce and sew leather, work normally performed by married women in their homes. Because these large machines required employees to leave home and children and work at the shoe-stitching factories, few married women would do so; here they are protesting their displacement.

to survive. And child labor in the 1850s differed fundamentally from child labor in the 1820s. The pace of the machines had become much faster by then, and the working environment more depressing.

Relatively few workers belonged to unions, but federations of craft unions sprang up in some cities, and during the boom that preceded the Panic of 1837, a National Trades Union representing a few northeastern cities managed to hold conventions. Early in the Jackson era, "workingmen's" political parties enjoyed a brief popularity, occasionally electing a few local officials. These organizations were made up mostly of skilled craftsmen, professional reformers, and even businessmen. They soon expired, destroyed by internal bickering over questions that had little or nothing to do with working conditions.

The flush times of the early 1850s caused the union movement to revive. Many strikes occurred, and a few new national organizations appeared. However, most unions were local institutions, weak and with little control over their membership. The Panic of 1857 dealt the labor movement another body blow. Thus there was no trend toward the general unionization of labor between 1820 and the Civil War.

This republican value system, along with the fluidity of society, the influx of job-hungry immigrants, and the widespread employment of women and children in unskilled jobs made labor organization difficult. The assumption was that nearly anyone who was willing to work could eventually escape from the wage-earning class. "If any continue through life in the condition of the hired laborer," Abraham Lincoln declared in 1859, "it is . . . because of either a dependent nature which prefers it, or improvidence, folly, or singular misfortune."

Foreign Commerce

Changes in the pattern of foreign commerce were less noticeable than those in manufacturing but were nevertheless significant. After increasing erratically during the 1820s and 1830s, both imports and exports leapt forward in the next 20 years. The nation remained primarily an exporter of raw materials and an importer of manufactured goods, and in most years it imported more than it exported. Cotton continued to be the most valuable export, in 1860 accounting for a record $191 million of total exports of $333 million. Despite America's own thriving industry, textiles still held the lead among imports, with iron products second. As in earlier days, Great Britain was both the best customer of the United States and its leading supplier.

The success of sailing packets, those "square-riggers on schedule," greatly facilitated the movement of passengers and freight. Fifty-two packets were operating between New York and Europe by 1845, and many more plied between New York and other American ports. The packets accelerated the tendency for trade to concentrate in New York and to a lesser extent in Philadelphia, Baltimore, and New Orleans. The commerce of Boston and smaller New England towns like Providence and New Haven, which had flourished in earlier days, now languished.

New Bedford and a few other southern New England towns shrewdly saved their prosperity by concentrating on whaling, which boomed between 1830 and 1860. The supply of whales seemed unlimited—as indeed it was, given the primitive hunting techniques of the age of sail. By the mid-1850s, with sperm oil selling at more than $1.75 a gallon and the country exporting an average of $2.7 million worth of whale oil and whalebone a year, New Bedford boasted a whaling fleet of well over 300 vessels and a population approaching 25,000.

The increase in the volume and value of trade and its concentration at larger ports had a marked effect on the construction of ships. By the 1850s the average vessel was three times the size of those built 30 years earlier. Startling improvements in design, culminating in the long, sleek, white-winged clipper ships, made possible speeds previously undreamed of. Appearing just in time to supply the need for fast transportation to the California gold fields, the clippers cut sailing time around Cape Horn to San Francisco from five or six months to three, the record of 89 days being held jointly by the *Andrew Jackson* and Donald McKay's famous *Flying Cloud*. Another McKay-designed clipper, *Champion of the Seas*, once logged 465 nautical miles in 24 hours, far in excess of the best efforts of modern yachts. To achieve such speeds, cargo capacity had to be sacrificed, making clippers uneconomical for carrying the bulky produce that was the mainstay of commerce. But for specialty goods, in their brief heyday the clippers were unsurpassed. Hong Kong merchants, never known for extravagance, willingly paid 75 cents a cubic foot to ship tea by clipper to London even though slower vessels charged only 28 cents. In the early 1850s clippers sold for as much as $150,000; with decent luck a ship might earn its full cost in a voyage or two.

Steam Conquers the Atlantic

The reign of the clipper ship was short. Like so many other things, ocean commerce was being mechanized. Steamships conquered the high seas more slowly than the rivers because early models were unsafe in rough waters and uneconomical. A riverboat could take on fuel along its route, whereas an Atlantic steamer had to carry tons of coal across the ocean, thereby reducing its capacity for cargo. However, by the late 1840s, steamships were capturing most of the passenger traffic, mail contracts, and first-class freight. These vessels could not keep up with the clippers in a heavy breeze, but their average speed was far greater, especially on the westward voyage against the prevailing winds. Steamers were soon crossing the Atlantic in less than ten days. Nevertheless, for very long voyages, such as the 15,000-mile haul around South America to California, fast sailing ships held their own for many years.

The combination of competition, government subsidy, and technological advance drove down shipping rates. Between the mid-1820s and the mid-1850s the cost of moving a pound of cotton from New York to Liverpool fell from 1 cent to about a third of a cent. Transatlantic passengers could obtain the best accommoda-

Giant Steamboats on the Levee at New Orleans (1853), a painting by Hippolyte Sebron, a Frenchman. A picture of stately elegance, these boats required unusually powerful engines to make way against the strong currents of the Mississippi. Improvements in engine design and iron casting helped boats meet the river's challenge.

tions on the fastest ships for under $200, good accommodations on slower packets for as little as $75.

Rates were especially low for European emigrants willing to travel to America on cargo vessels. By the 1840s at least 4,000 ships were engaged in carrying bulky American cotton and Canadian lumber to Europe. On their return trips with manufactured goods they had much unoccupied space, which they converted into rough quarters for passengers. Conditions on these ships were crowded, gloomy, and foul. Frequently epidemics took a fearful toll among steerage passengers. On one crossing of the ship *Lark*, 158 of 440 passengers died of typhus.

Yet without this cheap means of transportation, thousands of poor immigrants would simply have remained at home. Bargain freight rates also help explain the clamor of American manufacturers for high tariffs, for transportation costs added relatively little to the price of European goods.

Canals and Railroads

Another dramatic change was the shift in the direction of the nation's internal commerce and its immense increase. From the time of the first settlers in the Mississippi Valley, the Great River had controlled the flow of goods from farm to market. The completion of the Erie Canal in 1825 heralded a shift, speeded by the feverish canal construction of the following decade. In 1830 there were 1,277 miles of canal in the United States; by 1840 there were 3,326 miles.

Each year saw more western produce moving to market through the canals. In 1845 the Erie Canal was still drawing over two-thirds of its west-east traffic from within New York, but by 1847, despite the fact that this local business held steady, more than half of its traffic came from west of Buffalo, and by 1851 more than two-thirds. The volume of western commerce over the Erie Canal in 1851 amounted to more than twenty times what it had been in 1836, while the value of western goods reaching New Orleans in this period increased only two and a half times.

The first railroads did not compete with the canals for intersectional traffic. The through connections needed to move goods economically over great distances materialized slowly. Of the 6,000 miles of track operating in 1848, nearly all lay east of the Appalachians, and little of it had been coordinated into railroad systems. The intention of most early builders had been to monopolize the trade of surrounding districts, not to establish connections with competing centers. Frequently, railroads used tracks of different widths deliberately to prevent other lines from tying into their tracks.

Between 1848 and 1852 railroad mileage nearly doubled. Three years later it had doubled again, and by 1860 the nation had 30,636 miles of track. During this extraordinary burst of activity, four companies drove lines of gleaming iron from the Atlantic seaboard to the great interior valley. In 1851 the Erie Railroad, longest road in the world with 537 miles of track, linked the Hudson River north of New York City with Dunkirk on Lake Erie. Late the next year the Baltimore and Ohio reached the Ohio River at Wheeling, and in 1853 a banker named Erastus Corning

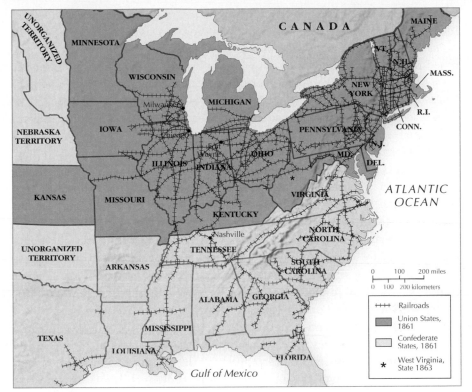

Railroads, 1860

This map shows trunk lines (lines carrying through-traffic) in operation in 1860. Certain towns and cities owed their spectacularly rapid growth to the railroad, Chicago being an outstanding example. The map suggests the strong influence of the railroads on the expansion and economic prosperity of smaller cities such as Fort Wayne, Milwaukee, and Nashville. At the outbreak of the Civil War in 1861, the relative lack of railroads in the South was a major disadvantage for the Confederacy.

consolidated eight short lines connecting Albany and Buffalo to form the New York Central Railroad. Finally, in 1858 the Pennsylvania Railroad completed a line across the mountains from Philadelphia to Pittsburgh.

In the states beyond the Appalachians, building went on at an even more feverish pace. By 1855 passengers could travel from Chicago or St. Louis to the east coast at a cost of $20 to $30, the trip taking, with luck, less than 48 hours. A generation earlier such a trip had required two to three weeks. Construction was slower in the South: Mississippi laid about 800 miles of track, Alabama 600.

Financing the Railroads

Railroad building required immense amounts of labor and capital at a time when many other demands for these resources existed. Immigrants or (in the South) slaves did most of the heavy work. Raising the necessary money proved a more complex task.

Private investors supplied about three-quarters of the money invested in railroads before 1860, more than $800 million in the 1850s alone. Much of this capital came from local merchants and businessmen and from farmers along the proposed rights-of-way. Funds were easy to raise because subscribers seldom had to lay out the full price of their stock at one time; instead they were subject to periodic "calls" for a percentage of their commitment as construction progressed. If the road made money, much of the additional mileage could be paid for out of earnings from the first sections built.

But many railroads that failed to find enough investors sought public money. Towns, counties, and the states themselves lent money to railroads and invested in their stock. Special privileges, such as exemption from taxation and the right to condemn property, were often granted, and in a few cases states built and operated roads as public corporations.

As with earlier internal improvement proposals, federal financial aid to railroads was usually blocked in Congress by a combination of eastern and southern votes. But in 1850 a scheme for granting federal lands to the states to build a line from Lake Michigan to the Gulf of Mexico passed both houses. The main beneficiary was the Illinois Central Railroad, which received a 200-foot right-of-way and alternate strips of land along the track 1 mile wide and 6 miles deep, a total of almost 2.6 million acres. By mortgaging this land and by selling portions of it to farmers, the Illinois Central raised nearly all the $23.4 million it spent on construction. The success of this operation led to additional grants of almost 20 million acres in the 1850s, benefiting more than forty railroads. Far larger federal grants were made after the Civil War, when the transcontinental lines were built.

Railroads and the Economy

The effects of so much railroad construction were profound. Although the main reason that farmers put more land under the plow was an increase in the price of agricultural products, the railroad helped determine just what land was used and how profitably it could be farmed. Much of the fertile prairie through which the Illinois Central ran had been available for settlement for many years before 1850, but development had been slow because it was remote from navigable waters and had no timber. In 1840 the three counties immediately northeast of Springfield had a population of about 8,500. They produced about 59,000 bushels of wheat and 690,000 bushels of corn. In the next decade the region grew slowly by the standards of that day: The three counties had about 14,000 people in 1850 and produced 71,000 bushels of wheat and 2.2 million bushels of corn. Then came the railroad and with it an agricultural revolution. By 1860 the population of the three counties had soared to over 38,000, wheat production had topped 550,000 bushels, and corn 5.7 million bushels. "Land-grant" railroads such as the Illinois Central stimulated agricultural expansion by advertising their lands widely and selling farm sites at low rates on liberal terms.

"OUR FIELD IS THE WORLD."

LIGHT DRAFT. SUPERIOR DESIGN.

CLEAN AND RAPID CUTTER.

McCormick Harvesting Machine Co., Chicago.

ESTABLISHED 1831.

An advertisement for the McCormick Reaper, so light that it could be pulled quickly by two horses.

Access to world markets gave the farmers of the upper Mississippi Valley an incentive to increase output. Land was plentiful and cheap, but farm labor was scarce; consequently agricultural wages rose sharply, especially after 1850. New tools and machines appeared in time to ease the labor shortage. First came the steel plowshare, invented by John Deere, a Vermont-born blacksmith who had moved to Illinois in 1837. The prairie sod was tough and sticky, but Deere's smooth metal plows cut through it easily. In 1839 Deere turned out ten such plows in his little shop in Moline, Illinois. By 1857 he was selling 10,000 a year.

Still more important was the perfection of the mechanical reaper, for wheat production was limited more by the amount that farmers could handle during the brief harvest season than by the acreage they could plant and cultivate. The major figure in the development of the reaper was Cyrus Hall McCormick. McCormick's horse-drawn reaper bent the grain against the cutting knife and then deposited it neatly on a platform, whence it could easily be raked into windrows. With this machine, two workers could cut fourteen times as much wheat as with scythes.

McCormick prospered, but despite his patents, he could not keep other manufacturers out of the business. Competition led to continual improvement of the machines and kept prices within the reach of most farmers. Installment selling

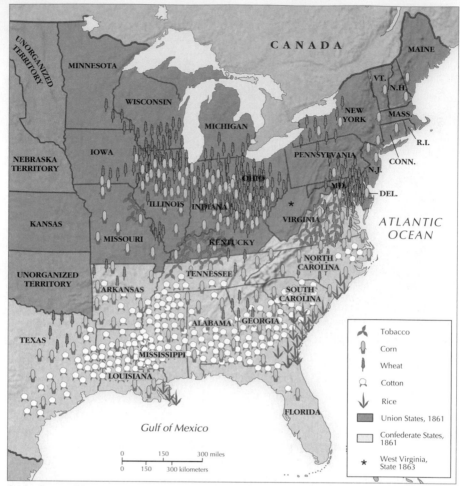

Agriculture, 1860

added to demand. By 1860 nearly 80,000 reapers had been sold; their efficiency helps explain why wheat output rose by nearly 75 percent in the 1850s.

The railroad had an equally powerful impact on American cities. The eastern seaports benefited, and so did countless intermediate centers, such as Buffalo and Cincinnati. But no city was affected more profoundly by railroads than Chicago.

In 1850 not a single line had reached there; five years later it was a terminal for 2,200 miles of track and controlled the commerce of an imperial domain. By extending half a dozen lines west to the Mississippi, it drained off nearly all the river traffic north of St. Louis. The Illinois Central sucked the expanding output of the prairies into Chicago as well. Most of this freight went eastward over the new railroads or on the Great Lakes and the Erie Canal. Nearly 350,000 tons of shipping plied the lakes by 1855.

The railroads, like the textile industry, stimulated other kinds of economic activity. They transformed agriculture, both real estate values and the buying and selling of land increased whenever the iron horse puffed into a new district. The railroads spurred regional concentration of industry and an increase in the size of business units. Their insatiable need for capital stimulated the growth of investment banking. Their massive size required the creation of complex structures and the employment of salaried managers.

The railroads consumed nearly half the nation's output of bar and sheet iron in 1860. Probably more labor and more capital were occupied in economic activities resulting from the development of railroads than in the roads themselves—another way of saying that the railroads were immensely valuable internal improvements.

The proliferation of trunk lines and the competition of the canal system (for many products the slowness of canal transportation was not a serious handicap) led to a sharp decline in freight and passenger rates. Cheap transportation had a revolutionary effect on western agriculture. Farmers in Iowa could now raise grain to feed the factory workers of Lowell and even of Manchester, England. Two-thirds of the meat consumed in New York City was soon arriving by rail from beyond the Appalachians. The center of American wheat production shifted westward to Illinois, Wisconsin, and Indiana. When the Crimean War (1853–1856) and European crop failures increased foreign demand, these regions boomed. Success bred success for farmers and for the railroads. Profits earned from carrying wheat enabled the roads to build feeder lines that opened up still-wider areas to commercial agriculture and made it easy to bring in lumber, farm machinery, household furnishings, and the settlers themselves at low cost.

Railroads and the Sectional Conflict

Increased production and cheap transportation boosted the western farmer's income and standard of living. The days of isolation and self-sufficiency, even for the family on the edge of the frontier, rapidly disappeared. Pioneers quickly became operators of businesses and, to a far greater extent than their forebears, consumers, buying all sorts of manufactured articles that their ancestors had made for themselves or done without. These changes had their costs. Like southern planters, they now became dependent on middlemen and lost some of their feeling of self-reliance. Overproduction became a problem. Buying a farm began to require more capital, for as profits increased, so did the price of land. Machinery was an additional expense. The proportion of farm laborers and tenants increased.

The linking of East and West had fateful effects on politics. The increased ease of movement from section to section and the ever more complex social and economic integration of East and West stimulated nationalism and thus became a force for the preservation of the Union. Without the railroads and canals, Illinois and Iowa would scarcely have dared to side against the South in 1861. When the

Mississippi ceased to be essential to them, citizens of the upper valley could afford to be more hostile to slavery and especially to its westward extension. Economic ties with the Northeast reinforced cultural connections.

The South might have preserved its influence in the Northwest if it had pressed forward its own railroad-building program. It failed to do so. There were many southern lines but nothing like a southern system. As late as 1856 one could get from Memphis to Richmond or Charleston only by very indirect routes. As late as 1859 the land-grant road extending the Illinois Central to Mobile, Alabama, was not complete, nor did any economical connection exist between Chicago and New Orleans.

This state of affairs could be accounted for in part by the scattered population of the South, the paucity of passenger traffic, the seasonal nature of much of the freight business, and the absence of large cities. Southerners placed too much reliance on the Mississippi: The fact that traffic on the river continued to be heavy throughout the 1850s blinded them to the precipitous rate at which their relative share of the nation's trade was declining. But the fundamental cause of the South's backwardness in railroad construction was the attitude of its leaders. Southerners of means were no more interested in commerce than in industry; their capital found other outlets.

The Economy on the Eve of Civil War

Between the mid-1840s and the mid-1850s the United States experienced one of the most remarkable periods of growth in the history of the world. Every economic indicator surged forward: manufacturing, grain and cotton production, population, railroad mileage, gold production, sales of public land. The building of the railroads stimulated business, and by making transportation cheaper, the completed lines energized the nation's economy. The American System that Henry Clay had dreamed of arrived with a rush just as Clay was passing from the scene.

Inevitably, this growth caused dislocations that were aggravated by the boom psychology that once again infected the popular mind. In 1857 there was a serious collapse. The return of Russian wheat to the world market after the Crimean War caused grain prices to fall. This checked agricultural expansion, which hurt the railroads and cut down on the demand for manufactures. Unemployment increased. Frightened depositors started runs on banks, most of which had to suspend specie payments.

People called this abrupt downturn the Panic of 1857. Yet the vigor of the economy was such that the bad times did not last long. The upper Mississippi Valley suffered most, for so much new land had been opened up that supplies of farm produce greatly exceeded demand. Elsewhere conditions improved rapidly.

The South, somewhat out of the hectic rush to begin with, was affected very little by the collapse of 1857, for cotton prices continued to be high. This gave planters the false impression that their economy was immune to such violent downturns. Some began to argue that the South would be better off out of the Union.

Before a new national upward swing could become well established, however, the sectional crisis between North and South shook people's confidence in the future. Then the war came, and a new set of forces shaped economic development.

1808	Congress bans further importation of slaves
1822	Thirty-seven slaves are executed when Denmark Vesey's "conspiracy" is exposed
1825	Erie Canal is completed, connecting East and Midwest
1830	Baltimore and Ohio railroad begins operation
1831	Nat Turner's slave uprising results in death of 57 whites
1837	Cyrus Hall McCormick invents reaper to harvest wheat
1839	John Deere begins manufacturing steel plows
1840–1857	Economy surges during boom in manufacturing, railroad construction, and foreign commerce
1846	Elias Howe invents sewing machine
1850	Congress grants land to aid construction of Illinois Central Railroad
1854	Clipper ship *Flying Cloud* sails from New York to San Francisco in 89 days
1857	Brief economic depression (Panic of 1857) collapses economy

The Coming of the Civil War

TWO-THIRDS OF AMERICANS INDICATE THAT TELEVISION IS THEIR main source of information about national politics. Around election time, 30-second television ads are the most ubiquitous (and dubious) source of information. (Such ads consumed most of the $1.2 billion cost of the 2004 presidential campaign.) Network news stories also inform voters about campaign issues, but over the past two decades such coverage has been condensed. In 1968, the average length of a quotation from a candidate on the evening news was 42 seconds; by 2000, such quotes had been reduced to 7 seconds. The term "sound bite" entered the political lexicon.

Televised debates provide a more sustained consideration of political issues. But the proportion of Americans who follow the debates has declined. In 1960, 77 percent of Americans watched the first televised debate between John F. Kennedy and Richard Nixon; even more tuned in to the 1980 debate between Ronald Reagan and Jimmy Carter. But during the 1996, 2000, and 2004 campaigns, fewer than one-third of Americans on the average watched the presidential debates.

We do not know precisely how many Americans gathered in the courthouse squares to listen to speeches and debates in the nineteenth century, yet we do know that politics then required a substantial investment of time. Unlike the visual medium of television, the spoken word takes time to digest. "Speak slowly," Lincoln advised a supporter who was to read a speech on his behalf. The seven influential debates between Abraham Lincoln and Stephen A. Douglas in 1858 each lasted over three hours.

During the 1850s the drumbeat of words grew faster and louder: Southern appeals for enforcement of the Fugitive Slave Act; Harriet Beecher Stowe's heartrending description of slavery in *Uncle Tom's Cabin*; the impassioned debates over "bleeding Kansas"; the Supreme Court's inflammatory decision in the Dred Scott case; the invective both for and against the manic crusade of John Brown. The din culminated in the superheated rhetoric of the 1860 presidential campaign. Then the words would be drowned out by the roar of cannon.

The Slave Power Comes North

The political settlement between North and South that Henry Clay designed in 1850 lasted only four years. One specific event wrecked it, but it was probably doomed in any case. Americans continued to migrate westward by the thousands, and as long as slaveholders could carry their human property into federally controlled territories, northern resentment would smolder. Slaves continued to seek freedom in the North, and the federal Fugitive Slave Act of 1850, which imposed fines for hiding or rescuing fugitive slaves, could not guarantee their capture and return. Abolitionists intensified their propaganda.

The new fugitive slave law encouraged more white Southerners to try to recover escaped slaves. Something approaching panic reigned in the black communities of northern cities when slave hunters arrived to seize former slaves. Thousands of blacks, not all of them fugitive slaves, fled to Canada, but many remained, and Northerners frequently refused to stand aside when such people were dragged off in chains.

Shortly after the passage of the act, James Hamlet was seized in New York City, convicted, and returned to slavery in Maryland without even being allowed to communicate with his wife and children. The New York black community was outraged, and with help from white neighbors it swiftly raised $800 to buy his freedom. Early in 1851 a Virginia agent captured Frederick "Shadrach" Jenkins, a waiter in a Boston coffeehouse. While Jenkins was being held for deportation, a mob of African Americans broke into the courthouse and hustled him off to Canada. That October a slave named Jerry, who had escaped from Missouri, was arrested in Syracuse, New York. Within minutes the whole town had the news. Crowds surged through the streets, and when night fell, a mob smashed into the building where Jerry was being held and spirited him away to safety in Canada.

Such incidents exacerbated sectional feelings. White Southerners accused the North of reneging on one of the main promises made in the Compromise of 1850, while the sight of harmless human beings being hustled off to a life of slavery disturbed many Northerners who were not abolitionists.

However, most white Northerners were not prepared to interfere with the enforcement of the Fugitive Slave Act themselves. Of the 332 blacks put on trial under the law, about 300 were returned to slavery, most without incident.

Uncle Tom's Cabin

Tremendously important in increasing sectional tensions and bringing home the evils of slavery to still more people in the North was Harriet Beecher Stowe's novel *Uncle Tom's Cabin* (1852). Stowe was neither a professional writer nor an abolitionist, and she had almost no firsthand knowledge of slavery. But her conscience had been roused by the Fugitive Slave Act. In gathering material for the book, she depended heavily on abolitionist writers, many of whom she knew. She dashed it off quickly; as she later recalled, it seemed to write itself. Nevertheless, *Uncle Tom's Cabin* was an enormous success: 10,000 copies were sold in a week; 300,000 in a year. It was translated into dozens of languages. Dramatized versions were staged in countries throughout the world.

Harriet Beecher Stowe was hardly a distinguished writer; it was her approach to the subject that explains the book's success. Her tale of the pious, patient slave Uncle Tom, the saintly white child Eva, and the callous slave driver Simon Legree appealed to an audience far wider than that reached by the abolitionists. She avoided the self-righteous, accusatory tone of most abolitionist tracts and did not seek to convert readers to belief in racial equality. Many of her southern white characters were fine, sensitive people, while the cruel Simon Legree was a transplanted Connecticut Yankee. There were many heart-rending scenes of pain, self-sacrifice, and heroism. The story proved especially effective on the stage: The slave Eliza crossing the frozen Ohio River to freedom, the death of Little Eva, Eva and Tom ascending to Heaven—these scenes left audiences in tears.

Southern critics pointed out, correctly enough, that Stowe's picture of plantation life was distorted, her slaves atypical. They called her a "coarse, ugly, long-tongued woman" and accused her of trying to "awaken rancorous hatred and malignant jealousies" that would undermine national unity. Most Northerners, having little basis on which to judge the accuracy of the book, tended to discount southern criticism as biased. In any case, *Uncle Tom's Cabin* raised questions that transcended the issue of accuracy. Did it matter if every slave was not as kindly as Uncle Tom, as determined as George Harris? What if only one white master was as evil as Simon Legree? No earlier white American writer had looked at slaves as people.

Uncle Tom's Cabin touched the hearts of millions. Some became abolitionists; others, still hesitating to step forward, asked themselves as they put the book down: Is slavery just?

Diversions Abroad: The "Young America" Movement

Clearly a distraction was needed to help keep the lid on sectional troubles. Some people hoped to find one in foreign affairs. The spirit of manifest destiny explains this in large part; once the United States had reached the Pacific, expansionists began to think of transmitting the dynamic, democratic U.S. spirit to other countries by aiding local revolutionaries, opening new markets, perhaps even annexing foreign lands. This became known as the "Young America" movement, whose

A poster advertising *Uncle Tom's Cabin* in 1852, the year of its publication. The following year, Harriet Beecher Stowe published *A Key to Uncle Tom's Cabin,* intended to provide documentary evidence in support of disputed details of her indictment of slavery.

adherents were confident that democracy would triumph everywhere, even if by conquest.

Some looked to Central America. The rapid development of California created a need for improved communication with the West Coast. A canal across Central America would cut weeks from the sailing time between New York and San Francisco. In 1850 Secretary of State John M. Clayton and the British minister to the United States, Henry Lytton Bulwer, negotiated a treaty providing for the demilitarization and joint Anglo-American control of any canal across the isthmus.

As this area assumed strategic importance to the United States, the desire to obtain Cuba grew stronger. In 1854 President Franklin Pierce instructed his minister to Spain to offer $130 million for the island. The State Department prepared a confidential dispatch suggesting that if Spain refused to sell Cuba, "the great law of self-preservation" might justify "wresting" it from Spain by force.

News of the dispatch—known as the Ostend Manifesto—leaked out, and it had to be published. Northern opinion was outraged by this "slaveholders' plot." Europeans claimed to be shocked by such "dishonorable" and "clandestine" diplomacy. The government had to disavow the manifesto, and any hope of obtaining Cuba or any other territory in the Caribbean vanished.

Stephen Douglas: "The Little Giant"

The most prominent spokesman of the Young America movement was Stephen A. Douglas. The senator from Illinois was the Henry Clay of his generation. Like Clay at his best, Douglas was able to see the needs of the nation in the broadest perspective. He held a succession of state offices before being elected to Congress in 1842 at the age of 29. After only two terms in the House, he was chosen U.S. senator.

The foundations of Douglas's politics were expansion and popular sovereignty. He had been willing to fight for all of Oregon in 1846, and he supported the Mexican War to the hilt, in sharp contrast to his one-term Illinois colleague in Congress, Abraham Lincoln. That local settlers should determine their own institutions was, to his way of thinking, axiomatic. Arguments over the future of slavery in the territories he believed a foolish waste of energy and time since he was convinced that natural conditions would keep the institution out of the West.

The main thing, he insisted, was to get on with the development of the United States. Let the nation build railroads, acquire new territory, expand its trade. He believed slavery "a curse beyond computation" for both blacks and whites, but he refused to admit that any moral issue was involved. He cared not, he boasted, whether slavery was voted up or voted down. This was not really true, but the question was interfering with the rapid exploitation of the continent. Douglas wanted it settled so that the country could concentrate on more important matters.

Douglas's success in steering the Compromise of 1850 through Congress added to his reputation. In 1851, he set out to win the Democratic presidential nomination, reasoning that since he was the brightest, most imaginative, and hardest-working Democrat around, he had every right to press his claim.

This brash aggressiveness proved his undoing. He expressed open contempt for James Buchanan and said of his other chief rival, Lewis Cass, who had won considerable fame while serving as minister to France, that his "reputation was beyond the C."

Stephen A. Douglas, dubbed the "Little Giant" for his height—he was 5 feet 4 inches tall—and his pugnacity. John Quincy Adams observed that during a debate Douglas worked himself into "such a heat that if his body had been made of combustible matter it would have burnt out."

At the 1852 Democratic convention Douglas had no chance. Cass and Buchanan killed each other off, and the delegates finally chose a dark horse, Franklin Pierce of New Hampshire. The Whigs, rejecting the colorless Fillmore, nominated General Winfield Scott, who was known as "Old Fuss and Feathers" because of his "punctiliousness in dress and decorum." In the campaign both sides supported the Compromise of 1850. The Democrats won an easy victory, 254 electoral votes to 42.

So handsome a triumph seemed to ensure stability, but in fact it was a prelude to political chaos. The Whig party was crumbling fast. The shifting amalgam of ethnic and cultural issues that held the party together at the local level dissolved as the slavery debate became more heated. The "Cotton" Whigs of the South, alienated by the antislavery sentiments of their northern brethren, were flocking into the Democratic fold. In the North the Whigs, divided between an antislavery wing ("Conscience Whigs") and another that was undisturbed by slavery, found themselves more and more at odds with each other. Congress fell overwhelmingly into the hands of proslavery southern Democrats, a development profoundly disturbing to northern Democrats as well as to Whigs.

The Kansas-Nebraska Act

Franklin Pierce was a youthful-appearing 48 years old when he took office. He was generally well liked by politicians. His career had included service in both houses of Congress. Alcohol had become a problem for him in Washington, however, and in 1842 he had resigned from the Senate and returned home to try to best the bottle, a struggle in which he was successful. His law practice boomed, and he added to his reputation by serving as a brigadier general during the Mexican War. Although his nomination for president came as a surprise, once made, it had appeared perfectly reasonable. Great things were expected of his administration, especially after he surrounded himself with men of all factions: To balance his appointment of a radical states' rights Mississippian, Jefferson Davis, as secretary of war, for example, he named a conservative Northerner, William L. Marcy of New York, as secretary of state.

Only a strong leader, however, can manage a ministry of all talents, and that President Pierce was not. The ship of state was soon drifting; Pierce seemed incapable of holding firm the helm.

This was the situation in January 1854 when Senator Douglas, chairman of the Committee on Territories, introduced what looked like a routine bill organizing the land west of Missouri and Iowa as the Nebraska Territory. Since settlers were beginning to trickle into the area, the time had arrived to set up a civil administration. The powerful southern faction in Congress would not go along with Douglas's proposal as it stood. Nebraska would presumably become a free state, for it lay north of latitude 36°30' in a district from which slavery had been excluded by the Missouri Compromise. Under pressure from the Southerners, led by Senator David R. Atchison of Missouri, Douglas agreed first to divide the region into two territories, Kansas and Nebraska, and then—a fateful concession—to repeal the part of the Missouri Compromise that excluded slavery from land north of 36°30'. Whether the new territories should become slave or free, he argued, should be left to the decision of the settlers in accordance with the democratic principle of popular sovereignty. The fact that he might advance his presidential ambitions by making concessions to the South must have influenced Douglas too, as must the local political situation in Missouri, where slaveholders feared being "surrounded" on three sides by free states.

Douglas's miscalculation of northern sentiment was monumental. It was one thing to apply popular sovereignty to the new territories in the Southwest, quite another to apply it to a region that had been part of the United States for half a century and free soil for 34 years. Word that the area was to be opened to slavery caused an indignant outcry; many moderate opponents of slavery were radicalized. A group of abolitionist congressmen issued what they called their "Appeal of the Independent Democrats" (actually, all were Free Soilers and Whigs) denouncing the Kansas-Nebraska bill as "a gross violation of a sacred pledge" and calling for a campaign of letter writing, petitions, and public meetings to prevent its passage. The unanimity and force of the northern public's reaction was like nothing in America since the days of the Stamp Act and the Intolerable Acts.

But protests could not defeat the bill. Southerners in both houses backed it regardless of party. Douglas, at his best when under attack, pushed it with all his power. The authors of the "Appeal," he charged, were "the pure unadulterated representatives of Abolitionism, Free Soilism, [and] Niggerism." President Pierce added whatever force the administration could muster. As a result, the northern Democrats split and the bill became law late in May 1854. In this manner the nation took the greatest single step in its march toward the abyss of secession and civil war.

Anthony Burns, the subject of this Boston poster, was the third runaway slave to be seized and returned to the South under the hated Fugitive Slave Act of 1850. The Burns case galvanized public opinion just when Congress was debating the Kansas-Nebraska Act. The passage of that bill further outraged Northerners.

The repeal of the Missouri Compromise struck the North like a slap in the face—at once shameful and challenging. Presumably the question of slavery in the territories had been settled forever; now, seemingly without justification, it had been reopened. On May 24, two days after the Kansas-Nebraska bill passed the House of Representatives, Anthony Burns, a slave who had escaped from Virginia by stowing away on a ship, was arrested in Boston. Massachusetts abolitionists brought suit against Burns's former master, charging false arrest. They also organized a protest meeting at which they inflamed the crowd into attacking the courthouse where Burns was being held. The mob broke into the building and a guard was killed, but federal marshals drove off the attackers.

President Pierce ordered the Boston district attorney to "incur any expense" to enforce the law. He also sent a revenue cutter to Boston to carry Burns back to Virginia. Thus Burns was returned to his master, but it required two companies of soldiers and 1,000 police and marines to get him aboard ship. As the grim parade marched past buildings festooned with black crepe, the crowd screamed "Kidnappers! Kidnappers!" at the soldiers. Estimates of the cost of returning this single slave to his owner ran as high as $100,000. A few months later, northern sympathizers bought Burns his freedom—for a few hundred dollars.

In previous cases Boston's conservative leaders, Whig to a man, had tended to hold back; after the Burns incident, they were thoroughly radicalized. "We went to bed one night old fashioned . . . Whigs," one of them explained, "and waked up stark mad Abolitionists."

Know-Nothings, Republicans, and the Demise of the Two-Party System

There were ninety-one free-state Democrats in the House of Representatives when the Kansas-Nebraska Act was passed, only twenty-five after the next election. With the Whig party already moribund, dissidents flocked to two new parties.

One was the American, or "Know-Nothing," party, so called because it grew out of a secret society whose members used the password "I don't know." The Know-Nothings were primarily nativists—immigration was soaring in the early 1850s, and the influx of poor foreigners was causing genuine social problems. Crime was on the rise in the cities along with drunkenness and other "diseases of poverty."

Several emotion-charged issues related to the fact that a large percentage of the immigrants were Irish and German Catholics also troubled the Know-Nothings. Questions such as public financing of parochial schools, lay control of church policies, the prohibition of alcoholic beverages, and increasing the time before an immigrant could apply for citizenship (the Know-Nothings favored 21 years) were matters of major importance to them. Since these were divisive issues, the established political parties tried to avoid them; hence the development of the new party.

The American party was important in the South as well as in the North, and while most Know-Nothings disliked blacks and considered them inherently inferior beings, they tended to adopt the dominant view of slavery in whichever section they were located. In the North most opposed the Kansas-Nebraska Act.

Operating often in tacit alliance with the antislavery forces (dislike of slavery did not prevent many abolitionists from being prejudiced against Catholics and immigrants), the northern Know-Nothings won a string of local victories in 1854 and elected more than forty congressmen.

Far more significant in the long run was the formation of the Republican party, which was made up of former Free Soilers, Conscience Whigs, and "Anti-Nebraska" Democrats. The American party was a national organization, but the Republican party was purely sectional. It sprang up spontaneously throughout the Old Northwest and caught on with a rush in New England.

Republicans presented themselves as the party of freedom. They were not abolitionists (though most abolitionists were soon voting Republican), but they insisted that slavery be kept out of the territories. They believed that if America was to remain a land of opportunity, free white labor must have exclusive access to the West. Thus the party appealed not only to voters who disapproved of slavery, but also to those who wished to keep blacks—free or slave—out of their states. In 1854 the Republicans won more than a hundred seats in the House of Representatives and control of many state governments.

The Whig party had almost disappeared in the northern states and the Democratic party had been gravely weakened, but it was unclear how these two new parties would fare. The Know-Nothing party had the superficial advantage of being a nationwide organization, but where slavery was concerned, this was anything but advantageous. And many Northerners who disliked slavery were troubled by the harsh Know-Nothing policies toward immigrants and Catholics. If the Know-Nothings were in control, said former Whig congressman Abraham Lincoln in 1855, the Declaration of Independence would read "all men are created equal, except negroes, *and foreigners, and catholics.*"

"Bleeding Kansas"

The furor over slavery might have died down if settlement of the new territories had proceeded in an orderly manner. Almost none of the settlers who flocked to Kansas owned slaves and relatively few of them were primarily interested in the slavery question.

When Congress opened the gates to settlement in May 1854, none of the land in the territory was available for sale. Treaties extinguishing Indian titles had yet to be ratified, and public lands had not been surveyed. In July Congress authorized squatters to occupy unsurveyed federal lands, but much of this property was far to the west of the frontier and practically inaccessible. The situation led to confusion over property boundaries, to graft and speculation, and to gen-

WAS THE CIVIL WAR AVOIDABLE?

Debating the Past

In 1855 Senator William H. Seward, New York's most prominent Whig, declared from the steps of the capitol in Albany that his party was dead. He advised supporters to join the new Republican party, which opposed slavery. Three years later Seward, a Republican, declared that conflict between the North and South was "irrepressible." Charles and Mary Beard used the term *irrepressible conflict* as a chapter title in their 1927 history text, arguing that antithetical economic systems—one based on free labor and the other on slavery—could not coexist. The argument was fleshed out by Arthur Cole in *The Irrepressible Conflict* (1934), who added that slavery was both outmoded and immoral. War had been inevitable, as was the South's defeat. In *The Repressible Conflict* (1939), Avery Craven dismissed Cole's book as a "belated abolitionist tract." War arose, Craven insisted, when northern "fanatics" whipped up sentiment against the South and southern politicians responded with equal vituperation. The "molders of public opinion" divided the nation by creating "the fiction of two distinct peoples." James G. Randall (1942) similarly saw no differences between the

North and South of sufficient magnitude to rip the nation apart. The leaders of both sides—he called them a "bungling generation"—should not have allowed overheated passions to ignite a civil war. In the 1970s and 1980s historians who embraced the "new political history," which focused on statistical analyses of voting behavior rather than the rhetoric of politicians, argued that war might have been avoided if the Whig party had not disintegrated. William Gienapp (1987) and Michael Holt (1999) credited the two-party system of the Whigs and Democrats with holding the nation together during difficult times; local coalitions on issues such as temperance and immigration had forestalled the divisive reckoning over slavery. It was the emergence of the Republican party in these contexts, not the economic tension between the sections, that made war "irrepressible."

Charles and Mary Beard, *The Rise of American Civilization* (1927), Arthur Cole, *The Irrepressible Conflict* (1934), Avery Craven, *The Repressible Conflict* (1939), James G. Randall, *The Coming of the Civil War* (1942), William Gienapp, *The Origins of the Republican Party* (1987), Michael Holt, *The Rise and Fall of the American Whig Party* (1999).

eral uncertainty, thereby exacerbating the difficulty of establishing an orderly government.

The legal status of slavery in Kansas became the focus of all these conflicts. Both northern abolitionists and southern defenders of slavery were determined to have Kansas. The New England Emigrant Aid Society was formed, with grandiose plans for transporting antislavery settlers to the area. The society transported only a hand-ful of New Englanders to Kansas. Yet the New Englanders were very conspicuous, and the society helped many midwestern antislavery settlers to make the move.

Doing so stirred white Southerners to action. The proslavery forces enjoyed several advantages in this struggle. The first inhabitants in frontier regions nearly always came from lands immediately to the east. In this case they were proslavery Missourians. When word spread that "foreigners" from New England were seeking to "steal" Kansas, many Missourians rushed to protect their "rights." "If we win we carry slavery to the Pacific Ocean," Senator Atchison boasted.

In November 1854 an election was held in Kansas to pick a territorial delegate to Congress. A large band of Missourians crossed over specifically to vote for a proslavery candidate and elected him easily. In March 1855 some 5,000 "border ruffians" again descended on Kansas and elected a territorial legislature. A census had recorded 2,905 eligible voters, but 6,307 votes were cast. The legislature promptly enacted a slave code and laws prohibiting abolitionist agitation. Antislavery settlers refused to recognize this regime and held elections of their own. By January 1856 two governments existed in Kansas, one based on fraud, the other extralegal.

By denouncing the free-state government located at Topeka, President Pierce encouraged the proslavery settlers to assume the offensive. In May, 800 of them sacked the antislavery town of Lawrence. An extremist named John Brown then took the law into his own hands in retaliation. By his reckoning, five Free Soilers had been killed by proslavery forces. In May 1856, together with six companions (four of them his sons), Brown stole into a settlement on Pottawatomie Creek in the dead of night. They dragged five unsuspecting men from their rude cabins and murdered them. This slaughter brought men on both sides to arms by the hun-dreds. Marauding bands came to blows and terrorized homesteads, first attempt-ing to ascertain the inhabitants' position on slavery.

Brown and his followers escaped capture and were never indicted for the mur-ders, but pressure from federal troops eventually forced him to go into hiding. He finally left Kansas in October 1856. By that time some 200 persons had lost their lives.

A certain amount of violence was normal in any frontier community, but it suited the political interests of the Republicans to make the situation in Kansas seem worse than it was. Exaggerated accounts of "bleeding Kansas" filled the pages of northern newspapers. The Democrats were also partly to blame, for although residents of nearby states often tried to influence elections in new territories, the actions of the border ruffians made a mockery of the democratic process.

However, the main responsibility for the Kansas tragedy must be borne by the Pierce administration. Under popular sovereignty the national government was supposed to see that elections were orderly and honest. Instead, the president acted as a partisan. When the first governor of the territory objected to the manner in which the proslavery legislature had been elected, Pierce replaced him with a man who backed the southern group without question.

Senator Sumner Becomes a Martyr for Abolitionism

As counterpoint to the fighting in Kansas there arose an almost continuous clamor in the halls of Congress. Red-faced legislators traded insults and threats. Epithets like "liar" were freely tossed about. Prominent in these angry outbursts was a new senator, Charles Sumner of Massachusetts. In the Kansas debates Sumner displayed an icy disdain for his foes. Colleagues threatened him with assassination, called him a "filthy reptile" and a "leper." He was impervious to such hostility. In the spring of 1856 he loosed a dreadful blast titled "The Crime Against Kansas." Characterizing administration policy as tyrannical, imbecilic, absurd, and infamous, he demanded that Kansas be admitted to the Union at once as a free state. Then he began a long and intemperate attack on both Douglas and the elderly Senator Andrew P. Butler of South Carolina, who was not present to defend himself.

Sumner described Butler as a "Don Quixote" who had taken "the harlot, slavery" as his mistress, and he spoke scornfully of "the loose expectoration" of Butler's speech. This was an inexcusable reference to the uncontrollable drooling to which the elderly senator was subject. While he was still talking, Douglas, who shrugged off most political name-calling as part of the game, was heard to mutter, "That damn fool will get himself killed by some other damn fool."

Such a "fool" quickly materialized in the person of Congressman Preston S. Brooks of South Carolina, a nephew of Senator Butler. Since Butler was absent from Washington, Brooks, who was probably as mentally unbalanced as Sumner, assumed the responsibility of defending his kinsman's honor. A southern romantic par excellence, he decided that caning Sumner would reflect his contempt more effectively than challenging him to a duel. Two days after the speech, Brooks entered the Senate as it adjourned. Sumner remained at his desk writing. Waiting until a talkative woman in the lobby had left so that she would be spared the sight of violence, Brooks then walked up to Sumner and rained blows on his head with a cane until Sumner fell, unconscious and bloody, to the floor. "I . . . gave him about 30 first-rate stripes," Brooks later boasted. "Towards the last he bellowed like a calf. I wore my cane out completely but saved the head which is gold." The physical damage suffered by Sumner was not life-threatening, but the incident so affected him psychologically that he was unable to return to his seat in Congress until 1859.

Both sides made much of this disgraceful incident. When the House censured him, Brooks resigned, returned to his home district, and was triumphantly reelected. A number of well-wishers sent him souvenir canes. Northerners viewed the affair as illustrating the brutalizing effect of slavery on southern whites and made a hero of Sumner.

Buchanan Tries His Hand

Such was the atmosphere surrounding the 1856 presidential election. The Republican party now dominated much of the North. It nominated John C. Frémont, "the Pathfinder," one of the heroes of the conquest of California during the war with Mexico. Frémont fit the Whig tradition of presidential candidates: a popular military man with almost no political experience. Unlike Taylor and Scott, however, he was articulate on the issue of slavery in the territories. Although citizens of diverse interests had joined the party, Republicans expressed their objectives in one simple slogan: "Free soil, free speech, and Frémont."

The Democrats cast aside the ineffectual Pierce, but they did not dare nominate Douglas because he had raised such a storm in the North. They settled on James Buchanan, chiefly because he had been out of the country serving as minister to Great Britain during the long debate over Kansas! The American party nominated former president Millard Fillmore, a choice the remnants of the Whigs endorsed.

In the campaign, the Democrats concentrated on denouncing the Republicans as a sectional party that threatened to destroy the Union. On this issue they carried the day. Buchanan won only a minority of the popular vote, but he had strength in every section. He got 174 electoral votes to Frémont's 114 and Fillmore's 8. The significant contest took place in the populous states just north of slave territory— Pennsylvania, Ohio, Indiana, and Illinois. Of these, Buchanan carried all but Ohio, although by narrow margins.

Personally, Buchanan was a bundle of contradictions. Dignified in bearing and by nature cautious, he could consume enormous amounts of liquor without showing the slightest sign of inebriation. A big, heavy man, he was nonetheless remarkably graceful and light on his tiny feet, of which he was inordinately proud. He wore a very high collar to conceal a scarred neck, and because of an eye defect he habitually carried his head to one side and slightly forward, which gave him, as his biographer says, "a perpetual attitude of courteous deference and attentive interest" that sometimes led individuals to believe they had won a greater share of his attention and support than was actually the case. In fact he was extremely stubborn and sometimes vindictive.

The Dred Scott Decision

Before Buchanan could fairly take the Kansas problem in hand, an event occurred that drove another deep wedge between North and South. Back in 1834 Dr. John Emerson of St. Louis joined the army as a surgeon and was assigned to duty at Rock Island, Illinois. Later he was transferred to Fort Snelling, in the Wisconsin Territory. In 1838 he returned to Missouri. Accompanying him on these travels was his body servant, Dred Scott, a slave. In 1846, after Emerson's death, Scott and his wife Harriet, whom he had married while in Wisconsin, with the help of a friendly lawyer brought suit in the Missouri courts for their liberty. They claimed that residence in Illinois, where slavery was barred under the Northwest Ordinance, and in the Wisconsin Territory, where the Missouri Compromise outlawed it, had made them free.

The future of Dred and Harriet Scott mattered not at all to the country or the courts; at issue was the question of whether Congress or the local legislatures had the power to outlaw slavery in the territories. After many years of litigation, the case reached the Supreme Court of the United States. On March 6, 1857, two days after Buchanan's inauguration, the high tribunal acted. Free or slave, the Court declared, blacks were not citizens; therefore, Scott could not sue in a federal court. This was dubious legal logic because many blacks were accepted as citizens in some states when the Constitution was drafted and ratified, and Article IV, Section 2, says that "the citizens of each state shall be entitled to all privileges and immunities of citizens in the several states." But the decision settled Scott's fate.

However, the Court went further. Since the plaintiff had returned to Missouri, the laws of Illinois no longer applied to him. His residence in the Wisconsin Territory—this was the most controversial part of the decision—did not make him free because the Missouri Compromise was unconstitutional. According to the Bill of Rights (the Fifth Amendment), the federal government cannot deprive any person of life, liberty, or property without due process of law.[1] Therefore, Chief Justice Roger

---

[1]*Some state constitutions had similar provisions, but the slave states obviously did not.*

Dred Scott and his wife and children, featured on the cover of *Frank Leslie's Illustrated Newspaper.* Historian Joshua Brown argues in *Beyond the Lines* (2002) that this publication was the precursor to today's popular newsmagazines. Its plentiful pictures were made possible by the new technology of mass-produced wood engraving.

B. Taney reasoned, "an Act of Congress which deprives a person . . . of his liberty or property merely because he came himself or brought his property into a particular Territory . . . could hardly be dignified with the name of due process of law."

In addition to invalidating the already repealed Missouri Compromise, the decision threatened Douglas's principle of popular sovereignty, for if Congress could not exclude slaves from a territory, how could a mere territorial legislature do so? Until statehood was granted, slavery seemed as inviolate as freedom of religion or speech or any other civil liberty guaranteed by the Constitution. Where formerly freedom (as guaranteed in the Bill of Rights) was a national institution and slavery a local one, now, according to the Court, slavery was nationwide, excluded only where states had specifically abolished it.

The irony of employing the Bill of Rights to keep blacks in chains did not escape northern critics. Now slaves could be brought into the Minnesota Territory, even into Oregon. In his inaugural address Buchanan had sanctimoniously urged the people to accept the forthcoming ruling, "whatever this may be," as a final settlement. Many assumed (indeed, it was true) that he had put pressure on the Court to act as it did and that he knew in advance of his speech what the decision would be. If this "greatest crime in the judicial annals of the Republic" was allowed to stand, Northerners argued, the Republican party would have no reason to exist: Its program had been declared unconstitutional! The Dred Scott decision convinced thousands that the South was engaged in an aggressive attempt to extend the peculiar institution so far that it could no longer be considered peculiar.

The Proslavery Lecompton Constitution

Kansas soon provided a test for northern suspicions. Initially Buchanan handled the problem of Kansas well by appointing Robert J. Walker as governor. Although he was from Mississippi, Walker had no desire to foist slavery on the territory against the will of its inhabitants. He was a small man, only five feet tall, but he had more political stature by far than any previous governor of the territory. A former senator and Cabinet member, he was also courageous, patriotic, and tough-minded, much like Douglas in temperament and belief.

The proslavery leaders in Kansas had managed to convene a constitutional convention at Lecompton, but the Free Soil forces boycotted the election of delegates. When this rump body drafted a proslavery constitution and then refused to submit it to a fair vote of all the settlers, Walker denounced its work and hurried back to Washington to explain the situation to Buchanan.

The president refused to face reality. His prosouthern advisers were clamoring for him to "save" Kansas. Instead of rejecting the Lecompton constitution, he asked Congress to admit Kansas to the Union with this document as its frame of government.

Buchanan's decision brought him head-on against Stephen A. Douglas, and the repercussions of their clash shattered the Democratic party. Principle and self-interest (an irresistible combination) forced Douglas to oppose the leader of his party. If he stood aside while Congress admitted Kansas, he not only would be abandoning popular sovereignty, but he would be committing political suicide as well. He was up for reelection to the Senate in 1858. All but one of the fifty-six newspapers in Illinois had declared editorially against the Lecompton constitution; if Douglas supported it, his defeat was certain. In a dramatic confrontation at the White House, he and Buchanan argued the question at length, tempers rising. Finally, the president tried to force him into line. "Mr. Douglas," he said, "I desire you to remember that no Democrat ever yet differed from an Administration of his own choice without being crushed." "Mr. President," Douglas replied contemptuously, "I wish you to remember that General Jackson is dead!" And he stalked out of the room.

Buchanan then compounded his error by putting tremendous political pressure on Douglas, cutting off his Illinois patronage on the eve of his reelection campaign. Of course Douglas persisted, openly joining the Republicans in the fight. Congress rejected the Lecompton bill.

Meanwhile, the extent of the fraud perpetrated at Lecompton became clear. In October 1857 a new legislature had been chosen in Kansas, antislavery voters participating in the balloting. It ordered a referendum on the Lecompton constitution in January 1858. This time the proslavery settlers boycotted the vote and the constitution was overwhelmingly rejected. When Buchanan persisted in pressing Congress to admit Kansas under the Lecompton constitution, Congress ordered another referendum. Kansans rejected it by a huge margin.

The Emergence of Lincoln

These were dark days. During the Panic of 1857 Northerners put the blame for the hard times on the southern-dominated Congress, which had just reduced tariff duties to the lowest levels in nearly half a century. As prices plummeted and unemployment rose, they attributed the collapse to foreign competition and accused the South of having sacrificed the prosperity of the rest of the nation for its selfish advantage. The South in turn read in its relative immunity from the depression proof of the superiority of the slave system, which further stimulated the running sectional debate about the relative merits of free and slave labor.

Dissolution threatened the Union. To many Americans, Stephen A. Douglas seemed to offer the best hope of preserving it. For this reason unusual attention was focused on his campaign for reelection to the Senate in 1858. The importance of the contest and Douglas's national prestige put great pressure on the Republicans of Illinois to nominate someone who would make a good showing against him. The man they chose was Abraham Lincoln.

After a towering figure has passed from the stage, it is always difficult to discover what he was like before his rise to prominence. This is especially true of Lincoln, who changed greatly when power, responsibility, and fame came to him. Lincoln was not unknown in 1858, but his public career had not been distinguished. He was born in Kentucky in 1809, and the story of his early life can be condensed, as he once said himself, into a single line from Thomas Gray's *Elegy:* "The short and simple annals of the poor." His illiterate father, Thomas Lincoln, was a typical frontier wanderer. When Abraham was seven years old, the family moved to Indiana. In 1830 they pushed west again into southern Illinois. The boy received almost no formal schooling.

However, Lincoln had a good mind, and he was extremely ambitious.[2] He cut loose from his family, made a trip to New Orleans, and for a time managed a general store in New Salem, Illinois. In 1834, when barely 25, he won a seat in the Illinois legislature as a Whig. Meanwhile, he studied law and was admitted to the bar in 1836.

---

[2]*His law partner, William Herndon, said that Lincoln's ambition was "a little engine that knows no rest."*

Lincoln remained in the legislature until 1842, displaying a perfect willingness to adopt the Whig position on all issues. In 1846 he was elected to Congress. While not engaged in politics he worked at the law, maintaining an office in Springfield and following the circuit, taking a variety of cases, few of much importance. He earned a decent but by no means sumptuous living. After one term in Congress, marked by his partisan opposition to Polk's Mexican policy, his political career petered out. He seemed fated to pass his remaining years as a small-town lawyer.

The revival of the slavery controversy in 1854 stirred Lincoln deeply. No abolitionist, he had tried to take a "realistic" view of the problem. The Kansas-Nebraska bill led him to see the moral issue more clearly. "If slavery is not wrong, nothing is wrong," he stated with the directness and simplicity of expression for which he later became famous. Compromises made in the past for the sake of sectional harmony had always sought to preserve as much territory as possible for freedom. Yet unlike most Free Soilers, he did not blame the Southerners for slavery. "They are just what we would be in their situation," he confessed.

Thus Lincoln was at once compassionate toward the slave owner and stern toward the institution. "A house divided against itself cannot stand," he warned. "I believe this government cannot endure permanently half slave and half free." Without minimizing the difficulties or urging a hasty or ill-considered solution, Lincoln demanded that the people look toward a day, however remote, when not only Kansas but the entire country would be free.

The Lincoln-Douglas Debates

As Lincoln developed these ideas his reputation grew. In 1855 he almost won the Whig nomination for senator. He became a Republican shortly thereafter, and in June 1856, at the first Republican National Convention, he received 110 votes for the vice presidential nomination. He seemed the logical man to pit against Douglas in 1858.

In July, Lincoln challenged Douglas to a series of seven debates. The senator accepted. The debates were well attended and widely reported, for the idea of a direct confrontation between candidates for an important office captured the popular imagination.

The choice of the next senator lay, of course, in the hands of the Illinois legislature. Technically, Douglas and Lincoln were campaigning for candidates for the legislature who were pledged to support them for the Senate seat. The two employed different political styles, each calculated to project a particular image. Douglas epitomized efficiency and success. He dressed in the latest fashion, favoring flashy vests and the finest broadcloth. He was a glad-hander and a heavy drinker—he apparently died of cirrhosis of the liver. Ordinarily he arrived in town in a private railroad car, to be met by a brass band, then to ride at the head of a parade to the appointed place.

How Lincoln aged during his term of office is evident in comparing Alexander Hesler's portrait, taken on June 3, 1860, with one by an unnamed photographer, taken April 10, 1865.

Lincoln appeared before the voters as a man of the people. He wore ill-fitting black suits and a stovepipe hat—repository for letters, bills, scribbled notes, and other scraps—that exaggerated his great height. He presented a worn and rumpled appearance, partly because he traveled from place to place on day coaches, accompanied by only a few advisers. When local supporters came to meet him at the station, he preferred to walk with them through the streets to the scene of the debate.

Douglas's strategy was to make Lincoln look like an abolitionist. He accused the Republicans of favoring racial equality and refusing to abide by the decision of the Supreme Court in the Dred Scott case. Himself he pictured as a heroic champion of democracy, attacked on one side by the "black" Republicans and on the other by Buchanan supporters, yet ready to fight to his last breath for popular sovereignty.

Lincoln tried to picture Douglas as proslavery and a defender of the Dred Scott decision. "Slavery is an unqualified evil to the negro, to the white man, to the soil, and to the State," he said. "Judge Douglas," he also said, "is blowing out the moral lights around us, when he contends that whoever wants slaves has a right to hold them."

However, Lincoln often weakened the impact of his arguments, being perhaps too eager to demonstrate his conservatism. "All men are created equal," he would say on the authority of the Declaration of Independence, only to add: "I am not, nor ever have been, in favor of bringing about in any way the social and political equality of the white and black races." He opposed allowing blacks to vote, to sit on juries, to marry whites, even to be citizens. He predicted the "ultimate extinction" of slavery, but when pressed he predicted that it would not occur "in less than a hundred years at the least." He took a fence-sitting position on the question of abolition in the District of Columbia and stated flatly that he did not favor repeal of the Fugitive Slave Act.

In the debate at Freeport, a town northwest of Chicago near the Wisconsin line, Lincoln asked Douglas if, considering the Dred Scott decision, the people of a territory could exclude slavery before the territory became a state. Unhesitatingly Douglas replied that they could, simply by not passing the local laws essential for holding blacks in bondage. "It matters not what way the Supreme Court may hereafter decide as to the abstract question," Douglas said. "The people have the lawful means to introduce or exclude it as they please, for the reason that slavery cannot exist . . . unless it is supported by local police regulations."

This argument saved Douglas in Illinois. The Democrats carried the legislature by a narrow margin, whereas it is almost certain that if Douglas had accepted the Dred Scott decision outright, the balance would have swung to the Republicans. But the so-called Freeport Doctrine cost him heavily two years later when he made his bid for the Democratic presidential nomination. "It matters not what way the Supreme Court may hereafter decide"—southern extremists would not accept a man who suggested that the Dred Scott decision could be circumvented, although in fact Douglas had only stated the obvious.

The campaign of 1858 marked Douglas's last triumph, Lincoln's last defeat. Elsewhere the elections in the North went heavily to the Republicans. When the old Congress reconvened in December, northern-sponsored economic measures (a higher tariff, the transcontinental railroad, river and harbor improvements, a free homestead bill) were all blocked by southern votes.

Whether the South could continue to prevent the passage of this legislation in the new Congress was problematical. In early 1859 even many moderate Southerners were uneasy about the future. The radicals, made panicky by Republican victories and their own failure to win in Kansas, spoke openly of secession if a Republican was elected president in 1860. Lincoln's "house divided" speech was quoted out of context, while Douglas's Freeport Doctrine added to southern woes. When Senator William H. Seward of New York spoke of an "irrepressible conflict" between freedom and slavery, white Southerners became still more alarmed.

Naturally they struck back. Led by such self-described "fire-eaters" as William L. Yancey of Alabama and Senators Jefferson Davis of Mississippi, John Slidell of Louisiana, and James H. Hammond of South Carolina, they demanded a federal slave code for the territories and talked of annexing Cuba and reviving the African slave trade.

John Brown's Raid

In October 1859, John Brown, the scourge of Kansas, made his second contribution to the unfolding sectional drama. Gathering a group of eighteen followers, white and black, he staged an attack on Harpers Ferry, Virginia, a town on the Potomac River upstream from Washington. Having boned up on guerrilla tactics, he planned to seize the federal arsenal there; arm the slaves, whom he thought would flock to his side; and then establish a black republic in the mountains of Virginia.

Simply by overpowering a few night watchmen, Brown and his men occupied the arsenal and a nearby rifle factory. They captured several hostages, one of them Colonel Lewis Washington, a great-grandnephew of George Washington. But no slaves came forward to join them. Federal troops commanded by Robert E. Lee soon trapped Brown's men in an engine house of the Baltimore and Ohio Railroad. After a two-day siege in which the attackers picked off ten of his men, Brown was captured.

No incident so well illustrates the role of emotion and irrationality in the sectional crisis as does John Brown's raid. After his ghastly Pottawatomie murders it should have been obvious to anyone that he was both a fanatic and mentally unstable: Some of the victims were hacked to bits with a broadsword. Yet numbers of high-minded Northerners, including Emerson and Thoreau, had supported Brown and his antislavery "work" after 1856. Some—among them Franklin B. Sanborn, a teacher; Thomas Wentworth Higginson, a clergyman; and the merchant George L. Stearns—contributed knowingly to his Harpers Ferry enterprise.

White Southerners reacted to Harpers Ferry with equal irrationality, some with a rage similar to Brown's. Dozens of hapless Northerners in the southern states were arrested, beaten, or driven off. One, falsely suspected of being an accomplice of Brown, was lynched.

Brown's fate lay in the hands of the Virginia authorities. Ignoring his obvious derangement, they charged him with treason, conspiracy, and murder. He was speedily convicted and sentenced to death by hanging.

Yet "Old Brown" had still one more contribution to make to the developing sectional tragedy. Despite the furor he had created, cool heads everywhere called for calm and denounced his attack. Most Republican politicians repudiated him. Even execution would probably not have made a martyr of Brown had he behaved like a madman after his capture. Instead, an enormous dignity descended on him as he lay in his Virginia jail awaiting death. Whatever his faults, he truly believed in racial equality. He addressed blacks who worked for him as "Mister" and arranged for them to eat at his table and sit with his family in church.

This conviction served him well in his last days. "If it is deemed necessary that I should forfeit my life for the furtherance of the ends of justice, and mingle my blood further with the blood of . . . millions in this slave country whose rights are

After John Brown's capture, Emerson called him "a martyr" who would "make the gallows as glorious as the cross." Brown's principled radicalism found favor during the Depression decade of the 1930s. John Stewart Curry's mural, completed in 1943, depicted the demented Brown in the pose of Christ on the cross. The image offended the Kansas legislature, which had commissioned Curry to portray Kansas history in a "sane and sensible manner."

disregarded by wicked, cruel, and unjust enactments," he said before the judge pronounced sentence, "I say, let it be done."

This John Brown, with his patriarchal beard and sad eyes, so apparently incompatible with the bloody terrorist of Pottawatomie and Harpers Ferry, led thousands in the North to ignore his past and treat him almost as a saint.

And so Brown, hanged on December 2, 1859, became to the North a hero and to the South a symbol of northern ruthlessness. Soon, as the popular song had it, Brown's body lay "a-mouldering in the grave," and the memory of his bloody act did indeed go "marching on."

The Election of 1860

By 1860 the nation was teetering on the brink of disunion. Radicals North and South were heedlessly provoking one another. Stephen A. Douglas was probably the last hope of avoiding a rupture between North and South. But when the Democrats met at Charleston, South Carolina, in April 1860 to choose a presidential candidate, the southern delegates would not support him unless he promised not to disturb slavery in the territories. Indeed, they went further in their demands. The North, William L. Yancey of Alabama insisted, must accept the proposition that slavery was not merely tolerable but right. Of course the Northerners would not go so far. "Gentlemen of the South," said Senator George E. Pugh of Ohio in replying to Yancey, "you mistake us—you mistake us! We will not do it!" When southern proposals were voted down, most of the delegates from the deep South walked out and the convention adjourned without naming a candidate.

In June the Democrats reconvened at Baltimore. Again they failed to reach agreement. The two wings then met separately, the Northerners nominating Douglas, the Southerners John C. Breckinridge of Kentucky, Buchanan's vice president. On the question of slavery in the territories, the Northerners promised to "abide by the decision of the Supreme Court," which meant, in effect, that they stood for Douglas's Freeport Doctrine. The Southerners announced their belief that neither Congress nor any territorial government could prevent citizens from settling "with their property" in any territory.

Meanwhile, the Republicans, who met in Chicago in mid-May, had drafted a platform attractive to all classes and all sections of the northern and western states. For manufacturers they proposed a high tariff, for farmers a homestead law providing free land for settlers. Internal improvements "of a National character," notably a railroad to the Pacific, should receive federal aid. No restrictions should be placed on immigration. As to slavery in the territories, the Republicans did not equivocate: "The normal condition of all the territory of the United States is that of freedom." Neither Congress nor a local legislature could "give legal existence to Slavery in any Territory."

In choosing a presidential candidate the Republicans displayed equally shrewd political judgment. Senator Seward was the front-runner, but he had taken too extreme a stand and appeared unlikely to carry the crucial states of Pennsylvania, Indiana, and Illinois. He led on the first ballot but could not get a majority. Then the delegates began to look closely at Abraham Lincoln. His thoughtful and moderate views on the main issue of the times and his formidable debating skills attracted many, and so did his political personality. "Honest Abe," the "Railsplitter," a man of humble origins (born in a log cabin), self-educated, self-made, a common man but by no means an ordinary man—the combination seemed unbeatable.

It also helped that Lincoln was from a crucial state and had an excellent team of convention managers. Taking advantage of the fact that the convention was meeting in Lincoln's home state, they packed the gallery with leather-lunged Chicago ward heelers who were assigned the task of shouting for their man. They also made a series of deals with the leaders of other state delegations to win additional votes. "I authorize no bargains and will be bound by none," Lincoln telegraphed the convention. "Lincoln ain't here and don't know what we have to meet," one of his managers remarked—and proceeded to trade off two Cabinet posts for the votes of key states.

On the second ballot Lincoln drew shoulder to shoulder with Seward, on the third he was within two votes of victory. Before the roll could be called again, dele-

THE UNDECIDED POLITICAL PRIZE FIGHT.

Modern scholars of the media have found that most news reporting of political campaigns focuses not on issues but on the contest itself. This cartoon, depicting Abraham Lincoln and Stephen A. Douglas as boxers during the 1860 presidential campaign, shows that Americans have long been attuned to the competitive aspects of politics.

gates began to switch their votes, and in a landslide, soon made unanimous, Lincoln was nominated.

A few days earlier the remnants of the American and Whig parties had formed the Constitutional Union party and nominated John Bell of Tennessee for president. "It is both the part of patriotism and of duty," they resolved, "to recognize no political principle other than the Constitution of the country, the union of the states, and the enforcement of the laws." Ostrichlike, the Constitutional Unionists ignored the conflicts rending the nation. Only in the border states, where the consequences of disunion were sure to be most tragic, did they have any following.

With four candidates in the field, no one could win a popular majority, but it soon became clear that Lincoln was going to be elected. Breckenridge had most of the slave states in his pocket and Bell would run strong in the border regions, but the populous northern and western states had a majority of the electoral votes, and there the choice lay between the Republicans and the Douglas Democrats. In such a contest the Republicans, with their attractive economic program and their strong stand against slavery in the territories, were sure to come out on top.

Lincoln avoided campaigning and made no public statements. Douglas, recognizing the certainty of Lincoln's victory, accepted his fate and for the first time in his career rose above ambition. "We must try to save the Union," he said. "I will go South."

Presidential Election, 1860

In the heart of the Cotton Kingdom, he appealed to the voters to stand by the Union regardless of who was elected. He was the only candidate to do so; the others refused to remind the people that their election might result in secession and civil war.

When the votes were counted, Lincoln had 1.866 million, almost a million fewer than the combined total of his three opponents, but he swept the North and West, which gave him 180 electoral votes and the presidency. Douglas received 1.383 million votes, so distributed that he carried only Missouri and part of New Jersey. Breckenridge, with 848,000 popular votes, won most of the South; Bell, with 593,000, carried Virginia, Tennessee, and Kentucky. Lincoln was thus a minority president, but his title to the office was unquestionable. Even if his opponents could have combined their popular votes in each state, Lincoln would have won.

The Secession Crisis

Only days after Lincoln's victory, the South Carolina legislature ordered an election of delegates to a convention to decide the state's future course. On December 20 the convention voted unanimously to secede, basing its action on the logic of Calhoun. "The State of South Carolina has resumed her position among the nations of the world," the delegates announced. By February 1, 1861, the six other states of the lower South had followed suit. A week later, at Montgomery, Alabama, a provisional government of the Confederate States of America was established. Virginia, Tennessee, North Carolina, and Arkansas did not leave the Union but announced that if the federal government attempted to use force against the Confederacy, they too would secede.

Why were white Southerners willing to wreck the Union their forebears had put together with so much love and labor? No simple explanation is possible. The danger that the expanding North would overwhelm them was for neither today nor tomorrow. Lincoln had assured them that he would respect slavery where it existed. The Democrats had retained control of Congress in the election; the Supreme Court was firmly in their hands as well. If the North did try to destroy slavery, secession would perhaps be a logical tactic, but why not wait until the threat materialized? To leave the Union meant abandoning the very objectives for which the South had been contending for over a decade: a share of the federal territories and an enforceable fugitive slave law.

One reason why the South rejected this line of thinking was the tremendous economic energy generated in the North, which seemed to threaten the South's independence. As one Southerner complained at a commercial convention in 1855:

> From the rattle with which the nurse tickles the ear of the child born in the South to the shroud which covers the cold form of the dead, everything comes from the North. We rise from between sheets made in Northern looms, and pillows of Northern feathers, to wash in basins made in the North. . . . We eat from Northern plates and dishes; our rooms are swept with Northern brooms, our gardens dug with Northern spades . . . and the very wood which feeds our fires is cut with Northern axes, helved with hickory brought from Connecticut and New York.

Secession, white Southerners argued, would "liberate" the South and produce the kind of balanced economy that was proving so successful in the North. Moreover, the mere possibility of emancipation was a powerful force for secession. "We must either submit to degradation, and to the loss of property worth four billions," the Mississippi convention declared, "or we must secede."

The years of sectional conflict, the growing northern criticism of slavery, perhaps even an unconscious awareness that this criticism was well founded, had undermined and in many cases destroyed the patriotic feelings of white Southerners. Because of the constant clamor set up by New England antislavery groups, the South tended to identify all Northerners as "Yankee abolitionists" and to resent them with increasing passion. "I look upon the whole New England race as a troublesome unquiet set of meddlers," one Georgian wrote. In addition, a Republican president would not need the consent of Congress to flood the South with unfriendly federal officials-abolitionists and perhaps even blacks. Such a possibility most white Southerners found unsupportable. Fear approaching panic swept the region.

Although states' rights provided the rationale for leaving the Union, and Southerners expounded the strict constructionist interpretation of the Constitution with great ingenuity, the economic and emotional factors were far more basic. The lower South decided to go ahead with secession regardless of the cost. "Let the consequences be what they may," an Atlanta newspaper proclaimed. "Whether the

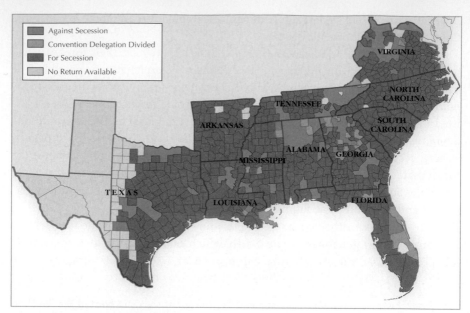

Secession of the South, 1860–1861

A comparison of this map with the one on page 353 shows the minimal support for secession in the mainly nonslave mountain areas of the Appalachians. The strong antisecession sentiment in the mountainous areas of Virginia eventually led several counties there to break from Virginia in 1863 and form the new state of West Virginia.

Potomac is crimsoned in human gore, and Pennsylvania Avenue is paved ten fathoms in depth with mangled bodies . . . the South will never submit."

Not every slave owner could contemplate secession with such bloodthirsty equanimity. Some believed that the risks of war and slave insurrection were too great. Others retained a profound loyalty to the United States. Many accepted secession only after the deepest examination of conscience. Lieutenant Colonel Robert E. Lee of Virginia was typical of thousands. "I see only that a fearful calamity is upon us," he wrote during the secession crisis. "There is no sacrifice I am not ready to make for the preservation of the Union save that of honour. If a disruption takes place, I shall go back in sorrow to my people & share the misery of my native state."

In the North there was a foolish but understandable reluctance to believe that the South really intended to break away. President-elect Lincoln was inclined to write off secession as a bluff designed to win concessions he was determined not to make. He also showed lamentable political caution in refusing to announce his plans or to cooperate with the outgoing Democratic administration before his inauguration.

The new southern Confederacy set vigorously to work drafting a constitution, choosing Jefferson Davis as provisional president, seizing arsenals and other federal property within its boundaries, and preparing to dispatch diplomatic representatives to enlist the support of foreign powers. Buchanan bumbled helplessly in Washington. And out in Illinois, Abraham Lincoln juggled Cabinet posts and grew a beard.

1850	Compromise of 1850 preserves Union
	U.S. and Great Britain sign Clayton-Bulwer Treaty on interoceanic travel
1851–1860	Northerners resist enforcement of Fugitive Slave Act
1852	Harriet Beecher Stowe publishes *Uncle Tom's Cabin*, a novel depicting slavery
	Franklin Pierce is elected president
1854	U.S. disavows secret Ostend Manifesto on Cuba
	Kansas-Nebraska Act repeals Missouri Compromise
1856–1858	Proslavery forces oppose Free Soilers in "Bleeding Kansas" Territory
1856	John Brown and followers murder five proslavery men in Pottawatomie Massacre
	South Carolina's Preston Brooks canes Senator Charles Sumner of Massachusetts on Senate floor
	James Buchanan is elected president
1857	U.S. Supreme Court issues decision in Dred Scott case, declaring slaves are not citizens
	Panic of 1857 collapses economy
1858	Abraham Lincoln loses Senate race to Stephen Douglas after Lincoln-Douglas debates, but wins national attention
1859	John Brown raids Harpers Ferry, Virginia, arsenal
1860	Abraham Lincoln is elected president
	South Carolina secedes from Union
1861	Seven southern states establish Confederate States of America

14 CHAPTER

The War to Save the Union

ON FEBRUARY 22, 2006, SUNNI INSURGENTS OVERWHELMED THE caretaker and staff of the Mosque of the Golden Dome in Samarra, 60 miles north of Baghdad, Iraq. The mosque was among the most revered Shiite shrines in the Middle East, visited by more than a million Muslims each year. The attackers placed explosive devices at the base of the dome and left the building. Moments later, an explosion collapsed the dome, shattering its 72,000 golden tiles.

If the purpose of the bombing were to ignite a civil war between Sunni and Shiite Muslims, it succeeded spectacularly. By sunset, Shiite militiamen bent on revenge had destroyed twenty-seven Sunni mosques, killed three imams—Islamic holy men—and assaulted hundreds of Sunnis. Over the next 12 months, the cycle of violence escalated, resulting in the deaths of over 34,000 Iraqi civilians. (This accounting is provided by the United Nations; other estimates are higher.) "The gates of hell are open in Iraq," declared Amr Moussa, head of the Arab League.

Americans have been baffled by such acts of "senseless violence"—the phrase used by President Bush after the attack on the Golden Dome. "Why do Sunnis kill Shiites?" asked Trent Lott, a Republican senator from Mississippi. "Why do they hate each other?" Bill O'Reilly, a TV commentator, provided a characteristically blunt answer: "There are so many nuts in the country—so many crazies." Why else would Iraqi kill Iraqi, and Muslim kill Muslim?

The reasons for any civil war are not so simple, as Americans were to learn in 1861. Brother fought brother; men intent on destroying each other prayed to the same God.

The U.S. Civil War moved forward, as wars do, impelled by its own terrible momentum. The first inconclusive battle led to others. More men were called to arms, often against their will. Farms and factories were diverted to the war effort. Lincoln emancipated slaves as a measure to weaken the South. The strains of the war fractured the political consensus. When the guns at last fell silent, a half million men lay dead.

President Abraham Lincoln, while touring the hospital wards after yet another gruesome battle, despaired at the horror of it all: "If there is a worse place than hell, I am in it."

Lincoln's Cabinet

The nomination of Lincoln had succeeded brilliantly for the Republicans, but was his election a good thing for the country? As the inauguration approached, many Americans had doubts. Honest Abe was a clever politician who had spoken well about the central issue of the times, but would he act decisively in this crisis? His behavior as president-elect was not reassuring. He spent much time closeted with politicians. Was he too obtuse to understand the grave threat to the Union posed by secession? People remembered uneasily that he had never held executive office, that his congressional career had been short and undistinguished. When he finally uprooted himself from Springfield in February 1861, his occasional speeches en route to Washington were vague, almost flippant. He kissed babies, shook hands, mouthed platitudes. Some people thought it downright cowardly that he let himself be spirited in the dead of night through Baltimore, where feeling against him ran high.

Everyone waited tensely to see whether Lincoln would oppose secession with force, but Lincoln seemed concerned only with organizing his Cabinet. William H. Seward, the secretary of state, was the ablest and best known of the appointees. Despite his reputation for radicalism, the hawk-nosed, chinless, tousle-haired Seward hoped to conciliate the South and was thus in bad odor with the radical wing of the Republican party. In time Seward proved himself Lincoln's strong right arm. Senator Salmon P. Chase, a bald, square-jawed, antislavery leader from Ohio, whom Lincoln named secretary of the treasury, represented the radicals. Chase was humorless and vain but able; he detested Seward. Many of the president's other selections worried thoughtful people.

Lincoln's inaugural address was conciliatory but firm. Southern institutions were in no danger from his administration. Secession, however, was illegal, the Union "perpetual." "A husband and wife may be divorced," Lincoln said, employing one of his homely and unconsciously risqué metaphors, "but the different parts of our country cannot . . . . Intercourse, either amicable or hostile, must continue between them." His tone was calm and warm. His concluding words catch the spirit of the inaugural perfectly:

> I am loath to close. We are not enemies, but friends. We must not be enemies. Though passion may have strained, it must not break, our bonds of affection. The mystic chords of memory, stretching from every battlefield and patriot grave to every living heart . . . will yet swell the chorus of the Union when again touched, as surely they will be, by the better angels of our nature.

Fort Sumter: The First Shot

While denying the legality of secession, Lincoln had taken a temporizing position. The Confederates had seized most federal property in the Deep South. Lincoln admitted frankly that he would not attempt to reclaim this property. However, two strongholds, Fort Sumter, on an island in Charleston harbor, and Fort Pickens, at Pensacola, Florida, were still in loyal Union hands. Most Republicans did not want to surrender them without a show of resistance. To do so, one wrote, would be to convert the American eagle into a "debilitated chicken."

Yet to reinforce the forts might mean bloodshed that would make reconciliation impossible. After weeks of indecision, Lincoln took the moderate step of sending a naval expedition to supply the beleaguered Sumter garrison with food. Unwilling to permit this, the Confederates opened fire on the fort on April 12 before the supply ships arrived. After holding out for 34 hours, Major Robert Anderson and his men surrendered.

The attack precipitated an outburst of patriotic indignation in the North. Lincoln issued a call for 75,000 volunteers; his request prompted Virginia, North Carolina, Arkansas, and Tennessee to secede. After years of crises and compromises, the nation chose to settle the great quarrel between the sections by force of arms.

The Southerners were seeking to exercise what a later generation would call the right of self-determination. How, they asked, could the North square its professed belief in democracy with its refusal to permit the southern states to leave the Union when a majority of their citizens wished to do so?

Lincoln took the position that secession was a rejection of democracy. If the South could refuse to abide by the result of an election in which it had freely participated, then everything that monarchists and other conservatives had said about the instability of republican governments would be proved true. "The central idea of secession is the essence of anarchy," he said. The United States must "demonstrate to the world" that "when ballots have been fairly and constitutionally decided, there can be no successful appeal except to ballots themselves, at succeeding elections."

Although abolition was to be one of the major results of the Civil War, the war was fought for nationalistic reasons, not to destroy slavery. Lincoln made this plain when he wrote in response to an editorial by Horace Greeley urging immediate emancipation: "I would save the Union. . . . If I could save the Union without freeing any slave, I would do it; and if I could save it by freeing all the slaves, I would do it; and if I could do it by freeing some and leaving others alone, I would also do that." He added, however, "I intend no modification of my oft-expressed personal wish that all men, everywhere, could be free."

The Blue and the Gray

In any test between the United States and the Confederacy, the former possessed tremendous advantages. There were more than 20 million people in the northern states (excluding Kentucky and Missouri, where opinion was divided) but only 9

Men Present for Service During the Civil War

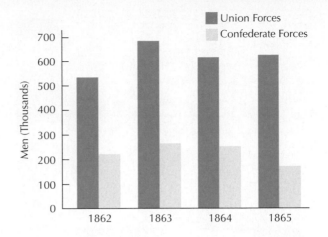

The North's economic capacity to wage war was even more preponderant. It was manufacturing nine times as much as the Confederacy (including 97 percent of the nation's firearms) and had a far larger and more efficient railroad system than the South. Northern control of the merchant marine and the navy made possible a blockade of the Confederacy, a particularly potent threat to a region so dependent on foreign markets.

The Confederates discounted these advantages. Many doubted that public opinion in the North would sustain Lincoln if he attempted to meet secession with force. Northern manufacturers needed southern markets, and merchants depended heavily on southern business. Many western farmers still sent their produce down the Mississippi. War would threaten the prosperity of all these groups, Southerners maintained. Should the North try to cut Europe off from southern cotton, the European powers, particularly Great Britain, would descend on the land in their might, force open southern ports, and provide the Confederacy with the means of defending itself forever. Moreover, the South provided nearly three-fourths of the world's cotton, essential for most textile mills. "You do not dare to make war on cotton," Senator Hammond of South Carolina had taunted his northern colleagues in 1858. "No power on earth dares to make war upon it. Cotton is king."

The Confederacy also counted on certain military advantages. The new nation need only hold what it had; it could fight a defensive war, less costly in men and material and of great importance in maintaining morale and winning outside sympathy. Southerners would be defending not only their social institutions but also their homes and families.

Luck played a part too; the Confederacy quickly found a great commander, while many of the northern generals in the early stages of the war proved either bungling or indecisive. In battle after battle Union armies were defeated by forces of equal or smaller size.

Young volunteers of the First Virginia Militia, in 1861. Why did they join the Confederate army? "It is better to spend our all in defending our country than to be subjugated and have it taken away from us," one explained, a sentiment that appeared often in the letters of Confederate soldiers. Soldiers on both sides believed that their cause was righteous.

There was little to distinguish the enlisted men of the two sides. Both, conscious of their forefathers of 1776, fought for liberty, though they interpreted the concept in opposite ways.

Both sides faced massive difficulties in organizing for a war long feared but never properly anticipated. After southern defections, the regular Union army consisted of only 13,000 officers and enlisted men, far too few to absorb the 186,000 who had joined the colors by early summer, much less the additional 450,000 who had volunteered by the end of the year. Recruiting was left to the states, each being assigned a quota; there was little central organization. Natty companies of "Fire Zouaves" and "Garibaldi Guards" in gorgeous uniforms rubbed shoulders with slovenly units composed of toughs and criminals and with regiments of farm boys from Iowa, Illinois, and Michigan. Unlike later conflicts in which men from all parts of the country were mixed in each regiment, Civil War units were recruited locally. Men in each company tended to have known one another or had friends in common in civilian life. But few knew even the rudiments of soldiering. The hastily composed high command, headed by the elderly Winfield Scott, debated grand strategy endlessly while regimental commanders lacked decent maps of Virginia.

The Confederacy faced far greater problems than the North, for it had to create an entire administration under pressure of war, with the additional handicap of the states' rights philosophy to which it was committed. The Confederate constitution explicitly recognized the sovereignty of the states and contained no broad authorization for laws designed to advance the general welfare. State governments repeatedly defied the central administration, located at Richmond after Virginia seceded, even with regard to military affairs.

The call to arms produced a turnout in the Confederacy perhaps even more impressive than that in the North; by July 1861 about 112,000 men were under arms. As in the North, men of every type enlisted, and morale was high. Some

Jefferson Davis sat for this portrait in 1863 in his mansion in Richmond. It is the only wartime portrait from the life of the Confederate president.

wealthy recruits brought slave servants with them to care for their needs in camp, cavalrymen supplied their own horses, and many men arrived with their own shot-guns and hunting rifles. Ordinary militia companies sporting names like Tallapoosa Thrashers, Cherokee Lincoln Killers, and Chickasaw Desperadoes marched in step with troops of "character, blood, and social position" bearing names like Richmond Howitzers and Louisiana Zouaves. ("Zouave" mania swept both North and South, prospective soldiers evidently considering broad sashes and baggy breeches the embodiment of military splendor.)

President Jefferson Davis represented the best type of southern planter, noted for his humane treatment of his slaves. In politics he had pursued a somewhat un-usual course. While senator from Mississippi, he opposed the Compromise of 1850 and became a leader of the southern radicals. After Franklin Pierce appointed him secretary of war, however, he took a more nationalistic position, one close to that of Stephen Douglas. Davis supported the building of a transcontinental railroad and spoke in favor of the annexation of Cuba and other Caribbean areas. He rejected Douglas's position during the Kansas controversy but tried to close the breach in Democratic ranks opened by the Kansas debacle. After the 1860 election he sup-ported secession only reluctantly, preferring to give Lincoln a chance to prove that he meant the South no harm.

The Test of Battle: Bull Run

"Forward to Richmond!" "On to Washington!" Such shouts propelled the armies into battle long before either was properly trained. On July 21 at Manassas Junction, Virginia, some 20 miles below Washington, on a branch of the Potomac called Bull

A dead young soldier. Eighteen-year-olds were the largest age group in the first year of the war in both armies. Soldiers were universally called "the boys"; and officers, even in their thirties, were called "old men." One of the most popular war songs was "Just Before the Battle, Mother."

Run, 30,000 Union soldiers under General Irvin McDowell attacked a roughly equal force of Confederates commanded by the "Napoleon of the South," Pierre G. T. Beauregard. McDowell swept back the Confederate left flank. Victory seemed sure. Then a Virginia brigade under Thomas J. Jackson rushed to the field by rail from the Shenandoah Valley in the nick of time, held doggedly to a key hill, and checked the advance. (A South Carolina general, seeking to rally his own men, pointed to the hill and shouted: "Look, there is Jackson with his Virginians, standing like a stone wall against the enemy." Thus "Stonewall" Jackson received his nickname.)

The Southerners then counterattacked, driving the Union soldiers back. As often happens with green troops, retreat quickly turned to rout. McDowell's men fled toward the defenses of Washington, abandoning their weapons, stumbling through lines of supply wagons, trampling foolish sightseers who had come out to watch the battle. Panic engulfed Washington. Richmond exulted. Both sides expected the northern capital to fall within hours.

The inexperienced southern troops were too disorganized to follow up their victory. Casualties on both sides were light, and the battle had little direct effect on anything but morale. Southern confidence soared, while the North began to realize how immense the task of subduing the Confederacy would be.

After Bull Run, Lincoln devised a broader, more systematic strategy for winning the war. The navy would clamp a tight blockade on all southern ports. In the West operations designed to gain control of the Mississippi would be undertaken. (This was part of General Scott's "Anaconda Plan," designed to starve the South into submission.) More important, a new army would be mustered at Washington to invade Virginia. Congress promptly authorized the enlistment of 500,000 three-year volunteers. To lead this army and—after General Scott's retirement in November—to command the Union forces, Lincoln appointed a 34-year-old major general, George B. McClellan.

McClellan was the North's first military hero. Units under his command had driven the Confederates from the pro-Union western counties of Virginia, clearing the way for the admission of West Virginia as a separate state in 1863. The fighting had been on a small scale, but McClellan, an incurable romantic and something of an egomaniac, managed to inflate its importance. "You have annihilated two armies," he proclaimed in a widely publicized message to his troops. Few Northerners noticed that they had "annihilated" only about 250 Confederates.

Paying for the War

After Bull Run, McClellan concentrated on training his troops and preparing them for a major offensive. By the fall of 1861 a real army was taking shape along the Potomac: disciplined, confident, adequately supplied. Northern shops and factories were producing guns, ammunition, wagons, uniforms, shoes, and the countless other supplies needed to fight a great war. Most manufacturers operated on a small scale, but with the armed forces soon wearing out 3 million pairs of shoes and 1.5 million uniforms a year and with men leaving their jobs by the hundreds of thousands to fight, the tendency of industry to mechanize and to increase the size of the average manufacturing unit became ever more pronounced.

At the beginning of the war Secretary of the Treasury Salmon P. Chase underestimated how much it would cost. He learned quickly. In August 1861 Congress passed an income tax law (3 percent on incomes over $800, which effectively exempted ordinary wage earners) and assessed a direct tax on the states. Loans amounting to $140 million were authorized. As the war dragged on and expenses mounted, new excise taxes on every imaginable product and service were passed, and still further borrowing was necessary. In 1863 the banking system was overhauled.

During the war the federal government borrowed a total of $2.2 billion and collected $667 million in taxes, slightly over 20 percent of its total expenditures. These unprecedented large sums proved inadequate. Some obligations were met by printing paper money unredeemable in coin. About $431 million in "greenbacks"—the term distinguished this fiat money from the redeemable yellowback bills—were issued during the conflict. Public confidence in all paper money vacillated with each change in the fortunes of the Union armies, but by the end of the war the cost of living in the North had doubled.

On balance, the heavy emphasis on borrowing and currency inflation was expensive but not irresponsible. In a country still chiefly agricultural, people had relatively low cash incomes and therefore could not easily bear a heavy tax load. Many Americans considered it reasonable to expect future generations to pay part of the dollar cost of saving the Union when theirs was contributing so heavily in labor and blood.

Politics as Usual

Partisan politics was altered by the war but not suspended. The secession of the southern states left the Republicans with large majorities in both houses of Congress. Most Democrats supported measures necessary for the conduct of the war but objected to the way the Lincoln administration was conducting it. The sharpest conflicts came when slavery and race relations were under discussion. The

Democrats adopted a conservative stance, as reflected in the slogan "The Constitution as it is; the Union as it was; the Negroes where they are." The Republicans divided into Moderate and Radical wings. Political divisions on economic issues such as tariffs and land policy tended to cut across party lines and, so far as the Republicans were concerned, to bear little relation to slavery and race. As the war progressed, the Radical faction became increasingly influential.

In 1861 the most prominent Radical senator was Charles Sumner, finally recovered from his caning by Preston Brooks and brimful of hatred for slaveholders. In the House, Thaddeus Stevens of Pennsylvania was the rising power. Sumner and Stevens were uncompromising on all questions relating to slaves; they insisted not merely on abolition but on granting full political and civil rights to blacks. Moderate Republicans objected vehemently to treating blacks as equals and opposed making abolition a war aim, and even many of the so-called Radicals disagreed with Sumner and Stevens on race relations.

At the other end of the political spectrum stood the so-called Peace Democrats. These "Copperheads" (apparently the reference was not to the poisonous snake but to an earlier time when some hard-money Democrats wore copper pennies around their necks) opposed all measures in support of the war. They hoped to win control of Congress and force a negotiated peace. Few were actually disloyal, but their activities at a time when thousands of men were risking their lives in battle infuriated many Northerners.

Lincoln treated dissenters with a curious mixture of repression and tolerance. He suspended the writ of habeas corpus in critical areas and applied martial law freely. Over 13,000 persons were arrested and held without trial, many, as it later turned out, unjustly. The president argued that the government dared not stand on ceremony in a national emergency. His object, he insisted, was not to punish but to prevent. Arbitrary arrests were rarely, if ever, made for purely political purposes, and free elections were held as scheduled throughout the war.

The most notorious domestic foe of the administration was the Peace Democrat Congressman Clement L. Vallandigham of Ohio, who was sent to prison by a military court. There were two rebellions in progress, Vallandigham claimed, "the Secessionist Rebellion" and "the Abolitionist Rebellion." "I am against both," he added. But Lincoln ordered him released and banished to the Confederacy. Once at liberty Vallandigham moved to Canada, from which refuge he ran unsuccessfully for governor of Ohio.

"Perish offices," he once said, "perish life itself, but do the thing that is right." In 1864 he returned to Ohio. Although he campaigned against Lincoln in the presidential election, he was not arrested. Lincoln was no dictator.

Behind Confederate Lines

The South also revised its strategy after Bull Run. Although it might have been wiser to risk everything on a bold invasion of the North, President Davis relied primarily on a strong defense to wear down the Union's will to fight. In 1862 the

Confederate Congress passed a conscription act that permitted the hiring of substitutes and exempted many classes of people (including college professors, druggists, and mail carriers) whose work could hardly have been deemed essential. A provision deferring one slave owner or overseer for every plantation of twenty or more slaves led many to grumble about "a rich man's war and a poor man's fight."

Finance was the Confederacy's most vexing problem. The blockade made it impossible to raise much money through tariffs. The Confederate Congress passed an income tax together with many excise taxes but all told they covered only 2 percent of its needs by taxation. The most effective levy was a tax in kind, amounting to one-tenth of each farmer's production. The South borrowed as much as it could ($712 million), even mortgaging cotton undeliverable because of the blockade, in order to gain European credits. But it relied mainly on printing paper currency; over $1.5 billion poured from the presses during the war. Considering the amount issued, this currency held its value well until late in the war, when the military fortunes of the Confederacy began to decline. Then the bottom fell out, and by early 1865 the Confederate dollar was worth less than 2 cents in gold.

Outfitting the army strained southern resources to the limit. Large supplies of small arms (some 600,000 weapons during the entire war) came from Europe through the blockade, along with other valuable matériel. As the blockade became more efficient, however, it became increasingly difficult to obtain European goods. The Confederates did manage to build a number of munitions plants, and they captured huge amounts of northern arms. No battle was lost because of a lack of guns or other military equipment, although shortages of shoes and uniforms handicapped the Confederate forces on some occasions.

Foreign policy loomed large in Confederate thinking, for the "cotton is king" theory presupposed that the great European powers would break any northern blockade to get cotton for their textile mills. Southern expectations were not realized, however. The European nations would have been delighted to see the United States broken up, but none was prepared to support the Confederacy directly. The attitude of Great Britain was decisive. The cutting off of cotton did not hit the British as hard as the South had hoped. They had a large supply on hand when the war broke out, and when that was exhausted, alternative sources in India and Egypt took up part of the slack.

Several times the Union and Great Britain came to the brink of war. In 1862 two powerful cruisers, the *Florida* and the *Alabama*, were built for the Confederates in English shipyards under the most transparent of subterfuges. Despite American protests, they were permitted to put to sea and were soon wreaking havoc among northern merchant ships. When two ironclad "rams" were also built in Britain for the Confederates, the United States made it clear that it would declare war if the ships were delivered. The British government then confiscated the vessels, avoiding a showdown.

Charles Francis Adams, the American minister in London, ably handled the many vexing problems that arose. However, the military situation determined

British policy; once the North obtained a clear superiority on the battlefield, the possibility of intervention vanished.

War in the West: Shiloh

After Bull Run no battles were fought until early 1862. Then, while McClellan continued his deliberate preparations to attack Richmond, important fighting occurred far to the west. Most of the Plains Indians sided with the Confederacy, principally because of their resentment of the federal government's policies toward them. White settlers from Colorado to California were mostly Unionists. In March 1862 a Texas army advancing beyond Santa Fe clashed with a Union force in the Battle of Glorieta Pass. The battle was indecisive, but a Union unit destroyed the Texans' supply train. The Texans felt compelled to retreat to the Rio Grande, thus ending the Confederate threat to the Far West.

Meanwhile, far larger Union forces, led by a shabby, cigar-smoking West Pointer named Ulysses S. Grant, had invaded Tennessee from a base at Cairo, Illinois. Making effective use of armored gunboats, Grant captured Fort Henry and Fort Donelson, strongholds on the Tennessee and Cumberland rivers, taking 14,000 prisoners. Next he marched toward Corinth, Mississippi, an important railroad junction.

To check Grant's advance, the Confederates massed 40,000 men under Albert Sidney Johnston. On April 6, while Grant slowly concentrated his forces, Johnston struck suddenly at Shiloh, 20 miles north of Corinth. Some Union soldiers were caught half-dressed, others in the midst of brewing their morning coffee. A few died in their blankets. "We were more than surprised," one Illinois officer later admitted. "We were astonished." However, Grant's men stood their ground. At the end of a day of ghastly carnage the Confederates held the advantage, but fresh Union troops poured in during the night, and on the second day of battle the tide turned. The Confederates fell back toward Corinth, exhausted and demoralized.

Grant, shaken by the unexpected attack and appalled by his losses, allowed the enemy to escape. This cost him the fine reputation he had won in capturing Fort Henry and Fort Donelson. He was relieved of his command. Although Corinth eventually fell and New Orleans was captured by a naval force under the command of Captain David Farragut, Vicksburg, key to control of the Mississippi, remained firmly in Confederate hands. A great opportunity had been lost.

Shiloh had other results. The staggering casualties shook the confidence of both belligerents. More Americans fell there in two days than in all the battles of the Revolution, the War of 1812, and the Mexican War combined. Union losses exceeded 13,000 out of 63,000 engaged; the Confederates lost 10,699, including General Johnston. Technology in the shape of more accurate guns that could be fired far more rapidly than the muskets of earlier times and more powerful artillery were responsible for the carnage. Gradually the generals began to reconsider their tactics and to experiment with field fortifications and other defensive measures.

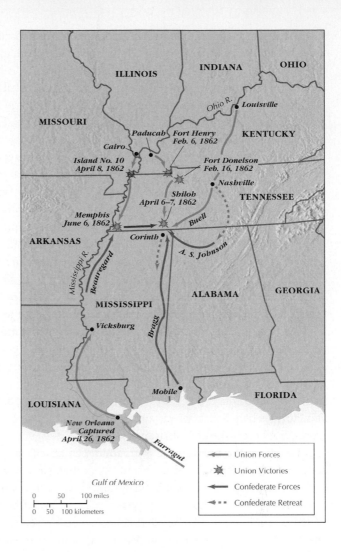

War in the West, 1862
Although Union forces ultimately took Shiloh in April 1862, the city of Vicksburg, and thus control of the Mississippi, remained in southern hands.

And the people, North and South, stopped thinking of the war as a romantic test of courage and military guile.

McClellan: The Reluctant Warrior

In Virginia, General McClellan, after unaccountable delays, was finally moving against Richmond. Instead of trying to advance across the difficult terrain of northern Virginia, he transported his army by water to the tip of the peninsula formed by the York and James rivers in order to attack Richmond from the southeast. After the famous battle on March 9, 1862, between the USS *Monitor* and the Confederate *Merrimack,* the first fight in history between armored warships, control of these waters was securely in northern hands.

McClellan began the Peninsula campaign in mid-March. Proceeding deliberately, he floated an army of 112,000 men down the Potomac and by May 14 had established a base at White House Landing, less than 25 miles from Richmond. A swift thrust might have ended the war quickly, but McClellan delayed, despite the fact that he had 80,000 men in striking position and large reserves. As he pushed forward slowly, the Confederates caught part of his force separated from the main body by the rain-swollen Chickahominy River and attacked. The Battle of Seven Pines was indecisive yet resulted in more than 10,000 casualties.

At Seven Pines the Confederate commander, General Joseph E. Johnston, was severely wounded; leadership of the Army of Northern Virginia then passed to Robert E. Lee. Although a reluctant supporter of secession, Lee was a superb soldier. During the Mexican War his gallantry under fire inspired General Scott to call him the bravest man in the army; another officer rhapsodized over his "daring reconnaissances pushed up to the cannon's mouth." He also had displayed an almost instinctive mastery of tactics. Admiral Raphael Semmes, who accompanied Scott's army on the march to Mexico City, recalled in 1851 that Lee "seemed to receive impressions intuitively, which it cost other men much labor to acquire."

Lee was McClellan's antithesis. McClellan seemed almost deliberately to avoid understanding his foes, acting as though every southern general was a genius. Lee, a master psychologist on the battlefield, took the measure of each Union general and devised his tactics accordingly. Where McClellan was complex, egotistical, perhaps even unbalanced, Lee was courtly, tactful, and entirely without McClellan's vainglorious belief that he was a man of destiny. Yet on the battlefield Lee's boldness skirted the edge of foolhardiness.

To relieve the pressure on Richmond, Lee sent General "Stonewall" Jackson, soon to be his most trusted lieutenant, on a diversionary raid in the Shenandoah Valley, west of Richmond and Washington. Jackson struck hard and swiftly at scattered Union forces in the region, winning a number of battles and capturing vast stores of equipment. Lincoln dispatched 20,000 reserves to the Shenandoah to check him—to the dismay of McClellan, who wanted the troops to attack Richmond from the north. But after Seven Pines, Lee ordered Jackson back to Richmond. While Union armies streamed toward the valley, Jackson slipped stealthily between them. On June 25 he reached Ashland, directly north of the Confederate capital.

Before that date McClellan had possessed clear numerical superiority yet had only inched ahead; now the advantage lay with Lee, and the very next day he attacked. For seven days the battle raged. Lee's plan was brilliant but too complicated for an army yet untested: The full weight of his force never hit the northern army at any one time. Nevertheless, the shock was formidable. McClellan, who excelled in defense, fell back, his lines intact, exacting a fearful toll. Under difficult conditions he managed to transfer his troops to a new base on the James River at Harrison's Landing, where the guns of the navy could shield his position. Again the loss of life was terrible: Northern casualties totaled 15,800; those of the South nearly 20,000 in the Seven Days' Battle for Richmond.

Lee Counterattacks: Antietam

McClellan was still within striking distance of Richmond, in an impregnable position with secure supply lines and 86,000 soldiers ready to resume battle. Lee had absorbed heavy losses without winning any significant advantage. Yet Lincoln was exasperated with McClellan for having surrendered the initiative and, after much deliberation, reduced his authority by placing him under General Henry W. Halleck. Halleck called off the Peninsula campaign and ordered McClellan to move his army from the James to the Potomac, near Washington. He was to join General John Pope, who was gathering a new army between Washington and Richmond.

To allow Halleck to pull back the troops was a bad mistake. When they withdrew, Lee seized the initiative. With typical decisiveness and daring, he marched rapidly north. Late in August his Confederates drove General Pope's confused troops from the same ground, Bull Run, where the first major engagement of the war had been fought.

Thirteen months had passed since the first failure at Bull Run, and despite the expenditure of thousands of lives, the Union army stood as far from Richmond as ever. Dismayed by Pope's incompetence, Lincoln turned in desperation back to

**War in the East,
1861–1862**

After the first battle at Bull Run, in July 1861, there was little action until the following spring, when McClellan launched his Peninsula campaign. The Battle of Antietam was the culmination of the fighting in the summer of 1862.

Antietam
Sept. 17, 1862

MARYLAND

McClellan

Winchester
May 25, 1862

Kernstown
Mar. 23, 1862

April

June

May

Potomac R.

Washington, D.C.

Bull Run
July 21, 1861
Aug. 29–30, 1862

Chesapeake Bay

Cedar Mountain
Aug. 9, 1862

Lee

Fredericksburg
Dec. 13, 1862

Cross Keys
June 8, 1862

Jackson

Lee

VIRGINIA

McClellan

Richmond

Yorktown
Besieged
Apr. 5–May 4,
1862

Seven Pines
May 31–June 1, 1862

Seven Days' Battles
June 25–July 1, 1862

James R.

Fortress Monroe ●

Monitor vs. Merrimac (Virginia)
Mar. 9, 1862

←	Union Forces
←	Confederate Forces
◄····	Confederate Retreat
✳	Union Victories
✳	Confederate Victories

0   25   50 miles

0   25   50 kilometers

McClellan. When his secretary protested that McClellan had expressed contempt for the president, Lincoln replied gently: "We must use what tools we have."

While McClellan was regrouping the shaken Union Army, Lee once again took the offensive. He realized that no number of individual southern triumphs could destroy the enormous material advantages of the North. Unless some dramatic blow, delivered on northern soil, persuaded the people of the United States that military victory was impossible, the South would surely be crushed in the long run by the weight of superior resources. Lee therefore marched rapidly northwest around the defenses of Washington.

Acting with even more than his usual boldness, Lee divided his army of 60,000 into a number of units. One, under Stonewall Jackson, descended on weakly defended Harpers Ferry, capturing more than 11,000 prisoners. Another pressed as far north as Hagerstown, Maryland, nearly to the Pennsylvania line. McClellan pursued with his usual deliberation until a captured dispatch revealed to him Lee's dispositions. Then he moved a bit more swiftly, forcing Lee to stand and fight on September 17 at Sharpsburg, Maryland, between the Potomac and Antietam Creek.[1] On a field that offered Lee no room to maneuver, 70,000 Union soldiers clashed with 40,000 Confederates. When darkness fell, more than 22,000 lay dead or wounded on the bloody field.

Although casualties were evenly divided and the Confederate lines remained intact, Lee's position was perilous. His men were exhausted. McClellan had not yet thrown in his reserves, and new federal units were arriving hourly. A bold northern general would have continued the fight without respite through the night. One of ordinary aggressiveness would have waited for first light and then struck with every soldier who could hold a rifle, for with the Potomac at his back, Lee could not retreat under fire without inviting disaster. McClellan, however, did nothing. For an entire day, while Lee scanned the field in futile search of some weakness in the Union lines, he held his fire. That night the Confederates slipped back across the Potomac into Virginia.

Lee's invasion had failed; his army had been badly mauled; the gravest threat to the Union in the war had been checked. But McClellan had let victory slip through his fingers. Soon Lee was back behind the defenses of Richmond, rebuilding his army.

Once again, this time finally, Lincoln dismissed McClellan from his command.

The Emancipation Proclamation

As the war progressed, the Radical faction in Congress gradually chipped away at slavery. In April 1862 the Radicals pushed through a bill abolishing slavery in the District of Columbia; two months later another measure outlawed it in the territo-

---

[1]*Southerners tended to identify battles by nearby towns, northerners by bodies of water. Thus Manassas and Bull Run, Sharpsburg and Antietam, Murfreesboro and Stone's River, and so on.*

ries; in July the Confiscation Act "freed" all slaves owned by persons in rebellion against the United States. Lincoln had resisted emancipation because he feared it would divide the country and injure the war effort, not because he personally disapproved. Indeed, he frequently cited Radical pressure as an excuse for doing what he wished to do on his own.

By the summer of 1862, however, he was convinced that for military reasons and to win the support of liberal opinion in Europe, the government should make abolition a war aim. "We must free the slaves or be ourselves subdued," he explained to a member of his Cabinet. The "victory" at Antietam Creek gave him his opportunity, and on September 22 he made public the Emancipation Proclamation. After January 1, 1863, it said, all slaves in areas in rebellion against the United States "shall be then, thenceforward, and forever free."

No single slave was freed directly by Lincoln's announcement, which did not apply to the border states or to those sections of the Confederacy, like New Orleans and Norfolk, Virginia, already controlled by federal troops. The proclamation differed in philosophy, however, from the Confiscation Act in striking at the institution, not at the property of rebels. Henceforth every Union victory would speed the destruction of slavery without regard for the attitudes of individual masters.

Southerners considered the Emancipation Proclamation an incitement to slave rebellion—as one of them put it, an "infamous attempt to . . . convert the quiet, ignorant, and dependent black son of toil into a savage incendiary and brutal murderer." Most antislavery groups thought it did not go far enough. Lincoln "is only stopping on the edge of Niagara, to pick up a few chips," one abolitionist declared. "He and they will go over together." Foreign opinion was mixed: Liberals tended to applaud, conservatives to react with alarm or contempt.

As Lincoln anticipated, the proclamation had a subtle but continuing impact in the North. Its immediate effect was to aggravate racial prejudices. Millions of whites disapproved of slavery yet abhorred the idea of equality for blacks. David Wilmot, for example, insisted that his famous proviso was designed to preserve the territories for whites rather than to weaken slavery, and as late as 1857 the people of Iowa rejected black suffrage by a vote of 49,000 to 8,000.

The Democrats spared no effort to make political capital of these fears and prejudices even before Lincoln's Emancipation Proclamation, and they made large gains in the 1862 election, especially in the Northwest. So strong was antiblack feeling that most of the Republican politicians who defended emancipation did so with racist arguments. Far from encouraging southern blacks to move north, they claimed, the ending of slavery would lead to a mass migration of northern blacks to the South.

When the Emancipation Proclamation began actually to free slaves, the government pursued a policy of "containment," that is, of keeping the former slaves in the South. Panicky fears of an inundation of blacks subsided in the North. Nevertheless, emancipation remained a cause of social discontent. In March 1863, volunteering having fallen off, Congress passed the Conscription Act. The law applied to all men between ages 20 and 45, but it allowed draftees to hire substitutes and even to buy exemption for $300, provisions that were patently unfair to the poor. During the remainder of the war 46,000 men were actually drafted, whereas 118,000 hired substitutes, and another 161,000 "failed to report." Conscription represented an enormous expansion of national authority, since in effect it gave the government the power of life and death over individual citizens.

The Draft Riots

After the passage of the Conscription Act, draft riots erupted in a number of cities. By far the most serious disturbance occurred in New York City in July 1863. Many workers resented conscription in principle and were embittered by the $300 exemption fee (which represented a year's wages). The idea of being forced to risk their lives to free slaves who would then, they believed, compete with them for jobs infuriated them. On July 13 a mob attacked the office where the names of conscripts were being drawn. Most of the rioters were poor Irish Catholic laborers who resented both the blacks and the middle-class Protestant whites who seemed to them responsible for the special attention blacks were suddenly receiving. For four days the city was an inferno. Public buildings, shops, and private residences were put to the torch. What began as a protest against the draft became an assault on blacks and the well-to-do. It took federal troops and the temporary suspension of the draft in the city to put an end to the rioting. By the time order was restored more than a hundred people (most of them rioters) had lost their lives.

Most white Northerners did not surrender their comforting belief in black inferiority, and Lincoln was no exception. Yet Lincoln was evolving. He talked about deporting freed slaves to the tropics, but he did not send any there. And he began to receive black leaders in the White House and to allow black groups to hold meetings on the grounds.

Many other Americans were changing too. The brutality of the New York riots horrified many white citizens. Over $40,000 was swiftly raised to aid the victims, and some conservatives were so appalled by the Irish rioters that they began to talk of giving blacks the vote. The influential *Atlantic Monthly* commented: "It is impossible to name any standard . . . that will give a vote to the Celt [the Irish] and exclude the negro."

The Emancipated People

To blacks, both slave and free, the Emancipation Proclamation served as a beacon. Even if it failed immediately to liberate one slave or to lift the burdens of prejudice from one black back, it stood as a promise of future improvement. "I took the proclamation for a little more than it purported," Frederick Douglass recalled in his autobiography, "and saw in its spirit a life and power far beyond its letter." Lincoln was by modern standards a racist, but his most militant black contemporaries respected him deeply. The *Anglo-African,* an uncompromising black newspaper (the position of which is revealed in an 1862 editorial that asked: "Poor, chicken-hearted, semi-barbarous Caucasians, when will you learn that 'the earth was made for MAN?'"), referred in 1864 to Lincoln's "many noble acts" and urged his reelection. Douglass said of him: "Lincoln was not . . . either our man or our model. In his interests, in his association, in his habits of thought and in his prejudices, he was a white man." Nevertheless, Douglass described Lincoln as "one whom I could love, honor, and trust without reserve or doubt."

As for the slaves of the South, after January 1, 1863, whenever the "Army of Freedom" approached, they laid down their plows and hoes and flocked to the Union lines in droves. Instead of referring to their workers as "servants" or "my black family," many owners began to describe them as "slaves" or "niggers."

African American Soldiers

A revolutionary shift occurred in white thinking about using black men as soldiers. Although they had fought in the Revolution and in the Battle of New Orleans during the War of 1812, a law of 1792 barred blacks from the army. During the early stages of the rebellion, despite the eagerness of thousands of free blacks to enlist, the prohibition remained in force. By 1862, however, the need for manpower was creating pressure for change. In August Secretary of War Edwin M. Stanton authorized the military government of the captured South Carolina Sea Islands to enlist slaves in the area. After the Emancipation Proclamation specifically authorized the enlistment of blacks, the governor of Massachusetts moved to organize a black regiment, the famous Massachusetts 54th. Swiftly thereafter, other states began to recruit black soldiers, and in May 1863 the federal government established a Bureau of Colored Troops to supervise their enlistment. By the end of the war one soldier in eight in the Union army was black.

Enlisting so many black soldiers changed the war from a struggle to save the Union to a kind of revolution. "Let the black man . . . get an eagle on his button and a musket on his shoulder," wrote Frederick Douglass, "and there is no power on earth which can deny that he has won the right to citizenship."

At first black soldiers received only $7 a month, about half what white soldiers were paid. But they soon proved themselves in battle; of the 178,000 who served in the Union army, 37,000 were killed, a rate of loss about 40 percent higher than that among white troops. The Congressional Medal of Honor was awarded to twenty-one blacks.

The higher death rates among black soldiers were partly due to the fury of Confederate soldiers. Many black captives were killed on the spot. After overrunning the garrison of Fort Pillow on the Mississippi River, the Confederates massacred several dozen black soldiers, along with their white commander. Lincoln was tempted to order reprisals, but he and his advisers realized that to do so would have been both morally wrong (two wrongs never make a right) and likely to lead to still more atrocities. "Blood can not restore blood," Lincoln said in his usual direct way.

Antietam to Gettysburg

It was well that Lincoln seized on Antietam to release his proclamation; had he waited for a more impressive victory, he would have waited nearly a year. To replace McClellan, he chose General Ambrose E. Burnside, best known to history for his magnificent side-whiskers (originally called burnsides, later, at first jokingly, sideburns). Unlike McClellan, Burnside was aggressive—too aggressive. He planned to ford the Rappahannock River at Fredericksburg. Supply problems and bad weather delayed him until mid-December, giving Lee time to concentrate his army in impregnable positions behind the town. Although he had more than 120,000 men against Lee's 75,000, Burnside should have called off the attack when he saw Lee's advantage; instead he ordered the troops forward. Crossing the river over pontoon bridges, his divisions occupied Fredericksburg. Then, in wave after wave, they charged the Confederate defense line while Lee's artillery riddled them from nearby Marye's Heights. Watching the battle from his command post on the heights, General Lee was deeply moved. Turning to General James Longstreet, he said: "It is well that war is so terrible—we should grow too fond of it!"

On December 14, the day following this futile assault, General Burnside, tears streaming down his cheeks, ordered the evacuation of Fredericksburg. Shortly thereafter General Joseph Hooker replaced him.

Gettysburg Campaign, 1863

Gettysburg, in July 1863, marked the turning point of the war; after this battle the South never again tried to invade the North.

Unlike Burnside, "Fighting Joe" Hooker was ill-tempered, vindictive, and devious. He proved no better than his predecessor, but his failings were more like McClellan's than Burnside's. By the spring of 1863 he had 125,000 men ready for action. Late in April he forded the Rappahannock and quickly concentrated at Chancellorsville, about 10 miles west of Fredericksburg. His army outnumbered the Confederates by more than two to one; he should have forced a battle at once. Instead he delayed, and while he did, Lee sent Stonewall Jackson's corps of 28,000 men across tangled countryside to a position directly athwart Hooker's unsuspecting flank. At 6 P.M. on May 2, Jackson attacked.

Completely surprised, the Union right crumbled, brigade after brigade overrun before it could wheel to meet Jackson's charge. At the first sound of firing, Lee had struck along the entire front to impede Union troop movements. If the battle had begun earlier in the day, the Confederates might have won a decisive victory; as it happened, nightfall brought a lull, and the next day the Union troops rallied and held their ground. Heavy fighting continued until May 5, when Hooker abandoned the field and retreated in good order behind the Rappahannock.

Chancellorsville cost the Confederates dearly, for their losses, in excess of 12,000, were almost as heavy as the North's and harder to replace. They also lost Stonewall Jackson, struck down by the bullets of his own men while returning from a reconnaissance. Nevertheless, the Union army had suffered another fearful blow to its morale.

Lee knew that time was still on the side of the North; to defend Richmond was not enough. Already federal troops in the West were closing in on Vicksburg, threatening to cut Confederate communications with Arkansas and Texas. Now was the time to strike, while the morale of the North was at low ebb. With 75,000 soldiers he crossed the Potomac again, a larger Union force dogging his right flank. By late June his army had fanned out across southern Pennsylvania in a 50-mile arc from Chambersburg to the Susquehanna. Grayclad soldiers ranged 50 miles *northwest* of Baltimore, within 10 miles of Harrisburg, Pennsylvania.

As Union soldiers had been doing in Virginia, Lee's men destroyed property and commandeered food, horses, and clothing wherever they could find them. They even seized a number of blacks and sent them south to be sold as slaves. On July 1 a Confederate division looking for shoes in the town of Gettysburg clashed with two brigades of Union cavalry northwest of the town. Both sides sent out calls for reinforcements. Like iron filings drawn to a magnet, the two armies converged. The Confederates won control of the town, but the Union army, now commanded by General George G. Meade, took a strong position on Cemetery Ridge, a hook-shaped stretch of high ground just to the south. Lee's men occupied Seminary Ridge, a parallel position.

On this field the fate of the Union was probably decided. For two days the Confederates attacked Cemetery Ridge, pounding it with the heaviest artillery barrage ever seen in America and sweeping bravely up its flanks in repeated assaults. During General George E. Pickett's famous charge, a handful of his men actually reached the Union lines, but reserves drove them back. By nightfall on July 3 the Confederate army was spent, the Union lines unbroken.

Glory

Glory (1989) tells the story of the 54th Massachusetts Volunteer Infantry, a black regiment, from its establishment in the fall of 1862 through its attack on Fort Wagner, South Carolina, on July 18, 1863.

"Historical accuracy," director Edward Zwick declared, was "the goal of everyone involved in the production." Filmmakers make such assertions, but Zwick proved that he had attended to the historical record. The peak of Shaw's cap was dyed the exact shade of medium green used by officers of the Massachusetts 54th; and when shoes were distributed to the recruits, there were no "lefts" or "rights": shoes were to shape themselves to either foot from wear. Few viewers could be expected to take note of such historical details, but Zwick included them nevertheless.

Zwick's evident commitment to history makes his deviations all the more interesting. Consider the opening scenes. The movie begins with a panoramic shot of rolling hills, dotted with tents. Fog blankets the valley and softens the morning light. The camera moves closer, focusing on Union soldiers around a campfire. Then the quiet is shattered by explosions: soldiers hasten to form ranks, trot toward a battlefield, and charge across it, a young officer in the vanguard. (He is Captain Robert Gould Shaw, played by Matthew Broderick.) The attackers are decimated. When Shaw turns to rally his troops, he sees that they are fleeing in terror. Then he is hit and loses consciousness.

Shaw is sent home to Boston to convalesce. At a reception, Governor Andrew offers the young officer command of the Massachusetts 54th, a black regiment being raised in Boston. Shaw hesitates for a moment. Then he confers privately with another officer, who is appalled.

"I knew how much you'd like to be a colonel, but a colored regiment?"

"I'm gonna do it," Shaw replies.

"You're not serious."

"Yeah."

These scenes contain truths without being entirely truthful. Governor Andrew did offer the commission and Shaw accepted it. But at the time Shaw was in Virginia. Andrew, in Boston, conveyed it through Shaw's father and young Shaw initially refused. Zwick has compressed the story chronologically, squeezing weeks into minutes; and he has rearranged it geographically to enable Andrew and young Shaw to meet. Such modifications are common in "reel history," and these do not impair historical understanding.

But *Glory* deviates from the historical record in more significant ways. It suggests, for example, that the Massachusetts 54th was composed mostly of former slaves whose hatred of slavery was based on personal experience. In truth, the Massachusetts 54th was recruited from blacks in northern states: Most had been born free.

The fiction that they had been slaves, however, made it possible for Zwick to examine a larger truth. Of the 178,000 blacks who served in the Union army, fewer than one-fifth were from the North; the great majority *were* former slaves. Nearly 100,000 were recruited from Louisiana, Mississippi, or Tennessee. *Glory* thus merges the story of the free blacks of the Massachusetts 54th with that of former slaves who were recruited from the Deep South.

Zwick exploited the dramatic potential of the latter groups. How did slaves respond when, having just received their freedom, they were placed under the absolute power of white officers?

Glory develops the question chiefly through the character of Trip (Denzel Washington), a former slave who hates all whites, including Shaw. Shaw illuminates the other side of the question. An inveterate abolitionist, he reluctantly decides that former slaves must be whipped (literally) into shape. When Trip sneaks off one night and is captured for desertion, Shaw orders him flogged. When Trip's back is bared, Shaw sees that it is laced with scars from whippings by slave masters. During the flogging, Trip fixes Shaw with a hateful stare, a powerful scene that underscores the movie's central irony: To end slavery, Shaw has superseded the plantation master while Trip has again become a slave.

Matthew Broderick, as Robert Gould Shaw in the movie *Glory,* and Robert Gould Shaw, Commander of the Massachusetts 54th.

Private Charles Arnum, a free black volunteer from Springfield, Massachusetts, and Denzel Washington as the former slave recruit Trip, in the movie *Glory.*

Whatever its dramatic merits, the scene is unhistorical. In 1861 Congress had outlawed flogging in the military. Disobedient soldiers were tied in a crouched position, or they were suspended by their thumbs, toes just touching the ground.

Physical punishment was one of the chief sources of contention between ex-slave soldiers and white officers. "I am no slave to be driven," one black recruit informed a brutish commander. When an officer of the 38th Colored Infantry tied a black recruit up by the thumbs, his friends cut him down and forced the officers back with bayonets: "No white son of a bitch can tie a man up here," they declared. The blacks were charged with mutiny and several were executed, an incident that shows that former slaves did not willingly submit to army discipline tainted with racism. Though African Americans constituted only 8 percent of the Union army, 80 percent of those executed for mutiny were black. Many white officers, as the movie suggests, did assert that former slaves must be treated like slaves. "I no longer wonder why slave drivers were cruel. I am," one white officer confided in a letter.

Could such soldiers—black recruits and white officers alike—have been good ones? The movie answers the question by recreating the actual attack on Fort Wagner. It shows the blacks of the Massachusetts 54th marching to the front of the line and forming up along a narrow beach. On Shaw's command, they charge forward. Unlike the white troops in the opening scene, the blacks follow him to the ramparts; when he falls, they continue onward until they are wiped out.

Were the soldiers of the Massachusetts 54th as courageous as those in the movie?

Shortly after the battle, Lieutenant Iredell Jones, a Confederate officer, reported: "The negroes fought gallantly, and were headed by as brave a colonel as ever lived." Of the 600 members of the 54th Massachusetts, 40 percent were casualties on that day, an extraordinarily high ratio. Did ex-slaves fight as courageously as the free blacks of the 54th? The answer to this question came not at Fort Wagner, but at other, less publicized battles. A few weeks earlier, for example, several companies of the Louisiana (Colored) Infantry, composed of former slaves who had been in the army only for several weeks, fought off a furious Confederate assault at Milliken's Bend near Vicksburg. The Confederate general was astonished when whites in the Union army fled but the blacks held their ground despite sustaining staggering casualties—45 percent—the highest of any single battle in the war.

Thus while *Glory* is a fictional composite—of free black and ex-slave recruits, and of the assault on Fort Wagner and Milliken's Bend—it conveys a broader truth about black soldiers. Howell Cobb, a Confederate senator from Georgia, declared: "If the black can make a good soldier, our whole system of government is wrong." *Glory* shows that although white officers and black recruits did not form a harmonious team, they together proved that slavery was doomed.

421

Questions for Discussion
- Was conscription during the Civil War a form of slavery?
- Would free blacks or former slaves more likely have been the better soldiers?

The following day was the Fourth of July. The two weary forces rested on their arms. Had the Union army attacked in force, the Confederates might have been crushed, but just as McClellan had hesitated after Antietam, Meade let opportunity pass. On July 5 Lee retreated to safety. For the first time he had been clearly bested on the field of battle.

Lincoln Finds His General: Grant at Vicksburg

On Independence Day, a day after Gettysburg, federal troops won another great victory far to the west. When General Halleck was called east in July 1862, Ulysses S. Grant resumed command of the Union troops. Grant was one of the most controversial officers in the army. At West Point he had compiled an indifferent record, ranking twenty-first in a class of thirty-nine. During the Mexican War he served well, but when he was later assigned to a lonely post in the West, he took to drink and was forced to resign his commission. Thereafter he was by turns a farmer, a real estate agent, and a clerk in a leather goods store. In 1861, approaching age 40, he seemed well into a life of frustration and mediocrity.

The war gave him a second chance. Back in service, however, his reputation as a ne'er-do-well and his unmilitary bearing worked against him, as did the heavy casualties suffered by his troops at Shiloh. Yet the fact that he knew how to manage a large army and win battles did not escape Lincoln. According to tradition, when a gossip tried to poison the president against Grant by referring to his drinking, Lincoln retorted that if he knew what brand Grant favored, he would send a barrel of it to some of his other generals.[2] Grant never used alcohol as a substitute for courage. "Old Ulysses," one of his soldiers said, "he don't scare worth a damn."

Grant's major aim was to capture Vicksburg, a city of tremendous strategic importance. Together with Port Hudson, a bastion north of Baton Rouge, Louisiana, it guarded a 150-mile stretch of the Mississippi. The river between these points was inaccessible to federal gunboats. So long as Vicksburg remained in southern hands, the trans-Mississippi region could send men and supplies to the rest of the Confederacy.

Vicksburg sits on a bluff overlooking a sharp bend in the river. When it proved unapproachable from either the west or the north, Grant devised an audacious scheme for getting at it from the east. He descended the Mississippi from Memphis to a point a few miles north of the city. Then, leaving part of his force behind to create the impression that he planned to attack from the north, he crossed the west bank and slipped quickly southward. Recrossing the river below Vicksburg, he abandoned his communications and supply lines and struck at Jackson, the capital of Mississippi. In a series of swift engagements his troops captured Jackson, cutting off

---

[2]Lincoln denied having said this, pointing out that it was a version of a remark about General James Wolfe attributed to King George II. When a critic remarked that Wolfe was a madman, the King is said to have replied: "I wish he would bite some of the others."

the army of General John C. Pemberton, defending Vicksburg, from other Confederate units. Turning next on Pemberton, Grant defeated him in two decisive battles, Champion's Hill and Big Black River, and drove him inside the Vicksburg fortifications. By mid-May the city was under siege. Grant applied relentless pressure, and on July 4 Pemberton surrendered. With Vicksburg in Union hands, federal gunboats could range the entire length of the Mississippi.[3] Texas and Arkansas were for all practical purposes lost to the Confederacy.

Lincoln had disliked Grant's plan for capturing Vicksburg. Now he generously confessed his error and placed Grant in command of all federal troops west of the Appalachians. Grant promptly took charge of the fighting around Chattanooga, Tennessee, where Confederate advances, beginning with the Battle of Chickamauga (September 19–20), were threatening to develop into a major disaster for the North. Shifting corps commanders and bringing up fresh units, he won another decisive victory at Chattanooga in a series of battles ending on November 25, 1863. This cleared the way for an invasion of Georgia. Suddenly this unkempt, stubby little man, who looked more like a tramp than a general, emerged as the military leader the North had been so desperately seeking. In March 1864 Lincoln summoned him to Washington, named him lieutenant general, and gave him supreme command of the armies of the United States.

Economic and Social Effects, North and South

Although much blood would yet be spilled, by the end of 1863 the Confederacy was on the road to defeat. Northern military pressure, gradually increasing, was eroding the South's most precious resource: manpower. An ever-tightening naval blockade was reducing its economic strength. Shortages developed that, combined with the flood of currency pouring from the presses, led to drastic inflation. By 1864 an officer's coat cost $2,000 in Confederate money, cigars sold for $10 each, butter was $25 a pound, and flour went for $275 a barrel. Wages rose too, but not nearly as rapidly.

The southern railroad network was gradually wearing out, the major lines maintaining operations only by cannibalizing less vital roads. Imported products such as coffee disappeared; even salt became scarce. Efforts to increase manufacturing were only moderately successful because of the shortage of labor, capital, and technical knowledge.

In the North, after a brief depression in 1861 caused by the uncertainties of the situation and the loss of southern business, the economy flourished. Government purchases greatly stimulated certain lines of manufacturing, the railroads operated at close to capacity and with increasing efficiency, the farm machinery business boomed because so many farmers left their fields to serve in the army, and bad harvests in Europe boosted agricultural prices.

---

[3]*Port Hudson, isolated by Vicksburg's fall, surrendered on July 9.*

Congress passed a number of economic measures long desired but held up in the past by southern opposition. The Homestead Act (1862) gave 160 acres to any settler who would farm the land for five years. The Morrill Land Grant Act of the same year provided the states with land at the rate of 30,000 acres for each member of Congress to support state agricultural colleges. Various tariff acts raised the duties on manufactured goods to an average rate of 47 percent in order to protect domestic manufacturers from foreign competition. The Pacific Railway Act (1862) authorized subsidies in land and money for the construction of a transcontinental railroad. And the National Banking Act of 1863 gave the country, at last, a uniform currency.

All these laws stimulated the economy. Whether the overall economic effect of the Civil War on the Union was beneficial is less clear. Since it was fought mostly with rifles, light cannon, horses, and wagons, it had much less effect on heavy industry than later wars would have. Although the economy grew, it did so more slowly during the 1860s than in the decades preceding and following. Prices soared beginning in 1862, averaging about 80 percent over the 1860 level by the end of the war. As in the South, wages did not keep pace. This did not make for a healthy economy; nor did the fact that there were chronic shortages of labor in many fields, shortages aggravated by a sharp drop in the number of immigrants.

As the war dragged on and the continuing inflation eroded purchasing power, resentment on the part of workers deepened. During the 1850s iron molders, cigar makers, and some other skilled workers had formed national unions. This trend continued through the war years. There were many strikes. Inflation and shortages encouraged speculation and fostered a selfish, materialistic attitude toward life. Many contractors took advantage of wartime confusion to sell the government shoddy goods. By 1864 cotton was worth $1.90 a pound in New England. It could be had for 20 cents a pound in the South. Although it was illegal to traffic in the staple across the lines, unscrupulous operators did so and made huge profits.

Yet the war undoubtedly hastened industrialization and laid the basis for many other aspects of modern civilization. It posed problems of organization and planning, both military and civilian, that challenged the talents of creative persons and thus led to a more complex and efficient economy. The mechanization of production, the growth of large corporations, the creation of a better banking system, and the emergence of business leaders attuned to these conditions would surely have occurred in any case, for industrialization was underway long before the South seceded. Nevertheless, the war greatly speeded all these changes.

Women in Wartime

Many southern women took over the management of farms and small plantations when their menfolk went off to war. Others became volunteer nurses, and after an initial period of resistance, the Confederate army began to enlist women in the medical corps. At least two female nurses, Captain Sally Tompkins and Kate

Women in the South playing croquet during the war, preserving the amenities of plantation life. By 1864 southern leaders were complaining that many southern women had lost their zeal for the Cause. Poor women engaged in bread riots; and well-to-do women held "incessant parties and balls." Through such actions, women registered their discontent with the war—and with the paternalist ethos of southern chivalry, which had manifestly failed to protect and defend southern womanhood.

Cumming, left records of their experiences that throw much light on how the wounded were treated during the war. Other southern women worked as clerks in newly organized government departments.

Southern "ladyhood" more generally was yet another casualty of the war. The absence or death of husbands or other male relations changed attitudes toward gender roles. When her husband obeyed a military order to abandon Atlanta to the advancing Union armies, Julia Davidson, about to give birth, denounced the "men of Atlanta" for having "run and left Atlanta" and their homes. Such women learned to fend for themselves. "Necessity," Davidson later wrote her husband, would "make a different woman of me."

Large numbers of women also contributed to the northern war effort. As in the South, farm women went out into fields to plant and harvest crops, aided in many instances by new farm machinery. Many others took jobs in textile factories; in establishments making shoes, uniforms, and other supplies for the army; and in government agencies. But as was usually the case, the low wages traditionally paid women acted as a brake on wage increases for their male colleagues.

Besides working in factories and shops and on farms, northern women, again like their southern counterparts, aided the war effort more directly. Elizabeth Blackwell, the first American woman doctor of medicine, had already founded the New York Infirmary for Women and Children. After war broke out she helped set

A family of a soldier in the 31st Philadelphia Infantry, camped near Washington, D.C. Although both armies discouraged women from following soldier-husbands, the practice was fairly common. Women proved indispensable as laundresses and cooks. Although women were initially excluded from army hospitals, the policy quickly changed and camp women often worked as nurses during battles.

up what became the U.S. Sanitary Commission, an organization of women similar to the Christian Commission dedicated to improving sanitary conditions at army camps, supplying hospitals with volunteer nurses, and raising money for medical supplies. Many thousands of women volunteers took part in Sanitary Commission and related programs.

An additional 3,000-odd women served as regular army nurses during the conflict. At the start the high command of both armies resisted the efforts of women to help, but necessity and a grudging recognition of the competence of these women gradually brought the generals around. Clara Barton, a schoolteacher and government clerk, was among the first women to dress wounds at forward stations on the battlefield. After she ran out of bandages at Antietam, she dressed wounds with green corn leaves. The chief surgeon declared her to be "the angel of the battlefield." The "proper sphere" of American woman was expanding, another illustration of the modernizing effect of the war.

Grant in the Wilderness

Grant's strategy as supreme commander was simple, logical, and ruthless. He would attack Lee and try to capture Richmond, Virginia. General William Tecumseh Sherman would drive from Chattanooga toward Atlanta, Georgia. Like a lobster's claw, the two armies could then close to crush all resistance. Early in May 1864 Grant and Sherman commenced operations, each with more than 100,000 men.

Grant marched the Army of the Potomac directly into the tangled wilderness area south of the Rappahannock, where Hooker had been routed a year earlier. Lee, having only 60,000 men, forced the battle in the roughest possible country, where Grant found it difficult to make efficient use of his larger force. For two days (May 5–6) the Battle of the Wilderness raged. When it was over, the North had sustained another 18,000 casualties, far more than the Confederates. But unlike his predecessors, Grant did not fall back after being checked, nor did he expose his army to the kind of devastating counterattack at which Lee was so expert. Instead he shifted his troops to the southeast, attempting to outflank the Confederates. Divining his intent, Lee rushed his divisions southeastward and disposed them behind hastily erected earthworks in well-placed positions around Spotsylvania Court House. Grant attacked. After five more days, at a cost to the Union army of another 12,000 men, the Confederate lines were still intact.

Grant had grasped the fundamental truth that the war could be won only by grinding the South down beneath the weight of numbers. His own losses of men and equipment could be replaced; Lee's could not. When critics complained of the cost, he replied doggedly that he intended to fight on in the same manner if it took all summer. Once more he pressed southeastward in an effort to outflank the enemy. At Cold Harbor, 9 miles from Richmond, he found the Confederates once more in strong defenses. He attacked. It was a battle as foolish and nearly as one-sided as General Pakenham's assault on Jackson's line outside New Orleans in 1815. "At Cold Harbor," the forthright Grant confessed in his memoirs, "no advantage whatever was gained to compensate for the heavy losses we sustained."

Sixty thousand casualties in less than a month! The news sent a wave of dismay through the North. There were demands that "Butcher" Grant be removed from command. Lincoln, however, stood firm. Although the price was fearfully high, Grant was gaining his objective. At Cold Harbor, Lee had to fight without a single regiment in general reserve while Grant's army was larger than at the start of the offensive. When Grant next swung around his flank, striking south of the James River toward Petersburg, Lee had to rush his troops to that city to hold him.

As the Confederates dug in, Grant put Petersburg under siege. Soon both armies had constructed complicated lines of breastworks and trenches, running for miles in a great arc south of Petersburg, much like the fortifications that would be used in France in World War I. Methodically the Union forces extended their lines, seeking to weaken the Confederates and cut the rail connections supplying Lee's troops and the city of Richmond. Grant could not overwhelm him, but by late June, Lee was pinned to earth. Moving again would mean having to abandon Richmond—tantamount, in southern eyes, to surrender.

Sherman in Georgia

The summer of 1864 saw the North submerged in pessimism. The Army of the Potomac held Lee at bay but appeared powerless to defeat him. In Georgia, General Sherman inched forward methodically against the wily Joseph E. Johnston, but

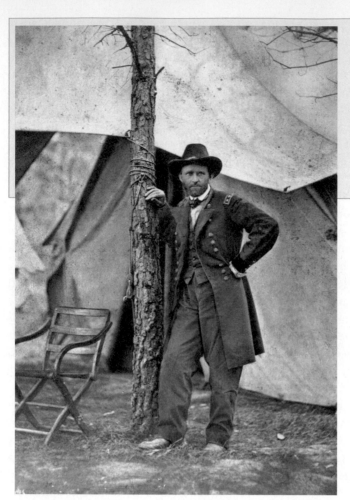

Ulysses S. Grant, shown at City Point, Virginia, during the siege of Petersburg. An 8.5-ton siege gun, mounted on a railroad flatcar, hurled 200-pound bombs onto Confederate positions during the siege. Trench warfare ensued, a chilling harbinger of World War I in early twentieth-century Europe.

when he tried a direct assault at Kennesaw Mountain on June 27, he was thrown back with heavy casualties. In July Confederate raiders under General Jubal Early dashed suddenly across the Potomac from the Shenandoah Valley to within five miles of Washington before being turned back. A draft call for 500,000 additional men did not improve the public temper. Huge losses and the absence of a decisive victory were taxing the northern will to continue the fight.

In June, Lincoln had been renominated on a National Union ticket, with the Tennessee Unionist Andrew Johnson, a former Democrat, as his running mate. He was under attack not only from the Democrats, who nominated General McClellan and came out for a policy that might almost be characterized as peace at any price, but also from the Radical Republicans, many of whom had wished to dump him in favor of Secretary of the Treasury Chase.

Then, almost overnight, the whole atmosphere changed. On September 2, General Sherman's army fought its way into Atlanta. When the Confederates coun-

Although Sherman's 100,000 Union soldiers marched to Atlanta, his men were supplied by sixteen railway trains from Chattanooga, Tennessee. After taking Atlanta late in the summer of 1864, Sherman pulled up the railway line and burned the depots. On his march to the sea, he destroyed several hundred miles of railroads.

tered with an offensive northward toward Tennessee,[4] Sherman did not follow. Instead he abandoned his communications with Chattanooga and marched unopposed through Georgia, "from Atlanta to the sea."

The march through Georgia had many objectives besides conquering territory. One obvious one was economic, the destruction of southern resources. "[We] must make old and young, rich and poor feel the hard hand of war," Sherman said. Before taking Atlanta he wrote his wife: "We have devoured the land. . . . All the people retire before us and desolation is behind. To realize what war is one should follow our tracks."

Another object of Sherman's march was psychological. "If the North can march an army right through the South," he told General Grant, Southerners will take it "as proof positive that the North can prevail." This was certainly true of Georgia's blacks, who flocked to the invaders by the thousands, women and children as well as men, all cheering mightily when the soldiers put their former masters' homes to the torch. "They pray and shout and mix up my name with Moses," Sherman explained.

Sherman's victories staggered the Confederacy and the anti-Lincoln forces in the North. In November the president was easily reelected, 212 electoral votes to 21. The country was determined to carry on the struggle.

---

[4]This force was crushed before Nashville in December by a Union army under General George Thomas.

At last the South's will to resist began to crack. Sherman entered Savannah on December 22, having denuded a strip of Georgia 60 miles wide. Early in January 1865 he marched northward, leaving behind "a broad black streak of ruin and desolation—the fences all gone; lonesome smoke-stacks, surrounded by dark heaps of ashes and cinders, marking the spots where human habitations had stood." In February his troops captured Columbia, South Carolina. Soon they were in North Carolina, advancing relentlessly. In Virginia, Grant's vise grew tighter day by day while the Confederate lines became thinner and more ragged.

To Appomattox Court House

On March 4 Lincoln took the presidential oath and delivered his second inaugural address. Photographs taken at about this time show how four years of war had marked him. Somehow he had become both gentle and steel-tough, both haggard and inwardly calm. With victory sure, he spoke for tolerance, mercy, and reconstruction. "Let us judge not," he said after stating again his personal dislike of slavery, "that we be not judged." He urged all Americans to turn without malice to the task of mending the damage and to make a just and lasting peace between the sections.

Now the Confederate troops around Petersburg could no longer withstand the federal pressure. Desperately Lee tried to pull his forces back to the Richmond and Danville Railroad at Lynchburg, but the swift wings of Grant's army enveloped them. Richmond fell on April 3. With fewer than 30,000 men to oppose Grant's 115,000, Lee recognized the futility of further resistance. On April 9 he and Grant met by prearrangement at Appomattox Court House.

It was a scene at once pathetic and inspiring. Lee was noble in defeat; Grant, despite his rough-hewn exterior, sensitive and magnanimous in victory. "I met you once before, General Lee, while we were serving in Mexico," Grant said after they had shaken hands. "I have always remembered your appearance, and I think I should have recognized you anywhere." They talked briefly of that earlier war, and then, acting on Lincoln's instructions, Grant outlined his terms. All that would be required was that the Confederate soldiers lay down their arms. They could return to their homes in peace. When Lee hinted (he was too proud to ask outright for the concession) that his men would profit greatly if allowed to retain possession of their horses, Grant agreed to let them do so.

Winners, Losers, and the Future

And so the war ended in 1865. It had cost the nation more than 600,000 lives, nearly as many as in all other American wars combined. The story of one of the lost thousands must stand for all, Union and Confederate. Jones Budbury, a tall, 19-

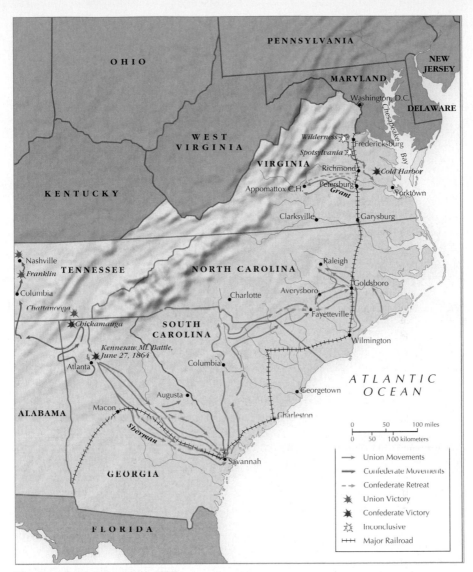

The Final Campaigns, 1864–1865

Grant's repeated and costly (60,000 casualties the first month) attempts to outflank Lee are detailed here. At Five Forks the long siege of Petersburg was broken; Richmond was evacuated. A week later, Lee surrendered. Sherman's campaign in Georgia and the Carolinas is also depicted.

year-old redhead, was working in a Pennsylvania textile mill when the war broke out, and he enlisted at once. His regiment first saw action at Bull Run. He took part in McClellan's Peninsula campaign. He fought at Second Bull Run, at Chancellorsville, and at Gettysburg. A few months after Gettysburg he was wounded in the foot and spent some time in an army hospital. By the spring of 1864 he had risen through the ranks to first sergeant and his hair had turned gray. In June he was captured and sent to Andersonville military prison, near Macon,

Debating the Past

WHY DID THE SOUTH LOSE THE CIVIL WAR?

The answer to this question had long been answered with numbers: The South had too few people and factories. But many have rebutted this point by noting that the South nearly *did* win. Moreover, while southern commanders were plagued with shortages, they lost no battles because they ran out of bullets or shells. In a study of industrial output, Emory Thomas (1979) concluded that southern leadership "outdid its northern counterpart in mobilizing for total war." The South's chief deficiency was, surprisingly, in food production. Frank L. Owsley (1925) blamed the South's defeat on "state's rights jealousy and particularism." Confederate states failed to coordinate financing and production and thus made the South's defeat "inevitable." Jeffrey Hummel (1996), however, has advanced the opposite argument: Jefferson Davis's centralization of power strangled the South with bureaucratic inefficiency and deprived it of ideological coherence. David Eicher (2006) adds that Davis interfered with generals and promoted incompetents. Folklore holds that the genius of southern generals, especially Robert E. Lee, overcame all southern deficiencies. But in *Attack and Die* (1982), a book

whose thesis is contained in its title, Grady McWhiney and Perry D. Jamieson insisted that Lee's audacity, and that of other southern generals, was ill-suited to the military technology of the day. Rifles were particularly effective at cutting down attacking armies. Detailed statistical analysis, however, has challenged this thesis: the North and South initiated attacks with nearly equal frequency and losses. Edward Channing (1925) proposed that the South was defeated because by 1865 Confederates "lost the will to fight." This is rather like saying that the South stopped fighting because it decided to stop fighting—an instance of circular reasoning. But many historians have found the argument, restated more subtly, to be persuasive. Herman Hattaway and Archer Jones (1986) proposed that while the Confederacy could field and equip an effective army for most of the war, "an insufficient nationalism" failed to "survive the strains imposed by lengthy hostilities." The scene above is of Richmond in April 1865.

Emory Thomas, *The Confederate Nation* (1979), Frank L. Owsley, *State Rights in the Confederacy* (1925), Grady McWhiney and Perry D. Jamieson, *Attack and Die* (1982), Edward Channing, *History of the United States* (1925), Herman Hattaway and Archer Jones, *How the North Won* (1986), Jeffrey Hummel, *Emancipating Slaves, Enslaving Free Men* (1996), David Eicher, *Dixie Betrayed* (2006).

Casualties of the Civil War

The Union death rate was 23 percent, the Confederate 24 percent. In general, twice as many soldiers were killed by disease as were killed by bullets.

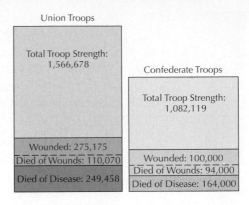

Union Troops

Total Troop Strength: 1,566,678

Wounded: 275,175
Died of Wounds: 110,070
Died of Disease: 249,458

Confederate Troops

Total Troop Strength: 1,082,119

Wounded: 100,000
Died of Wounds: 94,000
Died of Disease: 164,000

Georgia, but he fell ill and the Confederates released him. In March 1865 he was back with his regiment in the lines besieging Richmond. On April 6, three days before Lee's surrender, Jones Budbury was killed while pursuing Confederate units near Sailor's Creek, Virginia.

The war also caused enormous property losses, especially in the Confederacy. All the human and material destruction explains the eroding hatred and bitterness that the war implanted in millions of hearts. The corruption, the gross materialism, and the selfishness generated by wartime conditions were other disagreeable by-products of the conflict. Such sores fester in any society, but the Civil War bred conditions that inflamed and multiplied them. The war produced many examples of charity, self-sacrifice, and devotion to duty as well, yet if the general moral atmosphere of the postwar generation can be said to have resulted from the experiences of 1861 to 1865, the effect overall was bad.

What had been obtained at this price? Slavery was dead. Paradoxically, while the war had been fought to preserve the Union, after 1865 the people tended to see the United States not as a union of states but as a nation. After Appomattox, secession was almost literally inconceivable. In a strictly political sense, as Lincoln had predicted from the start, the northern victory heartened friends of republican government and democracy throughout the world. A better-integrated society and a more technically advanced and productive economic system also resulted from the war.

The Americans of 1865 estimated the balance between cost and profit according to their individual fortunes and prejudices. Only the wisest realized that no final accounting could be made until the people had decided what to do with the fruits of victory. That the physical damage would be repaired no one could reasonably doubt; that even the loss of human resources would be restored in short order was equally apparent. But would the nation make good use of the opportunities the war had made available? What would the former slaves do with freedom? How would whites, northern and southern, react to emancipation? To what end would the new technology and social efficiency be directed? Would the people be able to forget the recent past and fulfill the hopes for which so many brave soldiers had given their "last full measure of devotion"?

Milestones

1861	Confederates attack Fort Sumter; Lincoln calls for 75,000 volunteers
	First Battle of Bull Run (Virginia) boosts Confederate morale
	Lincoln appoints George B. McClellan Union commander
1862	Confederate Congress passes Conscription Act
	Battle of Glorieta Pass ends Confederate threat to Far West
	USS *Monitor* defeats Confederate *Merrimack* in battle of ironclads
	Robert E. Lee assumes command of Confederate Army of Northern Virginia
	Lee and Stonewall Jackson defeat huge Union army at Seven Days' Battle for Richmond
	Lee and Jackson defeat Union army at Second Battle of Bull Run
	Lee's northern advance is stopped at Battle of Antietam; 22,000 die
	Emancipation Proclamation frees slaves in 'areas of rebellion'
	Congress passes Homestead, Morrill Land Grant, and Pacific Railway acts
1863	Congress passes Conscription and National Banking acts
	Federal troops subdue draft riots in New York City
	Union army defeats Confederates at Gettysburg
	Union siege and capture of Vicksburg, Mississippi, gives Union control of entire Mississippi River
1864	Grant pushes deep into Virginia in costly battles of the Wilderness, Spotsylvania Court House, and Cold Harbor
	Sherman captures Atlanta, Georgia; marches to sea; captures Savannah
	Lincoln is reelected president
1864–1865	Grant takes Petersburg, Virginia, after 10-month siege
1865	Sherman captures Columbia, South Carolina
	Lee surrenders to Grant at Appomattox Court House, Virginia

CHAPTER 15

Reconstruction and the South

IN JANUARY 2007, CONGRESSMAN JOHN CONYERS OF MICHIGAN introduced a bill that would require the federal government to reimburse African Americans for the harm done to them by slavery and its aftermath. "It is a fact that slavery flourished in the United States and constituted an immoral and inhumane deprivation of African slaves' lives, liberty and cultural heritage," Conyers declared.

Why, doubters asked, should the nation make reparations to the *descendants* of slaves? Conyers responded that the legacy of slavery continued to inflict "great injustices" on "millions of African Americans today."

Although Conyers' bill (which he has submitted every year since 1989[1]) has yet to be passed by Congress, it encouraged Deadria Farmer-Paellman, a law school student, to file a lawsuit in 2002 against twenty railroad, tobacco, insurance, and textile companies. "These companies have amassed enormous wealth off the backs of enslaved Africans," Farmer-Paellman insisted. She held that they should be forced to make restitution to black Americans.

The lawsuits provided statistics on the unequal economic status of white and black Americans. In 2002, the median household income was $47,000 for whites and $29,000 for blacks. About one-fourth of all black households fell below the poverty line, twice as high a proportion as among whites. The median net worth for white households was $72,000, and for black households, $10,000.

Was the legacy of slavery responsible for these disparities? Conyers believed so. He had assigned his bill the number 40—a reference to General William Sherman's promise during the Civil War to provide free slaves with "40 acres and a mule."

---

[1] Conyers, who is black, was responding to a law passed by Congress in 1988 to make a lump sum payment of $20,000 to those who had suffered during the internment of Japanese by the United States during World War II.

But the promise after the Civil War went unfulfilled. At first, Radical Republicans in Congress did everything to elevate the ex-slaves (and to keep down former Confederates). For a time, Andrew Johnson, Lincoln's successor, stoutly resisted the Republican initiative—for which he was impeached and nearly removed from office. The Republican-dominated Congress then embarked on one of the most ambitious experiments in social engineering ever devised, an attempt to confer on ex-slaves political power over their former masters. Despite some major accomplishments, Reconstruction was undone by racial intransigence and violence, Republican mistakes, and persistent economic obstacles. In 1877, the experiment came to an end. Deprived of federal assistance, former slaves were obliged to make do on their own.

The Assassination of Lincoln

On April 5, 1865, Abraham Lincoln visited Richmond, Virginia. The fallen Confederate capital lay in ruins, sections blackened by fire, but the president was able to walk the streets unmolested and almost unattended. Everywhere black people crowded around him worshipfully; some fell to their knees as he passed, crying "Glory, Hallelujah," hailing him as a messiah. Even white townspeople seemed to have accepted defeat without resentment.

A few days later, in Washington, Lincoln delivered an important speech on Reconstruction, urging compassion and open-mindedness. On April 14 he held a Cabinet meeting at which postwar readjustment was considered at length. That evening, while Lincoln was watching a performance of the play *Our American Cousin* at Ford's Theater, a half-mad actor, John Wilkes Booth, slipped into the president's box and shot him in the back of the head with a small pistol. Early the next morning, without having regained consciousness, Lincoln died.

The murder was part of a complicated plot organized by die-hard pro-Southerners. Seldom have fanatics displayed so little understanding of their own interests, for with Lincoln perished the South's best hope for a mild peace. After his body had been taken home to Illinois, the national mood hardened; apparently the awesome drama was still unfolding—retribution and a final humbling of the South were inevitable.

Presidential Reconstruction

Despite its bloodiness, the Civil War had caused less intersectional hatred than might have been expected. Although civilian property was often seized or destroyed, the invading armies treated the southern population with forbearance, both during the war and after Appomattox. While confederate President Davis was ensconced in Richmond behind Lee's army, Northerners boasted that they would "hang Jeff Davis to a sour apple tree," and when he was captured in Georgia in May

1865, he was at once clapped into irons preparatory to being tried for treason and murder. But feeling against Davis subsided quickly. In 1867 the military turned him over to the civil courts, which released him on bail. He was never brought to trial. A few other Confederate officials spent short periods behind bars, but the only Southerner executed for war crimes was Major Henry Wirz, the commandant of Andersonville military prison.

The legal questions related to bringing the defeated states back into the Union were extremely complex. Since Southerners believed that secession was legal, logic should have compelled them to argue that they were out of the Union and would thus have to be formally readmitted. Northerners should have taken the contrary position, for they had fought to prove that secession was illegal. Yet the people of both sections did just the opposite. Senator Charles Sumner and Congressman Thaddeus Stevens, in 1861 uncompromising expounders of the theory that the Union was indissoluble, now insisted that the Confederate states had "committed suicide" and should be treated like "conquered provinces." Lincoln believed the issue a "pernicious abstraction" and tried to ignore it.

The process of readmission began in 1862, when Lincoln reappointed provisional governors for those parts of the South that had been occupied by federal troops. On December 8, 1863, he issued a proclamation setting forth a general policy. With the exception of high Confederate officials and a few other special groups, all Southerners could reinstate themselves as United States citizens by taking a simple loyalty oath. When, in any state, a number equal to 10 percent of those voting in the 1860 election had taken this oath, they could set up state government. Such governments had to be republican in form, must recognize the "permanent freedom" of the slaves, and must provide for education for blacks. The plan, however, did not require that blacks be given the right to vote.

The "Ten Percent Plan" reflected Lincoln's lack of vindictiveness and his political wisdom. He realized that any government based on such a small minority of the population would be, as he put it, merely "a tangible nucleus which the remainder . . . may rally around as fast as it can," a sort of puppet regime, like the paper government established in those sections of Virginia under federal control.[2] The regimes established under this plan in Tennessee, Louisiana, and Arkansas bore, in the president's mind, the same relation to finally reconstructed states that an egg bears to a chicken. "We shall sooner have the fowl by hatching it than by smashing it," he remarked. He knew that eventually representatives of the southern states would again be sitting in Congress, and he wished to lay the groundwork for a strong Republican party in the section. Yet he realized that Congress had no intention of seating representatives from the "10 percent" states at once.

The Radicals in Congress disliked the Ten Percent Plan, partly because of its moderation and partly because it enabled Lincoln to determine Union policy toward the recaptured regions. In July 1864 they passed the Wade-Davis bill, which

[2]By approving the separation of the western counties that had refused to secede, this government provided a legal pretext for the creation of West Virginia.

provided for constitutional conventions only after a majority of the others in a southern state had taken a loyalty oath. Confederate officials and anyone who had "voluntarily borne arms against the United States" were barred from voting in the election or serving at the convention. Besides prohibiting slavery, the new state constitutions would have to repudiate Confederate debts. Lincoln disposed of the Wade-Davis bill with a pocket veto and there matters stood when Andrew Johnson became president following the assassination.

Lincoln had picked Johnson for a running mate in 1864 because he was a border-state Unionist Democrat and something of a hero as a result of his courageous service as military governor of Tennessee. His political strength came from the poor whites and yeomen farmers of eastern Tennessee, and he was fond of extolling the common man and attacking "stuck-up aristocrats."

Thaddeus Stevens called Johnson a "rank demagogue" and a "damned scoundrel," and it is true that Johnson was a masterful rabble-rouser. But few men of his generation labored so consistently on behalf of small farmers. Free homesteads, public education, absolute social equality—such were his objectives. The father of communism, Karl Marx, a close observer of American affairs at this time, wrote approvingly of Johnson's "deadly hatred of the oligarchy."

Johnson was a Democrat, but because of his record and his reassuring penchant for excoriating southern aristocrats, the Republicans in Congress were ready to cooperate with him. "Johnson, we have faith in you," said Senator Ben Wade, author of the Wade-Davis bill, the day after Lincoln's death. "By the gods, there will be no trouble now in running the government!"

Johnson's reply, "Treason must be made infamous," delighted the Radicals, but the president proved temperamentally unable to work with them. Opposition was his specialty; he soon alienated every powerful Republican in Washington.

Radical Republicans listened to Johnson's diatribes against secessionists and the great planters and assumed that he was anti-southern. Nothing could have been further from the truth. He had great respect for states' rights and he shared most of his poor white Tennessee constituents' contempt of blacks. "Damn the negroes, I am fighting these traitorous aristocrats, their masters," he told a friend during the war. "I wish to God," he said on another occasion, "every head of a family in the United States had one slave to take the drudgery and menial service off his family."

The new president did not want to injure or humiliate all white Southerners. He issued an amnesty proclamation only slightly more rigorous than Lincoln's. It assumed, correctly enough, that with the war over most southern voters would freely take the loyalty oath; thus it contained no 10 percent clause. More classes of Confederates, including those who owned taxable property in excess of $20,000, were excluded from the general pardon. By the time Congress convened in December 1865, all the southern states had organized governments, ratified the Thirteenth Amendment abolishing slavery, and elected senators and representatives. Johnson promptly recommended these new governments to the attention of Congress.

Republican Radicals

Johnson's proposal had no chance in Congress. The Thirteenth Amendment had the effect of increasing the representation of the southern states in Congress because it made the Three-fifths Compromise meaningless. Henceforth those who had been slaves would be counted as whole persons in apportioning seats in the House of Representatives. If Congress seated the Southerners, the balance of power might swing to the Democrats. To expect the Republicans to surrender power in such a fashion was unrealistic. Former Copperheads gushing with extravagant praise for Johnson put them instantly on guard.

Southern voters had provoked northern resentment by their choice of congressmen. Georgia elected Alexander H. Stephens, vice president of the Confederacy, to the Senate, although he was still in a federal prison awaiting trial for treason! Several dozen men who had served in the Confederate Congress had been elected to either the House or the Senate, together with four generals and many other high officials. The southern people understandably selected locally respected and experienced leaders, but it was equally reasonable that these choices would sit poorly with Northerners.

Finally, the so-called Black Codes enacted by southern governments to control former slaves alarmed the North. These varied in severity from state to state, but all, as one planter admitted, set out to keep the blacks "as near to a state of bondage as possible." Blacks could not bear arms, be employed in occupations other than farming and domestic service, or leave their jobs without forfeiting back pay. The Mississippi code required them to sign labor contracts for the year in January, and, in addition, drunkards, vagrants, beggars, "common night-walkers," and even "mischief makers" and persons who "misspend what they earn" and who could not pay the stiff fines assessed for such misbehavior were to be "hired out . . . at public outcry" to the white persons who would take them for the shortest period in return for paying the fines. Such laws, apparently designed to get around the Thirteenth Amendment, outraged Northerners.

Congress Rejects Johnsonian Reconstruction

President Johnson's attitude speeded the swing toward the Radical position. Congress passed a bill expanding and extending the Freedmen's Bureau, which had been established in March 1865 to care for refugees. The bureau, a branch of the War Department, was already exercising considerable coercive and supervisory power in the South. Now Congress sought to add to its authority in order to protect the black population. Although the bill had wide support, Johnson vetoed it, arguing that it was an unconstitutional extension of military authority in peacetime. Congress then passed a Civil Rights Act that, besides declaring specifically that blacks were citizens of the United States, denied the states the power to restrict their rights to testify in court, to make contracts for their labor, and to hold property. In other words, it put teeth in the Thirteenth Amendment.

Once again the president refused to go along, although his veto was sure to drive more moderates into the arms of the Radicals. On April 9, 1866, Congress repassed the Civil Rights Act by a two-thirds majority, the first time in American history that a major piece of legislation became law over the veto of a president. This event marked a revolution in the history of Reconstruction. Thereafter Congress, not President Johnson, had the upper hand.

The president misread northern opinion. He believed that Congress had no right to pass laws affecting the South before southern representatives had been readmitted to Congress. However, in the light of the refusal of most southern whites to grant any real power or responsibility to the freedmen (an attitude that Johnson did not condemn), the public would not accept this point of view. Johnson placed his own judgment over that of the overwhelming majority of northern voters, and this was a great error, morally and tactically. By encouraging white Southerners to resist efforts to improve the lot of blacks, Johnson played into the hands of the Radicals.

The Radicals encountered grave problems in fighting for their program. Northerners might object to the Black Codes and to seating "rebels" in Congress, but few believed in racial equality. Between 1865 and 1868, Wisconsin, Minnesota,

Connecticut, Nebraska, New Jersey, Ohio, Michigan, and Pennsylvania all rejected bills granting blacks the vote.

Thus, while the Radicals sought partisan advantage in their battle with Johnson and sometimes played on war-bred passions in achieving their ends, they were taking large political risks in defense of genuinely held principles. One historian has aptly called them the "moral trustees" of the Civil War.

The Fourteenth Amendment

In June 1866 Congress submitted to the states a new amendment to the Constitution. The Fourteenth Amendment was, in the context of the times, a truly radical measure. Never before had newly freed slaves been granted significant political rights. For example, in the British Caribbean sugar islands, where slavery had been abolished in the 1830s, stiff property qualifications and poll taxes kept freedmen from voting. The Fourteenth Amendment was also a milestone along the road to the centralization of political power in the United States because it reduced the power of all the states. In this sense it confirmed the great change wrought by the Civil War: the growth of a more complex, more closely integrated social and economic structure requiring closer national supervision. Few people understood this aspect of the amendment at the time.

First the amendment supplied a broad definition of American citizenship: "All persons born or naturalized in the United States, and subject to the jurisdiction thereof, are citizens of the United States and of the State wherein they reside." Obviously this included blacks. Then it struck at discriminatory legislation like the Black Codes: "No State shall make or enforce any law which shall abridge the privileges or immunities of citizens of the United States; nor shall any State deprive any person of life, liberty, or property, without due process of law." The next section attempted to force the southern states to permit blacks to vote. If a state denied the vote to any class of its adult male citizens, its representation was to be reduced proportionately. Under another clause, former federal officials who had served the Confederacy were barred from holding either state or federal office unless specifically pardoned by a two-thirds vote of Congress. Finally, the Confederate debt was repudiated.

While the amendment did not specifically outlaw segregation or prevent a state from disenfranchising blacks, the southern states would have none of it. Without them the necessary three-fourths majority of the states could not be obtained.

President Johnson vowed to make the choice between the Fourteenth Amendment and his own policy the main issue of the 1866 congressional elections. He embarked on "a swing around the circle" to rally the public to his cause. He failed dismally. Northern women objected to the implication in the amendment that black men were more fit to vote than white women, but a large majority of northern voters was determined that African Americans must have at least formal legal equality. The Republicans won better than two-thirds of the seats in both houses, together with control of all the northern state governments. Johnson emerged from the campaign discredited, the Radicals stronger and determined to have their way. The southern states, Congressman James A. Garfield of Ohio said in February 1867, have "flung back into our teeth the magnanimous offer of a generous nation. It is now our turn to act."

The Reconstruction Acts

Had the southern states been willing to accept the Fourteenth Amendment, coercive measures might have been avoided. Their recalcitrance and continuing indications that local authorities were persecuting blacks finally led to the passage, on March 2, 1867, of the First Reconstruction Act. This law divided the former Confederacy—exclusive of Tennessee, which had ratified the Fourteenth Amendment—into five military districts, each controlled by a major general. It gave these officers almost dictatorial power to protect the civil rights of "all persons," maintain order, and supervise the administration of justice. To rid themselves of military rule, the former states were required to adopt new state constitutions guaranteeing blacks the right to vote and disenfranchising broad classes of ex-Confederates. If the new constitutions proved satisfactory to Congress, and if the new governments ratified the Fourteenth Amendment, their representatives would be admitted to Congress and military rule ended. Johnson's veto of the act was easily overridden.

Although drastic, the Reconstruction Act was so vague that it proved unworkable. Military control was easily established. But in deference to moderate Republican views, the law had not spelled out the process by which the new constitutions were to be drawn up. Southern whites preferred the status quo, even under army control, to enfranchising blacks and retiring their own respected leaders. They made no effort to follow the steps laid down in the law. Congress therefore passed a second act, requiring the military authorities to register voters and supervise the election of delegates to constitutional conventions. A third act further clarified procedures.

Still white Southerners resisted. The laws required that the constitutions be approved by a majority of the registered voters. Simply by staying away from the polls, whites prevented ratification in state after state. At last, in March 1868, a full year after the First Reconstruction Act, Congress changed the rules again. The constitutions were to be ratified by a majority of the voters. In June 1868 Arkansas, having fulfilled the requirements, was readmitted to the Union, and by July a sufficient number of states had ratified the Fourteenth Amendment to make it part of the Constitution. But it was not until July 1870 that the last southern state, Georgia, qualified to the satisfaction of Congress.

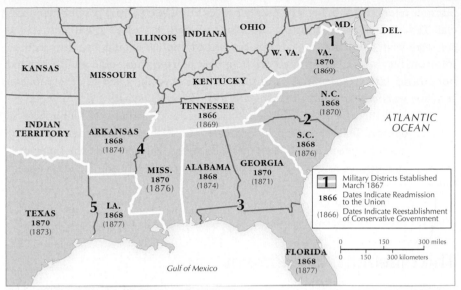

Military Districts Established March 1867

1866 Dates Indicate Readmission to the Union

(1866) Dates Indicate Reestablishment of Conservative Government

0   150   300 miles

0   150   300 kilometers

Return to the Union During Reconstruction

Congress Supreme

To carry out this program in the face of determined southern resistance required a degree of single-mindedness over a long period seldom demonstrated by an American legislature. A series of measures passed between 1866 and 1868 increased the authority of Congress over the army, over the process of amending the Constitution, and over Cabinet members and lesser appointive officers. Even the Supreme Court was affected. Its size was reduced and its jurisdiction over civil rights cases limited. Finally, in a showdown caused by emotion more than by practical considerations, the Republicans attempted to remove President Johnson from office.

The chief issue was the Tenure of Office Act of 1867, which prohibited the president from removing officials who had been appointed with the consent of the Senate without first obtaining Senate approval. In February 1868 Johnson "violated" this act by dismissing Secretary of War Edwin M. Stanton, who had been openly in sympathy with the Radicals for some time. The House, acting under the procedure set up in the Constitution for removing the president, promptly impeached him before the bar of the Senate, Chief Justice Salmon P. Chase presiding.

In the trial, Johnson's lawyers easily established that he had removed Stanton only in an effort to prove the Tenure of Office Act unconstitutional. They demonstrated that the act did not protect Stanton to begin with, since it gave Cabinet members tenure "during the term of the President by whom they may have been appointed," and Stanton had been appointed in 1862, during Lincoln's first term!

Nevertheless the Radicals pressed the charges (eleven separate articles) relentlessly. To the argument that Johnson had committed no crime, the learned Senator

Sumner retorted that the proceedings were "political in character" rather than judicial. Thaddeus Stevens, directing the attack on behalf of the House, warned the senators that although "no corrupt or wicked motive" could be attributed to Johnson, they would "be tortured on the gibbet of everlasting obloquy" if they did not convict him. Tremendous pressure was applied to the handful of Republican senators who were unwilling to disregard the evidence.

Seven of them resisted to the end, and the Senate failed by a single vote to convict Johnson. This was probably fortunate. The trial weakened the presidency, but if Johnson had been forced from office on such flimsy grounds, the independence of the executive might have been permanently undermined. Then the legislative branch would have become supreme.

The Fifteenth Amendment

The failure of the impeachment did not affect the course of Reconstruction. The president was acquitted on May 16, 1868. A few days later, the Republican National Convention nominated General Ulysses S. Grant for the presidency. At the Democratic convention Johnson had considerable support, but the delegates nominated Horatio Seymour, a former governor of New York. In November Grant won an easy victory in the Electoral College, 214 to 80, but the popular vote was close: 3 million to 2.7 million. Although he would probably have carried the Electoral College in any case, Grant's margin in the popular vote was supplied by southern blacks enfranchised under the Reconstruction acts, about 450,000 of whom supported him. On the other hand, Grant had carried Indiana by fewer than 10,000 votes and lost New York by a similar number. If blacks in these and other closely divided states had voted, Republican strength would have been greatly enhanced.

Suddenly Congress blossomed with suffrage amendments. After considerable bickering over details, the Fifteenth Amendment was sent to the states for ratification in February 1869. It forbade all the states to deny the vote to anyone "on account of race, color, or previous condition of servitude." Once again nothing was said about denial of the vote on the basis of sex, which caused feminists, such as Elizabeth Cady Stanton, to be even more outraged than they had been by the Fourteenth Amendment.

Most southern states, still under federal pressure, ratified the amendment swiftly. The same was true in most of New England and in some western states. Bitter battles were waged in Connecticut, New York, Pennsylvania, and the states immediately north of the Ohio River, but by March 1870 most of them had ratified the amendment and it became part of the Constitution.

The debates occasioned by these conventions show that partisan advantage was not the only reason why voters approved black suffrage at last. The unfairness of a double standard of voting, North and South, the contribution of black soldiers during the war, and the hope that by passing the amendment the strife of Reconstruction could finally be ended all played a part.

When the Fifteenth Amendment went into effect, President Grant called it "the greatest civil change and . . . the most important event that has occurred since the nation came to life." The American Anti-Slavery Society formally dissolved itself, its work apparently completed. "The Fifteenth Amendment confers upon the African race the care of its own destiny," Radical Congressman James A. Garfield wrote proudly after the amendment was ratified. "It places their fortunes in their own hands."

"Black Republican" Reconstruction: Scalawags and Carpetbaggers

The Radicals had at last succeeded in imposing their will on the South. Throughout the region former slaves had real political influence; they voted, held office, and exercised the "privileges" and enjoyed the "immunities" guaranteed them by the Fourteenth Amendment. Almost to a man they voted Republican.

The spectacle of blacks not five years removed from slavery in positions of power and responsibility attracted much attention at the time and has since been examined exhaustively by historians. But the real rulers of the "black Republican" governments were white: the "scalawags"—Southerners willing to cooperate with the Republicans because they accepted the results of the war and wished to advance their own interests—and the "carpetbaggers"—Northerners who went to the South as idealists to help the freed slaves, as employees of the federal government, or more commonly as settlers hoping to improve themselves.

The scalawags were by far the more numerous. A few were prewar politicians or well-to-do planters, men such as the Mississippi planter John L. Alcorn and Joseph E. Brown, the Confederate governor of Georgia. General James Longstreet, one of Lee's most important lieutenants, was another prominent Southerner who cooperated with the Republicans. But most were people who had supported the Whig party before the secession crisis and who saw the Republicans as the logical successors of the Whigs.

The carpetbaggers were a particularly varied lot. Most had mixed motives for coming south and personal gain was certainly among them. But so were opposition to slavery and the belief that blacks deserved to be treated decently and given a chance to get ahead in the world.

Many northern blacks became carpetbaggers: former Union soldiers, missionaries from northern black churches, and also teachers, lawyers, and other members of the small northern black professional class. Many of these became officeholders, but like southern black politicians their influence was limited.

Debating the Past

WERE RECONSTRUCTION GOVERNMENTS CORRUPT?

Racist depictions of Reconstruction were common. This one by Thomas Nast was entitled "Colored Rule in a Reconstructed (?) State" and appeared in the influential *Harper's Weekly* (1874). The harsh assessment of Reconstruction persisted. In 1902 Columbia historian William A. Dunning declared that free slaves were mere children, incapable of holding office. Such views informed D. W. Griffith's 1915 film, *The Birth of a Nation*. In 1910 W. E. B. Du Bois, an African American scholar, was the first to applaud Reconstruction for broadening educational opportunities and democratizing government, but few historians concurred. In the 1960s, as the civil rights movement was gaining momentum, more scholars came out in support of Reconstruction. Kenneth Stampp (1965) emphasized the Reconstruction governments' attempts to protect freedmen; that same year, Joel Williamson turned Dunning's thesis on its head and endorsed nearly all aspects of Reconstruction. More recent scholars have generally taken a moderate position: Reconstruction may have failed, but its accomplishments under difficult circumstances of white opposition were substantial; see, for example, Eric Foner (1988). Certain facts are beyond argument. Black officeholders during Reconstruction were neither numerous nor inordinately influential. None was ever elected governor of a state; fewer than a dozen and a half during the entire period served in Congress. Blacks held many minor offices and were influential in southern legislatures, although (except in South Carolina) they never made up the majority.

William A. Dunning, *Reconstruction and the Constitution* (1902), W. E. B. Du Bois, *Black Reconstruction in America* (1935), Kenneth Stampp, *The Peculiar Institution* (1965), Joel Williamson, *After Slavery* (1965), Eric Foner, *Reconstruction* (1988).

During Reconstruction, fourteen blacks won election to the House of Representatives and two, Hiram Revels and Blanche K. Bruce, served in the Senate. Revels, at far left, won the Mississippi Senate seat that Jefferson Davis had once held. He later became president of Alcorn University. Congressman R. Brown Elliot, at far right, had been educated at Eton in England.

In South Carolina and elsewhere, blacks proved in the main able and conscientious public servants: able because the best tended to rise to the top in such a fluid situation and conscientious because most of those who achieved importance sought eagerly to demonstrate the capacity of their race for self-government. Even at the local level, where the quality of officials was usually poor, there was little difference in the degree of competence displayed by white and black officeholders. In power, the blacks were not vindictive; by and large they did not seek to restrict the rights of ex-Confederates.

Not all black legislators and administrators were paragons of virtue. In South Carolina, despite their control of the legislature, they broke up into factions repeatedly and failed to press for laws that would improve the lot of poor black farm workers. And waste and corruption were common during Reconstruction governments, whether the politicians were black or white.

In fact, the Radical southern governments accomplished a great deal. They spent money freely but not entirely wastefully. Tax rates zoomed, but the money financed the repair and expansion of the South's dilapidated railroad network, rebuilt crumbling levees, and expanded social services. Before the Civil War, southern planters possessed a disproportionate share of political as well as economic power, and they spent relatively little public money on education and public services of all kinds.

During Reconstruction an enormous gap had to be filled, and it took money to fill it. The Freedmen's Bureau made a major contribution. Northern religious and philanthropic organizations also did important work. Eventually, however, the state governments established and supported hospitals, asylums, and systems of free public education that, while segregated, greatly benefited everyone, whites as well as blacks. Much state money was also spent on economic development: land reclamation, repairing and expanding the war-ravaged railroads, maintaining levees.

The former slaves grasped eagerly at the opportunities to learn. Schools and other institutions were supported chiefly by property taxes, and these, of course, hit well-to-do planters hard. Hence much of the complaining about the "extravagance" of Reconstruction governments concealed traditional selfish objections to paying for public projects. Eventually the benefits of expanded government services to the entire population became clear, and when white supremacy was reestablished, most of the new services remained in force, and the corruption and inefficiency inherited from the carpetbagger governments continued.

The Ravaged Land

The South's grave economic problems complicated the rebuilding of its political system. The section had never been as prosperous as the North, and wartime destruction left it desperately poor by any standard. In the long run the abolition of slavery released immeasurable quantities of human energy previously stifled, but the immediate effect was to create confusion. Freedom to move without a pass, to "see the world," was one of the former slaves' most cherished benefits of emancipation. Understandably, many at first equated legal freedom with freedom from having to earn a living, a tendency reinforced for a time by the willingness of the Freedmen's Bureau to provide rations and other forms of relief in war-devastated areas. Most, however, soon accepted the fact that they must earn a living; a small plot of land of their own ("40 acres and a mule") would complete their independence.

This objective was forcefully supported by the relentless Congressman Thaddeus Stevens, whose hatred of the planter class was pathological. "The property of the chief rebels should be seized," he stated. If the lands of the richest "70,000 proud, bloated and defiant rebels" were confiscated, the federal government would obtain 394 million acres. Every adult male ex-slave could easily be supplied with 40 acres. The beauty of his scheme, Stevens insisted, was that "nine-tenths of the [southern] people would remain untouched." Dispossessing the great planters would make the South "a safe republic," its lands cultivated by "the free labor of intelligent citizens." If the plan drove the planters into exile, "all the better."

Aside from its vindictiveness, the proposals of Stevens and other extremists were simplistic. Land without tools, seed, and other necessities would have done the freedmen little good. Congress did throw open 46 million acres of poor-quality federal land in the South to blacks under the Homestead Act, but few settled on it.

The Freedmen's Bureau built 4,329 schools, attended by some 250,000 former slaves, in the postwar South. Many of the teachers in these schools were abolitionists or missionaries from New England. The schools drew African Americans of all ages, from children to grandparents, who were eager for the advantages offered by education.

Establishing former slaves on small farms with adequate financial aid would have been of incalculable benefit to them. This would have been practicable, but extremely expensive. It was not done.

The former slaves therefore had either to agree to work for their former owners or strike out on their own. White planters, influenced by the precipitous decline of sugar production in Jamaica and other Caribbean islands that had followed the abolition of slavery there, expected freed blacks to be incapable of self-directed effort. If allowed to become independent farmers, they would either starve to death or descend into barbarism. Of course the blacks did neither. True, the output of cotton and other southern staples declined precipitously after slavery was abolished. Observers soon came to the conclusion that a free black produced much less than a slave had produced. "You can't get only about two-thirds as much out of 'em now as you could when they were slaves," an Arkansas planter complained.

However, the decline in productivity was not caused by the inability of free blacks to work independently. They simply chose no longer to work like slaves. They let their children play instead of forcing them into the fields. Mothers devoted more time to childcare and housework, less to farm labor. Elderly blacks worked less.

The family life of former slaves was changed in other ways. Male authority increased when husbands became true heads of families. (Under slavery the ultimate responsibility for providing for women and children was the master's.) When blacks became citizens, the men acquired rights and powers denied to all women, such as the right to hold public office and serve on juries. Similarly, black women became more like white women, devoting themselves to separate "spheres" where their lives revolved around housekeeping and child rearing.

Sharecropping and the Crop-Lien System

Quite swiftly, a new agricultural system known as sharecropping emerged. Instead of cultivating the land by gang labor as in antebellum times, planters broke up their estates into small units and established on each unit a black family. The planter provided housing, agricultural implements, draft animals, seed, and other supplies, and the family provided labor. The crop was divided between planter and laborer, usually on a fifty-fifty basis. If the landlord supplied only land and housing, the laborer got a larger share. This was called share tenancy.

Sharecropping gave blacks the day-to-day control of their lives that they craved and the hope of earning enough to buy a small farm. But few blacks succeeded in this goal. As late as 1880 blacks owned less than 10 percent of the agricultural land in the South, although they made up more than half of the region's farm population. Mississippi actually prohibited the purchase of farmland by blacks.

Many white farmers in the South were also trapped by the sharecropping system and by white efforts to keep blacks in a subordinate position. New fencing laws kept them from grazing livestock on undeveloped land, a practice common before the Civil War. But the main cause of southern rural poverty for whites as well as for blacks was the lack of enough capital to finance the sharecropping system. Like their colonial ancestors, the landowners had to borrow against October's harvest to pay for April's seed. Thus the crop-lien system developed.

Under the crop-lien system, both landowner and sharecropper depended on credit supplied by local bankers, merchants, and storekeepers for everything from seed, tools, and fertilizer to overalls, coffee, and salt. Crossroads stores proliferated, and a new class of small merchants appeared. The prices of goods sold on credit were high, adding to the burden borne by the rural population. The small southern merchants were almost equally victimized by the system, for they also lacked capital, bought goods on credit, and had to pay high interest rates.

Seen in broad perspective, the situation is not difficult to understand. The South, drained of every resource by the war, was competing for funds with the North and West, both vigorous and expanding and therefore voracious consumers of capital. Reconstruction, in the literal sense of the word, was accomplished chiefly at the expense of the standard of living of the producing classes. The crop-lien system and the small storekeeper were only agents of an economic process dictated by national, perhaps even worldwide, conditions.

Compared with the rest of the country, progress in the South was slow. Just before the Civil War cotton harvests averaged about 4 million bales. During the con-

After the Civil War, most blacks worked as sharecroppers on land owned by whites. In this photograph, black sharecroppers pick cotton, a major cash crop of the South with the owner of the land getting a share of the crop (crop-lien). The crop-lien system injured everyone. Diversified farming would have reduced the farmers' need for cash, preserved the fertility of the soil, and, by placing a premium on imagination and shrewdness, aided the best of them to rise in the world. Because the price for cotton remained low, sharecroppers often fell into debt and were tied to the land almost as tightly as under slavery.

flict, output fell to about half a million, and the former Confederate states did not enjoy a 4-million bale year again until 1870. In contrast, national wheat production in 1859 was 175 million bushels and in 1878, 449 million. About 7,000 miles of railroad were built in the South between 1865 and 1879; in the rest of the nation nearly 45,000 miles of track were laid.

But in the late 1870s, cotton production revived. It soon regained, and thereafter long retained, its title as "king" of the southern economy. This was true in large measure because of the crop-lien system.

The South made important gains in manufacturing after the war. The tobacco industry, stimulated by the sudden popularity of the cigarette, expanded rapidly. Virginia and North Carolina tobacco towns like Richmond, Lynchburg, and Durham flourished. The exploitation of the coal and iron deposits of northeastern Alabama in the early 1870s made a boomtown of Birmingham. The manufacture of cotton cloth increased, productive capacity nearly doubling between 1865 and 1880. Yet the mills of Massachusetts alone had eight times the capacity of the entire South in 1880. Despite the increases, the South's share of the national output of manufactured goods declined sharply during the Reconstruction era.

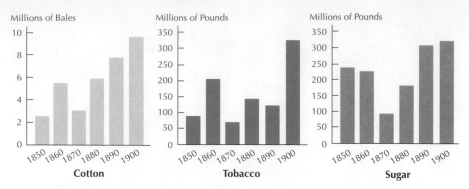

Southern Agriculture, 1850–1900
Cotton production recovered to its prewar level by 1880, but tobacco and sugar production lagged. Not until 1900 did tobacco growers have a better year than they had in 1860. The years following 1870 saw a general downward trend in wholesale prices for farm commodities. (Statistics are for the eleven states of the Confederacy.)

The White Backlash

Radical southern governments could sustain themselves only as long as they had the support of a significant proportion of the white population, for except in South Carolina and Louisiana, the blacks were not numerous enough to win elections alone. The key to survival lay in the hands of the wealthy merchants and planters, mostly former Whigs. People of this sort had nothing to fear from black economic competition. Taking a broad view, they could see that improving the lot of the former slaves would benefit all classes.

Southern white Republicans used the Union League of America, a patriotic club founded during the war, to control the black vote. Employing secret rituals, exotic symbols, and other paraphernalia calculated to impress unsophisticated people, they enrolled the freedmen in droves and marched them to the polls en masse.

Powerless to check the League by open methods, dissident Southerners established a number of secret terrorist societies, bearing such names as the Ku Klux Klan, the Knights of the White Camelia, and the Pale Faces. The most notorious of these organizations was the Klan, which originated in Tennessee in 1866. At first it was purely a social club, but by 1868 it had been taken over by vigilante types dedicated to driving blacks out of politics, and it was spreading rapidly across the South. Sheet-clad nightriders roamed the countryside, frightening the impressionable and chastising the defiant. Klansmen, using a weird mumbo jumbo and claiming to be the ghosts of Confederate soldiers, spread horrendous rumors and published broadsides designed to persuade the freedmen that it was unhealthy for them to participate in politics.

When intimidation failed, the Klansmen resorted to force. After being whipped by one group in Tennessee, a recently elected justice of the peace reported: "They said they had nothing particular against me . . . but they did not intend any nigger to hold office." In hundreds of cases the KKK murdered their opponents, often in the most gruesome manner.

Congress struck at the Klan with three Force Acts (1870–1871), which placed elections under federal jurisdiction and imposed fines and prison sentences on persons convicted of interfering with any citizen's exercise of the franchise. Troops were dispatched to areas where the Klan was strong, and by 1872 the federal authorities had arrested enough Klansmen to break up the organization.

Nevertheless the Klan contributed substantially to the destruction of Radical regimes in the South. Its depredations weakened the will of white Republicans (few of whom really believed in racial equality), and it intimidated many blacks. The fact that the army had to be called in to suppress it was a glaring illustration of the weakness of the Reconstruction governments.

Gradually it became respectable to intimidate black voters. Beginning in Mississippi in 1874, terrorism spread through the South. Instead of hiding behind masks and operating in the dark, these terrorists donned red shirts, organized into military companies, and paraded openly. Mississippi redshirts seized militant blacks and whipped them publicly. Killings were frequent. When blacks dared to fight back, heavily armed whites put them to rout. In other states similar results followed.

Before long the blacks learned to stay home on election day. One by one, "Conservative" parties—Democratic in national affairs—took over southern state governments. Intimidation was only a partial explanation of this development. The increasing solidarity of whites, northern and southern, was equally significant.

The North had subjected the South to control from Washington while preserving state sovereignty in the North itself. In the long run this discrimination proved unworkable. Many Northerners had supported the Radical policy only out of irritation with President Johnson. After his retirement their enthusiasm waned. The war was fading into the past and with it the worst of the anger it had generated.

Northern voters could still be stirred by references to the sacrifices Republicans had made to save the Union and by reminders that the Democratic party was the organization of rebels, Copperheads, and the Ku Klux Klan. "If the Devil himself were at the helm of the ship of state," wrote the novelist Lydia Maria Child in 1872, "my conscience would not allow me to aid in removing him to make room for the Democratic party." Yet emotional appeals could not convince Northerners that it was still necessary to maintain a large army in the South. In 1869 the occupying forces were down to 11,000 men. After Klan disruption and intimidation had made a farce of the 1874 elections in Mississippi, Governor Ames appealed to Washington for help. President Grant's attorney general, Edwards Pierrepont, refused to act. "The whole public are tired out with these autumnal outbreaks in the South," he told Ames. "Preserve the peace by the forces of your own state."

Nationalism was reasserting itself. Had not Washington and Jefferson been Virginians? Was not Andrew Jackson Carolina-born? Since most Northerners had little real love or respect for blacks, their interest in racial equality flagged once they felt reasonably certain that blacks would not be re-enslaved if left to their own devices in the South.

Another, much subtler force was also at work. The prewar Republican party had stressed the common interest of workers, manufacturers, and farmers in a free and mobile society, a land of equal opportunity where all could work in harmony. Southern whites had insisted that laborers must be disciplined if large enterprises were to be run efficiently. By the 1870s, as large industrial enterprises developed in the northern states, the thinking of business leaders changed—the southern argument began to make sense to them, and they became more sympathetic to the southern demand for more control over "their" labor force.

Grant as President

Other matters occupied the attention of northern voters. The expansion of industry and the rapid development of the West, stimulated by a new wave of railroad building, loomed more important to many than the fortunes of the former slaves. Beginning in 1873, when a stock market panic struck at public confidence, economic difficulties plagued the country. Heated controversies arose over tariff policy, with western agricultural interests seeking to force reductions from the high levels established during the war, and over the handling of the wartime greenback paper money, with debtor groups and many manufacturers favoring further expansion of the supply of dollars and conservative merchants and bankers arguing for retiring the greenbacks in order to return to a "sound" currency.

More damaging to the Republicans was the failure of Ulysses S. Grant to live up to expectations as president. His most serious weakness as president was his failure to deal effectively with economic and social problems, but the one that injured him and the Republicans most was his inability to cope with government corruption. The worst of the scandals—such as the Whiskey Ring affair, which implicated Grant's private secretary, Orville E. Babcock, and cost the government millions in tax revenue, and the corruption of Secretary of War William W. Belknap in the management of Indian affairs—did not become public knowledge during Grant's first term. However, in 1872 Republican reformers, alarmed by rumors of corruption and disappointed by Grant's failure to press for civil service reform, organized the Liberal Republican party and nominated Horace Greeley, the able but eccentric editor of the *New York Tribune,* for president.

The Liberal Republicans were mostly well-educated, socially prominent types—editors, college presidents, economists, along with a sprinkling of businessmen and politicians. Their liberalism was of the laissez-faire variety; they were for low tariffs and sound money, and against what they called "class legislation," meaning measures benefiting particular groups, whether labor unions or railroad companies or farm organizations. Nearly all had supported Reconstruction at the start, but by the early 1870s most were including southern blacks among the special interests that ought to be left to their own devices. Their observation of urban corruption and of unrestricted immigration led them to disparage universal suffrage, which, one of them said, "can only mean in plain English the government of ignorance and vice."

An 1872 Grant campaign poster of "Our Three Great Presidents." The poster was about two-thirds right.

The Democrats also nominated Greeley in 1872, although he had devoted his political life to flailing the Democratic party in the *Tribune*. That surrender to expediency, together with Greeley's temperamental unsuitability for the presidency, made the campaign a fiasco for the reformers. Grant triumphed easily, with a popular majority of nearly 800,000.

Nevertheless, the defection of the Liberal Republicans hurt the Republican party in Congress. In the 1874 elections, no longer hampered as in the presidential contest by Greeley's notoriety and Grant's fame, the Democrats carried the House of Representatives. It was clear that the days of military rule in the South were ending. By the end of 1875 only three southern states—South Carolina, Florida, and Louisiana—were still under Republican control.

The Republican party in the South was "dead as a doornail," a reporter noted. He reflected the opinion of thousands when he added: "We ought to have a sound sensible republican . . . for the next President as a measure of safety; but only on the condition of absolute noninterference in Southern local affairs, for which there is no further need or excuse."

The Disputed Election of 1876

Against this background the presidential election of 1876 took place. Since corruption in government was the most widely discussed issue, the Republicans passed over their most attractive political personality, the dynamic James G. Blaine, Speaker of the House of Representatives, who had been connected with some chicanery involving railroad securities. Instead they nominated Governor Rutherford B. Hayes of Ohio, a former general with an untarnished reputation. The Democrats picked Governor Samuel J. Tilden of New York, a wealthy lawyer who had attracted national attention for his part in breaking up the Tweed Ring in New York City.

In November early returns indicated that Tilden had carried New York, New Jersey, Connecticut, Indiana, and all the southern states, including Louisiana, South Carolina, and Florida, where Republican regimes were still in control. This seemed to give him 203 electoral votes to Hayes's 165, and a popular plurality in the neighborhood of 250,000 out of more than 8 million votes cast. However, Republican leaders had anticipated the possible loss of Florida, South Carolina, and Louisiana and were prepared to use their control of the election machinery in those states to throw out sufficient Democratic ballots to alter the results if doing so would change the national outcome. Realizing that the electoral votes of those states were exactly enough to elect their man, they telegraphed their henchmen on the scene, ordering them to go into action. The local Republicans then invalidated Democratic ballots in wholesale lots and filed returns showing Hayes the winner. Naturally the local Democrats protested vigorously and filed their own returns.

The Constitution provides (Article II, Section 1) that presidential electors must meet in their respective states to vote and forward the results to "the Seat of the Government." There, it adds, "the President of the Senate shall, in the Presence of the Senate and House of Representatives, open all the Certificates, and the Votes shall then be counted." But who was to do the counting? The House was Democratic, the Senate Republican; neither would agree to allow the other to do the job. On January 29, 1877, scarcely a month before inauguration day, Congress created a 15-member electoral commission to decide the disputed cases, The "neutral" vote was to be provided by Justice Joseph Bradley of New Jersey, a Republican.

Evidence presented before the commission revealed a disgraceful picture of election shenanigans. On the one hand, in all three disputed states Democrats had clearly cast a majority of the votes; on the other, it was unquestionable that many blacks had been forcibly prevented from voting.

In truth, both sides were shamefully corrupt. The governor of Louisiana was reported willing to sell his state's electoral votes for $200,000. The Florida election board was supposed to have offered itself to Tilden for the same price. "That seems to be the standard figure," Tilden remarked ruefully.

The Democrats had some hopes that Justice Bradley would be sympathetic to their case, for he was known to be opposed to harsh Reconstruction policies. On the eve of the commission's decision in the Florida controversy, he was apparently ready to vote in favor of Tilden. But the Republicans subjected him to tremendous political pressure. When he read his opinion on February 8, it was for Hayes. Thus, by a vote of 8 to 7, the commission awarded Florida's electoral votes to the Republicans.

The Compromise of 1877

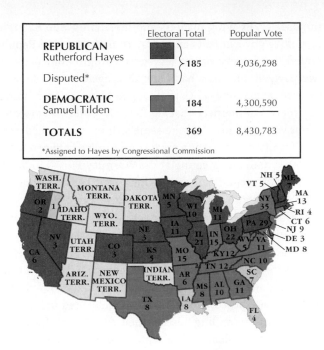

	Electoral Total	Popular Vote
REPUBLICAN Rutherford Hayes	⎫ 185	4,036,298
Disputed*	⎬	
DEMOCRATIC Samuel Tilden	184	4,300,590
TOTALS	369	8,430,783

*Assigned to Hayes by Congressional Commission

The rest of the proceedings was routine. The commission assigned all the disputed electoral votes (including one in Oregon where the Democratic governor had seized on a technicality to replace a single Republican elector with a Democrat) to Hayes.

Democratic institutions, shaken by the South's refusal to go along with the majority in 1860 and by the suppression of civil rights during the rebellion, and further weakened by military intervention and the intimidation of blacks in the South during Reconstruction, seemed now a farce. According to Tilden's campaign manager, angry Democrats in fifteen states, chiefly war veterans, were readying themselves to march on Washington to force the inauguration of Tilden. Tempers flared in Congress, where some spoke ominously of a filibuster that would prevent the recording of the electoral vote and leave the country, on March 4, with no president at all.

The Compromise of 1877

Forces for compromise had been at work behind the scenes in Washington for some time. Although northern Democrats threatened to fight to the last ditch, many southern Democrats were willing to accept Hayes if he would promise to remove the troops and allow the southern states to manage their internal affairs by themselves. Ex-Whig planters and merchants who had reluctantly abandoned the carpetbag governments and who sympathized with Republican economic policies hoped that by supporting Hayes they might contribute to the restoration of the two-party system that had been destroyed in the South during the 1850s. Ohio Congressman James A. Garfield urged Hayes to find "some discreet way" of showing these Southerners that he favored "internal improvements." Hayes replied: "Your views are so nearly the same as mine that I need not say a word."

Tradition has it that a great compromise between the sections was worked out during a dramatic meeting at the Wormley Hotel[3] in Washington on February 26. Actually the negotiations were drawn out and informal, and the Wormley conference was but one of many. With the tacit support of many Democrats, the electoral vote was counted by the president of the Senate on March 2, and Hayes was declared elected, 185 votes to 184.

Like all compromises, this agreement was not entirely satisfactory; like most, it was not honored in every detail. Hayes recalled the last troops from South Carolina and Louisiana in April. He appointed a former Confederate general, David M. Key of Tennessee, postmaster general and delegated to him the congenial task of finding Southerners willing to serve their country as officials of a Republican administration. But the alliance of ex-Whigs and northern Republicans did not flourish; the South remained solidly Democratic. The major significance of the compromise, one of the great intersectional political accommodations of American history, was that it ended Reconstruction and inaugurated a new political order in the South. More than the Constitutional amendments and federal statutes, this new regime would shape the destinies of the four million freedmen.

For most, this future was to be bleak. Forgotten in the North, manipulated and then callously rejected by the South, rebuffed by the Supreme Court, voiceless in national affairs, they and their descendants were condemned in the interests of sectional harmony to lives of poverty, indignity, and little hope. Meanwhile, the rest of the United States continued its golden march toward wealth and power.

---

[3]*Ironically, the hotel was owned by James Wormley, reputedly the wealthiest black in Washington.*

1863	Lincoln announces "Ten Percent Plan" for Reconstruction
1865	Federal government sets up Freedmen's Bureau
	Lee surrenders at Appomattox Court House
	Lincoln is assassinated; Andrew Johnson becomes president
	Johnson issues amnesty proclamation
	States ratify Thirteenth Amendment abolishing slavery
1865–1866	Southern states enact Black Codes
1866	Civil Rights Act passes over Johnson's veto
	Johnson campaigns for his Reconstruction policy
1867	First Reconstruction Act puts former Confederacy under military rule
	Tenure of Office Act protects Senate appointees
1868	House of Representatives impeaches Johnson
	Fourth Reconstruction Act requires a majority of Southern voters to ratify state constitutions
	Senate acquits Johnson
	States ratify Fourteenth Amendment extending rights to freed slaves
	Ulysses S. Grant is elected president
	Ku Klux Klan uses intimidation and force throughout South
1870	States ratify Fifteenth Amendment granting black suffrage
1870–1871	Force (Ku Klux Klan) Act destroys Klan
1872	Liberal Republican party nominates Horace Greeley for president
	Grant is reelected president
1876	Rutherford B. Hayes runs against Samuel Tilden in disputed presidential election
1877	Electoral Commission awards disputed votes to Rutherford B. Hayes, who becomes president
	Hayes agrees to Compromise of 1877

APPENDIX

The Declaration of Independence

The Constitution of the United States of America

Amendments to the Constitution

Supplementary Reading

Present-Day United States

Present-Day World

For additional reference material, including suggested websites, go to www.longmanamericanhistory.com

The Declaration of Independence

In Congress, July 4, 1776

The Unanimous Declaration
of the Thirteen United States of America,

When, in the course of human events, it becomes necessary for one people to dissolve the political bonds which have connected them with another, and to assume, among the powers of the earth, the separate and equal station to which the laws of nature and of nature's God entitle them, a decent respect to the opinions of mankind requires that they should declare the causes which impel them to the separation.

We hold these truths to be self-evident: That all men are created equal; that they are endowed by their Creator with certain unalienable rights; that among these are life, liberty, and the pursuit of happiness; that, to secure these rights, governments are instituted among men, deriving their just powers from the consent of the governed; that whenever any form of government becomes destructive of these ends, it is the right of the people to alter or to abolish it, and to institute new government, laying its foundation on such principles, and organizing its powers in such form, as to them shall seem most likely to effect their safety and happiness. Prudence, indeed, will dictate that governments long established should not be changed for light and transient causes; and accordingly all experience hath shown that mankind are more disposed to suffer, while evils are sufferable, than to right themselves by abolishing the forms to which they are accustomed. But when a long train of abuses and usurpations, pursuing invariably the same object, evinces a design to reduce them under absolute despotism, it is their right, it is their duty, to throw off such government, and to provide new guards for their future security. Such has been the patient sufferance of these colonies; and such is now the necessity which constrains them to alter their former systems of government. The history of the present King of Great Britain is a history of repeated injuries and usurpations, all having in direct object the establishment of an absolute tyranny over these states. To prove this, let facts be submitted to a candid world.

He has refused his assent to laws, the most wholesome and necessary for the public good.

He has forbidden his governors to pass laws of immediate and pressing importance, unless suspended in their operation till his assent should be obtained; and, when so suspended, he has utterly neglected to attend to them.

He has refused to pass other laws for the accommodation of large districts of people, unless those people would relinquish the right of representation in the legislature, a right inestimable to them, and formidable to tyrants only.

He has called together legislative bodies at places unusual, uncomfortable, and distant from the depository of their public records, for the sole purpose of fatiguing them into compliance with his measures.

He has dissolved representative houses repeatedly, for opposing, with manly firmness, his invasions on the rights of the people.

He has refused for a long time, after such dissolutions, to cause others to be elected; whereby the legislative powers, incapable of annihilation, have returned to the people at large for their exercise; the state remaining, in the mean time, exposed to all the dangers of invasions from without and convulsions within.

He has endeavored to prevent the population of these states; for that purpose obstructing the laws for naturalization of foreigners; refusing to pass others to encourage their migration hither, and raising the conditions of new appropriations of lands.

He has obstructed the administration of justice, by refusing his assent to laws for establishing judiciary powers.

He has made judges dependent on his will alone, for the tenure of their offices, and the amount and payment of their salaries.

He has erected a multitude of new offices, and sent hither swarms of officers to harass our people and eat out their substance.

He has kept among us, in times of peace, standing armies, without the consent of our legislatures.

He has affected to render the military independent of, and superior to, the civil power.

He has combined with others to subject us to a jurisdiction foreign to our constitution, and unacknowledged by our laws, giving his assent to their acts of pretended legislation:

For quartering large bodies of armed troops among us;

For protecting them, by a mock trial, from punishment for any murder which they should commit on the inhabitants of these states;

For cutting off our trade with all parts of the world;

For imposing taxes on us without our consent;

For depriving us, in many cases, of the benefits of trial by jury;

For transporting us beyond seas, to be tried for pretended offenses;

For abolishing the free system of English laws in a neighboring province, establishing therein an arbitrary government, and enlarging its boundaries, so as to render it at once an example and fit instrument for introducing the same absolute rule into these colonies;

For taking away our charters, abolishing our most valuable laws, and altering fundamentally the forms of our governments;

For suspending our own legislatures, and declaring themselves invested with power to legislate for us in all cases whatsoever.

He has abdicated government here, by declaring us out of his protection and waging war against us.

He has plundered our seas, ravaged our coasts, burned our towns, and destroyed the lives of our people.

He is at this time transporting large armies of foreign mercenaries to complete the works of death, desolation, and tyranny already begun with circumstances of cruelty and perfidy scarcely paralleled in the most barbarous ages, and totally unworthy the head of a civilized nation.

He has constrained our fellow-citizens, taken captive on the high seas, to bear arms against their country, to become the executioners of their friends and brethren, or to fall themselves by their hands.

He has excited domestic insurrection among us, and has endeavored to bring on the inhabitants of our frontiers the merciless Indian savages, whose known rule of warfare is an undistinguished destruction of all ages, sexes, and conditions.

In every stage of these oppressions we have petitioned for redress in the most humble terms; our repeated petitions have been answered only by repeated injury. A prince, whose character is thus marked by every act which may define a tyrant, is unfit to be the ruler of a free people.

Nor have we been wanting in our attentions to our British brethren. We have warned them, from time to time, of attempts by their legislature to extend an unwarrantable jurisdiction over us. We have reminded them of the circumstances of our emigration and settlement here. We have appealed to their native justice and magnanimity; and we have conjured them, by the ties of our common kindred, to disavow these usurpations, which would inevitably interrupt our connections and correspondence. They, too, have been deaf to the voice of justice and of consanguinity. We must, therefore, acquiesce in the necessity which denounces our separation, and hold them, as we hold the rest of mankind, enemies in war, in peace friends.

We, therefore, the representatives of the United States of America, in General Congress assembled, appealing to the Supreme Judge of the world for the rectitude of our intentions, do, in the name and by the authority of the good people of these colonies, solemnly publish and declare, that these United Colonies are, and of right ought to be, FREE AND INDEPENDENT STATES; that they are absolved from all allegiance to the British crown, and that all political connection between them and the state of Great Britain is, and ought to be, totally dissolved; and that, as free and independent states, they have full power to levy war, conclude peace, contract alliances, establish commerce, and do all other acts and things which independent states may of right do. And for the support of this declaration, with a firm reliance on the protection of Divine Providence, we mutually pledge to each other our lives, our fortunes, and our sacred honor.

JOHN HANCOCK

BUTTON GWINNETT
LYMAN HALL
GEO. WALTON
WM. HOOPER
JOSEPH HEWES
JOHN PENN
EDWARD RUTLEDGE
THOS. HEYWARD, JUNR.
THOMAS LYNCH, JUNR.
ARTHUR MIDDLETON
SAMUEL CHASE
WM. PACA
THOS. STONE
CHARLES CARROLL OF
  CARROLLTON
GEORGE WYTHE
RICHARD HENRY LEE
TH. JEFFERSON
BENJ. HARRISON

THOS. NELSON, JR
FRANCIS LIGHTFOOT LEE
CARTER BRAXTON
ROBT. MORRIS
BENJAMIN RUSH
BENJA. FRANKLIN
JOHN MORTON
GEO. CLYMER
JAS. SMITH
GEO. TAYLOR
JAMES WILSON
GEO. ROSS
CAESAR RODNEY
GEO. READ
THO. M'KEAN
WM. FLOYD
PHIL. LIVINGSTON
FRANS. LEWIS
LEWIS MORRIS

RICHD. STOCKTON
JNO. WITHERSPOON
FRAS. HOPKINSON
JOHN HART
ABRA. CLARK
JOSIAH BARTLETT
WM. WHIPPLE
SAML. ADAMS
JOHN ADAMS
ROBT. TREAT PAINE
ELDBRIDGE GERRY
STEP. HOPKINS
WILLIAM ELLERY
ROGER SHERMAN
SAM'EL HUNTINGTON
WM. WILLIAMS
OLIVER WOLCOTT
MATTHEW THORNTON

The Constitution of the United States of America

PREAMBLE

We the People of the United States, in Order to form a more perfect Union, establish Justice, insure domestic Tranquility, provide for the common defence, promote the general Welfare, and secure the Blessings of Liberty to ourselves and our Posterity, do ordain and establish this Constitution for the United States of America.

ARTICLE 1

Section 1

All legislative Powers herein granted shall be vested in a Congress of the United States, which shall consist of a Senate and House of Representatives.

Section 2

The House of Representatives shall be composed of Members chosen every second Year by the People of the several States, and the Electors in each State shall have the Qualifications requisite for Electors of the most numerous Branch of the State Legislature.

No Person shall be a Representative who shall not have attained to the Age of twenty five Years, and been seven Years a Citizen of the United States, and who shall not, when elected, be an inhabitant of that State in which he shall be chosen.

Representatives and direct Taxes shall be apportioned among the several States which may be included within this Union, according to their respective Numbers, *which shall be determined by adding to the whole Number of free Persons, including those bound to Service for a Term of Years, and excluding Indians not taxed, three fifths of all other Persons.** The actual Enumeration shall be made within three Years after the first Meeting of the Congress of the United States, and within every subsequent Term of ten Years, in such Manner as they shall by Law direct. The Number of Representatives shall not exceed one for every thirty Thousand, but each State shall have at Least one Representative; *and until such enumeration shall be made, the State of New Hampshire shall be entitled to chuse three, Massachusetts eight, Rhode-Island and Providence Plantations one, Connecticut five, New York six, New Jersey four, Pennsylvania eight, Delaware one, Maryland six, Virginia ten, North Carolina five, South Carolina five, and Georgia three.*

When vacancies happen in the Representation from any State, the Executive Authority thereof shall issue Writs of Election to fill such Vacancies.

The House of Representatives shall chuse their Speaker and other Officers; and shall have the sole Power of Impeachment.

Section 3

The Senate of the United States shall be composed of two Senators from each State, *chosen by the Legislature thereof,* for six Years; and each Senator shall have one Vote.

Immediately after they shall be assembled in Consequence of the first Election, they shall be divided as equally as may be into three Classes. The Seats of the Senators of the first Class shall be vacated at the Expiration of the second Year, of the second Class at the Expiration of the fourth Year, and of the third Class at the Expiration of the sixth Year so that one third may be chosen every second Year; and if Vacancies

---

**Passages no longer in effect are printed in italic type.*

happen by Resignation, or otherwise, during the Recess of the Legislature of any state, the Executive thereof may make temporary Appointments until the next Meeting of the Legislature, which shall then fill such Vacancies.

No Person shall be a Senator who shall not have attained to the Age of thirty Years, and been nine Years a Citizen of the United States, and who shall not, when elected, be an Inhabitant of that State for which he shall be chosen.

The Vice President of the United States shall be President of the Senate, but shall have no Vote, unless they be equally divided.

The Senate shall chuse their other Officers, and also a President *pro tempore,* in the Absence of the Vice President, or when he shall exercise the Office of President of the United States.

The Senate shall have the sole Power to try all Impeachments. When sitting for that Purpose, they shall be on Oath or Affirmation. When the President of the United States is tried the Chief Justice shall preside: And no Person shall be convicted without the Concurrence of two thirds of the Members present.

Judgment in Cases of Impeachment shall not extend further than to removal from Office, and disqualification to hold and enjoy any Office of honor, Trust or Profit under the United States: but the Party convicted shall nevertheless be liable and subject to Indictment, Trial, Judgment and Punishment, according to Law.

Section 4

The Times, Places and Manner of holding Elections for Senators and Representatives, shall be prescribed in each State by the Legislature thereof; but the Congress may at any time by Law make or alter such Regulations, except as to the Places of chusing Senators.

The Congress shall assemble at least once in every Year, *and such Meeting shall be on the first Monday in December, unless they shall by Law appoint a different Day.*

Section 5

Each House shall be the Judge of the Elections, Returns and Qualifications of its own Members, and a Majority of each shall constitute a Quorum to do Business; but a smaller Number may adjourn from day to day, and may be authorized to compel the Attendance of absent Members, in such Manner, and under such Penalties as each House may provide.

Each House may determine the Rules of its Proceedings, punish its Members for disorderly Behaviour, and, with the Concurrence of two thirds, expel a Member.

Each House shall keep a Journal of its Proceedings, and from time to time publish the same, excepting such Parts as may in their Judgment require Secrecy; and the Yeas and Nays of the Members of either House on any question shall, at the Desire of one fifth of those Present, be entered on the Journal.

Neither House, during the Session of Congress, shall, without the Consent of the other, adjourn for more than three days, nor to any other Place than that in which the two Houses shall be sitting.

Section 6

The Senators and Representatives shall receive a Compensation for their Services, to be ascertained by Law, and paid out of the Treasury of the United States. They shall in all Cases, except Treason, Felony and Breach of the Peace, be privileged from Arrest during their Attendance at the Session of their respective Houses, and in going to and returning from the same; and for any Speech or Debate in either House, they shall not be questioned in any other Place.

No Senator or Representative shall, during the Time for which he was elected, be appointed to any civil Office under the Authority of the United States, which shall have been created, or the Emoluments whereof shall have been encreased during such time, and no Person holding any Office under the United States, shall be a Member of either House during his Continuance in Office.

Section 7

All Bills for raising Revenue shall originate in the House of Representatives; but the Senate may propose or concur with Amendments as on other Bills.

Every Bill which shall have passed the House of Representatives and the Senate, shall, before it become a Law, be presented to the President of the United States; If he approve he shall sign it, but if not he shall return it, with his Objections to the House in which it shall have originated, who shall enter the Objections at large on their Journal, and proceed to reconsider it. If after such Reconsideration two thirds of that House shall agree to pass the Bill, it shall be sent, together with the Objections, to the other House, by which it shall likewise be reconsidered, and if approved by two thirds of that House, it shall become a Law. But in all such Cases the Votes of both Houses shall be determined by Yeas and Nays, and the Names of the Persons voting for and against the Bill shall be entered on the Journal of each House respectively. If any Bill shall not be returned by the President within ten Days (Sundays excepted) after it shall have been presented to him, the Same shall be a Law, in like Manner as if he had signed it, unless the Congress by their Adjournment prevent its Return, in which Case it shall not be a Law.

Every Order, Resolution, or Vote to which the Concurrence of the Senate and House of Representatives may be necessary (except on a question of Adjournment) shall be presented to the President of the United States; and before the Same shall take Effect, shall be approved by him, or being disapproved by him, shall be repassed by two thirds of the Senate and House of Representatives, according to the Rules and Limitations prescribed in the Case of a Bill.

Section 8

The Congress shall have Power To lay and collect Taxes, Duties, Imposts and Excises, to pay the Debts and provide for the common Defence and general Welfare of the United States; but all Duties, Imposts and Excises shall be uniform throughout the United States;

To borrow Money on the credit of the United States;

To regulate Commerce with foreign Nations, and among the several States, and with the Indian Tribes;

To establish an uniform Rule of Naturalization, and uniform Laws on the subject of Bankruptcies throughout the United States;

To coin Money, regulate the Value thereof, and of foreign Coin, and fix the Standard of Weights and Measures;

To provide for the Punishment of counterfeiting the Securities and current Coin of the United States;

To establish Post Offices and post Roads;

To promote the Progress of Science and useful Arts, by securing for limited Times to Authors and Inventors the exclusive Right to their respective Writings and Discoveries;

To constitute Tribunals inferior to the supreme Court;

To define and punish Piracies and Felonies committed on the high Seas, and Offences against the Law of Nations;

To declare War, grant Letters of Marque and Reprisal, and make Rules concerning Captures on Land and Water;

To raise and support Armies, but no Appropriation of Money to that Use shall be for a longer Term than two Years;

To provide and maintain a Navy;

To make Rules for the Government and Regulation of the land and naval Forces;

To provide for calling forth the Militia to execute the Laws of the Union, suppress Insurrections and repel Invasions;

To provide for organizing, arming, and disciplining, the Militia, and for governing such Part of them as may be employed in the Service of the United States, reserving to the States respectively, the Appointment of the Officers, and the Authority of training the Militia according to the discipline prescribed by Congress;

To exercise exclusive Legislation in all Cases whatsoever, over such District (not exceeding ten Miles square) as may, by Cession of particular States, and the Acceptance of Congress, become the Seat of the Government of the United States, and to exercise like Authority over all Places purchased by the Consent of the Legislature of the State in which the Same shall be, for the Erection of Forts, Magazines, Arsenals, dock-Yards, and other needful Buildings;—And

To make all Laws which shall be necessary and proper for carrying into Execution the foregoing Powers, and all other Powers vested by this Constitution in the Government of the United States, or in any Department or Officer thereof.

Section 9

The Migration or Importation of such Persons as any of the States now existing shall think proper to admit, shall not be prohibited by the Congress prior to the Year one thousand eight hundred and eight, but a Tax or duty may be imposed on such Importation, not exceeding ten dollars for each Person.

The Privilege of the Writ of Habeas Corpus shall not be suspended, unless when in Cases of Rebellion or Invasion the public Safety may require it.

No Bill of Attainder or ex post facto Law shall be passed.

No Capitation, or other direct, Tax shall be laid, unless in Proportion to the Census or Enumeration herein before directed to be taken.

No Tax or Duty shall be laid on Articles exported from any State.

No Preference shall be given by any Regulation of Commerce or Revenue to the Ports of one State over those of another: nor shall Vessels bound to, or from, one State, be obliged to enter, clear, or pay Duties in another.

No Money shall be drawn from the Treasury, but in Consequence of Appropriations made by Law; and a regular Statement and Account of the Receipts and Expenditures of all public Money shall be published from time to time.

No Title of Nobility shall be granted by the United States: And no Person holding any Office of Profit or Trust under them, shall, without the Consent of the Congress, accept of any present, Emolument, Office, or Title, of any kind whatever, from any King, Prince, or foreign State.

Section 10

No State shall enter into any Treaty, Alliance, or Confederation; grant Letters of Marque and Reprisal; coin Money; emit Bills of Credit; make any Thing but gold and silver Coin a Tender in Payment of Debts; pass any Bill of Attainder, ex post facto Law, or Law impairing the obligation of Contracts, or grant any Title of Nobility.

No State shall, without the Consent of the Congress, lay any Imposts or Duties on Imports or Exports, except what may be absolutely necessary for executing its inspection Laws: and the net Produce of all Duties and Imposts, laid by any State on Imports or Exports, shall be for the Use of the Treasury of the United States; and all such Laws shall be subject to the Revision and Controul of the Congress.

No State shall, without the Consent of Congress, lay any Duty of Tonnage, keep Troops, or Ships of War in time of Peace, enter into any Agreement or Compact with another State, or with a foreign Power, or engage in War, unless actually invaded, or in such imminent Danger as will not admit of delay.

ARTICLE II

Section 1

The executive Power shall be vested in a President of the United States of America. He shall hold his Office during the Term of four Years, and, together with the Vice President, chosen for the same Term, be elected, as follows:

Each State shall appoint, in such Manner as the Legislature thereof may direct, a Number of Electors, equal to the whole Number of Senators and Representatives to which the State may be entitled in the Congress: but no Senator or Representative, or Person holding an Office of Trust or Profit under the United States, shall be appointed an Elector.

The Electors shall meet in their respective States, and vote by Ballot for two Persons, of whom one at least shall not be an Inhabitant of the same State with themselves. And they shall make a List of all the

Persons voted for, and of the Number of Votes for each; which List they shall sign and certify, and trans-mit sealed to the Seat of the Government of the United States, directed to the President of the Senate. The President of the Senate shall, in the Presence of the Senate and House of Representatives, open all the Certificates, and the Votes shall then be counted. The Person having the greatest Number of Votes shall be the President, if such Number be a Majority of the whole number of Electors appointed; and if there be more than one who have such Majority, and have an equal Number of Votes, then the House of Representatives shall immediately chuse by Ballot one of them for President; and if no Person have a Majority, then from the five highest on the List the said House shall in like Manner chuse the President. But in chusing the President, the Votes shall be taken by States, the Representation from each State hav-ing one Vote; A quorum for this Purpose shall consist of a Member or Members from two thirds of the States, and a Majority of all the States shall be necessary to a Choice. In every Case, after the Choice of the President, the Person having the greatest Number of Votes of the Electors shall be the Vice President. But if there should remain two or more who have equal Votes, the Senate shall chuse from them by Ballot the Vice President.

The Congress may determine the time of chusing the Electors, and the Day on which they shall give their Votes; which Day shall be the same throughout the United States.

No person except a natural born Citizen, *or a Citizen of the United States, at the time of the Adoption of this Constitution,* shall be eligible to the Office of President; neither shall any Person be eligible to that Office who shall not have attained to the Age of thirty five Years, and been fourteen Years a Resident within the United States.

In Case of the Removal of the President from Office, or of his Death, Resignation, or Inability to discharge the Powers and Duties of the said Office, the Same shall devolve on the Vice President, and the Congress may by Law provide for the Case of Removal, Death, Resignation or Inability, both of the President and Vice President, declaring what Officer shall then act as President, and such Officer shall act accordingly, until the Disability be removed, or a President shall be elected.

The President shall, at stated Times, receive for his Services, a Compensation, which shall neither be encreased nor diminished during the Period for which he shall have been elected, and he shall not receive within that period any other Emolument from the United States, or any of them.

Before he enter on the Execution of his Office, he shall take the following Oath or Affirmation:— "I do solemnly swear (or affirm) that I will faithfully execute the Office of President of the United States, and will to the best of my Ability, preserve, protect and defend the Constitution of the United States."

Section 2

The President shall be Commander in Chief of the Army and Navy of the United States, and of the Militia of the several States, when called into the actual Service of the United States; he may require the Opinion, in writing, of the principal Officer in each of the executive Departments, upon any Subject relating to the Duties of their respective Offices, and he shall have Power to grant Reprieves and Pardons for Offences against the United States, except in Cases of Impeachment.

He shall have Power, by and with the Advice and Consent of the Senate, to make Treaties, pro-vided two thirds of the Senators present concur; and he shall nominate, and by and with the Advice and Consent of the Senate, shall appoint Ambassadors, other public Ministers and Consuls, Judges of the supreme Court, and all other Officers of the United States, whose Appointments are not herein otherwise provided for, and which shall be established by Law: but the Congress may by Law vest the Appointment of such inferior Officers, as they think proper in the President alone, in the Courts of Law, or in the Heads of Departments.

The President shall have Power to fill up all Vacancies that may happen during the Recess of the Senate, by granting Commissions which shall expire at the End of their next Session.

Section 3

He shall from time to time give to the Congress Information of the State of the Union, and rec-ommend to their Consideration such Measures as he shall judge necessary and expedient; he may, on extraordinary Occasions, convene both Houses, or either of them, and in Case of disagreement between them, with Respect to the Time of Adjournment, he may adjourn them to such Time as he shall think proper; he shall receive Ambassadors and other public Ministers; he shall take Care that the Laws be faithfully executed, and shall Commission all the officers of the United States.

Section 4

The President, Vice President and all civil Officers of the United States, shall be removed from Office on Impeachment for, and Conviction of, Treason, Bribery or other high Crimes and Misdemeanors.

ARTICLE III

Section 1

The judicial Power of the United States, shall be vested in one supreme Court, and in such inferior Courts as the Congress may from time to time ordain and establish. The Judges, both of the supreme and inferior Courts, shall hold their offices during good Behaviour, and shall, at stated Times, receive for their Services, a Compensation, which shall not be diminished during their Continuance in Office.

Section 2

The judicial Power shall extend to all Cases, in Law and Equity, arising under this Constitution, the Laws of the United States, and Treaties made, or which shall be made, under their Authority;—to all Cases affecting Ambassadors, other public Ministers and Consuls;—to all Cases of admiralty and maritime Jurisdiction;—to Controversies to which the United States shall be a Party;—to Controversies between two or more States;—*between a State and Citizens of another State;*—between Citizens of different States;—between Citizens of the same State claiming Lands under Grants of different States, and between a State, or the Citizens thereof, and foreign States, Citizens or Subjects.

In all Cases affecting Ambassadors, other public Ministers and Consuls, and those in which a State shall be Party, the supreme Court shall have original Jurisdiction. In all the other Cases before mentioned, the supreme Court shall have appellate Jurisdiction, both as to Law and Fact, with such Exceptions, and under such Regulations as the Congress shall make.

The Trial of all Crimes, except in Cases of Impeachment, shall be by Jury; and such Trial shall be held in the State where the said Crimes shall have been committed, but when not committed within any State, the Trial shall be at such Place or Places as the Congress may by Law have directed.

Section 3

Treason against the United States, shall consist only in levying War against them, or in adhering to their Enemies, giving them Aid and Comfort. No person shall be convicted of Treason unless on the Testimony of two Witnesses to the same overt Act, or on Confession in open Court.

The Congress shall have Power to declare the Punishment of Treason, but no Attainder of Treason shall work Corruption of Blood, or Forfeiture except during the Life of the Person attainted.

ARTICLE IV

Section 1

Full Faith and Credit shall be given in each State to the public Acts, Records, and judicial Proceedings of every other State. And the Congress may by general Laws prescribe the Manner in which such Acts, Records and Proceedings shall be proved, and the Effect thereof.

Section 2

The Citizens of each State shall be entitled to all Privileges and Immunities of Citizens in the several States.

A Person charged in any State with Treason, Felony, or other Crime, who shall flee from Justice, and be found in another State, shall on Demand of the executive Authority of the State from which he fled, be delivered up, to be removed to the State having Jurisdiction of the Crime.

No Person held to Service or Labour in one State, under the Laws thereof, escaping into another, shall, in Consequence of any Law or Regulation therein, be discharged from such Service or Labour, but shall be delivered up on Claim of the Party to whom such Service or Labour may be due.

Section 3

New States may be admitted by the Congress into this Union; but no new State shall be formed or erected within the Jurisdiction of any other State; nor any State be formed by the Junction of two or more States, or Parts of States, without the Consent of the Legislatures of the States concerned as well as of the Congress.

The Congress shall have Power to dispose of and make all needful Rules and Regulations respecting the Territory or other Property belonging to the United States; and nothing in this Constitution shall be so construed as to Prejudice any Claims of the United States, or of any particular States.

Section 4

The United States shall guarantee to every State in this Union a Republican Form of Government, and shall protect each of them against Invasion; and on Application of the Legislature, or of the Executive (when the Legislature cannot be convened) against domestic violence.

ARTICLE V

The Congress, whenever two thirds of both Houses shall deem it necessary, shall propose Amendments to this Constitution, or, on the Application of the Legislatures of two thirds of the several States, shall call a Convention for proposing Amendments, which, in either Case, shall be valid to all Intents and Purposes, as Part of this Constitution, when ratified by the Legislatures of three fourths of the several States, or by Conventions in three fourths thereof, as the one or the other Mode of Ratification may be proposed by the Congress; Provided *that no Amendment which may be made prior to the Year One thousand eight hundred and eight shall in any Manner affect the first and fourth Clauses in the Ninth Section of the first Article;* and that no State, without its Consent, shall be deprived of its equal Suffrage in the Senate.

ARTICLE VI

All Debts contracted and Engagements entered into, before the Adoption of this Constitution, shall be as valid against the United States under this Constitution, as under the Confederation.

This Constitution, and Laws of the United States which shall be made in Pursuance thereof; and all Treaties made, or which shall be made, under the Authority of the United States, shall be the supreme Law of the Land; and the Judges in every State shall be bound thereby, any Thing in the Constitution or Laws of any State to the Contrary notwithstanding.

The Senators and Representatives before mentioned, and the Members of the several State Legislatures, and all executive and Judicial Officers, both of the United States and of the several States, shall be bound by Oath or Affirmation, to support this Constitution; but no religious Test shall ever be required as a Qualification to any Office of public Trust under the United States.

ARTICLE VII

The Ratification of the Conventions of nine States, shall be sufficient for the Establishment of this Constitution between the States so ratifying the Same.

Done in Convention by the Unanimous Consent of the States present the Seventeenth Day of September in the Year of our Lord one thousand seven hundred and Eighty seven and of the Independence of the United States of America the Twelfth.[*] IN WITNESS whereof We have hereunto subscribed our Names,

GEORGE WASHINGTON
President and Deputy from Virginia

Delaware
GEORGE READ
GUNNING BEDFORD, JR.
JOHN DICKINSON
RICHARD BASSETT
JACOB BROOM

Maryland
JAMES MCHENRY
DANIEL OF ST. THOMAS JENIFER
DANIEL CARROLL

Virginia
JOHN BLAIR
JAMES MADISON, JR.

North Carolina
WILLIAM BLOUNT
RICHARD DOBBS SPRAIGHT
HUGH WILLIAMSON

South Carolina
JOHN RUTLEDGE
CHARLES COTESWORTH PINCKNEY
CHARLES PINCKNEY
PIERCE BUTLER

Georgia
WILLIAM FEW
ABRAHAM BALDWIN

New Hampshire
JOHN LANGDON
NICHOLAS GILMAN

Massachusetts
NATHANIEL GORHAM
RUFUS KING

Connecticut
WILLIAM SAMUEL JOHNSON
ROGER SHERMAN

New York
ALEXANDER HAMILTON

New Jersey
WILLIAM LIVINGSTON
DAVID BREARLEY
WILLIAM PATERSON
JONATHAN DAYTON

Pennsylvania
BENJAMIN FRANKLIN
THOMAS MIFFLIN
ROBERT MORRIS
GEORGE CLYMER
THOMAS FITZSIMONS
JARED INGERSOLL
JAMES WILSON
GOUVERNEUR MORRIS

---

[*]*The Constitution was submitted on September 17, 1787, by the Constitutional Convention, was ratified by the Convention of several states at various dates up to May 29, 1790, and became effective on March 4, 1789.*

Amendments to the Constitution

AMENDMENT I

Congress shall make no law respecting an establishment of religion, or prohibiting the free exercise thereof; or abridging the freedom of speech, or of the press; or the right of the people peaceably to assemble, and to petition the Government for a redress of grievances.

AMENDMENT II

A well regulated Militia being necessary to the security of a free State, the right of the people to keep and bear Arms, shall not be infringed.

AMENDMENT III

No Soldier shall, in time of peace be quartered in any house, without the consent of the Owner, nor in time of war, but in a manner to be prescribed by law.

AMENDMENT IV

The right of the people to be secure in their persons, houses, papers, and effects, against unreasonable searches and seizures, shall not be violated, and no Warrants shall issue, but upon probable cause, supported by Oath or affirmation, and particularly describing the place to be searched, and the persons or things to be seized.

AMENDMENT V

No person shall be held to answer for a capital, or otherwise infamous crime, unless on a presentment or indictment of a Grand Jury, except in cases arising in the land or naval forces, or in the Militia, when in actual service in time of War or public danger; nor shall any person be subject for the same offense to be twice put in jeopardy of life or limb; nor shall be compelled in any criminal case to be a witness against himself, nor be deprived of life, liberty, or property, without due process of law; nor shall private property be taken for public use, without just compensation.

AMENDMENT VI

In all criminal prosecutions, the accused shall enjoy the right to a speedy and public trial, by an impartial jury of the State and district wherein the crime shall have been committed, which district shall have been previously ascertained by law, and to be informed of the nature and cause of the accusation; to be confronted with the witnesses against him; to have compulsory process for obtaining witnesses in his favor, and to have the Assistance of Counsel for his defence.

AMENDMENT VII

In Suits at common law, where the value in controversy shall exceed twenty dollars, the right of trial by jury shall be preserved, and no fact tried by a jury, shall be otherwise re-examined in any Court of the United States, than according to the rules of the common law.

AMENDMENT VIII

Excessive bail shall not be required, nor excessive fines imposed, nor cruel and unusual punishments inflicted.

Amendment IX

The enumeration in the Constitution, of certain rights, shall not be construed to deny or disparage others retained by the people.

Amendment X*

The powers not delegated to the United States by the Constitution, nor prohibited by it to the States, are reserved to the States respectively, or to the people.

Amendment XI
[Adopted 1798]

The Judicial power of the United States shall not be construed to extend to any suit in law or equity, commenced or prosecuted against one of the United States by Citizens of another State, or by Citizens or Subjects of any Foreign State.

Amendment XII
[Adopted 1804]

The Electors shall meet in their respective states, and vote by ballot for President and Vice President, one of whom, at least, shall not be an inhabitant of the same state with themselves; they shall name in their ballots the person voted for as President, and in distinct ballots the person voted for as Vice President, and they shall make distinct lists of all persons voted for as President, and of all persons voted for as Vice President, and of the number of votes for each, which lists they shall sign and certify, and transmit sealed to the seat of the government of the United States, directed to the President of the Senate;—The President of the Senate shall, in the presence of the Senate and House of Representatives, open all the certificates and the votes shall then be counted;—The person having the greatest number of votes for President, shall be the President, if such number be a majority of the whole number of Electors appointed; and if no person have such majority, then from the persons having the highest numbers not exceeding three on the list of those voted for as President, the House of Representatives shall choose immediately, by ballot, the President. But in choosing the President, the votes shall be taken by states, the representation from each state having one vote; a quorum for this purpose shall consist of a member or members from two-thirds of the states, and a majority of all the states shall be necessary to a choice. And if the House of Representatives shall not choose a President whenever the right of choice shall devolve upon them, before *the fourth day of March* next following, then the Vice President shall act as President, as in the case of the death or other constitutional disability of the President.—The person having the greatest number of votes as Vice President, shall be the Vice President, if such number be a majority of the whole number of Electors appointed, and if no person have a majority, then from the two highest numbers on the list, the Senate shall choose the Vice President; a quorum for the purpose shall consist of two-thirds of the whole number of Senators, and a majority of the whole number shall be necessary to a choice. But no person constitutionally ineligible to the office of President shall be eligible to that of Vice President of the United States.

Amendment XIII
[Adopted 1865]

Section 1

Neither slavery nor involuntary servitude, except as a punishment for crime whereof the party shall have been duly convicted, shall exist within the United States, or any place subject to their jurisdiction.

---

*The first ten amendments (the Bill of Rights) were ratified, and their adoption was certified, on December 15, 1791.

Section 2

Congress shall have power to enforce this article by appropriate legislation.

AMENDMENT XIV
[ADOPTED 1868]

Section 1

All persons born or naturalized in the United States, and subject to the jurisdiction thereof, are citizens of the United States and of the State wherein they reside. No State shall make or enforce any law which shall abridge the privileges or immunities of citizens of the United States; nor shall any State deprive any person of life, liberty, or property, without due process of law; nor deny to any person within its jurisdiction the equal protection of the laws.

Section 2

Representatives shall be apportioned among the several States according to their respective numbers, counting the whole number of persons in each State, excluding Indians not taxed. But when the right to vote at any election for the choice of electors for President and Vice President of the United States, Representatives in Congress, the Executive and Judicial officers of a State, or the members of the Legislature thereof, is denied to any of the male inhabitants of such State, being twenty-one years of age, and citizens of the United States, or in any way abridged, except for participation in rebellion, or other crime, the basis of representation therein shall be reduced in the proportion which the number of such male citizens shall bear to the whole number of male citizens twenty-one years of age in such State.

Section 3

No person shall be a Senator or Representative in Congress, or elector of President and Vice President, or hold any office, civil or military, under the United States, or under any State, who, having previously taken an oath, as a member of Congress, or as an officer of the United States, or as a member of any State legislature, or as an executive or judicial officer of any State, to support the Constitution of the United States, shall have engaged in insurrection or rebellion against the same, or given aid or comfort to the enemies thereof. But Congress may by a vote of two-thirds of each House, remove such disability.

Section 4

The validity of the public debt of the United States, authorized by law, including debts incurred for payment of pensions and bounties for services in suppressing insurrection or rebellion, shall not be questioned. But neither the United States nor any State shall assume or pay any debt or obligation incurred in aid of insurrection or rebellion against the United States, or any claim for the loss or emancipation of any slave; but all such debts, obligations and claims shall be held illegal and void.

Section 5

The Congress shall have power to enforce, by appropriate legislation, the provisions of this article.

AMENDMENT XV
[ADOPTED 1870]

Section 1

The right of citizens of the United States to vote shall not be denied or abridged by the United States or by any State on account of race, color, or previous condition of servitude.

Section 2

The Congress shall have power to enforce this article by appropriate legislation.

Amendment XVI
[Adopted 1913]

The Congress shall have power to lay and collect taxes on incomes, from whatever source derived, without apportionment among the several States, and without regard to any census or enumeration.

Amendment XVII
[Adopted 1913]

The Senate of the United States shall be composed of two Senators from each State, elected by the people thereof, for six years; and each Senator shall have one vote. The electors in each State shall have the qualifications requisite for electors of the most numerous branch of the State legislatures.

When vacancies happen in the representation of any State in the Senate, the executive authority of such State shall issue writs of election to fill such vacancies: *Provided*, That the legislature of any State may empower the executive thereof to make temporary appointments until the people fill the vacancies by election as the legislature may direct.

This amendment shall not be so construed as to affect the election or term of any Senator chosen before it becomes valid as part of the Constitution.

Amendment XVIII
[Adopted 1919, Repealed 1933]

Section 1

After one year from the ratification of this article the manufacture, sale, or transportation of intoxicating liquors within, the importation thereof into, or the exportation thereof from the United States and all territory subject to the jurisdiction thereof for beverage purposes is hereby prohibited.

Section 2

The Congress and the several States shall have concurrent power to enforce this article by appropriate legislation.

Section 3

This article shall be inoperative unless it shall have been ratified as an amendment to the Constitution by the legislatures of the several States, as provided in the Constitution, within seven years from the date of the submission hereof to the States by the Congress.

Amendment XIX
[Adopted 1920]

The right of citizens of the United States to vote shall not be denied or abridged by the United States or by any State on account of sex.

Congress shall have power to enforce this article by appropriate legislation.

Amendment XX
[Adopted 1933]

Section 1

The terms of the President and Vice President shall end at noon on the 20th day of January, and the terms of Senators and Representatives at noon on the 3d day of January, of the years in which such terms would have ended if this article had not been ratified and the terms of their successors shall then begin.

Section 2

The Congress shall assemble at least once in every year, and such meeting shall begin at noon on the 3d day of January, unless they shall by law appoint a different day.

Section 3

If, at the time fixed for the beginning of the term of the President, the President elect shall have died, the Vice President elect shall become President. If a President shall not have been chosen before the time fixed for the beginning of his term, or if the President elect shall have failed to qualify, then the Vice President elect shall act as President until a President shall have qualified; and the Congress may by law provide for the case wherein neither a President elect nor a Vice President elect shall have qualified, declaring who shall then act as President, or the manner in which one who is to act shall be selected, and such person shall act accordingly until a President or Vice President shall have qualified.

Section 4

The Congress may by law provide for the case of the death of any of the persons from whom the House of Representatives may choose a President whenever the right of choice shall have devolved upon them, and for the case of the death of any of the persons from whom the Senate may choose a Vice President whenever the right of choice shall have devolved upon them.

Section 5

Sections 1 and 2 shall take effect on the 15th day of October following the ratification of this article.

Section 6

This article shall be inoperative unless it shall have been ratified as an amendment to the Constitution by the legislatures of three fourths of the several States within seven years from the date of its submission.

AMENDMENT XXI
[ADOPTED 1933]

Section 1

The eighteenth article of amendment to the Constitution of the United States is hereby repealed.

Section 2

The transportation or importation into any State, Territory, or possession of the United States for delivery or use therein of intoxicating liquors in violation of the laws thereof, is hereby prohibited.

Section 3

This article shall be inoperative unless it shall have been ratified as an amendment to the Constitution by conventions in the several States, as provided in the Constitution, within seven years from the date of the submission hereof to the States by the Congress.

AMENDMENT XXII
[ADOPTED 1951]

Section 1

No person shall be elected to the office of the President more than twice, and no person who has held the office of President, or acted as President, for more than two years of a term to which some other person was elected President shall be elected to the office of the President more than once. But this Article shall not apply to any person holding the office of President when this Article was proposed by the Congress, and shall not prevent any person who may be holding the office of President, or acting as President, during the term within which this Article becomes operative from holding the office of President or acting as President during the remainder of such term.

Section 2

This article shall be inoperative unless it shall have been ratified as an amendment to the Constitution by the legislatures of three-fourths of the several States within seven years from the date of its submission to the States by the Congress.

Amendment XXIII
[Adopted 1961]

Section 1

The District constituting the seat of Government of the United States shall appoint in such manner as the Congress shall direct:

A number of electors of President and Vice President equal to the whole number of Senators and Representatives in Congress to which the District would be entitled if it were a State, but in no event more than the least populous State; they shall be in addition to those appointed by the States, but they shall be considered, for the purposes of the election of President and Vice President, to be electors appointed by a State; and they shall meet in the District and perform such duties as provided by the twelfth article of amendment.

Section 2

The Congress shall have power to enforce this article by appropriate legislation.

Amendment XXIV
[Adopted 1964]

Section 1

The right of citizens of the United States to vote in any primary or other election for President or Vice President, for electors for President or Vice President, or for Senator or Representative in Congress, shall not be denied or abridged by the United States or any state by reason of failure to pay any poll tax or other tax.

Section 2

The Congress shall have the power to enforce this article by appropriate legislation.

Amendment XXV
[Adopted 1967]

Section 1

In case of the removal of the President from office or his death or resignation, the Vice President shall become President.

Section 2

Whenever there is a vacancy in the office of the Vice President, the President shall nominate a Vice President who shall take the office upon confirmation by a majority vote of both houses of Congress.

Section 3

Whenever the President transmits to the President pro tempore of the Senate and the Speaker of the House of Representatives his written declaration that he is unable to discharge the powers and duties of his office, and until he transmits to them a written declaration to the contrary, such powers and duties shall be discharged by the Vice President as Acting President.

Section 4

Whenever the Vice President and a majority of either the principal officers of the executive depart-ments or of such other body as Congress may by law provide, transmit to the President pro tempore of the Senate and the Speaker of the House of Representatives their written declaration that the President is unable to discharge the powers and duties of his office, the Vice President shall immedi-ately assume the powers and duties of the office as Acting President.

Thereafter, when the President transmits to the President pro tempore of the Senate and the Speaker of the House of Representatives his written declaration that no inability exists, he shall re-sume the powers and duties of his office unless the Vice President and a majority of either the prin-cipal officers of the executive department or of such other body as Congress may by law provide, transmit within four days to the President pro tempore of the Senate and the Speaker of the House of Representatives their written declaration that the President is unable to discharge the powers and duties of his office. Thereupon Congress shall decide the issue, assembling within 48 hours for that purpose if not in session. If the Congress, within 21 days after receipt of the latter written declaration, or, if Congress is not in session, within 21 days after Congress is required to assemble, determines by two-thirds vote of both houses that the President is unable to discharge the powers and duties of his office, the Vice President shall continue to discharge the same as Acting President; otherwise, the President shall resume the powers and duties of his office.

AMENDMENT XXVI
[ADOPTED 1971]

Section 1

The right of citizens of the United States, who are 18 years of age or older, to vote shall not be denied or abridged by the United States or any state on account of age.

Section 2

The Congress shall have the power to enforce this article by appropriate legislation.

AMENDMENT XXVII
[ADOPTED 1992]

No law, varying the compensation for the services of the Senators and Representatives shall take ef-fect, until an election of Representatives shall have intervened.

Supplementary Reading

PROLOGUE BEGINNINGS

During the 1990s the prehistoric era in North America has witnessed an explosion of interest, especially among archaeologists. A global perspective, focusing on geography as a causal force, is outlined in Jared Diamond, *Guns, Germs, and Steel* (1997). Another readable summary is Charles C. Mann, *1491* (2006). David Hurst Thomas, *Exploring Native North America* (2000), provides detailed analyses of representative archaeological sites.

A good survey of the first peoples of North America is David J. Meltzer, *Search for the First Americans* (1993). The "overkill hypothesis" is developed in Paul Martin and Richard Klein, eds., *Quaternary Extinctions* (1984). The best survey on the southwestern peoples is Linda S. Cordell, *Prehistory of the Southwest* (1997). See also J. J. Brody, *The Anasazi* (1990), David Roberts, *In Search of the Old Ones: Exploring the Anasazi World of the Southwest* (1995), R. Gwinn Vivian, *The Chacoan Prehistory of the San Juan Basin* (1990), John P. Andrews and Todd W. Bostwick, *Desert Farmers at the River's Edge: The Hohokam and Pueblo Grande* (1997), and, on early agriculture, R. G. Matson, *The Origins of Southwestern Agriculture* (1991). For a study of Hopewell peoples, see Bruce D. Smith, *Rivers of Change* (1992).

On the Mississippian societies, see Thomas E. Emerson, *Cahokia and the Archaeology of Power* (1997), Thomas E. Emerson and R. Barry Lewis, eds., *Cahokia and the Hinterlands: Middle Mississippian Cultures of the Midwest* (1991), Biloine W. Young and Robert Fowler, *Cahokia, The Great Native American Metropolis* (2000), Timothy Pauketat, *The Ascent of Chiefs: Cahokia and Mississippian Politics in Native North America* (1994), and Robert A. Birmingham and Leslie Eisenberg, *Indian Mounds of Wisconsin* (2000). For early peoples elsewhere, see Vance T. Holliday, *Paleoindian Geoarchaeology of the Southern High Plains* (1997) and Ruth Kirk and Richard D. Daugherty, *Hunters of the Whale* (1974), for the Makah of the Northwest.

For an overview of political structures, see Robert D. Drennan, *Chiefdoms in the Americas* (1987). That warfare was a product of gender tensions is explored in Bruce G. Trigger, *Natives and Newcomers* (1985). The contention that the early peoples of North America lived in perfect harmony with nature is rebutted in Shepard Krech, *The Ecological Indian* (1999). Another common assumption, based on Native American folklore, of the essentially peaceful character of Southwestern peoples has been challenged by recent studies such as Glen E. Rice and Steven A. Leblanc, eds., *Deadly Landscapes: Case Studies in Prehistoric Southwestern Warfare* (2001), and Tim D. White, *Prehistoric Cannibalism at Mancos* (1992). In *Eve's Seed: Biology, the Sexes and the Course of History* (2001), Robert S. McElvaine argues that men enshrined raids and warfare in response to women's increasingly important economic role in farming activities.

CHAPTER 1 ALIEN ENCOUNTERS: EUROPE IN THE AMERICAS

For a study of Columbus, see Miles Davidson, *Columbus Then and Now* (1997). David Stannard, *American Holocaust* (1992), and Kirkpatrick Sale, *The Conquest of Paradise* (1990), are highly critical of Columbus. The history of Spanish colonization in the Southwest is treated in David J. Weber, *The Spanish Frontier in North America* (1992) and, in the Southeast, in Paul E. Hoffman, *A New Andalucia and a Way to the Orient* (1991) and *Florida's Frontiers* (2002). Ned Blackhawk, *Violence over the Land* (2006), summarizes recent research on the cycle of violence attending colonization and slave raiding in the Southwest. For an imaginative attempt to reconstruct the Native American response, see Ramon Guitierrez, *When Jesus Came, The Corn Mothers Went Away* (1991).

Accounts of the English background of colonization can be found in Nicholas Canny, ed., *The Oxford History of the British Empire: The Origins of Empire* (1998). On French colonization, see William J. Eccles, *The French in North America, 1500–1765* (1998), Carl J. Ekberg, *French Roots in the Illinois Country* (1998), and Carole Blackburn, *Harvest of Souls* (2000), which focuses on the Jesuit Missionaries.

Contemporary scholarship on Indian-colonist relations focuses on their interactions. Important studies in that vein include Richard White, *Indians, Empires and Republics in the Great Lakes Region, 1650–1815* (1991), James Merrell, *Into the American Woods: Negotiators on the Pennsylvania Frontier* (1999), Jill Lepore, *Name of War: King Philip's War and the Origins of American Identity* (1999), and Karen Kupperman, *Indians and English: Facing Off in Early America* (2000).

The impact of the Europeans is discussed in the Debating the Past (p. 26). See also Alfred W. Crosby, *Ecological Imperialism: The Biological Expansion of Europe, 900–1900* (1993) and, though it deals with a later period, Robert Boyd, *The Coming of the Spirit of Pestilence: Introduced Infectious Diseases and Population Decline among Northwest Coast Indians* (1999). Joyce E. Chaplin, *Subject Matter: Technology, the Body, and Science on the Anglo-American Frontier, 1500–1676* (2001), argues that Europeans did not assume that they were racially superior until they saw how readily native peoples died of diseases.

For a general study of American slave trade, see David Eltis, *The Rise of African Slavery in the Americas* (2000). General surveys of slavery include Ira Berlin, *Many Thousands Gone* (1998), and Peter Kolchin, *American Slavery, 1619–1877* (1993).

On Virginia, see David H. Fischer and James C. Kelly, *Bound Away: Virginia and the Westward Movement* (2000), and Edmund S. Morgan, *American Slavery, American Freedom* (1975). Jack P. Greene, *Pursuits of Happiness* (1988), argues for the centrality of the Chesapeake in the formation of American identity. On Roanoke, see Ivor Noel Hume, *The Virginia Adventure* (1994). See also Everett Emerson, *Captain John Smith* (1993). For Maryland, consult Gloria T. Main, *Tobacco Colony* (1982), and A. C. Land, *Colonial Maryland* (1981); for Carolina, see Roger Ekirch, *Poor Carolina* (1981).

For the middle colonies, see Michael Kammen, *Colonial New York* (1975) and Donna Merwick, *Possessing Albany, 1630–1710: The Dutch and English Experiences* (1990). In addition to Merrell, see Mary Geiter, *William Penn* (2000);

On New England, Edmund Morgan's *The Puritan Dilemma: The Story of John Winthrop* (1958), long a classic, has been superseded by Francis J. Bremer, *John Winthrop: America's Forgotten Founding Father* (2003). The dispute over Anne Hutchinson has been enlivened by Michael P. Winship, *Making Heretics: Militant Protestantism and Free Grace in Massachusetts, 1636–1641* (2002), who notes that few at the time accused Hutchinson of antinomianism; see also his *Anne Hutchinson* (2005). Louise A. Breen, *Transgressing the Bounds: Subversive Enterprises among the Puritan Elite in Massachusetts, 1630–1692* (2001), draws a connection between religious dissenters such as Hutchinson and economic entrepreneurship. For Rhode Island, see Edwin S. Gaustad, *Liberty of Conscience: Roger Williams in America* (1991). William Bradford's classic, *Of Plymouth Plantation,* is also well worth sampling.

Chapter 2 American Society in the Making

Among general interpretations, D. J. Boorstin's *The Americans: The Colonial Experience* (1958), emphasizes the modern aspects of colonial society; Jon Butler's *Becoming America: The Revolution before 1776* (2000) similarly and more broadly emphasizes the rapid evolution of colonial society. Alan Kulikoff, *From British Peasants to Colonial American Farmers* (2000), underscores the importance of land in defining American life. Alan Taylor, *American Colonies* (2001), emphasizes the links between European and American societies.

On economic conditions, see John J. McCusker and Russell R. Menard, eds., *The Economy of British America, 1607–1789* (1991). For the economic growth of colonial New England, see Margaret Ellen Newell, *From Dependency to Independence* (1998). On the chronologically and geographically uneven development of slavery in America, consult Ira Berlin, *Generations of Captivity: A History of African-American Slaves* (2003), and *Many Thousands Gone* (1998). See also Philip D. Morgan, *Slave Counterpoint* (1998) and P. D. Curtin, *The Rise and Fall of the Plantation Complex* (1990). Alan Gallay, *The Indian Slave Trade* (2002) uncovers an issue that has long been overlooked.

On life in the colonial South, see T. W. Tate and David Ammerman, eds., *The Chesapeake in the Seventeenth Century* (1979), Allan Kulikoff, *Tobacco and Slaves* (1986), D. B. and A. H. Rutman, *A Place in Time* (1984), and Timothy H. Breen and Stephen Innes, *"Myne Owne Ground": Race and Freedom on Virginia's Eastern Shore* (1980).

Family and community life are surveyed in D. F. Hawke, *Everyday Life in Early America* (1988), and Edmund S. Morgan, *The Puritan Family* (1966). The places of women and children are effectively presented in Laurel T. Ulrich, *Good Wives: Image and Reality in the Lives of Women in Northern New England* (1982), and Philip Greven, *The Protestant Temperament: Patterns of Child-Rearing, Religious Experience, and the Self in Early America* (1980). Richard Godbeer, *Sexual Revolution in Early America* (2002), corrects the stereotype of the puritans as sexually repressive.

The works of Perry Miller remain the starting point for any serious study of the cultural life of colonial New England. Among them, *Errand into the Wilderness* (1956) provides a good introduction. More recent studies, most of which modify Miller's judgments, include D. D. Hall, *Worlds of Wonder, Days of Judgment* (1989), and Patricia U. Bonomi, *Under the Cope of Heaven* (1986). Some recent scholarship contends that Puritan practices complemented economic development: for example, John Frederick Martin, *Profits in the Wilderness* (1991), Stephen Innes, *Creating the Commonwealth* (1995), and Mark A. Peterson, *The Price of Redemption* (1997).

Larry D. Gragg, *The Salem Witch Crisis* (1992) provides a narrative account. Paul Boyer and Stephen Nissenbaum, *Salem Possessed* (1974), argue that the episode grew out of tensions between different factions within the community. Mary Beth Norton, *In the Devil's Snare: The Salem Witchcraft Crisis of 1692* (2002), views the crisis as a response to fear of Indians. The subject is considered more generally in John Demos, *Entertaining Satan: Witchcraft and the Culture of Early New England* (1982). On women and witchcraft, see Elizabeth Reis, *Damned Women* (1997), Elaine G. Breslaw, *Tituba, Reluctant Witch of Salem* (1996), and Carol F. Karlsen, *The Devil in the Shape of a Woman* (1987).

For an engaging overview of the ideology of gender authority in the seventeenth century, see Mary Beth Norton, *Founding Mothers and Fathers* (1996). On women and religion in New England, see also Susan Juster, *Disorderly Women* (1994). Karin Wolf, *Not All Wives* (2000), describes the range of women's activities in Philadelphia. For the role of women in Virginia, see Kathleen M. Brown, *Good Wives, Nasty Wenches and Anxious Patriarchs* (1996).

Educational and intellectual developments are treated in Bernard Bailyn, *Education in the Forming of American Society* (1960), and L. A. Cremin, *American Education: The Colonial Experience* (1970).

In the past decade there has been a profusion of studies on the interrelationship between settlers and Indians: Jane T. Merritt, *At the Crossroads: Indians and Empire on a Mid-Atlantic Frontier* (2003), Richard White, *The Middle Ground* (1991), Daniel K. Richter, *Ordeal of the Longhouse* (1992), Daniel H. Usner, *Indians, Settlers, and Slaves in a Frontier Exchange Economy* (1992), Colin G. Calloway, *New Worlds for All: Indians, Europeans, and the Remaking of Early America* (1997), Karen O. Kupperman, *Indians and English* (2001), and James F. Brooks, *Captives and Cousins* (2002).

CHAPTER 3 AMERICA IN THE BRITISH EMPIRE

A full analysis of the British imperial system can be found in the early volumes of L. H. Gipson's *British Empire Before the American Revolution* (1936–1968). See also James A. Henretta, *The Evolution of American Society* (1973), and Michael Kammen, *Empire and Interest* (1974). Jack P. Greene, *Peripheries and Center* (1989), describes how the colonists extended their control of political affairs. On colonial trade and the mercantilist system, see J. J. McCusker and R. R. Menard, *The Economy of British America* (1985), and P. J. Marshall, ed., *The Oxford History of the British Empire: The Eighteenth Century* (1998).

On the Great Awakening, Richard Bushman, *From Puritan to Yankee* (1967) emphasizes psychosocial factors while Frank Lambert, *Inventing the "Great Awakening"* (1999) focuses on the intersection of religion and economics. Catherine A. Brekus, *Strangers and Pilgrims: Female Preaching in America* (1998) addresses a long-neglected subject. See also P. U. Bonami, *Under the Cope of Heaven: Religion, Society, and Politics in Colonial America* (1986). For the Enlightenment, see H. F. May, *The Enlightenment in America* (1976); also Joyce E. Chaplin, *The First Scientific American: Benjamin Franklin and the Pursuit of Genius* (2006) and I. Bernard Cohen, *Science and the Founding Fathers* (1995). Fred Anderson, *The Crucible of War* (2000) is a readable and thorough narrative of the Great War for the Empire; see also his *A People's Army: Massachusetts Soldiers and Society in the Seven Years' War* (1984).

On the causes of the Revolution, see Pauline Maier, *From Resistance to Revolution* (1972), Edmund S. Morgan, *The Birth of the Republic* (1977), and Edward Countryman, *The American Revolution* (1985). Valuable local studies include T. H. Breen, *Tobacco Culture* (1985), on Virginia; Countryman's *A People in Revolution* (1989), on New York; and T. M. Doerflinger, *A Vigorous Spirit of Enterprise* (1986), on Philadelphia.

Bernard Bailyn's *The Ideological Origins of the American Revolution* (1967) and *The Origins of American Politics* (1968) are brilliant analyses of the political thinking and political structure of eighteenth-century America. Other seminal works include Gordon S. Wood, *The Radicalism of the American Revolution* (1992), and Edmund S. Morgan, *Inventing the People: The Rise of Popular Sovereignty in England and America* (1988). See also Pauline Maier, *The Old Revolutionaries* (1980). On Benjamin Franklin, in addition to Chapin (above), see two good recent biographies, by Edmund Morgan (2002) and Walter Isaacson (2003).

The full story of Eunice Williams/Gannenstenhawi is brilliantly told in John Demos, *The Unredeemed Captive* (1994); for the Indian perspective of the same event, see Evan Haefeli and Kevin Sweeney, *Captors and Captives: The 1704 French and Indian Raid on Deerfield* (2003).

Chapter 4 The American Revolution

Good brief surveys of the Revolutionary years are Edward Countryman, *The American Revolution* (1985), and E. S. Morgan, *The Birth of the Republic* (1977). David McCullough, *1776* (2005) provides a gripping account of that pivotal year. David Hackett Fischer's account of the battle of Lexington and Concord in *Paul Revere's Ride* (1994) shows why the colonists won the war; his *Washington's Crossing* (2004) outlines the importance of the New Jersey campaign. See also John W. Shy, *A People Numerous and Armed* (1990).

For a short biography of Washington, see James MacGregor Burns and Susan Dunn, *George Washington* (2004). Longer biographies include Richard Norton Smith, *Patriarch: George Washington and the New American Nation* (1993), and Henry Wiencek, *Imperfect God: George Washington, His Slaves, and the Creator of America* (2003). John E. Ferling, *Setting the World Ablaze* (2000) and his *A Leap in the Dark* (2003) provide a good overview of how Washington, Jefferson, and John Adams interacted. See also Joseph Ellis, *Founding Brothers: The Revolutionary Generation* (2000), and David McCullough *John Adams* (2001).

On the broader context of the Revolution, see Lester Langley, *The Americas in the Age of Revolution, 1750–1850* (1996); Eliga Gould emphasizes the continuity in America of British political culture, *The Persistence of Empire* (2000).

On the Continental Congress and the Articles of Confederation, see Jackson T. Main, *The Sovereign States* (1973) and Jack N. Rakove, *The Beginnings of National Politics* (1979). P. S. Onuf, *Statehood and Union* (1987), deals with the Northwest Ordinance. Eric Foner, *Tom Paine and Revolutionary America* (1976), is an excellent brief biography. James K. Martin makes a case for his subject in *Benedict Arnold, Revolutionary Hero* (1997).

The classic study of the Declaration of Independence is C. L. Becker, *The Declaration of Independence* (1922); for contemporary analysis see Pauline Maier, *American Scripture* (1997), and Jay Fliegelman, *Declaring Independence* (1993).

The early history of the state governments is covered in W. P. Adams, *The First American Constitutions* (1980). Edward Countryman, *A People in Revolution* (1982), deals with conditions in New York; for Maryland, see Jean B. Lee, *The Price of Nationhood* (1994). The development of political and social ideas, before, during, and after the Revolution, is admirably described and analyzed in G. S. Wood, *The Creation of the American Republic* (1969) and *The Radicalism of the American Revolution* (1992).

The effects of the Revolution on slavery are treated in W. D. Jordan, *White over Black* (1968), and on the Indians, in Colin G. Calloway, *The American Revolution in Indian Country* (1995). For an account of Indians, debtors, and slaves in Virginia, see Woody Holton, *Forced Founders* (1999). L. K. Kerber, *Women of the Republic* (1980), M. B. Norton, *Liberty's Daughters* (1980), and Joy Day Buel and Richard Buel, *The Way of Duty* (1984) discuss the effects of the Revolution on women and the family.

Chapter 5 The Federalist Era: Nationalism Triumphant

On the Constitution, in addition to the works cited in the Debating the Past (p. 168), see Reginald Horsman, *The New Republic* (2000), a good brief survey. Bernard Bailyn, *To Begin the World Anew* (2003) shows how the founders embraced ambiguity. For Madison's role, see Lance Banning, *The Sacred Fire of Liberty* (1995), Drew R. McCoy, *The Last of the Fathers* (1989), and Gary Rosen, *American Compact* (1999). On Hamilton, Ronald Chernow, *Alexander Hamilton* (2004) offers a balanced account while Richard Brookhiser's brief *Alexander Hamilton, American* (1999) is more partisan. See also Karl-Friedrich Walling, *Republican Empire: Alexander Hamilton on War and Free Government* (1999). The *Federalist Papers* of Hamilton, Madison, and Jay, available in many editions, are essential for the arguments of the supporters of the new government. For the Bill of Rights, consult Bernard Schwartz, *The Great Rights of Mankind* (1977).

For Washington, in addition to the works cited in the previous chapter, see Alexander De Conde, *Entangling Alliance: Politics and Diplomacy Under George Washington* (1958), Harry Ammon, *The Genet Mission* (1973), two volumes by S. F. Bemis, *Jay's Treaty* (1923) and *Pinckney's Treaty* (1926), Alexander De Conde, *The Quasi-War* (1966), and William Stinchcombe, *The XYZ Affair* (1980). On economic development, see E. J. Ferguson, *The Power of the Purse* (1968), and C. P. Nettels, *The Emergence of a National Economy* (1962), which puts this subject in the broader perspective of the period 1775–1815. On the radical western movements, see D. P. Szatmary, *Shays' Rebellion* (1980), and Thomas P. Slaughter, *The Whiskey Rebellion* (1986).

John Patrick Diggins, *John Adams* (2003) is a useful brief biography. Excellent full-length biographies include Joseph J. Ellis, *Passionate Sage* (1993), and David McCullough, *John Adams* (2001). Stanley Elkins and Eric McKitrick, *The Age of Federalism* (1993), and James Roger Sharp, *American Politics in the Early Republic* (1993), provide detailed accounts of the politics of this period. For the Alien and Sedition Acts, see J. M. Smith, *Freedom's Fetters* (1956), and L. W. Levy, *Freedom of Speech and Press in Early American History* (1963). Paul Nagel's collective biography, *The Adams Women* (1987), provides a superb account of a remarkable family.

CHAPTER 6 JEFFERSONIAN DEMOCRACY

No student interested in Jefferson's political and social philosophy should miss sampling his writings. A useful compilation is Merrill D. Peterson, ed., *Thomas Jefferson* (1984). The contradictory components of Jefferson's life and mind are best analyzed in Joseph Ellis, *American Sphinx: The Character of Thomas Jefferson*. See also Peter Onuf, *The Mind of Thomas Jefferson* (2007), and Christopher Hitchens, *Thomas Jefferson* (2005). On the issue of indebtedness, see Herbert Sloan, *Principle and Interest: Thomas Jefferson and the Problem of Debt* (1995), and Bruce H. Mann, *Republic of Debtors: Bankruptcy in the Age of American Independence* (2002).

For the election of 1800, see Bernard A. Weisberger, *America Afire* (2000). Arnold Rogow, *Fatal Friendship* (1998), describes the relationship of Hamilton and Burr; on Jefferson and Burr see Joseph Whelan, *Jefferson's Vendetta: The Pursuit of Aaron Burr and the Judiciary* (2005). See also Joanne B. Freeman, *Affairs of Honor* (2001) on politics and dueling more generally. On Jefferson and John Marshall see R. Kent Newmeyer, *John Marshall and the Heroic Age of the Supreme Court* (2001). A useful monograph is Anthony F. C. Wallace, *Jefferson and the Indians* (1999).

Thomas Fleming, *The Louisiana Purchase* (2003) is a brief, clear account; Jon Kukla, *A Wilderness So Immense: The Louisiana Purchase and the Destiny of America* (2003) argues that the region was acquired chiefly as a place for resettling Indians.Thomas P. Slaughter, *Exploring Lewis and Clark* (2003) is a scholarly examination of the explorers' writings.

CHAPTER 7 NATIONAL GROWING PAINS

On Madison, see Lance Banning, *Sacred Fire of Liberty* (1995), Jack N. Rakove, *James Madison and the Creation of the American Republic* (2007), and Richard Labunski, *James Madison and the Struggle for the Bill of Rights* (2006). On the War of 1812 from the American perspective, see A. J. Langguth, *Union, 1812* (2006). For the political issues, see Richard Buel, Jr., *America on the Brink* (2005). For accounts of key figures, see Winston Groom, *Patriotic Fire* (2006), about Andrew Jackson and the Battle of New Orleans, Allison Robert, *Stephen Decatur* (2005), and David C. Skaggs, *Oliver Hazard Perry* (2006).

For the postwar diplomatic settlements and the Era of Good Feelings, see James Lewis, *The American Union and the Problem of Neighborhood: The United States and the Collapse of the Spanish Empire, 1783–1829* (1998), George Dangerfield, *The Era of Good Feelings* (1952), and Harry Ammon, *James Monroe: The Quest for National Identity* (1971), and on his famous doctrine, Ernest May, *The Making of the Monroe Doctrine* (1976).

Merrill D. Peterson, *The Great Triumvirate* (1987), is an interesting study of Clay, Calhoun, and Webster. Other biographies of statesmen of the period include Paul C. Nagel, *John Quincy Adams* (1997), Robert Remini, *Daniel Webster* (1997), Irving Bartlett, *John C. Calhoun* (1993), Maurice Baxter, *Henry Clay and the American System* (1995), and C. C. Mooney, *William H. Crawford* (1974). On the Missouri Compromise, see Glover Moore, *The Missouri Controversy* (1953). See also P. C. Nagel, *One Nation Indivisible* (1965).

On Indians, in addition to the works cited in Debating the Past (p. 223) see John Sugden, *Tecumseh* (1998), R. David Edmonds, *The Potawatomis* (1978), and Michael N. McConnell, *A Country Between: The Upper Ohio Valley and Its Peoples* (1992).

CHAPTER 8 TOWARD A NATIONAL ECONOMY

On the consumer revolution, see especially Richard Bushman, *The Refinement of America* (1992). In addition to the works cited in Debating the Past (p. 269) on the market revolution, see Melvyn Stokes and Stephen Conway, eds., *The Market Revolution in America* (1996), and Christopher Clark, *The Roots of Rural Capitalism: Western Massachusetts, 1780–1860* (1991). See also Laurel Thatcher Ulrich, *The Age of Homespun* (2001).

On the industrial revolution in America, see A. D. Chandler, Jr., *The Visible Hand: The Managerial Revolution in American Business* (1977). On the role of inventors, see Carroll Pursell, *The Machine in America* (1995), and B. M. Tucker, *Samuel Slater and the Origins of the American Textile Industry* (1984).

The growth of cities in the Jacksonian era can be traced in Richard C. Wade, *The Urban Frontier* (1957), and Howard Chudacoff, *The Evolution of American Urban Society* (1981). Allen F. Davis and Mark Halle, eds., *The Peoples of Philadelphia* (1973), Oscar Handlin, *Boston's Immigrants* (1968 ed.), and P. R. Knights, *The Plain People of Boston* (1971), deal with individual cities.

Important new works on slavery include Steven Deyle, *Carry Me Back: The Domestic Trade in Slavery* (2005), Robert H. Gudmestad, *Troublesome Commerce* (2003), and Erskine Clarke, *Dwelling Place, Plantation Epic* (2005).

On immigration and ethnicity, see P. T. Knoble, *Paddy and the Republic* (1986), J. P. Dolan, *Immigrant Church: New York's Irish and German Catholics* (1982), and Stephan Thernstrom, ed., *Harvard Encyclopedia of American Ethnic Groups* (1980).

On changes in the nature of work, consult Paul Johnson, *A Shopkeeper's Millennium* (1978), Sean Wilentz, *Chants Democratic* (1984), Bruce Laurie, *Artisans into Workers* (1989), Norman Ware, *The Industrial Worker* (1990), and Anthony F. C. Wallace, *Rockdale* (1978); on women in the early factories, see Mary Blewett, *Men, Women, and Work* (1988), and Thomas Dublin, *Women at Work* (1979).

Peter L. Bernstein, *The Wedding of the Waters* (2005) is a thorough account of the Erie Canal; see also Evan Cornog describes the origins and impact of the Erie Canal in *The Birth of Empire* (1998). On canal building, consult R. E. Shaw, *Canals for a Nation* (1990). Two works by Carter Goodrich, *Government Promotion of American Canals and Railroads* (1960) and *Canals and American Economic Development* (1961), describe the role of government aid in canal construction authoritatively. John Lauritz Larson, *Internal Improvement: National Public Works and the Promise of Popular Government in the Early United States* (2001), blames Andrew Jackson for the abandonment of public support for transportation infrastructure.

R. Kent Newmyer, *John Marshall and the Heroic Age of the Supreme Court* (2001) is strongly supportive of Marshall's actions; see also G. Edward White, *The Marshall Court and Cultural Change* (1991), as well as the sources cited in previous chapters.

Chapter 9 Jacksonian Democracy

The nature of Jacksonian democracy was analyzed brilliantly by Alexis de Tocqueville, *Democracy in America* (1835–1840). Other commentaries by foreigners throw much light on Jacksonian democracy. See especially, in addition to Tocqueville, Frances Trollope, *Domestic Manners of the Americans* (1832), Michel Chevalier, *Society, Manners and Politics in the United States* (1961), Harriet Martineau, *Retrospect of Western Travel* (1838) and *Society in America* (1837), and F. J. Grund, *Aristocracy in America* (1859).

In addition to the works on Jackson cited in Debating the Past (p. 295), see Bray Hammond, *Banks and Politics in America from the Revolution to the Civil War* (1957), and J. M. McFaul, *The Politics of Jacksonian Finance* (1972). Peter Temin, *The Jacksonian Economy* (1969) minimizes the effects of Jackson's policies on economic conditions. Jill Norgren, *The Cherokee Cases* (1996) is critical of Jackson's policies toward Indians; Robert Remini is more supportive in *Andrew Jackson and His Indian Wars* (2001). For recent accounts of Indian resistance to removal, see Patricia W. Wickman *Osceola's Legacy* (2006), and Kerry Trask, *Black Hawk* (2006).

On the transformation of political parties, see Richard P. McCormick, *The Second American Party System* (1966), and Michael Holt, *The Rise and Fall of the American Whig Party* (1999), which focuses on variations at the state level. Gerald Leonard, *The Invention of Party Politics* (2002) provides a detailed study of Illinois.

On the nullification controversy, see R. E. Ellis, *The Union at Risk* (1987), and William W. Freehling, *The Road to Disunion* (1990), which stresses the close relationship between the nullifiers and the slavery issue.

For the Van Buren administration, see Ted Widmer, *Martin Van Buren* (2005), and Joel H. Silbey, *Martin Van Buren and the Emergency of American Popular Politics* (2002).

Louis Masur's *1831, Year of Eclipse* (2001), provides an interesting perspective on that pivotal year.

Chapter 10 The Making of Middle-Class America

On Tocqueville and his views of America, see Alexis de Tocqueville, *Democracy in America*, J. P. Mayer, ed. (1966 edition), and also Andre Jardin, *Alexis de Tocqueville* (1988). For an analysis of the middle class, see Stuart M. Blumin, *The Emergence of the Middle Class* (1989).

On the changing place of the family and the changes within it, see Mary P. Ryan, *Cradle of the Middle Class: The Family in Oneida, New York* (1981), Catherine E. Kelly, *In the New England Fashion: Reshaping Women's Lives in the Nineteenth Century* (1999), Nancy Cott, *The Bonds of Womanhood* (1977), and Carl Degler, *At Odds: Women and Family in America from the Revolution to the Present* (1980).

Fertility and the frontier is examined in Yasukichi Yasuba, *Birth Rates of the White Population in the U.S., 1800–1860* (1962), and John Modell, "Family and Fertility on the Indiana Frontier, 1820," in *American Quarterly* (1971).

The Second Great Awakening has been examined both as a religious and as a social phenomenon. Still useful is Whitney Cross, *The Burned-Over District* (1950), but see also Paul E. Johnson, *A Shopkeeper's Millennium* (1978). Mark A. Noll, *America's God: From Jonathan Edwards to Abraham Lincoln* (2002), provides a broader study of the religious dimension of reform movements. For the Shakers, see Stephen J. Stein, *The Shaker Experience in America* (1992). Richard Bushman, *Joseph Smith and the Beginnings of Mormonism* (1984), provides a good introduction to the subject. For a broader study see Leonard J. Arrington, *The Mormon Experience* (1992).

For the origins of feminism, see Nancy Cott, *The Grounding of Modern Feminism* (1987), Ellen C. DuBois, *Feminism and Suffrage: The Emergence of an Independent Women's Movement in America, 1848–1869* (1978), and Linda K. Kerber, *No Constitutional Right to Be Ladies* (1998). Bruce Dorsey, *Reforming Men and Women* (2002) shows how men often initiated reforms but women took control of them.

Accounts of the temperance movement include Barbara L. Epstein, *The Politics of Domesticity* (1981), and W. J. Rorabaugh, *The Alcoholic Republic* (1979).

For a general study of the context of abolitionism, see Richard S. Newman, *The Transformation of American Abolitionism* (2002). For sharply contrasting views of the abolitionist movement, see Stanley Elkins, *Slavery* (1975), and Lewis Perry and Michael Fellman, eds., *Anti-Slavery Reconsidered* (1979). Women's role in the movement is discussed in Julie Roy Jeffrey, *The Great Silent Army of Abolitionism* (1998).

The persistence of slavery in the North, a topic that is often overlooked, is examined in Joanne P. Melish, *Disowning Slavery* (1998). Biographical accounts include John L. Thomas, *The Liberator: William Lloyd Garrison* (1963), Gerda Lerner, *The Grimké Sisters from South Carolina* (1967), and Nathan Huggins, *Slave and Citizen: The Life of Frederick Douglass* (1980).

On Lydia Maria Child, see Carolyn L. Karcher, *The First Woman in the Republic: A Cultural Biography of Lydia Maria Child* (1994), Charles Capper, *Margaret Fuller* (1992), Elizabeth Griffith, *In Her Own Rights: The Life of Elizabeth Cady Stanton* (1984), and Kathryn K. Sklar, *Catharine Beecher* (1973), are solid biographies of important women in the era.

For Emerson and Thoreau, see the biographies by Robert D. Richardson, *Emerson: The Mind on Fire* (1995), and *Henry Thoreau: The Life of the Mind* (1986). For Poe, the biography by Kenneth Silverman (1991) is excellent. David S. Reynold's *Walt Whitman's America* (1995) examines the poet's relation to other trends in American life. See also Hershel Parker, *Herman Melville: 1819–1851* (1996) and *Herman Melville: 1851–1891* (2002).

On the cultural life of the South, see Bertram Wyatt-Brown, *Hearts of Darkness* (2003), and Drew Faust, *A Sacred Circle* (1977).

On education see Lawrence A. Cremin, *American Education: The National Experience* (1980), and C. F. Kaestle, *Pillars of the Republic* (1983). Jill Lepore, *A Is For American* (2002) is also useful.

CHAPTER 11 WESTWARD EXPANSION

For John Tyler, perhaps the least examined of the presidents, see Edgar Crapol, *John Tyler* (2006), and Dan Monroe, *The Republican Vision of John Tyler* (2003). For an overview of the politics of the era, see David P. Currie, *Constitution in Congress: Democrats and Whigs, 1829-1861* (2005); on the Whigs, see Michael F. Holt, *The Rise and Fall of the American Whig Party* (1999), and Daniel Walker Howe, *The Political Culture of the American Whigs* (1979).

On the debate over annexation of Texas, see Joel H. Silbey, *Storm over Texas: The Annexation Controversy and the Road to Civil War* (2005).

The course of western development is treated in R. A. Billington and Martin Ridge, *The Far Western Frontier* (1982). Important recent studies of the California gold rush include Malcolm J. Rohrbough, *Days of Gold* (1997), and Susan Lee Johnson, *Roaring Camp: The Social World of the California Gold Rush* (2000). On the effects of the settling of the Great Plains, see Elliott West, *The Contested Plains: Indians, Goldseekers and the Rush to Colorado* (1998) and J. D. Unruh, *The Plains Across* (1979). Francis Parkman's classic account, *The Oregon Trail* (1849), is absorbing.

For Polk, see two recent short biographies: Samuel W. Haynes, *James K. Polk* (2006), and John Siegenthaler, *James K. Polk* (2004). William Dusinberre, *Slavemaster President: The Double Career of James Polk* (2003), is sharply critical.

On the Mexican-American War, see Richard Bruce Winders, *Mr. Polk's Army* (1997), R. W. Johannsen, *To the Halls of the Montezumas* (1987), and K. J. Bauer, *The Mexican War* (1974). J. H. Schroeder, *Mr. Polk's War* (1973), discusses American opposition to the conflict. See also Randolph B. Campbell, *Sam Houston and the American Southwest* (2007). Randy Roberts and James S. Olson, *A Line in the Sand: The Alamo in Blood and Memory* (2001), is an accessible account.

For the Compromise of 1850, see John C. Waugh, *On the Brink of Civil War* (2003), and David M. Potter, *The Impending Crisis, 1848–1861* (1976). See also Robert Remini, *Daniel Webster: The Man and His Time* (1997), and Irving H. Bartlett, *John C. Calhoun* (1993).

CHAPTER 12 THE SECTIONS GO THEIR WAYS

Most of the volumes dealing with economic developments mentioned in earlier chapters continue to be useful for this period. On the Panic of 1857, see J. L. Huston, *The Panic of 1857 and the Coming of the Civil War* (1987). For a useful comparative study, see John Majewski, *A House Dividing: Economic Development in Pennsylvania and Virginia before the Civil War* (2000). On the economy of the South, see Gavin Wright, *The Political Economy of the Cotton South* (1978), and Michael Tadman, *Speculators and Slaves* (1989).

On slavery, in addition to the essential works listed in Debating the Past (p. 357), see Brenda Stevenson, *Life in Black and White* (1996), and Walter Johnson, *Soul by Soul: Life Inside the Antebellum Slave Market* (1999), which focuses on New Orleans. Recent evidence of slave resistance is documented in John Hope Franklin and Loren Schweninger, *Runaway Slaves* (1999), David Robertson, *Denmark Vesey* (1999), and Douglas R. Egerton, *Gabriel's Rebellion* (1993). An earlier study is Eugene D. Genovese, *From Rebellion to Revolution* (1979).

Excellent regional studies include Peter Coclanis, *The Shadow of a Dream* (1989), for South Carolina, as well as Charles E. Joyner, *Down by the Riverside: A South Carolina Slave Community* (1984), and Ann Patton Malone, *Sweet Chariot: Slave Family and Household Structure in Nineteenth-Century Louisiana* (1992).

Among specialized volumes, Bertram Wyatt-Brown, *Southern Honor* (1982), and Ira Berlin, *Slaves Without Masters* (1975), are important. Richard C. Wade, *Slavery in the Cities* (1964), contends that urban life eroded slavery, while Robert Starobin, *Industrial Slavery in the Old South* (1970), found that the institution could be adapted to industrial purposes. Most local studies take an intermediate position; see, for example, Midori Takagi, *"Rearing Wolves to Our Own Destruction": Slavery in Richmond, Virginia, 1782–1865* (1999).

Irish emigration is the subject of Tim Pat Coogan's expansive *Wherever Green Is Worn* (2000), and Edward Laxton, *The Famine Ships* (1997), as well as the scholarly collection edited by Arthur Gribben, *The Great Famine and the Irish Diaspora in America* (1999). J. Matthew Gallman, *Receiving Erin's Children* (2000), examines the arrival of Irish famine emigrants in Philadelphia. Although fewer sources on German emigration are available in English, see Marianne Wokeck, *Trade in Strangers* (1999).

On the New England shoe industry and labor organization, see Mary Blewett, *Men, Women and Work* (1988); for a more general study see her *Constant Turmoil: The Politics of Industrial Life in Nineteenth Century New England* (2000). For workingmen's political activities, Edward Pessen's *Most Uncommon Jacksonians* (1967) remains valuable.

CHAPTER 13 THE COMING OF THE CIVIL WAR

On the origins of the Civil War, in addition to the Debating the Past (p. 381), David M. Potter, *The Impending Crisis* (1976), remains useful. See also Don E. Fehrenbacher, *Sectional Crisis and Southern Constitutionalism* (1995), and Marshall De Rosa, *The Politics of Dissolution* (1998). In *States' Rights and the Union* (2000), as in his other works, Forrest McDonald affirms the South's right to secede. David Brion Davis, *Inhuman Bondage* (2006), provides a sweeping survey of the rise and fall of slavery. William A. Link, *Roots of Secession: Slavery and Politics in Antebellum Virginia* (2003), is a useful state study.

On slave resistance, see especially John Hope Franklin and Loren Schweninger, *Runaway Slaves* (1999), William Dusinberre, *Them Dark Days: Slavery in the American Rice Swamps* (1996), and Steven Weisenburger, *Modern Medea: A Family Story of Slavery and Child-Murder from the Old South* (1998).

On abolitionism in the north, see Sandra Petrulionis, *To Set this World Aright* (2006). Everyone should read Harriet Beecher Stowe's *Uncle Tom's Cabin*. Joan Hedrick's biography, *Harriet Beecher Stowe* (1994), is excellent.

For the foreign policy of the 1850s, see C. H. Brown, *Agents of Manifest Destiny* (1980), and P. B. Wiley and Korogi Ichiro, *Yankees in the Land of the Gods* (1990), which focuses on American involvement in Japan.

On Stephen A. Douglas, see James L. Huston, *Stephen A. Douglas* (2007). Sumner's role in the deepening crisis is brilliantly discussed in David H. Donald, *Charles Sumner and the Coming of the Civil War* (1960), and *Charles Sumner and the Rights of Man* (1970); a more recent, brief study is Frederick J. Blue, *Charles Sumner and the Conscience of the North* (1994). Jean Baker, *James Buchanan* (2004), is solid and concise. On Dred Scott, see Paul Finkelman, *Dred Scott v. Sandford* (1997).

For Lincoln's own well-crafted words, see Abraham Lincoln, *Selections* (2 vols., 1989). On his use of words, see Douglas L. Wilson, *Lincoln's Sword* (2006). Excellent biographies of Lincoln include David H. Donald, *Lincoln* (1995), and Mark Neely, *The Last Best Hope on Earth* (1993). Lincoln's early struggles are thoughtfully examined in Douglas L. Wilson, *Honor's Voice: The Transformation of Abraham Lincoln* (1998). W. E. Gienapp, *The Origins of the Republican Party* (1987), and Eric Foner, *Free Soil, Free Labor, Free Men* (1970), are excellent analyses of Republican ideas and policies. Allen Guelzo, *Lincoln's Emancipation Proclamation* (2004), is also useful.

John Brown remains controversial. Recent works include David S. Reynolds, *John Brown, Abolitionist* (2005), which is sympathetic, and Evan Carton, *Patriotic Treason* (2006), which is less so. See also James Oakes, *Radical and the Republican* (2007), on Frederick Douglass and Lincoln.

CHAPTER 14 THE WAR TO SAVE THE UNION

The best survey of the Civil War period is James M. McPherson, *Battle Cry of Freedom* (1988), but see also Russell F. Weigley, *A Great Civil War* (2000).

On the precipitating events of the war, see Maury Klein, *Days of Defiance: Sumter, Secession and the Coming of the Civil War* (1997), and Wallace Hettle, *The Peculiar Democracy: Southern Democrats in Peace and Civil War* (2001).

For Lincoln, in addition to books mentioned in previous chapters, see Richard Cawardine, *Lincoln* (2006), William Marvel, *Mr. Lincoln Goes to War* (2006), and Philip Paludan, *The Presidency of Abraham Lincoln* (1994). Mark E. Neely, *The Fate of Liberty* (1991), examines Lincoln's position on civil liberties. Frank Klement, *The Limits of Dissent* (1998), focuses on Clement Vallandigham. For the movement to make abolition a war aim and the reaction to it, see Michael Vorenberg, *Final Freedom* (2001).

On economic issues, see Heather Cox Richardson, *The Greatest Nation on Earth: Republican Economy Policies during the Civil War* (1997), and Bray Hammond, *Sovereignty and an Empty Purse: Banks and Politics in the Civil War* (1970).

On African Americans in the Union army, see Joseph T. Glatthaar, *Forged in Battle: The Civil War Alliance of Black Soldiers and White Officers* (1990); Peter Burchard, *One Gallant Rush* (1965), recounts the story of Robert Gould Shaw and the Massachusetts 54th. See also Martin H. Blatt, *Hope & Glory: Essays on the Legacy of the 54th Massachusetts Regiment* (2001).

For aspects of economic and social history, see Philip S. Paludan, *"A People's Contest": The Union at War* (1988). Edward L. Ayers, *In the Presence of Mine Enemies* (2003), examines the effect of the war on various communities. For women and the war, see Drew Gilpin Faust, *Mothers of Invention* (1997), Judith Ann Giesberg, *Civil War Sisterhood: The U.S. Sanitary Commission and Women's Politics in Transition* (2000), and Laura Edwards, *Scarlett Doesn't Live Here Anymore* (2000). Elizabeth Young considers the literary heritage of women and the war in *Disarming the Nation: Women's Writing and the American Civil War* (1999). See also Iver Bernstein, *The New York City Draft Riots* (1990).

For the Confederacy, see Gary W. Gallagher, *The Confederate War* (1997). See also his edited collection, *Lee the Soldier* (1996). On divisions within the Confederacy, see William W. Freehling, *The South vs. The South: How Anti-Confederate Southerners Shaped the Course of the Civil War* (2001). Important biographies include William Cooper, *Jefferson Davis, American* (2000). See also Mark Grimsley and Brooks D. Simpson, eds., *Collapse of the Confederacy* (2001), and Steven V. Ash, *When the Yankees Came: Conflict and Chaos in the Occupied South* (1995).

Gerald F. Linderman, *Embattled Courage* (1988), argues that the soldiers on both sides grew disillusioned with the fighting; the persistence of the initial ideals is a theme in James McPherson, *What They Fought For, 1861–1865* (1994), and Reid Mitchell, *The Vacant Chair* (1993). Bertram Wyatt-Brown,

The Shaping of Southern Culture: Honor, Grace and War, 1760s–1880s (2001), contends that while soldiers on both sides used the same rhetoric to defend their cause, they had different notions of what terms such as "honor" meant.

Among the biographies of Civil War generals, northern and southern, the following are especially noteworthy: Brooks D. Simpson, *Ulysses S. Grant: Triumph over Adversity, 1822–1865* (2000), Jean E. Smith, *Grant* (2001), William S. McFeely, *Grant* (1981), Michael Fellman, *The Making of Robert E. Lee* (2000), Douglass S. Freeman, *R. E. Lee* (1934–1935), James I. Robertson, *Stonewall Jackson* (1997), Stephen W. Sears, *George B. McClellan* (1988), Stanley P. Hirshson, *The White Tecumseh: A Biography of William T. Sherman* (1997), and Chester G. Hearn, *Admiral David Glasgow Farragut* (1998).

The diplomacy of the Civil War period is covered in two works by Howard Jones, *Union in Peril* (1992), on British intervention, and *Abraham Lincoln and a New Birth of Freedom* (1999), on issues of slavery. See also John Taylor, *William Henry Seward* (1991).

John C. Waugh, *Reelecting Lincoln* (1997) considers the election of 1864. The assassination of Lincoln and its aftermath is the subject of Jay Winik, *April 1865: The Month That Saved America* (2001).

The legacy of the Civil War is thoughtfully examined in David W. Blight, *Race and Reunion: The Civil War in American Memory* (2001), and Tony Horwitz, *Confederates in the Attic: Dispatches from the Unfinished Civil War* (1998).

CHAPTER 15 RECONSTRUCTION AND THE SOUTH

Lincoln's ideas about Reconstruction are analyzed in William C. Harris, *With Charity for All* (1997), and in many of the Lincoln volumes mentioned in earlier chapters. Hans Trefousse, *Andrew Johnson: A Biography* (1989), is a balanced account. See also Brooks D. Simpson, *The Reconstruction Presidents* (2001), and Howard B. Means, *The Avenger Takes His Place* (2006), an account of Johnson's pivotal struggle with the Radical Republicans.

A number of biographies provide information helpful in understanding the Radicals. The most important are Hans Trefousse, *Thaddeus Stevens* (1997), and David Donald, *Charles Sumner and the Rights of Man* (1970). J. M. McPherson, *The Struggle for Equality: Abolitionists and the Negro in the Civil War and Reconstruction* (1964), is also valuable. See also W. E. Nelson, *The Fourteenth Amendment* (1988).

Conditions in the South during Reconstruction are discussed in Edward Ayers, *The Promise of the New South* (1992). The Freedmen's Bureau is examined in Paul Cimbala, *Under the Guardianship of the Nation* (1997). See also R. H. Abbott, *The Republican Party and the South* (1986), Michael Perman, *Reunion Without Compromise* (1973), H. N. Rabinowitz, *Race Relations in the Urban South* (1978), J. L. Roark, *Masters Without Slaves* (1977), and Leon Litwack, *Been in the Storm Too Long* (1979). For recent general studies, see Don E. Fehrenbacher, *The Slaveholding Republic* (2001), and Pamela Brandwein, *Reconstructing Reconstruction* (1999). Daniel Stowell's *Rebuilding Zion* (1998) explores the religious dimensions of Reconstruction.

Of state studies see, for Virginia, Jane E. Dailey, *Before Jim Crow* (2000); for South Carolina, Julie Saville, *The Work of Reconstruction* (1994), and Thomas Holt, *Black over White: Negro Political Leadership in South Carolina* (1977); for Texas, Randolph B. Campbell, *Grass-Roots Reconstruction in Texas* (1997); and for Mississippi, Nicholas Lemann, *Redemption: The Last Battle of the Civil War* (2006). Much recent work on the Ku Klux Klan similarly focuses on particular states: see Lou F. Williams, *The Great South Carolina Ku Klux Klan Trials* (1996), Glenn Feldman, *Politics, Society and the Klan in Alabama* (1999), and Noel Fisher, *War at Every Door* (1997), which examines East Tennessee.

On the economic and social effects of Reconstruction, see G. D. Jaynes, *Branches Without Roots: Genesis of the Black Working Class* (1986), R. L. Ransom and Richard Sutch, *One Kind of Freedom: The Economic Consequences of Emancipation* (1977), Robert Higgs, *Competition and Coercion* (1977), and C. F. Oubre, *Forty Acres and a Mule* (1978). The ambiguities of dependence and independence as they relate to racial and gender issues are explored in Laura F. Edwards, *Gendered Strife and Confusion* (1997), and Amy Dru Stanley, *From Bondage to Contract* (1998).

Recent works on Grant include Josiah Bunting III, *Ulysses S. Grant* (2004), and Jean Edwards Smith, *Grant* (2001), though W. S. McFeely, *Grant* (1981) remains valuable.

David W. Blight, *Race and Reunion* (2001) considers the Civil War and Reconstruction in a deeper historical perspective.

CHAPTER 16 CONQUEST OF THE WEST

Recent historians of the West do not regard it as a frontier to be settled, but as a region where white settlers and Native American peoples converged, to the destruction of the latter's way of life. For the older view, see Frederick Jackson Turner's *The Frontier in American History* (1920), which has been updated in R. A. Billington and Martin Ridge, *Westward Expansion* (1982). For a summary of the newer interpretation, see Gregory H. Nobles, *American Frontiers* (1997). See also Patricia Nelson Limerick, *The Legacy of Conquest* (1987), Richard White, *"It's Your Misfortune and None of My Own"* (1991), and Elliott West, *Contested Plains: Indians, Goldseekers, and the Rush to Colorado* (1998).

The economic, political, and legal ideas current in this period are covered in David M. Wrobel, *Promised Lands* (2002), and Patricia Limerick, *Something in the Soil: Legacies and Reckonings in the New West* (2000).

On government policy and white attitudes toward Indians, see Robert F. Berkhofer, Jr., *The White Man's Indian* (1978), Robert Wooster, *The Military and U.S. Indian Policy* (1988), and Andrew C. Isenberg, *The Destruction of the Bison* (2000).

Two superb recent studies, in addition to Elliott West, cited above, have transformed our understanding of the California gold rush: Susan Lee Johnson, *Roaring Camp: The Social World of the California Gold Rush* (2000), and Malcolm J. Rohrbough, *Days of Gold: The California Gold Rush and the American Nation* (1997). For women on the frontier, see Deborah Lawrence, *Writing the Trail: Women's Narratives* (2006), John Mack Faragher, *Women and Men on the Overland Trail* (1979), and Sandra L. Myres, *Westering Women and the Frontier Experience* (1982).

For a compelling account of the development of transcontinental railroads see David Haward Bain, *Empire Express: Building the First Transcontinental Railroad* (1999).

On cattle ranching on the Plains, a good account is Lewis Atherton, *The Cattle Kings* (1961), but see also Don Worcester, *The Chisholm Trail* (1980).

CHAPTER 17 AN INDUSTRIAL GIANT

In addition to the works cited in Debating the Past (p. 500), see David Haward Bain, *Empire* Express (1999) on the construction of the transcontinental railroads. On railroad regulation, see Steven Usselman, *Regulating Railroad Innovation* (2002). On the ways that technology transformed the way people understood daily life, see David E. Nye, *Electrifying America* (1990), and Jill Jonnes, *Empires of Light* (2003). Sven Beckert, *The Monied Metropolis: New York City and the Consolidation of the American Bourgeoisie, 1850–1896* (2001), outlines the special significance of that city in the nation's economic development and cultural mores.

The nation's expansive economy in the 1990s sparked interest in the leading businessmen and inventors a century earlier. For a detailed study of the key investment figure, see Jean Strouse, *Morgan: American Financier* (1999). Other useful works include Harold C. Livesay, *Andrew Carnegie and the Rise of Big Business* (2007); Michael P. Malone, *James J. Hill* (1996); Ron Chernow, *Titan* (1998), on John D. Rockefeller and the oil industry; James A. Mackey, *Alexander Graham Bell: A Life* (1997); and Martin V. Melosi, *Thomas A. Edison and the Modernization of America* (2007).

For the radical critics, see John L. Thomas, *Alternative Americas: Henry George, Edward Bellamy, Henry Demarest Lloyd* (1983), and also the radicals' own writings.

On the growth of unions see David Montgomery, *Beyond Equality* (1967), Leon Fink, *Workingmen's Democracy: The Knights of Labor and American Politics* (1983), and Nick Salvatore, *Eugene V. Debs* (1982). Jo Ann Argersinger, *Making the Amalgamated* (1999), describes the relation of gender and ethnicity in the rise of the clothing workers' union in Baltimore. Robert E. Weird, *Knights Unhorsed* (2000), blames internal dissension for the Knights' rapid decline. Lawrence Blickman, *A Living Wage* (1997), insists that labor radicalism persisted even after unionized workers won steady wages. The important strikes and labor violence of the period are covered in David O. Stowell, *Streets, Railroads, and the Great Strike of 1877* (1999), Susan Hirsch, *After the Strike* (2003) on Pullman, Paul Avrich, *The Haymarket Tragedy* (1984), and Carl S. Smith, *Urban Disorder and the Shape of Belief* (1995). On the challenge confronting the unions, see David Montgomery, *The Fall of the House of Labor* (1987).

CHAPTER 18 AMERICAN SOCIETY IN THE INDUSTRIAL AGE

Henry Adams, *The Education of Henry Adams* (1918), is a fascinating if highly personal view of the period, and James Bryce, *The American Commonwealth* (1888), while primarily a political analysis, contains a great deal of information about social conditions. For two classic accounts of the settlement house movement, see Jane Addams, *Twenty Years at Hull House* (1910), and Lillian Wald, *The House on Henry Street* (1915). Addams's own life is the subject of two recent biographies: Jean Bethke Elshtain, *Jane Addams and the Dream of American Democracy* (2002), and Victoria Bissel Brown, *The Education of Jane Addams* (2004).

On the public character of nineteenth-century life, see Mary P. Ryan, *Civic Wars* (1997). On communities more generally, Robert Wiebe's *The Search for Order* (1967) shows how corporate and administrative bureaucracies overspread the nation, while Alan Trachtenberg, *The Incorporation of America* (1982), considers the cultural implications of Wiebe's insight. See also Gunther Barth, *City People* (1980).

On middle-class life and culture, see John Kasson, *Rudeness and Civility* (1990), Karen Halttunen, *Confidence Men and Painted Women* (1982), Burton Bledstein, *The Culture of Professionalism* (1976), and Mark C. Carnes, *Secret Ritual and Manhood in Victorian America* (1989). Karen Lystra, *Searching the Heart* (1989), emphasizes the close character of marriage, and Peter Gay, *The Bourgeois Experience* (1984–1997), argues that the middle classes throughout the Western world were not prudes. On contraception see Janet F. Brodie, *Contraception and Abortion in Nineteenth-Century America* (1994). On issues of consumption see Daniel Horowitz, *The Morality of Spending* (1985), William Leach, *Land of Desire: Merchants, Power, and the Rise of a New American Culture* (1993), and Elaine S. Abelson, *When Ladies' Go A-Thieving* (1989).

A broad survey on issues of disease is Gerald N. Grob, *The Deadly Truth: A History of Disease in America* (2002).

On working-class culture, Keith Peiss, *Cheap Amusements: Working Women and Leisure in Turn-of-the-Century New York* (1986), and Roy Rosenzweig, *Eight Hours for What We Will* (1983), are excellent. Kenneth T. Jackson, *Crabgrass Frontier* (1985), is a pioneering history of suburban development, and Jon C. Teaford, *The Metropolitan Revolution* (2007), gives weight to the accomplishments of the cities as well as to their inadequacies.

On the early development of intercollegiate sports, see Ronald A. Smith, *Sports and Freedom: The Rise of Big-Time College Athletics* (1988); on sports and modernization, see Melvin L. Adelman, *A Sporting Time* (1986), and Allen Guttmann, *From Ritual to Record* (1978).

CHAPTER 19 INTELLECTUAL AND CULTURAL TRENDS

The best overviews on intellectual trends include Louis Menand, *The Metaphysical Club* (2001), John Patrick Diggins, *The Promise of Pragmatism* (1994), and Jackson Lears, *No Place for Grace: Antimodernism and the Transformation of American Culture, 1880–1920* (1981). Gail Bederman, *Manliness and Civilization* (1995), is also stimulating.

On the impact of Darwin on late nineteenth-century America, see Richard Hofstadter's *Social Darwinism in American Thought* (1955), though his view has been substantially modified. See Robert C. Bannister, *Social Darwinism* (1979), Carl Degler, *In Search of Human Nature: The Decline and Revival of Darwinism in American Social Thought* (1991), and Paul Crook, *Darwinism, War and History* (1994). James Turner, *Without God, Without Creed: The Origins of Unbelief in America* (1996), contends that Darwinism promoted skepticism.

Thorstein Veblen, *The Higher Learning in America* (1918), is full of provocative opinions. Stimulating modern studies include Kim Townsend, *Manhood at Harvard* (1996), William McNeill, *Hutchins' University* (1992), on the University of Chicago, and Robert McCaughey, *Stand, Columbia* (2004), and George Marsden, *The Soul of the American University* (1994).

On law and the social sciences, see Morton Horwitz, *The Transformation of American Law, 1870–1960* (1992), and Dorothy Ross, *The Origins of American Social Science* (1991). For various figures, see Robert D. Richardson, *William James: In the Maelstrom of American Modernism* (2006), and William Gale, *The Philosophy of William James* (2005); Jay Martin, *Education of John Dewey* (2002), and Jerome Popp, *Evolution's First Philosopher* (2007), also on Dewey; Garry Wills, *Henry Adams and the Making of America* (2005).

On women, see Rosalind Rosenberg, *Beyond Separate Spheres: Intellectual Roots of Modern Feminism* (1982), and Regina Morantz-Sanchez, *Sympathy and Science: Women Physicians in American Medicine* (1985). See also Jane Hunter, *How Young Ladies Became Girls: The Victorian Origins of American Girlhood* (2003).

On Twain, see Everett Emerson, *Mark Twain: A Literary Life* (1999). On other leading figures, see Susan Goodman, *William Dean Howells* (2005); Leon Edel, *Henry James* (1985); and Edward Chalfant, *Better in Darkness* (1994), also on James; William McFeely, *Portrait: The Life of Thomas Eakins* (2007), and more generally, Kathleen Pyne, *Art and the Higher Life: Painting and Evolutionary Thought in Late Nineteenth-Century America* (1996).

A recent interpretation of the Chautauqua movement is John E. Tapia, *Circuit Chautauqua* (1997). On journalism, see especially David Nasaw, *The Chief: The Life of William Randolph Hearst* (2000), and Denis Brian, *Pulitzer: A Life* (2001).

Chapter 20 Politics: Local, State, and National

There are several superb analyses of the political system of the period written by men who studied it firsthand: James Bryce, *The American Commonwealth* (1888), and Woodrow Wilson, *Congressional Government* (1886). On the evolution of political parties, see Paul Kleppner, *The Third Electoral System, 1853–1892* (1979), and Michael E. McGerr, *The Decline of Popular Politics* (1986).

C. Vann Woodward, *Origins of the New South* (1951), is an important regional study. Following in Woodward's path are Heather Cox Richardson, *The Death of Reconstruction* (2001), and Michael Perman, *Struggle for Mastery: Disfranchisement in the South, 1888–1908* (2001), who focus on the 1890s as the pivotal decade for the defeat of Reconstruction. Samuel C. Hyde Jr., examines the tension between the old planting elite of the South and plain folk in *Pistols and Politics* (1996). Steven Hahn's *Nation Under Our Feet* (2003), is a superb study of black political struggles in the South for several generations after Reconstruction.

Among biographies of political leaders, the following are especially worth consulting: Ari Hoogenboom, *Rutherford B. Hayes* (1995), Ira Rutkin *James A. Garfield* (2006), Zachary Karabell, *Chester A. Arthur* (2004), H. Paul Jeffers, *An Honest President* (2000), on Cleveland, also Henry Graff, *Grover Cleveland* (2002), Charles W. Calhoun, *Benjamin Harrison* (2005), Michael Kazin, *Godly Hero: The Life of William Jennings Bryan* (2006), H. Wayne Morgan, *William McKinley and His Era* (2003), and Kevin Phillips, *William McKinley* (2003). See also Stephen D. Kantrowitz, *Ben Tillman and the Reconstruction of White Supremacy* (2000).

Populism has been the subject of intensive study. Richard Hofstadter, *The Age of Reform* (1955), takes a dim view of populism as a reform movement; Lawrence Goodwyn, *Democratic Promise: The Populist Movement in America* (1976), calls it "a people's movement of mass democratic aspiration." Elizabeth Sanders, *Roots of Reform* (1999), champions the farmers' political efforts, a position amplified by Gene Clanton, *Congressional Populism and the Crisis of the 1890s* (1998). Peter Argersinger, *The Limits of Agrarian Radicalism: Western Populism and American Politics* (1995), Sheldon Hackney, *Populism to Progressivism in Alabama* (1969), and Steven Hahn, *The Roots of Southern Populism* (1983), are more than local studies. Michael Kazin, *The Populist Persuasion* (1994), insists on the enduring legacy of the movement.

See also Gretchen Ritter, *Goldbugs and Greenbacks* (1997), and Ross Evans Paulson, *Liberty, Equality and Justice: Civil Rights, Women's Rights and the Regulation of Business, 1865–1932* (1997).

Chapter 21 The Age of Reform

The Progressive Era is surveyed in Michael McGerr, *A Fierce Discontent: The Rise and Fall of the Progressive Movement in America, 1870–1920* (2003), and David Traxel, *Crusader Nation: The United States in Peace and the Great War* (2006). Two recent scholars examine American progressivism in the context of reform movements elsewhere: Daniel T. Rodgers, *Atlantic Crossings: Social Politics in a Progressive Age* (1998), and Alan Dawley, *Changing the World: American Progressives in War and Revolution* (2003). The works cited in the Debating the Past feature (p. 597) are also essential.

The role of muckraking journalism is explored in David Nasaw, *The Chief: The Life of William Randolph Hearst* (2000). See also Louise K. Knight, *Citizen: Jane Addams* (2005).

For regional studies, see Dewey W. Grantham, *The South in Modern America* (1994), Nancy Unger, *Fighting Bob La Follette* (2000), and Bernard A. Weisberger, *The La Follettes of Wisconsin* (1994). Kenneth Finegold, *Experts and Politicians* (1995), compares the struggles between urban machines and reformers in New York, Cleveland, and Chicago. James J. Connolly, *The Triumph of Ethnic Progressivism* (1998), examines the political dynamics in Boston. J. Anthony Lukas, *Big Trouble* (1997), provides a detailed account of labor strife in Idaho and Colorado. Chuck Chalberg, *Emma Goldman* (2007), is accessible.

On the woman suffrage campaign, see Jean Baker, *Sisters: The Lives of America's Suffragists* (2005), Margaret Finnegan, *Selling Suffrage: Consumer Culture and Votes for Women* (1999), Ellen Carol DuBois, *Harriot Stanton Blanch and the Winning of Woman Suffrage* (1997), and Gayle Gullett, *Becoming Citizens: The Emergence and Development of the California Women's Movement, 1880–1911* (2000). Other useful works include Lynn D. Gordon, *Gender and Higher Education in the Progressive Era* (1990), Robyn Muncy, *Creating a Female Dominion in American Reform, 1890–1935* (1991), and Paula Baker, *The Moral Frameworks of Public Life: Gender, Politics and the State in Rural New York, 1870–1930* (1991).

Books treating special aspects of progressivism include Edward A. Purcell, *Brandeis and the Progressive Constitution* (2000), Tony Freyer, *Regulating Big Business: Antitrust in Great Britain and*

America, 1880–1990 (1992), James Weinstein, *The Corporate Ideal and the Liberal State* (1981), and Naomi Lamoreaux, *The Great Merger Movement in American Business, 1895–1940* (1985).

On African Americans, see David Levering Lewis, *W. E. B. DuBois: Biography of a Race, 1868–1919* (1993), and *W. E. B. DuBois: The Fight for Equality, 1919–1963* (2000).

H. W. Brands, *TR* (1997), and Kathleen Dalton, *Theodore Roosevelt: A Strenuous Life* (2003), offer concise narratives. Edmund Morris's *Theodore Rex* (2001) is engaging. An interesting critique of Roosevelt's environmental policies can be found in Karl Jacoby, *Crimes Against Nature* (2001). James Chace, *1912: Wilson, Roosevelt, Taft, and Debs—the Election that Changed the Country* (2004), describes that pivotal event.

The standard multi-volume biography of Wilson is Arthur S. Link, *Wilson* (1947–1965). Recent works include H. W. Brands, *Woodrow Wilson* (2003). See also David Steigerwald, *Wilsonian Idealism in America* (1996).

CHAPTER 22 FROM ISOLATION TO EMPIRE

Contemporary attitudes are reflected in Josiah Strong, *Our Country* (1885), and Alfred T. Mahan, *The Influence of Sea Power Upon History* (1890), which provides the clearest presentation of Mahan's thesis.

For post–Civil War diplomatic history the works cited in Debating the Past (p. 617) are essential. William Zimmermann, *First Great Triumph: How Five Americans Made Their Country a World Power* (2003), is an accessible study of the convergence of Theodore Roosevelt, John Hay, A. T. Mahan, Elihu Root, and Henry Cabot Lodge. See also Thomas D. Schoonover, *The United States in Central America* (1991), and David Healy, *U.S. Expansionism: The Imperialist Urge in the 1890's* (1970). Emily S. Rosenberg, *Financial Missionaries to the World: The Politics and Culture of Dollar Diplomacy, 1900–1930* (1999), shows how cultural and economic forces intersected to promote expansionism.

On Hawaiian annexation, see Merze Tate, *The United States and the Hawaiian Kingdom* (1965). On the Spanish-American War, see Paul T. McCartney, *Power and Progress: American National Identity, the War of 1898, and the Rise of American Imperialism* (2006), and John L. Offner, *An Unwanted War: The Diplomacy of the United States and Spain over Cuba, 1895–1898* (1992). John Lawrence Tone, *War and Genocide in Cuba: 1895–1898* (2006), is sharply critical.

For colonial problems in the Philippines, see Stuart Creighton Miller, *"Benevolent Assimilation": The American Conquest of the Philippines, 1899–1903* (1982), and H. W. Brands, *Bound to Empire: The United States and the Philippines* (1992). Barthelomew Sparrow, *The Insular Cases and the Emergence of American Empire* (2006), examines the role of the Court in American expansionist policy. On the Caribbean, see Thomas O'Brien, *The Revolutionary Mission: American Enterprise in Latin America, 1900–1945* (1996). David McCullough, *The Path Between the Seas* (1977), is excellent on the history of the Panama Canal.

CHAPTER 23 WOODROW WILSON AND THE GREAT WAR

On the American involvement with Mexico, see Eileen Welsome, *The General and the Jaguar: Pershing's Hunt for Pancho Villa* (2006), and Joseph A. Stout, *Border Conflict: Villistas, Carrancistas, and the Punitive Expedition, 1915–1920* (1999).

On Woodrow Wilson, in addition to the works discussed in previous chapters and in *Debating the Past* (p. 666), see H. W. Brands, *Woodrow Wilson* (2003), and, less critical, Arthur S. Link: *Woodrow Wilson and the Progressive Era* (1954), and *Wilson the Diplomatist* (1957).

The war on the home front is covered in David M. Kennedy, *Over Here: The First World War and American Society* (1980). Paul A. C. Koistinen, *Mobilizing for Modern War* (1997), examines the emergence of business and military ties during the war.

On American military participation, see Mark Meigs, *Optimism at Armageddon* (1997), and Gene Smith, *Until the Trumpet Sounds* (1998), on Pershing. On African-Americans and the war, see Mark Ellis, *Race, War and Surveillance* (2001), and Stephen L. Harris, *Harlem's Hell-Fighters* (2003). See also Herbert A. Johnson, *Wingless Eagle: U.S. Army Aviation through World War* (2001). Women's role with the AEF is examined in Susan Zeiger, *In Uncle Sam's Service* (1999).

On the peace settlement, in addition to the biographies of Wilson, consult Thomas J. Knock, *The War to End All Wars: Woodrow Wilson and the Quest for a New World Order* (1992), A. J. Mayer, *Politics and Diplomacy of Peacemaking* (1967), and John M. Cooper, *Breaking the Heart of the World* (2001).

On labor, see David Montgomery, *The Fall of the House of Labor: The Workplace, the State, and American Labor Activism, 1865–1921* (1987). For a detailed study of organized labor in the South, see Bryant Simon, *A Fabric of Defeat* (1998). Kathleen Kennedy, *Disloyal Mothers and Scurrilous Citizens*

(1999), examines the intersection of war, gender, and free speech. On radicalism and the red scare, see R. K. Murray, *The Red Scare* (1955), Stanley Coben, *A. Mitchell Palmer* (1963), David Brody, *The Steel Strike of 1919* (1965), and E. Anthony Lukas, *Big Trouble* (1997), on labor disturbances in the Far West. On the Spanish influenza epidemic, see John Barry, *Great Influenza* (2004), and Gina Kolata, *Flu: The Story of the Great Influenza Pandemic of 1918 and the Search for the Virus That Caused It* (1999).

CHAPTER 24 POSTWAR SOCIETY AND CULTURE: CHANGE AND ADJUSTMENT

In addition to the works cited in Debating the Past (p. 676), Ann Douglas, *Terrible Honesty: Mongrel Manhattan in the 1920s* (1995), emphasizes the positive aspects of urban life, and Stanley Coben, *Rebellion Against Victorianism* (1991), emphasizes its elements of change. David Goldberg's survey, *Discontented America* (1999), focuses on divisions of race, ethnicity, and class.

Nativism and immigration restriction are covered in Desmond King, *Making Americans* (2000). On changes in the family, see Steven Mintz and Susan Kellogg, *Domestic Revolutions* (1988); on other social trends, John D'Emilio and Estelle Freedman, *Intimate Matters* (1988), and Paula Fass, *The Damned and the Beautiful* (1977).

The "new" woman is discussed in Nancy F. Cott, *The Grounding of Modern Feminism* (1987), William Chafe, *The American Woman* (1972), Ellen Chesler, *Woman of Valor* (1992) (on Margaret Sanger and the birth control movement), Dorothy M. Brown, *Setting a Course: American Women in the 1920s* (1987), and Nancy Woloch, *Women and the American Experience* (1971). Peter N. Stearns, *Anxious Parents* (2003) is a survey of childrearing advice, with special emphasis on the early twentieth century.

On the evolution of celebrity in popular culture, see Charles L. Ponce de Leon, *Self-Exposure: Human-Interest Journalism and the Emergence of Celebrity in America, 1890–1940* (2002). On Hollywood, see Steven J. Ross, *Working-Class Hollywood: Silent Film and the Shaping of Class in America* (1998). On radio, see Hugh R. Slotten, *Radio and Television Regulation: Broadcast Technology in the United States* (2000). On the rise of consumer credit, see Lendol Calder, *Financing the American Dream* (1999).

Fundamentalism is treated in Joel A. Carpenter, *Revive Us Again: The Reawakening of American Fundamentalism* (1997); the Scopes trial in Edward J. Larson, *Summer for the Gods: The Scopes Trial and America's Continuing Debate over Science and Religion* (1997), and Paul Conkin, *When All the Gods Trembled* (1998). On prohibition, see Stanley Walker, *The Night Club Era* (1999). On the Klan, consult Nancy MacLean, *Behind the Mask of Chivalry: The Making of the Second Ku Klux Klan* (1994), and Jim Ruiz, *The Black Hood of the Ku Klux Klan* (1998).

Francis Russell, *Tragedy in Dedham* (1962), casts doubt on the innocence of Sacco and Vanzetti; see also Paul Avrich, *Sacco and Vanzetti: The Anarchist Background* (1991).

Milton C. Sernetet, *Bound for the Promised Land* (1997), emphasizes the religious dimensions of the black migration to the North. Alfred L. Brophy, *Reconstructing the Dreamland: The Tulsa Riot of 1921* (2002), is useful on that important episode. On blacks in Harlem, see Gilbert Osofsky, *Harlem: The Making of a Ghetto* (1965). The Harlem Renaissance is the subject of Steven Watson, *The Harlem Renaissance* (1995), and J. Martin Favor, *Authentic Blackness* (1999). Eric Porter, *What Is This Thing Called Jazz?* (2002), explores the connections between music and intellectual life.

The literature of the period is analyzed in Nathan Miller, *New World Coming: The 1920s and the Making of Modern America* (2003). See Jeffrey Meyers, *Scott Fitzgerald: A Biography* (1994), and also his *Hemingway: A Biography* (1999); also Carlos H. Baker, *Hemingway* (1956); on Mencken, William R. Manchester, *Disturber of the Peace* (1951); on Lewis, Mark Schorer, *Sinclair Lewis* (1961); on Wharton, R. W. B. Lewis, *Edith Wharton* (1975), and Shari Benstock, *No Gifts from Chance* (1994).

On Henry Ford, see Douglas Brinkley, *Wheels for the World* (2004); Clarence Hooker, *Life in the Shadows of the Crystal Palace 1910–1927* (1997), illuminates the role of labor at Ford. On the early history of General Motors, see David Farber, *Sloan Rules: Alfred P. Sloan and the Triumph of General Motors* (2002). On women and cars, see Virginia Scharff, *Taking the Wheel* (1991). Beth Bailey, *From Front Porch to Back Seat* (1988), considers the ramifications of the automobile on courtship.

On Lindbergh and early aviation, see Walter L. Hixon, *Charles A. Lindbergh: Lone Eagle* (2006).

CHAPTER 25 THE NEW ERA: 1921–1933

The political history of the 1920s is surveyed in Michael Parrish, *Anxious Decades: America in Prosperity and Depression, 1920–1941* (1992), and Geoffrey Parret, *America in the Twenties* (1982).

Robert K. Murray, *The Harding Era* (2000), relates the embattled president to his times. John Dean's *Warren G. Harding* (2004) is interesting in that the author was himself convicted of crimes connected with the Watergate burglary during the Nixon administration. See also David Greenberg, *Calvin Coolidge* (2007), and Robert Ferrell, *The Presidency of Calvin Coolidge* (1998). On Hoover, see Martin L. Fausold, *The Presidency of Herbert Hoover* (1985), and a narrower monograph, Kendrick A. Clements, *Hoover, Conservatives and Consumerism* (2000).

Barry Eichengreen, *Golden Fetters: The Gold Standard and the Great Depression* (1992), considers an important issue; Maury Klein, *Rainbow's End* (2001), examines the stock market crash of 1929. See also the works cited in the Debating the Past feature (p. 713).

Stephen Kneeshaw, *The Pursuit of Peace* (1991), examines the Kellogg-Briand pact. See also Manfred Jonas, *Isolationism in America, 1935–1941* (1990) and Charles De Benedetti, *Origins of the Modern Peace Movement* (1978).

CHAPTER 26 THE NEW DEAL: 1933–1941

The most important surveys of the New Deal are listed in the Debating the Past (p. 739). Jonathan Alter, *Defining Moment: FDR's Hundred Days and the Triumph of Hope* (2006), is an accessible introduction to that formative period. See also R. Alan Lawson, *Commonwealth of Hope* (2005), Maxwell Bloomfield, *Peaceful Revolution* (2000), Ronald Edsforth, *The New Deal* (2000), and Alan Brinkley, *Liberalism and Its Discontents* (1998). Robert Shogan, *Backlash: The Killing of the New Deal* (2006), recounts the mounting opposition of the late 1930s.

Of the many biographies of Roosevelt, Allan Winkler, *Franklin D. Roosevelt and the Making of Modern America* (2006), is concise; for longer studies, see Geoffrey Ward, *A First-Class Temperament: The Emergence of Franklin Roosevelt* (1989). On Eleanor Roosevelt, see Blanche W. Cook, *Eleanor Roosevelt* (1992–1999), and J. William T. Youngs, *Eleanor Roosevelt* (2006).

On the New Deal and agriculture, see David E. Hamilton, *From New Day to New Deal: American Farm Policy from Hoover to Roosevelt, 1928–1933* (1991); Donald Worster, *Dust Bowl* (2004), analyzes the calamity while Timothy Egan, *Worst Hard Time* (2006), describes its consequences in personal terms. Sarah T. Phillips, *This Land, This Nation* (2007), addresses the impact of the New Deal on farmers with a focus on conservation issues.

On the New Deal and economic policy, see William J. Barber, *Designs within Disorder* (1996), Morton Keller, *Regulating the New Economy: Public Policy and Economic Change in America* (1990) and *Regulating a New Society: Public Policy and Social Change in America, 1900–1933* (1994).

On workers and the New Deal, see Edwin Amenta, *Bold Relief: Institutional Politics and the Origins of Modern Social Policy* (1998), Gery Gerstle, *Working-Class Americanism: The Politics of Labor in a Textile City 1914–1960* (1989), Vicki Ruiz, *Cannery Women, Cannery Lives: Mexican Women, Unionization, and the California Food Processing Industry, 1930–1950* (1987), Lizabeth Cohen, *Making a New Deal: Industrial Workers in Chicago, 1919–1939* (1990), and Melvyn Dubofsky, *The State and Labor in Modern America* (1994). Bruce Nelson, *Divided We Stand: American Workers and the Struggle for Black Equality* (2001), describes a cleavage within the labor movement over racial issues. On the relation of private pensions and social security, see Jennifer Klein, *For All These Rights: Business, Labor, and the Shaping of America's Public-Private Welfare State* (2003).

On constitutional questions, see William E. Leuchtenburg, *The Supreme Court Reborn: The Constitutional Revolution in the Age of Roosevelt* (1995).

For the activities of the radical fringe, consult Michael Denning, *The Cultural Front: The Laboring of American Culture in the Twentieth Century* (1996), Donald R. McCoy, *Angry Voices: Left-of-Center Politics in the New Deal Era* (1958), and D. H. Bennett, *Demagogues in the Depression* (1969). On blacks during the 1930s, see Raymond Wolters, *Negroes and the Great Depression* (1970), Nancy J. Weiss, *Farewell to the Party of Lincoln* (1983), and Harvard Sitkoff, *A New Deal for Blacks* (1978).

On women and gender, apart from the works cited above, see Suzanne Mettler, *Dividing Citizens* (1998), Landon Storrs, *Civilizing Capitalism* (2000), Susan Ware, *Beyond Suffrage: Women in the New Deal* (1981), and *Partner and I* (1987), a life of Molly Dewson. Also Linda Gordon, *Pitied But Not Entitled: Single Mothers and the History of Welfare* (1994), and Susan Ware, *Holding Their Own: American Women in the 1930s* (1982). On New Deal Indian policy, see Kenneth R. Philip, *Termination Revisited: American Indians on the Trail to Self-Determination, 1933–1953* (1999).

On isolationism and the events leading to Pearl Harbor, see Justus D. Doenecke, *Storm on the Horizon: The Challenge to American Intervention, 1939–1941* (2000), and David Reynolds, *From Munich to Pearl Harbor: Roosevelt's America and the Origins of the Second World War* (2001).

On James J. Braddock, see Michael C. De Lisa, *Cinderella Man* (2005).

CHAPTER 27 WAR AND PEACE

The best history of the worldwide events leading to the Japanese attack on Pearl Harbor is Waldo Heinrichs, *Threshold of War* (1988), but for more detail see Akira Iriye, *Pearl Harbor and the Coming of the Pacific War* (1999), and Michael S. Stackman, *Target: Pearl Harbor* (1990). Charles C. Tansill, *Back Door to War* (1952), and Charles A. Beard, *President Roosevelt and the Coming of the War* (1948), are interesting interpretations by isolationists. Useful overviews include David M. Kennedy, *Freedom from Fear: The American People in Depression and War* (1999), Murray Williamson and Allan R. Millett, *A War to Be Won* (2000), and Warren F. Kimball, *Forged in War: Roosevelt, Churchill and the Second World War* (1997). Mark A. Stoler, *Allies and Adversaries* (2000), focuses on the Joint Chiefs of Staff. Thomas S. Fleming, *The New Dealers' War* (2001), is critical of Roosevelt.

Alan Schom, *Eagle and the Rising Sun* (2004), chronicles the war in the Pacific from 1941–1943. On aerial warfare, see Williamson Murray, *War in the Air, 1914–1945* (1999), and Geoffrey Peret, *Winged Victory* (1993); see also Michael S. Sherry, *The Rise of American Airpower* (1987). Paul Fussell, *Wartime: Understanding and Behavior in the Second World War* (1989), provides a realistic rendering of the carnage and chaos of modern warfare; Gerald F. Linderman, *The World Within War: America's Combat Experience in World War II* (1997), contends that the spectacle of war offers little sustenance to soldiers. The term "the greatest generation" is from Tom Brokaw's 1998 book by that title.

For a general, brief overview of the home front, see Lewis A. Erenberg and Susan E. Hirsch, *The War in American Culture: Society and Consciousness During World War II* (1996), Doris Kearns Goodwin, *No Ordinary Time* (1995), and Steven Mintz and Susan Kellogg, *Domestic Revolutions* (1988). The effects of the war on women are described in Margaret Paton-Walsh, *Our War Too* (2002), D'Ann Campbell, *Women at War with America* (1984), Karen Anderson, *Wartime Women* (1981), and Susan M. Hartmann, *The Home Front and Beyond* (1982). William M. Tuttle Jr., "Daddy's Gone To War": The Second World War in the Lives of America's Children* (1993), offers an interesting perspective. The impact of the war on radical politics is examined in Bill V. Mullen, *Popular Fronts: Chicago and African-American Cultural Politics, 1935–46* (1999).

African American participation is the subject of Maggie M. Morehouse, *Fighting in the Jim Crow Army* (2002), Nat Brandt, *Harlem at War* (1996), Neil A. Wynn, *The Afro-American and the Second World War* (1993), and Dominic J. Capeci, Jr., *Race Relations in Wartime Detroit* (1984). See also Maggie Rivas-Rodriguez, ed., *Mexican-Americans and World War II* (2007). On the Japanese internment, see Greg Robinson, *By Order of the President: FDR and the Internment of Japanese Americans* (2001).

Major biographies include Carlo D'Este, *Eisenhower: A Soldier's Life* (2002), Geoffrey Perret, *Eisenhower* (1999), and Ed Cray, *General of the Army: George C. Marshall* (1990).

Richard Rhodes, *The Making of the Atom Bomb* (1986), is superb. For the relationship among key Manhattan Project scientists, see Gregg Herken, *Brotherhood of the Bomb* (2002).

CHAPTER 28 THE AMERICAN CENTURY

General surveys include William Chafe, *The Unfinished Journey* (1986), James T. Patterson, *Grand Expectations: Postwar America, 1945–1974* (1996), David Halberstam, *The Fifties* (1993), H. W. Brands, *The Devil We Knew: Americans and the Cold War* (1993), John Patrick Diggins, *The Proud Decades, 1941–1960* (1989), and Michael S. Sherry, *In the Shadow of War* (1995).

The evolution of American policy toward nuclear weapons is debated in Gar Alperovitz, *Atomic Diplomacy: Hiroshima and Potsdam* (1985), Gregg Herken, *The Winning Weapon: The Atomic Bomb in the Cold War* (1982), and Melvyn P. Leffler, *A Preponderance of Power: National Security, the Truman Administration, and the Cold War* (1992). An accessible overview is Richard Rhodes, *Dark Sun: The Making of the Hydrogen Bomb* (1995).

The 1948 election is described in Gary Donaldson, *Truman Defeats Dewey* (1999). On the origins of the shift of the South away from the Democrats, see Kari Frederickson, *The Dixiecrat Revolt and the End of the Solid South, 1932–1968* (2001). On the cultural effects of the Cold War, see Elaine Tyler May, *Homeward Bound: American Families in the Cold War* (1988), and Paul Boyer, *By the Bomb's Early Light* (1986).

In addition to works cited in the previous chapter, see Donald R. McCoy, *The Presidency of Harry S Truman* (1984). David McCullough's *Truman* (1992), is accessible and sympathetic; Alonzo L. Hamby's *Man of the People: A Life of Harry S Truman* (1995), is scholarly and analytical.

Truman's foreign policy and the origins of the Cold War are examined in the Debating the Past feature for this chapter (p. 791). See also Robert L. Beisher, *Dean Acheson: A Life in the Cold War* (2006), and Michael J. Hogan, *The Marshall Plan* (1987). Roger C. Miller, *To Save a City: The Berlin Airlift* (2000), is a succinct account. See also John Lukas, *George Kennan* (2007).

The origins of the Korean War are now becoming clearer. In two volumes Bruce Cummings, *The Origins of the Korean War* (1981, 1990), emphasizes that the struggle was, at the outset, a civil war; William Stueck, *The Korean War: An International History* (1995), focuses on miscalculations by Stalin and Mao Zedong. For other perspectives, see Paul G. Pierpaoli Jr., *Truman and Korea* (1999), and Stanley Sandler, *The Korean War* (1999). On MacArthur, see Geoffrey Perret, *Old Soldiers Never Die* (1996).

On McCarthyism, see Tom Wicker, *Shooting Star: The Brief Arc of Joseph McCarthy* (2006). Ellen Schrecker, *Many Are the Crimes: McCarthyism in America* (1998), argues that the phenomenon was broader than McCarthy and became institutionalized in the FBI under J. Edgar Hoover. For different views of McCarthy himself, see Thomas C. Reeves, *Life and Times of Joe McCarthy* (1997), and Arthur Herman, *Joseph McCarthy* (2000). On the Hiss case, see Allen Weinsten, *Perjury: The Hiss-Chambers Case* (1978), and Sam Tanenhaus, *Whittaker Chambers* (1997). George Clooney, *Good Night, and Good Luck* (2006), includes the actor-director's thoughts on his movie about Edward R. Murrow and McCarthy, as well as the screenplay itself.

On the early history of the Civil Rights movement, see Mark Tushnet, *Making Civil Rights Law* (1994), and *Making Constitutional Law: Thurgood Marshall and the Supreme Court* (1997). The first volume of Taylor Branch's superb biography of Martin Luther King Jr., *Parting the Waters* (1988), covers 1959 through 1963. Thomas Borstelmann, *The Cold War and the Color Line* (2001), and Mary Dudziak, *Cold War Civil Rights* (2000), show how the civil rights movement became embroiled in foreign policy issues, especially with respect to African nations.

Recent (and increasingly positive) assessments of Dwight D. Eisenhower include Robert Bowie and Richard Immerman, *Waging Peace: How Eisenhower Shaped an Enduring Cold War Strategy* (1998), Craig Campbell, *Destroying the Village: Eisenhower and Thermonuclear War* (1998), and Ray Takeyh, *The Origins of the Eisenhower Doctrine* (2000) on Suez. See also Richard H. Immerman, *John Foster Dulles* (1999).

CHAPTER 29 FROM CAMELOT TO WATERGATE

On Kennedy, consult Robert Dallek, *Unfinished Life: John F. Kennedy, 1917–1963* (2003), Richard Reeves, *President Kennedy* (1992), and James Giglio, *The Presidency of John F. Kennedy* (1991). Barbara Leaming, *Jack Kennedy* (2006), focuses on the person rather than the presidency. On Kennedy's foreign policy, see Lawrence Freedman, *Kennedy's Wars* (2000), and William Taubman, *Khrushchev* (2003). The Kennedy style can be "heard" in Ernest R. May and Philip D. Zelikow, eds., *The Kennedy Tapes: Inside the White House During the Cuban Missile Crisis* (1997). Also on the Cuban missile crisis, see Sheldon M. Stern, *The Week the World Stood Still* (2005). Gerald Posner, *Case Closed: Lee Harvey Oswald and the Assassination of JFK* (1994), debunks the conspiracy theorists.

Robert Caro, *The Years of Lyndon B. Johnson: The Path to Power* (1982) and *Means of Ascent* (1990), are extremely critical; Robert Dallek, *Lone Star Rising: Lyndon Johnson and His Times, 1908–1960* (1991) and *Flawed Giant: Lyndon B. Johnson, 1960–1973* (1998), are more balanced. Michael Beschloss, ed., *Taking Charge: The Johnson White House Tapes, 1963–1969* (1997), provides a verbatim, previously secret, account.

For civil rights, in addition to works cited in the previous chapter, consult Taylor Branch's second and third volumes in his trilogy on Martin Luther King Jr., *Pillar of Fire* (1998) and *At Canaan's Edge* (2006). Diane McWhorter, *Carry Me Home* (2001), provides a gripping account of the civil rights struggle in Birmingham, Alabama. Raymond Arsenault, *Freedom Riders: 1961* (2006), examines that important movement. Nicholas Lemann, *The Promised Land: The Great Black Migration and How It Changed America* (1991), is also indispensable. Malcolm X, *Autobiography*, is a classic account of black alienation, but see also Robert Terrill, *Malcolm X* (2006). Joseph E. Peniel, *Waiting 'til the Midnight Hour* (2006), examines the Black Power movement. James T. Patterson, *Brown v. Board of Education* (2001), provides a thorough account of that Supreme Court decision.

For a concise biography of Nixon, see Herbert H. Parmet, *Richard M. Nixon* (2006). See also Richard Reeves, *Richard Nixon: Alone in the White House* (2001), and Joan Hoff, *Nixon Reconsidered* (1994). Allen J. Matusow, *Nixon's Economy* (1998), is excellent. Dean J. Kotlowski, *Nixon's Civil Rights* (2001), argues that Nixon's actions—if not his rhetoric—were mostly supportive; J. Brooks Flippen, *Nixon and the Environment* (2000), makes a similar point about Nixon and environmental issues.

Henry Kissinger's memoirs, *White House Years* (1979) and *Years of Upheaval* (1982), are important though, like most such works, self-serving. See also Christopher Hitchens, *The Trial of Henry Kissinger* (2001).

The literature on the war in Vietnam is enormous. See David E. Kaiser, *American Tragedy: Kennedy, Johnson and the Origins of the Vietnam War* (2000), Lawrence Freedman, *Kennedy's Wars: Berlin, Cuba, Laos, and Vietnam* (2000), A. J. Langguth, *Our Vietnam: The War: 1954–1975* (2000), and Robert D. Schulzinger, *A Time for War* (1997). Neil Sheehan, *A Bright and Shining Lie* (1988), an account of the war from one American adviser's perspective, provides the best explanation of why the war could not be won. See also Lloyd C. Gardner, *Pay Any Price: Lyndon Johnson and the Wars for Vietnam* (1995).

For the antiwar movement, see Robert Buzzanco, *Masters of War: Military Dissent and Politics in the Vietnam Era* (1996), Rhodri Jeffreys-Jones, *Peace Now!* (1999), and Mary Hershberger, *Traveling to Vietnam: American Peace Activists and the War* (1998) on the ending of the war. See also Michael S. Foley, *Confronting the War Machine: Draft Resistance during the Vietnam War* (2003).

The best analysis of the Watergate affair is Stanley I. Kutler, *The Wars of Watergate* (1990) and *Abuse of Power* (1997), but see also Carl Bernstein and Robert Woodward, *All the President's Men* (1974) and *Final Days* (1976), and John W. Dean, *Blind Ambition* (1976). On Ford's elevation to the presidency, see James Cannon, *Time and Chance* (2001).

CHAPTER 30 SOCIETY IN FLUX

Kenneth T. Jackson, *Crabgrass Frontier* (1985), is indispensable on the evolution of the suburbs. On Jackson's argument that home ownership contributed to political conservativism, see Becky M. Nicolaides, *My Blue Heaven: Life and Politics in the Working-Class Suburbs of Los Angeles, 1920–1965* (2002). Elaine Tyler May, *Homeward Bound: American Families in the Cold War* (1988), locates the rise of a conservative ideological mindset within the home. The environmental consequences of suburbanization are the subject of Adam Rome, *The Bulldozer in the Countryside* (2001). For the cities, see Robert M. Fogelson, *Downtown: Its Rise and Fall, 1880–1950* (2001).

On the effects of the automobile, see Jane H. Kay's history/manifesto, *Asphalt Nation* (1997), and Virginia Scharff's *Taking the Wheel: Women and the Coming of the Motor Age* (1992).

For a favorable account of New Left of the 1960s, by a former leader of the SDS, see Todd Gitlin, *The Sixties: Years of Hope, Days of Rage* (1987). Maurice Isserman and Michael Kazin, *America Divided: The Civil War of the 1960s* (2000), though sympathetic to the New Left, note that conservatives emerged from the decade victorious. David Burner, *Making Peace with the Sixties* (1996), argues that the New Left unwisely abandoned its Old Left origins, and thus slipped into self-destructive hedonism. Peter Collier and David Horowitz, *Destructive Generation: Second Thoughts about the '60s* (1989), contend that the decade's "hedonism" and "revolutionary passion" culminated in "tragic consequences." See also Roger Kimball, *The Long March: How the Cultural Revolution of the 1960s Changed America* (2000), Dominick Cavallo, *A Faction of the Past: The Sixties in American History* (1999), and David Farber, *Chicago 68* (1988). Ellen Fitzpatrick, *History's Memory: Writing America's Past, 1880–1980* (2002), is especially critical of historians of this period for neglecting their scholarly forebears.

For television, see Mary Ann Watson, *The Expanding Vista: American Television in the Kennedy Years* (1994), and two books by James L. Baughman, *The Republic of Mass Culture: Journalism, Filmmaking, and Broadcasting in America Since 1941* (2006), and *Same Time, Same Station: Creating American Television* (2007). On cultural issues, see Karal Ann Marling, *As Seen on TV: The Visual Culture of Everyday Life in the 1950s* (1994), and Josh Ozersky, *Archie Bunker's America: TV in an Era of Change* (2003).

On black radicalism, in addition to works cited in the previous chapter, see the first person accounts by Malcolm X, *Autobiography* (1966), Stokely Carmichael and C. V. Hamilton, *Black Power* (1967), and Eldridge Cleaver, *Soul on Ice* (1967). Modern studies include Robert Terrill, *Malcolm X* (2006), and, on the Black Power movement, Joseph Peniel, *Waiting 'til the Midnight Hour* (2006). Taylor Branch's three-volume biography of Martin Luther King Jr.—*Parting the Waters: 1954–1963* (1988), *Pillar of Fire: America in the King Years, 1963–1965* (1998), and *At Canaan's Edge* (1965–1968)—is a modern classic. The neglected role of women in the civil rights movement is addressed in Chana Kai Lee, *For Freedom's Sake: The Life of Fannie Lou Hamer* (1999), and Carolyn Wedin, *Inheritors of the Spirit: Mary White Ovington and the Founding of NAACP* (1998).

Ronald Takaki, *A Different Mirror: A History of Multicultural History* (1993), provides an overview of the contemporary immigrant experience. Rodolfo Acuna, *Occupied America: A History of Chicanos* (2000), Manuel Gonzales, *Mexicanos: A History of Mexicans in the United States* (1999), and Ernesto Vigil, *The Crusade for Justice* (1999) provide surveys of broad trends of Chicano history in the United States. See especially Dan La Botz, *César Chavez and La Causa* (2006). John W. Sayer, *Ghost Dancing the Law* (1997), examines the legal issues surrounding the Native American protests at Wounded Knee. See also Kenneth S. Stern, *Loud Hawk: The United States Against the American Indian Movement* (1994).

The literature on the women's movement is voluminous. Betty Friedan's *The Feminine Mystique* (1963), is essential, though her account must be modified in light of Daniel Horowitz, *Betty Friedan and the Making of The Feminine Mystique* (1998). Susan Oliver, *Betty Friedan: The Personal Is Political* (2007), is a concise account. On abortion, Rickie Solinger, *Wake Up Little Suzie: Single Pregnancy and Race before Roe v. Wade* (1992), considers the situation before 1973. On the *Roe* v. *Wade* decision itself, see Laurence H. Tribe, *Abortion: The Clash of Absolutes* (1990), and Linda Gordon, *Moral Property of Women: A History of Birth Control Politics in America* (2002). Andrea Tone, *Devices and Desires: A History of Contraceptives in America* (2001) is useful on contraception more generally.

James H. Jones, *Alfred C. Kinsey: A Public/Private Life* (1997), finds that Kinsey's odd behavior discredits his scholarship; Jonathan Gathorne-Hardy, *Alfred C. Kinsey: Sex the Measure of All Things* (1998), is less critical. On sexual trends more generally, see Beth Bailey, *Sex in the Heartland* (1999), on Kansas in the 1960s and 1970s.

The early history of the AIDS crisis is movingly told in Randy Shilts, *And the Band Played On* (1987). See also Elizabeth Fee and Daniel M. Fox, eds., *AIDS: The Making of a Chronic Disease* (1992).

CHAPTER 31 RUNNING ON EMPTY: THE NATION TRANSFORMED

Bruce J. Schulman, *The Seventies* (2001), surveys that decade, as Haynes Johnson, *Sleepwalking through History* (1992) does for the 1980s. James T. Patterson surveys a somewhat broader period in *Restless Giant: The United States from Watergate to Bush v. Gore* (2004). On Gerald Ford, the definitive account is Yanek Mieczkowski, *Gerald Ford and the Challenges of the 1970s* (2005).

Peter G. Bourne, *Jimmy Carter* (1997), relates his subject's life and policies. W. Carl Biven, *Jimmy Carter's Economy* (2002), examines that critical issue. Donald Spencer, *The Carter Implosion: Jimmy Carter and the Amateur Style of Diplomacy* (1988), contains its thesis in the title; Robert A. Strong, *Working the World: Jimmy Carter and the Making of American Foreign Policy* (2000), defends Carter's record.

On Reagan, in addition to the works cited in Debating the Past (p. 881), see two recent studies: Michael Schaller, *Right Turn: American Life in the Reagan-Bush Era* (2007), and John Patrick Diggins, *Ronald Reagan: Fate, Freedom, and the Making of History* (2007). Although Edmund Morris's *Dutch: A Memoir* (1999), which includes fictional characters and footnotes, is not what it purports to be, it nevertheless offers interesting observations. David A. Stockman, *The Triumph of Politics* (1986), contains a frank discussion of administration fiscal policies. Reagan's foreign policy remains controversial. Especially useful is Jack F. Matlock, *Reagan and Gorbachev* (2004). Peter Schweizer, *Victory: The Reagan Administration's Secret Strategy That Hastened the Collapse of the Soviet Union* (1994), summarizes its achievements; Frances FitzGerald, *Way Out There in the Blue: Reagan, Star Wars and the End of the Cold War* (2000), is sharply critical. See also Jay Winik, *On the Brink* (1996).

The early history of the AIDS crisis is movingly told in Randy Shilts, *And the Band Played On* (1987); see also Elizabeth Fee and Daniel M. Fox, eds., *AIDS: The Making of a Chronic Disease* (1992). John-Manual Andriote examines its impact on gays themselves in *Victory Deferred: How AIDS Changed Gay Life in America* (1999).

On the transformation of the economy, see Robert M. Collins, *More: The Politics of Economic Growth in Postwar America* (2000), Daniel Yergin, *The Prize: The Epic Quest for Oil, Money and Power* (1991), and Barry Bluestone and Bennett Harrison, *The Deindustrializing of America* (1982).

CHAPTER 32 MISDEMEANORS AND HIGH CRIMES

Haynes Johnson, *Divided We Fall: Gambling with History in the Nineties* (1994), notwithstanding its expansive title, discusses the first few years of the 1990s; for the end of the Cold War see Michael R. Beschloss and Strobe Talbot, *At the Highest Levels: The Inside Story of the End of the Cold War*, and John Lewis Gaddis, *The United States and the End of the Cold War* (1992).

David Courtwright, *Violent Land: Single Men and Social Disorder from the Frontier to the Inner City* (1996), argues that much of the nation's crime has come from single males; for a cultural analysis of the infatuation with aggression, see Richard Slotkin, *Gunfighter Nation: The Myth of the Frontier in Twentieth-Century America* (1992). Bruce Jacobs, *Dealing Crack* (1999), provides a case study of the drug problem.

On the Reagan and Bush administrations, see Michael Schaller, *Right Turn: American Life in the Reagan/Bush Era* (2007). For Bush see Tom Wicker, *George Herbert Walker Bush* (2004), and John R. Greene, *The Presidency of George Bush* (2000). Gary R. Hess provides a thoughtful comparison on war-making processes in *Presidential Decisions for War: Korea, Vietnam and the Persian Gulf* (2001).

On Clinton prior to his move to the White House, see David Maraniss, *First in His Class: A Biography of Bill Clinton* (1995). On the presidential years, see John F. Harris, *Survivor: Bill Clinton in the White House* (2005), as well as Clinton's memoir, *My Life* (2004). The *Starr Report* (1998), though hastily released and published, constituted the evidentiary base and set the tone for the subsequent impeachment debate. See also Richard A. Posner, *An Affair of State: The Investigation, Impeachment, and Trial of President Clinton* (1999). On foreign policy, see David Halberstam, *War in a Time of Peace: Bush, Clinton and the Generals* (2001).

On the advance of conservatism, see Godfrey Hodgson, *The World Turned Rightside Up: A History of the Conservative Ascendancy in America* (1996). On the defeat of the ERA, see Mary Francis Berry, *Why ERA Failed* (1986), and Donald G. Mathews and Jane Sherron De Hart, *Sex, Gender, and the Politics of E.R.A.* (1990).

On race and ethnicity, see David A. Hollinger, *Postethnic America: Beyond Multiculturalism* (1995), Andrew Hacker, *Two Nations: Black and White, Separate, Hostile, Unequal* (1992), and Stephen Thernstrom and Abigail Thernstrom, *America in Black and White: One Nation, Indivisible* (1997).

John Cassidy, *Dot.con* (2002), surveys the Internet economy. For a history of the Internet, see Janet Abbate, *Inventing the Internet* (1999). On the 2000 election, see David A. Kaplan, *The Accidental President* (2001), and Richard Posner, *Breaking the Deadlock* (2001).

The literature on terrorism is expanding rapidly. The *9/11 Commission* Report (2004) is a detailed assessment of multiple failures in intelligence and security. Lawrence Wright, *The Looming Tower: Al Qaeda and the Road to 9/11* (2006), is indispensable. Douglas Little, *American Orientalism: The United States and the Middle East since 1945* (2002), provides a useful overview of American policies, while Thomas L. Friedman, *From Beirut to Jerusalem* (1989) offers a thoughtful analysis of the complex problems of the region. See also George Packer, *The Assassin's Gate: The United States in Iraq* (2005).

Bob Woodward's three books provide the best account of George W. Bush after the terrorist attack of September 11, 2001. *Bush at War* (2002) applauds his leadership immediately after 9/11; *Plan of Attack* (2004), more critical, details Bush's campaign to oust Saddam Hussein of Iraq; *State of Denial* (2006) maintains that Bush was incapable of accepting that the war was failing.

Recent works on immigration include Gary Hytuck and Kristine Zentgraf, *America Transformed* (2008), and Reed Ueda and Mary Water, ed., *New Americans* (2007). On the effects of globalization on children, see Paula Fass, *Children of a New World* (2007).

In *Game of Shadows* (2006), Mark Fainaru-Wada and Lance Williams, reporters for the *San Francisco Chronicle*, leaked secret grand jury testimony and broke the scandal of steroid use in organized sports.

On global warming and climate change, see Ann Rappaport and Sarah Creighton, *Degrees that Matter* (2007). Al Gore, the Democratic candidate for President in 2000, published an influential polemic, *An Inconvenient Truth* (2006), which was made into a movie by that title. On Hurricane Katrina, Doug Brinkley, *The Great Deluge* (2006), is definitive.

A-43

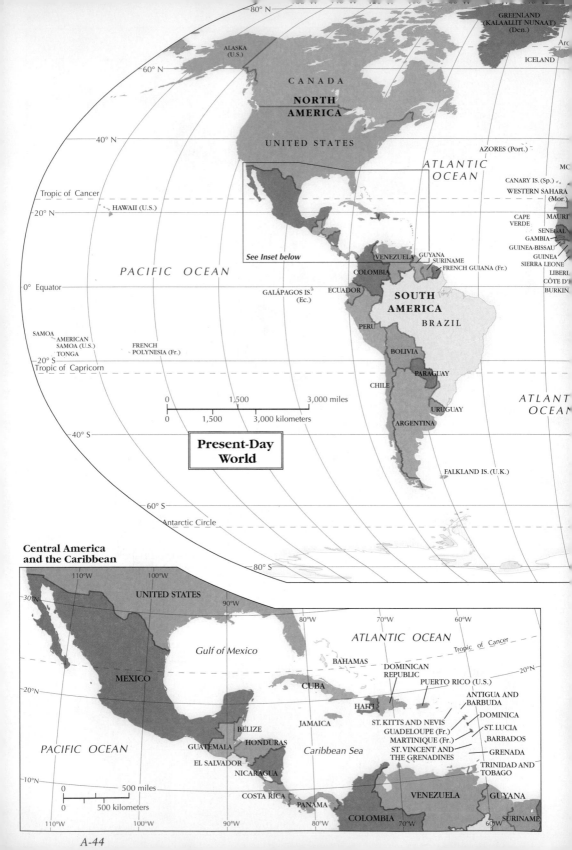

Present-Day World

Central America and the Caribbean

A-44

Europe

Southwest Asia

A-45

CREDITS

PROLOGUE   3 Jonathan Blair/Woodfin Camp & Associates. 6 Superstock, Inc. 7 Photo John Doebley/University of Wisconsin-Madison. 8 © Jerry Jacka Photography. 11 Cahokia Mounds State Historic Site, painting by Lloyd K. Townsend.

CHAPTER 1   21 The Bancroft Library, University of California. 26 Dorling Kindersley Media Library. 30 National Trust/Art Resource, New York. 33 National Portrait Gallery, Smithsonian Institution/Art Resource, New York. 35 Plimouth Plantation/Courtesy of the Plimouth Plantation, Plymouth, MA/www.plimoth.org. 39 The American Antiquarian Society. 43 Enoch Pratt Free Library Baltimore, MD. Photo courtesy of Maryland Department, Enoch Pratt Free Library. 46 Courtesy of the Pennsylvania Academy of the Fine Arts, Philadelphia. Gift of Mrs. Sarah Harrison (The Joseph Harrison, Jr. Collection) (1878.1.10). 50 (left) The British Museum/Dorling Kindersley Media Library. 50 (right) Oneida Indian Nation.

CHAPTER 2   56 Omni Photo Communications, Inc. 60 Library of Congress. 61 Library of Virginia. 64 Abby Aldrich Rockefeller Folk Art Museum, Williamsburg, VA. 69 Attributed to Freake-Gibbs, *The Mason Children—David, Joanna, & Abigail*, c. 1670, Fine Arts Museum of San Francisco. Gift of Mr. and Mrs. John D. Rockefeller 3rd (1979.7.3). 73 Unidentified artist. *Landscape (View of a Town)*, Worcester Art Museum, Worcester, MA. Gift of Dr. and Mrs. Kinnicut. 75 Photo by Mark Sexton/Peabody Essex Museum. 78 Kobal Collection. 79 Unknown Boston painter, *Mrs. Elizabeth Freake and Baby Mary (detail)*, c. 1670 Worcester Art Museum, Worcester, MA. Gift of Mr. and Mrs. Albert W. Rice.

CHAPTER 3   88 John Watson, *Portrait of Governor Lewis Morris* (detail). Brooklyn Museum of Art, Dick S. Ramsay Fund and John Hill Morgan. 90 John Greenwood, *Sea Captains Carousing in Surinam*, 1758. St. Louis Art Museum, Purchase. 94 Fenimore Art Museum, Cooperstown, NY. Richard Walker, Photo. 95 John Wallaston, *Portrait of George Whitfield*, c. 1742. The National Portrait Gallery, London. 99 White House Historical Association (White House Collection, 444). 103 Charles Willson Peale, *George Washington as Colonel of the Virginia Regiment*, 1772, Washington-Curtis-Lee Collection, Washington and Lee University, Lexington, VA. 108 Getty Images. 113 Hartley Greens, England. 119 Deposited by the City of Boston. Reproduced with permission. © 2002 Museum of Fine Arts, Boston, MA. All rights reserved. 120 Courtesy of the Massachusetts Historical Society (MHS Image #: 67). 122 The Library Company of Philadelphia.

CHAPTER 4 128 Concord Museum, Concord, MA. 132 The Granger Collection, New York. 133 William Walcott, *Pulling Down the Statue of George III at Bowling Green* (detail), c. 1857. Lafayette College Art Collection, Easton, PA. 135 The Granger Collection, New York. 139 The Pierpont Morgan Library/Art Resource, New York. 146 The Granger Collection, New York. 148 Photofest. 149 (top) Sir Joshua Reynolds, *Colonel Banastre Tarleton* (detail), 1782, National Gallery, London. 156 New York State Historical Association, Cooperstown, NY. 159 Alex Maclean/Landslides Aerial Photography.

CHAPTER 5 165 National Portrait Gallery, Smithsonian Institution/Art Resource, New York. 167 Creative Eye/Mira.com. 168 www.picturehistory.com. 170 Gilbert Stuart, *James Madison*, c. 1820. Mead Art Museum, Amherst College. Bequest of Herbert L. Pratt, Class of 1895 (1945.82). 177 © Collection of the New-York Historical Society (neg. No. 1371). 184 Frederick Kemmelmeyer, *Washington Reviewing the Western Army at Ft. Cumberland, October 18th, 1794* (detail), 1800. Courtesy, Winterthur Museum. 188 www.Picturehistory.com. 190 The Granger Collection.

CHAPTER 6 198 (left) © Paul Rocheleau Photography. 198 (right) Courtesy of the Massachusetts Historical Society. 204 Private Collection/Bridgeman Art Library. 205 Chicago Historical Society, G1932.0018. 207 Photo by Vincent Colabella Photography/Courtesy JP Morgan Chase Archives. 209 Clark Family Collection, William Clark Papers Voorhis #2/Missouri Historical Society, St. Louis. 211 National Maritime Museum, London. 214 Collection of the New-York Historical Society, (Neg. No. 7278).

CHAPTER 7 221 (left) Private collection. 221 (right) Library of Congress. 223 Getty Images. 225 Jacob Maentel, *General Schumacker*, c. 1812, Gift of Edgar William and Bernice Chrysler Garbisch, © 2003 Board of Trustees, National Gallery of Art, Washington, DC. 227 The Mariners' Museum, Newport News, VA. 230 The Granger Collection, New York. 235 (left) Courtesy of the National Park Service. 235 (right) Lee Snider/Photo Images/CORBIS. 244 Chicago Historical Society. 245 Hood Museum of Art, Dartmouth College, Hanover, New Hampshire, Gift of George C. Shattuck, Class of 1803. 247 National Portrait Gallery, Smithsonian Institution/Art Resource, New York.

CHAPTER 8 251 © 1992 Paul Rocheleau Photography. 255 The Granger Collection, New York. 260 © Bettmann/CORBIS. 265 Museum of Fine Arts, Boston, MA. 269 White House Historical Association (White House Collection). 270 New York Public Library/Art Resource, NY. 273 Boston Athenaeum.

CHAPTER 9 279 The Hermitage, Nashville, TN. 282 Memphis Brooks Museum of Art, Memphis, TN, Memphis Park Commission. 285 The Granger Collection, New York. 291 The Granger Collection, New York. 295 Library of Congress. 298 National Museum of American History/Smithsonian Institution, Washington, DC.

CHAPTER 10 303 Museum of Fine Arts, Boston, MA. Gift of Maxim Karolik for the M. and M. Karolik Collection. 305 Courtesy of the New Bedford Whaling Museum. 306 Gerry Images. 308 Prints and Photographs Collection, Library of Congress. 310 (left) Courtesy of